E. Clifford Nelson

The Trappe-Augustus
Lutheran Church,
built in 1743 near
present-day
Collegeville,
Pennsylvania, is the
oldest existing
Lutheran Church in
North America.
Aspects of the
Trappe church have
been photographed
and used to
identify the six
sections of this
volume. They express
the expansion of
the Lutheran church
in totality to its
present dimensions,
marked by new
modes of communication
and awareness.

Endpapers:
Front, Muhlenberg
graves at the Trappe
church.
Back, a worship service
as it is held today
in the later church
built in 1852
near the old Trappe
shrine.

The Lutherans in North America

Edited by
E. Clifford Nelson

in collaboration
with
Theodore G. Tappert
H. George Anderson
August R. Suelflow
Eugene L. Fevold
Fred W. Meuser

The
Lutherans
in
North
America

Fortress Press
Philadelphia

Contents

This book had its roots in a consultation of American Lutheran historians at the University of Chicago in June 1965. The host, Fortress Press, wondered whether it was time to undertake the writing of a new history of Lutherans in North America. Ever since the early 1930s the Press had been reissuing in revised editions the standard textbook written (1923) by the dean of historians doing American Lutheran history, Abdel Ross Wentz, now professor emeritus in the Lutheran Theological Seminary at Gettysburg, Pennsylvania. After considerable deliberation, the consultation delivered an opinion that the time had arrived to prepare a new history. This suggestion was not to be interpreted as a denigration of the earlier works—Wentz's book was not the sole contribution in this area—but as a recognition of the fact that a mass of new primary sources had been uncovered and that intensive research by numerous scholars had made it desirable to begin anew. The hope was expressed that the resulting work would be as useful and as durable as that of Professor Wentz.

A second suggestion by the consultation was that the new work should be a cooperative effort by several authors and that each writer be chosen with an eye not only to his scholarly and literary ability but also to his church affiliation. It was deemed wise that the three major Lutheran church bodies be represented on the team of writers.

A third suggestion was a proposal that the project consist of three volumes. The first would be a book of primary sources; the second would be a scholarly, interpretive volume; and the third would be a "popular" abridgement of the latter. For a variety of reasons, including rapidly rising publishing costs, the project had to be limited to one volume. The work, however, would make extensive reference to the most significant primary sources, use the results of the best scholarly research both recent and earlier, and would seek to interpret the materials in an historically responsible manner without sacrificing interest-evoking literary style and interpretive judgments. Whether or not this ambitious goal has been achieved is for others to assess.

In February 1966 the Press formally invited the undersigned to serve as editor of the project and to be one of the authors. When the remainder of the team had been selected, a number of meetings were held by the editor with the Press and the other authors. Among the numerous decisions reached two should be noted. First, a method of procedure was adopted. Each writer was to prepare a detailed outline of his assigned section. This was to be circulated for critical comment among the other writers and a number of recognized historians, non-Lutheran as well as Lutheran. The first draft was to be subjected to the same process. The final draft was to be in the editor's hands before the end of 1971. Circumstances beyond the control of those involved foreclosed the possibility of completing the project by the agreed date. After several postponements, the editor was able to present a completed manuscript to the Press in the early autumn of 1973.

The second notable decision recognized that one of the most prominent themes in American Lutheranism, as in Roman Catholicism, has been immigration. Consequently, it was determined that this sociological factor ought to be one of the main interpretive guides in attempting to tell the story of Lutherans in North America. On the other hand, recognition of the fact that Lutherans were also deeply rooted in the American colonial tradition and its subsequent development in the New World was an additional important historiographical factor. Although theology and denominationalism were clearly major forces in American Lutheranism, the book was not to be primarily a report of theological debate nor institutional foliation. Hence the writing of the story would seek to make clear that American Lutheran history could not be forced into a "frontier thesis" or some other popular theory of American historiography. Rather it should be seen as a natural outgrowth of the immigrant's cargo of European influence and his acculturation to the new North American environment.

The story, therefore, follows in a general way the movement of Lutheran people to the North American continent beginning in the seventeenth century. When the first wave of immigration came to an end during the American War of Independence, colonial Lutheranism numbered an estimated 40,000 (Roman Catholic, 25,000). Between the birth of the republic and 1840 immigration was little more than a trickle and contact with European mother churches was minimal. Because of these circumstances the orientation of the second "generation" was to America. Should Lutherans make common cause with other German-background (Reformed and sectarian) groups? Or should they give up both their "Germanism" and their Lutheranism and yield their life to the Anglo-American Protestantism which at the moment was the most prestigious religious element in American society? Lutherans faced an "identity crisis." The problem was resolved in a manner similar to that of the other bodies, that is, by adopting the completely new ecclesio-sociological form known as the American "denomination" which was neither "church" nor "sect" (à la Troeltsch) but had characteristics of both. Thus Lutheranism in America was a "free" voluntary association of like-minded people committed to a "churchly" confession which it held to be the true witness of Protestant Christianity. The temporary cessation of immigration (to ca. 1835) provided the opportunity to discover this identity. Although influenced by the language transition (German to English) and the modified and Americanized (Puritanized) Calvinism known as "American Evangelicalism," Lutheranism emerged consciously in this period as a particular confessional, denominational entity in the midst of the already evident American pluralism.

The remainder of the nineteenth century, with the exception of the Civil War years, was marked by a massive movement of people from Germany and Scandinavia. Again the immigrants confronted the attendant problems: the continuing quest for identity, the necessity for missions and institutionalization. By 1893 the "frontier" was gone, and the churches saw the necessity of "settling down" into the American environment, something which was to be accomplished in large measure during the twenties, a decade which still reverberated from the impact of World War I.

The powerful forces unleashed by the depression and the two world wars brought Lutheranism into the "mainstream of American life." By the sixties and seventies this communion faced another identity crisis, not unlike that in the early years of the nineteenth century. Numerous questions seemed to demand answers. For example: within the spectrum of American Christianity did Lutheranism have a viable future as a separate confessional church? In the face of the so-called great issues of the last third of the twentieth century was there anything unique, and therefore worthy of preservation, about Lutheranism? Did the staggering problems of the racial crisis, the Vietnam War, poverty, the Third World, political scandals, and the world energy crisis demand a "secular ecumenism" which minimized Lutheran particularity? Or could Lutherans under the lordship of Christ practice a fruitful coexistence and collaboration with others in the amelioration of the massive social, political, economic problems while remaining unabashedly and unapologetically "particular" and "confessional"? Much serious reflection and a plethora of words and activities during the past decade did not provide a resolution with sharply defined contours recognizably Lutheran, ecumenical, and practical. This remained unfinished business as the future rushed in upon the church.

The reader will recognize that the schema of periodization chosen by the writers follows roughly the sketch above. For the most part the sectional treatments cover natural time periods as far as Lutherans are concerned. At first glance the choice of 1900 as the terminus of one era may appear strained and unnatural. Admittedly there is nothing "Lutheran" about 1900; its choice, therefore, may be a bit artificial. Despite this, however, the writers encountered no major problems of transition, duplication, and coordination of materials and topics.

Some readers may question the wisdom of carrying the story to the present. It has often been said that to understand a piece of history that lies close at hand is a difficult if not impossible task. It is indeed easier to describe, and perhaps understand, a distant era if one assumes that it confronts us with a well-rounded, closed period of history. The question arises, however, whether there ever are in reality completely closed periods of history in isolation from the course of historical development. To make such an assumption is to remove life from history and to turn historiography into a sterile science dealing with objective facts that have no bearing on our own actions. As a matter of fact, this makes the writing of history all too easy! Rather, as Karl Barth once wrote, ". . . we are really concerned with what makes history different from science, we shall find no ideal conditions for historical knowledge in the immobility with which this or that distant event stands before us, nor shall we lament the degree of incompleteness, the topical urgency of the history that stands closest to us and so hampers our vision. The more difficult it is to see, observe, establish, the more urgently history asks questions of us and demands an answer, thus leaving no time for being a mere spectator, the more we have to do with real history." There is, therefore, a certain audacity and excitement in writing contemporary history, especially when one undertakes the task in full cognizance of the risk that the results may be vulnerable.

This consciousness is one of the main reasons for the editor's gratitude (he is the author of the last and "contemporary" section) to those who offered criticism and guidance along the way. It is also incumbent upon him to express the appreciation of the whole team of writers to numerous persons and institutions who offered encouragement and helpful criticism. Chief among these is the publisher, Fortress Press, which authorized and in part subsidized the project.

The manuscript was read as a whole, in part, or in outline by a number of scholars and churchmen whose critical comments proved invaluable. Special mention should be made of Professor Robert H. Fischer, Lutheran School of Theology, Chicago; Professor Robert T. Handy, Union Seminary, New York City; Professor Winthrop S. Hudson, Colgate Rochester Divinity School, Rochester, N.Y.; former president John Tietjen, Concordia Seminary, St. Louis, Mo.; and Professor Richard C. Wolf, Vanderbilt University, Nashville.

The staffs of libraries and archives in various parts of the country were invariably gracious and eager to be of assistance. The editor is particularly grateful to his faculty colleagues and to the administration of St. Olaf College for their gestures of encouragement; to Miss Charlotte Jacobson, assistant librarian, who prepared the index and did special editorial work on Section VI, and to Mrs. Mary Petersen and Miss Alma Roisum whose typing and editorial assistance contributed greatly in bringing the manuscript into shape for the publisher.

A special mention must be made of Dr. David L. Scheidt, pastor of St. Petri Ev. Lutheran Church of Tacony, Philadelphia. From the outset Dr. Scheidt has served as the liaison and chief consultant between Fortress Press and the team of writers. His many years of editorial experience, his sense of style, his wise judgments, and never-failing good humor have made him an indispensable member of the project-team. In fact, his literary skill, though invisible to the reader, has been brought to bear on a large section of the manuscript.

Permission to quote materials under copyright, gratefully acknowledged elsewhere, is only one sign of the authors' indebted-

ness to other historians. The knowledgeable reader will immediately recognize the wide-ranging use by the authors of materials from the hands of various and sundry practitioners of the
historian's craft. Although meticulous care has been exercised in
giving footnote credit to the writings of others, it may well be
that some sources have been inadvertently omitted in the notes.
If this has indeed happened, the editor and the writing team beg
indulgence for the oversight. Special mention should be made of
Augsburg Publishing House, Minneapolis, which gave permis-   xi
sion to use large segments of the editor's *Lutheranism in North
America 1914-1970* (1972) on which it holds the copyright.

These acknowledgments conclude on a sad note. Shortly before these lines were written, word was received of the death (on
Christmas Day, 1973) of one of the contributors, Theodore G.
Tappert, professor at the Lutheran Theological Seminary in
Philadelphia. We are deeply grieved that he did not live to see
the completion of a work that was close to his heart. The project
benefited by his scholarly expertise, his broad and profound
historical knowledge, his literary gifts, his high academic standards, and his kind but sharp and incisive criticisms. If this book
has any value, much of it is a reflection of Professor Tappert's
love of the Church, his knowledge of her history, and his special
mastery of the issues in Lutheranism. Though we mourn his
death, we rejoice that his works follow after him.

E. Clifford Nelson
St. Olaf College
Northfield, Minnesota
January 1974

Theodore G. Tappert

1   Colonists on the Hudson and the Delaware

lius F. Sachse, "The Earliest Attempt
German Colonization," *Proceedings of the
nsylvania German Society* 7 (1897):
–107, and the literature cited there.
rmán Arciniegas, *Germans in the Conquest
America: A Sixteenth Century Venture* (New
rk: Macmillan, 1943).

r example, Lars P. Qualben, *The Lu-
ran Church in Colonial America* (New
rk: Nelson, 1940), p. 117.

Long before Christopher Columbus reached North America in 1492 other seamen from Europe had set foot on the shores of the Western Hemisphere. It was not until after the exploit of Columbus, however, that permanent settlements were begun on the mainland. In the sixteenth and seventeenth centuries Spaniards, who were Roman Catholic, settled along the coasts of Florida and the Gulf of Mexico. Spanish possession was at first contested by the French, who were likewise Roman Catholic, but the chief French settlements were on the St. Lawrence River. The English claimed the Atlantic seaboard between New Spain in the south and New France in the north. This claim was supported by gradual colonization beginning with Jamestown, Virginia, in 1607 and Plymouth, Massachusetts, in 1620. In contrast to the Spaniards and the Frenchmen, English-speaking colonists were predominantly Protestant, while embracing a variety of beliefs and practices: Anglican (Episcopalian), Presbyterian, Congregational, Baptist, and Quaker. People of other nationalities were also attracted to what were, or became, the English colonies, and most were Protestants identified as Lutheran, Reformed, Moravian, Mennonite, etc.

Some Lutherans on the Periphery

Lutherans had early contacts with the New World. Some of these were peripheral to the story of Lutheranism in North America, but nevertheless deserve to be mentioned at least in passing.

In 1528 the banking house of the Welser family in Augsburg, Germany, received from Emperor Charles V, as security for a debt, the right to exploit a vast tract of land roughly comprising the present Venezuela, along the northern coast of South America. A small colony was promptly established there. Among the colonists were some Germans who were said to have embraced the new Lutheran faith. Within a few decades the enterprise collapsed and no trace of this early Lutheran presence in the Western Hemisphere remains.[1]

It has been said that shortly afterward there were Lutherans in what is now the state of Florida.[2] In 1564 some French Huguenots established Fort Caroline on the northeastern coast of Florida, where they were joined the following year by additional colonists from France. Less than a month later, Florida being considered Spanish territory, the Spanish captain-general Peter Menendez attacked the settlement and massacred all the Huguenots. He was reported to have explained, "I do this not as to Frenchmen but as to Lutherans [*Luteranos*]." In the sixteenth century Spaniards applied the term *Luteranos* to any and all Protestants and not merely to Lutherans. In this case the reference was to Calvinists rather than Lutherans. Failure to take this into account has produced the myth of an early Lutheran settlement in Florida.[3]

Like many others in his time, King Christian IV of the united kingdoms of Denmark and Norway was interested in discovering a northwest passage to the Orient. In 1619 he sent out two ships for this purpose under the command of Jens Munk, who sailed to what is now known as Churchill, on Hudson Bay in Canada. A chaplain, Rasmus Jensen, who accompanied the expedition, conducted services regularly, and since he and the seamen were Danes, Norwegians, and either Swedes or Germans, the services were Lutheran. Severe cold, shortage of food, and disease made heavy inroads among the settlers during the first winter. The chaplain himself died in April 1620. By summer there were only three survivors (including Munk, who afterward wrote an account of the expedition) and these returned to Denmark on the smaller of the two ships. Therefore no permanent settlement resulted.[4]

A generation later Lutheranism was permanently established in the West Indies. For purposes of trade a number of Danes and other Europeans (mostly Dutchmen) settled on those islands which for two and a half centuries were to be governed from Denmark and were accordingly known as the Danish West Indies. Beginning in 1665 a long succession of clergymen was sent from Denmark to minister to the colonists. The islands did not prosper, however, and in 1917 they were bought from Denmark by the United States for $25 million and were renamed the Virgin Islands. At the time of the transfer there were about three thousand Lutherans there; some were of Danish origin but more were Negroes.[5]

In 1743 some Dutch and German Lutherans in Berbice, a settlement in British Guiana (present-day Guyana), petitioned the colonial authorities for permission to introduce public worship according to their own faith. The colony in the northern part of South America was at the time under the government of the Netherlands and the established church was Dutch Reformed. The petition was nevertheless granted, but it was not until 1752 that the first pastor was secured from the Lutheran consistory in Amsterdam, and even longer before the first church building could be erected. Unfortunately there were long vacancies between pastorates during the subsequent century and a half and the Lutheran people repeatedly suffered from neglect. In 1890 a connection was finally established with Lutherans in Pennsylvania and this insured an uninterrupted ministry, financial assistance, and the formation of new congregations.[6]

The Dutch and Swedish Colonies

The Dutch Republic, which had secured its independence from Spain in 1581, quickly became a powerful nation. For reasons of trade and commerce Dutch merchants were interested in a new route to the Orient, and in 1609 Henry Hudson, an Eng-

3.
Michael V. Gannon, *The Cross in the Sand: The Early Catholic Church in Florida* (Gainesville, Fla.: University of Florida, 1965), pp. 20-29; William L. Saunders, ed., *The Colonial Records of North Carolina*, 9 vols. (Raleigh, N.C.: P. M. Hole, 1886-90), 2:763.
4.
Thorkild Hansen, *The Way to Hudson Bay: The Life and Times of Jens Munk* (New York: Harcourt, Brace & World, 1970).
5.
Jens Larsen, *Virgin Islands Story: A History of the Lutheran Church in the Danish West Indies* (Philadelphia: Fortress Press, 1968).
6.
Paul B. Beatty, Jr., *A History of the Lutheran Church in Guyana* (Georgetown, Guyana: Daily Chronicle, 1970); Henry S. Boner et al., *History of the Evangelical Lutheran Synod of East Pennsylvania* (Philadelphia: Lutheran Publication Society, 1893), pp. 309-22.

lishman, sailed under the Dutch flag to the West. After moving along the Atlantic coast from Newfoundland to Virginia, he entered New York Bay and sailed up the great river which was afterward named the Hudson River in his honor. He pursued the river beyond the present site of Albany in quest of a waterway to the Far East. Although he did not find what he was looking for, Hudson's explorations made Dutch merchants more aware of the possibilities of trade with the American Indians.

By 1614 a fort to protect traders was built where Albany now stands, and at about the same time huts were put on Manhattan Island for the use of transient traders. The way was prepared for colonization as well as trade when in 1621 a charter which conferred extensive powers and privileges was given by the States General in Holland to the newly formed Dutch West India Company.[7] However, it was not until 1624 that the first permanent settlers arrived from the Netherlands.[8] Others followed in subsequent years, and it has been estimated that by 1664 the total population of New Netherland was around ten thousand. By this time there were settlements along the Hudson River in such places as present-day Albany, Athens, Hackensack, and New York City. The settlers were of various nationalities, probably because foreigners, who had previously been drawn to the Netherlands by that country's growing prosperity, were now attracted by the opportunities which the New World was believed to offer. A visitor in 1643 was told by the director general (governor) of the colony that as many as eighteen languages were then spoken in New Netherland.[9]

At the time that the Hudson Valley began to be settled in 1624, the Dutch also landed a few colonists on the Delaware River to the south. The Dutch claim to the Delaware Valley was not supported, however, by extensive occupation. The resulting vacuum was filled by Sweden, whose king, Gustavus Adolphus, had become interested in American colonization but was prevented from carrying out his plans by his active participation in the Thirty Years' War. After his death on the field of battle in 1632, the king's intentions were fulfilled. The first colonists were sent to the Delaware Valley from Sweden in 1638 and were quickly followed by others.[10] Settlements appeared in such places as present-day Wilmington, Delaware, and Philadelphia. Altogether not more than four hundred colonists arrived while the colony was in Swedish hands, and these were not all Swedes by any means; in fact, the majority were Finns (Finland was then a dependency of Sweden), although they understood Swedish.

Despite the establishment of New Sweden, a few Dutch settlers remained on the Delaware, for the Delaware Valley was still claimed by the Dutch. The Swedish governor did not disturb the Dutch settlers, nor did the Dutch governor interfere with the Swedish colonists. The reason for this toleration was that in the Thirty Years' War—which was then being fought in Europe, Sweden, and the Netherlands—Protestants were allied against Roman Catholic powers. When the war ended in 1648 the cords of common interest soon came undone. In 1655 the

7.
For general orientation on the Dutch colony see Ellis R. Raesly, *Portrait of New Netherland* (New York: Columbia University, 1945); C. A. Weslager, *Dutch Explorers, Traders, and Settlers in the Delaware Valley* (Philadelphia: University of Pennsylvania, 1968); and Frederick J. Zwierlein, *Religion in New Netherland* (Rochester, N.Y.: J. P. Smith, 1910).

8.
The year cannot be fixed with absolute certainty, but the year 1624 is more probable than 1623, which used to be suggested. Cf. Alexander C. Flick, ed., *History of the State of New York*, 10 vols. (New York: Columbia University, 1933–37), 1:234–42.

9.
Isaac Jogues, "Novum Belgium," in *Narratives of New Netherland, 1706-1764*, ed. J. Franklin Jameson (New York: Barnes & Noble, 1909), p. 259.

10.
For general orientation on the Swedish colony see Amandus Johnson, *The Swedish Settlements on the Delaware*, 2 vols. (Philadelphia: University of Pennsylvania, 1911); Christopher Ward, *The Dutch and Swedes on the Delaware* (Philadelphia: University of Pennsylvania, 1930); and John H. Wuorinen, *The Finns on the Delaware* (New York: Columbia University, 1938).

Dutch governor, Peter Stuyvesant, sent six or seven hundred men against the much weaker New Sweden, which surrendered without firing a shot.

The whole territory now held by the Dutch had long been claimed by the English on the basis of earlier discoveries. Apart from this claim the English found it administratively awkward to have their colonies on the Atlantic coast divided, and the competition in trade and shipping which the Dutch provided was not appreciated. In 1664 several English warships appeared at Manhattan to demand surrender. Stuyvesant lacked the power to offer effective resistance and he capitulated without an exchange of fire. New Netherland was renamed New York because the colony was given by King Charles II to his brother, the duke of York. The English also conquered the former Swedish territory on the Delaware and thus gained control of the entire coast from Maine to Florida. Except for a brief interim (1673-74) when the Dutch reconquered their former colony, the English remained in possession until the Revolution.

Lutheran Beginnings on the Hudson, 1637-1703

Most of the inhabitants of New Netherland were Dutch Reformed in their religious adherence. This was natural inasmuch as the Dutch Reformed church was the state church in the mother country. In fact, a provisional order, issued at the time of the first settlement and subsequently repeated, called upon all colonists to observe the Reformed faith in public. Freedom of conscience was allowed in private, provided that those who dissented from the established religion did not assemble in conventicles, but every inhabitant was required to pay for the support of the Reformed churches and clergymen.[11] Such regulations were not rigidly enforced at first, as the Jesuit missionary Isaac Jogues observed during his visit in 1643: "No religion is publicly exercised but the Calvinist, and orders are to admit none but Calvinists, but this is not observed, for besides the Calvinists there are in the colony Catholics, English Puritans, Lutherans, Anabaptists (here called Mennonites), etc."[12] With the coming to New Netherland of Governor Peter Stuyvesant in 1647 and the conclusion of the Thirty Years' War in Europe the next year, the relaxed attitude toward dissenters ceased. Not even the "English Puritans" or Congregationalists (who, after all, were Reformed, too) were tolerated. That Baptists, Quakers, and Jews were dealt with more severely is less surprising.

Lutherans, a small minority in the New World as well as in Holland, were among those deprived of the free exercise of their religion. It is not possible to determine precisely when the first Lutherans arrived in New Netherland. The earliest specific reference to Lutherans along the Hudson River was the observation, already quoted, of Isaac Jogues in 1643. One may assume from this that there had been Lutherans along the Hudson River for some time before 1643; in fact, there is concrete evidence that some were there at least as early as 1637.[13] By 1649 they were numerous enough to justify a united appeal to their

11.
Hugh Hastings, ed., *Ecclesiastical Records, State of New York*, 7 vols. (Albany: James B. Lyon, 1901-16), 1:120, 121; cf. 2:884 (hereafter cited as *N.Y. Eccles. Records*).

12.
Jameson, *Narratives of New Netherland*, p. 260.

13.
Cf. Harry J. Kreider, *The Beginnings of Lutheranism in New York* (New York: New York Synod, 1949), pp. 8, 70.

fellow Lutherans in Amsterdam for a pastor.[14] Four years later they reported that there were about 150 Lutheran "heads of families" in New Netherland, "some having lived here somewhat longer than others."[15]

These Lutherans in the Dutch colony declared that they were "from divers lands of Europe."[16] Among them were people not only from the Netherlands but also from Germany, Denmark, Norway, Sweden, and even Poland.[17] It may well be, as already suggested, that those who were not Dutch had lived in the Netherlands for some time before embarking for the New World, and this seems to be substantiated by the fact that, whatever their national origin, all of them employed the Dutch tongue. In reply to the question whether a Dutchman or a German was preferred as pastor, the Lutherans on the Hudson wrote in 1656 to their fellow believers in Amsterdam: "This . . . is to inform you that, inasmuch as the Dutch language is most commonly used here and our children are also instructed therein, we desire, if possible, to have a Hollander."[18]

The petition for a pastor, first made in 1649, led to years of negotiation. The merchants of the Dutch West India Company at first seemed disposed to wink at the introduction of a Lutheran pastor and at Lutheran worship services,[19] for the prosperity of the colony depended on attracting more inhabitants. On the other hand, the Dutch Reformed ministers, both in the New World and in the Old, opposed the introduction of public worship by the Lutherans on the ground that "papists, Mennonites, and others" would soon make similar claims and the religious unity of the colony would be destroyed.[20] This is the view that finally prevailed, and in 1654 the Dutch West India Company informed Stuyvesant:

We have decided absolutely to deny the request made by some of our inhabitants, adherents of the Augsburg Confession, for a preacher and the free exercise of their religion . . . on account of the consequences arising therefrom, and we recommend to you also not to receive any similar petitions but rather to turn them off in the most civil and least offensive way and to employ all possible but moderate means in order to induce them to listen and finally to join the Reformed Church and thus live in greater love and harmony among themselves.[21]

This decision was repeated in subsequent years. Moreover, it was rigidly enforced in New Netherland by means of a new ordinance that forbade any but Reformed services and imposed fines on "all who presume to exercise the duties of a preacher, reader, or precentor" and on any "man or woman found at such a meeting."[22] Apparently unaware of the stiffening attitudes in the New World and evidently hopeful that the civil authorities would at least ignore the presence of a minister of the Augsburg Confession, the Lutheran consistory in Amsterdam chose a man, ordained him, and sent him abroad. This was John Ernest Gutwasser, a Saxon who had completed his study of theology. In late spring 1657 he sailed to New Netherland, and the Re-

14.
Arnold J. H. vanLaer, trans., *The Lutheran Church in New York, 1649-1772: Records in the Lutheran Church Archives at Amsterdam, Holland* (New York: New York Public Library, 1946), p. 13.

15.
Ibid., pp. 14-18.

16.
Ibid., p. 14.

17.
John O. Evjen, *Scandinavian Immigrants in New York, 1630-1674* (Minneapolis: Holter, 1916).

18.
VanLaer, *Lutheran Church in New York*, p. 21.

19.
Ibid., pp. 22, 23.

20.
Cf. *N.Y. Eccles. Records*, 1:386-88, where six reasons for not tolerating Lutherans are given by the Reformed clergymen.

21.
Ibid., p. 324.

22.
E. B. O'Callaghan, ed., *Laws and Ordinances of New Netherland, 1638-1674* (Albany: New York State, 1868), pp. 211, 212; Berthold Fernow, ed., *The Records of New Amsterdam from 1653 to 1674*, 7 vols. (New York: Knickerbocker, 1897), 1:20, 21.

formed clergymen there promptly reported his arrival in a joint
letter to their colleagues in the old country:

**The Lutherans here . . . requested the honorable director
and the council for permission . . . to hold their
conventicles to prepare the way for the pastor they
expected would be coming. . . . Although we could not
have believed that such permission had been given by
the lords directors [of the Dutch West India Company],
there nevertheless arrived here in July last, with the ship
"The Mill," a Lutheran preacher, Joannes Ernestus
Goetwater, to the great joy of the Lutherans but to the
special displeasure and uneasiness of the [Reformed]
congregation in this place. . . . We then demanded that
our authorities here should send back the Lutheran
preacher . . . in the same ship in which he had come in
order to put a stop to this work which they [the Lutheran
colonists] evidently intend to prosecute with a hard
Lutheran head in spite of and against the will of our
magistrates.[23]**

The consternation of the Reformed ministers at the arrival of
Gutwasser was not greater than the dismay of the Lutherans at
the treatment accorded their new minister. Gutwasser wrote to
the Lutheran consistory in Amsterdam:

**Together with the news of my safe arrival in New
Amsterdam and the great joy of the Christian
congregation, I hereby must and will write to your
reverences how the authorities here are beginning to use
all diligence to prevent us from exercising our true and
pure religion. Of the passing of ordinances and the
imposing of heavy fines against holding private and
public meetings, in order to throw a scare into the
congregation, there is no lack. When I appeared before
the honorable council, and especially before the
honorable director general Stuyvesant, they were not
inclined to listen to reason. They sent to my house two
ordinances according to which I must govern myself
precisely.[24]**

Gutwasser was forbidden to preach or to conduct any kind of
religious service during his stay in New Netherland. Moreover,
he was requested, and then ordered, to leave the colony at the
first opportunity. For two years the deportation was evaded on
one pretext or another in the hope that the authorities might
relent, but finally Gutwasser was compelled to return to Europe.

The English conquest of the Dutch colony in 1664 prepared
the way for a change in religious policy. The absence of Anglican churches in the predominantly Dutch Reformed colony
prevented the Church of England from becoming the established church in any exclusive sense. The situation required a
policy of religious toleration, and the articles of capitulation
provided that "the Dutch here shall enjoy the liberty of their
consciences in divine worship and church discipline."[25] When
the Lutherans inquired whether this provision applied to them
as well as to the Dutch Reformed, the English governor assured

23.
N.Y. Eccles. Records, 1:393, 394.
24.
VanLaer, *Lutheran Church in New York,*
pp. 48, 49.
25.
N.Y. Eccles. Records, 1:558, 572.

them "that they may have liberty to send for one or more pastors" and "that they may freely and publicly exercise their religion according to their conscience."[26]

Almost five years passed before a pastor was actually secured. Finally Jacob Fabritius, a native of Silesia who had been driven out of Hungary during the Turkish invasion, commended himself to the Lutherans in Amsterdam as suitable for America. He reached New York in 1669, took his oath of allegiance to the English governor, and received from the governor a license to perform the functions of a minister. Although he was regarded with suspicion by the Dutch Reformed clergymen, he set about his work with great energy. He installed elders and deacons as lay officers, planned for the building of "a small wooden church" in New York, and requested that catechisms and hymnals be sent from Holland.[27] However, within a year the congregation in New York was complaining to the Lutheran consistory in Amsterdam about the strange conduct of its pastor.

He does not behave himself or live as a pastor should. He is very fond of wine and brandy, and knows how to curse and swear too. In his apparel he is like a soldier, red from head to foot. He married a woman here with five children and has dressed them all in red. . . . He pays little attention to people, so that our opponents or neighbors have nothing else to talk about but the Lutheran pastor. . . . Our friendly request to your reverences is that you may please once more take the trouble to provide us with a capable pastor and, if possible, a young man who is not married.[28]

By the summer of 1671 a new minister arrived from the Netherlands, and Fabritius, who had for some time contemplated moving to the Delaware River, where his wife owned a house, secured permission to preach a farewell sermon and at the same time install his successor.[29] Laymen in New York described the new pastor, Bernard Arnzius, as "a capable man whose life conforms to his preaching," with the result that now "the mouths of our neighbors are stopped." Arnzius himself later reported to Amsterdam that the Lutheran congregations in New York and Albany were "in good and reasonably flourishing condition" and that his parishioners lived with one another "in Christian harmony, concord, and peace."[30]

During the pastorate of Arnzius churches and parsonages were built in New York and Albany, and between these areas he divided his time: summers in the former and winters in the latter. There continued to be some friction with the Dutch Reformed, and an Anglican clergyman reported that the Lutheran and the Reformed ministers "behaved themselves one towards the other as shyly and uncharitably as if Luther and Calvin had bequeathed and entailed their virulent and bigoted spirits upon them and their heirs forever." The Anglican reported his efforts to create a more congenial atmosphere:

I invited them both with their Vrows [wives] to a Supper one night unknown to each other, with an obligation that they should not speak one word in Dutch under the

9

26.
VanLaer, *Lutheran Church in New York,* pp. 48, 49.
27.
Ibid., pp. 64–75.
28.
Ibid., pp. 76, 77.
29.
N.Y. Eccles. Records, 1:607, 621.
30.
VanLaer, *Lutheran Church in New York,* p. 86; cf. p. 91.

penalty of a Bottle of Madeira, alleging I was so
imperfect in that Language that we could not manage a
sociable discourse, so accordingly they came, and at the
first interview they stood so appalled as if the Ghosts of
Luther and Calvin had suffered a transmigration, but the
amaze soon went off with a *salve tu quoque* and a Bottle
of Wine, . . . and so we continued our *Mensalla* the
whole meeting in Latin, which they both spoke so
fluently and promptly that I blush'd at my self with a
passionate regret that I could not keep pace with them.[31]

The absence of urgent correspondence suggests that the pastorate of Arnzius was a quiet and constructive one. It lasted twenty years, until his death in 1691. Another long vacancy then followed; this time it took eleven years to secure a pastor. Since the man who served after this long interim was one of the Swedish ministers on the Delaware River, we need to consider what had been happening among the Lutherans there.

Lutheran Beginnings on the Delaware, 1638–1703

The circumstances on the Delaware River were unlike those on the Hudson. The Lutherans on the Hudson were a small minority struggling for survival in what was often a hostile atmosphere, while the Lutherans on the Delaware comprised virtually the whole population and for several decades enjoyed the favor and support of the colonial government. When he left Sweden in 1642 Governor John Printz was instructed to "see to it that in all things a true and befitting worship . . . be paid to God the most high, and therefore take all good care that divine service be zealously performed according to the true Augsburg Confession, the Council of Upsala, and the ceremonies of the Swedish church."[32] The governor was at the same time instructed not to disturb the few Dutch settlers on the Delaware but rather to grant them freedom in "the exercise of the Reformed religion."[33] This generous attitude toward dissenters was probably dictated in part by the precarious military position of New Sweden, whose existence was threatened by both English and Dutch neighbors, but it was also an expression of that relaxed posture which a virtual religious monopoly produced both in the homeland and in New Sweden.

In any case, the consequence was that an ordered church life made its appearance more quickly among Lutherans on the Delaware than among Lutherans on the Hudson. Ministers were supplied from Sweden as long as the colony was in Swedish hands. The first was Reorus Torkillus, who conducted services regularly from 1639 until his death in an epidemic four years later. It was during his brief stay that the first log church was built near the present Wilmington, Delaware. John Campanius promptly replaced Torkillus and remained for six years. During his term Governor Printz reported to Sweden: "I caused a church to be built in New Gothenburg [Tinicum, Pa.] according to our Swedish fashion, so far as our resources and means would allow."[34] This second church was followed by a third in Philadelphia (then Wicaco), and so all the early churches were built

31.
N.Y. Eccles. Records, 1:720; Charles Wooley, "A Two Years' Journal in New York" (1680), reprinted in *Historic Chronicles of New Amsterdam, Colonial New York, and Early Long Island*, ed. Cornell Jaray, 1st ser. (Port Washington, N.Y.: Friedman, 1968), p. 56.
32.
Amandus Johnson, ed., *The Instruction for Johan Printz, Governor of New Sweden* (Port Washington, N.Y.: Friedman, 1969), pp. 94, 96. The decree of the Council of Uppsala, convened by the king of Sweden in 1593, reaffirmed adherence to the Augsburg Confession and repudiation of Roman ceremonies.
33.
Ibid., p. 96.
34.
Report of Printz to the West India Company, February 20, 1647, ibid., p. 131.

on the western shore of the river, where most of the Swedes and Finns then lived.

When the colony capitulated to the Dutch in 1655 there were only about four hundred Swedish and Finnish colonists. Although the Lutherans on the Hudson River were not granted freedom at this time to assemble for their own worship, the terms of the surrender permitted the Lutherans on the Delaware to continue to do so. The reason for this unexpected toleration was explained in a letter by the Dutch Reformed clergymen in New Amsterdam:

The Swedish governor made a condition in his capitulation, that they might retain one Lutheran preacher to teach these people in their own language. This was granted them the more easily, first, because new troubles had broken out at Manhattan with the Indians and it was desirable to shorten proceedings here and return to Manhattan to put things in order there, and, secondly, because there was no Reformed preacher here, nor any who understood their language, to be placed there.[35]

The Lutheran minister who was permitted to remain with his people was Lars Lock, a native of Finland who had been on the Delaware since 1647 and was to stay until his death forty years later in 1688. He seems to have combined faithfulness to his calling with a generous measure of churlishness, which may well have been exaggerated by the unfriendly Dutch Reformed dominies in New Amsterdam who wrote: "This Lutheran preacher is a man of impious and scandalous habits, a wild, drunken, unmannerly clown, more inclined to look into the wine can than into the Bible. He would prefer drinking brandy two hours to preaching one, and when the sap is in the wood his hands itch and he wants to fight whomsoever he meets."[36]

Lock continued to serve the Lutherans on the Delaware after the English conquest in 1664, whereupon the religious liberty granted to the Dutch was extended to the Swedes and Finns too. It was soon after this, in 1671, that Jacob Fabritius moved from New York. He assumed charge of the congregations on the upper Delaware (Philadelphia and Tinicum, Pa.) while Lock concentrated on the congregations on the lower Delaware (Wilmington and New Castle, Del.). Ill health plagued Lock. A successor reported that finally "he became too lame to help himself, and still less the churches, and therefore he did no service for some years before death ended all his sorrows in 1688."[37]

Evidence concerning the life and character of Fabritius remained ambiguous for a while. Four years after his transfer to the Delaware he was hauled into court for using "bad words which do not become a priest" and was charged with being one of several "ringleaders in causing a tumultuous disturbance."[38] About the same time, his parishioners complained that they could not understand Fabritius, who preached in German or Dutch and was slow in learning Swedish.[39] On the other hand, nine years later, when the parishioners who desired "a further

11

35.
Jameson, *Narratives of New Netherland*, pp. 395, 396.

36.
Ibid., p. 396; cf. p. 410.

37.
Israel Acrelius, *A History of New Sweden* (1759), trans. William M. Reynolds (Philadelphia: Historical Society of Pennsylvania, 1874), p. 177.

38.
N.Y. Eccles. Records, 1:673–75.

39.
G. B. Keen, trans., "Extracts from the Records of Gloria Dei," *Pennsylvania Magazine of History and Biography* 2 (1878): 342; *N.Y. Eccles. Records*, 1:676.

continuance of his service" in Philadelphia pledged contributions toward his salary, the response was generous, and he was commended for "pure doctrine and an exemplary life."[40] During his last nine years Fabritius was blind and "when he walked he was led by someone who went before him with a staff."[41] He ceased serving his congregations altogether by 1691 and died five years later.

The physical infirmities of both Lock and Fabritius and their subsequent deaths left the people on the Delaware without adequate spiritual care for almost a decade. They wrote to Sweden several times requesting pastors, but interest in the mother country had waned since the loss of the colony and no reply was received. A letter was also addressed to the Lutheran consistory in Amsterdam in which the consistory was requested, "in view of our blessed fellowship in the Lutheran religion," to secure a "suitable Swedish minister." Nothing came of this appeal either. For want of preachers, laymen read sermons from postils, but the churches became more and more deserted. A visitor from Sweden learned of these conditions and on his return reported what he had seen and heard. This ultimately came to the attention of the king, who made further inquiries. In reply Carl Springer, a lay reader who was "the most suitable among them to write Swedish and read Swedish writing," explained that there were almost 1,000 Lutherans on the Delaware, including a few Dutch and German persons intermarried with Swedes and Finns, and requested two ministers and a supply of Swedish Bibles, catechisms, and other books.[42]

Two young clergymen were selected, and in 1697 Andrew Rudman and Eric Bjork sailed across the Atlantic. Thus ecclesiastical relations were restored with Sweden. In fact, the congregations on the Delaware were now regarded as a mission of the Church of Sweden and treated as a chapter, or district, of the diocese of Skara or (after 1736) the archdiocese of Uppsala. Meanwhile, the congregational organization which had been transplanted from the Hudson to the Delaware by Fabritius (with elders and deacons now called "wardens" and "vestrymen" after the Anglican usage) was preserved and revitalized.[43]

Upon arriving in America, Rudman settled in Philadelphia and Bjork settled in Wilmington. One of the first things these two men did was set in motion plans for replacing the decayed wood churches with more permanent structures of brick and stone. Trinity Church in Wilmington was completed in 1699 and Gloria Dei in Philadelphia the following year, both buildings surviving to this day. It was the original intention that all Lutherans, no matter where they lived, should attend one or the other of these two churches, but this became increasingly inconvenient, and even impossible, as the population scattered. By 1704 a third church was built in what is now Swedesboro, New Jersey, on the eastern side of the Delaware, to which more and more people moved. Infrequent services were soon conducted by the ministers in other places as well—in Penn's Neck, Egg Harbor, and Maurice River, New Jersey; in Kingsessing, Upper Merion, and Douglasville, Pennsylvania; and even in Cecil

40.
Berthold Fernow, ed., *Documents Relating to the History of the Dutch and Swedish Settlements on the Delaware River* (Albany: Argus 1877), p. 539.
41.
Acrelius, *History of New Sweden*, p. 178.
42.
Ibid., pp. 179-95. On Springer see Jeannette Eckman, *Crane Hook on the Delaware* (Newark, Del.: University of Delaware, 1958), pp. 105-38.
43.
Cf. Willem J. Kooiman, *De Nederlandsche Luthersche Gemeenten in Noord-America, 1649-1772* (Amsterdam: Ten Have, 1946) pp. 21, 55.

County, Maryland—and in many of these localities churches were eventually built.

Growing Pains on the Hudson River, 1703–87

It was in the same year, 1691, in which Jacob Fabritius was compelled by his blindness and ill health to terminate his ministry on the Delaware that Bernard Arnzius died on the Hudson. During the six years that followed there was not a single Lutheran minister in all of continental North America. The restoration of connections between the Delaware and the Church of Sweden in 1697 still left the Lutherans on the Hudson unprovided for. However, when one of the new Swedish clergymen, Andrew Rudman, became ill and secured a replacement from Sweden, the Lutherans on the Hudson importuned Rudman to be their pastor at least for a time before his return to his native land. Rudman consented in 1702, and for more than a year he labored among the Lutherans in New York City and Albany. His strength was unequal to the task, however, and so he returned to Philadelphia, where he spent his few remaining years in semi-retirement.

Before leaving New York Rudman saw to it that his parishioners there would not be forsaken. He remembered an earnest young man in Philadelphia who had completed his theological studies in Germany but had crossed the ocean to Pennsylvania without ordination because he was reluctant to serve as a minister of the gospel. This was Justus Falckner, to whom Rudman wrote from New York: "What shall I do about forsaking my little flock? Looking everywhere, I find no one better fitted than you to whom I may safely entrust my sheep."[44] Falckner's resistance was finally broken down by the arguments of Rudman and his colleagues. "After much persuasion, also prompting of heart and conscience," he wrote to his former teacher August Herman Francke in Saxony: "I am staying as a regular preacher with a little Dutch Lutheran congregation, a state of affairs which I had so long avoided."[45] It was in 1703 that Falckner was ordained in Philadelphia by Rudman and his two Swedish colleagues, after Rudman had assured the hesitant Falckner of the propriety of this act.

Episcopal authority to consecrate churches, ordain, etc. has been delegated to me by the bishop [in Sweden] especially in a case of this kind. It has been done before in Pennsylvania among the Swedes by Domine Lars Lock, who ordained Avelius [Abelius Zetskoorn] there, etc. Moreover, you remember that Lutherans in Holland have no bishop and nevertheless have ordained by joint action of the presbyters. Henceforth let there be no doubt. . . .[46]

When Falckner arrived in Manhattan he found that during the long vacancy after the death of Arnzius many members had strayed into Reformed or Anglican parishes. The situation was made worse by the neglect and deterioration of the church building. But Falckner's immediate predecessor had at least been able to preserve the congregational organization and to

...nLaer, *Lutheran Church in New York*, p. ...1.

...lius F. Sachse, ed., "Missives to August ...erman Francke," *Proceedings of the Penn-...vania German Society* 18 (1909): 15.

...nLaer, *Lutheran Church in New York*, pp. ...1–2. Questions concerning the "regular-...." or "validity" of the ordination are ...rdly appropriate in the light of the Lu-...eran doctrine of the ministry; but see ...arry J. Kreider, *Lutheranism in Colonial ...w York* (New York, 1942), p. 31. Speak-...g of "defective orders" is not Lutheran ...t later Anglican; see Jehu Curtis Clay, ...nals of the Swedes on the Delaware, 2d ed., ...l. (Philadelphia: Pechin, 1835), p. 86.

13

keep alive the hope for the church's renewal. The situation was less favorable in Albany, where no organization had survived, the church building was dilapidated, and many of the former members had left to migrate southward. Falckner ministered to people not only in New York and Albany but also in other preaching points like Hackensack, New Jersey, and Athens, New York. As had been the case two generations earlier, the people who assembled for worship were of various nationalities. In 1704 Falckner wrote to Europe: "I learned the Dutch language in a short time, so that at times now I preach three times a week. . . . My few auditors are mostly Dutch in speech, but in extraction they are mostly High Germans, also Swedes, Danes, Norwegians, Poles, Lithuanians, Transylvanians, and other nationalities."[47]

During Falckner's pastorate the Lutheran population on the Hudson River was increased by the arrival, between 1708 and 1722, of more than two thousand Germans who had fled from their impoverished homelands.[48] In return for their passage from Europe land was provided for them by the colonial government about eighty miles up the river. Many left the places assigned to them, some migrating northwestward to the Mohawk and Schoharie valleys. Perhaps a third of all of these settlers were Lutheran, and they were ministered to by Joshua Kocherthal,[49] a Lutheran clergyman who had accompanied the newcomers from Germany, until his death in 1719. Falckner cooperated with Kocherthal in every possible way, and on the latter's death Falckner added to his own burdensome itinerary such Palatine settlements as Germantown, Newburgh, and Rhinebeck. Falckner's health was undermined by his incessant labors. In 1723, when he was only fifty-one years old and after he had completed almost twenty years of service on the Hudson River, he died.[50]

A request for a new pastor was promptly addressed to the Lutheran consistory in Amsterdam. None was available there, but a search made in Hamburg turned up William Christopher Berkenmeyer, a native of the German duchy of Lueneburg, who was ordained and sent to New York in 1725. He was soon caring for fourteen congregations scattered along the length of the Hudson Valley, a distance of about 150 miles. It quickly became apparent to Berkenmeyer that he alone could not provide the kind of ministry that the situation called for by covering so much territory as an itinerant. He therefore planned to divide the field into parishes of several congregations each and he appealed to various ecclesiastical authorities to furnish ministers for them. When his first appeals were unsuccessful and when the vacuum created by the lack of ordained ministers was in some cases filled by self-appointed "pretenders" who were lacking in competence as well as in ecclesiastical endorsement,[51] Berkenmeyer proposed to the Swedish clergymen on the Delaware, and then directly to Bishop Jesper Svedberg, that the Church of Sweden assume responsibility for all the Lutherans in America.

The first thing I urgently ask of you, Very Reverend Sir, is that I be honored by being received into the fellowship

47.
Sachse, "Missives to Francke," p. 17.
48.
For a fuller account of the Palatines see chapter 2.
49.
On the name of the minister see Heinz Schuchmann, "Der 1708 nach Amerika ausgewanderte Pfarrer Josua Kocherthal hiess ursprünglich Josua Harrsch," in *Mitteilungen zur Wanderungsgeschichte der Pfälzer* (Kaiserslautern, 1967), pp. 121–28.
50.
Delber W. Clark, *The World of Justus Falckner* (Philadelphia: Muhlenberg Press, 1946), pp. 175–78. Clark's account is somewhat romanticized.
51.
Among such men on the Hudson were John Bernard van Dieren, Daniel Falckner, and (a little later) John A. Langerfeld and John Spahler. Cf. John P. Dern, ed., *The Albany Protocol: W. C. Berkenmeyer's Chronicle, 1731-1750* (Ann Arbor, Mich., 1971), pp. 2, 48, 137, and passim.

of the Swedish consistory in Pennsylvania, that in the same way the congregations in New York and Albany, entrusted to me, be commended for their ecclesiastical oversight to the keeping of His Holy Majesty, the King of Sweden, and also that no one, at least in these colonies, be recognized as a Lutheran pastor unless his call can be demonstrated to the Swedish consistory to be lawful, as is becoming of brethren of the unaltered Augsburg Confession. . . . [I ask] that our congregations, and especially the pastors sent to them, may be protected from the ridicule of those who falsely pretend that they are Lutheran pastors but are disturbers and destroyers of ecclesiastical and civil peace.[52]

Nothing came of this overture, which was not very practical in any case because it called for absentee leadership, but the proposed division into parishes became a reality when the ministerium of Hamburg sent two young ministers to America. Michael Christian Knoll, who arrived in 1732, was installed in the parish of which New York City was the center. John August Wolf arrived two years later in response to a call from the Raritan parish centered around the present Oldwick, New Jersey. Berkenmeyer himself withdrew to the parish on the upper Hudson which embraced, among other places, Athens and Albany.

Although Berkenmeyer had now moved up the river, he continued to exercise leadership among the ministers and laymen along the entire length of the valley. He was not only respected as the oldest of the clergy in age and years of service but also deferred to because he assumed the role of agent for Amsterdam and Hamburg. His judgment was sometimes challenged, as it was by "pretenders." He also became involved in a long and disagreeable quarrel between Wolf and his parishioners on the Raritan. The people were at first pleased that Wolf had been sent to them, but within a month he began to read his sermons instead of preaching from memory, they said. Displeased by this change, many ceased coming to the church. They also complained that Wolf did not use the customary forms for baptism and other pastoral acts, whereupon he stopped teaching catechumens and seldom visited the sick. Wolf made countercharges to the effect that the promised parsonage was never completed and that firewood and candles were not supplied as stipulated.

When the contending parties rejected all private efforts looking toward reconciliation, Berkenmeyer called a meeting of ministers and lay representatives of the congregations on the Hudson. There was precedent among the Dutch Reformed for such a "classical assembly" (that is, a meeting of a classis, or district) when a serious problem arose that could not be resolved locally. It was just such an ad hoc meeting that was convened on the Raritan in the summer of 1735.[53] The grievances of Wolf and his parishioners were aired. It can hardly be said that there was an impartial investigation of these grievances, for Berkenmeyer saw to it that most of the blame fell on the laymen. The

52.
Simon Hart and Harry J. Kreider, trans., *Protocol of the Lutheran Church in New York City, 1702–1750* (New York: New York Synod, 1958), pp. 190, 191; cf. pp. 177, 202.

53.
The fact that Berkenmeyer sometimes referred to this "classical assembly" as a "synod" led some to conclude that it was the first meeting of a regularly constituted synod in the later sense of this term. Cf. Karl Kretzmann, "The First Lutheran Synod in America," *Concordia Historical Institute Quarterly* 8 (1935): 33–36, 76–84; and a rejoinder in Kreider, *Lutheranism in Colonial New York*, pp. 92–99.

result was that Wolf did not reform and remained in the parish for another decade. In this case Berkenmeyer revealed himself as the well-intentioned leader he was, but also as a man with clericalist leanings who thought in a legalistic and literalistic fashion. He continued his ministry in this vein until his death in 1751.

Another controversy grew out of a change in the complexion of the colonists during the first half of the eighteenth century. Dutchmen had long since ceased to come to the New World, and those of their descendants who were Lutheran were outnumbered more and more by later German immigrants. In New York City, where the Dutch language was still used in church if not at home, the German newcomers accommodated themselves for a long time to services in Dutch. Their growing dissatisfaction with this was suggested, however, when they declared that they were Lutherans whose faith,

being after the method and manner of the High Dutch [Germans], and in their language, [prevents their] assembling with the other Lutherans in their present church in the said city who vary much from them, and more so on account of their constant use and practice of their religion in the Low Dutch way, and who by reason of very many ancient people as well as young ones, most of them poor, likewise in respect of the tenderness of conscience, cannot be brought over to learn their language or exercise of religion in the Low Dutch way.[54]

In 1742 the German Lutherans were numerous enough in Manhattan to request the pastor, Michael C. Knoll, to conduct occasional services in their own language. By 1745 they went further and demanded that half the services be in German. The offensive tone of the demand evoked an obstinate response:

It was proposed in the church council that half of the services should be in Dutch and half in German. . . . Laurens van Boskerk said, "No, half of the services were not permitted in German." Mr. Charles Beekman said the same, also Jacobus van Boskerk. . . . It was asked if we should leave the decision to the members of the congregation who had come to the Lord's Supper during the past ten years and who had contributed to the pastor's salary. Laurens van Boskerk said, "No." Charles Beekman answered, "No." Jacobus van Boskerk said, "No, only to those who had signed the call." . . . Shall we leave it to one of our consistories? Laurens van Boskerk, Charles Beekman, and Jacobus van Boskerk said, "No."[55]

The resistance of the Dutch elders was countered by the temporary introduction of a German impostor, John L. Hofgut.[56] In 1749, after repeated attempts to hold services in their own language, a number of Germans called John F. Ries, who had just arrived from Germany by way of Philadelphia, and organized a separate German congregation. Not all the Germans forsook the old Dutch church (in which, it was now established, there had been eight times as many German communi-

54.
E. B. O'Callaghan, ed., *Documentary History of the State of New York*, quarto ed., 4 vols. (Albany: C. V. Benthuysen, 1850–51), 3:487–88.
55.
Hart and Kreider, *Protocol*, p. 453.
56.
Ibid., pp. 331–417, 442–57. Cf. August L. Graebner, *Geschichte der Lutherischen Kirche in Amerika* (St. Louis: Concordia, 1892), 214–32 (only one volume of this work was published).

cants as there had been Dutch),[57] but significantly no session of the "classical assembly" was called to help Knoll wrestle with the problem. He resigned in frustration. In 1751 he succeeded Berkenmeyer on the upper Hudson after the latter's death. Ries followed soon after to a succession of other parishes. Knoll (and he was not the only one) failed to recognize that Dutch Lutheranism was a thing of the past in the Hudson Valley.

Meanwhile, in 1745, the leading German Lutheran minister in Pennsylvania, Henry Melchior Muhlenberg, had been asked to help arbitrate the still unresolved quarrel between Wolf and his Raritan parish in northern New Jersey. Wolf was persuaded to resign in return for a sum of money and he disappeared from the scene.[58] In 1751, when schism resulted from the language controversy in New York City, Muhlenberg was called by the old Dutch congregation there. He spent two summers trying to reconcile the divided Lutherans and preaching to them not only in Dutch but also in German and English. Afterward he supplied the lower Hudson parish with pastors, the first of whom was John A. Weygand. Shortly before this the mid-Hudson congregations (Rhinebeck, Germantown, Manorton, Ancram, and Wurtemburgh) wrote to Hamburg, Germany, for a minister, and in 1746 John Christopher Hartwick was sent. He visited Muhlenberg in Philadelphia, and Muhlenberg in turn visited Hartwick's parish, as a result of which a basis for cooperation was established between the two men. In 1743 Peter N. Sommer also came directly from Hamburg, Germany, and took charge of churches in the Mohawk and Schoharie valleys west of Albany (Schoharie, Stone Arabia, Canajoharie, and Manheim). In time virtually all of the ministers on the Hudson with the notable exception of Sommer, a son-in-law of Berkenmeyer, looked to Pennsylvania for help and leadership. All told there were thirty-one ministers (including some pretenders) who served in the territory for a longer or shorter period of time between 1703 and 1787. Not one was Dutch by nationality.

The Dutch and the German congregations in New York City that had divided in the language controversy were reunited in 1784 with assistance from John C. Kunze, a son-in-law of Muhlenberg, who moved to New York from Philadelphia in the same year. He reported that within the first year of his pastorate he had confirmed 87 persons and that there were 300 families (equivalent to not fewer than 1,000 members) in the congregation.[59] The congregations that merged had long since become exclusively German, but for the sake of the young people who were beginning to be anglicized Kunze recognized that English services would also be desirable. Since his own attempts to preach in English were not very successful, he secured younger assistants to perform this task just before the turn of the century.

From Swedish to English on the Delaware, 1703–87

Before the end of the seventeenth century the king of England had made William Penn proprietor of the colony that was named Pennsylvania after him. Penn had to attract new settlers if the colony was to prosper. To this end he pursued a vigorous

57.
Hart and Kreider, *Protocol,* pp. 431, 432.
58.
Johann L. Schulze, in *Nachrichten von den vereinigten Deutschen Evangelisch-Lutherischen Gemeinen in Nord-America* (1787), ed. William J. Mann et al., new ed., 2 vols. (Allentown and Philadelphia: Brobst, Diehl & Co., 1886–95), 1:119–35.
59.
Ibid., 2:788, 790.

policy of recruitment in the framework of a broad toleration. The consequence was that early Swedish, Finnish, and Dutch colonists were soon vastly outnumbered on the Delaware by English, Welsh, German, Scotch-Irish, and other settlers. The religious diversity that resulted was described by Justus Falckner as early as 1702:

The few Christians who are here are divided among almost countless sects, which may preferably be called factions and rabble, such as the Quakers, Anabaptists, Naturalists, Libertines, Independents, Sabbatarians, and many others. . . . The Quakers are the most numerous because the governor is an adherent of this sect. . . . The Protestants [that is, the churches as distinguished from the sects] are here divided into three confessions and nationalities. According to their confession the Protestants here . . . are either Evangelical Lutheran or Presbyterian and Calvinist. So the Protestants are also divided here into three nationalities, an English Protestant church, a Swedish Protestant Lutheran church, and people of German nationality who are of the Evangelical Lutheran or the Reformed churches.[60]

The Swedish ministers had frequent contact with adherents of other national and religious groups. As far as possible they ministered to the needs of such people. Andrew Sandel, who in 1702 succeeded Rudman when the latter left for New York, apparently had good command of the English language and occasionally conducted services in vacant Anglican churches.[61] On the other hand, John Enneberg, who was ordained in London by a Swedish clergyman on instructions from Bishop Jesper Svedberg[62] (but was not ordained episcopally any more than Falckner had been), ministered to German Lutherans in and near Philadelphia before he became pastor in Wilmington in 1731. John Dylander, who died after only four years as a pastor in Philadelphia (1737–41), also extended his ministry beyond his parish. A Swedish traveler in America reported:

When Mr. Dylander first arrived here there was no German minister, though a large number of Germans had settled in this locality. Consequently he was requested to preach to them occasionally whenever the duties of his own parish would allow it. . . . In Philadelphia he delivered three sermons every Sunday: first, one in the morning in German, then at ten o'clock a second one in Swedish, and finally, after dinner, a third one in English. . . . As a result he had no opportunity to accomplish anything else during the short time he was here than continually to travel about preaching, baptizing, administering the sacrament of Holy Communion, etc. Once a month he went up to Lancaster to hold a [German] service, although this was far from Philadelphia. He had the German church in Germantown built and preached in it at least once a month. He often said that in one week he delivered sixteen sermons.[63]

60.
Letter to Heinrich Muhlen (1702), in Georg J. Fritschel, *Geschichte der Lutherische Kirche in Amerika*, 2 vols. (Gütersloh: Bertelsmann, 1896–97), 1:36.
61.
"Extracts from the Journal of Andreas Sandel," *Pennsylvania Magazine of History and Biography* 30 (1906): 445, 446, 449.
62.
Acrelius, *History of New Sweden*, p. 288.
63.
Adolph B. Benson, ed., *The America of 1750: Peter Kalm's Travels in North America*, vols. (New York: Wilson, 1937), 2: 670–71.

Between 1697, when relations between the Church of Sweden and the Lutherans on the Delaware were restored, and the outbreak of the American Revolution, twenty-five ministers were sent abroad from Sweden. As a rule these men did not cross the ocean with the intention of remaining in the New World, and so, unless they were overtaken by an early death, most of them returned to their homeland after five to ten years of service. In fact, before they embarked from their native soil they were "assured of their return after the lapse of some years," when they would be "graciously remembered in some suitable appointment" at home.[64] Replacements were not always readily available in the old country, and because of this, as well as the long voyage from Sweden, the churches were not supplied with an unbroken succession of clergymen. The consequence was described thus by one of the ministers:

The many and long vacancies which have taken place from time to time have produced no little injury in these churches. . . . The people were compelled to call upon the nearest English ministers for their assistance so that they might have some public worship. They were thus also rendered uncertain whether any minister was to be expected from Sweden, or any who would be suitable for the congregation, and so they doubted whether the church would continue to be Swedish.[65]

Such vacancies occurred in the parishes west of the Delaware River (Philadelphia and Wilmington) but more often in the third major center (Swedesboro, N.J.), where the parish was vacant for a total of twenty-one of the forty-six years between 1703 and 1749. During such vacancies church buildings tended to be neglected and the people scattered. Moreover, the absence of Swedish clergymen and services contributed to the people's estrangement from the language of their forefathers. When Peter Kalm was traveling in New Jersey in 1750 he observed that many of the descendants of early colonists no longer spoke or even understood Swedish: "Since English is the principal language in the land, all people gradually get to speak that, and they become ashamed to talk in their own tongue because they fear that they may not in such a case be real English, . . . so that it is easy to see that the Swedish language is doomed to extinction in America."[66]

By 1742 English services were introduced alongside Swedish services. In fact, at a congregational meeting held that year in an outparish in New Jersey it was decided that "after that day no Swedish service should be held any more in the church of Penn's Neck, but always English, with prayers and ceremonies according to the Church of England."[67] Actually, Swedish services were not discontinued that abruptly because most of the ministers who came from abroad lacked facility in the use of the English language. Israel Acrelius, who is remembered especially for his informative history of New Sweden, was reluctant to accept the call to America because he was, as he confessed, "entirely ignorant of the English language."[68] Although he tried

64.
Cf. the letter of King Charles of Sweden to the archbishop of Uppsala, February 22, 1696, in Acrelius, *History of New Sweden*, p. 370.

65.
Ibid., pp. 362, 363.

66.
Benson, *America of 1750*, 2:683.

67.
Amandus Johnson, ed., *The Records of the Swedish Lutheran Churches at Raccoon and Penns Neck, 1713-1786* (Elizabeth, N.J.: Works Progress Administration, 1938), p. 20.

68.
Horace Burr, trans., *The Records of Holy Trinity (Old Swedes) Church . . .* (Wilmington, Del.: Historical Society of Delaware, 1890), pp. 414, 415.

hard, he never did become comfortable in the use of English during his half-dozen years (1749–56) on the Delaware. On the other hand, the versatile Carl Magnus Wrangel, who was in America from 1759 to 1768, was reputed to be an eloquent preacher in German and English as well as in his native Swedish. He recognized that anglicization was inevitable and he took practical steps to help his people prepare for it.[69]

The last of the long line of clergymen sent to the Delaware from Sweden was Nicholas Collin, who arrived in 1770 and served, first in Swedesboro and then in Philadelphia, until his death sixty-one years later. He had an exceptional knowledge of English when he came, but "because of the extinction of the Swedish language" among the people it was manifestly no longer necessary or even desirable to secure ministers from Sweden. Since English-speaking ministers could not be supplied by neighboring German Lutherans at the time, the charter of the church in Philadelphia was amended in 1787 to provide that "the rector and other ministers shall be in the ministry of the Lutheran or Episcopal churches and hold their faith in the doctrine of the same." Similar action was taken in the other parishes. The way was thus prepared for the immediate de facto and the later de jure transfer of the Swedish Lutheran parishes to the Protestant Episcopal Church.[70]

69.
Cf. *Documentary History of the Evangelical Lutheran Ministerium of Pennsylvania, . . . 1748–1821* (Philadelphia: General Council Board of Publication, 1898), p. 62.
70.
Cf. Nicholas Collin's own accounts of 1791 in Johnson, *Records of the Swedish Churches*, pp. 208–22; and in Clay, *Annals of the Swedes*, pp. 118–33. Cf. also Nelson W. Rightmyer, *The Anglican Church in Delaware* (Philadelphia: Church Historical Society, 1947), pp. 106–10.

2 German Colonists on the Atlantic Seaboard

Cf. Friedrich Nieper, *Die ersten deutschen Auswanderer von Krefeld nach Pennsylvanien* (Neukirchen: Erziehungsverein, 1940); Samuel W. Pennypacker, *The Settlement of Germantown, Pa., and the Beginning of German Immigration to North America* (Philadelphia: W. J. Campbell, 1899), a reprint of *Proceedings of the Pennsylvania German Society*, vol. 9.

For general orientation see Albert B. Faust, *The German Element in the United States*, 2 vols. (New York: Steuben Society, 1927), 1:1–356. For the extensive literature on the subject see the monumental 636 double-column pages) work of Emil Meynen, *Bibliographie des Deutschtums der kolonialzeitlichen Einwanderung in Nordamerika, 1683–1933* (Leipzig: Harrassowitz, 1937).

Deut. 3:20, quoted in William L. Saunders, ed., *The Colonial Records of North Carolina*, 9 vols. (Raleigh, N.C.: P. M. Hole, 1886–90), 4:18.

Both in terms of their numbers and in terms of their influence Germans played a larger part in colonial America than the Dutch or the Swedes. Although there were a few Germans scattered in the colonies before the last decades of the seventeenth century, it was not until 1683 that the first German settlement was established. Named Germantown (then located just north of Philadelphia and later incorporated in that city), the original settlement was made up of religious dissenters from the lower Rhine Valley in Germany who had been attracted to Pennsylvania by William Penn's promise of religious freedom as well as material prosperity.[1] The way was thus opened for the growing stream of German colonists that poured into the New World at the end of the seventeenth and especially during the eighteenth century.[2]

Colonists were not sent from Germany as colonists were sent from the Netherlands, Sweden, or England. No colony was established in North America by a German government as were colonies under the auspices of the Dutch, Swedish, and English governments. One reason was that Germany bore the brunt of the Thirty Years' War (1618–48) and was suffering from the consequences of that war at the time that other nations were entering upon their colonial adventures. Moreover, Germany was then a geographical designation rather than a united nation, for it was divided into hundreds of territories whose rulers insisted on their own sovereignty and seldom acted in concert. But although no colony was carved out of the New World by any German government, large numbers of German people settled in the colonies governed from England. These Germans, most of whom were from the western parts of Germany and Switzerland, were attracted by the promise of freedom in a land beyond the ocean which was alleged to be "flowing with milk and honey"[3] at a time when their lives seemed to be restricted by poverty and oppression. On the other hand, the governors and landowners in the English colonies were aware that their own prosperity depended on new labor resources and consequently encouraged the coming of German colonists. Some of these were intentionally settled on the frontier, where they served the additional function of providing a buffer against hostile Indians, Frenchmen, or Spaniards.

Among the earliest German settlers in the New World were dissenters—Mennonites, German Quakers, Dunkers, etc.—who were attracted by promises of liberty exceeding anything they had known in Europe. After 1730—by which time only a few of the dissenters were left behind—most of the newcomers were Lutheran and German Reformed, together with a few Moravians.[4] The shift from "sect" to "church" in the religious complexion of the colonists was accompanied by a great increase in numbers. Perhaps five times as many German colonists crossed the Atlantic between 1730 and the beginning of the American Revolution as had crossed the Atlantic prior to that span of forty-five years. This means that the early preponderance of "sect people" (as Mennonites, Quakers, and others were often called) was soon replaced by a predominance of "church people," and among these, especially, were Lutherans. Inasmuch as these German Lutherans were not spread out evenly among the colonies, it is desirable to trace the circumstances of their settlement colony by colony and roughly in chronological order.

The "Palatines" in New York and North Carolina

The first large migration of Germans involved the "Palatines."[5] This designation was loosely applied by contemporaries in England and America to emigrants from various German lands, partly because the majority of emigrants at the time actually came from the Palatinate, a principality in the valley of the Rhine River, and partly because the geography of Germany was unfamiliar to outsiders, who took "Palatine" to be virtually synonymous with "German." In any case, the people called Palatines came not only from the Palatinate but also from such adjacent German lands as Alsace, Baden, Wuerttemberg, Nassau, and Franconia, and even from such more remote lands as Holstein and Silesia.

Three principal impulses may be mentioned as contributing to the emigration of the Palatines. One was the widespread devastation and suffering that resulted from a century of recurring wars, beginning with the Thirty Years' War and ending with the French plundering of southwestern Germany (1707) during the War of the Spanish Succession. A second cause of the exodus was the unprecedented severity of the winter of 1708–9, when wine was reported to have frozen solid in casks and bottles, when spit was said to have congealed during its fall from lips to the ground, and when people already suffering from the consequences of war were exposed to additional hardships. Contemporaries sometimes mentioned religious persecution as a third reason for emigration. In the Palatinate, as elsewhere, the ruler determined the religion of his subjects. Ever since the Reformation the princes had been either Reformed or Lutheran until the close of the seventeenth century, when a Roman Catholic became the elector of the Palatinate. Although on his accession he promised religious toleration, it was reported that he soon took steps to confiscate Protestant property and harass Protestant subjects. A pamphlet of the time recounted this incident, among others:

At Hackenheim, three quarters of an hour from Creutzenach, a Roman priest went into a Protestant church and not only pulled the minister out of the pulpit in which he was preaching but beat him out of the church as well, and he [the priest] and those that were

4.
For a contemporary account of the wave of colonization see William J. Mann et al., eds., *Nachrichten von den vereinigten Deutschen Evangelisch-Lutherischen Gemeinen Nord-America, absonderlich in Pennsylvanien* (1787), new ed., 2 vols. (Allentown and Philadelphia: Brobst, Diehl & Co., 1886–95), 2:194–204 (hereafter cited as *Hallesche Nachrichten*). This work is popularly known as the *Hallesche Nachrichten* because it was published serially in Halle, Saxony, from 1750 to 1787. Less than half the text, without appendixes of documents and notes, has been translated into English in *Reports of the United German Evangelical Lutheran Congregations in North America*, trans. Jonathan Oswald, 2 vols. (Philadelphia: Lutheran Publication Society, 1880–81).
5.
The best treatment of the subject is Walter A. Knittle's *Early Eighteenth Century Palatine Emigration* (Philadelphia: Dorrance & Co., 1937).

with him treated most barbarously those of the congregation who, being wounded, were obliged to go out of the church to have their wounds dressed.[6]

It seems that reports of this kind were exaggerated in order to secure the sympathy and support of other Protestants. The fact that a fair number of Roman Catholics joined the Protestants in leaving the Palatinate and adjacent territories suggests that religious persecution was not as important a cause of emigration as the war and severe weather.

The unfavorable conditions in their homelands would probably not have induced the Palatines to leave if it had not been for the strong attractions of the New World. William Penn had visited western Germany and apparently influenced the dissenters who settled in Germantown in 1683. After Penn's visits there appeared brochures and books in which various writers sang the praises of the English colonies in North America. Two of these, both written by Lutherans and both widely circulated in Germany, were Daniel Falckner's *Curieuse Nachricht von Pensylvania* (1702)[7] and Joshua Kocherthal's *Ausführlich und umständlicher Bericht von . . . Carolina* (1706). It was probably the second of these that was in the mind of a British parliamentary committee which was investigating the causes of Palatine emigration when it reported:

It appeared to the Committee that there were books and papers dispersed in the Palatinate with the Queen's picture before the books and the title pages in letters of Gold (which from thence were called the Golden Book) to encourage them to come to England in order to be sent to Carolina or other of her Majesty's Plantations to be settled there. The Book is chiefly a commendation of that country.[8]

Especially impressive must have been the glorification of the colonies in terms of their temperate climate, perpetual peace, religious freedom, fertile soil, and abundance of game.

The great exodus began when a small company of fifty-five Palatines set out in 1708 under the leadership of Joshua Kocherthal, the Lutheran minister who had written about America before he had ever seen it. In the following year, 1709, the original trickle became a veritable avalanche as about 13,500 people descended the Rhine. Gifts of charity received on the way made it possible for the emigrants to reach Rotterdam, from which they were transported to London at the reluctant expense of the English government. Alms were gathered to feed and house "the poor Palatines," and several ministers of Lutheran congregations in London did what they could to give the people physical as well as spiritual help in their temporary camps. Many proposals were made to dispose of the homeless Palatines. Some were settled in Ireland, others enlisted in the British army or navy, and a few were absorbed by English crafts and farms. More were transported on ten ships to New York City in 1710. Some two thousand were settled about eighty miles up the Hudson River, where towns like Newburgh, West

23

om a letter to an English gentleman reproduced in Hugh Hastings, ed., *Ecclesiastical Records, State of New York*, 7 vols. (Albany: James B. Lyon, 1901–16), 3:1456 ereafter cited as *N.Y. Eccles. Records*).

r a reproduction of this book in English well as in German see Julius F. Sachse, ., *Falckner's "Curieuse Nachricht von Pensylvania"* [sic] (Philadelphia, 1905), a reprint *Proceedings of the Pennsylvania German Society*, vol. 14.

Y. Eccles. Records, 3:1729.

Camp, Rhinebeck, and Germantown still mark those early settlements.

In return for their passage to America and in payment for their subsistence on the land assigned to them, the Palatines contracted to produce tar, hemp, and shipmasts for the British government. The covenant which the Palatines were required to sign stated:

We, the underwritten persons, natives of the lower
Palatinate of the Rhine, have been subsisted, maintained
and supported ever since our arrival in this Kingdom [of
England] by the great and christian charity of her
Majesty, the Queen [Anne], and of many of her good
subjects, and . . . her Majesty has been graciously
pleased to order and advance a loan . . . toward the
transporting, maintaining and settling of us and our
respective families in her Majesty's Province of New
York in America and toward the employing of us . . . in
the production and manufacture of all manner of needful
stores.[9]

9.
Ibid., p. 1814.
10.
Ibid., pp. 1811–12.

The Hudson River was selected because the Palatines were expected to protect the frontier "not only with regard to the French in Canada but against any Insurrection of the Scattered Nations of Indians" and because of the location there of "very great numbers of Pines fit for production of Turpentine and Tarr, out of which Rozin and Pitch are made."[10]

The German settlers, most of whom had been farmers and vinedressers in the old country, were unhappy with their new tasks. Presumably they were not very productive either, for the authorities were disappointed with the results. Within a few years the whole project was abandoned and the Palatines were told to shift for themselves. Some remained in their original habitations, but others migrated southward to New York City and northern New Jersey, and still others moved northward to the Schoharie Valley. Despite opposition from the colonial authorities several settlements were established (in 1712 and succeeding years) in and near the town of Schoharie, west of Albany, New York. Because of continued opposition some of the Palatines moved farther into the nearby Mohawk Valley and established settlements in such places as German Flats, Palatine, and Canajoharie. Others cut their way to the Susquehanna River, followed it southward to the Swatara and Tulpehocken creeks, and settled (1723) in and near Womelsdorf, a few miles west of Reading, Pennsylvania.

In addition to the Palatines who settled in New York after 1709 there were other Palatines, probably attracted by Kocherthal's book descriptive of the Carolinas, who found their way to the South. Under the leadership especially of Christopher von Graffenried, a native of Bern, Switzerland, an arrangement was made to secure a large parcel of land from the colonial government in North Carolina and another arrangement was made with representatives of Queen Anne to pay the cost of transporting 650 Palatines to that land. Supplemented by a smaller company of Swiss emigrants, the Palatines set sail from England

Vincent H. Todd and Julius Goebel,
s., *Christoph von Graffenried's Account of the
nding of New Bern* (Raleigh, N.C.:
rth Carolina Historical Commission,
20).

Y. Eccles. Records, 3:1737, 1747.

d., pp. 1708–9.

nrad Weiser's autobiography as quoted
Paul A. W. Wallace, *Conrad Weiser,
'end of Colonist and Mohawk* (Philadel-
ia: University of Pennsylvania Press,
45), p. 27.

in 1710. Those who survived the difficult crossing settled at the mouth of the Neuse River in the place thereafter named New Bern. The colonists suffered want and hunger as a result of miscalculations and experienced death or destruction at the hand of hostile Indians.[11] The survivors were scattered and in time lost their ethnic and religious identity.

Several attempts were made in England to determine the precise religious affiliation of the Palatine emigrants. The lists that were made are incomplete, but there is no reason to suppose that a complete religious census would have revealed different proportions. Roman Catholics, except for the few who were willing to renounce their faith, were refused aid by the self-consciously Protestant Queen Anne and were sent back to the Continent. Mennonites, Baptists, and others comprised only 1 percent of the total number of Protestants. The vast majority were Reformed and Lutheran, the former making up slightly more than half and the latter slightly less than half.[12]

Most of the colonists who settled in New Bern, North Carolina, and who were soon dispersed may be assumed to have been Reformed. Neither these nor the Lutheran minority among them had the services of ministers of their own tongue and faith. On the other hand, the Palatines who settled on the Hudson River were accompanied by a Reformed minister and a Lutheran minister. The former, John F. Haeger, was given an annual salary by the Society for the Propagation of the Gospel in Foreign Parts on condition that he submit to Anglican ordination. He did so and traveled from one Palatine settlement to another to minister to his own people. Kocherthal became a similar itinerant among the Lutherans on the Hudson after the British Board of Trade promised him financial support. The board had no precedent, it declared, for "a salary settled upon Foreign Clergymen in the Plantations."

However, as the said Kocherthal is very poor and not capable of maintaining himself, his wife and three children by his own labor and that the Lutherans who go over with him are not in a condition to make him any allowance, We humbly offer that Lord Lovelace have Directions to Grant to the said Minister a Reasonable portion of land for a glebe, not exceeding five hundred acres, And that he be permitted to sell a suitable Proportion thereof for his better Maintenance, 'till he shall be in a condition to live by the produce of the Rest.[13]

Kocherthal received some help from Justus Falckner, who was pastor of the Dutch Lutheran congregations on the Hudson, and when Kocherthal died in 1719 Falckner assumed the whole burden insofar as he was able. Thereafter William C. Berkenmeyer, Peter N. Sommer, and John C. Kunze were among the ministers on the Hudson. Some people seldom saw a minister of their own confession. So it was reported that in Schoharie "the people lived fairly peaceably for some years without preachers and without magistrates. Each man did what seemed right to him."[14] There may have been as many as ten thousand people of Lutheran background in New York by the time of the Revolution, but there were only twenty-five churches, including preaching points, to reach them.

The Coming of the German Redemptioners

After 1720 Germans continued to cross the Atlantic in even larger numbers. As before, some came from the Palatinate, but more came from other German lands. They responded to the pressing need in North America for labor and to their own desire for more favorable living conditions. The extravagant hopes that some were led to entertain are reported, for example, in this statement:

People were led to believe that all the fields in America are Elysian fields which seed themselves without effort and work, that the hills are full of pure gold and silver, that nothing but milk and honey bubbles out of the springs, etc. Whoever goes to America as a servant will become a lord, whoever goes as a maid will become a gracious lady, whoever goes as a farmer will become a nobleman, whoever goes as a townsman and craftsman will become a baron. The government is chosen by the people and can be deposed again at will.[15]

Attempts were made to counteract such propaganda of colonial land agents and shipmasters. A recent arrival from Germany warned that his countrymen would be "the biggest fools if they really believe that in America . . . roasted pigeons are going to fly into their mouths,"[16] that as a matter of fact they would have to work harder in America than in Europe. Few who had decided to emigrate seem to have been dissuaded by such warnings. So great was the attraction of the New World that many were willing to sell themselves into a period of bondage to pay for their passage across the ocean. Such persons were called indentured servants or redemptioners. Other nationalities were also involved in the system of "white servitude." As far as the Germans are concerned it has been estimated that somewhere between one-half and two-thirds of all the German colonists who arrived in North America between 1720 and 1775 came as redemptioners.[17]

The usual route taken by redemptioners was the same as that taken by other German emigrants. They descended the Rhine to Rotterdam or traveled in some other way to a port on the North Sea. If their homeland was as far away as Wuerttemberg or Switzerland this part of the journey sometimes took months and contributed to the impoverishment even of those who started out with some means. In the North Sea port they arranged with a shipmaster to transport them to the New World. Since most of the emigrants lacked the price for passage they agreed to work off the cost of their passage upon arriving in America. The voyage across the Atlantic often took eight to twelve weeks, depending on the winds. Passengers were said to be "packed into the ships as if they were herring."[18] Sickness (increased by the congestion), shipwreck, piracy, and shortage

15.
Report of Henry M. Muhlenberg (176[ ]) in *Hallesche Nachrichten*, 2:460.
16.
Gottlieb Mittelberger, *Journey to Pennsylvania* (1750), ed. and trans. Oscar Handlin and John Clive (Cambridge, Mass.: Harvard University Press, 1960), p. 21.
17.
Abbott E. Smith, *Colonists in Bondage: White Servitude and Convict Labor in America 1607-1776* (Chapel Hill, N.C.: University of North Carolina Press, 1947), pp. 32[ ]336.
18.
Report of Peter Brunnholz (1750) in *Hallesche Nachrichten*, 1:531.

of food and water were dangers not infrequently encountered at sea. A passenger in 1742 reported in his autobiography:

Today we had no wind at all, only calm. We took counsel together as to how to keep alive for several days without water. The captain said that . . . he had hidden several dozen bottles of vinegar and that when mixed with olive oil and taken in small quantities the liquid might help [to allay thirst]. When he showed us the place where the bottles were hidden, rat dirt was found there, crumbled corks or stoppers were lying on the floor nearby, and several bottles were open and half-empty. The mystery was solved by vigilant observation: a rat inserted its tail in an open bottle, withdrew it when it was sopping wet, and sucked off the vinegar [from the tail]. As far down as the tail reached the bottle was empty. Some insisted that this could not happen and that it must have been sorcery. But necessity is the mother of invention. After all, who taught the hordes of rats to enter our sleeping quarters at night, climb up on our beds, and lick the sweat off the people while they were asleep? . . . Thirst tormented the rats as much as the people.[19]

When a ship finally reached port in North America—Halifax, Boston, New York, Philadelphia, Annapolis, Baltimore, or Charleston—those unable to pay for their passage offered their service in return for the payment of their indebtedness. A typical advertisement inserted in a port newspaper by the captain of a ship on its arrival read:

German redemptioners! The Dutch ship "Miss Johanna," Captain H. H. Bleeker, has arrived from Amsterdam with a number of farmers, day laborers, and artificers whose stipulated time [of service] is to be sold. There are both male and female adults as well as some handsome boys and girls. All who wish to be provided with good servants are requested to apply to the shipmaster or captain.[20]

There was considerable inflation in the cost of the voyage across the Atlantic—from an average of £10 in 1722 to £20 in 1772. Generally adults could repay the amount advanced for their passage by working as servants for four or five years. Children often had to serve until they were twenty-one years of age. Members of families were sometimes separated. An observer reported:

Young people of both sexes are taken first, and their lot is either good or bad, better or worse, depending on the character of those who purchased them and the providence or permission of God. . . . Nobody wants to buy old married couples, widows, or infirm persons because there is already a surplus of poor and unusable people who are becoming a burden to the commonwealth. If they have healthy children, however, the passage of the old folks is added to that of their children, and the latter must serve just that much longer,

[i]nrich Melchior Mühlenberg, *Selbstbio-[gra]phie, 1711-1743*, ed. W. Germann (Al-[lent]own, Pa.: Brobst, Diehl & Co., 1881), [pp.] 98–99.

[qu]oted in Rudolf Cronau, *Drei Jahrhun-[dert]e deutschen Lebens in Amerika* (Berlin: D. [Re]imer, 1909), p. 119.

are accordingly sold at a higher price, and are scattered far and wide among all sorts of nationalities, languages, and tongues. The consequence is that the aged parents, and even their sons and daughters, almost never see one another the rest of their lives and forget their mother tongue.[21]

Germans in Pennsylvania and on Its Frontier

German colonists, whose number was greatly increased after 1720 by redemptioners, did not as a rule follow their Palatine forerunners by making their homes in New York or eastern North Carolina. Instead, most of them turned to Pennsylvania, probably not, as suggested, because the Palatines in the Hudson and Schoharie valleys warned their countrymen on the other side of the Atlantic that "their liberties and privileges were infringed upon" in New York,[22] but because since the time of William Penn the colony had received more and better publicity.[23] Precisely how many Germans arrived in Pennsylvania during the colonial period cannot be determined, in spite of the requirement that all immigrant ships and their passengers be registered in the port of Philadelphia. The lists of ships and passengers show that over 65,000 Germans entered the port between 1727 and 1775.[24] Not all known names are recorded, however, and so these ship lists are incomplete even for the limited years which they cover.[25]

In any case the increasing numbers of Germans in Pennsylvania alarmed some contemporaries. As early as 1717 Governor William Keith questioned whether the introduction into Pennsylvania of so many people who were strangers to the language and constitution of the colony might not be of "dangerous consequence." It was in this connection that shipmasters were first ordered to report the number of foreigners who had been brought into the colony and that such immigrants were required to testify by oath or otherwise that they were "well affected to his Majesty and his Government."[26] A decade later Governor Patrick Gordon expressed fear that the Germans, "being ignorant of our Language & Laws, & settling in a body together, [will] make, as it were, a distinct people from his Majesties Subjects."[27] Still later, in 1751, when Germans were streaming into Pennsylvania in even larger numbers, Benjamin Franklin put his misgivings into words which were afterward quoted against him by political opponents: "Why should the Palatine boors be suffered to swarm into our settlements and, by herding together, establish their language and manners to the exclusion of ours? Why should Pennsylvania, founded by the English, become a colony of aliens, who will shortly be so numerous as to Germanize us instead of our Anglifying them?"[28] Other opinions of Germans were not so negative. For example, Governor George Thomas declared that the flourishing condition of Pennsylvania in 1738 was due in large measure to the industry of the German inhabitants.[29]

Before the American Revolution, German immigrants and their descendants comprised somewhere between one-third and

21.
Report of Henry M. Muhlenberg (1769) in *Hallesche Nachrichten*, 2:461. For an evaluation of the whole system see Cheesman A. Herrick, *White Servitude in Pennsylvania* (Philadelphia: J. J. McVey, 1926), pp. 267–85.
22.
Adolph B. Benson, ed., *The America of 1750: Peter Kalm's Travels in North America*, vols. (New York: Wilson, 1937), 1:142–43; cf. 1:616.
23.
Cf. Knittle, *Palatine Emigration*, pp. 210–27; for the older theory see Sanford H. Cobb, *The Story of the Palatines* (New York: G. P. Putnam, 1897), pp. 263–303.
24.
Ralph B. Strassburger and William J. Hinke, eds., *Pennsylvania German Pioneers: Original Lists of Arrivals in the Port of Philadelphia from 1727 to 1808*, 3 vols. (Norristown, Pa.: Pennsylvania German Society, 1934).
25.
Cf. Smith, *Colonists in Bondage*, pp. 320–2
26.
Minutes of the Provincial Council of Pennsylvania (Harrisburg, Pa.: Theodore Fenn, 1851–52), 3:29.
27.
Ibid., pp. 282–83.
28.
In "Observations on the Increase of Mankind and the Peopling of Countries" (1751), in *The Writings of Benjamin Franklin*, ed. Albert H. Smyth, 10 vols. (New York: Macmillan, 1905–7), 3:197. Cf. Carl Van Doren, *Benjamin Franklin* (New York: Viking Press, 1938), pp. 218, 315.
29.
Minutes of the Provincial Council of Pennsylvania, 4:315.

30.
Cf. Herrick, *White Servitude*, p. 180.
31.
Report of Henry M. Muhlenberg, *Halle-sche Nachrichten*, 1:342.
32.
Diary of Baron George F. von Reck in George Fenwick Jones, ed., *Detailed Reports on the Salzburger Emigrants, 1733-1734* (Athens, Ga.: University of Georgia Press, 1968), p. 120.
33.
John Philip Fresenius, *Pastoral-Sammlungen* 12 (Spring 1752): 181–227. For an English translation see Henry Harbaugh, *The Life of Rev. Michael Schlatter* (Philadelphia: Lindsay & Blakiston, 1857), p. 201.
34.
Hallesche Nachrichten, 1:411. Cf. Theodore E. Schmauk, *A History of the Lutheran Church in Pennsylvania, 1638-1820* (Philadelphia: General Council, 1903), 1:28, 226–29 (this is the only volume published).
35.
Hallesche Nachrichten, 2:207.

one-half of the total population of Pennsylvania.[30] From Philadelphia, the port of entry for virtually all of them, they gradually spread farther and farther into the interior. Redemptioners who had completed their terms of service and had become freemen were especially eager to join other Germans and the Scotch-Irish in moving to the frontier. They appeared to the north in such towns as Easton and Allentown, to the west in such towns as Reading, Lancaster, and York, and in the open countryside between towns. In the year 1747 the following report was made:

For the most part our German Evangelical [Lutheran] inhabitants in Pennsylvania were the last to come into this colony. The English and German Quakers, the Inspired, the Mennonites, the Separatists, and members of other similar sects came during the first years while the land was still cheap. Such people chose the best and richest regions and since then have increased the value of their holdings. When in later years the poor Evangelical [Lutheran] people followed in their footsteps and came into this land in large numbers, a few still found some rich soil here and there. Most of them, however, are required to labor for several years as servants in order to pay for their passage and then have to be content with poor land on which to eat bread by the abundant sweat of their brows. Finally even poor land was no longer available. . . . Accordingly they are moving farther and farther into the uncultivated wilderness. Meanwhile those who still have some land of their own have large families, and some of the children are compelled to move away from their homesteads.[31]

The freedom that attracted people to Pennsylvania made this colony the home of a variety of churches and sects. A visitor to Pennsylvania, Baron George F. von Reck, wrote in his diary in 1734: "All religions and sects are represented here: Lutherans, Reformed, Episcopalians, Presbyterians, Catholics, Quakers, Dunkers, Mennonites, Sabbatarians, Seventh-Day Baptists, Separatists, Boehmists, Schwenkfelders, Tuchfelders, Wellwishers, Jews, heathen, etc."[32] How many Lutherans there were in colonial Pennsylvania cannot be stated with absolute certainty. The German Reformed leader Michael Schlatter estimated in 1751 that there were thirty-eight Reformed churches in the colony at that time with a total of 30,000 Reformed people.[33] Contemporaries thought it fair to suggest that there were again as many (that is, 60,000) Lutherans in Pennsylvania at the same time.[34] Not all of these were in organized congregations. The literature of the time abounds with references to dispersed and forsaken Lutherans. "Many thousands," it was reported, "must live wretchedly without preachers and books." Many "weep bitterly over their spiritual neglect."[35] When it was estimated therefore that there were 60,000 Lutherans in Pennsylvania in 1751 (and when we extend this figure and conjecture that there must have been 65,000 by the time of the Revolution) it must not be supposed that so many actually had access to churches and ministers, although with the passing of time more and more ministers came from Europe.

The earliest German Lutheran services in Pennsylvania were conducted occasionally by clergymen ministering to the Swedes. No permanent German congregation came into being until 1703, when people began to assemble for worship in New Hanover. There was a similar congregation in Germantown by 1728 and in Philadelphia by 1730. These were served by such men as Anthony J. Henkel, John C. Schulze, and John Caspar Stoever, Jr., who came to Pennsylvania uncalled and whose itinerant ministry extended to such places as Tulpehocken, New Holland, Lancaster, and York, Pennsylvania. The lay leaders of three congregations in southeastern Pennsylvania (Philadelphia, Trappe, and New Hanover) were not satisfied with existing conditions and decided in 1734 to unite for the purpose of making a joint appeal for pastors and financial aid from Germany.

These three congregations have united in the name of God and with prayers for God's gracious support and help in order to secure upright and able ministers, to build a church or meetinghouse in each place so that their services may hereafter be conducted decently and the Word of God may be proclaimed to them, and (not less important) to establish several accessible schools for the instruction of their children.[36]

After long and frustrating negotiations, Henry M. Muhlenberg was sent in 1742 by the foundation in Halle, Saxony, the result of the charitable impulses initiated by the pietist leader August Herman Francke (1663–1727). Muhlenberg gradually extended his influence beyond the congregations which had originally called him until he established contact, in person or by correspondence, with Lutherans in all parts of North America. He instilled new life in existing congregations and helped to found new ones. Such was his influence that he came to be called the patriarch of the Lutheran church in North America.[37]

The number of Germans in Pennsylvania did not continue to grow as rapidly after 1751 because many migrated to other colonies. It was natural that some should cross the Delaware River from Philadelphia and settle in southern New Jersey, as Swedes and Finns had done earlier. For example, after 1726 German Lutherans in and near Friesburg, New Jersey, were served from time to time by Swedish and then by German ministers.[38] About fifteen years before, some Germans who had participated in the great Palatine emigration of 1710 also began to migrate from New York City to such places in northern New Jersey as Hackensack, Oldwick, and Long Valley, where they had been preceded by the Dutch.[39] These people were related to New York City, even as those in southern New Jersey tended to look to Philadelphia for ecclesiastical assistance. Altogether there were twenty-two congregations in New Jersey, and there must have been eight thousand people of Lutheran heritage.

More extensive was the westward movement of Germans as far as the Allegheny Mountains in Pennsylvania and thence

36.
Ibid., 1:50.
37.
Cf. William J. Mann, *Life and Times of Henry Melchior Muhlenberg*, 2d ed. (Philadelphia: General Council, 1911); Paul A. W. Wallace, *The Muhlenbergs of Pennsylvania* (Philadelphia: University of Pennsylvania, 1950).
38.
Israel Acrelius, *A History of New Sweden* (1759), trans. William M. Reynolds (Philadelphia: Historical Society of Pennsylvania, 1874), pp. 252, 328; *Hallesche Nachrichten*, 1:269–70; *The Journals of Henry Melchior Muhlenberg*, ed. and trans. Theodore G. Tappert and John W. Doberstein, 3 vols. (Philadelphia: Muhlenberg Press, 1942–58), 2:280–86.
39.
John C. Honeyman, "Zion, St. Paul's, and Other Early Lutheran Churches in Central New Jersey," *Proceedings of the New Jersey Historical Society*, n.s. 13 (1928): 255–73.

southwestward to Maryland, Virginia, and the Carolinas. This migration began by 1730 and gradually increased. Muhlenberg referred to it in 1747, when he wrote:

I have noticed that within the five years that I have been here hardly half of the original members of my country congregations have remained. Some of those who left departed this life, but most of them have moved a great distance . . . to the frontier of Pennsylvania and to Maryland and Virginia. Meanwhile the congregations have not become smaller, but instead have grown, because every year more and more Germans are coming in.[40]

Seven years later the same writer explained that the continuing movement of Germans "into the wilderness" was caused by the fact that "the lands bordering on the ocean . . . have been filled up with inhabitants."[41]

Maryland, Virginia, and the Carolinas

A few Germans, coming directly from Europe and landing in Annapolis or Baltimore, settled on lands bordering on Chesapeake Bay. That some were Lutheran as well as Reformed is evident from the gathering of people for public worship in Baltimore. There the Lutherans were visited every other month by John G. Bager, pastor in York, Pennsylvania. It was not in the tidewater section of Maryland, however, that most of the Germans were found during the colonial period. The western frontier of the colony attracted land-hungry Germans, not only from eastern Maryland but also from Pennsylvania. Many of the latter pressed southwestward by way of York and Hanover, Pennsylvania, into the countryside around Frederick and Hagerstown, Maryland. They were encouraged by the governor of Maryland, who, "being Desirous to Increase the Number of Honest people within our Province of Maryland and willing to give suitable Encouragement to such as come and Reside therein," made liberal offers of land "on any of the back Lands on the Northern and Western Boundarys of our said province."[42] Beginning in 1734 John Caspar Stoever, Jr., made annual visits from Pennsylvania to minister to the Lutherans in western Maryland, and he was succeeded by other clergymen. By the eve of the American Revolution there were about 20,000 inhabitants of German background in Maryland. Perhaps as many as two-thirds of these were nominally Lutheran, but there were only twenty-one churches, all but one (the congregation in Baltimore) in western Maryland.

In Virginia, as in Maryland, only a few Germans settled in the tidewater areas during the colonial period. The first Lutheran congregation in Virginia was formed in Madison, just east of the Blue Ridge. John Caspar Stoever, Sr., was called as pastor there in 1733 but died five years later while returning from a collection tour in Europe. His place was taken by George S. Klug, who was called from Prussia and who served the congregation about thirty years.[43] Most of the Germans in Virginia settled west of the Blue Ridge, in the Shenandoah Valley, after

9.
Hallesche Nachrichten, 1:342.
1.
Ibid., 2:207.
2.
W. H. Browne et al., eds., *Archives of Maryland*, 65 vols. (Baltimore, 1883-1952), 3:25-26; quoted in Dieter Cunz, *The Maryland Germans* (Princeton: Princeton University Press, 1948), pp. 58-59. On the subject in general see also Abdel Ross Wentz, *History of the Evangelical Lutheran Synod of Maryland, 1820-1920* (Harrisburg, Pa.: Evangelical Press, 1920), pp. 11-38.
3.
A brief account by Stoever is reproduced in translation in William E. Eisenberg, *The Lutheran Church in Virginia, 1717-1962* (Roanoke, Va.: Virginia Synod, 1967), pp. 11-13. See also Klaus Wust, *The Virginia Germans* (Charlottesville, Va.: University of Virginia Press, 1969), pp. 3-89.

having migrated from Pennsylvania and journeyed southwestward through Maryland. In the valley the Lutherans lived alongside fellow Germans who were Reformed, Moravians, Mennonites, and Dunkers, and they assembled for worship in such towns as Winchester, Strasburg, Woodstock, and New Market, Virginia. Services were sometimes conducted by schoolmasters or other laymen, occasionally by itinerant ministers from Pennsylvania, and more often than not by impostors who "set themselves up as preachers and exercise the office without any ordination or examination whatsoever."[44] In spite of this neglect many Lutherans adhered tenaciously to the faith of their fathers. In 1772 Peter Muhlenberg, the patriarch's eldest son, became a resident pastor, and after the Revolution Christian Streit undertook the care of congregations in the valley. Of an estimated 25,000 Germans in colonial Virginia at this time, almost half may have had a Lutheran background, but there were only eighteen Lutheran churches.

Some of the Germans who migrated into the Valley of Virginia, as the Shenandoah Valley was also called, continued southward across the Dan River to the Yadkin Valley in the Piedmont section of North Carolina. The earliest of them settled near Salisbury and Cabarrus, North Carolina, in 1747. Shortly after this they built log churches—Lutherans often uniting with the Reformed in their construction—which were also used as schools. In the absence of ordained clergymen services were conducted by laymen, often by schoolmasters. Since there was no prospect of securing a minister from Pennsylvania, where there was a continuing shortage of clergymen, two laymen were sent to Europe in 1772 to get help. In response Adolph Nussmann was sent to North Carolina the next year by the Lutheran consistory of Hanover, in northwestern Germany. John G. Arndt was sent at the same time as schoolmaster, but within two years he was ordained because the need for ministers was greater than the demand for schoolmasters.[45] It has been estimated that by the time of the American Revolution there were 15,000 Germans in North Carolina,[46] of whom about 8,000 may be presumed to have been Lutheran. But there were only fifteen churches, including preaching points, and accordingly many of those who were nominally Lutheran remained unchurched.

Unlike the Germans in North Carolina, most of the Germans who settled in South Carolina entered the colony directly from the sea, Charleston serving as the port of entry. As elsewhere, not a few of these Germans arrived as indentured servants. For example, in 1751 the following advertisement appeared in a Charleston newspaper: "About 200 German *Passengers,* amongst them are several handicraft Tradesmen and Husbandmen, and likely young Boys and Girls: They are to be indented for a term of Years to any Person who will pay their Passages."[47] Germans settled not only in Charleston and its environs but also on the upper Congaree and Edisto rivers which flowed into the sea. Thus they pushed into the interior of the colony and settled in and near such places as Lexington, Newberry, and Ehrhardt. In

44.
Journals of Muhlenberg, 1:533; cf. William E. Eisenberg, *This Heritage: The Story of Lutheran Beginnings in the Lower Shenandoah Valley* (Winchester, Va.: Grace Church, 1954), pp. 22-40.
45.
Carl Hammer, Jr., *Rhinelanders on the Yadkin* (Salisbury, N.C.: Rowan Printing Co. 1943), pp. 35-52.
46.
Cf. Jacob L. Morgan et al., eds., *History of the Lutheran Church in North Carolina* (n.p., 1953), p. 18.
47.
Quoted in Warren B. Smith, *White Servitude in Colonial South Carolina* (Columbia, S.C.: University of South Carolina Press, 1961), p. 52.

1788 there were at least fifteen German churches in the interior of South Carolina; of these nine (not including the large church founded in Charleston in 1743) were Lutheran and the rest were Reformed.[48] By no means all of the nominal Lutherans in colonial South Carolina, comprising perhaps 3,000, were gathered up in these congregations.

The Salzburg Refugees and Others in Georgia

Except for the great Palatine emigration that brought many to New York and North Carolina between 1708 and 1710, most Germans who crossed the Atlantic in the eighteenth century made the voyage as families. It was also by families that the Germans migrated within the colonies from seaport to the interior or from New York to Pennsylvania and from Pennsylvania to Maryland, Virginia, and the Carolinas. Some of the Germans who settled in Georgia, however, arrived in large groups under government auspices. They were natives of Salzburg, a mountainous principality in present-day Austria. Subjects of a ruler who was a Roman Catholic archbishop, the emigrants belonged to a Lutheran minority and had again and again suffered persecution. In 1727 a new crisis occurred when Archbishop Leopold Anthony von Firmian became the ruler. He resolved to rid his land of dissenters and declared, "I would rather have thorns and thistles on my fields than Protestants in my land."[49] He introduced repressive measures. To his astonishment as many as 19,000 peasants defiantly registered as adherents of the Augsburg Confession. The archbishop thereupon prohibited public meetings, arrested Lutheran leaders in an attempt to undermine the opposition, and refused others the right to baptism, marriage, and burial. Finally, on October 31, 1731—the day commemorating the beginning of the Reformation—an "emigration patent" was published. By the terms of this official decree all Protestants were ordered to leave Salzburg promptly for having conspired against the ruler. Only by recanting and returning to the Catholic fold could expulsion be avoided.

Few took this recourse, and so the exodus began. In groups ranging from one hundred to one thousand the Salzburg Lutherans left their native villages to trudge northward. All together there were about 30,000 refugees. When groups of them reached Protestant soil they were received with great enthusiasm. Typical is a contemporaneous account of the arrival of five hundred Salzburgers in a town in Thuringia:

As the procession moved into the city all joined in singing "A Mighty Fortress Is Our God," "I Am a Poor Exile," and other hymns appropriate to the occasion. Townsmen broke ranks to lend a helping hand to the aged by grasping their arms and leading them on their way. Children were taken from the arms of their mothers, were kissed and embraced by welcoming townsfolk. . . . On the day following, Thursday, religious services were conducted for the honored guests and, as was customary, when they departed they were given money and personal apparel.[50]

8.
Cf. George D. Bernheim, *History of the German Settlements . . . in North and South Carolina* (Philadelphia: Lutheran Book Store, 1872), pp. 288–311. Cf. Paul G. McCullough et al., *A History of the Lutheran Church in North Carolina* (Columbia, S.C.: South Carolina Synod, 1971), pp. 11–149.

9.
Quoted in Georg Loesche, *Geschichte des Protestantismus im vormaligen und im neuen Oesterreich*, 3d ed. (Vienna: J. Klinkhardt, 1930), p. 274. Cf. Gerhard Florey, *Bischöfe, Ketzer, Emigranten* (Graz: Hermann Böhlau, 1967), pp. 97–173. The medieval principle of *cujus regio ejus religio*, "the religion of the people is determined by their ruler," was revived in the terms of the Peace of Westphalia (1648) which brought the Thirty Years' War to a formal close and was often applied by Protestants as well as Roman Catholics.

0.
Quoted in Carl Mauelshagen, *Salzburg Lutheran Expulsion and Its Impact* (New York: Vantage Press, 1962), p. 122.

It was about this time that a charter was granted (1732) to James Oglethorpe and some other philanthropists in England for the establishment of the new colony of Georgia. The colony was intended to serve as a buffer between the English in the Carolinas and the Spaniards in Florida. Oglethorpe was also interested, however, in providing a refuge abroad for English debtors and "for the distressed Salzburgers and other Protestants." The Society for the Promotion of Christian Knowledge (S.P.C.K.), a benevolent society formed in England a generation earlier, at once offered to pay for the transportation of some Salzburgers out of charitable gifts gathered from Protestants all over Europe. Englishmen had become aware of the Salzburgers when Samuel Urlsperger, senior of the Lutheran clergy in Augsburg and a corresponding member of the S.P.C.K. since his early ministry to German Lutherans in London, wrote an account of the exiles for his acquaintances in England. Thus Urlsperger became a mediator between Salzburgers who reached Augsburg in their flight northward and the English society which offered some of them free passage to Georgia. In fact, he selected those who were to go, provided them with instructions for the journey,[51] and remained their patron and supporter after their arrival in America.[52]

The first contingent of Salzburgers who accepted the offer to go overseas sailed from Rotterdam, and after a perilous voyage they arrived in Charleston in the spring of 1734. Two Lutheran ministers, John M. Boltzius and his assistant Israel C. Gronau, accompanied the first refugees. Within seven years four shiploads of Salzburgers arrived in Georgia, and some individual families followed in later years, bringing the total to about three hundred men, women, and children. Most of them eventually established a settlement, called Ebenezer, about twenty-five miles up the winding river from Savannah. It was a homogeneous community, and for years it was governed by the clergy in civil as well as religious matters.[53] Although the soil and the climate proved to be poor, John Wesley (who at this time was a young Anglican clergyman in Georgia) remarked on the progress made by the settlers when he visited them in 1737. "The industry of this people is quite surprising," he wrote.[54] Twelve years later Boltzius wrote to Wesley (who was now back in England):

We have two large houses for public worship, one in town, the other in the middle of our plantations; two schools in the same places; two corn-mills, one pounding mill for rice, and one saw-mill. . . . We are still in the favor of the honorable Society for Promoting Christian Knowledge, as also of many good Christians in Germany who love us, pray fervently for us, and contribute all in their power to promote our spiritual and temporal prosperity.[55]

By the time of the American Revolution there were about one thousand Salzburgers and their descendants in Georgia, not all of whom remained in Ebenezer. They began to be dispersed in adjacent regions, where the pastors occasionally tried to minis-

51.
Cf. George Fenwick Jones, ed., *Henry Newman's Salzburger Letterbooks* (Athens, Ga.: University of Georgia Press, 1966), pp. 348–50.
52.
Urlsperger edited and published reports from Georgia periodically in the two series, *Ausführliche Nachricht von den Saltzburgischen Emigranten* (Halle: Waisenhaus, 1735–52), and *Amerikanisches Ackerwerk Gottes* (Augsburg, 1754–67). A small part of the former work has been edited in translation by Jones in *Salzburger Emigrants*; some material not included in the German publication is supplied from original manuscripts in English translation, e.g., cf. 3:133–37, 271–321.
53.
Cf. Reba C. Strickland, *Religion and the State in Georgia in the Eighteenth Century* (New York: Columbia University Press, 1939), pp. 71–76.
54.
Nehemiah Curnock, ed., *The Journal of John Wesley*, 8 vols. (London: Epworth Press, 1938), 1:375.
55.
Ibid., 3:433–34.

ter to them. Germans other than Salzburgers also found their way to Georgia, and it has been estimated that there were five thousand in all by the time of the Revolution. Many of these were Reformed and Moravian, so it is not likely that there were more than two thousand nominal Lutherans, the largest concentrations in Savannah and Ebenezer. The Revolution itself hastened the decline of the Ebenezer community, and in time the church, which still stands, became an historical landmark rather than an active congregation.[56]

Settlements in New England and Nova Scotia

From the southernmost English colony we turn now to the far north, and first to New England. A few Germans who entered the colonies in early years through the port of Boston soon lost their identity. In 1749 the General Court of Massachusetts voted to encourage "foreign Protestants" to settle there,[57] but only a few traces can be found of the Germans who seem to have been attracted. More visible success attended an attempt at colonization in Maine, which was then a part of Massachusetts. When he was in Boston on other business, a German named Peter Waldo became interested in land speculation. Together with several associates he bought a tract of land in the present state of Maine and went to Germany to secure colonists for it. In 1740 he induced forty families from Saxony and Brunswick to settle in the place he named Waldoboro. Other Germans followed, but the intense cold of the winters and the hostility of neighboring Indians made life difficult. Most of the settlers were Lutheran. In early years a schoolmaster conducted services for them. The first Lutheran minister, John M. Schaeffer, arrived in 1762 and remained about a dozen years. Successors were difficult to secure in such a remote place, and in the long run the congregation was not able to maintain itself, although there remains a church building still standing today as a witness to former times.[58]

Germans appeared in larger numbers farther north in Nova Scotia. To keep this colony secure from the French, who disputed the British claim to possession, the latter recruited colonists from Europe. By 1750 there were German Lutherans and Reformed in Halifax, the principal town in the province. Lutherans assembled there for worship, at first in private houses and after 1758 in a church building. In the absence of an ordained minister services were conducted by laymen. Not until 1783 was a Lutheran pastor secured in the person of Bernard M. Hausihl, who left New York City with other "empire loyalists" who were unhappy about America's independence from England. Meanwhile a second town in Nova Scotia, Lunenburg, had an even larger proportion of Lutherans. Some of them were discharged British mercenaries who came originally from Brunswick and Lueneburg (whence the name Lunenburg). Others were redemptioners who paid for their passage by their service after reaching their destination. In 1765 the Lutherans and Reformed built a union church. Two years later they secured Paul Bryzelius from New Jersey as their pastor, but the

, P. A. Strobel, *The Salzburgers and Their
scendants* (Baltimore: T. Newton Kurtz,
55), pp. 201-308.

erbert L. Osgood, *American Colonies in the
ghteenth Century*, 4 vols. (New York: Co-
mbia University Press, 1924), 2:511-12.

enry N. Pohlman, "The German Col-
y and Lutheran Church in Maine,"
angelical Review 20 (1868): 440-42.

people were disappointed when they discovered that he had become an Anglican. The local schoolmaster wrote:

Immediately after Bryzelius had thrown off the mask under which he had come among us—for he had only been masquerading as a Lutheran minister—we began once more to hold our meetings in private houses as we had been doing before. . . . We engaged in devotional exercises, which consisted of reading a sermon, singing, and prayer. Then we consulted together among ourselves as to what should be done.[59]

After many pleas for help from the Lunenburgers, Frederick Schultz finally accepted a call in 1772 and journeyed north from New York. Some Lutherans lived in places other than Halifax and Lunenburg, but there could hardly have been more than fifteen hundred nominal Lutherans in Nova Scotia at the end of the colonial period.

Thus by the close of the War for Independence German Lutherans were scattered up and down the Atlantic coast and had penetrated the interior as far as the Allegheny Mountains. If we inquire how many there were all together we must reckon with the fact that we have few firm figures and generally only estimates, and often contradictory estimates at that. It may be helpful to begin with the number of Germans in the several states (1) as estimated by Faust for the year 1775[60] and (2) as deduced from surnames reported in the first United States census in 1790 (see table 1).[61] One might assume that the virtual cessation of immigration between these years would make the figures roughly comparable, although the high rate of natural increase must also be taken into account. Meanwhile one must not overlook the fact that both the figures derived from the census (deduced from the surnames of heads of families) and Faust's figures (based on an extrapolation from contemporary appraisals) are informed estimates, but estimates based on different kinds of information. On the assumption that between one-third and one-half of the German colonists were of Lutheran background, these figures would suggest that from 80,000 to 130,000 were nominal Lutherans.

Another way to approach the problem is to ask how many Lutheran churches there were. This question is easier to answer because most of the congregations continued to exist into the twentieth century. On the basis both of contemporary evidence and of later survivals it is safe to assert that there were at least three hundred Lutheran congregations at the close of the American Revolution.[62] If Faust had been correct about his estimate of the relation of religious adherents to the number of congregations,[63] there would have been 200,000 nominal Lutherans. This figure is certainly too high. A fairer estimate, based on what appear to be reasonable appraisals, state by state, would suggest that there were about 120,000 nominal Lutherans. These were not evenly divided among the states, for more than half of the total number were in Pennsylvania. The fact that only 151 Lutheran ministers (including 38 Swedish minis-

59.
D. Luther Roth, *Acadie and the Acadians*, 2d ed. (Utica, N.Y.: Childs & Son, 1891), p. 280.
60.
Faust, *The German Element*, 1:285.
61.
Walter F. Willcox et al., "Report on Linguistic and National Stocks in the Population of the United States . . . ," in *Annual Report of the American Historical Association for the Year 1931* (Washington, D.C.: U.S. Government Printing Office, 1932), 1:103–441.
62.
Cf. Frederick L. Weis, *The Colonial Churches and the Colonial Clergy of the Middle and Southern Colonies, 1607-1776* (Lancaster, Mass.: Society of Descendants of Colonial Clergy, 1938), p. 18; G. L. Kieffer, "An Analysis of Colonial Enumerations," in *Lutherans in Colonial Days*, ed. Nathan R. Melhorn (Philadelphia: United Lutheran Publication House, 1926), pp. 71–92. The estimates in Edwin Scott Gaustad, *Historical Atlas of Religion in America* (New York: Harper & Row, 1962), pp. 17–19, appear to be too low. This is also true of William Warren Sweet, "Church Membership," in *Dictionary of American History*, ed. James T. Adams, 5 vols. (New York: Scribner's, 1940), 1:372.
63.
Faust, *The German Element*, p. 284.

36

Table 1

**Lutherans
In the Total
German Population**

	Germans Estimated by Faust for 1775	Germans Suggested by 1790 Census	Lutheran Churches 1790	Estimated Nominal Lutherans 1790
New England	1,500	4,120	1	**500**
New York	25,000	25,800	25	**10,000**
New Jersey	15,000	15,640	18	**8,000**
Pennsylvania	110,000	140,980	191	**65,000**
Maryland and Delaware	20,500	24,920	27	**12,000**
Virginia	25,000	27,850	18	**12,000**
North Carolina	8,000	13,590	15	**8,000**
South Carolina	15,000	7,010	13	**3,000**
Georgia	5,000	4,020	4	**2,000**
Nova Scotia (Canada)	. . . .	. . . .	2	**1,500**
Total	225,000	263,930	314	122,000

Note: Not included are the 13,000
Germans believed to have been living in
Kentucky and Tennessee by 1790.

ters) have been identified as having served in all of North America between 1638 and 1775[64]—not simultaneously but cumulatively—would in itself demonstrate that only a portion of the 120,000 nominal Lutherans could possibly have been "churched" in any meaningful sense of the term. Just what it meant, however, to be Lutheran in the colonial period, or to be a member of a Lutheran church at that time, must occupy our attention further.

64.
Weis, *Colonial Churches and the Clergy*, p. 17

3 Laymen, Ministers, and Church Organization

1.
George Fenwick Jones, ed., *Henry New-man's Salzburger Letterbooks* (Athens, Ga.: University of Georgia Press, 1966), p. 503.

As we have seen, Lutheran people in North America were of diverse national origins. They spoke different languages and observed somewhat different styles of life. But there were similarities beyond their common confessional identity, for circumstances compelled them to accommodate themselves to one another and to their new environment. Thus we can treat the Lutherans during the period from 1637 to 1787 as a unit.

The People and How They Came to America

All Lutherans came to North America in much the same way. The sailing vessels on which they crossed the Atlantic hardly changed during the century and a half. Typical was one of the ships on which Salzburgers made the voyage to Georgia in 1734. The ship owner described it thus:

The Ship's Burthen is 200 Tuns, built on purpose to carry with Conveniency a great number of Passengers; she is 6½ foot high in the Steerage, and 5 feet high between Decks. So large a Ship and of such a Built might contain very easily 150 Common Passengers, whose Passage is paid upon the common footing; if they were to be heaped upon one another as the Palatines it might have contain[ed] 300, and these pay however as much as Saltzburgers.[1]

These lines were written to counteract charges that the passengers had been given inadequate accommodations, and reference was made to the notoriously less humane treatment of many of the so-called Palatines when they crossed the ocean. The fact is that even at best the voyage involved hardship and danger. Movement depended on favorable winds, and often ships were becalmed and remained motionless for days and even weeks. An anticipated six weeks at sea was in many instances extended to ten, twelve, or more weeks. By that time food and water would spoil or the supply would be exhausted. A Lutheran schoolmaster and organist who made such a journey in 1750 described the consequences.

During the journey the ship is full of pitiful signs of distress—smells, fumes, horrors, vomiting, various kinds of sea sickness, fever, dysentery, headaches, heat, constipation, boils, scurvy, cancer, mouth-rot, and similar afflictions, all of them caused by the age and the highly salted state of the food, especially of the meat, as well as by the very bad and filthy water, which brings about the miserable destruction and death of many. . . . There are so many lice, especially on the sick people, that they have to be scraped off the bodies. All this

misery reaches its climax when in addition to everything else one must also suffer through two to three days and nights of storm, with everyone convinced that the ship with all aboard is bound to sink. In such misery all the people on board pray and cry pitifully together.[2]

In heavy storms ships sometimes sprang leaks and sank, or capsized and disappeared without a trace. A worse fate threatened passengers who encountered pirates on the high sea. Even apart from these dangers the overcrowded conditions on board, as well as the food and drink, produced a variety of diseases, not a few of them fatal.[3]

Lutherans found their way to the New World in relatively small numbers at first. By the year 1700 there were about 1,000 Swedish and Finnish Lutherans on the Delaware and perhaps 300 Dutch Lutherans on the Hudson. In addition there must have been at least 500 Lutherans of other nationalities, mostly German. If these estimates are reasonably correct, there were at best only 2,000 Lutherans in a total white population of 300,000 in 1700; they therefore represented fewer than 1 percent. The proportion changed during the eighteenth century, when large numbers of German Lutherans made their way across the ocean. By 1790 as many as 120,000 of them had settled along the Atlantic seaboard and represented more than 4 percent of the total white population of 2,800,000 at that time.

When we inquire what kind of people these were who came to North America in large numbers despite grave hardships and dangers it will become clear to us that in many respects there was no fundamental difference between Lutherans of Dutch, Swedish, Finnish, or German background. All came from predominantly agricultural environments in Europe, and what most attracted them to the New World was the opportunity to improve their lot and possess and cultivate their own land. Officials in Sweden were instructed to attract Finnish settlers by making them understand that on the Delaware River "there is a choice and fruitful land, overgrown with all kinds of beautiful forests, and that there are all sorts of wild animals in plenty."[4] Several generations later potential German colonists were appealed to by this description of a colony in the New World:

South Carolina is one of the most fruitful countries to be found. . . . Two crops of Indian corn may be raised in a season. No better rice is raised in any land. . . . Much may be expected from the raising of cotton. . . . All sorts of domestic animals may be raised. Cattle need not be housed in winter, which in South Carolina has the temperature of April or October in Germany. Swine may be raised with scarcely any cost since the forests abound in acorns. . . . Generally the climate is very healthful. The Indians frequently used to attain the age of 100.[5]

Before their departure from Europe or on their arrival in America the occupations of new settlers were sometimes listed, and such lists indicate that the great majority were "husbandmen and vinedressers" and only a few were tanners and shoe-

40

2.
Gottlieb Mittelberger, *Journey to Pennsylvania* (1750), ed. and trans. Oscar Handlin and John Clive (Cambridge, Mass.: Harvard University Press, 1960), pp. 12, 13.
3.
Minutes of the Provincial Council of Pennsylvania (Harrisburg, Pa.: Theodore Fenn, 1851–52), 6:173–75.
4.
Quoted in E. A. Louhi, *The Delaware Finn* (New York: Humanity Press, 1925), pp. 36, 37.
5.
Quoted in Henry Eyster Jacobs, *The German Emigration to America, 1709–1740* (Lancaster, Pa.: Pennsylvania German Society, 1898), pp. 6, 7.

Hugh Hastings, ed., *Ecclesiastical Records, State of New York,* 7 vols. (Albany: James B. Lyon, 1901–16), 3:1747, 1748, 1824 (hereafter cited as *N.Y. Eccles. Records*).

William J. Mann et al., eds., *Nachrichten von den vereinigten Deutschen Evangelisch-Lutherischen Gemeinen in Nord-America, absonderlich in Pennsylvanien* (1787), new ed., 2 vols. Allentown and Philadelphia: Brobst, Diehl & Co., 1886–95), 2:725; cf. 1:78, 106, 522; 2:170, 183, 184 (hereafter cited as *Hallesche Nachrichten*).

Ibid., 1:105, 106, 526, 529; Samuel Urlsperger, ed., *Ausführliche Nachricht von den saltzburgischen Emigranten* (Halle: Waisenhaus, 1735–52), 4th continuation, pp. 193, 2213; 6th continuation, pp. 25, 190, 212; 7th continuation, p. 615; 8th continuation, p. 722; 11th continuation, p. 2079; 12th continuation, p. 2141; and passim.

Adolph B. Benson, ed., *The America of 1750: Peter Kalm's Travels in North America,* 2 vols. (New York: Wilson, 1937), 1:142; cf. 2:626, 627.

Amandus Johnson, *The Journal and Biography of Nicholas Collin, 1746-1831* (Philadelphia: New Jersey Society of Pennsylvania, 1936), p. 299.

Acta historico-ecclesiastica, oder gesammelte Nachrichten von den neuesten Kirchen-Geschichten, 20 vols. (Weimar, 1735–58), 20:845.

makers, weavers and tailors, butchers and bakers.[6] Most were, accordingly, peasants and laborers. They are frequently referred to in the literature of the time as "poor people," and it is clear that this was not a metaphorical expression. They "did not belong to the upper class in the old world," Henry Melchior Muhlenberg once put it, "but were generally descendants of poor, despised, oppressed, and to some extent persecuted people."[7] Large numbers, as noted earlier, were unable to pay for their passage to North America and hence came as indentured servants.[8] In time they were free to secure land of their own which had to be cleared before it could be put under cultivation. As a rule it was not until the second or third generation that a measure of prosperity was achieved. Because Dutch, Swedish, and Finnish colonists had settled in America before Germans arrived in significant numbers, the latter generally remained poorer even to the close of the colonial period.

When they arrived in North America, Lutheran colonists found themselves in a new and strange land. Even if they had been glad to leave their homelands, as many were, it was a cultural shock for them to face the New World. Not only was the topography of the land different but they encountered unfamiliar animals and insects, crops and people, customs and tongues. Under these circumstances they often became more deeply attached to the particular manners and mores brought with them from the other side of the ocean. To these they clung tenaciously and did what they could to cultivate and perpetuate them.

The Problems Attending Language Transition

There were three major language groups among colonial Lutherans. The first was Dutch, originally the language of all official transactions in the Dutch colony on the Hudson and the language to which all nationalities there accommodated themselves. After the conquest by England there was a change, and by the middle of the eighteenth century a traveler in New York reported that, although some older people still spoke Dutch, "most of the young people now speak English and would even take it amiss if they were called Dutchmen and not Englishmen."[9] The second major language group was Swedish, and the early settlers on the Delaware quite uniformly understood and spoke this tongue. "Some families who were originally Dutch," a clergyman reported, "have long been regarded as Swedes since they have learned the Swedish language."[10] Here again, however, Swedish speech gave way before the middle of the eighteenth century to the English of the rapidly growing majority. A Swedish minister wrote to his parents in 1743: "Everything that is Swedish here will not be able to remain so very long, for most of our people are ashamed of the Swedish language and despise it. Many understand English as well as Swedish, but when I try to speak to them in Swedish they do not answer me and act as if they do not understand."[11]

The third major language group was German. Because for the most part Germans came to North America after the Dutch and Swedish-speaking colonists, and continued to come until the Revolution, they were not only the largest group by far but also most likely to preserve their mother tongue longest. A church elder who lived in Germantown, Pennsylvania, warned as early as 1748 that the Germans would have the same experience as the Swedes: "It seems that the Swedish language is disappearing entirely in Pennsylvania. . . . The young people know little, and most of them nothing at all, of their mother tongue. Exactly the same thing is going to happen to our German language."[12] A quarter of a century later Muhlenberg observed that young people in Philadelphia "gradually become ashamed of the German language and waver between the two [German and English] until the old people are out of the way."[13] He recommended that children should be encouraged to learn English, "for this is the predominant language and is employed in trade, social intercourse, and the courts."[14]

The process of anglicization was not uniform. The mother tongue—whether Dutch, Swedish, or German—survived longest in isolated settlements where there was little contact with English-speaking people. In 1749, for example, a traveler reported that Swedish speech was preserved with relative purity in a remote village in southern New Jersey. "It was inhabited only by Swedes, and not a single Englishman or people of any other nation had settled it. Therefore they have preserved their native Swedish tongue there better than elsewhere and mixed but few English words with it."[15] On the other hand, it was frequently remarked that German servants indentured at an early age to English-speaking masters gradually lost the ability to express themselves in their native language.[16] As a rule, marriage to an English-speaking spouse also resulted in the adoption of English by the entire family.[17] In cities a bilingual compromise was sometimes attempted with potentially disastrous consequences, as in Charleston, South Carolina, where the proposal was "German for our religion and English for temporal and civic welfare."[18] In rural areas, especially, the spoken language was often corrupted. In 1772 a layman declared that he came from a little place called Mondschein (or Moonshine). The mystery was soon unraveled.

The old Germans, who are otherwise discerning, spoil the English language and in time produce a third language, which is neither English nor German. The district is said to be called _Mount Joy_ in English, and from this our Germans get _Mondschein_ because the sound is somewhat similar. Even so, they call the agent of the king (in English the _King's Attorney_) the king's _Saturnus_ because they find the word in the calendar and the sound is almost identical with _attorney_.[19]

The process of anglicization can be traced in the change of Swedish proper names from Cock to Cox, Kyn to Keen, and Joccom to Yocum or the change of German names from Jung to Young, Schwarzwaelder to Blackwelder, Ries to Reese, and Mohr to Moore.

Every threat to the continued use of Dutch, Swedish, or German was met with stout resistance. In early years the Swed-

12.
Letter of John Nicholas Grössmann in *Hallesche Nachrichten*, 1:187.
13.
The Journals of Henry Melchior Muhlenberg, ed. Theodore G. Tappert and John W. Doberstein, 3 vols. (Philadelphia: Muhlenberg Press, 1942–58), 2:528.
14.
Ibid., 3:372.
15.
Benson, *America of 1750*, 1:295, 296.
16.
Cf. *Hallesche Nachrichten*, 1:16.
17.
Cf. Israel Acrelius, *A History of New Sweden* (1759), trans. William M. Reynolds (Philadelphia: Historical Society of Pennsylvania, 1874), p. 360.
18.
Journals of Muhlenberg, 2:588.
19.
Ibid., p. 515.

20.
"Instructions for the Swedish Mission in America, 1758," trans. Milan von Lany, *Lutheran Church Quarterly* 13 (1940): 76.

21.
Kirchen-Agende der Evangelisch-Lutherischen Vereinigten Gemeinen in Nord-America (Philadelphia: Steiner, 1786), p. 7. Cf. Henry Eyster Jacobs, *A History of the Evangelical Lutheran Church in the United States* (New York: Christian Literature Co., 1893), p. 338.

22.
Theodore G. Tappert, "Language and Legislation," *The Lutheran*, November 15, 1939, pp. 11–19; Robert A. Faer, "Official Use of the German Language in Pennsylvania," *Pennsylvania Magazine of History and Biography* 76 (1952): 394–405. Acceptance of the myth in Europe is indicated in Werner Elert, *Morphologie des Luthertums*, 2 vols. (Munich: C. H. Beck, 1932), 2:251, 271.

23.
Henry M. Muhlenberg, "Opinion on the Introduction of English in the Swedish Churches," trans. Henry P. Suhr, *Lutheran Church Quarterly* 13 (1940): 82.

ish clergy on the Delaware were repeatedly instructed to "take special care to preserve the Swedish language and not to deviate from it in their official acts, except in cases of emergency."[20] Lutheran ministers seemed more reluctant than laymen to adopt English, perhaps because most clergymen came directly from Europe while more and more of their parishioners were native Americans of the second or third generation. On the other hand, the laymen were mostly of peasant stock, deterred less by cultural impediments and, because of their occupations, thrown together more with English-speaking people. Propaganda for the cultivation of the language and institutions of forefathers found a place even in the general prayer of the Pennsylvania liturgy of 1786:

Inasmuch as it has pleased Thee, chiefly by means of the Germans, to transform this state into a blooming garden and the desert into pleasant pasturage, help us not to deny our nationality but to endeavor that our dear youth may be so educated that German churches and schools may not only be preserved but may attain a still more flourishing condition.[21]

Somewhat similar sentiment underlies the hardy myth that German would have become the official language of Pennsylvania (or, as some versions had it, of the new United States of America) if a proposal to that effect had not been defeated by a single vote.[22] Although the men who ministered to colonists in Dutch, Swedish, or German quite understandably had emotional attachments to their native tongues, the best of them placed their Christian mission above national loyalty. Muhlenberg put it this way when he replied to an inquiry which his Swedish colleagues addressed to him:

We Germans would also like to retain our mother tongue in order to propagate our religion more fittingly. However, many of our young people annually marry English people, speak English in their families, and teach their children this language. Accordingly we preach in our churches, wherever it is necessary, in English as well as German. . . . We should look at language as we look at a bridge over a river. Whether it is made of oak or of birch bark is not important, so long as it holds and enables us to get across and toward our goal.[23]

Clergymen and Pretenders from Europe

Unfortunately there were not enough clergymen to meet the need. To be sure, the Church of Sweden supplied the Lutherans on the Delaware with pastors almost to the time of the American Revolution, but the ministers were too few for the scattered population, and there were frequent vacancies between pastorates. The Lutheran consistory of Amsterdam, in the Netherlands, cooperated with the ministerium of Hamburg, in Germany, to supply the Lutherans on the Hudson with pastors to the middle of the eighteenth century, but the people were even more scattered and the vacancies were even longer. The so-called Palatines who settled in New York and Virginia in the early decades of the eighteenth century secured temporary help from the English Society for the Propagation of the Gospel. The Salzburgers in Georgia were sponsored by Samuel Urlsperger, of Augsburg in Germany, who published extensive diaries and reports by the Salzburgers in order to awaken interest in and secure financial support for the ministers sent to the Savannah River.[24]

24.
See chapter 2, n. 52.
25.
Hallesche Nachrichten, 1:52.
26.
See chapter 2, n. 4.
27.
Ralph B. Strassburger and William J. Hinke, eds., *Pennsylvania German Pioneers: Original Lists of Arrivals in the Port of Philadelphia from 1727 to 1808*, 3 vols. (Norristown, Pa.: Pennsylvania German Society, 1934), 1:xvii, xli, xlii. Cf. *Journals of Muhlenberg*, 3:350, 358, 359.
28.
Hallesche Nachrichten, 2:205; cf. 1:427.
29.
Journals of Muhlenberg, 1:296, 381.

Beginning in 1733 some German Lutherans in southeastern Pennsylvania entered into correspondence with Gotthilf A. Francke, head of the charitable foundations established in Halle, Saxony, by his father, the recently deceased August Herman Francke, and Frederick M. Ziegenhagen, pastor of one of the German Lutheran churches in London. The Pennsylvanians reported that several thousand of them, "poor and destitute of all means, arrived there and settled down in the wilderness, scattering here and there. As a consequence they have unfortunately continued to live without a church, without the services of a regularly ordained preacher, and without the administration of the holy sacraments, even as lost sheep."[25] During the half-century beginning in 1742 Halle sent a succession of twenty-four ministers. Reports and correspondence concerning the churches "in North America, especially in Pennsylvania," were published in the "Halle Reports," whose circulation in Europe helped to finance the mission.[26] Still other ministers were sent from Germany. In 1772 two laymen from North Carolina appealed in person to the Lutheran consistory in Hanover, Germany, and in response a half-dozen ministers were in time supplied by Hanover and adjacent Brunswick.

In addition to the men who were thus sent to North America were some who came of their own accord without ecclesiastical endorsement. A few, like Joshua Kocherthal among the early Palatines in New York, came as leaders of groups of colonists. Some were chaplains who accompanied German mercenaries and chose to remain in America when the soldiers were demobilized after one or another of the colonial wars.[27] Some crossed the Atlantic as indentured servants, and it was said of such men in 1754: "When these men arrive their passage is paid by disorderly Lutherans and thus they are redeemed from the ship. In return they must preach and administer the sacraments to the people for a specified period of time, whether or not they have been ordained. Afterward they take their leave, and new men are bought free."[28] Most of those who crossed the ocean as indentured servants and set themselves up as clergymen were hardly qualified to perform the duties of the office. This was also true of others who had either been deposed from the ministry in Europe for reasons of incompetence or immorality, or had never prepared themselves for that profession at all. The activity of men like this gave Lutheran ministers the reputation of being "squabblers and wranglers."[29] "Well meaning Evangelical [Lutheran] Christians have to put up with many an offense and blasphemy on the part of fellow Christians who claim their name (I refer to the disorderly groups and their scandalous preachers who call themselves Lutherans) and they are almost forced to be ashamed of their Lutheran name."[30]

All these men who came to America on their own authority, whether they insinuated themselves into Lutheran or other churches, were commonly called "pretenders" because, as an Anglican put it, they are persons "that run before they are sent and pretend they are ministers of the Gospell that never had a legal call or ordination."[31] Sometimes the designation "vagabond preachers" was used because they wandered from place to place. They appeared among the Swedish-speaking people on the Delaware, the Dutch-speaking people on the Hudson, and the German-speaking people in many other places.[32] The appearance of pretenders can be accounted for not only by the absence of effective ecclesiastical supervision but also by the great shortage of clergymen. Often Lutherans were confronted by a choice between a vagabond preacher or no preacher at all.[33] The situation was described by a minister in North Carolina: "The absence of good preachers caused the people, who after all had a longing for the gospel and would gladly have heard the Word of God, to take their refuge to such men who, like roaming knights, traverse the land and, after they were no longer able to make their living because of evil conduct in their [other] profession, became preachers."[34]

Immediately on his arrival in Pennsylvania Henry M. Muhlenberg had conflicts with pretenders. He thought he could get rid of them by sapping the source of their income. After preaching one day in 1743 he announced that the people should stop making contributions to the pastor when they receive the Lord's Supper or have their children baptized.

Since those vagabonds are concerned only to get a few shillings for a baptism and the offerings at the Lord's Supper and thus produce much strife, thereby giving the sects good cause for slander, I have abolished the abominable custom, considering that there is no need to pay the pastor his salary just at the occasion of the services.[35]

That this measure did not succeed in solving the problem is apparent from the fact that less than a dozen years later, in 1754, Muhlenberg tried to get help from the civil authorities. He wrote to Governor Robert Morris, mentioned several vagabonds, and then continued:

There are many more of the same sort whom we shall never get rid of, nor reduce the people to proper order, until our gracious superiors are pleased to demand proper credentials of all who exercise the ministry and no longer suffer vagabonds to laugh at us who are regular clergymen by saying it is a free country and by turning liberty into licentiousness.[36]

In the long run colonial government officials did not have the power to curb pretenders, who simply filled places left vacant by the failure of Lutheran churches in Europe, especially in Germany, to supply enough competent ministers. Under these circumstances schoolmasters and others who could read and write

30.
Ibid., p. 381.
31.
John Yeo (1676) quoted in H. Shelton Smith, Robert T. Handy, and Lefferts A. Loetscher, eds., *American Christianity: An Historical Interpretation with Representative Documents*, 2 vols. (New York: Scribner's, 1960–63), 1:54. The Duke's Laws of New York in 1665 referred to "scandalous and ignorant pretenders to the ministry": see *N.Y. Eccles. Records,* 1:571.
32.
E.g., Acrelius, *History of New Sweden*, pp. 212, 213, 315–19; Simon Hart and Harry J. Kreider, trans., *Protocol of the Lutheran Church in New York City, 1702–1750* (New York: New York Synod, 1958), pp. 263–96, 409–18, 442–51, 462, 463.
33.
Journals of Muhlenberg, 1:533.
34.
William K. Boyd and Charles A. Krummel, "German Tracts Concerning the Lutheran Church in North Carolina During the Eighteenth Century," *North Carolina Historical Review* 8 (1930): 128.
35.
Journals of Muhlenberg, 1:84.
36.
Samuel Hazard, ed., *Pennsylvania Archives,* 10 vols. (Philadelphia: J. Severns, 1853–54), 2:183–84.

were often drafted into emergency service, and Muhlenberg himself was in time persuaded by experience to condone the practice.

Let him who can, provide regular preachers. . . . But at a time when there is a great shortage of such ministers in all parts of the world let us not bind the hands and feet of the poor souls who are swimming in the water and thus make them drown. Let us rather give them our hands and extend poles to them so that they have something to take hold of. [37]

Education and Ordination of Ministers in America

It was recognized in Europe as well as in America that "co-workers" would have to be prepared on this side of the ocean to minister to the increasing numbers of Lutheran colonists. [38] A step in this direction was taken when, for want of a school of theology, some ministers took students into their homes and tutored them privately. In addition to what such students learned from books and recitations, they also became acquainted with practical parish work by observing and assisting their tutors, among whom Carl M. Wrangel, Henry M. Muhlenberg, and Justus H. C. Helmuth were especially active. After submitting to "a brief examination in the ancient languages and theology" a candidate could be licensed "to preach, to catechize, and to administer the holy sacraments" for only one year and only in a designated place or places. [39] The license could be renewed annually until the candidate was believed to be ready for a more demanding examination and subsequent ordination as a minister of the gospel. In time the requirements were relaxed because the demand for ministers continued to grow. Knowledge of "the oriental and occidental languages, with which the studious youth is so sorely detained and tormented," was no longer insisted upon, provided there was evidence of "righteousness of the heart and personal experience of repentance, faith, and devotion." [40]

The example of Presbyterians and others was cited to demonstrate how important a school would be in providing ministers. [41] In 1749 Muhlenberg took advantage of an opportunity to secure forty-nine acres near Philadelphia on which he hoped to establish, among other institutions, a theological seminary. He was compelled to abandon this project for want of funds. Again and again the need for a school was mentioned, and Muhlenberg wrote to Halle that "at least a sort of seminary" ought to be established in America. [42] Although "the Reverend Fathers" in Halle looked with disfavor on the plan, [43] the idea did not die. In 1773 John C. Kunze founded an academy in Philadelphia "to furnish the preparation preliminary to the further training of young men for the office of the ministry." The occupation of Philadelphia by British troops in 1777 quickly put an end to this school. [44] After the Revolution, in 1787, Lutheran and German Reformed leaders united in the founding of Franklin (later Franklin and Marshall) College in Lancaster, Pennsylvania, but it was not until the early decades of the nineteenth century

37.
Journals of Muhlenberg, 2:369; cf. 1:533.
38.
Hallesche Nachrichten, 2:586.
39.
Documentary History of the Evangelical Lutheran Ministerium of Pennsylvania . . . 1748-1821 (Philadelphia: General Council Board of Publication, 1898), p. 174.
40.
Journals of Muhlenberg, 3:369.
41.
Ibid., 2:181, 295, 313; 3:687.
42.
Hallesche Nachrichten, 2:627.
43.
Journals of Muhlenberg, 2:318; but cf. *Hallesche Nachrichten*, 2:586.
44.
Cf. Theodore G. Tappert, *History of the Lutheran Theological Seminary at Philadelphia, 1864-1964* (Philadelphia: Lutheran Theological Seminary, 1964), pp. 3-9; Abdel Ross Wentz, *Gettysburg Lutheran Theological Seminary . . . 1826-1965,* 2 vols. (Gettysburg, Pa.: Lutheran Theological Seminary, 1965), 1:18-29. Carl F. Haussmann *Kunze's Seminarium* (Philadelphia: Americana Germanica Press, 1917), pp. 70-84.

that Lutheran schools of theology came into being. Until then students for the ministry continued to be tutored privately.

It was only natural that the education of candidates for the ministry should be followed by ordination. Lutheran colonists would probably have found it difficult to explain just what ordination was, but it was part of their churchly heritage from Europe to expect a minister to be ordained. Certainly it was not that they thought of ordination as conferring any inherent power or effecting any personal change. Muhlenberg himself once wrote: "Experience shows that neither episcopal nor presbyterial ordination infuses any natural or supernatural qualities, else there would not be so many counterfeit ministers."[45] Muhlenberg and his colleagues had no qualms about approving the ministry of unordained men in an emergency. Often such ministry expressly included the administration of Holy Communion, and even in Europe no theological objection was raised to forbid this exceptional practice.[46] The normal procedure was to ordain, however, and ordination was understood as a formal and public authorization of certain persons to perform ministerial functions. It was in order to secure at least the appearance of such authorization that self-appointed pretenders often ordained one another. For example, John C. Schulze, who had himself been ordained privately, in turn ordained John Caspar Stoever, Jr., in 1733. In contrast to such private ordinations by individuals were the public acts of ecclesiastical bodies.

It was in keeping with what Kunze called "the settled practice" of the Lutheran church that ordination should be the prerogative of a corporate assembly and not of an individual.[47] When Falckner was ordained in 1703 (as described above in chapter 1) this was therefore done by the Swedish clergymen on the Delaware as a body, with the approval of the official of the Church of Sweden who was their superior. In fact, one of the fruits of the restoration of ties with the old country in 1697 was that the Swedes on the Delaware constituted a chapter with a dean, or provost, at its head.[48] With some interruptions, the clergy of this chapter met at least once a year under the chairmanship of the dean, whose function it was to supervise the ministers and their parishes and to report to and receive instructions from his bishop in Sweden. A much looser union of Lutheran churches was formed in 1733 by the German congregations in Philadelphia, Trappe, and New Hanover, Pennsylvania. They formed what they called "the united congregations" and proceeded to make joint appeals to Europe for ministers and financial assistance.[49] Nine years later Muhlenberg was sent in response to these appeals. He and the associates who soon joined him established cordial relations with the Swedish clergy, whose chapter meetings the German ministers were invited to attend. For example, Peter Tranberg, minister of the Swedish church in Wilmington (Christina), Delaware, recorded in 1754:

On the Fourth Sunday after Easter, May 12, a meeting of clergy was held in Christina, when there were present the senior minister of the German Lutherans, Mr. Henric Muhlenberg; Mr. Matthias Heinzelmann, assistant pastor

45.
Journals of Muhlenberg, 3:255, 256.

46.
Cf. ibid., 1:533; ibid., 3:495. See also, letter of Gotthilf A. Francke, March 26, 1749, in *Hallesche Nachrichten*, 1:324; cf. pp. 495–97.

47.
Letter of John C. Kunze in *Journals of Muhlenberg*, 3:411.

48.
Horace Burr, trans., *The Records of Holy Trinity (Old Swedes) Church . . .* (Wilmington, Del.: Historical Society of Delaware, 1890), pp. 157, 250, 251; Acrelius, *History of New Sweden*, pp. 213, 219, 273, 336, 363, 364.

49.
The correspondence is reproduced in *Hallesche Nachrichten*, 1:50–70.

of the German church in Philadelphia; Magister Olof Parlin, the [Swedish] pastor in Wicaco [South Philadelphia]; Mr. Eric Unander, the [Swedish] pastor in Raccoon and Penn's Neck [N.J.]. . . . We received the Lord's Supper together on Sunday. . . . The remainder of our meeting was spent in conversation about various matters of conscience which often come up in all our congregations.[50]

The "classical assembly" of 1735, convoked in northern New Jersey by William C. Berkenmeyer, also reflected the need for mutual consultation, although it met only once (see chapter 1).

Clergymen of other religious persuasions also met in associations of one kind or another. Some Presbyterian ministers met in 1701 to ordain a man to the ministry. Four years later a half-dozen of them met in Philadelphia to participate in the organization of the first American presbytery. Ever since 1736 the Dutch Reformed ministers on the Hudson River contemplated forming an association, but it was not until 1747 that a coetus was finally organized with clerical and lay delegates from every congregation. The same year a similar coetus was formed in Philadelphia among German Reformed churches under the leadership of Michael Schlatter. Earlier, a leading German Reformed layman, Henry Antes, had become interested in bringing about greater unity among all the many German-speaking churches and sects in Pennsylvania. When the Moravian leader, Count Nicholas Zinzendorf, crossed the ocean in the fall of 1741 he was welcomed by Antes, whose vision of church union Zinzendorf embraced. In fact, in 1742 the count became the leading figure in a series of seven monthly meetings (called synods) which were intended to gather all German-speaking religious bodies into a Congregation of God in the Spirit. The meetings were attended by more than a hundred persons, mostly laymen, of Lutheran, Reformed, Moravian, Mennonite, Dunker, Schwenkfelder, and other backgrounds. At one of the sessions Zinzendorf set forth what he and others hoped to accomplish:

The proper object of this assembly of all religious denominations is that henceforth a poor inquirer for the way of life may not be directed in twelve different ways but only in one, let him ask whom he will. But if any one should take fancy to him who directed him in the way and should wish to travel on the same according to his method, he has full liberty to do so, provided he be as yet in no connection with any religious society.[51]

Within six months the effort to achieve unity collapsed, and by 1748 the "synods" were transformed into the Unity of the Brethren, or the Moravian Church.

It was in part to counteract the influence of Zinzendorf and the Moravians that a union of the Swedish and the German Lutherans was suggested. Two prominent Philadelphia merchants, Peter Kock, a Swede, and Henry Schleydorn, a German, pressed for such a union in 1744.

50.
Burr, *Records of Holy Trinity*, p. 455.
51.
Quoted in A. J. Lewis, *Zinzendorf: The Ecumenical Pioneer* (Philadelphia: Westminster Press, 1962), p. 145; cf. John Joseph Stoudt, "Count Zinzendorf and the Pennsylvania Congregation of God in the Spirit," *Church History* 9 (1940): 366-80.

48

The proposal was made that they [the ministers] should hold yearly meetings together, and that in these a few of the elders of the congregations, Germans as well as Swedes, should also be included. They should there consult together in regard to the best establishment of each congregation, for the circumstances in their affairs required that they should shake hands with one another and fight their common enemy, the Zinzendorfians.[52]

52.
Acrelius, *History of New Sweden*, p. 246.
53.
Hallesche Nachrichten, 1:84.
54.
Theodore G. Tappert, "John Caspar Stoever and the Ministerium of Pennsylvania," *Lutheran Church Quarterly* 21 (1948): 180–84.
55.
August L. Graebner, *Geschichte der Lutherischen Kirche in Amerika* (St. Louis: Concordia, 1892), p. 313.

The proposal was for church union on confessional grounds, not on the basis of common nationality assumed by the earlier Congregation of God in the Spirit. The plan was premature, however, for Swedes and Germans "did not understand each other's language," and the former feared that they would lose control of their greater wealth by being outvoted by the far more numerous Germans. Although union with the Swedes did not materialize, the German Lutheran ministers who were sent from Halle conferred among themselves in "Christian harmony," looked upon Muhlenberg as their "elder brother,"[53] and continued to be invited to attend the Swedish conferences.

The Ministerium of North America

Such were the gropings among Lutherans as among others for some form of organizational expression. By January 20, 1747, Muhlenberg had decided to call German Lutheran clergymen and laymen together,[54] but it was not until August 26, 1748, that such a meeting was finally held, and it is with some justice that it has been called "the most important event in the history of the Lutheran Church in America."[55] Six ministers were present, including the dean of the Swedish chapter and a minister from upper New York. There were lay representatives from the original "united congregations" (Philadelphia, Trappe, and New Hanover) and from congregations more recently added to their number (Germantown, Upper Saucon, Zionsville, Stouchsburg, Bernville, Lancaster, and New Holland, Pa.). Both Peter Kock and Henry Schleydorn were present and must have rejoiced that their dream was fulfilled in some measure at least. Advantage was taken of the occasion to dedicate a new church building in Philadelphia, to inquire into the condition of parishes and schools, and to approve a proposed form of worship. The principal purpose, however, was to examine and ordain one or two men who had studied theology in Halle, had been sent to Pennsylvania as catechists in 1745, and had served since then as schoolmasters and supply preachers. A contemporaneous account made the priority clear.

In order that, even if only one preacher can be sent, aid may be given to several congregations, it was deemed good to ordain to the ministry Mr. [John Nicholas] Kurtz and Mr. [John H.] Schaum, who had hitherto been assistants. . . . For this purpose, as well as for the closer union of the preachers and the united congregations among themselves, . . . a meeting of the preachers, elders, and deacons of all the frequently mentioned

49

Inasmuch as Schaum was unable to reach Philadelphia from York, his ordination was postponed a year, but Kurtz was carefully examined and ordained by the assembled clergymen. A circumstantial report of these transactions pleased Gotthilf A. Francke in Halle, who wrote that hardly one in ten candidates for ordination in Germany would have been able to answer questions as well as Kurtz.[57] Although this high standard was not adhered to long, the preparation of and oversight over ministers to supply the growing number of congregations remained the principal purpose of the organization which, with a few exceptions, met annually during the remainder of the colonial period. During the early years the body was variously called: general conference, association of pastors, synod, coetus, consistory. The most common designation was "ministerium," and this accurately described the organization, for it really was a body of ministers. Until the end of the colonial period, lay representatives of local churches were consultants rather than voting members. Decisions were made by the ministers alone.

Although most of these ministers served in Pennsylvania, membership was not limited to that colony. So this descriptive title is encountered: "The united preachers of the Evangelical Lutheran congregations of German nationality in these American colonies, especially Pennsylvania."[58] From time to time there were ministers in New York, New Jersey, Maryland, Virginia, and the Carolinas who were enrolled, and when the first written constitution was adopted in 1781 the ambitious name there given to the body was "Evangelical Lutheran Ministerium in North America."[59] The inclusiveness suggested in this name was more than geographical, for during the first quarter of a century of the organization's existence Swedish clergymen attended its sessions regularly.[60] In fact, Muhlenberg could refer to "the Swedish and German Ministerium" with only slight exaggeration, and when meetings were discontinued for a few years it was the Swedish dean Carl Magnus Wrangel who "affectionately admonished" Muhlenberg to revive the organization.[61] It was during Wrangel's stay in America that relations between Germans and Swedes were closest.[62]

When the Ministerium was first organized it had no officers. At the third annual meeting in 1750, however, Peter Brunnholz was elected "superintendent," and the following year John F. Handschuh was chosen "president or superintendent." In 1760 it was formally decided to elect a president every year with the duty of overseeing congregations between annual meetings as well as presiding at these meetings. A secretary was also chosen to record minutes, but there was neither treasurer nor treasury until later. Muhlenberg was chosen president most frequently. Even when he did not fill this office "he did most of the talking" at meetings, it was quaintly reported,[63] and he was the acknowledged leader and counselor between meetings. He once complained, "Pennsylvania will miss me sorely when I die, for I am

56.
Hallesche Nachrichten, 1:150; *Documentary History, Ministerium of Pa.*, p. 3.
57.
Hallesche Nachrichten, 1:324.
58.
Cf. *Documentary History, Ministerium of Pa.*, p. 42.
59.
Ibid., p. 165.
60.
Cf. ibid., pp. 3, 33, 35, 42, 46, 59, 69, 138.
61.
Journals of Muhlenberg, 1:532; 3:623.
62.
Nils Jacobsson, *Bland Svenskamerikaner och Gustavianer: Ur Carl Magnus Wrangels Levnadshistoria, 1727-1786* (Stockholm: Svensk Kyrkans Diakonistyrelses Bokförlag, 1953), pp. 78-84, 98-106, 126-47, 161-66, 182-91, 298-302.
63.
Documentary History, Ministerium of Pa., pp. 25, 38.

almost like a privy to which all those with loose bowels come running from all directions to relieve themselves."[64] He was sought out in part because of his knowledge and judgment but also in part because of his personal relationship to the "fathers and patrons" in Halle. In their eyes he was the "senior" of the German ministers who had been sent to America and who continued to be supported from abroad. This designation was more than a recognition of the fact that Muhlenberg was the oldest of the ministers sent from Halle; it was an ecclesiastical title, current in Germany, which indicated that he had responsibility for oversight not unlike that of the dean of the Swedish clergy on the Delaware.

51

Congregations were admonished to maintain friendship and harmony not only with one another in America but also with their "spiritual fathers and patrons" on the other side of the ocean.[65] In the early years the dependence of the American churches on Europe was often emphasized—as it was, for example, at the annual meeting of the Ministerium in 1750, where the statement was made that "without the knowledge and permission of our Fathers in Europe we were not authorized to make any changes."[66] With the passing of years the Ministerium gradually became more independent of Europe. The authority of the Ministerium over the ministers and congregations associated with it was also asserted again and again in the early years. When Kurtz was ordained in 1748 he pledged "to undertake nothing important . . . without communicating with the reverend association of pastors, receiving their opinion about it, and acquiescing in their good counsel and instruction."[67] In applying for a pastor the same year the congregation in Stouchsburg (Tulpehocken), Pennsylvania, solemnly promised "to recognize the aforesaid association of pastors of the Evangelical Lutheran congregations in Pennsylvania as a true and regular presbytery and ministerium, and especially as our chief pastors, and to regard and respect them as such. Nor will we do, decide, resolve, or alter anything without their previous knowledge and consent."[68] Such submissiveness could not last in the free atmosphere of colonial America. Although the shortage of ministers tended to make congregations defer to the Ministerium, it was acknowledged that the people could not be forced to accept a minister they did not want.[69]

When the Ministerium was organized in 1748 it had no constitution. Business was conducted, it was suggested in 1754, in a "childlike, simple, edifying manner and without the least imperiousness."[70] Rules and procedures developed gradually from experience or from observation of the practice in neighboring church bodies. By 1772 there was talk of "a better plan and constitutional regulations," whereupon Kunze was asked to draft some proposals. The comment was made that "a poor father would be foolish to insist that his twenty- and thirty-year-old children should continue to wear clothes that fitted when they were three, six, or nine years old."[71] A constitution was completed by the summer of 1777, and the text was amended

64.
Journals of Muhlenberg, 2:268.
65.
E.g., *Hallesche Nachrichten*, 1:264.
66.
Documentary History, Ministerium of Pa., p. 31.
67.
Ibid., p. 21; cf. *Hallesche Nachrichten*, 1:135.
68.
Hallesche Nachrichten, 1:140; cf. *Documentary History, Ministerium of Pa.*, p. 22.
69.
Journals of Muhlenberg, 1:191; *Hallesche Nachrichten*, 2:166. To call this a "hierarchical tendency" appears to be an overstatement; see Graebner, *Geschichte*, pp. 320–22.
70.
Documentary History, Ministerium of Pa., p. 43.
71.
Journals of Muhlenberg, 2:515.

and presumably adopted by a vote of the Ministerium the following year. It was not until 1781, however, that this constitution was signed and transcribed into the minutes.[72]

In accordance with an earlier proposal, the constitution of 1781 provided for a geographical division into districts or conferences so that "preachers who live nearest together" might confer with one another between annual meetings. Such conferences became substitutes for sessions of the Ministerium in the case of men who lived too far from the place of meeting. One of the districts defined comprised the state of New York, where Frederick A. Muhlenberg, the patriarch's second son, planned to hold a "minister's conference" as early as 1775.[73] It appears probable that it was to this kind of district conference that Kunze referred when he wrote:

To the late Dr. Henry Muhlenberg, who died in the year 1787, belongs the immortal honor of having formed in Pennsylvania a regular ministry, and, what is somewhat remarkable, to one of his sons, who officiated as Lutheran minister from the year 1773 to 1776 in the city of New York, that of having formed the evangelical ministry of New York State.[74]

It was not until 1786 that, under the leadership of Kunze, who had moved from Philadelphia to New York City in 1784, a meeting of three ministers and two laymen was finally held in Albany. Several proposals were there made looking to the formation of a new synod or ministerium independent of the one centering in Pennsylvania. The Pennsylvania constitution of 1781 was tentatively recommended insofar as it would be applicable. Noteworthy was a new proposal to give lay delegates votes as well as seats: "That every congregation of the Evangelical Lutheran faith in this state be entitled to send a delegate to such meeting who, like the preacher, is to have seat and vote, except in the examination of the theological standing of a candidate or the orthodoxy of a preacher who is accused of false teachings."[75] Similar proposals were made in Pennsylvania and incorporated in 1792 in a new constitution. It was in this same year that the New York Ministerium met for the first time after its organizational meeting six years before.[76] It may therefore be said that in 1792 both the Ministerium of New York and the Ministerium of Pennsylvania and Adjacent States became synods made up of clerical and lay delegates, although sentimentally the name "ministerium" was still adhered to.

The Pattern of Congregational Organization

The relation of local congregations to the Ministerium was in some respects ambiguous. Congregations were occasionally referred to as asking to be "incorporated with the united congregations," to "join our number," to "ask for union with us," or to be "regarded as united with the Ministerium."[77] Yet actual membership was expressly limited to ministers. The "united congregations" existed, as it were, alongside the "united ministers." The former were the objects of the latter's care. An examination of the minutes of the annual meetings shows that the

52

72.
Ibid., 3:59, 188; *Documentary History, Ministerium of Pa.*, pp. 165–76, 180, 183.
73.
Documentary History, Ministerium of Pa., pp. 119, 128, 175, 190, 191; *Journals of Muhlenberg*, 2:663.
74.
John Christopher Kunze, ed., *Hymn and Prayer-Book* . . . (New York: Hurtin & Commardinger, 1795), appendix, p. 143. Cf. letter of Frederick A. Muhlenberg to Emanuel Schulze, October 1774, in manuscript PM99, Z1, Krauth Memorial Library Archives, Lutheran Theological Seminary, Philadelphia. For a different view see Robert Fortenbaugh, *The Development of the Synodical Polity of the Lutheran Church in America to 1829* (Philadelphia, 1926), pp. 64–67; Christian O. Kraushaar, *Verfassungsformen der lutherischen Kirchen Amerikas* (Gütersloh: Bertelsmann, 1911), pp. 259–62.
75.
Harry J. Kreider, *History of the United Lutheran Synod of New York and New England, 1786-1860* (Philadelphia: Muhlenberg Press, 1954), p. 18.
76.
Ibid., p. 21; *Documentary History, Ministerium of Pa.*, pp. 223, 240, 241, 244, 253, 254.
77.
Documentary History, Ministerium of Pa., pp. 22, 30, 35, 79, 159.

78.
On this subject see Beale M. Schmucker, "The Organization of the Congregation in the Early Lutheran Churches in America," *Lutheran Church Review* 6 (1887): 188–226; Willem J. Kooiman, "Die Amsterdamer Kirchenordnung," *Evangelische Theologie* 16 (1956): 225–38; Kraushaar, *Verfassungsformen*, pp. 1–26, 44–57; Rudolf Schomerus, *Die verfassungsrechtliche Entwicklung der lutherischen Kirche in Nordamerika von 1638 bis 1792* (Göttingen: Robert Kleinert, 1965), pp. 15–125.

79.
Hallesche Nachrichten, 1:514.

80.
Schomerus, *Die verfassungsrechtliche Entwicklung*, pp. 55–64. There is a partial text of the New York constitution in Karl Kretzmann, "The Constitution of the First Lutheran Synod in America," *Concordia Historical Institute Quarterly* 9 (1936): 3–9, 83–90. Cf. John P. Dern, ed., *The Albany Protocol: Wilhelm Christoph Berkenmeyer's Chronicle, 1731–1750* (Ann Arbor, Mich., 1971), passim, s.v. "church constitution."

ministers and the Ministerium, individually and corporately, existed for the sake of the congregations and their members, however paternalistic the relation may often have been.

In terms of chronology, it was Lutheran lay people who arrived in North America first, as a rule, and now and then they assembled for public worship without benefit of clergy and thus formed primitive congregations. Then ministers came from Europe, either on their own initiative or in response to appeals of colonists, and these ministers expedited the gathering of Lutheran people and the formation of congregations. Finally congregations united with one another for mutual encouragement and service, and this led in time to the organization of synods and larger ecclesiastical bodies. Having become acquainted to some extent with Lutheran lay people and their pastors in colonial America, we need now to look more closely at the congregations which they organized.

The model which shaped congregational structure came directly or indirectly from the Netherlands.[78] There Lutherans comprised only a small minority of the population and were consequently compelled to exist without control or support from the civil government. This was a unique situation for Lutherans, whose churches in most other European lands were established by law as state churches. In 1597 the congregation in Amsterdam, which was by far the largest Lutheran church in the Netherlands, prepared a church order, or constitution, to govern itself. With subsequent revisions this was adopted by other congregations in the Netherlands during the early decades of the seventeenth century. The pattern of organization set forth in this constitution was introduced, although probably not at first in written form, in the early Dutch churches on the Hudson River. When Muhlenberg visited New York a century later he reported:

As far as the external order, the usages, and the ceremonies of public worship are concerned, the aforementioned preachers [among the Dutch and German settlers] introduced a church order, prepared according to the model of the church order used in the Evangelical Lutheran church in Amsterdam, and subscribed it together with the elders and deacons. Up to the present they have also used the liturgy of Amsterdam, which has been adapted to American conditions in a very appropriate and edifying way.[79]

When the constitution was finally put into writing in New York it was drafted by William C. Berkenmeyer in 1735. Like the Amsterdam church order, it provided for a church council, or consistory, made up of a pastor and lay elders and deacons. In keeping with Berkenmeyer's clericalist tendencies, the lay officers were chosen by the church council rather than by the congregation as a whole.[80] The pastor was called by the church council, too, rather than, as in Amsterdam, by the congregation. Oversight over the externals of church life was in any case entrusted to the council. Prior to this there is mention of lay officers in the Swedish churches on the Delaware, and it is probable that when Jacob Fabritius transferred from the Hudson to the Delaware in 1672 he took the Dutch pattern of organization with him. Meanwhile the Amsterdam church order had been adapted for use in St. Mary's (Savoy) Lutheran Church in London, where Lutherans were likewise a small minority. From London this constitution was carried by the Salzburgers to Georgia, and Muhlenberg became acquainted with it not only in London and in Georgia when he first made his way to Pennsylvania in 1742 but also in New York a decade later. In this way the substance of the Amsterdam church order spread until its main features were commonly used throughout America.

The Lutheran congregational organization in the Netherlands had to some extent been patterned after Reformed models, and the influence of Dutch and German Reformed polity may be presupposed in America too. At all events the activity of elders and deacons in the German congregations in southeastern Pennsylvania before the arrival of Muhlenberg can most easily be accounted for in this way. With the passing of years experience suggested changes. The appointment of elders by a minister instead of their election by a congregation proved to be unacceptable. Life tenure of lay officers was in time rejected in favor of two-year or three-year terms and rotation in office. The church council, whose function it was at first to advise the pastor, gradually became a decision-making body. The practice of giving the pastor two votes as over against one for each elder and deacon was soon abandoned.[81]

The direction in all these changes was toward more participation by the laity. It was increasingly recognized that conditions in America required Lutheran congregations to organize as free churches. "The place in which we live and the times, customs, and conditions . . . ," a Swedish clergyman stated as early as 1714, "have rendered it necessary to proceed in a different manner than if we could have help from any government or court."[82] It took a long time before the implications of this insight were realized. Not only did ministers have to acknowledge that "one cannot use force in this country" to impose decisions on the people,[83] but lay officers who temporarily grasped dictatorial power also had to be willing to share their power in the interest of all. Finally Peter Brunnholz and Henry M. Muhlenberg, with help from Carl M. Wrangel, collaborated on the framing of a new congregational constitution which incorporated the fruit of decades of experience. This was adopted in 1762 by St. Michael's Church in Philadelphia. Muhlenberg spoke of the "long desired and necessary constitution" as one "which we may confidently hold up before God and all Christendom."[84] The importance which he attached to the instrument is apparent from his account of its adoption.

I said that I was going to sign my name to this constitution and, if need be, sacrifice my last hours for it, just as it pleased God, and that anyone who was of one mind with me should now do the same. After I had

54

81.
Cf. Schomerus, *Die verfassungsrechtliche Entwicklung*, pp. 87–94.
82.
Burr, *Records of Holy Trinity*, p. 167.
83.
Journals of Muhlenberg, 1:191.
84.
Ibid., p. 561; cf. p. 481.

signed, Mr. Handschuh followed, then the elders and deacons, and then the members pressed forward and signed, in all more than 270. But since this took a long time, many left—not, however, because they did not agree, but with the intention of signing on another occasion.[85]

The constitution declared that the congregation had the permanent right and freedom to elect its officers and ministers by majority vote. In addition to trustees, required by civil law to hold and transfer property, there was provision for a church council of six elders and six deacons. The duties of the former were defined at first as primarily spiritual and of the latter as primarily temporal, but this distinction soon fell away. The elders and deacons, totaling twelve men, were elected by the congregation from thirty-six nominees submitted by the church council. Elders served for three years and deacons for two.

55

When great and important matters occur in the congregation, no matter what they may be called, whether they exist in the church or outside of it, whether they concern the parsonage or the schoolhouse, the cemetery or the place of burial, such a matter is under no circumstances to be decided by the preachers alone, nor by the trustees alone, nor by the six elders and six deacons alone, but it must be given full and mature consideration by the whole church council and decided by at least a two-thirds vote of the entire council. Afterward the matter must be reported to the congregation and, according to the custom of the country, must be approved by two-thirds of the communing members of the congregation.[86]

It was also according to custom that women were excluded from the right to vote. They were usually dismissed before a congregational meeting began, but because women "in many homes rule more than men" the Swedish dean Israel Acrelius permitted them on at least one occasion to stay and listen.[87]

The congregational constitution of 1762 became the model for other congregations along the whole length of the Atlantic seaboard. It gave laymen vote as well as voice on the local level which the Ministerium withheld from them on the provincial and national level until the end of the colonial period. The resulting polity was not "congregational," as has been supposed, for the form of organization was adapted to circumstances in America and was not determined by any theological or biblical prescription. Besides, relations with Lutheran ecclesiastical authorities in Europe and with the united ministers and united congregations in America were testimonies to the belief that the church existed beyond the limits of local congregations. The constitution of 1762 was nevertheless a major landmark in the transformation of a European into an American church, of a state church into a free church. The Lutheran church became a free church not only in the sense that it was independent of state control but also in the sense that membership in the church

85.
Ibid., pp. 561, 562.
86.
Hallesche Nachrichten, 2:439; the full text of the constitution is reproduced on pp. 435–41.
87.
Cf. *Journals of Muhlenberg*, 1:561; 3:334; Burr, *Records of Holy Trinity*, pp. 436, 437.

was voluntary rather than an automatic accompaniment of citizenship.

The Number of Lutherans in the Colonies

We can now return to the question raised earlier (in chapter 2) concerning the number of Lutherans in North America at the close of the colonial period. Part of the answer is related to differences between Europe and America. Henry M. Muhlenberg often referred to the Lutheran church in the colonies as an *ecclesia plantanda* (a church that still had to be planted). He used this Latin expression not as a slogan or motto (the church must be planted!), as has sometimes been suggested,[88] but rather as a descriptive phrase contrasted with another which Muhlenberg also used, *ecclesia plantata* (the church that had already been planted). The latter was applied to Europe and the former to America. In Europe people had been gathered into parishes and church buildings had been erected for their use, and there were enough educated and ordained ministers who had proper oversight and received adequate salaries. Generally the church and its ministry were readily accessible to all people. It was not so in North America, where people were poor and left to their own devices, where Lutheran churches were nowhere built with state subsidies, and where Lutheran ministers were not paid out of government funds.

Access to churches of their own confession was made difficult by the fact that often Lutheran people did not settle together. Except in towns, which were neither numerous nor large, Lutherans tended to disperse.

In the countryside the houses were not close together, as they are in the villages of Germany. There are always several thousand acres together. . . . At first such a region is nothing but forest. . . . When one travels on the road one is constantly moving through woods. Here stands a house, and several miles farther on there is another house near the road.[89]

Because the people were scattered it was not possible to provide everybody with convenient access to a church. In exceptional cases frontiersmen were reported to travel "a hundred or two hundred English miles to hear a sermon and receive the sacraments and weep bitterly over their spiritual neglect."[90] People in rural areas near more populous places were visited on weekdays by ministers from adjacent towns. In 1760 John F. Handschuh, pastor in Philadelphia at the time, made such a preaching tour thirty miles across the Delaware River into southern New Jersey.

Early on Tuesday, June 24, I set out . . . for Cohansey [Friesburg, N.J.]. The following day, Wednesday, a large number of people gathered there, some of them traveling about 36 miles to reach the place. By 9 o'clock in the morning all were there. . . . I conducted the preparatory service with a penitential admonition, preached, baptized twelve children of various ages who cried like lambs during the act of baptism, and administered Holy

88.
E.g., Gerhard E. Lenski in *The Encyclopedia of the Lutheran Church*, ed. Julius Bodensieck, 3 vols. (Minneapolis: Augsburg Publishing House, 1965), 2:1672. Cf. Theodore G. Tappert, "Was Ecclesia Plantanda Muhlenberg's Motto?" *Lutheran Quarterly* 5 (1953): 308–11.
89.
Letter of 1743 in *Hallesche Nachrichten*, 1:14, 15.
90.
Joint report of ministers in Pennsylvania (1754) in ibid., 2:207.

Communion to some 120 persons. Since everything proceeded with unexpected quiet and order my chief task was done by 3 o'clock. . . . On Thursday, when we were ten miles from Cohansey on the return journey, we were asked to stop at a house along the road in order to baptize several children. Within an hour so many people assembled there that we had a fair-sized congregation. Not only were seven children brought forward for baptism but nineteen or twenty persons eagerly desired Holy Communion; they excused themselves for not going to Cohansey on the ground that it was too far and they were too old for such a journey.[91]

Such itinerant ministry to preaching points or outparishes was common practice. A parallel example may be seen in the visits made by pastors among the Salzburgers to Lutherans in Savannah, Georgia, and Purisburg, South Carolina.[92] In the case of Friesburg there was a church building, but for a long time no resident minister, and services could be held only once or twice a year. No constitution had been adopted, and it appears that elders and deacons were inactive if they existed at all. It would be wrong, however, to deny that these people were Christians, or Lutherans, merely because they were not attached to a certain kind of organization. To be sure, prolonged absence of the preaching of the gospel and the administration of the sacraments exposed them to the danger of losing their Christian and Lutheran identity.

Throughout the land there are many thousands who, according to their baptism, training, and confirmation, ought to be Lutherans, but many of them have strayed away. . . . So wretched is the condition and the deterioration of our poor Lutheran people that it can hardly be sufficiently lamented with tears of blood. The children are growing up, and the parents often allow them to live on without baptism, without instruction, and without knowledge, and so they lapse into paganism.[93]

One might presume that half the colonists who had Lutheran roots in Europe ceased to practice the faith of their fathers. This is only a guess, however. The absence of membership rolls and the careless reporting of pastoral acts[94] frustrate attempts to establish the number of adherents beyond such generalizations as have been mentioned.

91.
bid., pp. 278, 279.

92.
Urlsperger, *Ausführliche Nachricht*, 9th continuation, pp. 1099, 1116, 1120, 1143, 1162, and passim; Samuel Urlsperger, ed., *Americanisches Ackerwerk Gottes, oder zuerlässige Nachrichten . . . von Saltzburgischen Emigranten . . . in Georgien*, 4 parts (Augsburg, 1754–67), 1:24, 81, 99, 117, 147, 175, 192, and passim.

93.
Henry M. Muhlenberg (1743) in *Hallesche Nachrichten*, 1:17.

94.
Cf. ibid., 2:57; *Documentary History, Ministerium of Pa.*, pp. 196, 202.

4 Colonists in Church and in Society

When colonial Lutherans first assembled for worship they did so in private homes, in barns, and sometimes in vacant shops. In time, however, church buildings were erected, and except in large towns they were usually designed and constructed by the parishioners themselves. William C. Berkenmeyer reported from the Hudson Valley in 1734: "When I speak of the churches here in the country I always mean a house made of logs, or, if it is high, put together with boards and covered on the outside with plaster. Only our church in New York City is made of stone."[1]

The Building and Financing of Churches

Log churches, although they could be erected quickly, did not last long. Before long the ground timbers rotted and the roof began to leak. In 1760 it was reported that the church in Cohansey (Friesburg, N.J.) "was on the point of collapse because the ground timbers were rotten. Moreover, it was in such condition that one could no longer sit in it and remain dry when it was snowing or raining."[2] One of the most ambitious of all the colonial log churches was completed in 1741 by the Salzburgers in Ebenezer, Georgia. Their senior pastor, John Martin Boltzius, described it:

The walls consist of logs, six inches thick and just as wide, hewn smooth and fitted together so tightly that no wind or rain can penetrate. . . . Because we have no stones and are not now in a position to construct a brick building, the churches, like our houses, had to be erected on thick tree trunks set two feet in the ground and one foot above the ground. They will not last very long, it is true. . . . On the inside the room is 13 feet high from floor to ceiling, 45 feet long, and 30 feet wide. . . . The church has 16 large windows, four on each wall. . . . In the center of each of the long walls is a door. . . .[3]

The average life of a log church was twenty to thirty years, and it was often easier to build a new one than to repair the old. Many congregations accordingly erected three or four log churches, one after another, in less than a century. The constant repairing and rebuilding caused log churches to fall into disfavor, and as soon as a congregation felt equal to the financial burden it undertook the building of a more durable structure. Sometimes this consisted of a stone or brick foundation supporting a weatherboarded building. More often the structure was made entirely of stone or brick.

In the case of town churches, an architect or master builder was consulted, and after the church council and the congrega-

1.
Simon Hart and Harry J. Kreider, trans., *Lutheran Church in New York and New Jersey, 1722-1760: Records in Hamburg* (New York: New York Synod, 1962), p. 56.
2.
Report of John F. Handschuh (1760) in William J. Mann et al., eds., *Nachrichten von den vereinigten Deutschen Evangelisch-Lutherischen Gemeinen in Nord-America* (1787), new ed., 2 vols. (Allentown and Philadelphia: Brobst, Diehl & Co., 1886-95), 2:278 (hereafter cited as *Hallesche Nachrichten*).
3.
Samuel Urlsperger, ed., *Ausführliche Nachricht von den Saltzburgischen Emigranten* (Halle: Waisenhaus, 1735-52), 3d continuation, p. 1914.

tion gave their approval the minister often had to organize and oversee the work. For example, when in 1698 the construction of Trinity Church was begun in Wilmington, Delaware, Eric Bjork, the pastor, cosigned a contract with a mason. After the stonework was finished Bjork called in a carpenter "to talk over the matter of the gable ends." He was interested, as he put it, in making the upper part "look more like a church building." Then he added, "In the meantime we were consulting someone to whitelime and plaster the church within." In turn, a roofer, a glazier, a sawyer, and another carpenter to finish the interior were called upon. In addition to work contracted for, members of the congregation donated labor. So it was decided that "those who can best do the carting shall, of their own free will and at their own expense, haul the stone."[4] The experience with Gloria Dei (Swedish) and St. Michael's (German) churches in Philadelphia was similar, although these churches were built of brick instead of stone. Local stone was most frequently used in rural churches, and these buildings were occasionally distinguished from wood buildings by the popular designation "stone church." Whether the churches were of brick, stone, or wood, the workmen paused according to custom to celebrate the completion of each stage. Congregational ledgers contain items such as those for "rum and sugar for the mason," "a treat to the carpenters . . . on finishing the banisters," "two quarts of rum for the masons and carpenters when they set the door jambs."[5]

As far as the interior of the churches is concerned, balconies were often erected on three sides to accommodate growing congregations. The pulpit was the most conspicuous piece of furniture, and it was elevated when galleries were added so that the preacher would be visible from every seat. An altar or table was placed just below the pulpit and often surrounded by a rail. The pews were made of plain boards and were sometimes enclosed. Foot warmers in the form of heated stones were used by women at times, for the churches were not heated in winter. In 1770 the Swedish church in Wilmington was the first among Lutherans to introduce a wood stove.[6] During the eighteenth century most churches, from Nova Scotia to Georgia, acquired bells; these were usually hung in small belfries and rung to summon the scattered people for public worship, funerals, and the like.[7]

Funds for construction were raised in various ways. Lutherans in every colony appealed for and secured financial assistance from the Netherlands, Sweden, Germany, Denmark, or England, and in some cases solicitors were sent to Europe in person. Books and money were sent from abroad, and some of the Bibles, prayerbooks, and hymnals were sold in America to pay building debts. In addition, contributions were solicited from charitably inclined citizens of various religious persuasions in America. The minutes of the Supreme Executive Council of Pennsylvania record:

A petition from the Minister of the Lutheran church in the city of Albany, praying liberty to collect monies from the pious and benevolent in this State, for the purpose of

4.
Horace Burr, trans., *The Records of Holy Trinity (Old Swedes) Church . . .* (Wilmington, Del.: Historical Society of Delaware, 1890), pp. 17-56.

5.
Amandus Johnson, ed., *The Records of the Swedish Lutheran Churches at Raccoon and Penn's Neck, 1713-1786* (Elizabeth, N.J.: Works Progress Administration, 1938), pp. 119, 202. Cf. manuscript PM95, Z6, p. 11 from back, Krauth Memorial Library Archives, Lutheran Theological Seminary, Philadelphia.

6.
Burr, *Records of Holy Trinity*, pp. 487, 492.

7.
Cf. Theodore G. Tappert and John W. Doberstein, eds., *The Journals of Henry Melchior Muhlenberg*, 3 vols. (Philadelphia: Muhlenberg Press, 1942-58), 1:85; 2:56, 57.

building a house for public worship, was read, and thereupon

Resolved, That the said Minister be informed that Council have no objection to his setting on foot a subscription for the purposes mentioned in the petition.[8]

Similar appeals were made to fellow Lutherans. In response, to mention only a few instances, the Salzburgers in Georgia sent a gift to the church in Trappe, Pennsylvania, Lutherans in the Virgin Islands sent money to their fellow believers in Albany, New York, and parishioners in Philadelphia and Lancaster, Pennsylvania, gathered gifts for the building of a church on the frontier of Pennsylvania.[9] Lotteries were not uncommon in colonial America and Lutherans sometimes borrowed this method of raising money, but laymen as well as clergymen frequently had misgivings about it.[10] The example of Anglicans and Presbyterians was also followed in the widespread adoption of a system of pew rentals. Often the land on which a church was built was donated, and in a few cases the donor's name came to be attached to the building: Follmer's Church, Grubb's Church, Bindnagel's Church. When in 1772 Henry W. Stiegel provided land for a church in Manheim, Pennsylvania, he stipulated payment of ground rent of "one red rose in the month of June, yearly forever hereafter, if the same shall be lawfully demanded." Since 1892 the congregation has observed an annual "festival of the red rose," when a rose is given to a descendant of Stiegel.[11]

In the last analysis money for building churches came chiefly from the parishioners themselves, and subscriptions or pledges were gathered annually by church councilmen.[12] The cost of construction was sometimes reduced, however, by erecting union churches. Union churches were cooperative ventures in which two congregations of different denominations (usually German Reformed and Lutheran) shared ownership and use of property. The idea was imported by colonists from the upper Rhine Valley, where the religious complexion of some territories became mixed and where Lutheran and Reformed people (occasionally also Roman Catholics) used the same building for public worship. Such a union church was called a *simultaneum,* that is, an arrangement for "simultaneous religious exercises of different communions in the same church building."[13] Sometimes services were actually conducted simultaneously in different parts of a building, but more often they were held at different hours.

Reformed and Lutheran people, who migrated together from their homelands on the Rhine and settled down side by side in the new world, built union churches in America as an economy measure. Such churches appeared along the whole Atlantic seaboard, and perhaps half the churches erected in the colonial period were built originally as union churches. They were found most often in rural areas where the population was scattered. When the building of a union church was begun it was customary for the congregations to adopt articles of agreement. In time these became more and more elaborate, but the substance was

60

8.
Minutes of the Supreme Executive Council of Pennsylvania, 16 vols. (Harrisburg, Pa.: T. Fenn, 1852-53), 15:14.
9.
Urlsperger, *Ausführliche Nachricht,* 4th continuation, pp. 2223, 2233; Simon Hart and Harry J. Kreider, trans., *Protocol of the Lutheran Church in New York City, 1702-1750* (New York: New York Synod, 1958), pp. 80-83; *Journals of Muhlenberg,* 2:389.
10.
William J. Mann, *Die gute alte Zeit in Pennsylvanien* (Philadelphia: I. Kohler, 1880), pp. 27, 28.
11.
George L. Heiges, *Henry William Stiegel and His Associates* (Lancaster, Pa., 1948), pp. 176-82.
12.
Cf. John P. Dern, ed., *The Albany Protocol: W. C. Berkenmeyer's Chronicle, 1731-1750* (Ann Arbor, Mich., 1971), pp. 512-16.
13.
In Latin, *"simultaneum exercitium diversae religionis in eadem ecclesia."* Cf. Kurt Rosendorn, *Die rheinhessischen Simultankirchen* (Speyer: Joeger, 1958).

14.
William J. Hinke, *A History of the Goshen-hoppen Reformed Charge, 1727-1819* (Lancaster, Pa.: Pennsylvania German Society, 1920), pp. 143, 144.

15.
Report of Henry M. Muhlenberg to Halle (1745) in *Hallesche Nachrichten*, 1:115.

16.
Hart and Kreider, *Protocol*, p. 311.

17.
Burr, *Records of Holy Trinity*, pp. 114-16.

usually similar to the agreement entered into by Lutheran and Reformed people in Goshenhoppen, Pennsylvania, in 1744.

1. Unitedly and with burning hearts we implore the almighty and gracious God that he may not allow any discord or dissension to arise among us but may preserve us in love and unity in order that the Christian work undertaken by us may have a happy issue.

2. No congregation, either Lutheran or Reformed, shall have any preference as to the [time of] divine services, nor shall either congregation have more rights in the church than the other, but everything shall be done in love, without confusion and disorder, nor shall either congregation disturb the divine services of the other.

3. Mainly and earnestly we stipulate that no false teacher, suspected of heresy and adhering to neither Lutheran nor Reformed doctrines, shall under any circumstances be permitted or tolerated in our house of God, but in such a case either congregation shall have authority, right, and power to close and lock the church against such a false teacher.[14]

Lutherans who did not come from the upper Rhine Valley in Germany were unacquainted with union churches and looked with less favor on them. Muhlenberg, among others, recognized that there were dangers as well as economic advantages in joint ownership and use of church property.

Not surprisingly, the income for building and maintaining churches was in many respects parallel to the sources of income for supporting ministers. Here, too, the chief resource was within the congregations, and money was raised by appealing to members annually for subscriptions. Parishioners were sometimes reluctant to pledge fixed sums in advance because their minister might turn out to be unsatisfactory or might even venture to rebuke them.

There are still quite a few rough codgers like this, and if we come too close home to their consciences they let loose and cry, "What right does this parson have to order me about? Of course I pay him by the year. If he does not preach according to my liking I'll go to another church and get my preaching for nothing."[15]

The method of raising money for salaries by subscription had disadvantages for the ministers too. It made them feel, as they often said, as if they were hirelings, "like cowherds in Germany." Hiring on an annual basis was said to invite people "to drive out pious pastors when the year is up."[16] Even when parishioners were well disposed they were often too poor to pay the salary promised. During most of the colonial period the announced salaries were somewhere between £50 and £100 a year, variations resulting in part from fluctuation in the value of currency from colony to colony. Seldom were the salaries paid in full. "I live worse than a common laborer," Eric Bjork complained.[17]

Fortunately, salaries were not the only income of clergymen. As a rule they were provided with a parsonage, and those who lived in the country, as most did, had the use of a glebe or other adjacent land for growing grain and vegetables and for grazing cattle (for food) and horses (for travel). Firewood, tallow candles, and fodder were supplied. Although cash was often in short supply, parishioners were generous with farm products, as Muhlenberg testified: "One man brings me a sausage, another a piece of meat, a third a chicken, a fourth a loaf of bread, a fifth some pigeons, a sixth rabbits, a seventh eggs, an eighth some tea and sugar, a ninth some honey, a tenth some apples, an eleventh partridges, and so forth."[18] In the course of a later year Muhlenberg received such gifts as a pair of shoes, a bottle of Rhine wine and some plums, a dozen herring, a cake, confections, a pair of new boots and slippers, a half-cord of hickory wood, two pairs of stockings, and varying amounts of money.[19] Lutheran ministers had additional income in the form of perquisites for the performance of pastoral acts. It was customary to announce a schedule of payments: for example, in New York, one shilling for a child's funeral and six shillings for an adult's funeral, but twelve shillings more if a funeral address was desired; three shillings for proclaiming the banns, six shillings for a wedding, and one shilling for churching a woman after childbirth. When, in spite of all these sources of income, most ministers complained that they received barely enough to feed and clothe their families, to say nothing of buying and maintaining horses, they usually blamed this on the fact that "the majority of the people are poor" and on a basic "unwillingness of the people."[20]

Orthodoxist and Pietist Types of Lutherans

Neither the external design of the churches nor the methods of supporting them were determined to a significant extent by the religious professions of the people. Because other things were so affected, however, we need to look into these professions more closely.

The early Dutch Lutherans on the Hudson River fought for a long time to preserve their faith and identity, and when Justus Falckner became the pastor there he wrote a book in which he set forth what he regarded as the fundamental difference between the Dutch Reformed and the Lutheran understandings of the Christian faith.[21] When the consistory in Amsterdam called a successor to Falckner in 1724 it was made explicit that he was to expound "the pure doctrine of God's Word, which is founded on the canonical books of Holy Scripture and contained in . . . the Augsburg Confession and its Apology, the Smalcald Articles, Luther's Catechisms, and the Formula of Concord; faithfully to warn his hearers against all false doctrine; to administer the holy sacraments as instituted by Christ and according to the custom in that church. . . ."[22] Although the Swedish clergymen on the Delaware were less rigid, they were reminded of their adherence to the "unaltered Augsburg Confession," whose faith they were "to expound clearly and purely, without any admixture of superstition and false doctrine."[23] Similar attachment to the doctrinal standards of the Lutheran church was affirmed in the constitutions of 1733 and 1774 which were in force among

18.
Journals of Muhlenberg, 1:91.
19.
Ibid., pp. 481–614, passim.
20.
Hart and Kreider, *Lutheran Church*, p. 66; Amandus Johnson, *The Journal and Biography of Nicholas Collin, 1746-1831* (Philadelphia: New Jersey Society of Pennsylvania, 1936), p. 220.
21.
Grondlycke Onderricht van Sekere Voorname Hoofd-stucken der waren, lautern, selikmakende Christelycken Leere (New York: W. Bradfordt, 1708).
22.
Arnold J. H. vanLaer, trans., *The Lutheran Church in New York, 1649-1772: Records in the Lutheran Church Archives at Amsterdam, Holland* (New York: New York Public Library, 1946), pp. 121, 122.
23.
Thomas Campanius [Holm], *Short Description of the Province of New Sweden* (1702), trans. Peter S. DuPonceau (Philadelphia: McCarty & Davis, 1834), pp. 94-96.

24.
Cf. P. A. Strobel, *The Salzburgers and Their Descendants* (Baltimore: T. Newton Kurtz, 1855), pp. 94, 170, 171; G. D. Bernheim, *History of the German Settlements . . . in North and South Carolina* (Philadelphia: Lutheran Book Store, 1872), pp. 251, 266, 301.
25.
Documentary History of the Evangelical Lutheran Ministerium of Pennsylvania . . . 1748-1821 (Philadelphia: General Council Board of Publication, 1898), pp. 21, 175. For further discussion of the subject see Theodore E. Schmauk, *The Confessional Principle and the Confessions of the Lutheran Church* (Philadelphia: General Council Board of Publication, 1911), pp. 859-73.

the Salzburgers in Georgia and in the constitutions used in North and South Carolina.[24] The same was true of congregations connected directly and indirectly with the Ministerium of North America, where candidates for ordination promised to teach and preach only "what harmonizes with the Word of God and the Confessions of the Evangelical Lutheran Church."[25] Insofar as formal statements are concerned, therefore, all the Lutheran churches and all acknowledged Lutheran ministers subscribed to the Lutheran faith and the official standards which were the historical witnesses to it.

63

Actually there were some variations within this general conformity. Lutherans in North America inherited from Europe some tensions between strict and loose interpreters of the confessions. The former were usually called orthodoxists because they were representatives of the tendency to stress correct doctrine which was dominant in the seventeenth century. The latter were usually called pietists because they were representatives of a reaction which emphasized Christian life and piety rather than Christian doctrine and belief and which was dominant in the eighteenth century. Philip Jakob Spener (1635-1705) and August Herman Francke (1663-1727) were the early leaders of pietism in Germany, and from there the movement spread into the Scandinavian countries. It had the warm support of some rulers and members of the nobility, but it was sternly opposed by others, especially in areas bordering on the North Sea. When pietists met for the cultivation of holiness in assemblies (*collegia pietatis*) outside of churches, these meetings were often suppressed by civil authorities as dangerous conventicles. Pietists did not gain friends among their critics when they denounced the theater, dancing, and other "worldly pleasures." On the other hand orthodoxists were charged with making the Christian faith a matter of knowledge rather than experience and with substituting intellectual assent for heartfelt trust.

There were echoes of this conflict in North America. Some of the Lutheran colonists came to America with orthodoxist convictions while others came with pietist inclinations. Significantly it was the pietist circles in Europe that responded most quickly and generously to appeals for help from America: Jesper Svedberg, bishop of the Church of Sweden, who was largely responsible for the "golden age" of the Swedish mission on the Delaware; Gotthilf A. Francke, who sent men and money from Halle to Pennsylvania and other colonies; Samuel Urlsperger, senior of the ministerium in Augsburg, who supplied the Salzburgers in Georgia with continuing assistance; and Frederick M. Ziegenhagen, Lutheran pastor in London, who was a key contact for colonists and their ministers—all were critics of orthodoxism and representatives of pietist emphases. On the other hand, the consistory in Amsterdam and the ministerium in Hamburg, both of which helped the Lutherans on the Hudson, were orthodoxist in tendency. Men who came on their own initiative and became clergymen in America were sometimes pietists, like John C. Hartwick, and sometimes orthodoxists, like John Caspar Stoever, Jr., but the dominant influence among Lutherans in North America was pietistic. The impulse that went out from the Franckean institutions in Halle, Saxony, was especially great both in terms of the number of ministers sent abroad and in terms of the shaping of a style of life.

Evidence of the tension between pietists and orthodoxists can be seen when, in 1748, Muhlenberg and his associates did not invite to the first sessions of the Ministerium of North America the ministers with whom, it was said, "we can have no fellowship and close brotherhood" because "they decry us as pietists without reason." A dozen years later opponents spread rumors to the effect that "the preachers sent from Halle were pietists, secret Zinzendorfians, teachers of error, no true Lutherans, but seducers and dangerous people." In New York William C. Berkenmeyer called Hartwick a "crypto-Herrnhuter," or secret Moravian, attacking him in a booklet published in 1749.[26] Charges were preferred against Carl M. Wrangel by some of his Swedish colleagues on the Delaware on account of his pietistic leanings and his support of the English evangelist George Whitefield. An Anglican echoed the charges:

Mr. Whitefield . . . has thrown the Clergy and laity in the country into a very great consternation. . . . Mr. Duchée, one of the assistant Ministers in Christ Church in Philadelphia, and Mr. Wrangel, the Swedish Minister, have appeared more openly than the others in preaching up his Doctrine and espousing his cause—they have set up private Meetings in Town, where they admit of none but such as they deem converted.[27]

One of the criticisms that orthodoxists and others had of Muhlenberg was that his standards of conduct were too rigorous. "Since we have to hire a preacher for money," one of them put it, "let's have a jolly one, for this Muhlenberg is too strict for us." In 1751 he visited New York City and remarked that his auditors noticed a difference between his preaching and the orthodoxist preaching of Berkenmeyer and others to which they had been accustomed. He reported that "whatever is said that does not sound like the old doctrine but urges conversion to God and living faith in the Lord Jesus seems dangerous to them."[28] Ten years later, when Muhlenberg was charged with heterodoxy and unchristian conduct, he defended himself with vigor:

I herewith challenge Satan and all his servile, lying spirits to prove against me the least point that would be repugnant to the teachings of the apostles and prophets and our symbolical writings. . . . Again and again I have stated orally and in writing that . . . in our Confessions I discover no error, blemish, or defect.[29]

The trouble with the orthodoxists, Muhlenberg was fond of saying, was that they tried to adhere to the unaltered Augsburg Confession with unaltered hearts.[30]

Before the end of the colonial period the influence of English deism, French skepticism, and the German Enlightenment began to raise doubts concerning religion in the minds of some colonists. A Lutheran minister ventured to say that the apostles had corrupted the teachings of Jesus, and to prevent the spread

26.
Documentary History, Ministerium of Pa., pp. 11, 50; Dern, *Albany Protocol,* pp. xlvi, xlvii.
27.
William Stevens Perry, ed., *Papers Relating to the History of the [Anglican] Church in Pennsylvania, 1680-1778* (Philadelphia, 1871), p 354. Cf. Nils Jacobsson, *Bland Svenskamerikaner och Gustavianer: Ur Carl Magnus Wrangels Levnadshistoria, 1727-1786* (Stockholm: Svenska Kyrkans Diakonistyrelses Bokförlag, 1953), pp. 192-95.
28.
Journals of Muhlenberg, 1:97, 278.
29.
William J. Mann, "The Conservatism of Henry Melchior Muhlenberg," *Lutheran Church Review* 7 (1888): 33.
30.
Journals of Muhlenberg, 2:387; 3:427. For an overall view of German pietism see F. Ernest Stoeffler, *The Rise of Evangelical Pietism* (Leiden: E. J. Brill, 1969); and idem, *German Pietism During the Eighteenth Century* (Leiden: E. J. Brill, 1973).

of such notions it was proposed that no minister should be called from Germany until there was improvement in the situation there.[31] Not until later did this new way of thinking gain a real footing among some Lutherans in America.

The Atmosphere of Public Worship

The dominant pietistic mood affected the atmosphere of public worship, but there was some diversity of practice. On the Delaware, primitive conditions did not at first permit the introduction of the entire Swedish liturgy, but after the restoration of relations with the old country in 1697 and the erection of permanent church buildings this ideal was more nearly approached. The church year was observed, and Christmas, Easter, and Pentecost were special festivals. The main features of the services consisted of confession and absolution, Scripture lessons, the Apostles' Creed, the sermon, hymns, prayers, and benediction. The intoning of parts of the service and the participation of the congregation in liturgical responses were regarded by English-speaking neighbors as singular. "Divine service is performed without let or hindrance according to the prescriptions of the Church of Sweden. . . . The genuine Swedes are also greatly attached to their church usages. . . . The singing of the Creed seems strange to the English."[32]

In the Dutch Lutheran churches on the Hudson, public worship was simpler. The model for it was the Amsterdam church order.[33] The same order, as revised for use in the Savoy Lutheran Church in London, was employed among the Salzburgers in Georgia. "In our public services and pastoral acts," it was reported, "we use the London church order as our guide in all respects." Worship on Sundays and festivals began there with "prayer from the London liturgy." The service also included Scripture lessons, hymns, sermon, "extemporaneous prayer" ending with the Lord's Prayer, and benediction.[34] Typical of many pietists was the scrupulosity with respect to ceremony expressed by John Martin Boltzius:

Among other things we have taken pains to guard our congregation against the *opus operatum* and to lead them always from such external ceremonies and practices (insofar as they are edifying they are carefully used among us) to the chief content of Christianity. In public services, in the Lord's Supper, and in the preparation for this we therefore arrange things as simply and edifyingly as God's grace enables us.[35]

The Amsterdam-London liturgy was also used in Nova Scotia and North Carolina. Here and there a German translation of a few parts of the Anglican *Book of Common Prayer* were also used.[36] When a form of worship was prepared in 1748 for adoption at the first meeting of the Ministerium in Philadelphia, Muhlenberg wrote in his diary with reference to Peter Brunnholz, John F. Handschuh, and himself:

To adopt the Swedish liturgy did not appear either suitable or necessary since most of our congregations came from the districts on the Rhine and the Main and

31.
Journals of Muhlenberg, 2:569; 3:637. Correspondence of Henry M. Muhlenberg in manuscript PM95, A1783–84, pp. 17, 21, 56, Krauth Memorial Library Archives.

32.
Israel Acrelius, *A History of New Sweden* (1759), trans. William M. Reynolds (Philadelphia: Historical Society of Pennsylvania, 1874), p. 359.

33.
Hallesche Nachrichten, 1:514.

34.
Urlsperger, *Ausführliche Nachricht,* 2d continuation, pp. 889, 890; Strobel, *The Salzburgers,* pp. 175, 176.

35.
Letter to Gotthilf A. Francke (1735) in Urlsperger, *Ausführliche Nachricht,* 1st continuation, p. 474.

36.
Hallesche Nachrichten, 1:576; 2:111; *Documentary History, Ministerium of Pa.,* p. 98.

considered the singing of collects to be papistical. Nor yet could we select a liturgy with regard to every individual's accustomed use, since almost every country town and village has its own. We therefore took the liturgy of the Savoy Church in London as the basis, cut out parts and added to it according to what seemed to us to be profitable and edifying in these circumstances.[37]

66

The liturgy of 1748 borrowed from several German orders as well as from the London liturgy. Handwritten copies were made by ministers, and in this form the liturgy had limited circulation.[38] It must not be supposed that all services actually adhered to the proposed form in spite of admonitions to conform. The liturgy was used more in town congregations than in rural congregations. Even where the liturgy was used, the responses of the congregation were very limited, but the traditional elements were present: confession, collect, hymns, lessons, sermon, prayer, and benediction. As the eighteenth century advanced, the tendency was to depart more and more from the standard proposed in 1748.

In order to get a better impression of what Lutheran worship was like we need to take into account that the minister may have worn a white surplice or alb if he was among the Swedes or a black gown, with or without bands, if he was among the Dutch or Germans. This was likely to be so only in town churches, for ministers found it inconvenient to carry vestments with them when riding on horseback from one country church to another, especially in rain or snow. For example, in North Carolina, Arnold Roschen reported, "We preach in a black suit and collar, usually, however, without a gown."[39] Paraments were used on altars and pulpits, especially in the Swedish churches, but altar linens were mentioned in Dutch and German churches as well. Adornments of any kind on interior walls were rare. The Swedes noted that English-speaking Protestants regarded crucifixes and representations of saints as idolatrous. An exception was a German church in York, Pennsylvania, that was reported to have "all kinds of paintings, including one of the blessed Dr. Luther, which is life-size and fairly recognizable because his name is written underneath in large letters."[40] As a rule, therefore, people assembled in churches that were unadorned, the men on one side and the women on the other, to listen and to sing.

Vigorous hymn-singing was inherited from Europe. When Boltzius visited John Wesley in Savannah in 1737, the Englishman praised the hymns of the Salzburgers.[41] Shortly after this, Muhlenberg wrote that on a missionary journey in Pennsylvania he preached in their own tongues to German and English settlers who had not had an opportunity to hear the gospel for a long time. "The English people were very attentive and much moved. . . . The English were amazed at our singing and almost went into raptures over it, for some of the people had fine musical voices and knew how to sing in harmony."[42] Hymns

37.
Journals of Muhlenberg, 1:193, 194.
38.
Ibid., 1:647, 653; 2:121. For a translation of the liturgy see *Documentary History, Ministerium of Pa.*, pp. 13–18. For an evaluation see Beale M. Schmucker, "The First Pennsylvania Liturgy," *Lutheran Church Review* 1 (1882): 16–27, 161–72.
39.
William K. Boyd and Charles A. Krummel, "German Tracts Concerning the Lutheran Church in North Carolina During the Eighteenth Century," *North Carolina Historical Review* 8 (1930): 334.
40.
Acrelius, *History of New Sweden*, p. 359; *Journals of Muhlenberg*, 2:394.
41.
Urlsperger, *Ausführliche Nachricht*, 3d continuation, p. 1092.
42.
Journals of Muhlenberg, 2:246; cf. 2:442.

were sung not only during church services but also by families at home, by workers in fields and shops, and by ministers making pastoral visits. The important place which hymns occupied in the lives of the people is suggested by the fact that not a few of the ministers were authors of hymns. Justus Falckner wrote several that found their way into such collections of the time as the Halle and Moravian hymnals. Best known later in English translation is his "Rise, Ye Children of Salvation." Henry M. Muhlenberg wrote hymns of a more occasional character, notably a hymn of thirty-six stanzas composed for the dedication in 1752 of St. Michael's Church in Germantown, Pennsylvania. His youngest son, Gotthilf H. E. Muhlenberg, wrote a special hymn for confirmands, and some hymns by John C. Kunze and Justus H. C. Helmuth were included in the *Erbauliche Liedersammlung* (1786) which they helped to edit.[43]

Instrumental accompaniment for hymns in church services seems to have been unknown in the seventeenth century. In 1701 Falckner wrote to a friend in Germany that an organ was much to be desired. The Swedish churches on the Delaware were the first Lutheran churches in North America to have organs. It was reported that in 1740 "a small, new, and fine organ was set up" in Gloria Dei Church in Philadelphia.[44] In 1751 three German churches in Philadelphia, Trappe, and New Hanover, Pennsylvania, got organs which were transported from Germany under the supervision of the schoolmaster and organist Gottlieb Mittelberger. Because Quakers and others objected to instrumental music in public worship, it was deemed necessary to publish a dedicatory program in which the use of organs was justified.[45] In the second half of the eighteenth century organs were built in larger numbers in America, and more and more churches, especially in towns, secured such instruments. Some churches derived their fame from the possession of organs, and the so-called "organ churches" in Rowan County, North Carolina, and East Pikeland, Pennsylvania, are examples of this. In lieu of an organ (or to supplement organ music) harps, trumpets, French horns, oboes, and other instruments were occasionally employed to accompany hymns.

Preaching and the Lord's Supper

Although vibrant singing was a prominent feature of colonial Lutheran worship, it was the preaching that was responsible for its distinctive character. From the point of view of the preachers there was much preaching, for in addition to conducting services where they resided they usually traveled to preach on weekdays where there were no ministers. From the point of view of the laity there was too little preaching, for, unless laymen lived in large towns where ministers had their residences, services were conducted nearby only once every three weeks (as in Frederick, Md.), once every six weeks (as in Easton, Pa.), three times a year (as in Hackensack, N.J.), or even less often. It was frequently remarked that people who seldom had an opportunity to hear a sermon traveled great distances to do so and were

43.
Cf. Don Yoder, *Pennsylvania Spirituals* (Lancaster, Pa.: Pennsylvania Folklife Society, 1961), pp. 122, 123.
44.
Julius F. Sachse, *Justus Falckner, Mystic and Scholar* (Philadelphia, 1903), pp. 44–46; Acrelius, *History of New Sweden*, p. 238.
45.
Hallesche Nachrichten, 2:69. On this subject see William H. Armstrong, *Organs for America: The Life and Work of David Tannenberg* (Philadelphia: University of Pennsylvania, 1967).

especially attentive. In 1745 Brunnholz was urgently requested to preach to some Germans in Chester, Pennsylvania, about sixteen miles from Philadelphia. He reported:

Most of the Germans who assembled there were servants, indentured to English masters, and as a consequence they spoke half German and half English. . . . They stood around me like children, or like famishing sheep that had no shepherd, and began to weep. . . . In Germany there are very few who appreciate the opportunity of hearing one, two, or even three sermons every Sunday, but here there are many who are glad if they hear a sermon once a year. It is six years since these people in Chester have been able to hear an Evangelical [Lutheran] sermon in German.[46]

Sermons, often prepared in the saddle, averaged between three-quarters of an hour to a full hour in length. Sometimes sermons were even longer. John S. Gerock's sermon at the dedication of a new church in New York City "lasted two hours and made a sharp impression," and John C. Hartwick "usually could not or would not cut his sermons down to less than two hours." The liturgy of 1748 prescribed that the sermon should ordinarily be "three-quarters of an hour or at most one hour" in length, but some elders feared that the liturgy in addition to the sermon would make the service too long, "especially in the cold winter."[47] In the Swedish church in Wilmington in 1753 an hourglass was placed on the pulpit to help the preacher regulate the length of his sermon.[48] Country congregations seem to have been less impatient with long sermons than town congregations, partly because services were held less frequently in rural areas and partly because the people often traveled great distances to get to church and wished their trip to be worthwhile. This is not to suggest that the auditors were uncritical. It was hard to please everybody, August H. Schmidt reported from Easton, Pennsylvania. If he preached without notes he was called a Quaker, but if he used notes he was charged with a lack of personal religious experience and piety. If he preached only a half-hour it was not worthwhile going to church, but if he preached for an hour the people complained, "Will he never finish?"[49]

The quality and effectiveness of preaching naturally varied from one minister to another. Exposition of segments of the Scriptures played a large part in sermons, but the ultimate goal was not instruction so much as it was edification. When the best method of preaching was being discussed at a meeting of the Ministerium in Philadelphia in 1706 it was said:

One should not affect erudition but descend to the level of the people. . . . The attempt should be made not simply to amass materials but rather to work them out and lay them on the hearts of hearers. . . . This must be done in a practical rather than in a dry way, and the Christian religion should be presented as a pleasure rather than as a burden.[50]

Peter Brunnholz declared that his purpose was achieved "not only by publicly proclaiming the Word of God in its purity but

46.
Report of Peter Brunnholz (1745) in *Hallesche Nachrichten,* 1:108.
47.
Journals of Muhlenberg, 1:283; 2:329; 3:177; *Hallesche Nachrichten,* 1:210, 212; Dern, *Albany Protocol,* p. 119.
48.
Burr, *Records of Holy Trinity,* pp. 451, 452.
49.
Heinrich Philipp Conrad Henke, *Archiv für die neueste Kirchen-Geschichte,* 6 vols. (Weimar, 1795-99), 5:239-42.
50.
Journals of Muhlenberg, 1:448, 449; *Hallesche Nachrichten,* 2:371.

68

especially by bringing it faithfully to bear in its saving power on the souls of his hearers."[51] It was characteristic of the pietistic tradition that was dominant among colonial Lutherans to regard Christianity as a matter of the heart rather than of the head. Preaching was therefore addressed to the consciences of people with the intention of producing evidences of conversion. This is what Muhlenberg had in mind when he said: "Theoretical knowledge, without practice and experience, leaves one in the lurch when a test comes."[52]

Catechization was associated with preaching. Among the Swedes on the Delaware it was customary during the summer months to have sermons on the Catechism, whereupon the preacher "went through the aisles and repeated his sermon and also examined the people on what had been said." Several times a year similar catechization was conducted among small clusters of families in private homes. The practice was scarcely different among Dutch and German Lutherans. Adults were sometimes timid about answering questions in public, but the intention was to fix in the minds and hearts of adults as well as children what was believed to be essential in the Christian faith. It was observed that "the people grasp and understand a presentation in question and answer much better than they do a connected discourse in a sermon that sometimes rushes past them."[53]

Many ministers in the eighteenth century meticulously recorded in their diaries, reports, and correspondence what effects their preaching seemed to have. Abundant evidence was available because that was an age in which people carried their hearts on their sleeves. Parishioners were often seen to weep and sob during a sermon. Individuals who were "awakened"—that is, persons who became conscious of their sin and who repented—were sometimes invited publicly to a conference with the pastor for additional counsel. In town congregations larger prayer meetings, or assemblies for the cultivation of holiness, also met at times in private homes. Here "awakened" individuals were sometimes "converted"—that is, brought to a dramatic experience of God's pardon. In a series of letters Helmuth described what once happened in Lancaster, Pennsylvania, under his ministry.

As far as the inner condition [of the congregation] is concerned, an uncommonly blessed awakening is in progress. Old and dead sinners are coming to life again and are crying out with tears for grace. Sinners for whom I have often given up hope are now being moved mightily. In fact, quite a few of them have been converted to Christ. . . . Those who have come to a better understanding have drawn closer together and have met two or three times a week in various houses to sing together, pray, read a chapter of the Bible and in Arndt's _True Christianity_, and review the sermon [of the previous Sunday].[54]

This description is parallel to accounts of revivals in Germany and Scandinavia as well as in a variety of denominations during the Great Awakening in eighteenth-century America. A conta-

69

51.
Report of Peter Brunnholz (1745) in _Hallesche Nachrichten_, 2:73.
52.
Journals of Muhlenberg, 1:498.
53.
Acrelius, _History of New Sweden_, pp. 218, 243, 244; Urlsperger, _Ausführliche Nachricht_, 2d continuation, pp. 583, 584, 590, 618, and passim; _Hallesche Nachrichten_, 1:407; 2:43–45.
54.
Letters of Justus H. C. Helmuth to Halle (1772, 1773) in _Hallesche Nachrichten_, 2:689, 693.

gion of emotion seems to have played a part, as may be seen in an instance connected with the evangelist George Whitefield (1714–70).

One time when the sainted Mr. Whitefield was preaching forty miles from Philadelphia a German woman undertook to go there and went on foot. On her return she asserted that never in all her life had she had such a quickening, awakening, and edifying experience as when she listened to this man. To be sure, she understood nothing of his English sermon. . . .[55]

55.
Journals of Muhlenberg, 2:696.
56.
Samuel Urlsperger, ed., *Americanisches Ackerwerk Gottes, oder zuverlässige Nachrichten . . . von Saltzburgischen Emigranten . . . in Georgien* (Augsburg, 1754–67), 1:5.
57.
Journals of Muhlenberg, 1:307; *Hallesche Nachrichten,* 2:121. On the whole subject see Gottfried Fritschel, "Die Praxis der Väter und Gründer der lutherischen Kirche Amerikas bei der Verwaltung des heiligen Abendmahls," *Theologische Monatshefte* 1(1868): 321–37, 353–72.

In addition to preaching, the Lord's Supper was administered from time to time. On such occasions it was not unusual for the minister to preach on the meaning of the sacrament. The views of Quakers, Mennonites, Baptists, and others were counteracted by emphasizing that the sacrament is a means of grace. An observation such as this was made:

In this dangerous land it is necessary that our auditors, both adults and children, are carefully instructed in the wholesome teaching of our church concerning baptism and the Lord's Supper, for both sacraments of the New Testament have many opponents here, some of whom despise them in theory and practice and others of whom attach a false meaning to them.[56]

Over against mainline Protestants a more tolerant and unpolemical stance was taken. To an audience consisting of Reformed and Lutheran people Muhlenberg once preached on the sacrament in such a way that neither party was offended. He preached, he said, in the manner of Queen Elizabeth I, who was reported to have declared:

It was the Lord that spake it;
He took the bread and brake it;
And what the Word did make it,
That I believe and take it.[57]

This is not to suggest that intercommunion was practiced, for as a rule participation in the sacrament was limited to members of a particular confession, even in union churches.

Frequency of communion was not determined chiefly by "pioneer conditions," as has sometimes been said, but rather by the understanding of the sacrament, and this was inherited from Europe. It is true that the Lord's Supper was administered only once or twice a year in most country churches, but even in town churches in which services were held every Sunday the sacrament was not available much more frequently. In the Swedish churches on the Delaware the Lord's Supper was normally administered four to six times a year, among the Salzburgers in Georgia about six times, among the Dutch in New York City three times, and among the Germans in Philadelphia three to six times. Even at that, records indicate that communicants did not throng to the altars. Neither pastors nor people took reception of the sacrament lightly. Parishioners should not rush to the table of the Lord, it was said, but "should examine themselves outwardly and inwardly, get down on their knees, and continue to pray and beseech God until they attain a true change of heart and faith in the Lord Jesus; only then will they be fit guests at his table."[58] Drunkards and others who violated accepted norms of behavior were admitted only after public reproof. A couple who had given offense by "sporting and dancing" were refused. The "unworthy" were not welcome, and many who regarded themselves as unworthy because of their scruples avoided the sacrament. Not untypical was this pastoral advice:

N. wished to go to the table of our Lord, but in accordance with my counsel he stayed away. His wife also wished to receive the sacrament on her sickbed, but I did not give it to her because she is full of unbelief, love of the world, and unwillingness to be reconciled with those who offended her, although she does not think so. . . . On her account the husband should postpone his use of the Lord's Supper.[59]

Christian Conduct and Service of Fellow Men

Pastoral ministry was obviously related closely to the observance of the sacrament. Administration of the Lord's Supper was uniformly preceded by the parishioners' announcement of their intention to commune, and this provided opportunity for personal inquiry into their spiritual condition. There were other occasions, too, for visits to the pastor and for visits of the pastor to the homes of the people. The purpose of these calls were not social. Ministers seized every opportunity for "edifying conversation," as they were fond of expressing it. They asked parishioners to relate the story of their lives and the circumstances of their awakening or conversion. They looked for "evidences of the grace of God working in people," for "traces of the power of godliness," or for "a true change of heart."[60] The test of true conversion could be detected in subsequent conduct, it was believed, and the Christian life tended to be described in negative terms. Fairs, horse-racing, card-playing, and other forms of amusement were frowned upon as ungodly. The singing of secular songs was criticized. With few exceptions, dancing and "frolicking" were denounced. A typical, if extreme, example was the apparent commendation of a young woman who, "when she was in the company of other young people, never laughed but testified that she found no pleasure in any conversation that was not concerned with Jesus."[61]

A great deal of attention was given to the sick and the dying. It may be said, in fact, that it was characteristic of pietistic otherworldliness to prepare more for death than for life. Not that the bodies of the sick were neglected, for at a time when medical knowledge was primitive and good physicians were rare, the diaries of clergymen reveal that they often prescribed for fevers, ague, pleurisy, "running fire," colic, dysentery, smallpox, malaria, epilepsy, rheumatism, etc. For the most part, the Lutheran ministers limited themselves to the use of medicines prepared according to private recipes in Halle and sent abroad in considerable quantities.[62] Sickness was interpreted as a visitation from God. Accordingly, ministers spent hours at the bedsides of the sick, confronting the impenitent with the law and

58.
Urlsperger, *Ausführliche Nachricht,* 2d continuation, p. 838.
59.
Ibid., 4th continuation, p. 2190.
60.
Hallesche Nachrichten, 1:380, 386, 481; 2:21, 39, 40, 44, 161, 162; Urlsperger, *Ausführliche Nachricht,* 6th continuation, p. 49; 8th continuation, pp. 726, 831.
61.
Hallesche Nachrichten, 2:41; *Journals of Muhlenberg,* 1:229, 268, 382; 2:89, 637; 3:309, 573, 619, 746.
62.
Heinrich M. Mühlenberg, *Selbstbiographie, 1711-1743,* ed. W. Germann (Allentown, Pa.: Brobst, Diehl & Co., 1881), pp. 209, 210; cf. Stevenson W. Fletcher, *Pennsylvania Agriculture and Country Life, 1640-1840* (Harrisburg, Pa.: Historical and Museum Commission, 1950), pp. 427-33.

comforting believers with the gospel. For the edification of others they recorded numerous case studies ("remarkable examples") of their ministry to the sick and dying.[63]

These were not the only objects of concern. From early times parishioners on the Delaware and Hudson rivers were encouraged to contribute toward the relief of the poor, the assumption being that each congregation would take care of its own needy. Extreme poverty usually resulted from some calamity, such as the incapacity or death of a husband and father, and throughout the colonial period there was compassion for widows and orphans. In 1737 the Salzburgers in Georgia, with help from abroad, erected an orphans' home. Actually it housed half-orphans as well as orphans, and forsaken adults as well as children. The evangelist George Whitefield was much impressed by the institution when he visited it.[64] A few years later Swedish layman Peter Kock proposed the establishment of an orphanage, "like the orphan house at Halle," in Philadelphia. Neither this nor the proposal in 1773 that a house be erected outside of Philadelphia for the aged and orphans was realized at this time. In 1750 the Lutheran Ministerium took action to protect orphaned children who arrived in the port of Philadelphia.

A guardian shall be appointed in Philadelphia for the orphans who have just arrived and whose passage has been paid, although their parents were lost at sea. He shall see to it that they are not deprived of their rights by deceivers and unjust persons. For this position John Eberle, of Philadelphia, was appointed. During the past year he was used for this purpose by Pastor Brunnholz [in St. Michael's Church] and by his diligence prevented much mischief.[65]

The inhuman treatment of many passengers, especially indentured servants, on their voyage to America required more than a guardian for orphans. In 1764 a number of prominent Germans in Philadelphia met in the local Lutheran schoolhouse and organized the German Society of Pennsylvania with Henry Keppele, Lutheran merchant, as the first president. A large proportion of the original and the later members were Lutheran. Through concerted action reforms were gradually introduced in the transport of colonists, and the society also made a variety of other charitable and cultural contributions. A similar society was formed in 1766 in Charleston, South Carolina.[66] Meanwhile, Lutheran ministers visited patients in hospitals and almshouses. They ministered to prisoners. Congregations occasionally raised money for the relief of refugees on the frontier, and their ministers interceded in behalf of persons in one kind of trouble or another.[67]

Concern for fellow men, fostered especially where pietistic influence was felt, extended to the American Indians. The Swedish governors on the Delaware were instructed to live in peace with the Indians and bear witness among them to the Christian faith. Indians sometimes attended the services conducted by John Campanius, who was pastor on the Delaware from 1643 to 1648, and called him "big mouth" because "they

63.
Cf. *Hallesche Nachrichten*, 2:445–93, 501–20, 588–615, 637–48, 672–80, 722–30.
64.
Urlsperger, *Ausführliche Nachricht*, 4th continuation, pp. 2206-8. Cf. Albert D. Belden, *George Whitefield, the Awakener* (Nashville, Tenn.: Cokesbury, 1930), p. 48.
65.
Documentary History, Ministerium of Pa., pp. 31, 32; *Hallesche Nachrichten*, 1:472.
66.
Oswald Seidensticker, *Geschichte der Deutschen Gesellschaft von Pennsylvanien* (Philadelphia: I. Kohler, 1876), pp. 7–50; George J. Gongaware, *The History of the German Friendly Society of Charleston, S.C.* (Richmond, Va.: Garrett, 1935).
67.
Cf. *Journals of Muhlenberg*, 1:655; 2:8, 17, 39, 84, 242, 265; 3:27, 28, 79, 604.

68.
Campanius, *Description of New Sweden*, pp. 75, 76; cf. p. 140.

69.
Acrelius, *History of New Sweden*, p. 283. The title of the catechism, a facsimile edition of which was published in Stockholm on the tercentenary of the founding of the colony in 1938, is *Lutheri Catechismus, öfwersatt pa American-Virginiske Spraket* (Stockholm: J. J. Genath, 1696). On the whole missionary effort see Nils Jacobssen, *Svanskar och Indianer* (Stockholm: Svenska Kyrkans Diakonistyrelses Bokförlag, 1922).

70.
VanLaer, *Lutheran Church in New York*, p. 70.

71.
The text of the will is reproduced in Henry H. Heins, *Throughout All the Years: The Bicentennial Story of Hartwick in America, 1746-1946* (Oneonta, N.Y.: Hartwick College, 1946), pp. 148-57.

72.
Urlsperger, *Ausführliche Nachricht*, 4th continuation, pp. 2277, 2278.

73.
E.g., Ellis B. Burgess, *Memorial History of the Pittsburgh Synod . . .* (Greensville, Pa.: Beaver, 1925), pp. 23-27; *Hallesche Nachrichten*, 2:247.

greatly wondered that he had so much to say, and that he stood alone and talked so long while all the rest were listening in silence. . . . [Gradually] he gained their affection, and they visited and sent for him very frequently. This induced him to exert himself to learn their language."[68] Campanius reduced to writing the sounds of the Indian speech which he heard, and then he laboriously translated Luther's Small Catechism into the dialect of the Lenapes. He undoubtedly used this text in experiments with the Indians, but after his return to Sweden he improved it. In this revised form it was printed in 1696 at royal expense, and five hundred copies were dispatched to the Delaware. Some missionary efforts were made with the use of the translation but virtually nothing was accomplished.[69]

Quite independently of what happened on the Delaware, Jacob Fabritius reported to the Netherlands from New York in 1669, "I am also instructing some Indians and heathen," but there is no evidence of any fruit.[70] Nicholas Sommer is reported to have baptized Indians in the Mohawk and Schoharie valleys of New York. Better authenticated is the interest of John C. Hartwick in the Indians, for in 1750 and again in 1761, when he was pastor in central New York, he bought from the natives a huge tract of land, and in his will (he died in 1796) provided that "a school of theology for the propagation of the Evangelical [Lutheran] Christian religion among the heathen" should be established on this land.[71] In Georgia the Salzburgers were visited again and again by Indians, and this stirred missionary interest, but the ministers were too preoccupied with their own people to do anything. John M. Boltzius wrote to Europe in 1739:

If somebody had the gifts and a call from God to learn their language and devote himself entirely to their service, it would probably not be without blessing. It would require, however, that a man should devote himself entirely to this and give all his time to the learning of different Indian tongues, for not one alone is spoken. He would also have to live among them altogether, gain their respect through his word and conduct so that they have confidence in him, . . . and then with God's help and support he may be able to accomplish something with the children.[72]

Henry M. Muhlenberg learned about the Indians especially from his father-in-law, Conrad Weiser, who was an Indian agent, but neither he nor his colleagues in Pennsylvania and adjacent colonies engaged in any serious missionary effort. As the years passed and more colonists came from Europe, the Indians withdrew farther and farther to the west. They appear in the Lutheran records of the latter half of the eighteenth century mostly in connection with hostile incursions on the frontier.[73]

Lutherans came into more frequent contact with Negroes because there were more of them in their immediate environment. Although there were a few black slaves in the Swedish colony, it was not until the descendants of the early colonists had become more prosperous that slavery became an accepted institution. Baptisms and marriages of the slaves of Lutheran masters were recorded again and again. In 1724 "a Negress named Peggy was bought for the parsonage" in Wilmington, Delaware, for £40. She was referred to as "part of the inventory at the parsonage." Two children of hers were baptized later, although there is no mention of a father. After eighteen years, by which time she was referred to as an "old, contumacious Negress," she was sold at auction for only seven shillings.[74] There were also slaves among the Dutch Lutherans on the Hudson and among the Germans who followed them there. Fabritius appears to have baptized the first black man in 1669, and Falckner baptized or married a number of Negroes in Albany, New York City, and northern New Jersey. Uncommon was the case of the black man who married two German women in succession, and also uncommon is the fact that William C. Berkenmeyer owned two Negro slaves. It was Berkenmeyer who inserted in the church constitution of 1735 a provision that baptism does not "dissolve the tie of obedience."[75]

Slavery was at first forbidden in Georgia, and Boltzius wrote in 1740, "It is a great, though in part unrecognized, blessing that no black slaves may be imported into our colony." The shortage of labor altered the opinion of the Salzburgers as well as of others. Slavery was justified on the ground that Negroes were spiritually and physically better off as slaves in America than as freemen in Africa. Slaves were accordingly bought by the Ebenezer community and by individuals in it. Attempts were made to convert them to Christianity, but the success was limited. When Muhlenberg was in Georgia in 1774 he observed: "A number of the members of the Ebenezer congregation have purchased young Negroes and brought them to school and church, but they have had little success in giving them Christianity. It is like writing Hebrew text with points and accents on coarse blotting paper."[76]

When Muhlenberg had originally arrived in Charleston, South Carolina, in 1742 he encountered black slaves for the first time and was not pleased by what he learned. "I wonder if it will not produce severe judgments if people who pretend to be Christians use their fellow creatures, who have been redeemed along with themselves, as mere body slaves and do not concern themselves about their souls. This the future will show."[77] During subsequent years Muhlenberg and other German-speaking Lutherans instructed, baptized, and united in marriage numerous slaves in many colonies. The fact that some of these spoke "a fair German" suggests that their masters were German-speaking and presumably Lutheran. The congregation in Culpepper, Virginia, used part of the money gathered on a collection tour in Europe to buy several slaves who were to support the pastor by cultivating his farm. Muhlenberg refused the gift of a slave, but his son Peter owned several.[78] In general there were fewer slaveholders among German families than among families of other nationalities.[79] This is probably to be accounted for by relative poverty as much as by objection to slavery.

74.
Burr, *Records of Holy Trinity*, pp. 285, 289, 293, 301, 380; Acrelius, *History of New Sweden*, pp. 284, 287, 289, 295.
75.
VanLaer, *Lutheran Church in New York*, p. 70; *Hallesche Nachrichten*, 1:96; 2:50, 51; Dern, *Albany Protocol*, pp. 160, 183, 271, 286, 309, 343, 439; Harry J. Kreider, *Lutheranism in Colonial New York* (New York, 1942), p. 56.
76.
Urlsperger, *Ackerwerk Gottes*, 1:4, 250, 252–54, 276, 328, 360–63; 3:469–74, 492; *Journals of Muhlenberg*, 2:638.
77.
Mühlenberg, *Selbstbiographie*, p. 105.
78.
Hallesche Nachrichten, 1:578, 579; 2:88; *Journals of Muhlenberg*, 2:362, 576, 675; 3:552.
79.
S. N. D. North, *A Century of Population Growth* (Washington, D.C.: U.S. Government Printing Office, 1909), pp. 123, 124. Only 3.7 percent of German families owned slaves in 1790 as compared with 11.3 percent of English, 16 percent of Scottish, 27.9 percent of Dutch families, etc.

Lutheran ministers and their parishioners were interested in the education of their own children and generally established schools alongside of their churches. Where the churches were union churches the schools were usually maintained jointly by Lutheran and Reformed people. More than a hundred schools were established in the colonial period, but not all of these were kept open continuously because of the shortage of competent schoolmasters. In 1753 the Lutheran ministers in and near Philadelphia reported to Europe:

The school work in our congregations is still in a very poor condition because able and upright schoolmasters are rare, the salaries are totally inadequate, the church members live too far from one another, most of them are poor, the roads are too bad in winter, and the children are needed too much for work in summer. . . . The great majority of our so-called Christian people in America are pitifully neglected in their youth.[80]

Since most of the schools were conducted under congregational auspices, religion was taught as well as reading, writing, and arithmetic, and there was a tendency to continue this pattern when public schools supplanted church schools early in the nineteenth century.

Colonial Lutherans in Civil Life

Lutherans made contributions to the civil life of colonial America. Since most of them were farmers, their activity centered in the clearing of land and making it productive for the benefit of their contemporaries and their descendants. A few colonists achieved prominence in other areas. Paul Schrick, whose business involved him in numerous voyages between the New World and the Old in the time of Dutch rule, was a leading Lutheran layman on the Hudson. Gustave Hesselius, brother of a Lutheran clergyman, arrived on the Delaware in 1711 and distinguished himself as a portrait painter. Conrad Weiser, whose daughter married Henry M. Muhlenberg, was employed by several colonial governments as an Indian agent and was credited with maintaining peace with the natives. Henry William Stiegel, popularly called "Baron," was the designer and manufacturer of famous glassware and iron products. Peter Kock and Henry Schleydorn have already been mentioned in another connection as prominent Swedish and German merchants, respectively, in Philadelphia. Henry Keppele, also a well-to-do merchant, not only was elected the first president of the German Society of Pennsylvania but also served in the Pennsylvania assembly, and Michael Kalteisen occupied a parallel position in Charleston, South Carolina. Bodo Otto was a physician in southern New Jersey who was appointed surgeon-general of the army in the American Revolution.[81] Charles F. Wiesenthal, also a surgeon in the Revolution, later founded the first medical school in Baltimore.

When England conquered the Dutch and Swedish colonies in 1664 the inhabitants on the Hudson and Delaware rivers were required to take an oath of allegiance to the sovereign of Eng-

30.
Hallesche Nachrichten, 1:696.

31.
Cf. James E. Gibson, *Dr. Bodo Otto and the Medical Background of the American Revolution* (Springfield, Ill.: C. C. Thomas, 1939). For sketches of some mentioned here and below see William J. Finck, *Lutheran Landmarks and Pioneers in America* (Philadelphia: United Lutheran, 1913); and Ira O. Nothstein, *Lutheran Makers of America* (Philadelphia: United Lutheran, 1930).

land. A similar requirement was imposed on German colonists after 1717. This oath did not make them citizens, however, and therefore they did not have the right to vote or to own and transfer property. Such rights were conferred in another way. The early Palatines and the Salzburgers were naturalized by special acts of the English parliament before they sailed for America. Others were naturalized after their settlement by similar acts of colonial legislatures. Although in this way many secured the right to vote, Lutherans were often reluctant to exercise their franchise, probably on account of pietistic other-worldliness. When the Quakers, who controlled the Pennsylvania assembly, decided in 1748 against raising levies for defense, and the Anglicans and Presbyterians maintained "in speech and printed word that defense is not contrary to God's Word," the Lutheran ministers refused to take sides and "mix in political affairs." Six years later, when the Quakers rejected a plea for soldiers to protect frontiersmen from hostile Indians, the Lutheran ministers again felt that they could not "interfere in such critical, political affairs."[82] Shortly after this, however, the church council of St. Michael's Church in Philadelphia called a meeting, and Muhlenberg reported that when it was "unanimously decided that it would be a good thing if several German citizens were elected to the Assembly, I approved it because we German citizens are not bastards but His Majesty's loyal subjects and naturalized children."[83] Like Muhlenberg in Pennsylvania, so Christian Rabenhorst in Georgia remained aloof from the public protests against the Stamp Act which were forerunners of the Revolution.[84]

When the War of Independence began Muhlenberg was at first an opponent of the war and an apologist for England. Later he tried to pursue a hazardous course of neutrality.[85] This position was not shared by his oldest son, Peter, who promptly gave up his pastorate in Woodstock, Virginia, to serve as a colonel and ultimately as a lieutenant-general in the American army. The story that at a service he dramatically removed his clerical gown to expose his army uniform underneath is as lacking in contemporary evidence as the statement that on this occasion he said that there is a time to pray and a time to preach but that the time had now come to fight.[86] The second Muhlenberg son, Frederick, also demitted the ministry; he entered politics and eventually was chosen the first speaker of the United States House of Representatives. John A. Treutlen, a layman among the Salzburgers, was elected governor of revolutionary Georgia. John Hanson, of Swedish heritage but questionable Lutheran adherence, was representative from Maryland to the Continental Congress and its chairman for a year.[87] Christian Streit served as chaplain and Christopher Ludwig, a member of St. Michael's Church in Philadelphia, was baker-general of the army.

Because the country as a whole was divided in its sentiments, it is not surprising to find as many opponents as supporters of the Revolution among Lutheran ministers and laymen. Christopher Triebner was a Tory clergyman who fled from Georgia to

82.
Journals of Muhlenberg, 1:212; 2:55.

83.
Ibid., 2:192.

84.
Ibid., 2:373, 374, 678. For the context see Dietmar Rothermund, *The Layman's Progress: Religious and Political Experience in Colonial Pennsylvania, 1740-1770* (Philadelphia: University of Pennsylvania, 1961), pp. 37-143.

85.
Theodore G. Tappert, "Henry Melchior Muhlenberg and the American Revolution," *Church History* 11 (1942): 284-301.

86.
Klaus Wust, *The Virginia Germans* (Charlottesville, Va.: University of Virginia Press, 1969), pp. 75-81, 264. For the traditional view see Edward W. Hocker, *The Fighting Parson of the American Revolution* (Philadelphia, 1936).

87.
An extravagant account is available in Jacob A. Nelson, *John Hanson and the Inseparable Union* (Boston: Meador, 1943).

England with the retreating British soldiers in 1782. Nicholas Collin was arrested as a British sympathizer in New Jersey but was released on the intervention of a layman. John L. Voigt refused to replace the traditional prayer for the king with a prayer for the American Congress. Peter N. Sommer, whose parish was in the Mohawk Valley of New York, supported the crown until all hope for victory was lost. John S. Schwerdfeger moved from New York to Ontario at the close of the Revolution and took most members of his congregation with him as "empire loyalists." Bernard M. Hausihl was also an empire loyalist and moved to Nova Scotia, where he not only lived under the flag of England but identified himself with the Church of England.

77

Little needs to be added to what has already been said about the relations of Lutherans to people of other confessions. Anglicans had more in common with Lutherans in the eighteenth century than later, when the Oxford Movement altered the character of Anglicanism. Many attempts were made to absorb Lutherans into the Church of England, but these overtures were resisted.[88] Although there was often friction between Dutch Reformed and Lutheran ministers and people, this was not generally so in the case of the German Reformed. Michael Schlatter, who was Muhlenberg's counterpart among the German Reformed, was a close friend and collaborator of the Lutheran leader. Relations with William Tennent and other Presbyterian ministers were also cordial. On the whole the Lutherans who were under pietistic influence tended not to inquire what the denominational labels of others were, but rather acknowledged as fellow Christians all who, like themselves, professed to be converted.

88.
There is a judicious summary in Henry Eyster Jacobs, *A History of the Evangelical Lutheran Church in the United States* (New York: Christian Literature Co., 1893), pp. 78–88.

George Anderson

5   Achieving Identity

1.
John C. Kunze, "Short Account of the Lutheran Church," in *Hymn and Prayer-Book* . . . (New York: Hurtin & Commardinger, 1975), pp. 9, 143, in Microfilm Corpus of American Lutheranism (hereafter cited as *MCAL*), reel 1. The statement is accurate if one remembers that Maine was still a part of Massachusetts in 1795, so the Waldoboro congregation would account for the inclusion of the latter state. A useful survey of the period 1790–1840 is Marcus Cunliffe's *The Nation Takes Shape* (Chicago: University of Chicago Press, 1959), where further bibliography may be found. On westward movement see Ray A. Billington, *Westward Expansion: A History of the American Frontier* (New York: Macmillan, 1949), chaps. 8ff. Maps of settlement are in *Statistical Atlas* (Washington: U.S. Census Office, 1903). Cf. Roy H. Johnson, "The Lutheran Church and the Western Frontier, 1789 to 1830," *Lutheran Church Quarterly* 3 (July 1930): 225–48.
2.
William J. Finck, ed., "A Chronological Life of Paul Henkel," typescript (1935–37), pp. 142, 147; North Carolina Synod, *Proceedings . . . 1813,* pp. 32, 33; cf. A. Fries, ed., *Records of the Moravians in North Carolina* (Raleigh, N.C.: North Carolina Historical Commission, 1941), 5:2269, and passim.

The first sketch of Lutheran history written after the Revolution could boast that "in all the United States of America there are Lutheran congregations, except New-Hampshire, Vermont, Rhode-Island, and Connecticut."[1] Far from being a bit of proud exaggeration, the statement was much too modest. While it was true that Lutherans had spread to every corner of the United States except New England, they had already expanded even beyond the borders of the new nation and were forming congregations in Upper Canada and the Northwest Territory. A period of vigorous expansion was just dawning.

Crossing the Appalachians

Before the Revolution there had been little settlement of the trans-Appalachian frontier. The ranges of mountains and the hostile Indian tribes had acted as a dam, turning the tide of migration southward into Virginia and the Carolinas. By the end of the Revolution, however, several usable routes had opened through the mountains and a series of military actions soon cleared the Indian threat from all territory east of the Mississippi. Settlers poured into this newly opened land by the thousands. Kentucky became a state by 1792, and Tennessee followed four years later. By 1800 Kentucky alone would have over 200,000 inhabitants.

The Germans and Scotch-Irish living along the eastern slopes of the Appalachians were among the first to take advantage of the opening of the West. Many North Carolinians followed their neighbor Daniel Boone through the Cumberland Gap to Kentucky, while others joined Virginians and South Carolinians on the new wagon road to Knoxville, Tennessee. Pennsylvania Germans moved along former military roads to Pittsburgh and the upper Ohio River; New Yorkers bought land from numerous speculation companies operating in the western part of their state. By 1797 the Ministerium of Pennsylvania took official notice of the population shift by resolving that its annual convention be held in the western half of the state every third year.

The settlers often moved in groups, taking land near former neighbors from the East. Later, when missionaries from the older states came asking for German families, they would discover whole communities of settlers from the same county in some seaboard state. Occasionally a missionary would meet adults whom he had baptized as children years before across the mountains to the east.[2] In at least one instance, a colony of sixty families was brought over directly from Germany for settlement in western New York. Dissatisfaction with arrangements for them prompted their leader, William Berczy, to take the entire group to Canada. They finally settled northeast of Toronto near Markham, Ontario, in 1794. Apparently they brought their own pastor, but he maintained only nominal residence in the frontier colony and spent most of his time near Montreal, 250 miles away.[3]

The meager pastoral services available to those settlers in Ontario were better, however, than the usual predicament of German-speaking pioneers in the West. Frontier Lutherans presented a vast and fertile field in which many congregations could have taken root, but there was no leadership. Families that disappeared from church records in the East never found their way into Lutheran congregations in the West. What little was known of Lutheran settlement came almost by accident, as a group of pious folk here or there petitioned eastern clergy to send them a pastor or to visit them once a year. More ominous were those petitions which presented the names of unreliable or uneducated men for ordination.

Much critical material is available on uneducated frontier preachers, but in some cases they worked faithfully, did what they could, and did not presume to replace more educated men. A strapping wagon-maker named John Stough [Stauch] has left a simple record of the steps that led him to begin preaching on the frontier:

As I had been chosen to lead and read sermons, and uniformly to lead in our religious services, it was consequently thought that I should marry [a couple]. I accordingly did it backwoods style without any license myself or asking them for one. Others came on the same business, and I served them also. . . . But now another difficulty more formidable than the first awaited us. It was the baptism of our children. I would always find some way to have my own baptized. But others thought it impossible for them. They wanted me to baptize their children. But I declined. They also wanted the Lord's Supper administered, and wanted me to do it. . . . The duty of preaching became more impressed on my mind than ever before, and my brethren thought that I could and must preach for them and others. . . . My thoughts continued to trouble me more and more. . . . Sometimes it seemed to me the learned and accomplished in the church would upbraid me for transcending my proper sphere. . . . After many prayers and much consideration . . . I formed a fixed resolution by the grace of God I would preach Jesus and trust God for good results.[4]

In 1794 Stough came east to be licensed as a catechist by the Ministerium, and after ten years he was ordained. Like Stough, six out of the seven pioneer pastors in western Pennsylvania began their ministries before they had been recognized by any synod.[5]

3.
An introduction to Canadian Lutheran history and historiography is Erich R. W. Schultz's "Tragedy and Triumph in Canadian Lutheranism," *Concordia Historical Institute Quarterly* 38 (July 1965): 55–72; for general orientation see Carl R. Cronmiller, *A History of the Lutheran Church in Canada* (Toronto: Synod of Canada, 1961), pp. 102–3. A useful study of one region, which also introduces pertinent secular literature, is Welf H. Heick's "The Lutherans of Waterloo County, Ontario, 1810-1959: A Historical Study" (M.A. thesis, Queen's University, Kingston, Ont., 1959), pp. 34–54. Marion Gilroy's "Loyalists and Land Settlement in Nova Scotia," Public Archives of Nova Scotia, Publication No. 4 (Halifax, N.S., 1937), lists settlers and settlements in Nova Scotia.
4.
John Stough [Stauch], "Autobiography," in Ellis B. Burgess, *Memorial History of the Pittsburgh Synod* . . . (Greenville, Pa.: Beaver, 1925), pp. 31–32; for a fuller account of Stough, and for other places where the "Autobiography" has been printed, see Willard D. Allbeck, "John Stough: Founder of Ohio Lutheranism," *Lutheran Quarterly* 12 (February 1960): 25–43.
5.
Burgess, *Memorial History,* pp. 48–49. Another frontier missionary's account is in Willard D. Allbeck, "A Journal of John Samuel Mau," *Lutheran Quarterly* 13 (May 1961): 155–64.

Synodical Organization

The cry for pastoral leadership, the demand for more qualified clergy in all areas of the country, and the simple need for common consultation and fellowship combined to stimulate the rapid organization of synodical bodies in the United States. Within six years of 1787, pastors organized synods or conferences in South Carolina (1787), North Carolina (1791), New York (1792), and Virginia (1793). In addition, the Ministerium of Pennsylvania went through a major reorganization in 1792, so it is no exaggeration to say that the polity of North American Lutheranism experienced a revolution of its own from 1787 to 1793.

The organization in South Carolina was the earliest, the most unusual, and the shortest lived. It was occasioned by the opportunity for incorporation of congregations afforded by the first constitution of the state. Seven pastors of the Lutheran and Reformed churches in the central part of the state met in November 1787 to form a "ministerial society" and to draft petitions for incorporation of the various congregations. A constitution was adopted in which sweeping powers rested with a "directory" composed of the clergymen and two lay delegates from each congregation. This "*Unio Ecclesiastica* of the German Protestant Churches in the State of South Carolina" intended to hold meetings twice a year, but meetings became less frequent as its clerical members moved away or died. Later writers claim it lasted until at least 1794.[6]

North Carolina pastors were originally to have been a part of the *Unio Ecclesiastica* but additions to their number in 1788 made an independent organization possible. Adolph Nussman and Gottfried Arndt, the two missionaries who had arrived just before the Revolution, had written Europe for more help, and their request was answered by a mission society formed expressly for that purpose by John C. Velthusen of the University at Helmstedt. Within five years the Helmstedt society had sent over two thousand books and provided two youthful missionaries. Much encouraged by this help, the North Carolina pastors formed a "conference" in 1791, resolving to meet at six-month intervals. Their first order of business was the ordination of two young men from southern Germany who were assisting with pastoral work in the state. This conference of pastors in North Carolina apparently existed without an official title. Although some of its early members were lost by death or distance, three of its pastors survived to participate in the formation of the North Carolina Synod in 1803. In 1794 their number had been increased by the ordination of Robert Johnson Miller, a Scotsman who had connected himself with the Episcopal Church after a period of work for the Methodists. The four Lutherans who ordained him stated on his certificate that he was being ordained to the ministry of "ye Protestant Episcopal Church," but since Episcopalians were not yet strong in the western part of North Carolina, Miller continued his affiliation with the

he constitution and accounts of the early eetings of the *Unio* are in George D. ernheim, *History of the German Settlements . in North and South Carolina* (Philadelhia: Lutheran Book Store, 1872), pp. 39–302.

German Lutherans for more than twenty years. He became president of the North Carolina Synod, served as frontier missionary for that body, and was usually called an "English" or "English Lutheran" minister by his Lutheran colleagues. He joined the Protestant Episcopal Church in 1821.[7]

The increasing number of pastors in New York State raised the possibility of a new organization there, independent of the Ministerium of Pennsylvania. Several vacancies in the state had been filled by pastors who retained their membership in the Ministerium, and the Ministerium itself exerted efforts to bring congregations in northern New Jersey under its wing, so it is conceivable that New York could have become a special conference of the Ministerium. On the other hand, differences of doctrinal and ecclesiastical attitudes going back to the difficulties between William C. Berkenmeyer and Henry M. Muhlenberg continued to keep New York pastors aloof from the Ministerium. Distance also made a local synod attractive. Attempts to set up an independent Ministerium in New York were made in 1773 and again in 1786, but they did not gather enough members to survive.

The decisive steps toward organizing the Ministerium of New York came as the result of the work of Muhlenberg's son-in-law, John Christopher Kunze. It was Kunze who called the key meetings, invited the delegates to meet in his church, and eventually wrote the new synod's constitution. If Muhlenberg's mantle fell on anyone after the patriarch's death, it must have fallen on Kunze. He had come to America as a twenty-six-year-old missionary just before the Revolution, arriving on the same boat with Muhlenberg's two sons who had been studying at Halle. Within a year Kunze had further identified himself with the Muhlenbergs by marrying one of the patriarch's daughters. He soon distinguished himself as a teacher, conducting a school of his own and teaching the ancient languages to German-speaking students at the University of Pennsylvania. After having received an honorary doctorate from the university, Kunze moved to New York City in 1784 to serve Trinity and Christ congregations. By the time of Muhlenberg's death he was known and respected from Nova Scotia to Savannah. He served simultaneously as Senior of the Ministeriums of Pennsylvania and New York, wrote constitutions for both bodies, and conducted correspondence with Europe for both groups. In addition to his pastoral and ecclesiastical leadership he found time to serve as a German translator in Congress and as a faculty member at Columbia University. He was the first leader of his generation among Lutherans to see the necessity for providing hymnals and catechisms in English. More than any other individual, Kunze typified the transitional character of the post-revolutionary decade.[8]

Kunze had tried to organize the pastors in New York as early as 1786, but only three participants appeared at that "ministers' meeting." A second attempt in 1792 brought an equally small response, even though the delegates came from a wider area. Despite its size, the little group decided to proceed toward

7.
The basic source for North Carolina Lutheran history in this period is Bernheim's *History*. Biographies of the early pastors are in Eberhard Pellens, *Die Beziehungen der ev. luth. Kirchen von Hannover und Braunschweig zur ev. luth. Kirche in North Carolina in der 2. Hälfte des 18. Jahrhunderts (Hilfe und Einfluss)* (Hamburg: Evang.-Theologische Fakultät der Universität Hamburg, 1961). Reports of North Carolina pastors to Europe during this period are translated by William K. Boyd and Charles A. Krummel, "German Tracts Concerning the Lutheran Church in North Carolina During the Eighteenth Century," *North Carolina Historical Review* 7 (January and April 1930). Material on the conference organized in 1791 is in H. George Anderson, "The First Lutheran Synodical Organization in North Carolina," *Lutheran Quarterly* 24 (August 1972): 280-85.
8.
For a fuller biography and bibliography see Allen Johnson, ed., *Dictionary of American Biography*, 21 vols. (New York: Scribner's, 1943), 10:512-13.

organization and asked Kunze to write a constitution. The document, when completed, served the Ministerium for the next forty years. The organization steadily widened its influence among pastors in the state so that by the turn of the century it included eleven pastors, representing thirty-nine congregations in New York, New Jersey, and Canada.[9]

Other Protestant bodies in America were organizing during the same period. The Episcopalians and Methodists had set up structures independent of their English brethren in 1784. Presbyterians adopted their Form of Government and Book of Discipline in 1789. The Dutch Reformed Church completed a gradual process of separation from Holland by adopting a translation of its articles of doctrine in English by 1792. The German Reformed Church stated its independence from European leadership in 1791 and convened its first synod two years later.

In contrast to most of these denominations the Lutheran synods did not organize to achieve independence from European authority. They were singularly interested in maintaining contacts with Europe and in soliciting European support. One of the first acts of the pastors who assembled in New York in 1792 was to direct Kunze "to correspond with Europe in order to provide whatever support is possible for the Evangelical Lutheran Church life in New York, as the Ministerium of Pennsylvania is furnished by the Halle Orphan House and the North Carolinians by the praiseworthy society of Helmstedt professors." Pastors in both North and South Carolina had hoped that the organization of synods, far from severing connections with Germany, would actually help in "making a special plea for them among their friends in their mother country." Through the 1790s the money, materials, and pastors continued to come. Every major settlement of Lutherans benefited from the continued relationship with England and the Continent.[10]

Naturally, the formation of new synodical bodies around 1790 affected the character and scope of the Ministerium of Pennsylvania. Although its latest constitution was barely ten years old, events of the intervening decade demanded a new document. Several important changes were incorporated in the Ministerium's new constitution, which was written by Kunze and printed in 1792.

The impetus for a new constitution came from a request that lay delegates be given seat and vote in the Ministerium's meetings. Since that request originated with the large Philadelphia congregation of Zion and St. Michael's it carried weight. There was little debate on the need for the change. The principle of lay representation grew directly out of the revolutionary experience, where sentiments of "no taxation without representation" and distrust of hierarchy became articles of faith. Both the Ministerium of New York and the *Unio Ecclesiastica* in South Carolina had provisions for lay delegates. Other denominations that were organizing in the United States after the Revolution also incorporated the same principle.[11]

A few problems arose from the inclusion of laymen in synodical meetings. It did not seem proper for laymen to sit in judg-

85

9.
Minutes of the Evangelical Lutheran Ministerium of New York, 1786-1818 (1786-1806 translated by Theodore E. Palleske in 1957; 1807-18 transcribed by Harry J. Kreider), in *MCAL*, reel 18. A general treatment of synodical developments in New York is Harry J. Kreider's *History of the United Lutheran Synod of New York and New England, 1786-1860* (Philadelphia: Muhlenberg Press, 1954), vol. 1. Details on pastors and individual congregations are in J. Nicum, *Geschichte des Evangelisch-Lutherischen Ministeriums vom Staate New York* (New York: Verlag des New York-Ministeriums, 1886).
10.
Nicum, *Geschichte*, p. 403; *North Carolina Historical Review* 7 (January 1930): 109.
11.
Documentary History of the General Council of the Evangelical Lutheran Church in North America (Philadelphia: General Council Pub. House, 1912), pp. 24-41. A general study of synodical polity through this period is Robert Fortenbaugh's "The Development of the Synodical Polity of the Lutheran Church in America to 1829" (Ph.D. diss., University of Pennsylvania, 1926).

ment on questions concerning the fitness of men for the ministry and the discipline of clergy. Furthermore, the pastors were just as afraid of lay domination as the laymen were of domination by the clergy. The presence of delegates from vacant congregations raised the possibility that pastors at any given meeting would be outnumbered by laymen. A third issue concerned finances. Who would pay the expenses of the lay delegates? Host congregations had traditionally provided food and lodging for clergymen who attended, but the size of a convention with lay delegates would tax the hospitality of even the largest congregations.

The 1792 constitution solved these issues by directing that laymen should furnish food and lodging for themselves and their horses, that they should never outnumber the clergy present at a convention, and that some questions should be reserved for a "ministerial meeting" which would convene after the regular synod and which would be restricted to clergymen and licensed candidates. It is significant that the ministerial meeting was officially designated as the "most important" part of the annual convention. In reality the constitution just modified the old Ministerium which had been composed exclusively of clergymen by opening some of its sessions to laymen.[12]

In rewriting its constitution to include lay delegates, however, it was possible for the Ministerium to make some other significant changes. These changes centered around needs arising from Lutheran growth and the scarcity of qualified clergy. A new title symbolized changes required by Lutheran growth. The constitution no longer belonged to *the* "Ministerium of the Evangelical Lutheran Church in North America," as the old synodical title ran, but simply to the "German Evangelical Lutheran Congregations in Pennsylvania and Adjacent States." The existence of other synodical bodies was recognized, and their members were even given voice and vote in meetings of the Pennsylvania Ministerium. A member of the Ministerium could still maintain his voting rights in Pennsylvania while being affiliated with some other Lutheran body. In fact, Kunze himself remained a member of the Pennsylvania Ministerium while serving as president of its sister body in New York.

Growth in the East and expansion toward the West stretched the communication lines of the Ministerium nearly to the breaking point. By 1800 there were over thirty pastors and candidates serving congregations from New Jersey to Tennessee. To meet this need the constitution provided for a new system of "special conferences" so that pastors who lived in the same area could meet together to plan for the care of existing congregations and the planting of new ones. Acting immediately, the four leading pastors in northern Virginia met in January 1793 to organize the Virginia Conference of the Ministerium.[13] During the next decade, the Virginia Conference would be the most active of the Ministerium's new subdivisions, although six other conferences were officially recognized. In all cases the special conferences were considered arms of the Ministerium and not substitutes for it. They cared for local needs of

12.
The constitution is printed in *Documentary History of the Evangelical Lutheran Ministerium of Pennsylvania . . . 1748-1821* (Philadelphia: General Council Board of Publication, 1898), pp. 248–58. A few additions were made in 1793; see ibid., pp. 259, 263.

13.
Although the minutes of the Virginia Special Conference are lost, what can be known of its work is summarized in William E. Eisenberg, *The Lutheran Church in Virginia, 1717-1962* (Lynchburg, Va.: J. P. Bell, 1967), pp. 79–80, 107.

congregations and their schools, but they had no power to examine or to ordain clergy.

In addition to communication difficulties, growth also intensified the need for properly qualified clergy. The existence of congregations far from other Lutheran pastors invited the attention of fee-hungry imposters. Yet the supply of clergymen from Europe had dwindled to a trickle and native-born candidates were hard to find. Not a single candidate was ordained by the Ministerium for the eight years between 1792 and 1800. Each year, it is true, three or four men would apply to the Ministerium, but many of them had educational backgrounds so weak that they could not be entrusted with the unsupervised leadership of a congregation until they had completed further study. To meet this situation the new constitution of the Ministerium set up the office of "catechist." In contrast to "licensed candidates" who were under the general supervision of the Ministerium and who had voting power in synodical meetings, a catechist had no vote and remained under the supervision of one particular pastor who was to be his "instructor and father." To qualify as a catechist a young man had to be at least twenty years old, demonstrate a "blameless" character, have a systematic knowledge of Christian doctrine and ethics, and possess some knowledge of human nature, a gift for speaking, and "above all things," evidence of personal religious experience. The need for clergy soon prompted other synods to adopt the office of catechist too.

In speaking of the synodical organizations in existence between the end of the Revolution and the end of the century it is important to remember that they differed widely from each other and from the modern Lutheran synod or district. They varied in size from four pastors in North Carolina to about thirty in the Ministerium of Pennsylvania. Those that were too small to survive a sharp drop in membership soon disappeared, as was the case in both Carolinas. In contrast, the Ministerium of Pennsylvania grew so large that subdivision into special conferences became necessary. South Carolina's "directory" was highly centralized, able to regulate "reception and dismission of preachers, their election, examination, ordination and induction, the establishment and regulation of churches and schools . . . the manner of Divine service . . . the collections in the churches, and . . . in what manner a fund may be collected gradually for several necessary expenses." On the other hand, even as late as 1803 in North Carolina the synod ceased to exist between annual conventions and officers presided only over the actual sessions.[14] Even the official titles varied from "corpus," "assembly," and "conference" to "synod," "ministerium," and "united congregations." No one plan of organization fit all circumstances, and so there was a great deal of experimentation and improvisation.

Despite their variety, however, the synods showed some characteristics which distinguish them sharply from their modern counterparts. They were primarily concerned with the quality and supply of clergymen. Synodical business centered largely on

14.
Bernheim, *History,* pp. 292-93; *Minutes of the Evangelical Lutheran Synod of North Carolina, 1803-1826* (Newberry, S.C.: Aull & Houseal, 1894), p. 4. The latter work should be compared with the original German minutes where possible, since some editing has occurred.

reading and replying to letters from congregations and clergy-men. The congregations either wanted a pastor or wanted to get rid of one. The clergy generally requested admission as members of the synod or brought complaints against a congregation that had argued too much or paid too little. When the ministers met separately, they tended to concentrate on cases of discipline or on the assignment of theological students to individual pastors for instruction. In general, synods did not handle appeals for funds or projects which would require a central treasury. The Ministerium of Pennsylvania specifically rejected the role of fund raiser in 1788, and not until a decade later did any synod feel the need for a treasurer. Even then his funds were to be used for such essential items as "paper, postage, etc." Control was not as expensive as action.[15]

Of course, the preoccupation with problems of a qualified ministry was only natural. The synods existed in a sea of self-appointed preachers and renegades from Europe. To establish a list of qualified men took time and courage. Experience had taught the synods that an ordination certificate or a diploma from Europe did not guarantee that a man had the personal standards required in a minister. The Ministerium of Pennsylvania often noted that it "would have nothing to do" with some dubious petitioner, and even pastors recently arrived from Europe had to demonstrate their competence during a probationary period before gaining membership. In one case the Ministerium forced a petitioner to renounce an illegal ordination and to come up through the ranks as a licensed candidate before he could become a member.[16]

Indian Missions and the Hartwick Bequest

The possibility of educating candidates for the ministry on a systematic basis came one step nearer realization through one man's interest in missionary work among the Indians. Around the year 1793 John Christopher Hartwick (1714-96) wrote a remarkable will which set aside his immense land holdings for the establishment of the theological seminary for training missionaries to "Red or Black Heathens." Hartwick had acquired his land from the Indians and had always been on good terms with them. He felt that they often were confused by the bickering of missionaries who preached their own "heretical Sectarian Philosophical opinions," so he planned a seminary which would inculcate the "pure and simple religion of the Gospel." Upon his death in 1796 the estate was in such a tangle that the executors decided to defer establishment of the seminary on the designated site, some sixty-five miles west of Albany, and to use the available income to pay two pastors for the instruction of any ministerial candidates who presented themselves.[17]

One of the appointed pastors was Anton Braun, who also had a long-standing interest in Indian missions. Braun was a former Roman Catholic mission supervisor who had worked for his church in Canada during the Revolution. While there he had begun to serve a Lutheran congregation and after the war he appeared in New York City with recommendations from the

15.
Documentary History, Ministerium of Pa., p. 220. New York was the first synod to elect a treasurer (1798); see Nicum, *Geschichte,* p. 407.

16.
Documentary History, Ministerium of Pa., pp. 240, 306.

17.
Contemporary copies of Hartwick's will and the records of the executors are in the Krauth Memorial Library Archives, Lutheran Theological Seminary, Philadelphia. The quotations above appear on pp. 51, 52, and 62 of the manuscript copy. For Hartwick Seminary see John W. Schmitthenner, "The Origin and Educational Contribution of Hartwick Seminary" (Ph.D. diss., New York University, 1934); and Henry H. Heins, *Throughout All the Years: The Bicentennial Story of Hartwick in America, 1746-1946* (Oneonta, N.Y.: Hartwick College, 1946). This was the first Lutheran theological seminary founded in America. Gettysburg (1826) was to be the first seminary established by action of an official church body.

Canadian congregation. Successful completion of a month-long investigation by Kunze permitted Father Braun to become Pastor Braun in 1790. He expressed strong interest in continuing his missionary work among the Indians and drafted a thorough plan for carrying out the project. Lutheran resources seemed too thin to underwrite the program, however, so an appeal was made to President Washington for federal assistance. Washington declined aid. That ended Braun's hopes, and he became pastor of the congregation in Albany.[18]

Since the projected seminary on Hartwick's lands was fairly close to Albany and Braun's interest in Indian missions would fit in well with the terms of the bequest, his choice as a teacher seemed logical. The executors of Hartwick's will, among whom was Kunze, instructed Braun to teach prospective missionaries and also to "instruct such Indians in the Christian Religion as may offer themselves to him. . . ." There is no record, however, of any Indian catechumens. Thus, while the Indian mission project seemed unlikely to succeed, it had provided money, a site, and a teacher for the education of clergymen in America. The idea of a seminary was closer to becoming reality.

Worship and the Use of English

Worship practices continued to vary from synod to synod. Even the materials in use reflected the diverse origin of Lutheran colonists. Canadians and South Carolinians remained faithful to the Marburg Hymnal, which had served both Lutheran and Reformed immigrants. North Carolina Lutherans published a small collection of hymns in 1797 for the use of congregations. Only the New York Ministerium made an effort to simplify the liturgical confusion. In 1796 it adopted the hymnal and liturgy of the Ministerium of Pennsylvania. However, even that small step toward unity in worship must be qualified by noting that synodical action did not guarantee that congregations would actually use the recommended materials. Widespread illiteracy and local traditions continued to make any standardization of forms impossible. In 1811 a missionary in North Carolina visited a church where there had been "neither instruction, confirmation or communion" for thirty years.[19]

In New York City the growing use of English among the youth had prompted Kunze to publish an English translation of Luther's catechism—without the explanations—as early as 1785. He followed this first effort with an English hymnal in 1795 and an English liturgy in 1796.[20] In the latter year a survey among pastors of the Pennsylvania Ministerium showed that most had opened English schools in their parishes. The demand for English hymnals and catechisms would certainly increase.

The quality of English materials, however, was far from adequate. Kunze's translations proved so awkward that they were almost immediately supplanted by a new hymnal and liturgy produced by his native-born assistant in 1797.[21] As the Swedish congregations along the Delaware moved toward English services they adopted the Book of Common Prayer of the Episcopal Church. The use of English was still rare enough to cause little

18.
Letter of John C. Kunze, November 1, 1790, Krauth Memorial Library Archives.
19.
Finck, "Henkel," p. 149. An analysis of the North Carolina hymnal is in Pellens, *Beziehungen,* p. 64. South Carolina's materials were prescribed by the *Unio Ecclesiastica* in 1788; see Bernheim, *History,* p. 294. For Canada see Cronmiller, *History,* p. 87. New York's action is in *Minutes . . . 1796,* p. 10.
20.
Kunze, *Hymn and Prayer-Book.*
21.
George Strebeck, *A Collection of Evangelical Hymns* (New York: Tiebout, 1797), in *MCAL,* reel 1; *Documentary History, Ministerium of Pa.,* pp. 285-86.

89

alarm but the trend had obviously begun. For the moment, however, there were more pressing problems to occupy the attention of the church.

The Fight Against Deism

The great enemy of religion in this decade was deism. "Deist principles have been prevalent for several years," wrote a North Carolina pastor in 1796. "A book by Thomas Paine, entitled *Age of Reason*, which is quite widely read, causes much unwholsomeness in religious thinking." The alarm sounded from every state where Lutherans had much strength. Was it coincidence that a terrible plague of yellow fever struck Philadelphia, the city "where a certain class of people, had associated themselves for the avowed purpose of blaspheming our blessed Savior"? wondered one pastor in that city. The "wrath to come" would be revealed against all who "deny the divine character of Jesus Christ, and treat his name with the most insulting and opprobrious epithets; deny the divine inspiration . . . burlesque, and vilify the Scriptures," warned a preacher in New York. Even more dangerous were those who claimed to believe in the divine nature of Christ but who taught a doctrine of universal salvation. These universalists could lead astray many of the faithful who would never be tempted by the more radical ideas of the deists.[22]

In common with other denominations, the synods took precautions to protect themselves from contagion by deist tendencies. Prospective clergymen faced a thorough screening. When a pastor from the West Indies applied for reception into the New York Ministerium in 1793, he had to affirm his belief in the Bible and the Lutheran confessions, "and especially that the Lord Jesus was True God and man in one person."[23] Five years later the Ministerium of Pennsylvania checked on the orthodoxy of prospective clergymen by asking them for "a brief disquisition" on the text "He who believes in the Son has eternal life; he who does not obey the Son shall not see life, but the wrath of God rests on him" (John 3:36). The Ministerium could hardly have made the point more forcefully.[24]

The most popular defense against error, however, was the strenuous exercise of "experimental religion." The latter term implied an individual experience of the struggle against sin and its eventual conquest through the power of Christ. The Ministerium of Pennsylvania made "experimental religion" a constitutional requirement for its clergy. Its ministerial meetings were to occupy themselves with "mutual edification" and the "consideration of Bible truths."[25] The ideal Christian would be known by his fruits; the efforts to produce those fruits would leave no time for dalliance with the speculations of deists and universalists.

Preaching aimed at the same target. When young candidates for the ministry presented sample sermons that lacked practical value the older ministers suggested that they "aim more at edification and popularity than at oratorical art, for if they preach sermons like the outlines presented, their congregations

90

22.
For general orientation to deism in America see Herbert Montfort Morais, *Deism in Eighteenth Century America* (New York and London, 1934). For Lutheran reactions see: letter of C. A. G. Storch, January 20–February 25, 1796, in *North Carolina Historical Review* 20 (October 1943): 340; Finck, "Henkel," p. 14; *Six Sermons, Preached by the Late Mr. Laurence Van Buskirk, B.A.* (New York: T. Kirk, 1797), p. 13, in *MCAL*, reel 1; J. H. C. Helmuth, *A Short Account of the Yellow Fever in Philadelphia for the Reflecting Christian* (Philadelphia: Jones, Hoff & Derrick, 1794), p. 18, in *MCAL*, reel 1; George Strebeck, *The Wrath to Come, Discussed in Three Sermons* . . . (New York: L. Nichols, 1803), pp. 23–24, in *MCAL*, reel 4.
23.
New York Ministerium, *Minutes . . . 1793*, p. 5.
24.
Documentary History, Ministerium of Pa., p. 301.
25.
Ibid., pp. 250, 252, 257; cf. J. H. C. Helmuth, "A Sermon Preached at Kingsess, November 15, 1789," Krauth Memorial Library Archives.

are to be sincerely pitied." Preachers could find lively themes in the corrupt state of the youth, the prevalence of sabbath-breaking, and the rise of theatrical exhibitions, luxury, and dissipation. Surely the "days were evil" and there was much for true Christians to do.[26]

Relationships to Other Denominations

The threat of a common enemy and the challenge of a common task led Lutherans into closer cooperation with other Protestant bodies. In areas where German language and culture remained strong, relations between Lutherans and the German Reformed Church were cordial, as they had been during most of the eighteenth century. Relations with the Moravians had improved since Muhlenberg's conflict with Zinzendorf fifty years earlier. In areas where German Lutherans came in daily contact with the English language, patterns of cooperation developed with the Episcopal Church, and, in a more fragile way, with the Methodists. These relationships presupposed the distinctiveness of each denomination but at the same time they recognized that there were substantial areas of agreement where Lutherans could benefit from closer ties with other Protestant church bodies. "The time is over, my brethren," wrote Kunze in 1801, "when Protestant parties could exclude each other for the sake of unessential dissentions, from the . . . affections of the common Lord."[27]

In his *Hymn and Prayer Book* of 1795 Kunze included a "Short Account of the Lutheran Church" that helps us understand how a Lutheran leader understood his denomination's place in Protestantism.[28] He describes the Lutheran church from its beginnings in Germany and then shows how a division developed between Luther and Zwingli over the doctrine of the Lord's Supper. This gap widened, he wrote, as Calvin added a concept of "divine absolute predestination to life and damnation" to Zwingli's teachings. Since that time there have been two Protestant churches—the Lutheran and the Reformed. The churches have often quarreled but Kunze rejoices in the fact that "such times are past." He is certain that every "true Christian" would wish the "present union of the two churches . . . to be indissoluble."

The union, already expressed in common church buildings and schools, had been made more secure by the founding of Franklin College, Lancaster, Pennsylvania, in 1787, as a Lutheran-Reformed joint project. In the Carolinas, too, where both denominations were strong, cooperation was also common. Lutheran pastors took candidates of both traditions into their homes for theological instruction, and even taught confirmation classes for Reformed congregations from the Heidelberg Catechism. The *Unio Ecclesiastica* in South Carolina was specifically designed to keep German Reformed and Lutheran members from being separated.[29]

Such staunch and widespread unity, however, did not stop each denomination from publishing its own hymnals, liturgies, and catechisms. Kunze's own synod in New York took special

26.
Documentary History, Ministerium of Pa., p. 281; *Six Sermons*, pp. 13, 53; Helmuth, *Short Account*, pp. 12ff.
27.
John C. Kunze, *King Solomon's Great Sacrifice at the Dedication of His Temple* (New York, 1801), p. 28, in *MCAL*, reel 1.
28.
Kunze, *Hymn and Prayer-Book*, pp. 134–43.
29.
Documentary History, Ministerium of Pa., p. 218; Finck, "Henkel," p. 24; G. William Welker, "Early German Reformed Settlements in North Carolina," *The Colonial Records of North Carolina* (Raleigh, N.C.: Josephus Daniels, 1888), 8:731; Bernheim, *History*, p. 292.

action prohibiting the breaking of the host in the Lord's Supper, which was a Reformed custom, since it would lead to a "symbolic" interpretation of the sacrament.[30]

Kunze also advocated warm relationships with the Moravians. He believed that they had come from a healthy revival of Lutheranism under the leadership of Spener and Francke. They accepted the Augsburg Confession; Lutherans naturally would "consider them as their brethren." In North Carolina they often supplied vacant congregations and practically adopted the Lutheran pastor Paul Henkel as one of their own. Kunze himself relied heavily on a Moravian Hymnal in preparing the collection of hymns that accompanied his "Account of the Lutheran Church."[31]

A later document from Kunze's hand clarifies the relationship he saw between Lutherans and Episcopalians:

The thirty-nine articles fully agree with the Augustan [Augsburg] Confession and every Lutheran can subscribe them. . . . At the accession of George the I the agreement of both churches was, by a conference of English and German divines investigated into and pronounced to be as perfect as possible, which removed the doubts of this king, who is said to have declared that he would not renounce his religion for a crown. The bishops of London, therefore, have never made a difficulty to ordain Lutheran divines, when called to congregations; which, on account of being connected with English episcopalians [sic], made this ordination requisite. Thus by bishops of London the following Lutheran ministers were ordained: Bryselius, Pet[er] Muhlenberg, Illing, Hauseal, and Wagner. . . . I have these twenty four years, that is, as long as I have instructed students of divinity for my church, uniformly and constantly held out this and no other language to them. . . .[32]

These comments, written in November 1797, take on added significance when seen in the light of an action taken by Kunze's Ministerium of New York just two months earlier. In an effort to halt the tendency of English-speaking Lutherans to form new congregations, the Ministerium resolved that no English Lutheran congregation would be recognized in a place where an Episcopal congregation already existed. In effect, this resolution said it was better for English-speaking Lutherans to join the Episcopal Church than to form a new congregation for themselves. If, as Kunze believed, there was full doctrinal agreement between the two denominations, then it certainly made sense to suggest that a change in language did not warrant putting two congregations where one would suffice.[33]

Since the Methodist movement grew out of Episcopal roots and shared much of the emphasis on "experimental religion" that dominated Lutheran piety, one might expect that Lutherans would cooperate fully with them. However, Methodists never received from Lutherans the wholehearted recognition achieved by the other denominations we have considered. The

92

30.
New York Ministerium, *Minutes . . . 1796,* p. 11.
31.
Numerous instances of cooperation are cited in Fries, *Records of the Moravians,* passim; Finck, "Henkel," pp. 25, 42.
32.
John C. Kunze in the preface to *Six Sermons,* pp. v–vi. A similar view is taken by Paul Henkel, *Die ersten ein und zwanzig Artikel der ungeänderten Augsburgischen Confession* (Hagerstown, Md.: John Gruber, 1805), p. 4. This attitude also accounts for the Lutheran ordination of an Episcopalian in North Carolina in 1794; see Bernheim, *History,* p. 339.
33.
New York Ministerium, *Minutes . . . 1797,* p. 13. This action has been used to make sweeping generalizations about the "unionism" of the Ministerium; cf. Abdel Ross Wentz, *A Basic History of Lutheranism in America,* rev. ed. (Philadelphia: Fortress Press, 1964), pp. 70–71. A more accurate estimate of the situation may be gained by remembering that the action grew out of a schism in Kunze's own congregation in New York City. See New York Ministerium, *Minutes . . . 1804,* p. 36. See also Harry J. Kreider, "The English Language Schism in the Lutheran Church in New York City, 1794–1810," *Lutheran Church Quarterly* 21 (January 1948): 50–60, for quotations from congregational records.

reason lay in Methodism's distinctive doctrines and in its tendency to attract "awakened" members out of existing denominations. In a letter written in 1790, Kunze complains that after his preaching had awakened some members of the congregation they stopped coming to church and began to meet with one of their number who was designated by the Methodists as a "leader of a class." Even a letter from Wesley himself failed to bring them back. Kunze continued to meet with the group privately, but they were lost to his congregation. His particular objection, beyond that of the loss of members, was the Methodist teaching on the possibility of reaching perfection.[34]

Although Kunze's opposition to the Methodists stemmed partly from their threat to his congregation, his attitude toward them was shared by other Lutherans. The frontier preacher John Samuel Mau noted in his journal that he had attended a meeting conducted by a Methodist in Martinsburg, West Virginia, and that when he was asked to speak to the group he questioned the purity of their motives. When George Strebeck, himself a former Methodist, published a hymnal for the use of English-speaking Lutherans in New York City, he carefully concealed the authorship of hymns written by the Wesley brothers, although he felt free to publish the names of other non-Lutheran authors, such as Watts and Doddridge.[35]

Later Lutheran historians, writing out of the bitter confessional struggles of the nineteenth century, have stressed the seeming indifference of the post-revolutionary generation to the historic Lutheran confessions.[36] The facts present a mixed picture for the 1790s. While it is certainly true that no doctrinal sections were included in the constitutions that were written during this period for the Pennsylvania and New York Ministeriums, it is also clear that the author of those documents, Kunze, had a strong sense of the distinctive doctrines of the Lutheran church. There is no attempt in his writings to ignore or dismiss the differences between Lutherans and other denominations. He had hoped to print the Augsburg Confession in his *Hymn and Prayer Book* of 1795 but he was prevented from carrying out the plan because of lack of space. In the Ministerium of New York candidates for the ministry had to sign a statement indicating their assent to the symbolical books before they could be ordained. The most interdenominational of the new synodical organizations of this period was the *Unio Ecclesiastica* of South Carolina, but all of the Lutheran clergymen involved in the body were "sworn on the Symbolical Books." There is at least a hint that the Ministerium of Pennsylvania began to dispense with the signing of a pledge of loyalty to the confessions by 1792, but no reasons are given. In general, the picture seems to indicate that the confessions were taken for granted rather than being deliberately ignored.[37]

In retrospect, it is clear that some significant decisions were made in the decade between the ending of the revolutionary war and the beginning of the nineteenth century. Geography forced the abandonment of Muhlenberg's dream of a united

34.
Letter of John C. Kunze, January 27, 1790, Krauth Memorial Library Archives.

35.
Allbeck, "Journal of John Samuel Mau," p. 162; Strebeck, *Hymns,* passim.

36.
Henry Eyster Jacobs, *A History of the Evangelical Lutheran Church in the United States* (New York: Christian Literature Co., 1893), pp. 309ff.; August L. Graebner, *Geschichte der Lutherischen Kirche in Amerika* (St. Louis: Concordia Publishing House, 1892), pp. 525ff.; Wentz, *Basic History,* pp. 70–72.

37.
New York Ministerium, *Minutes . . . 1793,* p. 5; Bernheim, *History,* p. 301; Samuel S. Schmucker, *The American Lutheran Church,* 2d ed. (Springfield, Ohio: D. Harbough, 1851), p. 371, where the "minister" referred to is his father.

Lutheran church in North America. Instead, a number of smaller bodies organized, each with its own form of government, style of ministry, and tradition of worship. A spirit of goodwill and brotherhood knit these local units to each other, of course, so that ministers found no difficulty in moving from one synod to another. But the pattern of local autonomy was established and it would continue to dominate Lutheran thinking for a century.

Another decisive step was the attempt to place Lutheranism within the spectrum of denominations in the New World. Two lines of definition began to emerge. On the one hand, Lutherans could be identified with the "churchly" Protestant groups over against the "sects" and the "deists." This view would see the Lutherans as more closely allied with Episcopalians, Presbyterians, Moravians, and German Reformed than with Methodists, Baptists, Unitarians, and Universalists. Another view, however, would identify Lutherans with their cultural heritage, especially the German language. In this perspective the German Reformed churches, union schools, and German societies were to be preferred to any extensive fraternization with English-speaking denominations. By 1800 the problem had not been solved but the alternatives had been stated. It remained for time and testing to decide which view would prevail. That decision would occupy the next generation.

The years 1800–1817 have been considered the darkest hours in the history of North American Lutheranism by some historians. They see this period as a time of rampant rationalism, unionism, and liturgical ignorance.[1] Parish records seem to have been kept less carefully; clergymen did not have the advantages of formal education; the "Lutheran consciousness" of the church appears to have reached a new low. In short, the less said about this period, the better.

Viewed in another way, however, the period from 1800 to 1817 was crucial to the future of Lutheranism in North America. During these years the church faced decisive questions about its identity and role on the North American scene. How could a church with a German tradition minister to its own youth, who literally "spoke a different language"? If one translated the pietism of the fathers into English what would be distinctively Lutheran in the result? How was a church with a parish-oriented clergy going to cope with the mobile population of this new land? How could the high standards of theological education, which most Lutheran leaders considered necessary, be maintained in the face of a pressing need for clergymen and an obvious lack of interest in establishing a school to educate them?

Any one of these questions could have crippled the church in its response to the others. Yet one generation managed to deal effectively with them all. It is little wonder that parish records suffered. The real surprise is that so many significant steps could be taken within seventeen years.

The Problem of Language

The dominant issue confronting Lutherans in the first decades of the nineteenth century was the place of English in their churches. Behind every other problem loomed the language question. At the beginning of the century the question was how to provide English services for the younger generation. Twenty years later the question was how to preserve German from extinction.

At first, English seemed a natural addition which would accommodate those members of the congregations who no longer knew German or who married into the church. The New York Ministerium led the way in this accommodation, partly because it was already accustomed to dealing with both Dutch and German, so it had experience with the use of two languages. John C. Kunze had begun the introduction of English into his New York City congregation in the 1790s, at first by preaching in English himself, and later through the use of assistants who

---

1.
Chapter titles in the standard histories are instructive: J. Nicum, *Geschichte des Evangelisch-Lutherischen Ministeriums von Staate New York* (New York: Verlag des New York-Ministeriums, 1886), "Apostacy from the Teaching and Practice of the Fathers," pp. 87–123; August L. Graebner, *Geschichte der Lutherischen Kirche in Amerika* (St. Louis: Concordia Publishing House, 1892), "The Period of Decline," pp. 525–50; Henry Eyster Jacobs, *A History of the Evangelical Lutheran Church in the United States* (New York: Christian Literature Co., 1893), "Deterioration," pp. 309–47. Abdel Ross Wentz, *A Basic History of Lutheranism in America* (Philadelphia: Fortress Press, 1964), more objectively uses the chapter title "Problems of Faith and Language" (pp. 69–73), but the content of the chapter tends to mix evidence for "unionism" with charges of "rationalism," and the impression on the reader remains negative.

spoke English as their native tongue. But the experiments in New York led to schism and the formation of separate, all-English congregations. It seemed that English and German, like oil and water, just did not mix.[2]

The experience of the Swedish congregations in Delaware and southeastern Pennsylvania proved even more alarming. As the supply of clergymen from Sweden was cut off and the younger generation expected services in English, the only way out seemed to be to employ Episcopalian assistants to provide adequate leadership. These younger assistants took over the parishes as the years passed and eventually brought the congregations formerly affiliated with the Church of Sweden into the Protestant Episcopal Church.[3]

This process of gradual departure from Lutheranism occurred virtually next door to the most influential Lutheran clergyman of the period, and he never forgot its lesson. The clergyman was Justus Henry Christian Helmuth (1745–1825), senior pastor of the prestigious congregations of Zion and St. Michael's in Philadelphia. Helmuth had come to America just before the Revolution. After ten years as pastor in Lancaster, Pennsylvania, he received a unanimous call to Philadelphia, where he served for forty-one years. Many young candidates for ordination studied with him during those decades. Although not a tall or handsome man, Helmuth was a powerful preacher whose homiletic style carried conviction, passion, and directness. A contemporary estimated that he was probably the most popular Lutheran preacher in the United States through most of his ministry.

Helmuth was a conservative force among the Lutheran clergy of this period. His educational background was similar to Muhlenberg's—Halle pietism. His many publications aimed at revitalizing the personal faith of his readers and educating the young in the traditions of their fathers. Helmuth believed that a principal means of preserving his Lutheran heritage was through the continued use of German. While in Philadelphia he served as professor of German and Oriental languages at the University of Pennsylvania for eighteen years. He preached exclusively in German. Soon after the close of the revolutionary war he led the German pastors in Philadelphia to issue a pamphlet urging their congregations to uphold German "religious institutions and language." The pairing of the terms "religious institutions" and "language" indicates how closely linked he thought they were.[4]

It is not surprising, then, that when the language question arose in his Philadelphia congregation at the turn of the century Helmuth moved immediately to prohibit English services. A fire in 1794 had forced the rebuilding of Zion Church, and from that time on, influential members of the congregation began to urge the introduction of English. The pastor and a majority of the congregation vigorously opposed the suggestion. The minority brought the case before the Ministerium in 1804, 1805, and 1807, but the general body, under Helmuth's presidency, steadily refused to allow bilingual services. If the minority wanted to

2.
For general orientation on the language issue see Richard C. Wolf, "The Americanization of German Lutherans in America, to 1829" (Ph.D. diss., Yale University, 1947). For studies of the issue in certain areas see: Armin George Weng, "The Language Problem in the Lutheran Church in Pennsylvania, 1742–1870," *Church History,* December 1936 (condensation of his Ph.D. diss., Yale University, 1927); Harry J. Kreider, "The English Language Schism in the Lutheran Church in New York City, 1794–1810," *Lutheran Church Quarterly* 21 (January 1948): 50–60; William H. Gehrke, "The Transition from the German to the English Language in North Carolina," *North Carolina Historical Review* 12 (January 1935): 1–19.

3.
Amandus Johnson, *The Journal and Biography of Nicholas Collin, 1746–1831* (Philadelphia: New Jersey Society of Pennsylvania, 1936), pp. 79–83; J. H. C. Helmuth, *Denkmal der Liebe und Achtung . . . Herrn. D. Heinrich Melchior Muhlenberg* (Philadelphia: Steiner, 1788), p. 11.

4.
For biography of Helmuth see: Allen Johnson, ed., *Dictionary of American Biography,* 21 vols. (New York: Scribner's, 1943), 8:515–16; C. R. Demme, *The Christian Minister's Last Honor from a Christian Congregation* (Philadelphia: German-American Bookstore, 1825), Microfilm Corpus of American Lutheranism (hereafter cited as *MCAL*), reel 6; M. L. Stoever, "Reminiscences of Lutheran Clergymen," *Evangelical Review* 6 (1854): 2–10; W. B. Sprague, ed., *Annals of the American Lutheran Pulpit* (New York, 1869), pp. 51–54; Theodore G. Tappert, "Pastoral Heroism in a Time of Panic: Helmuth and the Yellow Fever Epidemic in Philadelphia, 1793," *Lutheran Church Quarterly* 13 (April 1940): 162–75. Much Helmuth material, including ninety manuscript volumes of his diary, is located in the Krauth Memorial Library Archives, Lutheran Theological Seminary, Philadelphia. For his published writings see Robert C. Wiederaenders, "A Bibliography of American Lutheranism,

form another congregation that would be permissible, and the new congregation could even send its pastor and delegates to meetings of the Ministerium. But the presence of such delegates was not to change the language of the Ministerium; it "must remain a German-speaking Ministerium."[5]

Attempts to keep English out of the church proved futile. The introduction of English moved forward rapidly in the cities and on the frontier. The Philadelphia insurgents, led by General Peter Muhlenberg, formed an English-speaking congregation (St. John's) in 1806. In the next year English became the official language of the New York Ministerium. Even while the Pennsylvania Ministerium was asserting that it would remain German-speaking its missionaries were preaching in English in Virginia, West Virginia, and Ohio. One of its strongest congregations was urging that all candidates for the ministry be trained in both languages. From Albany to the Carolinas English rapidly supplanted German as the language of records and public worship. Even the Ministerium of Pennsylvania was allowing English services at its convention by 1810, just five years after it had taken its stand for German.[6]

The process was inexorable. Where Germans formed a minority, as in the cities, in the South, in Maine, and on the frontier, they had to learn the language of the dominant culture. Their speech became "checkered with English words" and they began to disguise their German background. They anglicized their names; "Zimmermanns" and "Schneiders" became "Carpenters" and "Taylors." They sent their children to English schools, and thus they broke out of a cultural framework in which language, literature, and religion were intertwined. A contemporary complaint read:

First evangelical teaching gradually disappears, and our children grow up without hymns, without prayer, without catechism, and therefore without religious instruction; for you know that nothing of the sort is done in the English schools. . . . Next we gradually lose our German customs, diligence, and thrift, replacing them with English styles which frequently degenerate into pride, laziness, and extravagance. . . . And finally, through neglect of our mother tongue, we lose our majestic hymns, prayerbooks, and edifying literature—an unspeakable loss![7]

The last stage of this process of cultural transition involved a change in religion. An observer noted in 1813:

Those people who spend the whole week in the company of lawyers, judges, and people of quality will also attend church with them on Sundays. Those who look for orderly worship, if they have no worship services of their own, attend the Presbyterian Church, to which they become accustomed in the course of time. Those who are fervent in their Christianity visit the Methodists, and are soon captivated.[8]

In other cases, the transition from German meant an end to any religious affiliation. A missionary to Virginia reported that Ger-

1624–1850," mimeographed, ca. 1964; available at Concordia Historical Institute, St. Louis, and several other Lutheran libraries.
5.
Documentary History of the General Council of the Evangelical Lutheran Church in North America (Philadelphia: General Council Pub. House, 1912), pp. 352–53, 378; J. H. C. Helmuth, "Nachricht von Gemeinen," *Evangelisches Magazin* 1 (January-March 1812): 106–7 (hereafter cited as *Ev. Mag.*), in *MCAL*, reel 28; "Zuruf an die Deutschen in Amerika," ibid. 2 (1812–13): 43–47, 65–71, 174–77, 193–97; *Trial of Frederick Eberle and Others . . . 1817*, in *MCAL*, reel 5.
6.
"Zuruf," p. 67; William J. Finck, ed., "A Chronological Life of Paul Henkel," typescript (1935–37), pp. 96, 97, 110–11, 187; Nicum, *Geschichte*, p. 468; North Carolina Synod, *Proceedings . . . 1812*, p. 15; ibid. *1813*, p. 14, in *MCAL*, reel 27; *Documentary History of the Evangelical Lutheran Ministerium of Pennsylvania . . . 1748-1821* (Philadelphia: General Council Board of Publication, 1898), pp. 409, 466.
7.
Daniel Kurtz and John George Lochman, *Ansprache an die deutschen Einwohner Virginiens* (n.p., 1815), p. 5.
8.
"Zuruf," p. 68; cf. ibid., p. 70; North Carolina Synod, *Proceedings . . . 1813*, pp. 27, 32.

mans he met on the frontier seemed to "leave religion behind with the German language."[9]

Many church leaders felt they were at a crossroads. A choice had to be made. Either they would preserve the German language or they would have to abandon the faith to inevitable extinction. When the question was posed in those stark alternatives it was not difficult to choose. All that remained to be decided was how best to maintain the culture of their fathers.

Two lines of defense developed: German newspapers and German schools. Both methods show clearly how the preservation of religious patterns was interwoven with the defense of German culture in general. In fact, proposals for newspapers and schools tended to include all German-speaking people, whether they were Lutheran, Moravian, or Reformed. Confessional differences among Germans dwindled before the great gulf separating them all from the English-speaking denominations around them. Readers were warned that "the Episcopal Church is not Lutheran, as many uninformed people think; nor are the Presbyterians Reformed; they all differ from us in their confessions of faith."[10]

An ambitious publishing project, the *Evangelisches Magazin,* was launched in 1811. Its editors were the aging Helmuth and John George Schmucker, one of Helmuth's most articulate students. Although both its editors were Lutheran, the first issue stressed that the magazine was for "brothers of all denominations." Contributors from other German-speaking denominations were welcomed, especially the Moravians.[11] The periodical appeared quarterly for three years, but its circulation did not increase as rapidly as its planners had hoped. Consequently it became an annual publication in 1815 and ceased altogether two years later. While Helmuth and Schmucker contributed the majority of articles, a representative number of other clergymen also provided material. Its contents ranged from poetry and edifying hymns—often written by Helmuth—to articles for children, church news, biblical studies, and sermons. Although its brief life spanned only six years, the publication provided a means of communication for all those church leaders who sought a way to preserve the German language and promote their German schools.[12]

In the final analysis those who tried to save the German language felt that the only workable method was the continuation of German schools. "Send your children to German schools," wrote an author in the *Evangelisches Magazin.* "There they still will read hymns, prayers, scripture and catechism, while in English schools they read newspapers, stories, and fables." Some synods urged their congregations to sponsor German schools, and occasionally delegates were asked to report on the number of schools in their parish. It gradually became clear, however, that children would have to learn English in order to succeed in an English-speaking country. By 1813, therefore, advocates of German schools were suggesting that children have the benefit of instruction in both languages, and even the re-

9.
North Carolina Synod, *Proceedings . . . 1811,* p. 11; cf. Finck, "Henkel," p. 174; *Ev. Mag.* 1 (October-December 1811): 2.
10.
"Zuruf," p. 68.
11.
The Reformed Synod (Eastern) voted approval in 1812; see James Isaac Good, *History of the Reformed Church in the United States* (Reading, Pa.: D. Miller, 1899).
12.
Ev. Mag. 1 (October-December 1811): 1-5, contains the editors' prospectus. For information on size, issues, etc., see Frederick G. Gotwald, "Pioneer American Lutheran Journalism, 1812-1850," *Lutheran Quarterly* 42 (April 1912): 161-204; the article was later reprinted and published separately with some illustrations.

doubtable Helmuth was describing German as principally a "religious language."[13]

Worship and Catechetics

The most enduring result of this common concern for German was the publication in 1817 of a hymnal designed for use by both Lutheran and Reformed church members. It was the *"Gemeinschaftliche Gesangbuch"*—the "Common Songbook," and it proudly carried the official endorsement of the Reformed Synod and of all three Lutheran synods. Its foreword noted that there was hardly a family which did not have members of both denominations as a result of intermarriage. Both in family devotions and church services a common hymnal would eliminate "awkwardness" and would serve to remove the "wall of separation" caused by unfounded prejudice. Evidently the hymnal, with its more "modern" choice of hymns, filled a need, for it was reprinted within a year and went through many subsequent editions.[14]

Other materials for worship also were published during this period. A survey of activities in 1811 would find the New York Ministerium appointing committees to produce hymnals and liturgies in both English and German, the Pennsylvania Ministerium hearing a report that a collection of tunes to two hundred hymns was in preparation, the North Carolina Synod adopting a burial service, and the Ohio Conference deciding that congregational singing would be improved if an inexpensive hymnal could be made available. Not all the projects proved feasible, but the New York Ministerium did publish an English hymnal and a liturgy, and Helmuth succeeded in completing a collection of 266 hymn tunes for the use of church organists. Hymnals were also published in the Ohio Conference and in Virginia. Even Lutherans in Nova Scotia obtained a new liturgy and prayer book through the efforts of their scholarly pastor. Most of the books showed the defects which one would associate with first efforts—lack of originality, simplicity of form, and occasional inaccuracies. The New York Hymnal and Helmuth's tune book, however, continued to enjoy wide popularity for decades.[15]

It is clear that the Ministerium of Pennsylvania played a major role in preserving the use of traditional worship materials. When a group of pastors "of different denominations" in the western part of the state asked for a brief hymnal that would include hymns of the Lutheran and Reformed churches, the Ministerium rejected the idea in 1814 and prohibited its members from cooperating. Viewed in the light of the generally warm relationships between the two denominations, and the publication of the Common Songbook three years later, such an action seems calculated only to preserve the use of existing hymnals. A more precise example of the same tendency can be seen in the response of the Ministerium to a letter from the North Carolina Synod which suggested closer cooperation between the two synods. The letter, written in 1812, came at a

13.
Pleas for German schools may be found in "Zuruf," pp. 45ff., 67, 71, 195; *Ansprache an die gesammten Glieder der Deutsch Ev. Luth. Gemeinen in Pennsylvanien und den benachbarten Staaten* (1811) and *Ansprache an die deutschen Einwohner Virginiens* (1815), both pamphlets in the Archives of the Ministerium of Pennsylvania, Krauth Memorial Library. Synod actions are in *Documentary History, General Council,* p. 451; North Carolina Synod, *Proceedings . . . 1814,* p. 5; and ibid. *1815,* pp. 5, 10. Cf. *Ev. Mag.* 1 (January-March 1812): 107; ibid. 1 (July-September 1812): 194.

14.
Das Gemeinschaftliche Gesangbuch zum gottesdienstlichen Gebrauch der Lutherischen und Reformirten Gemeinden in Nord-America (Baltimore: Schaeffer & Maund, 1817); the second edition gives a longer list of official endorsements. For studies of hymnals of the period see G. Everett Arden, "The Interrelationships Between Cultus and Theology in the History of the Lutheran Churches in America" (Ph.D. diss., University of Chicago, 1944); Carleton Y. Smith, "Early Lutheran Hymnody in America from the Colonial Period to the Year 1850" (Ph.D. diss., University of Southern California, 1956); and Edward C. Wolf, "Lutheran Church Music in America During the Eighteenth and Early Nineteenth Centuries" (Ph.D. diss., University of Illinois, 1960; University Microfilms, 61-218).

15.
A Collection of Hymns and a Liturgy (Philadelphia: G. & D. Billmeyer, 1814), in *MCAL,* reel 5, for the liturgy and *MCAL,* reel 6, for the 1824 edition of the hymnal; J. H. C. Helmuth, ed., *Choral-Buch für die Erbauliche Lieder-Sammlung der deutschen Evangelisch-Lutherischen Gemeinden in Nord Amerika* (Philadelphia: C. Zentler & G. Blake, 1813); *Das Neue Gesangbuch . . . Zum Druck verordnet durch eine Special Conferenz der Evangelisch Lutherischen Prediger im westlichen Theil von Pennsylvanien und dem Staat Ohio* (Pittsburgh: Jacob Schnee, n.d.); Paul Henkel, *Church Hymn Book* (New Market, Va.: Solomon Henkel, 1816); Conrad Temme, *Evangelische-Lutherische Kirchen-*

time when the Henkel Press in Virginia had already published two German hymnals and two catechisms. In his reply to the letter, Helmuth urged that the North Carolina Synod use the catechism "as it is printed in most places in Pennsylvania" and that no further catechisms be introduced unless agreed upon by both bodies. He further advised that both synods print the Augsburg Confession as a common reading book in their schools and that the hymnal of the Ministerium become standard in North Carolina. He artfully concluded, "How lovely it would sound to a travelling German if he heard exactly the same tunes and words sung in Philadelphia that were so thrilling to his heart in North Carolina."[16]

While the form of worship may have varied from place to place it was usually simple in structure. It required little from the congregation beyond attention and the singing of a few hymns. In this respect it did not differ greatly from the forms of worship used by other Protestant bodies. The following outline was considered typical in 1818:

The beginning is made by a few passages of scripture, or by a short ejaculation, and by singing a hymn. Prayers are then read, consisting of confession of sins— praise and thanksgiving—petition—and intercession; or the minister may pray extempore. A portion of scripture is then read, which may be either the gospel and epistle of the day, or any other portion suited to the occasion, and relating to the subject, on which the sermon is to be preached. Another hymn is sung. Then the sermon is preached, which should not take up more than three quarters of an hour. Before the sermon a short prayer *may* be offered up, but after the sermon it is considered necessary to pray.—Another hymn is sung, during which, or before which, the alms are collected. The congregation is dismissed with the benediction. In some congregations a doxology is sung after the benediction.[17]

In spite of the numerous citations of efforts to cooperate with other denominations, the record indicates that most clergy and congregations made heroic efforts to preserve their identity and distinctive doctrines in the face of widespread illiteracy, poverty, and scarcity of printed materials. One index to that determination is the steady stream of catechisms which appeared. In the twenty years between 1801 and 1820 no less than twenty-two German editions of Luther's Small Catechism were printed and, presumably, sold—a rate of better than one per year. During the same period English translations of the catechism were made in New York, Pennsylvania, and Virginia. Paul Henkel was the publisher in Virginia. From his family press at New Market came five editions of the catechism in five years. Those books were then shipped southward into the Carolinas and westward to Ohio, Kentucky, and Tennessee. It is true that many of these editions, like those in other states, altered sections of the catechism to conform with imagined "improvements" in use or application. In general, however, the changes were not

Agende . . . in der Lutherischen Kirche, zu Luneberg, in Nova Scotia (Philadelphia: G. & D. Billmeyer, 1816). An introduction to Helmuth's tune book and to literature on church music of this period is Edward C. Wolf's "America's First Lutheran Chorale Book," *Concordia Historical Institute Quarterly* 46 (Spring 1973): 5-17.

16.
Documentary History, General Council, pp. 469, 476; North Carolina Synod, *Proceedings . . . 1811-12*, p. 9; *Ev. Mag.* 2 (October-December 1812), pp. 17-18.

17.
John George Lochman, *The History, Doctrine, and Discipline of the Evangelical Lutheran Church* (Harrisburg, Pa.: John Wyeth, 1818), pp. 151-52, in *MCAL*, reel 5.

made with an eye to diluting the Lutheran faith or accommodating it to other denominations.[18]

Westward Migration

Second only to the language question was the problem of westward migration. The issue of language would have arisen even if the westward movement had not occurred, but the needs of the frontier hastened the transition to English and presented a set of circumstances similar to those faced by the first generation of colonists a century earlier.

The westward flow of population that had begun after the Revolution continued strong through the early decades of the nineteenth century. Ohio was the chief beneficiary of the migration. It became a state in 1803 and rapidly achieved the settled look of much older states to the east. By 1814 a meeting of Lutheran pastors in Ohio could report sixty congregations and thirty-seven church buildings. Lutherans settled in three sections of the young state: along the border of Pennsylvania northwest of Pittsburgh, in the center of the state just south of Columbus, and somewhat farther west near Dayton. Meanwhile, the frontier raced on westward. By the time of the 300th anniversary of the Reformation in 1817 Lutherans were settling in south central Illinois and crossing the Mississippi River to take up land in southeastern Missouri. A writer of that period estimated that there were "about six hundred and fifty" congregations in the United States,[19] to which should be added about ten congregations and preaching points in Canada.

Canada also opened up a second center of Lutheran strength to match, and later to surpass, the older center of settlement in Nova Scotia. Colonists loyal to England had fled the newly-independent United States and had helped to open the northern shore of Lake Ontario to settlement. This area in the present province of Ontario—or "Upper Canada" as a decree of 1791 called it—proved an attractive location for Lutherans. While some Loyalists had moved northeastward to the older Lutheran colony in Nova Scotia, the overwhelming growth of the church occurred among those Loyalists who moved northwestward into Ontario. The continued flow of population into this area permitted the construction of church buildings in Lennox and Addington counties and in Markham Township near Toronto between 1800 and 1817. Ministers for the congregations usually came from the Ministeriums of Pennsylvania and New York.[20]

The manpower for these migrations to the West and Northwest came chiefly from already established centers of Lutheran strength in the East. Some of those centers were so drained of their human resources that they would never recover. Few immigrants from Europe came to replace the lost population since the Napoleonic wars had interrupted the complex system of travel that brought farmers from the Palatinate to Pennsylvania. As a result, the initial effect of the westward migration was a thinning of Lutheran resources on both sides of the Appalachians. Lutherans moved out of their compact little communities in Pennsylvania and Virginia into a vast new area where

18.
For materials on catechisms see M. Reu, "Luther's Catechism in the United States," in *Dr. Luther's Small Catechism* (Chicago: Wartburg Press, 1929), pp. 275-93; Beale M. Schmucker, "Luther's Small Catechism," *Lutheran Church Review* 5 (April and June 1886): 102-4, 165, 171; microfilm copies of several catechisms are in *MCAL*, reels 4, 5. A list of extant catechisms has been prepared by Frederick Weiser and may be obtained through the Abdel Ross Wentz Library, Lutheran Theological Seminary, Gettysburg, Pa.

19.
Ray Billington, *Westward Expansion: A History of the American Frontier* (New York: Macmillan, 1949); Lochman, *History*, p. 71. On early work in Kentucky and Illinois see Martin L. Wagner, *The Chicago Synod and Its Antecedents* (Waverly, Iowa: Wartburg, 1909), pp. 23-24; on western New York see Harry J. Kreider, *History of the United Lutheran Synod of New York and New England, 1786-1860* (Philadelphia: Muhlenberg Press, 1954), pp. 57-58. Ellis B. Burgess, *Memorial History of the Pittsburgh Synod . . .* (Greenville, Pa.: Beaver, 1925), pp. 57-63, has some biographical material and character sketches of early Lutheran pastors in western Pennsylvania from 1806 to 1820.

20.
Carl R. Cronmiller, *A History of the Lutheran Church in Canada* (Toronto: Synod of Canada, 1961), pp. 44-45, 50-51, 75ff., 90-91, 104.

their German language and their catechisms were curiosities. At the same time, the older congregations in the East found their numbers dwindling and their traditional ways challenged by a younger generation. As a symptom of this weakness, fewer churches were built between 1800 and 1817 than had been constructed in the ten years prior to 1800.

The Ministeriums of Pennsylvania and New York felt the effects of this westward flow in their synodical meetings. Pastors began to ask to be excused from the annual gatherings because of distance. In an effort to meet this problem both bodies resorted to strengthening smaller units called conferences or districts. In New York the district plan did not work well and was finally abandoned in 1815. The Ministerium of Pennsylvania, however, succeeded in strengthening its five conferences and enabled them to maintain a more or less active program. The Ohio and the Maryland-Virginia conferences proved especially viable, since they served the needs of pastors far removed from the more populous areas of the Ministerium. By 1814 the Ohio Conference received permission to assign parishes to its own young candidates for the ministry. It also was granted the right to send one representative to the annual Ministerium meetings so that all the pastors in Ohio would not be required to make the long trip every year. While the parent body retained the right to examine candidates for ordination and to maintain discipline over the clergy, it is clear that a decentralization process had begun. Eventually it would lead to the formation of new synods on both sides of the Appalachians.

Traveling Preachers

Who was to provide pastoral services to these thinly spread pioneers in their mountain valleys and forest-walled farmlands? For the twenty-five years preceding 1806, there were never more than three Lutheran pastors in the relatively thickly populated areas of western Pennsylvania and eastern Ohio.

In 1804 the Ministerium of Pennsylvania, acting on a plan submitted by its Lancaster Conference, provided for "traveling preachers" to visit vacant congregations. The North Carolina Synod adopted a similar plan for "traveling missionaries" in 1810. The synods would often choose pastors serving parishes near the frontier for this task, although young men preparing for ordination would sometimes combine a missionary tour with a search for a vacant pulpit which they might later fill on a permanent basis. The tours would last up to four months and would begin as soon as roads were passable in the spring. The synods guaranteed a certain amount of money to their missionaries but the pastors were expected to earn most of that sum through offerings collected on the tour. Synods would then pay the difference between the amount collected and the amount guaranteed. Within a decade of its inauguration, the plan produced enough congregations in Ohio to keep "six to eight" resident pastors busy.[21]

21.
Burgess, *Memorial History,* pp. 55–57. Cf. Willard D. Allbeck, *A Century of Lutherans in Ohio* (Yellow Springs, Ohio: Antioch Press, 1966), pp. 38–56.

The traveling preachers followed a fairly uniform plan of action. After locating a settlement of Germans they held a worship service in any convenient structure—house, barn, school, church, or courthouse. The service was announced from house to house by the servants or children of the missionary preacher's host. Occasionally a Communion service, in which a small percentage of those present would participate, followed. After the service, the missionary asked all who wished instruction in Luther's catechism to step forward and give their names to him or to his helpers. The next days were spent in catechization of those who had enrolled. At the end of the instruction period, which would usually be a week or ten days, a service of confirmation and a second Communion service climaxed the missionary's visit. In some cases, the instruction process was delegated to a local schoolmaster or lay leader and the missionary would continue on his way after the classes had been well begun. If a congregation organized it would send a letter requesting regular pastoral services back to the synod which had sent the missionary. In this way up to fifteen congregations were admitted to a synod in a given year.[22] Here, in the missionary's own words, is a typical example of what occurred:

This was a hard day for me. The weather was warm and the people came from afar. A large dwelling house served as our church; all the rooms were filled and many stood outside. I took my place at the door in order to take advantage of the air. I first preached to the Germans on Isaiah 45:22. As this was the first German sermon at this place it received much attention and aroused much curiosity, particularly on the part of the young people. The Germans were very quiet and well-behaved, but it was very difficult for the English to remain in order. The sermon had considerable effect on many of the Germans. I was astonished that the young people were so deeply moved. As soon as the German sermon was finished I turned to the English. . . . With their bad habits and wild nature those in the house were unable to sit still and much less those outside. After much talking I finally succeeded in making a beginning but had to permit myself to engage in digressions and droll speeches in order to make them attentive. . . . My sermon was on Proverbs 1:23. The sermon lasted a full hour and a half. It is true that the sermon was not approved by all nor was it openly condemned by anyone. It seemed as if many were unaccustomed to hear the plan of salvation explained in this way. A friend informed me that certain listeners had threatened to attack me when opportunity should offer because of infant baptism. However, everything was quiet after the sermon ended, and I came away in peace. After the sermon I baptized a child and received 13 shillings and six pence. . . . Here my work for the day ended. God be

22.
North Carolina Synod, *Proceedings . . . 1813,* pp. 12, 28; *Documentary History, General Council,* p. 465.

praised I find that I am not so very tired even though I preached two long sermons and helped to row the nine miles against the stream in order to bring us here. May He add his blessing to the work I did according to the best of my knowledge and understanding.[23]

Now and then the missionaries would encounter a congregation with a preacher who belonged to no synod. Some of these irregular ministers lacked both character and education to qualify for the pastoral office. In earlier days the synods would have ignored these men, but the needs for manpower were so vast that rules were bent. The local preachers became members of a synod even though membership often meant a demotion from the lofty, if self-assumed, title of "pastor" to the lowly status of "catechist." None of the synods seemed happy with this arrangement and as time went on standards gradually rose to eliminate the most obviously unfit candidates.[24]

Theological Education

Although the need for adequately trained men increased, the supply of clergy from Europe continued to dwindle. In 1790 a majority of the Lutheran ministers connected with synods in North America had received university educations in Germany. By 1810 university graduates were in the minority. In a young land without a strong university system Lutherans had to find methods of education which would keep standards high but would not require extensive formal education. The apprentice system seemed the best answer, and during the early years of the nineteenth century most synods devoted their energies to improving and regulating the quality of education obtained through study in the homes of individual pastors. The Ministeriums of New York and Pennsylvania designated certain pastors as qualified to teach candidates for the ministry. In addition they stipulated which subjects should be included in examinations for ordination. They asked that students be able to translate passages from the original languages of the Bible at sight and that they be familiar with "exegesis, church history, and dogmatics." Spelling and composition of sermons also received major emphasis. In the southern states standards were less definite and synods simply assigned students to the nearest pastor for instruction in theology.[25]

Even this somewhat informal system of theological education in the New World was incapable of meeting the need for clergy. Other denominations, accustomed to an educated clergy, were facing the same problem because the pace of westward expansion made tremendous demands on leadership resources. What was to be done? Pastors in Ohio pleaded for some means of education in their own state. North Carolina leaders considered founding a seminary. Pennsylvania clergy weighed the possibilities of a diaconate which would recognize service in a parish as the equivalent of a theological education.[26] Finally, in New York, a long-awaited step was taken. In 1815 the executors of John C. Hartwick's will, after years of financial wrangling, opened Hartwick Academy with one professor and nineteen

23.
Finck, "Henkel," pp. 71–72. For a biography of this noted missionary see R. Baur, "Paul Henkel, Pioneer Lutheran Missionary" (Ph.D. diss., State University of Iowa, 1968), available in microfilm no. 790d, Concordia Historical Institute, St. Louis; and B. H. Pershing, "Paul Henkel, Frontier Missionary," *Lutheran Church Quarterly* 7 (April 1934): 125–51; William J. Finck, "Paul Henkel, the Lutheran Pioneer," *Lutheran Quarterly* 56 (July 1926). Henkel materials are located at University of Virginia; Lutheran Theological Seminary, Gettysburg, Pa.; Lutheran Theological Seminary, Philadelphia; Concordia Historical Institute, St. Louis; and Winchester Historical Society, Winchester, Va.
24.
On the need see "Zuruf," p. 66. On synodical actions see, e.g., North Carolina Synod, *Proceedings . . . 1814*, p. 10.
25.
Documentary History, General Council, pp. 345, 400, 406, 407, 444–45. For a list of pastors and their pupils see Benjamin Sadtler, "The Education of Ministers by Private Tutors, Before the Establishment of Theological Seminaries," *Lutheran Church Review* 13 (July 1894): 177–84. Jacobs, *History*, p. 353, notes that Columbia College (N.Y.), the University of Pennsylvania, Dickinson College, Jefferson College, and Princeton University had students who later became Lutheran clergymen.
26.
North Carolina Synod, *Proceedings . . . 1813*, pp. 8, 33; *Documentary History, General Council*, pp. 444, 482–83.

students.[27] Although its location near Cooperstown, New York, made it inaccessible to theological candidates of other synods, the tiny "academy" proved that a theological seminary could be established and maintained. Its example made the founding of other seminaries easier. A significant milestone had been passed.

The new academy also presented a break with the tradition of accepting clergy from Europe. The rise of rationalism and "neology" in Germany aroused fear of contamination in the hearts of Lutheran leaders on this side of the Atlantic. In 1805 Kunze wrote in alarm to his fellow clergy in New York State: "Dreadful as it may seem, it is nevertheless the result of my continuing to read German publications and of my continued German correspondence that I assert, should we send for ten candidates to place them in our vacant congregations, it is highly probable that we would have . . . nine despisers, yea, blasphemers of Christ. . . ."[28] A year earlier a Georgia pastor had complained that "in Germany both Protestant Churches [Lutheran and Reformed] have become measurably corrupt, through false teachers creeping into the church. . . . These teachers impiously deny all the fundamental doctrines of our salvation, which is in Jesus Christ. The Germans who have come to this country in late years have imbibed these false principles. . . ."[29]

The Hartwick Academy would provide an alternative to importing clergymen who might deny Christ. Kunze assured his colleagues that they, combined with the Lutheran clergy of Pennsylvania, could support the new institution just as "some faithful servants of God" in Germany had "associated themselves for instructing young candidates for the pulpit, in order to counteract the academical poison they may have imbibed" at German universities.

The Continued Fight Against Deism

It is clear from Kunze's letter that the battle against deism which began in the 1790s was still being fought. Deist principles had gained ground in the meantime, especially after the turn of the century when Thomas Jefferson and James Madison brought deism to the highest circles of government. Faced with the rise of deism in their communities and their congregations, Lutheran leaders fought back with two strategies. A very few leaders tried to meet the rationalistic opponents on their own ground by demonstrating that there was no conflict between reason and Christianity. However, the greatest number of clergy, and most of the laymen, preferred a strategy of frontal attack, questioning the deist axiom that reason was the standard by which all religion should be judged.

The most prominent of the small group who tried to answer reason by reason was the man who succeeded Kunze as president of the New York Ministerium. In 1807 Frederick Henry Quitman, a graduate of Halle and a vigorous writer, became the second president of the Ministerium. He had arrived in New York twelve years earlier and was almost immediately elected

27.
Source material on Hartwick Academy (later Hartwick Seminary) is in the Hartwick Seminary Archives, Hartwick College, Oneonta, N.Y. A detailed treatment of Hartwick's background and early years is given in John W. Schmitthenner, "The Origin and Educational Contribution of Hartwick Seminary" (Ph.D. diss., New York University, 1934), and an expansion of that dissertation, "The Hartwick Seminary: The Oldest Lutheran School in America," in the archives of the Metropolitan New York Synod. Published studies are found in Henry H. Heins, *Throughout All the Years: The Bicentennial Story of Hartwick in America, 1746-1946* (Oneonta, N.Y.: Hartwick College, 1946).
28.
Letter to the Ministerium of New York, quoted in Henry Eyster Jacobs, "The Confessional History of the Ministerium of Pennsylvania," *Lutheran Church Review* 17 (April 1898): 365-66.
29.
Letter of John Ernest Bergman, July 4, 1804, quoted in P. A. Strobel, *The Salzburgers and Their Descendants* (Baltimore: T. Newton Kurtz, 1855), p. 238. Cf. *Ev. Mag.* 1 (July-September 1812): 213-14.

secretary of the Ministerium. Already fluent in German and Dutch, he soon became a leader in the movement to provide English hymnals and catechisms for the rapidly changing congregations in New York.[30]

Quitman has been accused of unitarianism and rationalism, but his actual position within the theological spectrum of his day was more nearly that of the so-called biblical supernaturalism. This school, represented in Germany by Gottlob Christian Storr (1746–1805) and the Old Tuebingen school, held that both reason and revelation were authoritative for the Christian. Reason alone could not plumb the divine depths. Therefore, the biblical revelation, validated by reason, was necessary. In his catechism, published in 1814, Quitman asks if the creative activity of God can be understood by the human mind. He answers, "No, it surpasses all human understanding, and is a matter of faith solely." Left to itself, reason produces the "madness" of infidelity. While admitting there are rational proofs for God's existence, Quitman begins his list of evidences with "the testimony of the holy scriptures, and in particular that of our Lord Jesus, who, as the only begotten Son of God has declared him."[31]

Standing between the thoroughgoing rationalists on the one hand and evangelistic American Protestantism on the other, Quitman presents a hybrid theology. His statements sometimes seem contradictory, as when he asserts that man has not been deprived of his "free moral agency," and then goes on to declare that it is the Holy Spirit who provides "every good quality of which the Christian is possessed." In an early work he attacks local superstition about spirits and demons on grounds that would argue equally well against miracles; he condemns the "miracles" of Pharaoh's sorcerers but does not question the miracles of Moses. His catechism does not deal explicitly with the divinity of Christ, yet it refers to him as "the only begotten Son of God" in several places. His definition of faith and his explanation of the Lord's Supper show an almost complete misunderstanding of Luther. In short, Quitman presents no finished Lutheran theological system; he simply tries unsuccessfully to restate traditional beliefs in a rationalistic language and manner.

Quitman's attempt to fight deism with its own rational weapons failed to stimulate widespread imitation among his fellow Lutherans. His catechism did not sell well; an edition of Luther's Catechism, published at about the same time, was far more popular. Even Quitman's students and stepsons hesitated to give reason the central place it had occupied in his theology. The New York Ministerium continued to respect him personally, electing him regularly to its presidency from 1806 to 1825, but it did not follow his theological leadership.[32] The fortifications against "infidelity" were being erected on a different, more aggressive plan.

The most successful war on deism was not waged through the printed word, but by the human voice, raised day and night in

30.
For biographical material on Quitman see Sprague, *Annals,* pp. 115–21; J. F. H. Claiborne, *Life and Correspondence of John A. Quitman* (New York: Harper & Bros., 1860), 1:15–24, 29–35, 47–48, 66, 131–33; Stoever, "Reminiscences," *Evangelical Review* 10 (October 1858): 189; Nicum, *Geschichte,* pp. 96–99.

31.
The most thorough study of Quitman's theological position is Raymond M. Bost, "The Reverend John Bachman and the Development of Southern Lutheranism" (Ph.D. diss., Yale University, 1963), pp. 18–60. For Quitman's works see *MCAL,* reels 4, 5. The traditional view of Quitman as a thoroughgoing rationalist is in Kreider, *History,* pp. 41–47.

32.
Nicum, *Geschichte,* p. 99, quotes Quitman in 1824 as saying that he still had 200 copies of the catechism and that he "had every reason to expect that the books would not remain unsold so many years." His stepsons, Philip and Frederick Mayer, are judged "more conservative" by the conservative Nicum (ibid., p. 95) and this judgment is substantiated by an examination of Philip Mayer, "Notes on the Order of Salvation . . . " (1808), in *MCAL,* reel 4. The theology of one of Quitman's (and Mayer's) pupils, John Bachman, is described in Bost, "Bachman," pp. 115–20.

forest clearings along the farming frontier. A North Carolina pastor wrote with amazement of an early camp meeting:

Christians of all denominations assemble in the woods from four to six or sometimes 10 thousand strong. They pitch tents, sing, pray, and preach day and night for five, six or even eight days. I have been an eyewitness to occurrences at such "big meetings" that I cannot explain. I saw young and old, weak and strong, white and black, in short, men of every age, rank and station fall to the ground as though they had been struck by lightning, and then lie for a time without speaking, some without breathing or moving. As they began to recover, one heard them cry out bitterly and flee to God for grace. After three or more hours spent in this fashion, they stood up, praised God, began to pray in an unusual way, exhorted sinners to come to Jesus, etc. Many of those thus "exercised" were previously godless men in whom one could recognize a true and noticeable change. *Even Deists were brought to confession in this way.*[33] (Italics added)

After noting that various observers of these meetings attributed them to God, to the devil, or to natural causes, the pastor concluded, "The matter has disturbed me greatly. It has not yet evidenced itself in our German congregations."

Lutherans never entered wholeheartedly into the camp-meeting movement, but they did share its conviction that the way to fight infidelity was through a vigorous proclamation of human sin and God's grace. This focus on personal religious experience paralleled the pietism of Muhlenberg and the other Halle missionaries. It emphasized individual commitment over denominational distinction at a time when relatively few Lutheran congregations enjoyed the exclusive services of a Lutheran pastor.[34]

Most of the interest in camp meetings and their methods arose in areas where regular pastoral services were infrequent; the occasional visit of a traveling preacher or missionary would provide opportunity for a concentrated series of services leading to commitments that would carry the new members through until the next visitation. The North Carolina Synod overcame doubts about revivals and began to utilize revivalistic methods among its constituency. A three-day preaching program in conjunction with the Moravians and the German and English Reformed churches was adopted by the synod in 1810, and three years later the synod allowed adults to be confirmed "without much instruction" when the pastor was satisfied that their life and faith were "conformable to the Gospel." John Stough cooperated with Reformed preachers in southwestern Pennsylvania in a week-long revival where "men and women in perfect health were involuntarily often suddenly jerked about like persons afflicted with St. Vitus dance, while others fell down and appeared in a state of syncope."[35]

The spread of interest in revivals prompted the Ministerium

33.
Letter of C. A. Storch to Velthusen, February 25, 1803, quoted in Eberhard Pellens, *Die Beziehungen der ev. luth. Kirchen von Hannover und Braunschweig zur ev. luth. Kirche in North Carolina in der 2. Hälfte des 18. Jahrhunderts (Hilfe und Einfluss)* (Hamburg: Evang.-Theologische Fakultät der Universität Hamburg, 1961), pp. 54–55. See Finck "Henkel," pp. 41–43, for a critical account.

34.
For a general survey of the camp meetings see Charles A. Johnson, *The Frontier Camp Meeting: Religion's Harvest Time* (Dallas: SMU Press, 1955), and Bernard A. Weisberger, *They Gathered at the River* (Boston: Little, Brown, 1958), chap. 2, and the bibliographies in both books.

35.
Willard D. Allbeck, "John Stough: Founder of Ohio Lutheranism," *Lutheran Quarterly* 12 (February 1960): 33; cf. Paul H. Eller, "Revivalism and the German Churches in Pennsylvania, 1783–1816" (Ph.D. diss., University of Chicago, 1933). North Carolina Synod, *Proceedings . . . 1806,* p. 8; ibid. *1810,* pp. 10–11; ibid. *1814,* p. 3.

of Pennsylvania to advise its frontier missionary "to have no dealings with camp meetings, if he should find such departures from our Evangelical ways" in Ohio, Kentucky, Virginia, and Tennessee.[36]

Although the more dramatic methods of camp meetings did not capture the attention of Lutherans, the success of these methods in converting unbelievers coincided exactly with the goals of Lutheran leadership. The result was that the emotional side of their pietistic heritage resurfaced in the use of conversion-centered methods and theology. In the process, it was possible to make common cause with other German-speaking groups, and, to a lesser extent, with English denominations.[37]

A key figure in Lutheran adoption of the methods and goals of evangelical American Protestantism was John George Schmucker (1771-1854), the father of Samuel S. Schmucker (see chapter 7). An immigrant to Virginia, he was converted at the age of eighteen and licensed to preach three years later. In the meantime he had studied under Helmuth and Jacob Goering of York. After seven years of ministry at Hagerstown, Maryland, he was ordained in 1800. He moved back to York after the death of Goering and spent the remaining twenty-six years of his life in that center of Pennsylvania Lutheranism. He was an able, aggressive, learned, and respected pastor, fearless in controversy and uncompromising in principle.[38]

John G. Schmucker's affinity for "American Evangelicalism" came out of his own background and interests. He considered "infidelity, and the illustration of natural truths, without any reference to God or his word" to be the "fountainhead . . . of all moral degeneracy and confusion." Reason was not the gateway by which he had entered the church. His own conversion experience had convinced him that one must reach the heart to reach the man. The Bible was true because experience proved it so, not because it conformed to reason. Schmucker's major literary work concentrated on recounting the historical fulfillment of biblical prophecy in order to demonstrate that the Bible was able to authenticate itself.[39]

As co-editor with Helmuth of the *Evangelisches Magazin*, Schmucker could urge his fellow Lutherans to join with all true Christians in the common battle against infidelity. The magazine printed accounts of converted deists, universalists, and "awakened" congregations where "days of special blessing" resulted from vigorous preaching and solemn instruction of the young. The enemy was being driven back by Christians banded together in a last great counterattack. Schmucker saw "revivals of religion, a spirit for forming Missionary Societies, evangelical tract-societies, societies to support Sunday Schools . . . ," and "a disposition to *union among believers* of all parties" as "the first indication of the morning dawn of the Millennian day." He carried this hope into action by serving as senior vice-president of the American Tract Society and as a local officer in the Temperance and Bible and Sunday School societies.[40]

Many Lutherans shared Schmucker's interest in revivals. A Maryland pastor reported that in 1809 he completed his confir-

108

36.
Documentary History, General Council, p. 428.
37.
General studies dealing with Protestant attempts to oppose "infidelity" are: Vernon Stauffer, *New England and the Bavarian Illuminati* (New York: Columbia University Press, 1918), and Howard M. Jones, *America and French Culture, 1750-1848* (Chapel Hill, N.C.: University of North Carolina Press, 1927), chaps. 10-12.
38.
For biographical material see Luke Schmucker, *The Schmucker Family and the Lutheran Church in America* (Luke Schmucker, 1937), pp. 12-20; Abdel Ross Wentz, *Pioneer in Christian Unity: Samuel Simon Schmucker* (Philadelphia: Fortress Press, 1967), pp. 2-3; and James Lawton Haney, "The Religious Heritage and Education of Samuel Simon Schmucker: A Study in the Rise of 'American Lutheranism'" (Ph.D. diss., Yale University, 1968) pp. 189-200, available in microfilm no. 790d, Concordia Historical Institute, St. Louis.
39.
For John George Schmucker's theology see Haney, "Religious Heritage," pp. 276-307. Schmucker's works in English are: "Catechism for the Use of Those Who Prepare for Confirmation," Krauth Memorial Library Archives; and *The Prophetic History of the Christian Religion Explained . . .* , 2 vols. (Baltimore: Schaeffer & Maund, 1817-21). He also wrote many unsigned articles in *Ev. Mag.* A partial list of these German articles may be found in Gotwald, "Lutheran Journalism," p. 168.
40.
Ev. Mag. 1 (January-March 1812): 114; ibid. 1 (July-September 1812): 226ff.; ibid. 3 (October-December 1813): 41; *Prophetic History*, 2:227, quoted in Haney, "Religious Heritage," pp. 219-20.

mation instruction of six children by talking with them about the condition of their souls. He began to pray for them and "in a very few minutes their weeping and crying for grace made it impossible for me to hear my own voice."[41] Most of them continued to pray for an hour or more by themselves. Other accounts indicate that a display of intense emotion upon the completion of confirmation instruction was encouraged, as an external sign of conversion.

Relations with Other Protestant Groups

The common battle against infidelity promoted generally good relationships with other denominations. Communion was opened to members of other denominations by specific action of the North Carolina Synod; the Ministerium of Pennsylvania permitted its pastors to commune any Protestant "in an emergency." The president of the Ministerium, Helmuth, recommended the American Bible Society to member congregations from central New York State to Virginia, and in 1813 the Ministerium urged candidates for ordination to season their preaching "with the spirit of true Evangelical Christianity."[42] A writer in the *Evangelisches Magazin* noted that there was more tolerance of other beliefs in America than there had been in Germany. Those who criticized their neighbors were judged either to lack genuine Christian love or to be weak in understanding. The German denominations particularly began to share worship services in areas where neither Lutherans nor Reformed had their own clergy available. Then intermarriage further blurred the lines of distinction.

The English congregations—the Presbyterians and especially the Quakers—are far behind us in this regard. The Mennonites took a long time to forget the pain which the persecuting spirit of European Catholics and Protestants had caused them, but in our time they too have become more cooperative and at least are not nearly so bigoted as the Baptists. The Lutheran and Reformed churches are so interwoven and bound together here that their minor difference in doctrine is almost forgotten through the similarity in their church organization and worship.[43]

Relations with the Reformed and the Moravians were close throughout the period. Both groups shared a concern for maintaining the German language with Lutherans, and thus they became major partners in efforts to provide and maintain schools, printed materials, and periodicals. In Pennsylvania and on the Ohio frontier, Reformed pastors and congregations became the chief ally. In North Carolina the Moravians served in the same capacity. In fact, a Moravian, Gottlieb Shober, became successively secretary and president of the North Carolina Synod.[44]

Relationships to English-speaking bodies and German sectarian groups varied from time to time and from place to place. Episcopalians in Canada, New York, Pennsylvania, and Delaware were receiving former Lutheran congregations into their

41.
Ev. Mag. 1 (October–December 1811): 8–20.
42.
North Carolina Synod, *Proceedings . . . 1809,* p. 10; *Documentary History, General Council,* pp. 397, 405, 437, 459. Cf. Finck, "Henkel," p. 117.
43.
Ev. Mag. 3 (January–March 1814): 67–68. The author is probably John George Schmucker.
44.
On Reformed: *Documentary History, General Council,* pp. 456–57, 469, 476; Ohio Conference, *Reports . . . 1812,* in *MCAL,* reel 29; North Carolina Synod, *Proceedings . . . 1810,* p. 11; ibid. *1815,* pp. 10–12. Cf. Donald H. Yoder, "Lutheran-Reformed Union Proposals, 1800–1850: An Experiment in Ecumenics," *Bulletin of the Theological Seminary of the Evangelical and Reformed Church* 17 (January 1946)): 39–77. This is expanded in his "Church Union Efforts of the Reformed Church in the United States to 1934" (Ph.D. diss., University of Chicago, 1948). Another study is Harold C. Fry's "Union Churches in Southeastern Pennsylvania" (S.T.D. diss., Temple University, 1937). On Moravians: North Carolina Synod, *Proceedings . . . 1813,* pp. 12–13; ibid. *1814,* pp. 5, 12–15; Finck, "Henkel," p. 141; *Ev. Mag.* 1 (October–December 1811): 1, 3.

communion. As a result, the New York Ministerium rescinded its agreement to allow this process in 1804, and the Pennsylvania Ministerium noted that only the ignorant would call Episcopalians "Lutheran" or "English Lutheran." Cooperation with Episcopalians continued only in areas where the Episcopal Church was weaker than the Lutheran church, such as in western North Carolina. Methodist clergy occasionally joined Lutheran synods after careful deliberations on both sides, although Methodist missionary activity continued to threaten Lutherans. The "New Reformed" or United Brethren were generally considered as rivals for members on the frontier, and therefore Lutherans had little to do with them.[45]

Baptists were the one denomination with which Lutherans continued to disagree. This opposition did not arise out of conflicts concerning revivals; it lay in the basic theological question of the meaning and mode of baptism. As early as 1802 a Lutheran catechism added questions defending infant baptism to Luther's traditional format. Later catechisms followed suit. Lutheran preachers on the frontier were challenged by hecklers during their sermons and occasionally fights threatened to erupt. The missionary preachers returned the fire with vehemence and occasional humor. While preaching on Jesus' command to "baptize all nations," one missionary in western Pennsylvania noted that the only three cases of total immersion he discovered in Scripture were the victims of the Flood, the army of Pharaoh, and the swine of the Gadarenes.[46]

The 300th Anniversary of the Reformation

As the 300th Anniversary of the Reformation approached in 1817, the synodical bodies exchanged notices of plans for the celebration. The respective arrangements for that occasion sum up the variety of viewpoints present in Lutheranism by 1817.

In New York, Quitman prepared two sermons which stressed the Reformation's contribution to "religious knowledge," liberty, and toleration. The carefully constructed addresses reflect Quitman's interest in the power of human reason to "shed new light upon received doctrines" and to set "the rules by which all religious questions are to be decided." Nearby, in New York City, the Episcopal Church continued a tradition of friendship with Lutherans by inviting Frederick Christian Schaeffer of that city to preach a Reformation sermon in St. Paul's Church. An overflow crowd attended.[47]

Farther down the Atlantic seaboard, in Baltimore, Schaeffer's brother David was preaching to a more conservative congregation from several Protestant denominations. Here in the Middle Atlantic states reason was less important than revelation, as indicated by the words of one of the hymns written for the occasion:

Far hence, each superstition vain,
Wild offspring of the human brain,
The truths that fill thy hallow'd page
My happier choice great God engage.

45.
On Episcopalians: New York Ministerium, *Minutes . . . 1804*, p. 36; *Documentary History, General Council*, pp. 359, 483. On Methodists: New York Ministerium, *Minutes . . . 1805*, pp. 39-40; *Documentary History, General Council*, pp. 371, 383. On New Reformed: Ohio Conference, *Reports . . . 1813*; Finck, "Henkel," pp. 112, 113, 115, 116.
46.
Dr. Martin Luther's Catechism for Children and Young People (Philadelphia: Henry Sweitzer, 1802), p. 16. Cf. Mayer, "Notes on the Order of Salvation," in *MCAL*, reel 4, and Paul Henkel, *The Christian Catechism*, 2d ed. (New Market, Va.: Ambrose Henkel, 1811), pp. 68-73, in *MCAL*, reel 4. The missionary's experience is cited in Burgess, *Memorial History*, pp. 60-61.
47.
Frederick H. Quitman, *Three Sermons . . .* (Hudson, N.Y.: William E. Norman, 1817), in *MCAL*, reel 5. Frederick C. Schaeffer, *A Sermon Preached in St. Paul's Church, in the City of New York . . .* (New York: Kirk & Mercein, 1817).

David Schaeffer emphasized that the Reformation had exalted the Bible and had induced Christians to work together in defense of received doctrines. "All agree," he pointed out, "that the Bible should be read and diligently studied, that true repentance, faith in Christ Jesus, sanctification by the spirit, are prerequisites for our admission into the mansions of future bliss." In Philadelphia, Helmuth addressed a congregation which included invited representatives of the Reformed, Moravian, Episcopal, and Presbyterian churches on a similar theme.[48]

In the South, Lutheran cooperation with other Protestants had gone even further. The Reformation anniversary in North Carolina was marked by the appearance of a book on Luther written by a Moravian. Its author was the Gottlieb Shober mentioned earlier as the secretary and president of the North Carolina Synod. Both his book and his position reflect the close friendship which had developed between the two churches of German background in an area where the English denominations were increasing in power.[49]

By 1817 Lutherans had begun to cope with the problems of language and westward expansion. The question of the future language of the church was settled in favor of English. Although many congregations in regions of heavy German settlement would continue to worship in German, synodical business was increasingly carried on in English. The flow of settlers to the West now was accompanied by traveling preachers who laid the foundations for future congregations. The church had not succumbed to the dilution of its strength caused by the westward movement. It had leaped the mountains successfully and would soon organize along the former frontier.[50]

In the process of their adjustment to new conditions, Lutherans also advanced in their plans to provide for the needs of the church in North America. An "academy" was opened in New York, catechisms began to flow from presses in Philadelphia and Virginia, revised hymnals and liturgies gained acceptance, and a religious newspaper enjoyed brief popularity. Not all the projects survived; many of them did not deserve a larger influence. The crisis, however, had been passed. The Lutheran church was not swallowed up by other denominations, as it had been along the Delaware, nor did it go into hibernation, as its Moravian neighbors would do. It began the long process of rethinking its tradition and its distinctiveness in a new environment.

Naturally, the process of adaptation produced strains and revealed unresolved issues among Lutherans. The proper extent of cooperation with other denominations, for example, had not been determined, nor had agreement been reached on the desirability of emotional methods of evangelism. No one had yet stated clearly how Lutherans should view their confessions and their pietistic heritage. These issues, together with some serious problems raised by the culture in which they lived, remained as unfinished business for the next generation of Lutherans.

48.
David F. Schaeffer, *Historical Address Commemorative of the Blessed Reformation* . . . (1818), in *MCAL*, reel 5. J. H. C. Helmuth, *Gedächtnisz-Predigt* . . . (Philadelphia: G. & D. Billmeyer, 1817).

49.
Gottlieb Shober, *A Comprehensive Account of the Rise and Progress of the Blessed Reformation of the Christian Church* . . . (Baltimore: Schaeffer & Maund, 1818).

50.
There is little evidence that the War of 1812 had any great effect on church life. The New York Ministerium omitted its meeting that year, but the chief result in the literature is that many sermons drew on the uncertain times to warn of God's judgment: *Documentary History, General Council*, pp. 456–57; North Carolina Synod, *Proceedings . . . 1813*, pp. 18, 21; Jacob Fry, *The History of Trinity Lutheran Church, Reading, Pa.* (Reading, Pa., 1894), p. 142.

111

7   Synodical Growth and the General Synod, 1817–1840

Two factors accelerated the pace of westward expansion after 1817. Improved transportation made the journey west easier and raised the cash value of crops. The Erie Canal, opened in 1825, proved that spectacular returns could be made on investments in transportation routes to the center of the continent. Railroads soon began to compete with the canals, and the federal government even ventured into the transportation business with the first interstate highway, the National Road from Maryland to central Ohio. Canada's Huron Road performed a similar function by opening up the land between Lake Ontario and Lake Huron.

A second impetus to expansion came from government determination to push the Indians out of the way. Troops made resistance by the Indians impossible; treaties consolidated the gains and promised Indians that they would be left undisturbed on new lands farther west. But treaty followed treaty and the white man edged onto lands recently "reserved" for Indian occupation. During the eight years of Andrew Jackson's presidency (1829–37), ninety-four treaties were concluded with the Indians. Maps which had shown the location of Cherokees, Creeks, Miamis, and Choctaws in 1820 were replaced by others which ignored the tribes or covered them all with the single phrase "Indian territory"—and that territory lay farther west on each succeeding map.

The Moving Frontier

The frontier moved westward with increasing speed. For the first 150 years of colonial history the frontier had crept inland at the average rate of two miles per year. A visitor in 1831 reported, however, that the current rate had risen to seventeen miles per year. Indiana, Illinois, Missouri, Arkansas, and Louisiana were fully settled by 1840, and the area beyond them was organized into territories. The center of population also moved rapidly westward, crossing the main ranges of the Appalachians between 1820 and 1840. The good farming land of Canada north of Lake Erie went under the plow during this period, but the rocky wilderness farther to the west discouraged settlement and turned pioneers southward into the United States.

A generation earlier this increased expansion would have been disastrous to an already overextended church, but by 1820 the West had become a challenge instead of a threat. One reason for the new attitude was that there were enough people to maintain congregations at home and populate the new territories at the same time. Population in Upper Canada nearly trebled in the twenty years after 1820 and United States census

1.

For a firsthand description of missionary travels in this period see the autobiographical account of "Father" J. F. C. Heyer incorporated in William A. Lambert, *Life of Rev. J. F. C. Heyer, M.D.* (Philadelphia: General Council Pub. House, 1903). Other sources on Heyer are in the Krauth Memorial Library Archives, Lutheran Theological Seminary, Philadelphia; a popular biography is E. Theodore Bachmann's *They Called Him Father* (Philadelphia: Muhlenberg Press, 1942).

2.

New York Ministerium, *Minutes . . . 1823*, pp. 23–24.

3.

For a biographical sketch of Hazelius, with bibliographical note, see Egil Grislis, "Ernest L. Hazelius: Ecumenical Theologian [sic] of the Southern Lutheran Church," *Lutheran Theological Seminary [Gettysburg] Bulletin* 45 (August 1965): 22–39. Hazelius's theological views are in his *Materials for Catechization . . .* (1823) in Microfilm Corpus of American Lutheranism (hereafter cited as *MCAL*), reel 6. His missionary work for the New York Ministerium is summarized in Harry J. Kreider, *History of the United Lutheran Synod of New York and New England, 1786–1860* (Philadelphia: Muhlenberg Press, 1954), pp. 47, 58, 61. Personal reminiscences are in W. B. Sprague, ed., *Annals of the American Lutheran Pulpit* (New York, 1869), pp. 132–41.

figures doubled during the same period. Most of the Canadian growth, and much of the increase in the United States, came from a renewed flow of immigrants from Europe. Twice as many immigrants entered the United States during six years (1831–37) as had come into the country in the thirty years prior to 1820.

In addition to numerical strength, Lutheran synods could also rely on a fairly well-developed system of missionary work to aid in serving the frontier. Every synod meeting devoted a major portion of its time to hearing petitions from clusters of families who desired the services of a minister; when possible, a pastor was designated to visit them and to report on the prospects of a permanent organization. Funds raised by subscription helped to pay the traveling costs of the missionaries. The succeeding decades would see little change in this basic strategy, although some significant improvements would increase the system's effectiveness.[1]

The first step was to put someone in charge of surveying the needs of vacant congregations and supervising the tours of traveling preachers. Usually one or two pastors were named by synods for this function, and then, in 1823, the Ministerium of New York set up a Committee on Home Missions. The committee was to find out about vacant congregations, determine where missionaries should be sent and how much to pay them, and act on mission matters when the synod was not in session. It could even draw money needed to support its work from the Missionary Fund.[2] This committee represented a significant new stage in synodical development. Formerly, synods had transacted their business at annual conventions. The only work done between conventions was limited to previously authorized ordinations and specific tasks of appointed committees. Now an important function had been delegated to a committee which could carry out its work without waiting for synodical approval. Of course, the actions of the committee would be subject to review by the synod at its subsequent meeting, but the precedent of an independently operating agency with power to spend money on its own had been set.

The chief proponent of this new structure was the mission-oriented professor at Hartwick Seminary, Ernest Lewis Hazelius. Originally a Moravian, born and educated in Europe, Hazelius had left a teaching post with the Moravians in Pennsylvania when they had not permitted him to marry. He served a Lutheran parish in Germantown, New Jersey, before being selected as professor at Hartwick. Hazelius was much more conservative in his theology than was Quitman of the Ministerium of New York. In fact, it may have been the latter's indifference to missionary needs that prompted Hazelius to suggest a Committee on Home Missions.[3]

Once the committee was established, Hazelius became its most active missionary. Not only did he urge Hartwick students to use their summer vacations for mission work, but he often went along with them or made trips by himself. In 1824 he reached Lake Ontario; two years later he visited congregations on the Canadian side of the lake. In 1827 he visited all the congregations of northern New York and most of the congregations in Upper Canada.

The next step was to find enough money to keep the mission program alive. Synods asked their ministers to set aside one Sunday a year for the offering of funds for missions. When this method proved inadequate to meet the needs, Hazelius had another suggestion. He urged the Ministerium of New York to form itself into a missionary society, modeled on the many other voluntary societies that were being formed in the 1820s. These societies focused on one particular problem, such as home missions, foreign missions, or the distribution of tracts and Bibles. Members of the society contributed to its work directly, rather than through the channels of a synodical treasury. Local branches of the society held meetings to excite interest, to inform members of the need, and to collect contributions. The method was an effective one, and the Ministerium of New York decided to adopt it in 1827.[4]

The Ohio and Maryland-Virginia Synods

Although it was not as well-organized in mission work as its sister to the northeast, the Ministerium of Pennsylvania had continued to grow in numbers and territory. In fact, the Ministerium had become so large that it could not fully serve the needs of congregations on its western and southern fringes. "Special conferences" held in these areas, of course, had been providing opportunities to consider local problems, and so it was natural for the conferences to assume greater responsibilities. Between 1817 and 1820 the Ohio and Maryland-Virginia special conferences severed their last tenuous connections with the Ministerium and became independent synods. The organization of an independent synod for Ohio seemed almost inevitable. Presbyterians, Methodists, and Quakers had already formed jurisdictional units in the state by 1817 and the Episcopalians and German Reformed would act by 1820.

Special conferences of the Pennsylvania Ministerium had been held in Ohio and western Pennsylvania at least once a year since 1812. The "mother synod" had smiled on this development and had encouraged her western offspring to care for all local business except the examination and ordination of pastors. In 1817 even this last thin connection was dissolved. The way for this action had been cleared by a decision of the Ministerium in 1816 that, since deacons were being ordained by the laying on of hands, "no further laying on of hands shall be necessary to advance them to the office of a pastor." A "simple declaration of the assembled pastors" would be sufficient. According to this instruction, the Ohio Special Conference declared a deacon to be a pastor "by a handclasp" at its meeting in the fall of 1817. Significantly, it sent no delegate to the Ministerium meeting the next spring—the first time it had omitted that symbol of unity and dependence.[5]

4.
New York Ministerium, *Minutes . . . 1827,* p. 35.
5.
The standard history is Willard D. Allbeck's *A Century of Lutherans in Ohio* (Yellow Springs, Ohio: Antioch Press, 1966); pages 50–60 describe the early years of the synod. Minutes of the special conferences and of the Ohio Synod for this period are in *MCAL,* reel 29. Also useful for names of early pastors in western Pennsylvania and Ohio is Ellis B. Burgess's *Memorial History of the Pittsburgh Synod . . .* (Greenville, Pa.: Beaver, 1925), pp. 51–54. Brief biographies of the founders and summaries of synodical actions are in Clarence V. Sheatsley, *History of the Evangelical Lutheran Joint Synod of Ohio and Other States* (Columbus, Ohio: Lutheran Book Concern, 1918), pp. 11–82. An excellent reference work for all synods is Robert C. Wiederaenders and W. G. Tillmanns, *The Synods of American Lutheranism* (St. Louis: Concordia Print Shop, 1968).

The first convention of the new body indicated its potential strength. Four pastors and six licensed candidates met at Somerset, Ohio, in September 1818 to organize. Seven more pastors were listed as "absent." The unusually large number of candidates shows that young men from the area were already being prepared for leadership. In fact, the only pastors among the founders of the synod who had their roots in the East were John Stough and Paul Henkel. In order to insure a continued supply of qualified leaders, the convention assumed the responsibility of organizing and supporting an academy where candidates could learn Latin and Greek as well as "all other sciences and learning which are necessary for this important pastoral office."[6]

Separation from the Ministerium of Pennsylvania was not considered a criticism of the parent body since the new synod adopted the Ministerium's constitution almost without change. It did abolish the grade of deacon in its clergy list so that a licensed candidate would be ordained directly into the pastorate instead of into a diaconate. In other respects, the Ohio Synod proved to be a cooperative child. The synod continued the use of German in its sessions, sent regular correspondence to the Ministerium, and was treated with respect by its parent body.[7]

The Maryland-Virginia Synod grew up in a similarly smooth fashion. There had been a Virginia Special Conference of the Pennsylvania Ministerium for over twenty-five years. Its membership included pastors from Maryland as well as from Virginia; in fact the conference might better have been called the "Potomac Conference," since it drew most of its members from the area north and west of Washington, D.C. Churches farther south in Virginia tended to affiliate with the North Carolina Synod.[8]

At its meeting in the spring of 1820, the Pennsylvania Ministerium received a petition from members of the Virginia Special Conference requesting permission to form a synod. The Ministerium had "no objection whatever" and a convention met within six months. The eleven ministers and seven laymen who convened in Winchester, Virginia, were the largest group to organize a Lutheran synod up to that time. They represented congregations from the mountain frontier to Baltimore. Some of the ministers still preached exclusively in German; others preached exclusively in English; most were bilingual. Over half the clergy were in their twenties. The leading force in their organization was undoubtedly David F. Schaeffer, pastor in Frederick and the only university graduate in the group. Several of the younger clergy were his pupils, although he was only thirty-five years old himself. He became the first secretary of the new synod, a position to which he was often reelected.

After speedily compiling a constitution on the basis of the constitutions of the Ministeriums of Pennsylvania and New York, the young synod declared all its deacons to be fully recognized pastors. In effect this removed the grade of deacon—an

The interest in an academy may reflect the growing discussion in the Ministerium of Pennsylvania about a joint seminary with the Reformed. Since the projected location would have been Lancaster in central Pennsylvania, the Ohio pastors may have decided to try to erect an educational institution closer to home. The venture failed, however, within a year.

Wallbeck, *Century*, p. 53, quotes Andrew Henkel, a contemporary, who observed that younger men in Ohio were the principal agitators for the organization of a new synod. A similar dynamic was involved with the Henkel family role in the North Carolina-Tennessee Synod schism; see below, pp. 117-18.

The standard history is Abdel Ross Wentz's *History of the Evangelical Lutheran Synod of Maryland, 1820-1920* (Harrisburg, Pa.: Evangelical Press, 1920). A more recent study of the organizational years is William E. Eisenberg's *The Lutheran Church in Virginia, 1717-1962* (Lynchburg, Va.: J. P. Bell, 1967), pp. 80-82, 141-50.

action equivalent to that taken by the Ohio Synod two years earlier. The delegates also decided to investigate the possibility of publishing a religious periodical and writing a "discipline" which would set forth the beliefs and standards required of Lutherans.

The convention's primary item of business, however, concerned a great project involving the Ministeriums of Pennsylvania and New York, together with the North Carolina Synod. The meeting in Winchester had been carefully timed to occur less than two weeks before a significant convention in Hagerstown, where the constitution of a General Synod for all Lutherans in North America would be discussed. The Maryland-Virginia Synod, which sent its officers as delegates to that convention, would soon become the most vigorous and steadfast advocate of a General Synod.[9]

The "Proposed Plan"

The multiplication of synods around 1820 revived interest in the need for some way by which Lutherans could move forward on a common basis. Already questions were arising about the proper number of grades in the ministry, and even about the correct posture for prayer. As early as 1812 the North Carolina Synod had inquired about the possibility of better intersynodical cooperation. Other matters seemed more pressing at the time, however, so the various synods contented themselves with an informal and haphazard exchange of delegates. The constitutions of the Ministeriums in Pennsylvania and New York permitted visiting clergymen to have both voice and vote in synodical affairs, and that courtesy seemed to afford adequate communication between the two largest synods.

In 1818, the same year in which the Ohio Synod organized, the Ministerium of Pennsylvania expressed interest in devising a plan by which the various synods could "stand in some way or another in closer connection with each other." Letters went out to all points of the compass, inviting the other synods to send representatives to the Ministerium's 1819 convention in Baltimore.[10] The response proved encouraging. When the Ministerium convened in June there were letters from New York and North Carolina expressing approval of a closer union. In fact, the secretary of the North Carolina Synod, Gottlieb Shober, had come in person—and he had even brought a suggested plan. Taking the project seriously, the Ministerium appointed its senior pastors to confer with Shober and report back with a specific proposal.

Shober's original plan, which reportedly resembled the constitution of the General Assembly of the Presbyterian Church, was modified by reducing the power of the new central body. Even at that, the plan as finally presented to the Ministerium outlined a fairly tight structure, to be called "The General Synod," which would meet every third year to regulate publications, modes of worship, and the formation of new synods. In addition, the General Synod would fix grades of the ministry and hear appeals.[11]

9.
Eisenberg, *Lutheran Church in Virginia,* p. 153; Wentz, *Synod of Maryland,* pp. 162-6.
10.
Documentary History of the Evangelical Lutheran Ministerium of Pennsylvania . . . 1748-1821 (Philadelphia: General Council Board of Publication, 1898), pp. 517, 522. Although there is no full history of the General Synod, much information on its early years may be gained from Charles Philip Krauth, "Our General Synod," *Evangelical Review* 5 (October 1853): 239-80; Charles Porterfield Krauth, "Th General Synod: Theological Characteristics of the Era of Its Formation," *Lutheran and Missionary,* May 3, 1866, p. 110; Edmund J. Wolf, "History of the General Synod," *Lutheran Quarterly* 19 (July 1889) 420-58; and J. W. Early, "The Ministerium of Pennsylvania and the Organizatio of the General Synod," *Lutheran Church R view* 11 (January and April 1892): 61-70 172-86. See also Henry Eyster Jacobs, *A History of the Evangelical Lutheran Church in the United States* (New York: Christian Li erature Co., 1893), pp. 351-72; and Friedrich Bente, *American Lutheranism* (St. Louis: Concordia Publishing House, 1902), 2:12-79. The latter is a strongly antagonistic view. Selected documents ar in Richard C. Wolf, *Documents of Lutheran Unity in America* (Philadelphia: Fortress Press, 1966), pp. 49-94.
11.
Samuel S. Schmucker, "Extracts from N Lectures on the History of the General Synod," quoted in Robert Fortenbaugh, "The Development of the Synodical Pol ity of the Lutheran Church in America, to 1829" (Ph.D. diss., University of Pen sylvania, 1926), pp. 148-49.

Shober's plan was presented on Monday, June 7. The committee reported back on Wednesday afternoon, no doubt after much discussion in and out of the committee itself. When the matter finally reached the floor of the Ministerium on Thursday morning, it passed by a vote of better than five to one. Copies of the "Proposed Plan" (called "*Plan Entwurf*" in German) were printed and distributed from Pennsylvania to North Carolina so that congregations could have an opportunity to express themselves on the idea and thus assist other synods to vote on the project. If three of the four synods then in existence informed the president of the Ministerium that they had adopted the plan "at least in its spirit and substance," the president was to designate a place and time for the ratifying synods to gather and form the General Synod.[12]

It took a year for all the returns to come in. The Ohio Synod, meeting just two months after the Ministerium of Pennsylvania, adopted the Proposed Plan, although President John Stough wrote that "some members" had opposed it. The next month New York considered the Plan. Apparently no copies had been sent to the congregations so the only person with a text was Quitman. He had to read it twice to the convention and then the delegates decided that some of its points took away powers expressly granted to their own body so they rejected the Plan. They preferred to strengthen the existing system of exchanging delegates. The following spring the North Carolina Synod ratified the Plan. That action provided the necessary three-fourths majority among the synods, so a meeting to organize the general body was called for October 1820 in Hagerstown, Maryland.[13]

Conflict Over the General Synod

Although it seemed that the proposed plan had found general approval, except among the cautious congregations in New York, a widespread undertone of opposition was developing. No synod had approved the Plan unanimously and in North Carolina efforts to hurry its adoption opened a fateful breach among the clergy.

For several years tension had been mounting in North Carolina between Secretary of Synod Shober and David Henkel, the most brilliant and aggressive of Paul Henkel's six sons. Despite his talents and obvious ability as a minister, David Henkel encountered delay after delay in his progress from catechist to deacon to pastor. The official reason given by the synod was his youth; he was only twenty-four in 1819. Behind that fact, however, lurked the alarm with which Shober, who was still Moravian in his theology, viewed Henkel's emphasis on Lutheran particularity. When Henkel supposedly claimed that marriage between Lutherans and Reformed was like mating cows with horses, for example, Shober was ready to exercise synodical discipline. Henkel, on the other hand, criticized Shober for his arbitrary control of synodical business and his lack of concern for traditional Lutheran teaching.[14]

Everyone's worst suspicions were confirmed at the 1819 North Carolina Synod convention. Shober, eager to participate

12.
For an account of the process see *Documentary History, Ministerium of Pa.*, pp. 527, 528, 537, 538. The plan was published as *Plan-Entwurf zu einer Central-Verbindung der Evangelisch-Lutherischen Kirche in den Vereinigten Staaten von Nord-Amerika* (Baltimore: Schaeffer & Maund, 1819). A translation is in *Documentary History, Ministerium of Pa.*, pp. 541–44; an abbreviated version appears in Wolf, *Documents*, pp. 56–58.
13.
Fortenbaugh, "Synodical Polity," pp. 164–66; Kreider, *History*, pp. 62–65; New York Ministerium, *Minutes . . . 1819*, pp. 8–12.
14.
L. L. Lohr, "David Henkel, Pioneer Missionary of the Lutheran Church in the South," *Lutheran Church Visitor*, October 5, 1916, pp. 4–6. David Henkel's struggle to obtain ordination is summarized in Raymond M. Bost, "The Reverend John Bachman and the Development of Southern Lutheranism" (Ph.D. diss., Yale University, 1963), pp. 177–78. The charges against Henkel may be gleaned from the David Henkel Papers, especially those from 1819, Abdel Ross Wentz Library, Lutheran Theological Seminary, Gettysburg, Pa. For Shober's views on union among denominations, see Gottlieb Shober, *A Comprehensive Account of the Rise and Progress of the Blessed Reformation of the Christian Church . . .* (Baltimore: Schaeffer & Maund, 1818). For Shober's life see Sprague, *Annals*, pp. 141–45, and "Gottlieb Shober," *Evangelical Review* 8 (January 1857): 404–15.

in the Pennsylvania Ministerium discussion of a General Synod, secured the consent of the aged and blind synod president to convene the synod six weeks ahead of the stated time. When it met, David Henkel was present, but once again he was not able to secure his long-awaited ordination. Instead, he was tried for making statements critical of non-Lutherans and then placed on probation. The synod also delegated Shober to represent it at the Ministerium's coming meeting.[15]

Six weeks later, at the original time set for the convention, David Henkel's father and brother appeared, accompanied by their delegates and asserting that the earlier synod meeting was "untimely" and unconstitutional. They opened the "real" synod convention, ordained David Henkel a pastor, and exonerated him of all charges. A few months later they met to organize a "conference" in Greene County, Tennessee, where David's brother Philip served several congregations. When the North Carolina Synod convened in 1820 the Henkels attempted to obtain recognition of *their* meeting as the only legitimate meeting of the synod in 1819. The attempt failed, so they severed connection with the older body and organized the Evangelical Lutheran Tennessee Synod in July 1820. Because of the Henkel family's leadership, members of the Tennessee Synod were popularly called "Henkelites." Shober's connection with the Proposed Plan made the project anathema to the Henkels and their associates. They opposed it in Virginia, where Paul Henkel resided, and in Tennessee, Ohio, and North Carolina, where his sons were pastors. Their attacks set off a decade of controversy over the value of a General Synod.[16]

The earliest grounds for opposition to the Plan seem designed more to touch sensitive nerves than to explore the issues. Would Pennsylvania dominate the smaller synods? they asked. Did the power to recognize new synods mean that the individual pastors no longer had the right to organize synods without approval from above? Wasn't that "papacy"? Did the "exclusive right" to prescribe orders of service violate the seventh article of the Augsburg Confession, where uniformity of ceremonies is called unnecessary to the unity of the church? Would the power to set up grades of the ministry multiply ranks until the president of the General Synod would resemble "a sceptered monarch . . . [with] delegates for his life-guard, presidents his emissaries, pastors his common people, deacons his servants, candidates and catechetes his outposts, and congregations his footstool"? Would the General Synod be English-speaking, so that German pastors and delegates would be handicapped? Didn't the power to hear appeals, recognize ordinations, introduce new books, and charter synods belong to congregations and synods rather than to a large and ill-defined national church? Lutherans ought to beware of "buying a pig in a poke." "To be sure, we see its outward form clearly to some extent through the sack, and conclude from that that it is not worth what it will cost us."[17]

The outcome of the conflict remained in doubt as the time for the organizing meeting of the General Synod approached. At its convention in August 1820 the New York Ministerium debated

15.
North Carolina Synod, *Minutes . . . 1819*, p. 12.
16.
The Tennessee Synod version of events is recounted in David Henkel, *Carolinian Herald of Liberty, Religious and Political* (Salisbury, N.C.: Kreider & Bingham, 1821), *MCAL*, reel 6; cf. Socrates Henkel, *History of the Evangelical Lutheran Tennessee Synod* (New Market, Va.: Henkel & Co., 1890).
17.
David Henkel, *Carolinian Herald*, p. 14; *Kurze Nachrichten von den Berrichtungen der ersten Conferenz . . . gehalten in dem Staate Tennessee, den 17ten Julius, 1820 . . .* part of which is translated in Wolf, *Documents*, pp. 60-65.

for hours before agreeing to send a delegation. The next month, however, the Ohio Synod bowed to pressure from some of its pastors and rescinded its former action favoring the new body. That reversal reduced the number of synods endorsing the general synod from three to two. The move jeopardized the legality of further efforts to organize, since "three-fourths" of the synods no longer supported the Plan. At the last minute, though, barely ten days before the appointed time, the Maryland-Virginia Synod came into being and heartily endorsed the Plan. The idea of a General Synod stayed alive.

When the delegates met in Hagerstown they demonstrated that they were aware of the most vulnerable points in the Proposed Plan. The constitution which they proposed for the General Synod limited its powers at precisely those points where the Plan had been most criticized. Instead of giving the General Synod "exclusive right" to regulate orders of worship and the publication of new hymnals, the constitution limited the synod to proposing materials which might or might not be adopted by individual synods. In accordance with the Augsburg Confession the General Synod was forbidden to prescribe religious ceremonies.

The same reduction in power occurred at other places in the new constitution. Instead of "fixing grades in the ministry" the General Synod was to give "well considered advice" so that "unpleasant and unfriendly collisions" between synods over ministerial ranks could be prevented. Where the Proposed Plan had proposed that the new general body would serve as the court of final appeal in disputes between synods or even in problems arising within a synod, the constitution explicitly denied the General Synod this power; it might only give "advice or opinion" in cases referred to it.[18]

The power of the new body was further limited in its relation to the formation of new synods and the recognition of ordinations. The Proposed Plan had seen the General Synod as the controlling agent in the organization of new synods. It was to protect existing synods against the sort of splintering which had just occurred in the secession from the North Carolina Synod to found the Tennessee Synod. Furthermore, according to the Plan, ordinations by synods not recognized by the General Synod would be invalid, and ministers who attempted to transfer out of a synod without that synod's permission would likewise be considered unordained. The constitution took a milder line. It omitted references to transfers and to ordination. It also provided that synods formed over the objections of existing synods would not be "recognized," but it did not deny that they could be formed.

While these changes tended to make the General Synod no more than an advisory body, the Hagerstown convention also added some powers which would allow the General Synod to function in a coordinating capacity. It was empowered to "devise plans for seminaries of education and missionary institutions, as well as for the aid of poor ministers, and the widows and orphans of ministers, and endeavor, with the help of God, to

18.
Constitution of the Evangelical Lutheran General Synod in the United States of North America: Together with the Proceedings of the Convention in Which It Was Formed, translated from the German (Lancaster, Pa., n.d.); quoted partially in Wolf, *Documents,* pp. 66–72. Wolf also has a brief comparison of the Plan and the constitution on pp. 65–66. A fuller analysis is in Fortenbaugh, "Synodical Polity," pp. 153–58.

carry them into effect." A further addition was the power to "institute and create a treasury." These clauses established a broad foundation for the cooperative development of projects and institutions which would be of service to all member synods. The convention showed that it intended to move forward immediately on such projects by appointing committees to begin planning for a seminary, a missionary program, and an aid fund.

One other significant point should be noted. Some critics had attacked the Plan's apparent interest in cooperative work with other Christian denominations. On this front, at least, the writers of the General Synod constitution did not retreat. They added a section which stated that the new body should constantly be attentive to every evidence of "unity of sentiment among Christians in general, of whatever kind or denomination, in order that the blessed opportunities . . . to promote general concord and unity, may not pass by neglected and unavailing."

It is clear that a significant change occurred in the direction of the General Synod at the Hagerstown convention. It moved from a regulatory role to an advisory one. At the same time it gained a mandate to assist synods in cooperative projects for theological education, missionary work, and ministerial aid. In short, the synods had refused to delegate their traditional control of their own clergy and worship to the General Synod. They had, however, agreed to utilize the new body as their common agent in cooperative and interdenominational activities. The pattern set here in 1820 would prevail as the standard for subsequent general bodies among Lutherans for one hundred and fifty years.

Samuel Simon Schmucker and the General Synod

The man who would become the guiding genius of the General Synod sat through its constituting convention as an observer. He would be present at every subsequent meeting for the next fifty years. His name was Samuel Simon Schmucker (1799–1873), the twenty-one-year-old son of John George Schmucker, president of the Ministerium of Pennsylvania. Samuel had just been licensed by the Ministerium to serve congregations near New Market, Virginia, and he was awaiting official word that the congregations had called him as their pastor. He would soon begin that work, marry, and enter upon a career of leadership that would span more than forty years.

Samuel Schmucker combined a boundless capacity for work with an unyielding seriousness. He was slender, with a hawklike nose and piercing eyes. His mind dispassionately weighed every emotion, every argument, and every friend. When visiting a fellow pastor in New York, Samuel confided to his journal that the young minister was "orthodox . . . tolerable interesting, somewhat severe, but much defective in solemnity. Prayed very lightly for the heathen in the afternoon, not at all in the morning." Schmucker himself was certainly not "defective in solemnity." A former student wrote of him:

Dr. Schmucker was the severest moralist I ever knew. . . . He did not know one card from another. I do not suppose he ever had a dice-box in his hand, even for amusement. He knew nothing of checkers, or back-gammon or chess. He never was in a theatre or circus, never heard an opera. He even doubted the propriety of Christians going to hear famous vocalists in a concert hall, especially if they had appeared on the operatic stage. He never used tobacco in any form. He never drank a drop of strong liquor as a beverage. He never conformed to any modern fashion in dress for fashion's sake, however neat and appropriate it might be.

19.
Paul Anstadt, *Life and Times of Rev. S. S. Schmucker, D.D.* (York, Pa.: P. Anstadt & Sons, 1896), incorporates material from Schmucker's own journal, now lost. For a modern biography with notes on related studies see Abdel Ross Wentz, *Pioneer in Christian Unity: Samuel Simon Schmucker* (Philadelphia: Fortress Press, 1967). James Lawton Haney, "The Religious Heritage and Education of Samuel Simon Schmucker: A Study in the Rise of 'American Lutheranism'" (Ph.D. diss., Yale University, 1968), explores the theological influences up to 1820. O. J. Jorgenson and V. K. Smith, "Collected Papers of Samuel Simon Schmucker," mimeographed, July 1965, is a useful guide to the collection at the archives of the Lutheran Theological Seminary at Gettysburg. The quotation on Schmucker's morality is from a delightful memoir in John G. Morris, *Fifty Years in the Lutheran Ministry* (Baltimore: James Young, 1878), p. 129.
20.
General Synod, *Minutes . . . 1820*, p. 14.

Schmucker's mind had been sharpened by the best education open to pastors of his generation. In addition to theological instruction from his own father, he spent two years at the University of Pennsylvania and nineteen months at Princeton Seminary. Although the length of study seems short by modern standards, it was considered adequate in Schmucker's day. Few clergymen had even that much formal education.[19]

The theology of Samuel Schmucker displayed characteristics gathered from each of his educational environments. At the University of Pennsylvania he became convinced that pure Christianity had nothing to fear from rigorously disciplined thought. Through his learned father he discovered the classic Lutheran authors of earlier centuries. His favorites may be detected in the names given his sons: Mosheim, Melanchthon, and Spener. His father's vigorous opposition to rationalism also became a permanent part of Samuel's thought. Princeton gave him significant help in the areas of church history and church government, as well as a respect for denominations other than his own.

Samuel Schmucker had great plans for the Lutheran church. He first wanted to purge it of every trace of deism. That would require stronger discipline within the synods, coupled with a conscious return to the fundamental doctrines of Lutheran Christianity. Then the education of clergymen should receive attention, and that would demand a Lutheran seminary and college as good as—or better than—Princeton. The General Synod would become his instrument for achieving these goals.

It is clear that the members of the constituting convention in Hagerstown anticipated opposition to their newly christened "Evangelical Lutheran General Synod of the United States of North America." The provisions for ratifying the constitution left room for skeptical synods to suggest improvements. The hesitant Ohio Synod was to receive a "friendly letter" urging cooperation. To forestall criticism on the language question, each minister of the synods involved was to be supplied with two copies of the constitution, one in German and one in English.[20]

At first it appeared that the caution was unnecessary. The Ministerium of Pennsylvania, the North Carolina Synod, and the Maryland-Virginia Synod ratified the constitution by large majorities within a year. But when the General Synod met again in 1821, its timid resolutions betrayed the fact that trouble was brewing. Only ten delegates attended; New York and Ohio still hesitated to join. Plans for a seminary were "deferred, for several years"; an appeal from a pastor was referred politely back to his own synod; instead of providing a central agency for home missions the General Synod urged synods to do their own missionary work.[21]

Opposition was mounting from two sources. The Tennessee Synod continued a steady barrage of letters and pronouncements against the General Synod. Its minutes contained resolutions and essays condemning the body; David and Philip Henkel traveled as far as Indiana to discourage participation in it; and David corresponded with pastors and laymen in Kentucky, Ohio, Indiana, and Missouri regarding the evils of a central power. In Kentucky a pastor gathered lay delegates from two states in the hope that a "Kentucky Synod" could block further progress of the General Synod in the West. After meetings in 1822 and 1823, however, the movement dissolved, probably for lack of additional ministerial leadership. Much of the appeal for these efforts of opposition in the West arose from a widespread mistrust of the larger, older, and wealthier synods in the East— especially of the Ministerium of Pennsylvania.[22]

Ironically, it was within the Ministerium of Pennsylvania itself that the other sources of opposition to the General Synod began to appear. In Pennsylvania the Lutheran and Reformed churches were tightly woven together by language, intermarriage, and geography. At the time of the founding of the General Synod, the Reformed church was going through the agony of a schism over the issues of seminaries and centralization. By 1822 the Reformed were giving up plans for a seminary in a fruitless attempt to prevent the establishment of a "free synod." This controversy ignited similar emotions among the Lutherans. Charges of domination by clergy and fears of a powerful national body combined to turn many of the rural parishes against the General Synod. Other congregations feared that prospects for union with the Reformed church would be shattered by a closer union among Lutherans. When the Ministerium of Pennsylvania met in 1823 it became clear that the only way to avoid a "free church" split among the Lutherans was to bow before the anti–General Synod feeling. In a long, painful explanation the Ministerium declared that its motives in favoring a General Synod had been misjudged by "the congregations." But, "for the sake of preserving universal love and harmony," it resolved to send no more delegates to the General Synod "until somehow in the future the congregations themselves became aware of their misunderstanding of our true purposes." The officers of the Ministerium were obviously embarrassed by this action and did all within their power to assure the other synods that the setback was only temporary.[23]

Even though it might have been temporary, the withdrawal of the Ministerium of Pennsylvania left a shattered General Synod. The Ministerium listed over seventy pastors, deacons, and candidates on its rolls—over twice the number of clergy in

122

21.
Ibid. *1821,* pp. 8, 9, 11; cf. Fortenbaugh, "Synodical Polity," pp. 181–82. For actions of New York see New York Ministerium, *Minutes . . . 1821,* pp. 9–10; for Ohio see Allbeck, *Century,* pp. 65–66.
22.
Tennessee Synod, *Minutes . . . 1822,* p. 6; ibid. *1825,* pp. 8–9, 11; Martin L. Wagner, *The Chicago Synod and Its Antecedents* (Waverly, Iowa: Wartburg, 1909), pp. 41–47, 63–64.
23.
Jacobs, *History,* pp. 360–61; James I. Good, *History of the Reformed Church in the United States in the Nineteenth Century* (New York: Board of Publication of the Reformed Church in America, 1911), pp. 21–46; Wolf, *Documents,* pp. 77–82; New York Ministerium, *Minutes . . . 1824,* pp. 31–32. Sources for the conflict in Pennsylvania are: Carl Gock, *Die Vertheidigung der freyen Kirche in Nord-Amerika* (Reading, Pa., 1822); idem, *Politische Ansicht und Fortsetzung der Vertheidigung der freyen Kirche in Nord-Amerika* (Reading, Pa., 1822); and J. C. Goszler, *Carl Gock's . . . Rechtfertigung der Hoch-Deutschen Luth. und Ref. Synoden von Nord-Amerika* (Reading, Pa.: Carl A. Bruckman, 1823).

24.
Allbeck, *Century*, p. 67; Fortenbaugh, "Synodical Polity," p. 168.

25.
Anstadt, *Schmucker*, p. 126; Wentz, *Pioneer*, pp. 126–27. The standard history is Adam Stump and Henry Anstadt, eds., *Centennial History of the Evangelical Lutheran Synod of West Pennsylvania, 1825–1925* (Chambersburg, Pa.: J. R. Kerr & Bro., 1925).

the two synods remaining in the General Synod. In what sense could a synod be called "general" when it contained only two of the six existing synods and only a fraction of the active clergy? It seemed as though the General Synod had suffered a mortal blow. Pastors in central Pennsylvania decided to hold a conference of their own on the date in October formerly announced for the 1823 convention of the General Synod. Leaders in Ohio and North Carolina heard of the Ministerium's action and decided it was useless to send delegates or observers.[24]

At that moment, Samuel Simon Schmucker moved into action. Shaking off the grief which had weighed on him after the death of his young bride, he feverishly wrote letters to men whom he knew to be supporters of the General Synod. "I have within the last six weeks written sixteen letters to different parts of our church," he wrote in his diary. There were letters to North Carolina, urging the synod to send delegates at the appointed time to Frederick, Maryland, in spite of the action of the Pennsylvania Ministerium. He wrote his uncle Peter in Ohio to insure at least a token representation from that region. His greatest efforts, however, focused on his own father and other leaders of the West Pennsylvania Conference. These men had been granted permission by the Ministerium to form a new synod. Many of them were favorable to the General Synod. Schmucker argued that they could save the organization if they held their conference meeting two weeks ahead of schedule, so that they could organize a synod, elect delegates, and send them to Frederick in time for the General Synod convention. He even drafted a German address to the members of the West Pennsylvania Conference in behalf of the revised meeting plan. Personal visits to key leaders added weight to Schmucker's influence. When the West Pennsylvania Conference did meet early, it passed a series of resolutions favoring the General Synod. The resolutions had been framed by Samuel Schmucker.[25]

The General Synod convened in Frederick, Maryland, on the appointed day, with delegates or observers present from the new West Pennsylvania Synod, and from Maryland-Virginia, North Carolina, and Ohio. Although little more was accomplished at that meeting, the General Synod had been saved. It now faced the long and difficult tasks of negotiating with non-member synods, attracting new synods as they were organized, and carrying out its own agenda of projects.

The conflict over the General Synod left its mark on synodical development over the next decade. Pamphlets, synodical resolutions, and pastoral letters circulated among Lutheran families from the Atlantic to the frontier. The North Carolina Synod, already weakened by the withdrawal of the Tennessee Synod, suffered another loss in 1824 when the controversy prompted members of the synod living in South Carolina to ask for permission to form a new synod. The reason given for this request was that the "fulminating pamphlets" had begun to spread "censure, contention, party-spirit, destruction in congregations," and other "infective venom." When organized, the South Carolina Synod adopted a neutral attitude on the General Synod question. In Virginia the attempt to avoid conflict came too late. Although pastors in the Shenandoah region separated from the Maryland-Virginia Synod in 1829, they brought the General Synod conflict with them. Their 1830 meeting split over whether or not they should remain affiliated with the general body. When the decision to withdraw was made, four of the ten pastors left the convention and rejoined the Maryland Synod. The infant Virginia Synod, badly crippled, barely managed to stay alive for the next few years.[26]

Even the Ministerium of New York, which had attempted to avoid involvement in the General Synod, found the question divisive. After repeated efforts to bring the Ministerium into the larger body, a number of pastors resolved to form a new synod which would more nearly reflect their point of view. These men, serving congregations clustered to the west of Albany, also shared interest in prayer meetings and a more aggressive home missions policy. They found leadership and support from Hazelius, who was serving as the president of the Ministerium in 1830. Under his chairmanship they initiated organization of the Hartwick Synod. Soon thereafter (1830), Hazelius left the New York Ministerium to become a professor at the General Synod's Gettysburg Seminary, founded in 1826. In the meantime, some tension had developed between the older Ministerium and the new Hartwick Synod. When it became apparent, however, that the younger body was not likely to conflict with Ministerium churches in the larger cities but was going to pursue its missionary work in villages and smaller towns, reconciliation was soon achieved. The Hartwick Synod's constituting convention in 1830 adopted a constitution similar to the one recommended by the General Synod, and it became a member of the General Synod the following year.[27]

Migration and Immigration

Conflict over the General Synod did not inhibit the growth and spread of Lutheranism between 1830 and 1840. In 1831 the Ohio Synod subdivided into two districts, Eastern and Western. From that time it was known as the Evangelical Lutheran Joint Synod of Ohio and Adjacent States, popularly referred to as the Joint Synod of Ohio. By 1833 the Joint Synod of Ohio ranked second in size to the much older Ministerium of Pennsylvania. Synod reports from 1830 show that, even then, the New York Ministerium had pastors in Canada, Maine, and Pennsylvania; the North Carolina Synod listed pastors in Virginia, Tennessee, and Illinois; the South Carolina Synod reached into Georgia and Alabama. In the words of the president of the South Carolina Synod, the challenge was to "follow the tide of emigration which is now hurrying westwardly, and will only be checked by the Rocky Mountains, or probably only by the Pacific Ocean itself."[28]

Men and money were poured into the effort to provide religious services for the settlers. All of the synods sent traveling missionaries into the new states to preach, to baptize, and to organize congregations. In the early 1830s congregations were

26.
Raymond M. Bost in *A History of the Lutheran Church in South Carolina* (Columbia, S.C.: R. L. Bryan Co., 1971), pp. 158–59; Eisenberg, *Lutheran Church in Virginia*, pp. 157–63.
27.
Kreider, *History*, pp. 70–86, 128–30, 209. He also cites the older literature.
28.
Allbeck, *Century*, pp. 60–61; South Carolina Synod, *Minutes . . . 1830*, p. 24; Frank L. Oswley, "The Pattern of Migration and Settlement on the Southern Frontier," *Journal of Southern History* 11 (May 1945): 169–72.

29.
Wagner, *Chicago Synod*, pp. 9–30, 47–51;
Bost, *Lutheran Church in South Carolina*, p.
262; Kreider, *History*, pp. 190–200; C. W.
Sifferd, "The Lutheran Church in Southern Illinois," *Lutheran Quarterly* 41 (July
1911): 412–16; Hualpha M. Lentz, *A History of the Lutheran Churches in Boone County
Kentucky* (York, Pa.: P. Anstadt & Sons,
1902).
30.
Quotation from Kreider, *History*, pp.
189–90. Annual figures on immigration
are in U.S., Congress, Senate, *Report of
Immigration Commission*, 61st Congress, 3d
sess., 1910–11, Senate Document no. 756.
A general survey of causes for emigration
from Germany and of the changing character of the immigrants is Marcus Lee
Hansen's *The Atlantic Migration, 1607–1860*
(Cambridge: Harvard University Press,
1940), pp. 106–98. See also Peter B.
Sheridan, Jr., "The Immigrant in Philadelphia, 1827–1860: The Contemporary
Published Report" (Ph.D. diss., Georgetown University, 1957). Early German
pastors in Indiana are listed in Wagner,
Chicago Synod, pp. 51–52.
31.
Carl R. Cronmiller, *A History of the Lutheran Church in Canada* (Toronto: Synod of
Canada, 1961), pp. 83–115.

established along the Wabash River on the border between
Indiana and Illinois. Five years later missionaries were crisscrossing the southern halves of both states. Western Georgia and
central Alabama benefited from sporadic visits by part-time
missionaries, although the first permanent congregation in western Georgia did not organize until 1840. Western New York
State received attention from both the Ministerium of New
York and the Hartwick Synod. The latter body raised over a
thousand dollars for its home mission program in 1835.[29]

A major concern of the new missionary enthusiasm was the
rising number of immigrants from Germany. In 1836 a home
missionary in New York reported that German immigrants "are
to be met with in every city, town and village. In the city of New
York alone there is estimated to be not less than 200,000; in the
state at large they cannot fall far short of treble that number."
This observation is significant in its concentration on cities because it accurately reflects the urban character of the new immigrants. In contrast to the farmers of previous generations,
these immigrants were shopkeepers, tradesmen, or industrial
workers. They first settled in cities from Buffalo and Kitchener
(called Berlin in those days) to Charleston and Mobile. They
were the leading edge of a wave of immigrants who would create
and shape the great Midwestern cities of St. Louis, Chicago, and
Milwaukee. In number they would far surpass the Lutherans
who had arrived before the Revolution, but in the 1830s they
seemed merely to be a promising mission field for the established synods.[30]

While the earlier wave of immigrants had come without
clergy, this new immigration included Reformed and Lutheran
ministers and Union ministers who considered themselves capable of serving congregations of either denomination. Some of the
clergy came as seekers of a better living, some as missionaries of
European societies, and others as fugitives from discipline. They
settled among the new immigrants and preached to them,
thereby forcing existing synods to decide whether to recognize
them, screen them, or exclude them. The question would lead
to irritation on both sides and eventually contribute to the
further fragmentation of Lutherans in North America.

In Canada, the immigration reversed a trend toward assimilation that might have erased a Lutheran presence north of the
Great Lakes. Canadian Lutherans had no organization of their
own. Lunenburg in Nova Scotia received clergymen who had
been educated in Europe. Most congregations in Ontario were
served by missionaries from the synods in New York State,
although the area around Waterloo received missionaries from
Pennsylvania. Other congregations were led by independent
clergymen or by ministers of other denominations.

In the 1830s German Reformed, Anglican, and Methodist
clergy began to wean parishes away from Lutheranism, but
renewed immigration strengthened the hands of members who
tried to maintain the traditions of their fathers. The new settlers
assured a strong basis for Lutheran growth between Kitchener
and the Niagara River.[31]

The General Synod Conflict Continues

Westward growth reopened the question of the General Synod. As new mission fields developed, congregations began to organize new synods. Should these new bodies affiliate with the General Synod or remain independent? Naturally, pastors tended to maintain attitudes toward the General Synod that they had formed before their move to the West, so "Generalists" and "Anti-generalists" competed for control of the new synods.

The most obvious conflict occurred in the fall of 1835 when two synods with opposite views organized in Indiana and Kentucky. During a brief visit, Philip Henkel had gathered several churches in Indiana, and his son Eusebius soon settled there. Other Tennessee Synod pastors who had constantly opposed the General Synod were already in the state. A missionary reported: "Many of the Lutherans in Indiana have emigrated from North Carolina and Tennessee, where they have imbibed prejudices against everything connected with the General Synod." Although earlier attempts by the Anti-generalists to form a synod in Kentucky had failed, they began to discuss organization of a synod in Indiana. On August 15, 1835, pastors and laymen from ten congregations in Indiana and Missouri gathered in a small log church south of Indianapolis and formed the Evangelical Lutheran Synod of Indiana.[32]

Seven weeks later a slightly smaller group of Generalists met in Louisville, Kentucky, and adopted the title "Evangelical Lutheran Synod of the West." The new body, comprising congregations in Kentucky, Tennessee, and Indiana, joined the General Synod in 1841. Efforts to merge with the Indiana Synod failed over the General Synod issue.[33]

Similar tensions produced another synod in Ohio—the beginning of a tangled web of synodical relationships in that state. As noted earlier, in 1831 the Ohio Synod, aware of encroachment on its traditional territory from Pennsylvania, decided to divide into Eastern and Western districts. The two districts lay on either side of a line drawn southward from Cleveland and about fifty miles west of the Ohio-Pennsylvania border. Each district was to meet annually for two years and in the third year they were to meet together in what came to be known as the "Joint Synod of Ohio."[34]

The growing use of English precipitated formation of a third district in 1836. Called the "English District," the new body had over forty congregations spread across the state. Pastors of the English District grew increasingly friendly with the General Synod at the same time that their relationships with the Eastern and Western Ohio districts cooled. A clumsy attempt by Joint Ohio to bring them into harmony with the other two districts precipitated a schism in which a few pastors remained loyal to the English District of the Joint Synod while a large majority formed a new English Synod. The English Synod, organized in 1840, joined the General Synod three years later.[35]

While the conflict sputtered on in the West, synods in the East were regaining interest in the General Synod. The chief

32.
Allbeck, *Century,* pp. 128-30; Wagner, *Chicago Synod,* pp. 44-47, 63-65, 70-72. The quotation is from Bachmann, *They Called Him Father,* p. 91.
33.
Allbeck, *Century,* pp. 125-28; Wagner, *Chicago Synod,* pp. 72-77.
34.
Allbeck, *Century,* pp. 72-82.
35.
Ibid., pp. 111-17; Arthur H. Smith, *A History of the East Ohio Synod of the General Synod of the Evangelical Lutheran Church, 1836-1920* (Columbus, Ohio: Lutheran Book Concern, 1924). Emanuel G. Greenwald, *The Evangelical Lutheran English Synod of Ohio* (Baltimore: Publication Rooms, 1841), is a contemporary criticism of the English Synod.

reason for this change of heart seems to lie in the conviction that the General Synod did not really pose a threat to local programs and usages. The South Carolina Synod, for example, had hesitated to join the general body because it feared the loss of control over its newly founded (1830) seminary. After extended debate it agreed to apply for membership in the General Synod, provided that the larger body would remain advisory, would not dictate the use of specific hymnals or catechisms, and would not control the seminary. When John Bachman, the South Carolina Synod's delegate, reached the convention of the General Synod in 1835, he was elected president of the body and selected to help revise its constitution along the desired lines. Since the Ministerium of New York had asked for the same assurance that South Carolina had requested, the General Synod complied with the wishes of both groups. Its advisory nature was guaranteed. Both the South Carolina Synod and the Ministerium of New York promptly joined. In 1839 the Virginia Synod, also assured by the new guarantees, brought the total number of member bodies in the General Synod to seven.[36]

By 1840 Lutheran synods stretched from the Atlantic seaboard to the western banks of the Mississippi River. These synods had attempted to find a common basis for union, but the efforts had failed. Much of the previous twenty years had been spent in argument over the existence of the General Synod. After a brief period when it seemed that some general organization would be possible, most Lutherans abandoned the idea in favor of local autonomy or union with the Reformed church. Strenuous efforts by Samuel S. Schmucker and others kept the General Synod alive, however, and by 1835 the tide began to turn. Paul and David Henkel, two of the chief opponents of the General Synod, were dead. Newly organized synods in Ohio and the West applied for membership. Earlier fears of centralization subsided when the General Synod revised its constitution to stress its purely advisory function, and the way was opened for additional synods to join. Although the two largest synods—the Ministerium of Pennsylvania and the Joint Synod of Ohio—remained aloof, the General Synod was clearly growing.

Lutheran population was growing too, chiefly through rising immigration from Germany. The new immigrants posed problems, however, because their background was so different from the "Americanized" Lutherans who had lived in the New World for several generations. They proved to be a significant factor in the debate over what was truly Lutheran in faith and practice. The next chapter will describe that debate.

36.
Bost, *Lutheran Church in South Carolina*, pp. 195–99; Kreider, *History*, p. 124; Eisenberg, *Lutheran Church in Virginia*, pp. 164–69.

8   Doctrine and Practice, 1820–40

On February 9, 1825, four young pastors gathered at Martinsburg, Virginia, for a district conference. All of the pastors served parishes within twenty miles of Martinsburg. Two of the group were licensed but not yet ordained. The other two, Charles Philip Krauth and Benjamin Kurtz, were both under thirty. Their imaginations had been captured by a sermon preached by Samuel S. Schmucker at the previous convention of their synod. The twenty-four-year-old pastor had described his own experience in educating candidates for the ministry and had pleaded for a seminary which would be supported by the entire church. The General Synod, already committed to the idea of a seminary, had postponed action as inexpedient.

These young men, however, were ready to try again. They determined to "begin at once" to "engage in the important work of founding a theological seminary to be under the direction and for the benefit of the Evangelical Lutheran Church." A collection on the spot yielded five dollars. They further resolved to urge the Maryland-Virginia Synod to take action, and, in case details should be requested, they forewarned Schmucker to come to the synod meeting with a plan in his pocket. At the synod meeting their plan proved successful. Under the chairmanship of Schmucker, Kurtz and Krauth served on a committee which secured synodical approval for a seminary.[1] Schmucker, Kurtz, and Krauth thus began a long drama in which they would play leading, but differing, roles. With the seminary as the backdrop, their lives would unfold a complex story which came to dominate Lutheran church life for four decades.

A New Seminary

The seminary project proved workable. After approval by the Maryland-Virginia Synod, the plan received favorable response from the General Synod at its meeting in November 1825. Kurtz and Krauth were both elected as directors of the seminary, and, after the board had met, Schmucker was selected as professor. By March 2, 1826, just about thirteen months after the young men in Martinsburg had begun their project, Charles Philip Krauth was elected secretary of the seminary board of directors, Benjamin Kurtz was commissioned to raise funds from Lutherans in Germany, and Samuel Schmucker was sent to Gettysburg, Pennsylvania, to open the seminary in a building provided by the community.

Gettysburg Seminary, although younger than the Hartwick Seminary in New York State, soon became the principal institution for educating Lutheran ministers. Private instruction of

1.
Abdel Ross Wentz, *Pioneer in Christian Unity: Samuel Simon Schmucker* (Philadelphia: Fortress Press, 1967), pp. 127–28; idem, *History of the Gettysburg Theological Seminary . . . 1826-1926* (Philadelphia: United Lutheran Publication House, 1926). Primary documents are: *Constitution of the Theological Seminary . . .* (Philadelphia: W. Brown, 1826), in Microfilm Corpus of American Lutheranism (hereafter cited as *MCAL*), reel 32; Samuel S. Schmucker, *An Inaugural Address Delivered Before the Directors of the Theological Seminary . . . Together with the Charge Delivered to Him by the Rev. D. F. Schaeffer* (Carlisle, Pa: Tizzart & Crever, 1826), in *MCAL*, reel 7. *Catalog of the Officers and Students . . .* (Gettysburg, Pa.: Neinstedt, 1827); *General Catalog and Constitution of the Theological Seminary . . .* (Gettysburg, Pa.: Neinstedt, 1840). Biographical material on Krauth is in Allen Johnson, ed., *Dictionary of American Biography*, 21 vols. (New York: Scribner's, 1943), 10:501–2; and John G. Morris, *Fifty Years in the Lutheran Ministry* (Baltimore: James Young, 1878), pp. 101–19. Material on Kurtz is in *Dictionary of American Biography*, 10:544; Morris, *Fifty Years*, pp. 137–46; and L. S. Straley, "Benjamin Kurtz: Theologian and Churchman" (B.D. thesis, Gettysburg Seminary, 1929). See also Charles A. Hay, *Memoirs of Rev. Jacob Goering, Rev. George Lochman, D.D., and Rev. Benjamin Kurtz, D.D., LL.D.* (Philadelphia: Lutheran Publication Society, 1887), pp. 107–211.

theological candidates continued in every synod, but Gettysburg was recognized as the seminary of all synods south of New York. Even synods which did not belong to the General Synod, such as the Ministerium of Pennsylvania, sent their candidates to Gettysburg. In an effort to remind prospective students that there was another seminary available, Hazelius of the Hartwick Seminary addressed a letter to every synod in 1830, urging them to consider sending candidates to his institution. The South Carolina Synod, however, already had been led by John Bachman to develop plans for a seminary of its own; and the Ohio Synod decided to educate its pastors locally. As a result, two new seminaries were organized in 1830, making the period 1825–30 a fruitful one for Lutheran theological education.[2]

Seminary education in those days was relatively unstructured. Few students stayed for the entire three-year course. After a year or so of education they would find a suitable parish and apply for ordination. If the synodical committee appointed to examine them felt that they had a firm enough grasp of the elements of theology and of spelling and sermon structure, they would be ordained. Many students presented themselves at seminary with little or no background in higher academic study. In such cases the professor would have to give the student private instruction in languages or in composition. Given the shortness of the average stay and deficiencies of the average candidate, courses of study for students would vary widely. The published curricula were always more of a goal than a reality.

To help remedy the problem of inadequate preparation, a "classical school" was set up in connection with the seminary. Of course, this school demanded more time from Schmucker, so a younger man was employed to help with the teaching. The classical school grew to be a major responsibility, prompting its charter in 1832 as a separate institution for college-level work, Pennsylvania College; later the name was changed to Gettysburg College. Meanwhile, the need for German instruction in the seminary made the calling of a second professor advisable. After several arrangements had been tried, the college post and the second professorship were given to one man. He was Charles Philip Krauth, one of the original advocates of the seminary. Krauth came to Gettysburg in 1833 as professor in both the college and the seminary, but within a few months he became president of the college and served in that capacity, along with his seminary work, for seventeen years. The remaining years of his life were spent in seminary teaching, where he worked with Schmucker in the preparation of hundreds of students for the Lutheran ministry.[3]

Schmucker's "Popular Theology"

Given the brief and varied preparation of candidates, it is difficult to assert what theological positions they represented. As early as 1826, the year he began teaching at Gettysburg, Samuel Schmucker had translated a fairly recent German textbook, Gottlob Christian Storr's *Lehrbuch der Christlichen Dogmatik* (Handbook of Christian Dogmatics), which represented the

2.
Summaries of the founding of the Canton (later Columbus), Ohio, seminary may be found in Clarence V. Sheatsley, *History of the Evangelical Lutheran Joint Synod of Ohio and Other States* (Columbus, Ohio: Lutheran Book Concern, 1918), pp. 81–98; and Allbeck, *A Century of Lutherans in Ohio* (Yellow Springs, Ohio: Antioch Press, 1966), pp. 70–75. Histories of the seminary are: George H. Schodde, *Historical Sketch of the Theological Seminary of the Evangelical Lutheran Joint Synod of Ohio and Other States* (n.p., 1905); and Clarence V. Sheatsley, *History of the First Lutheran Seminary of the West, 1830–1930* (Columbus, Ohio: Lutheran Book Concern, 1930). Descriptions of the founding of the seminary in South Carolina are in Raymond M. Bost in *A History of the Lutheran Church in South Carolina* (Columbia, S.C.: R. L. Bryan Co., 1971), pp. 167–75; and Gilbert P. Voigt, *A Historical Sketch: Lutheran Theological Southern Seminary* (Columbia, S.C.: Board of Trustees, 1955). Developments at Hartwick, including a sample curriculum, are in Harry J. Kreider, *History of the United Lutheran Synod of New York and New England, 1786–1860* (Philadelphia: Muhlenberg Press, 1954), pp. 52–56, 214–16; also, Henry H. Heins, *Throughout All the Years: The Bicentennial Story of Hartwick in America, 1746–1946* (Oneonta, N.Y.: Hartwick College, 1946).
3.
Wentz, *Pioneer*, pp. 141–54, gives a picture of Schmucker's teaching situation at Gettysburg. See ibid., pp. 137–39, and Samuel G. Hefelbower, *History of Gettysburg College* (Gettysburg, Pa.: Gettysburg College, 1932), for development of the college. Primary documents are: *The Charter of Pennsylvania College . . .* (Gettysburg, Pa.: Neinstedt, 1834); *Statutes of Pennsylvania College . . .* (Gettysburg, Pa.: Neinstedt, 1834); and *Regulations of Pennsylvania College . . .* (Gettysburg, Pa.: Robert Harper, 1839). Further description of the teaching influence of Schmucker is in E. Theodore Bachmann in *Sons of the Prophets: Leaders in Protestantism from Princeton Seminary*, ed. Hugh Kerr (Princeton: Princeton University Press, 1963), pp. 39–68.

"biblical supernaturalism" of the Old Tuebingen school. However, Schmucker soon found that the work was too technical for the needs of his students, so he produced a textbook of his own, *Elements of Popular Theology,* in 1834. Since every one of the hundreds of students who studied under Schmucker after 1834 was required to use the *Popular Theology,* its position may be taken as representative of many pastors in the period.[4]

It is clear that Schmucker accepted the general axiom that all "orthodox" Christian bodies—and Roman Catholics were excluded from that group—held a common faith based on the "fundamental doctrines of Scripture." "The ground held by them in common should be considered fundamental, and the points of difference regarded in a secondary light as legitimate subjects for free and friendly inquiry," he wrote. Even the early church did not enjoy "entire harmony of opinion" when the apostles were present, so why should it be necessary later? Of course, "fundamental errorists" like Unitarians, Romanists, and deists, should be excluded; so some creeds were required. "The error of creeds," he explained, "lies not in their being reduced to paper, but in their undue length, and rigour of construction on those minor points which ought not to be embraced in them." In that light, the Augsburg Confession served a useful purpose because it contained the fundamental doctrines of Scripture in a manner that was "substantially" correct. Schmucker used the first twenty-one Articles of the Augsburg Confession as the outline for his *Popular Theology.*[5]

The chief theological opponents of Schmucker's day ranged from the Unitarians, who were just becoming a vocal part of the theological debate, through the Campbellites, or Disciples of Christ, who challenged the use of any creeds or the requirement of any theological education, to the Baptists, who disagreed with Lutherans over the propriety and effectiveness of infant baptism. A continued battle with Roman Catholics also required attention. Students of the *Popular Theology* were prepared to meet these opponents. Schmucker used almost a quarter of his book to examine the doctrine of God, especially in reference to the basis for rational belief in the Trinity. Another section defended the practice of infant baptism and questioned the need for immersion. Schmucker even risked violating his own canon against detailed creeds in order to publish that part of the Augsburg Confession which listed abuses "which had crept into the Roman Church," since that list "is seldom found annexed to the modern editions of the Confessions" and since he felt it was not "entirely superfluous" for readers of his own day.

On at least two points Schmucker seemed to allow so much latitude that the reader wonders how Lutherans would differ from other Protestant denominations. In the Lord's Supper, Schmucker contented himself with describing four views of Christ's presence in the sacrament, ranging from His "actual" presence to the opinion that "there is no presence of the human nature of the Saviour of any kind." While noting that most Lutheran clergy in America would agree with neither extreme, Schmucker concludes: "After a protracted and unprofitable

4.
Samuel S. Schmucker, *An Elementary Course of Biblical Theology Translated from the Work of Professors Storr and Flatt,* 2 vols. (Andover, Mass.: Flagg & Gould, 1826), in *MCAL,* reel 7; Samuel S. Schmucker, *Elements of Popular Theology, with Special Reference to the Doctrines of the Reformation* (Andover, Mass.: Gould & Newman, 1834), in *MCAL,* reel 33.
5.
Schmucker, *Popular Theology,* pp. iii-vi. Schmucker shared the prevailing anti-Roman animus present among Protestant "American Evangelicals." The introduction to Schmucker's *Popular Theology* makes derogatory reference to Roman Catholics. Some of the later Lutheran immigrants experienced similar criticism by American "nativists." The conflict between "American Lutherans" and immigrant Scandinavian Lutherans in Illinois (1850s) had stong "nativist" overtones, which contributed in part to the withdrawal of the latter in order to establish their own Scandinavian Augustana Synod (1860).

struggle, the Lutheran Church has long since settled down in the happy conviction, that on this, as on all other subjects not clearly determined by the inspired volume, her sons shall be left to follow the dictates of their own conscience, having none to molest them or make them afraid."[6]

On baptism he is similarly vague about what benefits the sacrament confers. At one point he speaks about its symbolic portrayal of "the process of spiritual purification," its initiatory significance in making a person part of the visible church of Christ, and its "federal" character in establishing a covenant between the believer and God. Later, however, he remarks that baptized infants who die before receiving any instruction have "in God's appointed way been *brought within the pales of covenanted hope,* have received the seal of membership in God's visible people; and are in exactly the same state" as circumcised children were in Israel. Whether that meant they were "saved" or not is impossible to determine from Schmucker's comments.[7]

One may wonder what value or special benefit Schmucker found in retaining the identity of a Lutheran. The answer to this question lies in his conviction that the Augsburg Confession said just enough to insure the rejection of fundamental error but that it wisely left other questions open. In matters such as the presence of Christ in the Lord's Supper, it is true, he would have been happier if the Augsburg Confession had been less specific; but he was willing to accept a few controversial points for the sake of his major goal. In contrast to Presbyterians who argued over predestination and Baptists who made a fetish of immersion, the Lutheran church wisely concentrated on "the ground held . . . in common" while choosing to regard "the points of difference . . . in a secondary light as legitimate subjects for free and friendly inquiry." It is therefore totally consistent with his esteem for the Augsburg Confession that Schmucker used its outline in 1838 when he suggested an "Apostolic, Protestant Confession" as a model creed for greater unity among Protestant denominations.[8]

Schmucker's views fit in well with the prevailing spirit among Lutherans of his day. His concentration on the "fundamental" doctrines of Scripture echoed the thought of his father's generation in its fight against deism. Even in Ohio, where the General Synod was not popular, a fairly broad attitude toward doctrine prevailed. An examining committee noted that, since the candidates for ordination "were neither infected by the poison of Rationalism nor inflamed by the wildfire of Fanaticism," the synod "need not hesitate to receive them." Creeds, said the new professor at Hartwick in 1831, "are no better than a Chinese shoe, by which the living foot being cramped, never attains its proper shape. . . ."[9]

Relations with the Reformed Church

In Europe, the king of Prussia was attempting to open a new perspective on traditional beliefs. In 1817, on the 300th anniversary of the Reformation, King Friedrich Wilhelm III urged his subjects to abandon their Lutheran or Reformed liturgies and

6.
Ibid., p. 225. John Nevin and Philip Schaff, Reformed theologians at Mercersburg, charged Schmucker with being neither Lutheran nor Calvinist. Rather, they said, he was a Zwinglian. See J. H. Nichols, *Romanticism in American Theology* (Chicago: University of Chicago Press, 1961), pp. 92–93.
7.
Schmucker, *Popular Theology*, pp. 201, 225–26.
8.
Ibid., pp. iv–v; Samuel S. Schmucker, *Fraternal Appeal to the American Churches with a Plan for Catholic Union, on Apostolic Principles* . . . (New York: Gould & Newman, 1838). The "enlarged" 1839 edition is available in *MCAL*, reel 34, and edited with an introduction by Frederick K. Wentz (Philadelphia: Fortress Press, 1965).
9.
Ohio Synod, *Minutes . . . 1832*, p. 28. Quoted in Vergilius Ferm, *The Crisis in American Lutheran Theology* (New York: Century Co., 1927), p. 102. This work discusses the growing tensions over doctrine in the pre-Civil War era; pp. 71–116 cover the period 1820–40.

131

celebrate the anniversary with a new "Evangelical" form. For Lutherans this change meant they would no longer hear the minister say, "Take, eat, this is the true body of our Lord Jesus Christ." Instead, the communicant would be told, "Jesus Christ says, 'This is my body.'" The effect would be to leave the interpretation of Christ's presence in the sacrament up to the individual believer. Other traditional forms, such as the use of candles, were also discouraged. After more than a decade of urging, the king decreed in 1831 that ministers who still refused to use the new liturgy of the "Prussian Union" would be guilty of flagrant disobedience to the crown.[10]

Some of the effects of this Prussian Union were felt in the New World. Mission societies in the Prussian lands, especially the Rhenish Missionary Society, began to send pastors with "Union" views to America. One of the early missionaries of the Union was Frederick Bindemann, who was sent to Pennsylvania but later moved to Canada, where he settled in the Waterloo area and remained for over thirty years. Other Union ministers worked among the German immigrants from New York to New Orleans.[11]

In such a climate, it is surprising that unions between Lutheran and Reformed bodies did not take place. Of course there had been talk of union in Pennsylvania for years. Cordial relationships existed almost everywhere. Reformed clergymen were uniformly welcomed to synodical conventions and given the privilege of the floor. Communion services often included representatives of both denominations. At the meeting of the General Synod in 1837, the secretary recorded with satisfaction: "The brethren, united with many followers of Christ, of our own as well as of sister-churches, celebrated the Lord's Supper." In Ohio a union of the two bodies occupied synodical agendas for four years. The editor of a church paper pleaded for it. Yet no mergers took place. It is likely that, in the absence of theological reasons for maintaining separate denominations, the old traditions of worship and polity resisted change. The simple difference of saying the Lord's Prayer in a "Lutheran" or "Reformed" word order may have proved to be as powerful a mark of identity in that period as the unaltered Augsburg Confession would become for a later generation.[12]

The Augsburg Confession

In the meantime, the use of the Augsburg Confession became more general. Schmucker undoubtedly helped to "raise it up out of the dust" but its popularity was too widespread to attribute entirely to his efforts. The founders of the Tennessee Synod, of course, had stressed the Augsburg Confession as the true standard of Lutheran belief in opposition to the prevailing attitudes in the North Carolina Synod. In fact, when trouble developed in the Tennessee Synod over a proper constitution, Philip Henkel suggested that the synod simply be governed by the Augsburg Confession. The Ohio Synod also became more explicit in its adherence to the confession, especially after 1830, when its leadership shifted to a younger generation. Its patri-

10.
For summaries of the Prussian Union and its effects on migration to North America see Fred W. Meuser, *The Formation of the American Lutheran Church* (Columbus, Ohio: Wartburg Press, 1958), pp. 14ff.; and W. O. Forster, *Zion on the Mississippi* (St. Louis: Concordia Publishing House, 1953), pp. 16–26.
11.
Welf H. Heick, "The Lutherans in Waterloo County, Ontario, 1810–1959: A Historical Study" (M.A. thesis, Queen's University, Kingston, Ont., 1959), pp. 44–51; on the Rhenish Missionary Society see L. von Rohden, *Geschichte der Rheinschen Missionsgesellschaft* (Barmen: J. F. Steinhaus, 1856). On a Union "German Evangelical" congregation see Malcolm Shutters, "History of the Lutheran Church in the District of Columbia, 1769–1909" (B.D. thesis, Gettysburg Seminary, 1939).
12.
General Synod, *Minutes . . . 1837*, p. 3; Ohio Synod, *Minutes . . . 1833*, p. 9; Kurtz in *Lutheran Observer*, November 11, 1836, p. 46. Documents relating to union movements from 1818–25 in Pennsylvania are in Richard C. Wolf, *Documents of Lutheran Unity in America* (Philadelphia: Fortress Press, 1966), pp. 77–84. Lutheran: "*Vater unser*"; Reformed: "*Unser Vater*."

arch, John Stough, apparently had never mentioned any of the Lutheran confessions in his writings; the synod's constitution of 1833, however, specified that pastors were to preach "according to the doctrine of the Symbolical Books of the Evangelical Lutheran Church." Three years later the synod tightened the reins even further by declaring that it would "strictly adhere to the Augsburg Confession of faith, and admit no one to membership . . . who shall deny any part thereof."[13]

Member synods of the General Synod, however, did not tend to accept the confession as wholeheartedly, since the synod's constitution did not require any specific doctrinal assertion until 1839, and then the only requirement was to hold "the fundamental doctrines of the Bible as taught by our Church." However, there was much interest in the confession and its teaching. The South Carolina Synod made it the "point of union in our Church" at its organization in 1824. Its Discipline included a translation of the confession by Hazelius. George Lochman of Harrisburg, Pennsylvania, used the confession as the basis for one section of his *History, Doctrine and Discipline of the Evangelical Lutheran Church* (1818) and the Hartwick Synod published an edition of it "with Explanatory Notes" in 1837. Thus the Augsburg Confession became the center of curiosity and discussion, even though it was far from being the norm of doctrine. None of the arguments before 1840 was carried on with real scholarship, since the participants had not fully realized the issues at stake. The debate was often marked by more heat than light.[14]

The "Lutheran Observer"

One of the most strident voices to enter the controversy belonged to Benjamin Kurtz, one of the founders of Gettysburg Seminary. Kurtz entered the fray through the editorship of the *Lutheran Observer,* a biweekly newspaper which he took over in 1833 from its previous editor and founder, John G. Morris. In the course of his many years as editor, he increased the circulation from about 700 to many thousands, and he changed the publication to a weekly. A friend wrote that Kurtz was "a hard man to preach to, and seldom listened to any other man's sermons with any degree of patience." The same aggressive intolerance characterized his style as an editor. A close friend of Schmucker, he had none of the scholar's care for balanced argument. He made the *Observer* into a partisan paper, fiercely loyal to the General Synod, to the broad confessional position of his friends, and to the principles of a "practical Christianity." "It has had more friends, and, I may say, more enemies, too, than any paper ever printed in the church," said a contemporary. Kurtz's paper was a fresh and powerful force in Lutheranism.[15]

The *Observer* was not the first Lutheran periodical in English. That honor belongs to the *Lutheran Intelligencer,* published by a pastor in Frederick, Maryland, from 1826 to 1831. A second entry was another monthly, the *Lutheran Magazine,* published in Schoharie, New York, by a group of pastors from 1827 to 1831. Both of these publications appeared at about the same time and

3.
Letters of Philip Henkel to David Henkel, March 14, 1820, and October 19, 1826, quoted in Friedrich Bente, *American Lutheranism* (St. Louis: Concordia Publishing House, 1919), 1:150–52. Willard D. Alleck, "John Stough, Founder of Ohio Lutheranism," *Lutheran Quarterly* 12 (February 1960): 42; Ohio Synod, *Minutes . . . 1833,* pp. 18, 27–28; ibid. *1836,* p. 8.

4.
General Synod, *Minutes . . . 1839,* p. 49; Bost, *Lutheran Church in South Carolina,* pp. 59–60; Ernest L. Hazelius, *Discipline, Articles of Faith and Synodical Constitution as Adopted by the Evangelical Lutheran Synod of South Carolina* (Baltimore: Publication Rooms, 1841); John George Lochman, *The History, Doctrine, and Discipline of the Evangelical Lutheran Church* (Harrisburg, Pa.: John Wyeth, 1818), pp. 80ff., in *MCAL,* reel 5; *The Augsburg Confession with Explanatory Notes and Observations . . .* (Troy, N.Y.: Hartwick Synod, 1837).

5.
Morris, *Fifty Years,* p. 312.

shared the same fate. The English-speaking audience for which they were intended did not care for a steady diet of "Historical, Biographical and Religious Memoirs with Essays on the Doctrines of Luther; and Practical Remarks and Anecdotes for the Edification of Pious Persons of all Denominations." Circulation dwindled and debts increased. A German monthly, *Das Evangelisches Magazin,* fared even more poorly. Three successive editors, including Schmucker and Hazelius, were not able to keep it alive. It lasted only from 1829 to 1833.

Efforts to launch other papers, in German or English, proved fruitless. The only successful competitor to the *Observer* was the *Lutheran Standard,* which appeared in 1843 as a counterbalance to the revival-oriented *Observer.* For more than a decade the Joint Synod of Ohio had squirmed under the virtually unchallenged "fanaticism" of the *Observer.* As early as 1832 the synod had decided "that the signs of the times and the prevailing spirit of the religious papers which either advocate the cause of new measures and fanaticism, or vacillate like Lot's wife, between Sodom and Zoar, make it necessary that we establish a religious paper, under the exclusive control of our synod." After favoring German-language papers for a while, synodical leaders began preparation for a rival paper in English.[16]

Language Tensions

The rise of English newspapers gives a clue to the changing linguistic pattern during the 1820s and 1830s. Many areas of the church, such as New York and South Carolina, were almost exclusively English-speaking by 1830. Most of the other areas had come to accept bilingual arrangements, printing synodical minutes in German and English. A few strongly German districts remained, however, especially in Pennsylvania, Ohio, and Tennessee. The Ministerium of Pennsylvania still contained an overwhelming majority of pastors who preached in German; the Joint Synod of Ohio grudgingly allowed an "English District" to be formed by a small group of pastors in 1836, but instruction in its seminary was in German until 1840. Although the rising number of German immigrants flowing into the country began to reverse the trend toward English, it was clear that Lutherans would have to accustom themselves to two languages, at least.[17]

The existence of two linguistic traditions aggravated other tensions in the Lutheran church. Partisans of each language accused the others of endangering the future of the church. Advocates of English claimed that, by clinging to German, traditionalists "drove the young away and death took the old, and that left their churches in desolation." German-speaking leaders retorted that there were no reliable Lutheran textbooks in English. The courses at Gettysburg Seminary, for example, used texts written by members of other denominations. "If the knowledge of the German language be lost," wrote David Henkel, "the peculiar doctrines of our church will also be forgotten in another generation, provided there be no accurate translations." Thus the question of language reflected the larger question of the importance of the "peculiar doctrines" of the Luther-

16.
Frederick G. Gotwald, "Pioneer American Lutheran Journalism, 1812-1850," *Lutheran Quarterly* 42 (April 1912): 161-204, reviews names and statistics of periodicals in this era; cf. Morris, *Fifty Years,* pp. 311-13; and Sheatsley, *Joint Synod of Ohio* (Columbus, Ohio: Lutheran Book Concern, 1919), p. 103. Other synodical actions on newspapers may be found in Allbeck, *Century,* pp. 105-6, 164; and William E. Eisenberg, *The Lutheran Church in Virginia, 1717-1962* (Lynchburg, Va.: J. P. Bell, 1967), p. 169.

17.
The only synods which printed their minutes entirely in English were Hartwick, New York, Synod of the West, and South Carolina. The transition problems in Ohio are covered in Allbeck, *Century,* pp. 84-90, 136. Carl R. Cronmiller, *A History of the Lutheran Church in Canada* (Toronto: Synod of Canada, 1961), p. 94, notes that the Dundas congregation had moved entirely to English by 1837. Linguistic problems in the Tennessee Synod in 1826 are documented in Bente, *American Lutheranism,* 1:150-51. Cf. Bost, *Lutheran Church in South Carolina,* p. 182.

an church. Ought they be preserved by the use of German? Or were they, like German, only incidental trappings of the "fundamental doctrines of Scripture," useful for a time but destined to fall away in the interests of broader cooperation among all Christians?[18]

New Measures

The issues of doctrine, language, and the future of the church converged in the most hotly debated question of the period— "new measures." The term referred, in general, to revival meetings, but more specifically it referred to specialized techniques for bringing individuals through an emotional conversion experience. The necessity for these methods was clearly stated by Charles G. Finney, the most famous advocate of their use: "God has found it necessary to take advantage of the excitability there is in mankind, to produce powerful excitements among them, before he can lead them to obey. Men are so spiritually sluggish . . . that it is necessary to raise an excitement among them, till the tide rises so high as to sweep away the opposing obstacles."[19] The method included holding meetings day after day in a given church or community, and "protracting" them as long as interest remained. These "protracted meetings" could last from a few days to several weeks. The preaching was focused on convincing listeners that they were sinful and in need of immediate help. Little time was spent in generalities or theological polemic. All controversial points were avoided, because the listener must be forced to consider only one theme: his need for immediate repentance. All aspects of the meeting supported this single purpose. Prayers were to be short and direct. "Urge the Christians present," wrote Finney, "to pray in such a way as to make sinners feel that they are expected to repent immediately." Solemn hymns, especially those concerning judgment, were more appropriate than "that joyful kind of singing that makes everybody feel comfortable."[20]

The capstone of the system and the climax of the process was the "anxious seat" or the "mourner's bench." An area at the front of the church stood ready to receive those listeners who felt the need for special prayer and help in conversion. These mourners became the objects of intensive prayer and exhortation by the ministers and by other members of the congregation:

They are, as it were, on the turning point, balancing on a pivot. On the decision they come to in many, very many instances depends their eternal destiny. If they submit, if they resolve to believe in Jesus Christ, if they close in with the overtures of mercy and declare on the side of religion, their conversion is accomplished and their salvation sure. But if they hesitate and waver, . . . then they are thrown further away from God and heaven than they ever had been. . . .[21]

Ministers would come down from the pulpit and address the mourner personally; members of the congregation would pray aloud; someone might start a hymn. Quite often, these measures would be sufficient to bring the mourner to an intense emotional

18.
Lutheran Observer, December 16, 1836; David Henkel, *Carolinian Herald of Liberty, Religious and Political* (Salisbury, N.C.: Kreider & Bingham, 1821), p. 43, in *MCAL*, reel 6.
19.
Quoted in F. Seilhamer, "The 'New Measure' Movement in the Lutheran Church in America, 1820–1860" (B.D. thesis, Gettysburg Seminary, 1959), p. 7. This essay, somewhat abridged, appeared as "The New Measure Movement Among Lutherans" in *Lutheran Quarterly* 12 (May 1960): 121–43. For general orientation see William Warren Sweet, *Revivalism in America* (New York: Scribner's, 1944); Bernard A. Weisberger, *They Gathered at the River* (Boston: Little, Brown, 1958); W. G. McLoughlin, *Modern Revivalism: Charles Grandison Finney to Billy Graham* (New York: Ronald Press Co., 1959). A useful regional study is Whitney R. Cross's *The Burned-over District* (Ithaca, N.Y.: Cornell University Press, 1950).
20.
Seilhamer, "New Measure Movement Among Lutherans," pp. 122–25.
21.
Ibid., p. 125.

experience, frequently signaled by tears or cries. The sinner would be "brought through."

The protracted meetings actually moved the frontier camp meetings indoors. They adapted the time schedule, the surroundings, and the process to small-town congregations, but the atmosphere remained the same. Emotions may have been somewhat better controlled, especially among Lutherans, who shunned the more extreme physical jerkings and howlings of the camp meetings. Meetings seldom continued past midnight. But cooperative preaching by clergy of several denominations, emotional emphasis on the conversion experience, and direct appeals for immediate decision all reflected the influence of camp meetings.

To many Lutheran leaders of the early nineteenth century these dramatic methods seemed to offer an effective way to combat rationalism, indifference, and apathy. Older methods of catechization had often included emotional elements; Muhlenberg considered tears to be a certain sign of repentance and he often noted in his journal when a conversation had brought someone to tears. Thus it was easy to move gradually toward an emphasis on emotion rather than on understanding. If the goal of catechetical instruction was the personal conversion of the sinner, then why not concentrate on the goal, regardless of the means? Instruction dwindled and exhortation increased. The times required not a "religion of imitation but of experience, not of the letter but of the spirit, not of human wisdom but divine grace. . . ."[22]

Adoption of the new measures seemed most common in English-speaking areas of the church. In South Carolina it was reported that the seminary students, as well as two-thirds of the pastors in the synod, participated in revivals. At a four-day revival in 1831 "hundreds were bathed in tears, a profound solemnity pervaded the whole assembly, more than one hundred individuals accepted the invitation given to those who desired to be personally conversed with on the subject of their soul's salvation." North Carolina and Virginia shared these sentiments. The Hartwick Synod, in the counties bordering New York's "Burned-over District," heard that "upwards of 1000 souls" had been converted in its first year. The Maryland and West Pennsylvania synods reported countless revivals during the period under study, although many of the reports came from the same congregations year after year. In all the other states, and in Upper Canada, individual congregations experienced "seasons of refreshing." Benjamin Kurtz of the *Lutheran Observer* gladly spread accounts of these revivals across the pages of his paper.[23]

Opposition to new measures was fully as emotional as the revivals themselves. An irate reader wrote Kurtz:

Instead of less of that disgusting stuff about go-up Revivals, Screaming, Clapping of Hands at the Hypocrite's Bench, you have more of it every week. You and the other Revival-Boys are advocating this Rail-Road christianity according to which they become

22.
Quoted in ibid., p. 139.
23.
South Carolina: *Lutheran Observer*, December 15, 1831, and July 21, 1843; Virginia: Eisenberg, *Lutheran Church in Virginia*, p. 168; Hartwick Synod, *Minutes . . . 1832*, p. 21; New York Ministerium, *Minutes . . . 1834*, pp. 9–10, and ibid. *1840*, p. 8; see Seilhamer, "New Measure Movement Among Lutherans," p. 140, for a list of communities reporting revivals; Canada: Cronmiller, *History*, p. 86; Ohio: Allbeck, *Century*, pp. 90–98.

sinlessly perfect in an hour, for the same reason for which the Presbyterians have adopted it, that our people might not desert to the Methodists . . . Altar [sic], for the Lutheran Church's sake, the name of your paper; call it *New Measure, Fanatical, Methodistical, Anti-Lutheran Engine, or Advocate of Screaming, Falling, Clapping of Hands, of Hypocrisy and Lies.*[24]

The letter makes several points which were typical of critics of new measures. They claimed that the method was not Lutheran, chiefly because it seemed to rely on human efforts for conversion rather than on the lifelong work of the Holy Spirit. It also minimized the place of confirmation instruction since a convert could "become sinlessly perfect in an hour." Another fault stressed by critics was the emotionalism associated with the new measures. Was a "heated imagination" really to be taken for "godly notions," and human passions conceived to be divine impulses? Finally, the critics pointed out that many of the converts did not remain faithful, so that the "mourner's bench" could be more properly termed "the hypocrite's bench."

Defenders of new measures retorted by claiming that their position had been misrepresented. Emotions among Lutherans did not become as "fanatical" as opponents liked to imply. Usually accounts of revivals noted that a "dreadful solemnity" had prevailed throughout the services. Weeping and earnest conversation rather than "screaming and falling" seemed to be typical. Furthermore, they did not intend to substitute human efforts for God's grace any more than those who claimed grace came through the preaching of the Word. It was merely a question of taking the style of preaching more seriously. As far as the genuineness of the conversions was concerned, there was plenty of evidence that the Old Lutheran way of confirmation did not produce perfect results either. The debate went on, even after the peak of the revival movement in the early 1840s.[25]

Worship

The new emphasis which the new-measure men put on preaching was typical of most worship services in this period. Whether English or German, the pattern of worship stressed hymns, prayer, and preaching. Most English-speaking congregations used the New York Hymnal which had originally appeared in 1814. It really had no full liturgical form for the Sunday service; it simply provided a selection of prayers, confessions of sins, and benedictions. Each pastor could adapt these resources to his own form of worship. German congregations followed a similar procedure. As late as 1842 a new liturgy suggested the following outline:

The minister rises and pronounces a benediction, or some other devotional passage of Scripture, and then gives out the hymn that is to be sung. After the singing he goes to the altar, and calls upon the congregation to confess their sins, or reads one of the general prayers for Sunday. The prayer is followed by the reading of a portion of Scripture, such as the Gospels, the Epistles,

4.
Quoted in Allbeck, *Century*, p. 106.

5.
[W]eilhamer, "New Measure Movement [A]mong Lutherans," pp. 131–40; D. F. [B]ittle, *Remarks on New Measures* (Staunton, [V]a.: K. Harper, 1839). Conflict over re-[v]ivals initiated an extended controversy in [S]outh Carolina. See Godfrey Dreher, *A [F]air and Candid Statement . . . in Reference to [D]ifficulties . . . Between the Lutheran Synod of [S]outh Carolina and Godfrey Dreher* (Colum-[b]ia, S.C.: I. C. Morgan, 1842).

or some other suitable passage. After this the minister announces a hymn adapted to his sermon, and whilst it is sung, ascends the pulpit. After the close of the hymn he prays, preaches, and prays again; whereupon the congregation, having sung another hymn, is dismissed with the benediction.

Before these simple rules were laid down, pastors either copied forms of worship out of books belonging to others or composed liturgies of their own.[26]

Some efforts in the period sought to provide new hymnals and liturgies but they did not really change the basic hymn-prayer-hymn-preach pattern. The most successful new publication was the hymn book of the General Synod. It had sold out more than thirty editions by 1843 and it came to replace the New York Hymnal as the standard among English-speaking congregations.[27] Catechisms did not sell as well in this period of interest in revivals and sudden conversions, although editions were produced by the General Synod (1825), Henry Pohlman in New Jersey (1826), David Henkel (1828), and John G. Morris (1832). German catechisms were published also, chiefly in Pennsylvania. The struggle, however, was uphill all the way. As a pastor near the "Burned-over District" put it:

I state with regret that I have found it extremely difficult to collect together a class of young persons for catechetical instruction. This I attribute to the practice so widely pursued at present, . . . of admitting persons into the church . . . whilst ignorant of the very first principles of Christianity. The influence of this practice is severely felt among us, and in the minds of many catechetical instruction and formality in religion are inseparably linked together.[28]

Sunday Schools

Sunday schools, however, fit in well with the goals of both revivalists and traditionalists. Naturally, the revival-oriented congregations felt freer to join the American Sunday School Union and other interdenominational agencies, but traditional congregations often developed Sunday schools on an independent basis. One of the compelling reasons for acceptance of Sunday schools by conservative groups lay in their adaptation to instruction in the German language. A "missionary" for the Sunday school movement sent out by the Ministerium of Pennsylvania to work among its churches reported: "If the children had not had the opportunity on Sunday, they would probably never have learned to read German. So generally are the people now in favor of the Sunday school that the church council does not hesitate to use the alms collected after each Communion service toward purchasing the necessary textbooks." The conservative Joint Synod of Ohio directed its clergy to announce the Sunday school plan from their pulpits.[29]

Schmucker noted with satisfaction that although many "brethren and churches" would not join the General Synod

26.
A Collection of Hymns and a Liturgy (Philadelphia: G. & D. Billmeyer, 1814); cf. *MCAL*, reels 5, 6. This hymnal was reissued in 1834. Hazelius, *Discipline*, pp. 131–61, follows the New York Hymnal closely. Allbeck, *Century*, pp. 158–63, lists hymnals and liturgies used in Ohio; the quotation is from pp. 160–61.
27.
Hymns, Selected and Original for Public and Private Worship (Baltimore: Lucas & Deaver, 1828), to which was added *Liturgy for the Use of the Evangelical Lutheran Church* (Baltimore: Lucas & Deaver, 1832). Charles Henkel also provided a *Liturgy or Formulary for the Use of Evangelical Lutheran Churches* (Lancaster, Ohio: John Herman, 1830). The *Erbauliche Lieder-Sammlung* of the Ministerium of Pennsylvania, together with the Lutheran-Reformed *Gemeinschaftliches Gesangbuch*, remained popular among Germans. A selection of hymns from both these sources was published by authorization of the General Synod in 1834: *Evangelische Lieder-Sammlung genommen aus der Liedersammlung und dem Gemeinschaftlichen Gesangbuch* (Gettysburg, Pa., 1834).
28.
New York Ministerium, *Minutes . . . 1835*, p. 7. About eight editions of Luther's catechism in German were published between 1820 and 1840. Seventeen English editions appeared in the same period, including four editions of the General Synod's catechism. See Henry N. Pohlman, *Catechism for the Use of Evangelical Lutheran Churches* (Morristown, N.J.: Jacob Mann, 1826), and John G. Morris, *Catechetical Exercises . . .* (Baltimore: Wright, 1832).
29.
On the Sunday school movement in general see E. W. Rice, *The Sunday School Movement, 1780–1917, and the American Sunday School Union, 1817–1917* (Philadelphia: Union Press, 1917). For the broader relationships and effects of this and other voluntary movements see: C. I. Foster, *An Errand of Mercy: The Evangelical United Front, 1790–1837* (Chapel Hill, N.C.: University of North Carolina Press, 1960). Foster, however, omits any references to Lutheran participation. On Lutheran Sunday

they "continued to afford their substantial and increasing aid to every good work undertaken by this synod." One of those "good works" was the Lutheran Sunday School Union, established in 1829 by the General Synod as a Lutheran counterpart to the American Sunday School Union which had been organized five years earlier. The Lutheran Union, in turn, encouraged the formation of synodical unions to help promote the Sunday school cause in local congregations, and many synods complied.[30]

The pattern of Sunday school instruction is worth noting because it differs from the usage to which we are accustomed. Here is a description of the plan developed by the Ohio Synod in 1828:

The pastor with the advice of the church council shall appoint a capable person to act as superintendent, and as many male and female teachers as conditions require. (Boys and girls may come to the same school, although lady teachers should instruct the girls.) . . . The pupils should be separated into classes of 8 to 10 members. And here age should not be the determining factor, but the ability and progress of the pupil. . . . The school should be held in the church, school house or some suitable building and, where possible, every Sunday; it should begin at a definite time and continue at least two hours. . . . The duties of the superintendent are, among others, the following: To open and close the school with singing and prayer, or at least to see that this is done. . . . The teachers shall make it their special duty to see that their pupils learn to spell, commit to memory and get hold of the fundamentals of our precious religion.[31]

The material to be committed to memory usually consisted of Bible verses, the catechism, or sections taken from the uniform Selected Scripture Lessons. Where opposition to this plan remained, it usually stemmed from a dislike of involving lay leadership or from suspicion of projects that might require cooperation with other denominations, usually the German Reformed Church. The majority of congregations sponsored Sunday schools by 1840.[32]

Closely allied with the Sunday school movement in terms of cooperation with other denominations was the budding interest in foreign missions. Home missions, of course, absorbed most of the attention and energy of synods. The foreign mission field, however, was becoming popular among other denominations, which had set up national boards to direct their work. In 1836 the Maryland Synod urged its delegates to bring the challenge of foreign missions before the General Synod, and the result was an imaginative plan for cooperation with other German-speaking bodies in a "Foreign Mission Society of the Evangelical German Churches in the United States." While the project never sent out a missionary, it did bring the foreign mission enterprise before Lutherans.[33]

chools see R. H. Thurau, "A Study of the Lutheran Sunday School in America to 1865" (Ph.D. diss., University of Pittsburgh, 1946), copies of which are available at Krauth Memorial Library, Lutheran Theological Seminary, Philadelphia, and Wittenberg College Library, Springfield, Ohio. See also E. Theodore Bachmann, *They Called Him Father* (Philadelphia: Muhlenberg Press, 1942), p. 64; and Sheatsley, *Joint Synod of Ohio*, pp. 80–81.

30.

Samuel S. Schmucker, *Retrospect of Lutheranism in the United States . . .* (Baltimore: Publication Rooms, 1841), p. 19. Schmucker strongly advocated Sunday schools; see his *A Plea for the Sabbath School System* (Gettysburg, Pa.: Neinstedt, 1830), in *MCAL*, reel 32, and his *A Sermon . . . "The Happy Adaptation of the Sabbath School System to the Peculiar Wants of Our Age and Country"* (Philadelphia: American Sunday School Union, 1839), in *MCAL*, reel 34. For organization see General Synod, *Minutes . . . 1829*, pp. 8–9; Maryland Synod, *Minutes . . . 1830*, printed in *Lutheran Intelligencer*, December 1830, p. 294; New York Ministerium, *Minutes . . . 1830*, p. 19; Hartwick Synod, *Minutes . . . 1832*, p. 15; Bost, *Lutheran Church in South Carolina*, p. 227; Allbeck, *Century*, p. 180; New York Sunday School Society, *Constitution and Regulation* (New York: A. Paul, 1817).

31.

Quoted in Sheatsley, *Joint Synod of Ohio*, pp. 80–88.

32.

S. W. Harkey, *The Lutheran Sunday School Question Book . . .* (Fredericktown, Md.: Hughes & Levely, 1838); Pennsylvania Ministerium, *Kleines Liederbuch für Sonntagschulen . . .* (Gettysburg, Pa.: Neinstedt, 1828); Charles Philip Krauth, *Hymns . . . for Sunday Schools . . .* (Philadelphia: Brown, 1838); cf. Kreider, *History*, pp. 166–68; Ohio Synod, *Minutes . . . 1833*, p. 4; General Synod, *Minutes . . . 1831*, p. 29; Allbeck, *Century*, p. 130.

33.

General Synod, *Minutes . . . 1837*, p. 39; the Virginia Synod set up an auxiliary to this body (see Eisenberg, *Lutheran Church in*

Temperance and Sabbath Observance

In common with many other Protestant denominations in America, Lutherans believed that a life of faith would express itself in certain outward characteristics. Prominent among these signs of Christian faith were strict attitudes toward alcoholic beverages and the proper observance of Sunday. Some Lutherans opposed these outward manifestations of piety, however, so no unanimity was achieved. In general, those synods most fully Americanized and English-speaking adopted the standards of their Protestant neighbors. German-speaking synods tended to avoid taking public stands on these issues, usually because their own membership was divided on whether or not temperance and Sunday observance were infallible indexes to a person's faith.

The period from 1820 to 1840 saw a fundamental change occur in the temperance movement. The name "temperance" implies moderate use, and that had been the goal of earlier generations. By 1830, however, the objective had really become total abstinence, although the term "temperance" was still universally employed.[34] The transition in goals was both understandable and confusing. It was obvious that "moderation" in the use of alcoholic beverages was difficult to define. "Moderation" meant stopping before one became intoxicated, but at what point did that occur? John Stough, an early advocate of temperance in Ohio, wrote:

We tried to define the term "drunk" according to the notions of the people, but never could do it. . . . One thing was evident to me, as long as a drinker could keep up his head, he would not admit that he was drunk, and when he could no longer reel to and fro, but was compelled to lie down and sleep in filth like a hog in the sty, he had not sense enough to know that he was drunk. Hence I preached that the only safe way was to refrain from it entirely.

In 1836 the American Temperance Union distributed a new pledge which substituted total abstinence for "temperance." But the new move proved confusing. Formerly, the pledge was considered in reference only to distilled liquor or "ardent spirits"; fermented drinks, such as cider, beer, and wine, were not included. Some temperance advocates, including Benjamin Kurtz of the *Lutheran Observer,* had maintained the distinction, opposing the use of distilled beverages while permitting the use of fermented ones. In fact, Kurtz had suggested that drinkers of "hard" liquors might well break their habit by consuming greater quantities of fermented drinks. Bowing to the trend of public thinking, however, Kurtz rejected all alcoholic beverages by 1837. Students at Pennsylvania College were also confused by the shifting terminology. In 1834 two campus temperance societies appeared—the second one had hastily organized when some students realized that the first one opposed only distilled spirits and did not reject wine as well.[35]

Another confusing aspect of the total abstinence position was

Virginia, p. 169); New York: Kreider, *History*, pp. 221, 223–24; Ohio: Allbeck, *Century*, p. 182; cf. *Annual Report of the Missionary Society of the Sunday Schools of St. John's* . . . (Philadelphia: T. U. Baker, 1839); the South Carolina Synod found that support of home missions took all its resources, so it did not cooperate (South Carolina Synod, *Minutes . . . 1835*, p. 7).
34.
For general orientation, see A. F. Tyler, *Freedom's Ferment: Phases of American Social History to 1860* (Minneapolis: University of Minnesota Press, 1944), pp. 315–28; Timothy L. Smith, *Revivalism and Social Reform in Mid-Nineteenth-Century America* (Nashville: Abingdon Press, 1957); L. L. Lehman, "Lutherans and the Movement for Temperance (1827–1859)" (B.D. thesis, Gettysburg Seminary, 1961), pp. 48–54, gives locations of articles on temperance in English-language Lutheran periodicals.
35.
The Stough quotation is from Sheatsley, *Joint Synod of Ohio*, pp. 29–30. See Hartwick Synod, *Minutes . . . 1836*, pp. 33–36; *Lutheran Observer*, March 15, 1832, pp. 247–48; ibid., May 30, 1834, p. 279; ibid., May 8, 1835, p. 145; ibid., May 26, 1837, p. 157. On Pennsylvania College see *Lutheran Observer*, June 11, 1834, p. 303, and June 18, 1834, p. 307.

its implications for the use of wine in Communion. Some Protestant bodies were already calling for the use of unfermented grape juice since it was widely believed that just one sip of wine would send reformed drinkers back to their cups. In 1835 the Virginia Synod opposed that suggestion and retorted that the exclusion of wine from the sacrament was "unreasonable, unwarrantable, and wholly opposed to the spirit of that ordinance of our religion." When the same question came up later in the Hartwick Synod, the use of unfermented liquid was recommended "if possible."[36]

141

The 1830s also saw the attack on alcohol broadened to include manufacturers and distributors. Formerly, temperance had been a matter for the individual conscience, but opponents soon began to attempt blocking the problem at its source. Just as opponents of slavery were turning their attention to the slave trade, opponents of alcohol began to point out that the making and selling of liquor was "inconsistent with Christian character." Both the Maryland and the Hartwick synods took action in this vein just before 1840.[37]

The promotion and inculcation of the temperance cause utilized the same channels that had proven so effective for the Sunday schools. Synods set up temperance societies to publicize and direct the work. These societies, in turn, attempted to organize local societies in congregations or communities. All the English-language Lutheran newspapers urged the formation of societies and the Franckean Synod actually included total abstinence as one of its constitutional requirements for all clergy. Societies were linked together regionally, and a general merger of all temperance-oriented bodies brought the American Temperance Union into existence in 1833.[38]

Crusades against labor on the Sabbath seemed much less popular with Lutherans than with some other Protestants. Government regulations in 1825 which required certain post offices to stay open on Sunday evoked steady petitions and complaints from various Christian groups, but there is little evidence that societies were organized or that synods took strong action. Four synods passed resolutions against the misuse of Sunday in 1839—one employing the phrase "entire abstinence"—and the General Synod made a broad suggestion that ministers and members ought to observe "this holy day" in 1843; the emphasis in all synodical actions, however, is on personal behavior rather than public action.[39]

Slavery

Although Lutherans reflected general Protestant attitudes on many subjects of social concern, they found the question of slavery too difficult to manage. The broad cooperative spirit we have noted among the English-speaking synods that became part of the General Synod began to shatter under the pressure of abolition.[40]

The relation of the Lutheran church to slavery received official notice in 1809 when the North Carolina Synod authorized its pastors to baptize slaves—provided the owners did not object.

36.
Lutheran Observer, December 11, 1835, p. 62, and January 1, 1836, p. 74; cf. ibid., May 30, 1834, p. 279. Kreider, *History*, p. 90. Spirits for "medicinal purposes" were usually allowed.
37.
Maryland Synod, *Minutes . . . 1838*, p. 21; Hartwick Synod, *Minutes . . . 1839*, p. 21.
38.
Maryland Synod, *Minutes . . . 1830*, printed in *Lutheran Intelligencer*, December 1830, p. 294; *Lutheran Observer*, September 12, 1834, p. 11; Franckean Synod action is quoted in Kreider, *History*, pp. 115-16. Efforts in Ohio were less successful; see Allbeck, *Century*, pp. 103-4.
39.
Hartwick Synod, *Minutes . . . 1836*, p. 21, and ibid. *1839*, p. 20; Franckean Synod, *Minutes . . . 1838*, p. 17; and *Lutheran Herald*, June 16, 1839, p. 91. Eisenberg cites the Virginia Synod action in *Lutheran Church in Virginia*, p. 168; for English Synod in Ohio see Allbeck, *Century*, p. 103. See also General Synod, *Minutes . . . 1843*, p. 22. Further information may be found in G. L. Huff, "A Historical Study of the Sabbatarian Issue in the Lutheran Church in America, 1830-1860" (B.D. thesis, Gettysburg Seminary, 1961); and Frederick L. Bronner, "The Observance of the Sabbath in the U.S., 1800-1865" (Ph.D. diss., Harvard University, 1937).
40.
For general orientation see Sydney A. Ahlstrom, *A Religious History of the American People* (New Haven: Yale University Press, 1972), pp. 648-69, together with the bibliography, pp. 1117-18. For Lutherans see Robert Fortenbaugh, "American Lutheran Synods and Slavery, 1830-1860," *Journal of Religion* 13 (January 1933): 72-92.

A subsequent resolution in 1814 urged slave owners to permit instruction and baptism. Pastors of the synod dwelling in South Carolina spelled out the implications of this program a year later, and their proposals became the basis for a five-point program. The program suggested that elders in each congregation see that some place be set aside for the instruction of slaves. After adequate instruction and demonstration of good conduct, the slaves could be baptized. Then, in contrast to white members, blacks would undergo an additional probationary period during which they were to receive more instruction. Then, after an unspecified time, the slaves could be admitted to Communion, but only at their masters' churches. Slaves could have their children baptized and could stand as sponsors at baptism. The most awkward rule concerned marriage. Slaves were to remain faithful to their spouses "as long as they are not separated by their masters, in being removed to a distance." In that case, they were not to marry again until given permission by the minister or by their owners. Under this plan, slaves did become members of the Lutheran church. St. John's, Charleston, had ninety-two black members by 1825 and the number steadily increased. By the time of the Civil War, about one-fourth of the Lutherans in South Carolina were black.[41]

At least one synod took action opposing slavery at a very early date. In 1822 a delegate from Washington County, Tennessee, asked the Tennessee Synod if it did not consider slavery to be "a great evil." The synod responded that it did indeed and that it wished "that government, if possible, would devise some means as an antidote to this evil." Lest it be thought that this synod had no slaveholders in its ranks—and there were certainly only a few in Eastern Tennessee—it is important to mention that the synod instructed its ministers to admonish "every master to treat his slaves well. . . ."[42]

By 1825 colonization plans had been devised in order to remove blacks from the nation. The Ohio Synod was asked in 1827 to support the Ohio Society, which sponsored a colonization scheme, and, although it approved the purpose of the society, the synod referred action on the matter to individual consciences. An interesting chapter in the colonization story involved Jehu Jones, a young black man who had been recommended to the New York Ministerium by John Bachman of Charleston, South Carolina. Jones was to go to the new colony of Liberia as a missionary. Although he was ordained by the Ministerium, Jones went to Philadelphia instead of Africa. A subsequent request by him for support from the Ministerium drew a sharp rebuke for his failure to connect himself with "this or any other Lutheran ministerium."[43]

In 1834 Samuel S. Schmucker realized that voluntary colonization would never solve the slavery question. He suggested that Christians could continue to support colonization projects but "at the same time also maintain the justice and necessity of *gradual* and *entire* abolition by legislative provision in the various states." His shift in thinking paralleled the sentiments of many other leaders. Although Schmucker advocated "gradual" abo-

41.
Bost, *Lutheran Church in South Carolina*, pp. 238-45.
42.
Tennessee Synod, *Minutes . . . 1822*, p. 13.
43.
Allbeck, *Century*, p. 174; Kreider, *History*, pp. 152-53.

lition and disavowed the radical abolitionist goals of the American Anti-Slavery Society, his new ideas were in step with the times. Abolition of slavery became the goal, just as total abstinence had become the goal of the temperance movement. The "abolitionists" soon were mailing literature into the South and in 1835 some of their materials reached South Carolina. A mob broke into the Charleston post office and removed the literature. Later than same year the South Carolina Synod passed resolutions expressing their "strongest disapproval of the conduct of the Northern Abolitionists." The synod consoled itself by noting that none of the ministers of the Lutheran church had adopted abolitionist sentiments.[44]

Their pleasure proved short-lived. The next year a resolution was introduced in the Hartwick Synod expressing "the abhorrence of this body relative to the system of slavery in the United States." The synod declined to adopt the resolution and voted instead to postpone the subject indefinitely. Its action precipitated the formation of a new synod.[45]

The Franckean Synod

In 1837 four pastors of the Hartwick Synod, dissatisfied with the quality and quantity of pastoral leadership available to the smaller congregations, and upset over the synod's silence on the slavery question, met about fifty-five miles northwest of Albany "to form another synod in the Evangelical Lutheran Church." They called themselves the Franckean Synod, after the great pietist leader, August Herman Francke.[46]

The formation of the Franckean Synod marks the extremity of many of the movements and causes we have considered in this chapter. In its public statements and in its newspaper, the *Lutheran Herald,* the Franckean Synod took the most advanced positions of any contemporary synod. In a sense, it may be seen as the logical consequence of many of the trends we have mentioned.[47]

In terms of revivals, temperance attitudes, Sabbath observance, and abolition, for example, the synod had no rivals. Its constitution required ministers to sign a pledge of "total abstinence from intoxicating liquors" and to oppose slavery "as it exists in these United States." In 1842 the synod sent an appeal to every other synod in the United States, calling for them to express themselves on the abolition issue. The next year it published the results of its survey and revealed that no other synod had chosen to take a public stand. The Franckean Synod had already ordained a black pastor, Daniel Payne, who later became a bishop in the African Methodist Episcopal Church and a president of Wilberforce University.[48]

On other social issues the synod took equally strong stands. It considered "travelling on the Sabbath, paying social visits, operating post-offices, delivering and receiving letters and papers, running stages and investing money in Sabbath-breaking establishments" "violations of the Sabbath and sins against God." Its views on war were so pronounced that it later forbade its clergy to act as chaplains in military parades. In short, members and

44.
Wentz, *Pioneer,* p. 319; South Carolina Synod, *Minutes . . . 1835,* pp. 8, 30–31; ibid. *1836,* p. 20; ibid. *1837,* pp. 9, 10, 33, 37. North Carolina Synod, *Minutes . . . 1837,* p. 12.
45.
Kreider, *History,* p. 92.
46.
Ibid., pp. 94–98.
47.
Ibid., p. 105.
48.
Ibid., pp. 112–18.

ministers were to lead lives of "holiness" and "deep-toned piety."[49]

The emphasis on piety was cultivated through vigorous and unrestrained revivals. In contrast to a general Lutheran reluctance to encourage noisy, protracted meetings, the Franckean Synod pastors rejoiced over loud weepings and audible shouts for mercy. On the other hand, the Lord's Supper and baptism became less significant as means of grace. Church membership did not depend upon baptism but on public evidence of a conversion experience. Even more, the proper qualifications for a minister were not the number of years he had spent in school but the level of his piety and the intensity of his religious experience. Doctrine, after all, could be learned from reading the Bible; it was not encased in creeds or confessions. The Augsburg Confession, although valuable insofar as it agreed with Scripture, was not binding on anyone—in fact the synod declared that it "frankly and candidly" did not believe everything in the confession.[50]

Although it might seem that these views differed only in degree from those held by members of the General Synod, the combination of radical social and religious beliefs proved to be too strong for the latter body. The Franckean Synod had voted to join the General Synod, but it was roughly rejected in 1839. Pairing it with the ultra-conservative Tennessee Synod, the General Synod resolved "to exhort the churches in our connection . . . to beware of the efforts of these men to cause divisions and offenses contrary to the spirit of the Gospel." The Franckeans retorted by suggesting that the General Synod should "repent of its sins."[51]

Thus, by 1840 some significant strains were developing among North American Lutherans. By far the deepest lay along the linguistic border separating predominately German synods from predominately English synods. This stress would increase as the number of immigrants continued to multiply. Other strains, however, were becoming apparent within the membership of the General Synod. The slavery issue, dormant and ignored for the moment, remained unresolved. Division over the place of the Augsburg Confession in defining Lutheran identity ran through almost every synod and would ultimately divide Schmucker from Krauth at Gettysburg. The Franckean Synod was only the first tremor of an earthquake that would one day shake apart the carefully constructed compromises of the General Synod.

49.
Ibid., pp. 120–22, 106.
50.
Ibid., pp. 106–12.
51.
Ibid., pp. 100–101; General Synod, *Minutes . . . 1839*, p. 17.

III

Following the Frontier

August R. Suelflow and E. Clifford Nelson

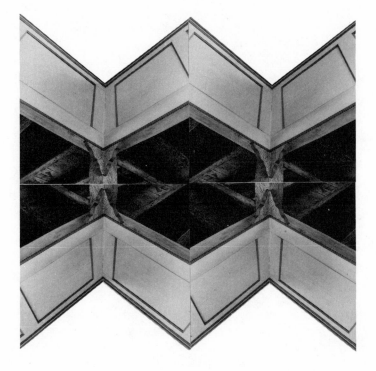

9 To the Promised Land

1.
Edwin Scott Gaustad, *A Religious History of America* (New York: Harper & Row, 1966), p. 207.
2.
Ibid.
3.
Ibid., pp. 203–5.

In his autobiography, *Seventy Years of Life and Labor,* English-born Samuel Gompers, one of the founders and long-time president of the American Federation of Labor, quotes a song which was popular among workers in the days of his boyhood.

To the west, to the west, to the land of the free,
Where the mighty Missouri rolls down to the sea,
Where a man is a man, if he's willing to toil,
And the humblest may gather the fruits of the soil,
Where children are blessings, and he who has most
Has aid for his fortune and riches to boast.
Where the young may exult and the aged may rest,
Away, far away, to the land of the west.[1]

"The song," Gompers writes, "expressed my feeling of America and my desire to go there rose with the ringing chorus: 'Away! far away, let us hope for the best,/And build up a home in the land of the west.' "[2] Millions of others in Europe shared that feeling about America during the nineteenth century, and many of those millions, looking upon America as the promised land of freedom and opportunity, crossed the ocean in the hope of building a new and better life.

It is estimated that during the three decades from 1781 to 1820 approximately 250,000 immigrants came to America. During the next decade another 143,389 crossed the ocean, followed by 599,125 between 1831 to 1840; 1,713,251 from 1841 to 1850; and 4,913,038 between 1851 and 1870.[3] Many of the earlier immigrants were from the British Isles and France. Beginning in the 1830s and culminating in the late 1880s, immigrants came largely from Germany, Scandinavia, and Ireland. For Lutheranism these immigrations marked not only great numerical growth but also long decades of doctrinal controversy, the proliferation of synodical bodies reflecting national origin and theological leanings, and the often painful process of transition from the language, traditions, and outlooks of the old homeland to those of the new.

Several factors played a role in stimulating migration to America. One was the confusion and disillusionment which followed the defeat of Napoleon at Waterloo in 1815. To bring order out of chaos the Congress of Vienna changed and shifted the boundaries of nations. New nations, such as the kingdom of the Netherlands, were created; other nations and territories were placed under other rule and sovereignty. Norway, for example, was separated from Danish rule and ceded to Sweden. In Germany, where the number of sovereign states had been reduced considerably, Prussia became the chief beneficiary of Napoleon's defeat. In compensation for eastern territories lost to

Russia and as a reward for its part in overthrowing the Corsican, Prussia's borders were extended from Memel on the Baltic coast to Westphalia and to the Rhineland.

In light of these conditions it is not surprising that the ideals of political liberalism inspired earlier by the American and French revolutions again began to take hold in many quarters in Europe. To be sure, the excesses which followed the overthrow of French King Louis XVI had brought these ideals into disrepute, but only for a time. Sweden (1809) and Norway (1814) had incorporated many of these ideals into their constitutions. The common man, however, derived little real or immediate benefit from such constitutions, for while the Swedish constitution provided wider extension of the electoral franchise, the franchise was based on income. Elsewhere in Europe the introduction of constitutional government had slower, more tedious progress. In the German kingdom of Saxony student uprisings in Leipzig and Dresden (1830) helped to hasten the adoption of a constitution which provided for a bicameral parliament and a limited monarchy.

For many in Europe, however, the political changes they hoped for were too slow and too painful in coming. Disappointed and often disgruntled, they began to look to America with longing eyes, hoping—often quite unrealistically—to find there what they had little, if any, immediate prospect of realizing at home.

A second factor which contributed to the mass immigration to America was economic. The Industrial Revolution was taking firm and irreversible hold upon the economic structures of Europe. New methods of travel (e.g., the steamboat and railroad) and communication (government-operated postal services and the telegraph) brought nations and peoples closer together both in community and in rivalry. For the common man, however, economic changes often brought more bane than blessing at the outset. The rural populace, especially farmers, of western Europe felt the changes most painfully. For the most part these farmers were barely emerging from the final stages of medieval feudalism. Suddenly a new society created by steam-powered industrialization was making the old-style guild craftsman obsolete, the factory was putting an end to home-based manufacture, and changes in agricultural methods and machinery deprived many of present livelihood and future security.

By the 1830s in Germany, particularly in the Saxon territories where the ancient guild system still prevailed, the home-based textile industry was increasingly hard-pressed by competition from British factories. Moreover, widespread crop failures in Saxony and elsewhere inflicted severe blows upon the heavily agricultural German economy. In Sweden, where 80 percent of the population lived in rural areas and farmed for a living, farm consolidation forced the children of large land-holding families to seek their livelihood elsewhere. For them as well as for already poorly situated field hands and tenant farmers, the future held little in store but want and poverty. Many of those who moved to the industrialized cities discovered that they had simply exchanged their roles as "slaves of the land" for those of "slaves of iron monsters," or joined the ranks of the unemployed.

A third factor which played a role in the immigration was religious. The successors to the Lutheran Reformers, in their polemics with the Roman Catholics and the Calvinists, had produced precise, exact, and systematic doctrinal formulations. These formulations, which presupposed the verbal, historical, and scientific inerrancy of Scripture, were transmitted to and perpetuated among the faithful by means of hymn and prayer books, preaching, and catechetical instruction. This orthodox theology, both in its content and method, became not only an accepted and respected academic discipline but also the form and content of the faith itself. So far as orthodox Lutheran dogmaticians were concerned, the range of theological inquiry and answer had been fixed by the church's confessions.

But for many correctness of doctrine was a cold and sterile matter. The long decades of warfare, famine, and pestilence of the sixteenth and early seventeenth centuries had produced a yearning for the kind of religion that warmed the heart and set the soul on fire with assurance and certainty. The movement known as pietism met that need. Far more concerned with a faith that could be lived with zeal and certainty than with a doctrinal system, pietism produced in both the Lutheran and Reformed churches an attitude and disposition which minimized the doctrinal differences between the two and stressed instead an underlying unity rooted in personal religious experience.

One of the chief characteristics of pietism as it took institutional form in Germany and Scandinavia was the conventicle, a small group of Christians who met apart from the regular worship of the congregation for Bible study, prayer, and mutual edification. In these groups the externals of liturgical worship as well as the sacramental means of grace were subordinate to the experience of awakening and conversion. While not fundamentally anticlerical or antichurch, pietism was characterized by strong lay leadership and lay involvement in the works of evangelism, missions, and mercy.

Pietism broke the hold of orthodoxy, but in so doing left the intellectual field in Germany and Scandinavia open to the inroads of English deism and French skepticism. The resulting Enlightenment had the overall effect of promoting among intellectuals both a critical-literary approach to Scripture and the view that biblical truths are essentially the same as those of natural religion and morality.

Although radically different from each other in their approach to and understanding of Scripture and of the Christian religion, pietists and the rationalists of the Enlightenment had at least one thing in common: they tended to minimize doctrinal differences between the Lutheran and Reformed churches. Both viewed the confessional standards of the two churches as human testimonies. For the pietist such testimonies were to be tested by God's word, i.e., the written text of Scripture read and interpreted uncritically. For the rationalist Scripture itself was subject to test, that of human reason.

By the nineteenth century the rationalism of the Enlightenment was strongly entrenched among the Protestant clergy. In general, rationalism dismissed traditional Protestant Christianity (e.g., vicarious atonement, justification by faith) as untenable. Preaching in rationalistic pulpits shifted from traditional religious concerns and themes to homilies on current events, scientific discourses, advice on stall feeding, the evils of drunkenness and careless bathing, the necessity of planting trees, and the importance of public sanitation.

Rationalistic views and sentiments were propagated not only in university classrooms but also in the Protestant pulpits of northern Europe, particularly in Germany. Among the lay people there were, of course, those who did not think or care about what their ministers preached. Others quite possibly welcomed the change in homiletical theme. Still others, by strong personal conviction as well as by natural conservatism, clung tenaciously to the faith of their fathers as their fathers had held it.

Reaction to rationalism developed along two major lines. One line issued from a division in rationalist ranks. Among the enlightened there were those who were unwilling to abandon supernatural revelation. Religious truth, they maintained, was to be proved by Scripture, which they held to be superior to reason. Nonetheless, reason was for them the tool by which Scripture's teaching was to be established. In Germany this position became known as supra-rationalism or rationalistic supernaturalism. Among the major figures identified with this movement were Gottlieb Jakob Planck (1751–1830), Franz Volkmar Reinhard (1753–1812), and Gottlob Christian Storr (1746–1805), who was co-author of a handbook of Christian dogmatics later translated by Samuel S. Schmucker (*An Elementary Course of Biblical Theology* [1826]) and used by him as the basis of instruction at the General Synod's Gettysburg Seminary (see above, chapter 8). The other line of reaction was the confluence of the number of factors which led to what has been variously termed "Old Lutheranism" or "confessionalism," a blending of scholastic orthodoxy and pietistic individualism.

A major factor in blending orthodoxy and pietism was the so-called Prussian Union of the Lutheran and Reformed churches. In part this union (later reflected in the German Evangelical Synod of North America) was facilitated by a wave of nationalism during the Napoleonic era. To a large extent the union was made possible by the pietistic revivals which broke out in northern Europe during this period. Fearful of the present and terrified of the future, many were stricken with a sense of sinfulness and of the need for divine forgiveness. They turned intently to Bible reading, to prayer, and to a kind of urgent, conversion-oriented preaching which spoke to their anxious condition. Essentially sporadic and unorganized, these revivals frequently were sparked by earnest, often gifted, preachers, both lay and ordained.

On this revival see Theodore G. Tappert, ed., *Lutheran Confessional Theology in America, 1840-1880* (New York: Oxford University Press, 1972).

Wilhelm Loehe, *Three Books About the Church*, trans. James L. Schaaf (Philadelphia: Fortress Press, 1969).

August Vilmar, *Die Theologie der Thatsachen wider die Theologie der Rhetorik*, 3d ed. (Stuttgart: Verlag von S. G. Liesching, 1864).

The nineteenth-century revivals, like the pietism of an earlier era, together with national feeling, fostered an indifference toward doctrinal distinctions between the Lutheran and Reformed churches. The Prussian Union, which joined the two bodies, at first was looked upon as both a natural union and an antidote to rationalism. The union, however, soon came under severe attack and criticism. From the Reformed side there was objection to liturgical aspects and to the role of the king of Prussia in creating the union. Lutherans, particularly those influenced by the revivals, became convinced that the emphases of the revivals were in essence those of the Lutheran confessions, which they began to see threatened by the union's doctrinal indifference. Thus spiritual awakening led to a revival of confessional consciousness among Lutherans.[4]

The confessional revival—fostered and abetted by the publication of the writings of Luther (e.g., the Erlangen edition, 1826), tercentennial celebrations (1817, 1830), and publication of a new edition of the Augsburg Confession (1819)—issued in three not entirely dissimilar movements. The first advocated a theology of repristination. The chief formulator and advocate of this theology was Ernst Wilhelm Hengstenberg (1802-69), whose Old Testament studies were translated into English and whose influence extended into Scandinavia through his professorship at the University of Berlin. Through his widely read *Evangelische Kirchenzeitung* (especially after 1850), Hengstenberg defended the immunity of the Scriptures to literary criticism and called for a return to the authority of the seventeenth-century fathers under the aegis of a thoroughgoing biblicism.

Closely related to Hengstenberg's repristinationism was the Neo-Lutheranism represented by Wilhelm Loehe (1808-72) and August Vilmar (1800-1868). Influenced by German nationalism and the romantic movement, Neo-Lutheranism was a Lutheran churchly revival akin to the Oxford Movement in England. Loehe stressed that the Lutheran church, as defined by its confessions, conformed exactly to the New Testament church.[5] Vilmar stressed the ordained ministry as the means through which Christ works in and through the church.[6] Loehe in particular was widely suspected of crypto-Catholicism because of his liturgical emphasis, his exaltation of the Lord's Supper, and his stress upon the catholic character of Lutheranism and its confessions.

The third movement to issue out of the confessional revival was the Erlangen school associated with Adolph von Harless (1806-79), most of whose teaching career was spent at the University of Erlangen. Others identified with this theology were Gottfried Thomasius (1802-75), Johann C. K. von Hofmann (1810-77), and Franz H. R. von Frank (1827-94). The major organ of the Erlangen school was the *Zeitschrift für Protestantismus und Kirche*, founded by von Harless in 1838. Unlike the other movements which emerged from the confessional revival, the Erlangen school did not regard the confessions as rigid, inflexible interpretations of the Christian faith but rather as expressions of the religious experience of the church in its conflict with error and its search for truth. The Erlangen school's adherents were, therefore, neither repristinators nor confessional romantics. They held that Christianity is not an inherited doctrine about man's relationship to God, but the relationship itself, i.e., a personal experience of regeneration. Thus, the Erlangen school may be characterized as a theology of organic progress.

The Lutheran churches in Europe were deeply and permanently affected by the confessional revival in its several forms. So was Lutheranism in America. The waves of mid-nineteenth-century immigrations brought scores of thousands of Lutherans to America from Germany, Sweden, and Norway (Danes, Finns, and others will be considered in section 4). With them these immigrants brought a kind of confessional Lutheranism generally quite different from that which had developed in America over the preceding century-and-a-half, and laid the groundwork for more than another century of conflict, division, rivalry, realignment, and rapprochement.

7.
Quoted in English in Carl S. Meyer, ed., *Moving Frontiers: Readings in the History of the Lutheran Church—Missouri Synod* (St. Louis: Concordia Publishing House, 1964), p. 48. Used by permission.
8.
Ibid., p. 59.

Emigration Movements

Germany
As early as 1788 church historian Gottlieb Jakob Planck (1751–1833) asserted:

Not only the forms, but also the basic ideas of the older [theologians] had been almost universally abandoned. We are aware that we have departed from them. And no one any longer fears that the spirit of our theology could on its own ever return to or even be forced back to them. For this reason these ideas are regarded as entirely inconsequential antiques.[7]

Thus, with religion emphasizing the subjective, idealistic, naturalistic, and rational, the traditional distinctions between the Lutheran and Reformed churches were all but totally erased. Furthermore, the struggle against Napoleon, which sounded the call for German political unity, revived an old dream, that of a union of the German Protestant churches on the basis of doctrinal standards comprehensive enough to include Protestants of all views. Such a religious union was as dearly desired as was the political unification of Germany, not least because of the political threat presented by Catholic Austria.

Prussian King Friedrich Wilhelm III had attempted, without success, as early as 1798 to unite Lutherans and Reformed. In 1817 he utilized the 300th anniversary of the Reformation as the occasion for a union Communion service in the palace at Potsdam. In his decree of September 27, 1817, he referred to the proposed union of Lutherans and Reformed as "this God-pleasing work," but was careful to add: "But no matter how strongly I desire the Reformed and Lutheran churches in my territories to share my well-grounded conviction, I respect their rights and freedom and have no intention of forcing anything upon them by my decree and decision."[8]

The king changed his approach for the celebration of the tricentennial of the Augsburg Confession. In a decree issued

9.
bid., p. 61.
10.
bid.
11.
bid., pp. 62-63.
12.
bid., p. 66.
13.
bid., p. 68.
14.
bid.
15.
bid., p. 71.

April 4, 1830, he authorized the application of the state's power to enforce the use of a union Agenda (liturgy) and particularly to introduce the Reformed practice of the breaking of bread in the Communion "as a symbolical expression of concurrence in the union. . . ."[9] Superintendents of the churches were instructed "to give attention and support to the abandonment both by the clergy and by the congregations of those proper names which differentiate the two evangelical congregations."[10] Because of Prussia's preeminence among the German states, the influence of the union decrees, their intent and method, spread throughout Germany. So did the opposition.

153

Franz Volkmar Reinhard's Reformation Day sermon of 1800 decried the state of Protestantism in his day as a departure from Luther.[11] Claus Harms (1778-1855), in his *Ninety-Five Theses,* published in 1817, lamented that "Lutheranism is reformed into paganism, and Christianity is reformed out of this world."[12] Reason, he wrote, was running wildly through the Lutheran church; Christ was torn from the altar and pulpit; the water of baptism was defiled with the slime of heresy, and priest and people were being driven out of the sanctuary. More to the point, Harms attacked the whole principle of union: "To say that time has removed the wall of separation between Lutheran and Reformed is not to speak correctly. The question is: Who have fallen away from the faith of their church, the Lutheran or the Reformed? Or both?"[13] For Harms and others of his persuasion it was unthinkable that Lutheranism, as they held it, could be wrong:

The structure of the Lutheran Church is complete and perfect; only one thing needs to be corrected and that is that the ultimate authority and final decision even in essentially spiritual matters is in the hands of the prince who does not belong to the clergy. This error was made in haste and disorder and should be corrected in an orderly manner.[14]

In recalling the revival of confessionalism among his contemporaries in Bavaria in the early nineteenth century, Thomasius wrote in *The Reawakening of the Evangelical Life in the Lutheran Church of Bavaria:*

As soon, however, as we began to ask questions about the way God had led us, or about the witness from which our faith had grown, or about the historical roots of our contemporary situation in the church's past, we became conscious that we stood in the center of Lutheranism. . . . From then on, to value them [the confessions] highly and to confess our agreement with them became itself a matter of faith and conscience. We blessed the Church for this; we were glad that we belonged to it. *Thus we became Lutherans, freely, from within.*[15]

Johann Gottfried Scheibel (1783-1843) of Breslau in Silesia was suspended from the exercise of his ministerial office for his opposition to the Union. He represented a minority group of confessional Lutherans including Henrik Steffens (1773-1845), rector of the University of Breslau, and Edward Huschke (1801–86) who had petitioned in 1830 for recognition of a Lutheran church separate and apart from the state Evangelical (Union) church. The petition, however, was denied. The following year the Breslau Lutherans petitioned for: (1) an independent Lutheran church; (2) a presbyterial constitution; (3) the election of officials and teachers by the congregation; (4) use of the Wittenberg Agenda; and (5) freedom to teach according to the Lutheran confessions. This petition also was denied. By 1835 those pastors who had refused to conduct services and perform ministerial acts according to the Union Agenda were imprisoned. Dissenters consequently began to hold conventicle services led by laymen. Government pressure and prosecution not only had failed to crush opposition to the Union, but even helped to unify its opponents and extend their influence into areas such as Pomerania, where revival movements had made many receptive to the pietistic orthodoxy represented by confessionalism.

Seeing no hope for a happy resolution of their difficulties, Prussian and other dissenters began to consider seriously the possibility of emigration to the United States. The idea of religious liberty and political equality, not to mention the availability of cheap land, held strong appeal for them. Furthermore, books such as Gottfried Duden's *Report of a Visit to the Western States of North America* heightened interest in America.[16] A host of emigration plans took shape and some were even carried out. In June 1838, Andreas L. C. Kavel (1798–1860) led 690 emigrants to Australia. They were followed in 1841 by 274 emigrants led by Gotthard Daniel Fritzsche (1797–1863).

The largest Prussian movement, however, emigrated to America under the leadership of Johannes Andreas August Grabau (1804–79). Grabau had studied at Halle. Ordained in 1834, he became involved in open opposition to the Union in 1836 while serving a parish in Erfurt. He took strong exception to the formula of the distribution of the Lord's Supper in the Union Agenda: "Jesus says, 'This is my body . . . blood.'" His refusal to use the Agenda led to his imprisonment of 1837. With the help of two laymen who later served as Lutheran ministers in America, Friedrich Miller and Heinrich von Rohr, Grabau escaped from prison and the trio made their way to Berlin. There and in Pomerania Grabau ministered clandestinely to small groups, frequently making his escape from a service just one jump ahead of police raiders. In 1838 he was apprehended and returned to prison.

During Grabau's second imprisonment he became convinced that emigration was the only solution for opponents to the Union. He was asked by members of the congregation in Magdeburg to accompany them to America following his release. By this time government authorities had concluded that the emigration of dissenters would rid them of a serious problem and issued the necessary emigration permits. Bureaucratic procedures were tediously slow; moreover, in January 1839 Grabau was so seriously ill that friends feared for his life. He recovered

16.
A partial translation of this account is published in *Missouri Historical Review*, vols. 12 and 13.

and on March 12 was released from custody; within another month he had his emigration permit.

The negotiations and arrangements for the emigration were carried on by laymen. Approximately one thousand members of the emigrant party traveled by canal boat from Halle to Hamburg. From Hamburg the party sailed to Liverpool, where between June and August 1839 they boarded five vessels and sailed for America. From New York City they traveled by steamer to Albany, then by canal boat to their destination, Buffalo. A small group, however, had remained in Albany; meanwhile, some forty families pushed on into Wisconsin and established the community of Freistadt near Milwaukee. The leadership of the Freistadt congregation soon became the responsibility of another "Old Lutheran," Leberecht Friedrich Ehregott Krause (1804–85).[17]

At the same time that Grabau and his company of dissenters were organizing and emigrating, another emigration movement was taking shape in Saxony under Martin Stephan, pastor of St. John's Church in Dresden. Because the royal family of Saxony was Roman Catholic, Protestant affairs were governed by an ecclesiastical council which was also responsible for the educational system and institutions of mercy. Although the ordination oath pledged Lutheran ministerial candidates to the Lutheran confessions, rationalism was very prevalent among the clergy. A new order of worship, strongly influenced by rationalist tenets, had been introduced in 1812. Here, too, conservative reaction and resistance set in, a large part of it looking to Stephan for leadership.

Born in Moravia of parents converted from Roman Catholicism, Stephan had studied at Halle and Leipzig. After a brief pastorate in Bohemia he was called to St. John's, Dresden, which had been founded during the Thirty Years' War by Bohemian refugees. This congregation enjoyed a semi-independent relationship to the state church, including the right to call its own pastor, a privilege which continued long after the membership had become thoroughly German. Strongly conservative in his theology and pietistic in outlook, Stephan attracted a large following among like-minded laymen. Among those drawn to him was a group of students at the University of Leipzig. Having experienced the emptiness of rationalism, these young men had turned to pietism. To this group belonged the Walther brothers, Otto Hermann and Carl Ferdinand Wilhelm, Ottomar Fuerbringer, Theodore J. Brohm, Ernst G. W. Keyl, Ernst M. Buerger, and Johann F. Buenger. With deeply disturbed and shaken consciences these students together searched for the certainty of salvation. Avidly they read the classic writers of pietism, Arndt, Spener, Francke, and Bogatsky. Half a century later C. F. W. Walther described their search:

The less a book invited to faith, and the more legalistically it urged contrition of the heart and total mortification of the old man before conversion, the better a book we held it to be. And even these books we read

7.
. F. E. Krause, *The Chronicle of Pastor*
. *F. E. Krause, First Lutheran Pastor to Work n Wisconsin*, ed. and trans. Roy A. Suelflow (St. Louis: Lutheran Historical Conference, 1973).

only so far as they described the sorrows and exercises of repentance; when this was followed by a description of faith and comfort for the penitent, we usually closed such a book; for we thought this did not as yet concern us.[18]

At the suggestion of Brohm, C. F. W. Walther had written to Stephan of his spiritual plight. When Stephan's reply was received, Walther was afraid to open the letter. But his fear was turned into joy upon reading Stephan's assurance that even Walther was forgiven through the blood of Christ. Acknowledging his debt to Stephan and demonstrating the adulation in which he was held, Walther later wrote:

When I read his reply, I felt as though I had been translated from hell to heaven. Tears of distress and sorrow were converted into tears of heavenly joy. . . . He [Stephan] directed me to the Good Samaritan and showed me what faith in Christ means. . . . Peace and joy entered my heart. . . . He applied the Gospel to my own soul.[19]

Despite legal sanctions against conventicles decreed in 1820, Stephan began to conduct such meetings, often for just a select company who looked upon him as the champion of orthodoxy and the defender of the true faith. Forster summarizes the esteem in which Stephan was held by his followers:

They firmly asserted that the means of grace were dependent upon his person and that if he were silenced, the Lutheran Church would cease to exist in Saxony. Stephan's doctrine was unerringly true, his solution of a question inevitably correct. Any criticism of or opposition to the Dresden pastor was condemned in the harshest terms. Stephan became an oracle, and all who disagreed with him or with whom he disagreed, were wrong. Since Stephan eventually disagreed with almost everyone, the simple conclusion was that all other views represented in the Church were false; only Stephanism was right. In fact the claim was finally made not only that Stephanism was the only right church . . . but that it alone was a Church. The Stephanites were the Church![20]

Not everyone shared this opinion, however. Members of his congregation were strongly opposed to Stephan. Other pastors criticized and attacked him for his insistence upon a literal interpretation of the Bible and the Lutheran confessions. His pastoral methods also came under criticism. Nor did the police hold Stephan in high regard. Rumor and complaint of his conventicle meetings, held with mixed company and until late hours, gave the police cause to take action. On February 1, 1836, gendarmes raided the house in which Stephan was meeting with his followers and arrested him. The case involved long, complex, and expensive litigation.

The action of the police persuaded Stephan and others that emigration was the only solution to their problem. For some years the possibility had been discussed among his followers. In fact, in 1827, when Benjamin Kurtz of the General Synod was

156

18.
C. F. W. Walther, *Kurzer Lebenslauf . . . J. F. Buenger* (St. Louis: F. Dette, 1882), pp. 17–18; English text in W. G. Polack, *The Story of C. F. W. Walther* (St. Louis: Concordia Publishing House, 1947), p. 15, and used by permission.
19.
Walter O. Forster, *Zion on the Mississippi* (St. Louis: Concordia Publishing House, 1953), p. 29. Used by permission.
20.
Ibid., pp. 63–64.

in Germany, Stephan had met with him and discussed the matter in general terms. In 1833 Stephan wrote to Kurtz inquiring about places of settlement in America. Kurtz's son proposed the area of the Missouri River because of the reported clear air, pleasant climate, and cheap land in the area. He also referred Stephan to Gottfried Duden's book.

In 1836 an emigration society was formed by Stephan's followers. The society formulated detailed sets of regulations prescribing a confession of faith and set forth the objectives of the emigration and a code of general conduct.[21] These regulations further prescribed maximum and minimum land purchases, forbade theaters, dance halls, and profane language, and dealt with matters of attire. A common treasury and credit fund were also established. At bottom the Stephanites envisaged the establishment in America of a theocratic community whose religious and secular head would be the bishop or primate. The regulations specifically stated: "The chief management of all affairs of the entire society shall be exercised by its primate, who accordingly will combine in his person the supreme authority in spiritual and civil matters."[22]

Early in November 1838 the first two of a five-ship flotilla left Bremen for New Orleans. The other three followed in rapid succession and all but one, which was lost at sea with its cargo of books, musical instruments, and other supplies, arrived in New Orleans in January 1839 with almost 700 passengers. Here Stephan was formally invested with the office of bishop. Shortly thereafter the immigrants traveled up the Mississippi by steamboat to St. Louis. A few months later some 10,000 acres of land in Perry County, Missouri, were purchased. While a number of the party remained in St. Louis, the rest began to clear the purchased land and to lay the foundations of settlements at Wittenberg, Altenburg, Frohna, and Dresden.

Considerable interest in the condition of German Lutheran immigrants in America was aroused in Germany by Friedrich C. D. Wyneken (1810-76). An immigrant himself, Wyneken had served a congregation in Baltimore and later became a zealous home missionary with headquarters in Fort Wayne, Indiana. A confessional Lutheran who spoke English with comfort and fluency, Wyneken had come to America in 1838 with the intention of serving his countrymen. He was received into the Ministerium of Pennsylvania and was sent by its mission society to serve the territory of northwestern Ohio, southern Michigan, and northern Indiana. His frequent travel through this territory, coupled with his experience as a home missionary, gave Wyneken a firsthand knowledge of the deplorable spiritual condition of German immigrants in the Midwest. When he returned to Germany in 1841 for medical treatment he also sought help for his countrymen in the New World. His published appeal was graphic:

Enter into the large cities; you will find thousands of people who have made their home there, either compelled by bodily necessity or deluded by the prince of darkness with the prospect of carnal liberty and

21.
Ibid., pp. 566-68.
22.
Ibid., p. 72.

157

outward comfort. A great many of them, sunk in the mire of baseness already in the old country, gave rein to their animal drives without any awe for that which is holy, no longer restrained even outwardly by any discipline. Even now as I write this, horror and dismay still fill me, as I remember the shamelessness with which vice strutted about not only in the darkness of night but in the broadest daylight, and how there I found the grossest indecency as well as the most abominable dens of vice owned by Germans. Others, happy to have cast off the fetters of the church as well as of the state, do indeed live in outward decency, yet without God, without the church, without hope, alas, without any longing for anything higher.[23]

Turning to the frontier, Wyneken described the lot of settlers:
Come now, step into the settlements and log cabins of your brethren! Behold, husband, wife, and children must work hard to fell the giant trees, to clear the underbrush, plow, sow and plant, for their little bit of money is running out or is already gone. There must be bread; no one gives to them but the ground which they till. . . . Small wonder then that everybody works to stay alive, that there is no difference between Sunday and weekday, especially since no church bell calls them to the house of God. . . . Bible and prayerbooks have often been left at home, since people have unfortunately lost their taste for them because of the enlightenment and it's not worth the effort to stretch out your hand for the revised hymnbooks. No preacher comes to rouse them from their earthly thoughts and pursuits, and for a long time the voice of the sweet Gospel has no longer been heard.[24]

Rhetorically but passionately he continued:
But who gives instruction to those who have been baptized: How can the washing of regeneration continue its action, grow and become powerful, when preaching or instruction is missing? Who will confirm the children? Who will administer Holy Communion to them afterwards? Perhaps their parents of German extraction are themselves heathen, unbaptized; just imagine— German heathen. . . . Help, in the name of Jesus, help! . . . [25]

Wilhelm Loehe in Neuendettelsau heard Wyneken's plea. In addition to funds, two volunteer helpers were sent to America in 1842: Adam Ernst (1815-95), a cobbler by trade, and George Burger (1816-47). Both men studied at the seminary of the Joint Synod of Ohio in Columbus. Burger accepted a call to Hancock County, Ohio; Ernst, who became a member of the Joint Synod of Ohio served pastorates in Ohio and Ontario, Canada. Both of these men found that Wyneken's account of the situation in America was true.

Beginning in 1845 Loehe promoted the establishment of German colonies in the Saginaw Valley of Michigan, where one of

23.
Meyer, *Moving Frontiers*, pp. 91-92.
24.
Ibid., p. 93.
25.
Ibid., p. 96.

158

the early Michigan synods was intensely concerned about the theological training begun in Europe and continued at the seminary in Columbus, Ohio. In their commissioning documents Loehe's men were solemnly enjoined to eschew fellowship with "all sects and false churches," to hold to the Lutheran confessions, observing the old regulations, and to accept a call only from a Lutheran congregation.[26] Reports of the activities of these missionaries were published by Loehe in his *Kirchliche Mittheilungen,* which aroused sustained interest on the Continent in German compatriots in America. Loehe also prepared and published a map to encourage the gravitation of immigrants toward existing congregations of German Lutheran immigrants.

159

Norway

During the early nineteenth century Norway was experiencing much the same theological transition as was Germany.[27] Orthodoxy had tended more and more in the direction of correct doctrine intellectually asserted and defended. In turn, the subjective nature of pietism was challenged by the same kind of rationalism which came to prevail in Germany.

In rapid succession three major events took place which radically changed the complexion of Norwegian Lutheranism. The first of these was the revival movement which centered in Hans Nielsen Hauge (1771–1824), a powerful lay preacher.[28] Between 1796 and 1804 Hauge preached his message of repentance and regeneration throughout Norway, reviving the backsliders and strengthening and encouraging the faithful. From 1804 to 1811 he was imprisoned not only for his criticisms of church and clergy, but for his violation of the anticonventicle act of 1741.

The second factor to influence Norwegian Lutheranism and closely allied to the Hauge revival was the establishment of the national university at Christiania (now Oslo) in 1811. The new institution was tantamount to a declaration of independence from the Church of Denmark, for prior to this most Norwegian pastors had been educated at the University of Copenhagen. The first two faculty members, Svend Borchmann Hersleb (1784–1826) and Stener Johannes Stenersen (1789–1835), had studied at the University of Copenhagen and were admirers of Hauge. They also enjoyed the friendship of Nicolai F. S. Grundtvig (1783–1872),[29] the controversial Danish theologian who at an early stage of his career was as highly esteemed by pietists as he was deprecated by rationalists, and whose later theological position found acceptance by some Norwegians.

The third factor at work in Norwegian Lutheranism was the blending of pietism and orthodoxy, particularly by Gisle Johnson (1822–94). He held a professorship at the University of Christiania where his teaching aimed at awakening the spiritual life of the Norwegian people and preserving confessional Lutheranism against the inroads of sectarianism and Grundtvigianism. Strongly influenced by confessionalism while a student of Adolf von Harless at Leipzig, Johnson sought to imbue his students with a spirit of orthodoxy which blended the passion

26.
Ibid., pp. 98–101, gives the English text of Loehe's "General Instructions for Our Friends in America."
27.
On the background and development of Norwegian-American Lutheranism see E. Clifford Nelson and Eugene L. Fevold, *The Lutheran Church Among Norwegian-Americans,* 2 vols. (Minneapolis: Augsburg Publishing House, 1960).
28.
On Hauge see G. Everett Arden, *Four Northern Lights* (Minneapolis: Augsburg Publishing House, 1964), pp. 51–76.
29.
On Grundtvig see ibid., pp. 79–113.

and subjectivity of a revival preacher with the intellect of an orthodox systematician. Johnson succeeded in merging elements of the Haugean revival with the confessional awakening and in exerting an influence on his students.

The characteristic Norwegian pattern of voluntary religious organizations independent of the state church took form during Johnson's era. Prior to his leadership in national religious life, the Norwegian [foreign] Mission Society (1842) had been established. By mid-century numerous inner mission societies, dedicated to evangelism in the homeland, had sprung up. Under Johnson's leadership these societies merged into the Norwegian Luther Foundation, whose purposes included distribution of Christian literature, fostering family devotions, assisting young men preparing for the ministry or teaching, and supporting "inner mission" work in general. Unlike many ministers of the state church, Johnson was not antagonistic to lay preaching. On the contrary, he emphasized that where an emergency existed a nonordained person could engage in public preaching. This principle was to become significant among Norwegian Lutherans in America.

Another effect of Johnson's work was a first though hesitant reformatory step toward separating the administration of the church from the state and providing for a national church assembly or synod. Concomitantly, Johnson endeavored to grant the congregations more rights and authority in the selection of their pastors. This latter point followed especially in the wake of objections raised by younger clergymen who found it difficult to enter the service of a state church which made confirmation mandatory but failed to exercise church discipline. Although these and other reforms were not completely realized, it is important to note that Norwegian immigrants brought with them to America the seminal concepts of a voluntary church independent of the state.

And come to America they did. From 1820 to 1865 some 77,874 Norwegians came to America, joined by another 110,896 between 1866 and 1873. In large part the exodus from Norway can be attributed to political, cultural, and economic factors rather than religious motives. Norwegian farmers, who constituted 90 percent of the nation's population, deeply resented the cultural and religious domination which had built up over the long years of Danish rule. Nor did the ceding of Norway to Sweden bring about any radical change. Danish influences were still felt and Swedish influences began to assert themselves. Deep and bitter resentment against all foreign influence as well as against the affluence of the Norwegian upper classes combined to intensify the dissatisfaction of the rank and file. Thus, when famine or other economic calamity struck, Norwegians became infected with "America fever,"

. . . that contagion of excitement about the New World which spread over the entire country, touching every district, every hamlet, almost every family. This was no casual episode, no passing phenomenon but a great social and economic force generated by a combination

of the magnetic attraction of America with fundamental changes in the national economy of Norway. It was a folk movement. . . . [30]

Such a movement was not easily stopped by appeals to reason or fear or even to sentiment. Bishop Jacob Neumann (1772–1848) of Bergen, hoping to deter his people from emigration, issued a pastoral letter which he concluded emotionally by saying:

Here in Norway rest the ashes of your fathers; here you first saw the light of day; here you enjoyed many childhood pleasures, here you received your first impressions of God and of His love; here you are still surrounded by relatives and friends who share your joy and your sorrow, while there when you are far away from all that has been dear to you, who shall close your eyes in the last hour of life? A stranger's hand! And who shall weep at your grave? Perhaps—no one.[31]

The bishop's appeal was not notably successful.

The first Norwegians to arrive in America were the "Sloopers," so called because of the kind of ship in which they arrived. By no means representative of Norwegian immigration, this group, including one Quaker and some Haugeans with Quaker sympathies, arrived in October 1825, and settled in Orleans County, New York. One of the first Norwegian settlements in America was established in the Fox River Valley of Illinois, some seventy miles southwest of Chicago. Beginning in 1834 with only six families, the community was enlarged by the arrival of new immigrants. When the lay preacher Elling Eielsen (1804–83) arrived in 1839, he established his headquarters among these Haugeans. Under his leadership the first house of worship for Norwegian Lutherans in America was constructed. Eielsen's ordination on October 3, 1843, made him the first Norwegian Lutheran pastor to be ordained in America. Other major Norwegian settlements were Jefferson Prairie (1839), Rock Prairie (1839), Muskego (1839), and Koshkonong (1840) in Wisconsin. These areas were selected chiefly because they reminded the immigrants of their beloved meadowlands in Norway. Many of these settlers were Haugeans.

Of the first clergymen to serve these communities, Claus Laurits Clausen (1820–92), a Dane, is of special interest.[32] He had come to America at the prompting of one Tollef O. Bache, a moderately wealthy Haugean. The Muskego settlers, among whom was Bache's son Soren, had called Clausen in 1843 to be a teacher of religion. Shortly he was to become Muskego's first pastor. Enroute to Wisconsin from New York, he was introduced to J. A. A. Grabau in Buffalo, and discussed with the leader of the Prussian immigrant church, later known as the Buffalo Synod, the religious situation among the Norwegians in Wisconsin. Grabau, who laid great stress upon the office of the ordained ministry, expressed concern that the Norwegian settlements were being served by lay preachers rather than by ordained pastors. As a result of these conversations Grabau wrote a letter introducing Clausen to L. F. E. Krause, pastor of the

30.
Theodore C. Blegen, *Norwegian Migration to America: The American Transition* (Northfield, Minn.: Norwegian-American Historical Assoc., 1940), p. 455.
31.
Jacob Neumann, "A Word of Admonition to the Peasants," trans. and ed. Gunnar J. Malmin, in *Norwegian-American Studies and Records* 1 (1926): 108–9.
32.
On Clausen, see Enok Mortensen, *The Danish Lutheran Church in America* (Philadelphia: Board of Publication, LCA, 1967), pp. 28–34.

Old Lutheran settlement at Freistadt, Wisconsin. Clausen discussed with Krause his desire to be ordained and satisfied the latter as to his qualifications for the ministry. The ordination took place on October 18, 1843, in a haymow in Muskego. Krause gives this account of the examination which preceded the ordination:

The local church elders, who had been asked to come as witnesses, came to the local parsonage. The examination was conducted strictly according to the order as set forth in the *Corpore iuris ecclesiastici Saxonici* . . . of the year 1580. In this examination Mr. Clausen gave detailed evidence of his orthodox agreement with the confessions, namely, the symbolical books of the Lutheran Church based on the Word of God, with the result that we acknowledge him fit for the ministry, in the conviction that he is pure in doctrine and, as we hope to God, that he will be subject to this pure doctrine with all his heart.[33]

One of the Norwegian settlers present at the examination noted in his diary: ". . . We went upstairs to hear the examination. There we sat as stiff as wooden images. I did not understand the language. Furthermore I was so sleepy that I had a terrible time keeping my eyes open."[34]

The "state church element" of Norwegian Lutheranism was introduced into America with the arrival of Johannes Wilhelm Christian Dietrichson (1815–83), who came in 1844 to serve the Koshkonong settlement, the largest of the Norwegian settlements. Like Eielsen and Clausen, Dietrichson served numerous other Norwegian settlements, namely the four in Dane County and one in Jefferson County, Wisconsin. But in contrast to Eielsen and Clausen, Dietrichson came as a representative of the Norwegian state church and had been ordained by Bishop Sorenssen of Christiania. In 1850 he returned to Norway.

Over the next few years the ranks of Norwegian clergymen were reinforced. Hans A. Stub (1822–1907), a graduate of the University of Christiania, replaced Clausen at Muskego in 1847 when the latter moved to Luther Valley. Adolph C. Preus arrived in 1850 and succeeded Dietrichson at Koshkonong. Herman A. Preus, who arrived in 1851, was called to serve the congregation at Spring Prairie, Columbia County, Wisconsin. That same year Nils Brandt was sent as a missionary to Iowa, while G. F. Dietrichson, a cousin of J. W. C. Dietrichson's father, succeeded Clausen at Luther Valley, Wisconsin. The following year, Jacob A. Ottesen began his service at Manitowoc, Wisconsin. On Christmas Day, 1853, Ulrik V. Koren embarked on a long pastorate at Washington Prairie near Decorah, Iowa.

As it had for the German immigrants, a pietistic-orthodox theology served the Norwegians as a common bond. Lay preaching, strongly advocated by Eielsen, was accepted by many of the early immigrants, if only as an emergency measure. Nonetheless, other elements, which set the future course of Nor-

162

33.
Meyer, *Moving Frontiers*, pp. 130–31.
34.
Quoted in Nelson and Fevold, *Lutheran Church Among Norwegian-Americans*, 1:90.

wegian organizational structure in America, were present even during the earliest phase of the immigration.

Elling Eielsen had a dislike for both the state church clergy and Grundtvigianism, and had little appreciation of order. Since Dietrichson and Eielsen could not agree, they indulged in mutual faultfinding. Clausen, also influenced by Grundtvigianism, occupied a middle ground. On this background can be traced the course which led to the organization of several synods among Norwegian pioneers.[35]

Sweden

Like Norway, Sweden, too, experienced a rash of "America fever."[36] During the reign of Karl Johan the nation's predominantly agricultural economy was ruled by a relatively small group of aristocratic landholders. America had land, and land meant the kind of future for which Swedes could not hope at home. Moreover, Swedes found America's disregard for social and class distinctions, on which so much stress was laid in the homeland, appealing to their sense of human dignity. Thus, combined with a host of other factors such as heavy and inequitable taxes and compulsory military service, Swedes began to emigrate to America in increasingly larger numbers. During the 1840s, when Sweden's population numbered some 3,000,000 emigration was but a trickle. By the end of the American Civil War the number of Swedish immigrants to America rose to as many as 10,000 a year. It has been estimated that by 1870 the Swedish population in America stood at approximately 97,000, climbing each year until the 1880s and continuing until World War I.

Church membership in Sweden was often tenuous at best. The Swedish theologian Bishop Jesper Svedberg (1635–1735) described the relationship: "People go to church and at times to holy communion, but at the same time live in all manner of sins and deeds of the flesh; no one dare say but that they are good Lutherans and Christians and will without question be saved."[37] It is, then, no surprise that not all Swedish immigrants attached themselves to a Lutheran church in their new home. Those who did hold to the church in America were, for the most part, "Old Lutherans" in the sense that their religious life and outlook was fashioned by a blending of conservative, orthodox theology and pietistic influences, particularly those which issued out of the Evangelical Movement of the nineteenth century. At that time in its life the state church of Sweden was in great need of renewal. Arden describes the church's condition:

The National [state] Church had absorbed elements of rationalism, secularism, and formalism. By reason of its close political ties with the State, the Church often found it difficult to maintain the kind of freedom which would enable it to live close to the common people. Political consideration, local as well as national, rather than the spiritual needs of the people, frequently determined the

35.
Juergen L. Neve, *History of the Lutheran Church in America*, 3d ed., rev. (Burlington, Iowa: Lutheran Literary Board, 1934).
36.
On the background and development of Swedish-American Lutheranism in the nineteenth century see Oscar N. Olson, *The Augustana Lutheran Church in America: Pioneer Period, 1846 to 1860* (Rock Island, Ill.: Augustana Book Concern, 1950).
37.
Quoted in ibid., p. 10.

ecclesiastical attitudes and action. The clergy, supported by public taxation imposed by the State, were so often preoccupied with the details of official record keeping and government reports that they had little time for real pastoral care. Furthermore, especially in the far-flung rural areas, the parishes were so extensive and the distances were so vast that it was difficult for pastors to visit their people, or for the people to attend public worship with any regularity.[38]

164

One of the early protesters against encroaching rationalism in the church was Anders Nohrborg (1725–67). Others who joined in the protest, thereby sparking revivals of personal religion of the heart, were Henrik Schartau (1757–1825), Peter Lorents Sellergren (1769–1839), Jacob Otto Hoof (1768–1839), Pehr Nynan (1794–1856), and Lars Laestadius (1800–1861). Each was a gifted and popular preacher. Schartau, an orthodox pietist, concentrated on the conversion and sanctification of the individual, laying great emphasis upon the church's worship. Educational in his approach, Schartau's catechetical lectures drew large crowds. Sellergren preached repentance and grace and was an advocate of lay preaching. Hoof, something of a mystic and an ascetic, demanded self-denial as evidence of conversion and new life. His sermons were widely read by Swedes in America. Nynan was a revivalist-type preacher whose unconventional manner and language held great appeal for the common man. Laestadius, whose influence was felt mostly among the Finns, was a profoundly emotional, moralistic, and effective preacher of repentance, given to ecstatic trances and the practice of public absolution with the laying-on of hands.

To these revivals, which emphasized the virtues of sobriety and abstinence, was added another element, that of foreign and sectarian influences: Moravianism from Germany, Methodism from England, and Mormonism from the United States. Scottish Congregationalists John Patterson and Ebenezer Henderson preached in Sweden and were instrumental in the formation of Bible societies and the promotion of Bible reading. George Scott, an English Methodist, brought to Sweden an emphasis on sanctification through radical personal reform.

Among those influenced by Scott and who later exerted an influence upon Swedish Lutherans in America were Carl Olof Rosenius (1816–68)[39] and Peter Fjellstedt (1802–81). Orthodox, introspective, and ascetic, Rosenius stressed a theology of "objective justification" which he personalized by emphasis on Bible study and soul-searching favored by the many conventicle groups which had sprung up. Rosenius's influence was also strong in western Norway and among Norwegian-Americans. Fjellstedt later headed a society which recruited ordained ministers and candidates for service among the Swedes in America; he was also the author of a three-volume commentary on the Bible read widely by laymen.

Those for whom the revival movement held appeal were often severely critical of the state church. The movement was, in many respects, a vehicle of protest against what those caught

38.
G. Everett Arden, *Augustana Heritage: A History of the Augustana Lutheran Church* (Rock Island, Ill.: Augustana Press, 1963), p. 5.
39.
On Rosenius see Arden, *Four Northern Lights*, pp. 115–50.

up by the revival regarded as dead formalism, hierarchical intolerance, and the worldliness of many pastors and leaders. Few of the movement's adherents, however, were separatists. Those who leaned in that direction joined the Methodists and Baptists; a few became Mormons. The attitude of the state church toward the revival movement was less than cordial, and on occasion the censorship and anticonventicle laws of an earlier era were invoked, but with little effect. Moreover, like the Church of Norway, the Church of Sweden took a dim view of the increasing rate of emigration, regarding the emigrants as dissenters and sectarians eager to escape the boundaries and mores of their fatherland and mother church. Little assistance was offered from official quarters of the church to those who struck out for the promised land. At first Swedish emigration was a matter of isolated, individual (occasionally family) undertakings. The publication of books about America served to spread the "America fever." Moreover, some of the American states sent representatives abroad to enlist settlers for their territories. Companies of emigrants were formed and ships engaged.

An attempt at Swedish colonization in Kansas around the year 1857 had failed. More successful for a time was the colony at New Uppsala, Pine Lake, Wisconsin, and at Bishop Hill, near Andover, Illinois. The latter, a communistic community, was established by a party led by Erik Janson (1808–50). In Sweden Janson had undergone a second conversion which turned him against pietistic literature. He read only the Bible and soon began to preach, an offense for which he was arrested and fined. Janson became intrigued with the idea of emigration at a temperance rally at which America's religious liberty was portrayed in glowing terms. An advance agent was sent to America and on the basis of his report Janson's company decided on the Illinois site, arriving during the summer of 1846. Over the next few years the colony was augmented by almost fifteen hundred new immigrants; nonetheless, the venture collapsed in 1860.

Another major Swedish settlement developed at Andover, Illinois, where a party of 146 led by Lars P. Esbjorn (1808–70) settled in 1849. The experience of this group with unscrupulous real-estate agents was not uncommon. One agent showed them a colored chart depicting the city of Andover. On the chart the gullible newcomers saw a lovely settlement on the broad banks of the Edwards River, a tributary of the Mississippi, with steamboats trafficking the harbor. The agents offered them the entire town and money for a church in the bargain. The manner in which the site was described suggested that the immigrants were about to take possession of the land of milk and honey. Arden describes the reality they found:

The neat city on the agent's chart turned out to be in fact only a tiny settlement of nondescript houses and shacks, while the broad, deep-flowing Edwards River was in truth little more than a small brook meandering through the hills and marshland, but which nevertheless

**had proved difficult enough to cross without bridges.
The only steamboats which would ever traffic on that
stream were on the real estate map in New York.**[40]

The colony was established however, and it survived despite much sickness and death.

Esbjorn had left Sweden with both royal and episcopal permission. At home he had been strongly influenced by Scott, Rosenius, and Peter Wieselgren (1800-1877). He had been commissioned by the pietistic Swedish Missionary Society to serve as pastor to the group with which he emigrated. This he did faithfully until his return to Sweden in 1863. He conceived his task in America to be to keep Swedish immigrants faithful to the Lutheran church, to make the Lutheran faith vital and real through conscious fellowship with God, and to gather his countrymen into Lutheran congregations. True to his pietistic convictions and in harmony with the voluntary character of the churches in America, Esbjorn insisted upon experience of conversion and a Christian life as conditions of church membership.

Other Swedish settlements and communities grew up at New Sweden, Swede Bend, Stratford, Bergholm (Munterville), Burlington, and McGregor in Iowa; Moline, Rock Island, Genesco, Galesburg, Rockford, and Chicago in Illinois; Lafayette and Attica in Indiana. Chisago Lake (now Center City), St. Paul, Vasa, and Taylors Falls in Minnesota were also the locations of Swedish settlements. Hans Mattson, an early immigrant, left this account of the religious interest in Vasa in 1854:

**One fine Sunday morning . . . all the settlers met under
two oak trees on the prairie . . . for the first religious
service in the settlement. It had been agreed that some
of the men should take turns reading one of Luther's
sermons at each of the gatherings, and I was selected
as reader the first day. Some prayers were said, and
Swedish hymns sung, and seldom did a temple contain
more devout worshippers than did that little
congregation on the prairie.**[41]

While this description is not necessarily typical, that by Eric Norelius (1833-1916) of the Swedes at Chisago Lake is.[42] He described them as thrifty and industrious. The men made tools, farm implements, and furniture while the women tended to spinning and weaving. Their clothing was simple and homespun; their footgear of wood. Swedes in Rockford, Illinois, according to Norelius, were

**. . . poor and living in shabby houses on the east side of
the river . . . full of hope and happy in expectation of
better times. They were very eager to hear the Word of
God. On Sunday we held services in a schoolhouse in
which many window panes were broken; it was cold and
uncomfortable, but all were glad to have some place to
meet.**[43]

In Pecatonica, Illinois, however, the Swedish congregation was very small. Moreover, it was especially resentful of Olof Christian Telemak Andren's preaching against drunkenness.

166

40.
Arden, *Augustana Heritage*, pp. 31-32.
41.
Hans Mattson, *Reminiscences: The Story of an Immigrant* (St. Paul, Minn., 1891), quoted by Olson, *Augustana Church*, p. 81.
42.
On Norelius and his work see G. Everett Arden, ed., *The Journals of Eric Norelius* (Philadelphia: Fortress Press, 1967).
43.
Quoted in English in Olson, *Augustana Church*, p. 184.

Of the early Swedish clergymen one of the most significant was Eric Norelius. As a young man in Sweden he had hoped to become a minister, but his family did not have the means to provide him with the necessary education. On the advice of a pastor he decided to come to America in the hope of acquiring the education and advancement which he could not hope for in Sweden. He landed in New York on October 31, 1850, after a sea voyage that lasted seventy-five days. Like many other Swedish immigrants, his destination was Andover, Illinois. There he spent several months in the home of Esbjorn, who became a lifelong friend. Through Esbjorn young Norelius achieved his ambition of entering the ministry following studies at Capital University in Columbus, Ohio. He spent the next sixty years as a missionary pastor, evangelist, publisher, humanitarian, and churchman. Like most of his ministerial colleagues, Norelius was not a profound thinker. For him Christianity is an experience of the power of the Holy Spirit whereby the gospel becomes the good news of life and salvation appropriated through faith in Christ. Theologically, then, he stood in that tradition in which orthodox doctrine was merged with pietistic warmth.

167

Adjusting to America

The ships on which the immigrants came to America were by no means luxury-liners. While passage was cheap enough—often as low as twenty-five dollars—the passengers were responsible for their own provisions. They provided bedding and other personal necessities, including food (hardtack, butter, cheese, and dried meats), and prepared their meals on deck. Weather permitting, craftsmen plied their trade on deck while the women knitted, sewed, and cooked and the children played or were taught. Needless to say, the decks were frequently the sites of less profitable and more raucous activities during the transatlantic voyages which often lasted three months. Sickness, birth, and death were constant companions during the voyage, as were the crude and unlovely traits of human character and disposition.

Arrival in America was always a confused and chaotic experience. For the most part the immigrants spoke and understood little or no English and were dependent on the self-appointed interpreters and agents who swarmed over the landing docks and railroad stations and were more concerned for their own profit than the welfare of the newly arrived. Blegen describes these scenes quite vividly:

In all the principal cities of this country, but perhaps more so in New York and Chicago, the emigrants on arriving are beset by a number of sharpers and swindlers, mostly of their own countrymen, who attempt in every way to impose upon them and cheat them. Such men are usually runners for emigrant boarding houses, expressmen, hackmen, and exchange brokers. They flock around the emigrants, hurry them about, and by pretended interest, friendship or authority obtain their

baggage checks, get them loaded on to wagons and hurried off to boarding houses, when it is really their desire to go to the next station in order to proceed on their journey, or get their little gold and silver exchanged for them below its real value.[44]

In many instances the newcomers did not realize they had been cheated and hoodwinked until they were hundreds of miles away from the scene of the crime.

Most of these immigrants came seeking land to farm. They got what they came for. Others earned their living by plying trades and crafts learned in the old country. Many Swedes found employment with railroad construction gangs, in logging camps, or as hired farmhands. Few immigrants, according to Forster, were as well prepared to earn their living in America as were the Saxons who had emigrated with Stephan's company. Until they could purchase, clear, and develop the land on which they expected to establish their Zion, Stephan's people had to obtain work in St. Louis. Even after the land had been purchased only a part of the company left the city to establish the settlements. Those who remained were able to work as craftsmen in a city where skilled workers were much needed. This company was also fortunate in that they escaped much of the ire of American nativists, if only because they did not offend the non-German population of St. Louis as did other German elements, which often and loudly talked about a German state.

So far as opposition was concerned, the northern European immigrants often experienced more difficulty from their own countrymen than from native-born Americans. The Saxons in Missouri were repeatedly attacked in the columns of *Der Anzeiger des Westens,* a widely read newspaper of the day. Heinrich Koch, editor of the *Anzeiger,* was an antireligious, anticlerical radical who took particular delight in attacking the Saxons because of their hierarchical polity and fealty to Stephan. Such articles from the *Anzeiger* were widely quoted in Germany. Elsewhere, German immigrants were caught in the conflict between those who were churchly and those who for primarily political reasons had left the fatherland but still carried the torch of their political convictions, ideals, and prejudices in the New World. Among this latter group there was a pronounced hostility toward religion in general and the church in particular.

Of the Swedes in Swede Bend (Stratford), Iowa, Magnus Haakanson, a lay preacher, reported: "To begin with they lead a godless life; not only neglecting religion, but also conducting themselves quite badly in civic matters."[45] In Chicago revival-minded Erland Carlsson and his congregation had to contend with a rough, dissolute, and ungodly element among their countrymen, many of whom disturbed worship services by breaking windows, kicking doors open, and other contemptuous and hostile acts.

More serious than the hostility of fellow countrymen, however, were the divisive factors at work among the churchly immigrants themselves. For the Saxons the chief problem was their leader Martin Stephan. The entire emigration in its reli-

44.
Theodore C. Blegen, "Minnesota's Campaign for Immigrants," in *Swedish Historical Society of America Year Book, 1926,* p. 33.
45.
Olson, *Augustana Church,* p. 105.

gious and financial aspects was under Stephan's absolute control. His authority was absolute to the point that he even censored sermons preached by the clergymen in his group. At first Stephan was challenged on confessional grounds when he excluded from the Emigration Society all who did not subscribe to his episcopate or obey him without question. A number of key individuals began not only to resent Stephan's high-handedness, but to suspect serious mismanagement (if not outright dishonesty) of the society's funds. The bishop, however, was able to silence disgruntlement and challenges to his authority because they were voiced only by individuals whom he could overwhelm by the force of his personality. Stephan's overthrow was enabled when the ministers in his company pressed charges of moral offenses against him. After much maneuvering and with serious misgiving (they stood in fear of Stephan), the man on whose word they had staked their souls was deposed and expelled from their presence and their fellowship. Stephan's deposition, however, was only the first of a series of difficulties which preceded the founding of the Lutheran Church—Missouri Synod.[46]

Among the churchly Swedes internal dissension was promoted by those who had converted to other denominations. Their efforts to win adherents among the Swedish immigrants frequently caused confusion, dissension, and division. One of the major representatives of non-Lutheran work among the Swedes was Gustaf Unonius (1810–1902).[47] A native of Finland, Unonius was discouraged by the lack of unity among Lutherans in America and unsympathetic to Swedish pietism as well as American sects and denominations. He became attracted to the high-church wing of the Episcopal Church, in which he saw a kinship to the state church of Sweden. Although the archbishop of Uppsala discouraged this interest, Unonius received ordination as an Episcopal priest. This did not prevent his serving congregations of Swedish Lutherans, chiefly in Chicago and in Pine Lake, Wisconsin. Although he established a relationship of a kind between the congregations he served and the Episcopal Church, the members were adamant about maintaining their Lutheran identity. Unonius's efforts to win Swedish immigrants to the Episcopal Church were unsuccessful.

Most of the dissension and division was fostered by the work of Methodists Olaf and Jonas Hedstrom and Baptist Gustav Palmquist. Olaf Hedstrom, based in New York City, was in an excellent position to meet newly arrived Swedes and he conducted Methodist services there. It was through him and his brother Jonas that Janson and his people were directed to Illinois. For a time Palmquist exerted a powerful influence over Magnus Haakanson, the Lutheran lay-preacher of New Sweden, Iowa. That influence was so strong that Haakanson actually submitted to rebaptism, but later recanted and returned to the Lutherans.

Contact with American churches and denominations was unavoidable and often confusing for the immigrants. The Saxons conducted their Lutheran services in a church lent by Epis-

169

46.
Forster, *Zion*, pp. 390–442, treats the deposition of Stephan in detail, quoting in English translation from memoirs, letters, and other documents, the autographs of which are in the Concordia Historical Institute, St. Louis.

47.
On Unonius see Arden, *Augustana Heritage*, pp. 22–23; and Gustaf Unonius, *A Pioneer in Northwest America 1841–1858: The Memoirs of Gustaf Unonius*, trans. J. O. Backlund (Minneapolis, 1950), vol. 1.

copalians. This was a welcomed gesture because the German congregation which they found in St. Louis was patterned along the lines of the nonconfessional unionism from which they had fled, and the Saxons wanted no part of such a church. Then, too, the hostile editor of the *Anzeiger,* despite his personal aversion to the church, had considerable influence in that congregation's affairs. The arrangement with the English-speaking Episcopalians was far more comfortable and cordial. With respect to their relationships to native American Lutheranism, particularly to synodical bodies, the Saxons were understandably aloof. They were primarily too occupied with their own immediate situation to become involved with others whom they did not know and of whom they were instinctively suspicious.

The Swedes, however, had a different approach to the religious environment of America. While they were confessionally orthodox, they were also ecumenical in a pietistic sense. For this reason Esbjorn, Tuve Nilsson Hasselquist (1816–91), and others could accept financial support from the Congregationalist-Presbyterian American Home Mission Society. Such financial support did not compromise the Lutheranism of those who accepted it. In a letter to the society Hasselquist made his position clear:

I am with all my heart attached to the Lutheran Confessions, but not so that I should draw back from fellow laboring with brethren of other denominations and oppose them, who do not only wish to make disciples to themselves. I regard the different denominations as members of the body of Jesus Christ, where each of them has its gifts which it must not root out but let it serve to "profit withal." With these principles it is . . . easy to unite faithfulness to my own confessions and love toward them who do not think in all things the same as I.[48]

Swedish contacts with American Lutherans in the East were neither frequent nor intimate. Gettysburg professor William Reynolds was very interested in the welfare of Swedish immigrants and had some contact with those in Chicago, where he was instrumental in exposing the Episcopalianism of Unonius. A Pastor Schweitzerbarth, of Zelienople, Pennsylvania, corresponded with his brother-in-law Fjellstedt in Sweden with the result that a Scandinavian professorship was established at Capital University. Paul Andersen, pastor of a Norwegian congregation in Chicago, had joined the Franckean Synod. Esbjorn had attended a meeting of that synod in 1850 but was not impressed by it. During the spring of 1851 Esbjorn also attended sessions of the Joint Synod of Ohio, the Pittsburgh Synod, and the Ministerium of Pennsylvania in a fund-raising tour which opened the eyes of Eastern Lutherans to the mission task in the west. In a letter to William A. Passavant he said: "I have the hope that a Lutheran Synod may be opened in Illinois and I would be pleased to unite with the same, unless it 'throws away the Augsburg Confession.' I openly confess that I can never unite with a synod which does so."[49]

48.
Quoted in Olson, *Augustana Church,* p. 129.
49.
Ibid., p. 132.

Esbjorn and a Swedish lay delegate were present at the organizing meeting of the Synod of Northern Illinois. At that meeting Esbjorn played a prominent role, insisting for himself and on behalf of the Swedish churches that the synod affirm that the Old and New Testaments are the inspired Word of God; that what the Scriptures do not contain or what cannot be proven by them should not be binding upon faith or practice; that symbols, resolutions, and the like be maintained only insofar as they agreed with the Word of God; and that the confessions of the Lutheran church contain "a correct summary and exposition of the divine word. . . . "[50] Two years later, however, Esbjorn was becoming disenchanted with the Northern Illinois Synod. His increasing tendency toward theological conservatism, his insistence upon controlling the synod's Scandinavian professorship at Illinois State University, and the general Scandinavian unhappiness with the "Americanized" elements of the synod, especially on the question of confessional subscription, paved the way for the Swedes and the Norwegians to withdraw from the synod to establish a body of their own in 1860. To indicate their confessional concern they named the new church the Scandinavian Evangelical Lutheran *Augustana* Synod of North America.

The waves of immigration during the period covered by this section had three distinct and long-lasting effects upon North American Lutheranism. First, immigration had pronounced effect upon Lutheran numerical growth. The influx of so many Lutherans from abroad constituted a gigantic home mission task. Until well into the twentieth century German and Scandinavian immigrants and their offspring were the chief concern of Lutheran home mission effort and the major reservoir upon which the Lutheran churches drew for numerical growth.

Second, the immigration had the effect of establishing and institutionalizing on American soil the Lutheranism of nineteenth-century Europe. Except for those synods in the East (chiefly the Ministeriums of Pennsylvania and New York) whose constituencies still included a number of German-speaking pastors and congregations, the established American synods were linguistically ill-equipped to meet the mission task imposed by the immigration of Germans. For mission work among the Scandinavians they were not at all equipped. The task of churching the immigrants and their offspring, then, fell chiefly to the immigrants themselves. Sharing the common ties of language, heritage, and strangeness in a new land, it was inevitable and necessary that the new Americans organize their own synods and conferences along lines not only of language and nationality but also of theological outlook and religious attitude and custom to which they had adhered in the homeland.

Third, immigration had an isolating and introverting effect upon Lutherans in their relationships to each other and to other American Protestants. In part this was due to the barrier of language. Beside German, the use of which was greatly reenforced by the immigration, two other languages, Norwegian and Swedish, were introduced in America as media of Lutheran

50.
Synod of Northern Illinois, *Minutes . . . 1851*, p. 5, quoted in Olson, *Augustana Church*, pp. 244-45.

worship and communication. In part the isolation was caused by theological differences (real, imagined, and superficial) which became entangled with the emotional problems and struggles of acculturation. The Lutheranism these immigrants found in America was looked upon with suspicion, and other forms of Protestantism were rejected out of hand. Thus, for most of the next century Lutherans were preoccupied with gathering and meeting the (often parochial) needs of their own people, and with overcoming the barriers which separated them from each other.

10   Expansion and Concern

1.
Andrew M. Greeley, *Why Can't They Be Like Us?* (New York: E. P. Dutton & Co., 1971), p. 54.

Andrew M. Greeley, a noted contemporary American sociologist, defines the second phase of immigrant assimilation as consisting of "organization and emerging self-consciousness." He continues: " . . . The immigrant group begins to become organized; its clergy, its precinct captains, the leaders of its fraternal organizations, its journalists, become the key figures in the communities."[1] The developments among the German and Scandinavian Lutheran immigrants of the nineteenth century substantiated Greeley's conclusion. Under the dual pressures of assimilation and self-preservation affecting the immigrants' culture and theology, new church organizations quickly appeared between 1840 and 1875. Almost sixty independent church bodies were organized (see table 2). As expected, the religiously inclined immigrants gravitated toward their own ethnic groups and at the same time produced variations in polity and theology as they established their separate organizations. Some of the immigrant synods patterned their structures after the churches in their homelands, while others endeavored to create new and independent bodies, some of which reflected theological emphases differing from the mother churches.

In a general way, Lutherans in America prior to the 1840s had established "state synods." Such a pattern corresponded roughly with the European concept of territorial or provincial churches though independent of the civil authority. The formation of a single Lutheran church in America with geographical or district synods as envisioned by the General Synod in the 1820s seemed a logical extension of the idea, but some of the new immigrants found this unacceptable. Ethnic and theological particularities, therefore, led to the establishment of independent synodical structures.

The organization of church bodies by the German and Scandinavian Lutherans put an ecclesiastical capstone on the immigration. The German synods included Ohio (1818), Buffalo (1845), Missouri (1847), Wisconsin (1850), and Iowa (1854). The Scandinavian groups were the Eielsen Synod (1846), the Norwegian Synod (1853), the Scandinavian Augustana Synod (1860), the Norwegian-Danish Augustana Synod (1870), the Norwegian-Danish Conference (1870), and the Danish Evangelical Lutheran Church in America (1872).

Most of these frontier synods emerged in the Mississippi Valley. Their growth and expansion were rapid and extensive. After the first organizational processes had been completed, these synods, as well as the Eastern Lutherans, launched aggressive mission programs. These included home missions, work among the American Indians, support of fellow Lutherans in

Canada, and work in foreign fields. The need for training a native ministry led them to establish theological seminaries. Existing needs for church books produced a variety of publication ventures culminating in modern publishing programs.

The Joint Synod of Ohio[2]

The Synod of Ohio had been organized as a conference in 1812. At the turn of the century German-speaking missionaries had been sent into Ohio by the Pennsylvania Ministerium. John Stough [Stauch] (1762–1845), who later became the first president of the Ohio Synod, was the leading figure among the early missionaries in the state. At the time of its formal organization at Somerset, Ohio, in 1818, the new synod counted seventeen pastors and approximately seventy-five parishes. Peacefully separating from its mother, the Pennsylvania Ministerium, the new synod adopted the Ministerium's constitution in its entirety with the exception of the name. As noted earlier, the Ohio Synod came to be known as the Joint Synod of Ohio after 1831 (see chapter 7). Since the new church body was bilingual, it experienced rapid growth. As time went on, Ohio became increasingly conservative and confessional.

These developments, together with the language problem, created difficulties, especially with respect to Ohio's seminary at Columbus. Founded in 1830, the school had originally been established at Canton, Ohio, with Wilhelm Schmidt as instructor. After one year it was moved to Columbus, Ohio, where it has remained to the present. William Reynolds (1812–76) became its first president. A preparatory department was added in 1850 when the institution was renamed Capital University. Until 1959 both the college and seminary were operated as a joint institution. Among its early leaders were William F. Lehmann, its president for many years, and Matthias Loy. The synod's attempt to pursue a bilingual course created two opposing forces: one (the German) clamored for greater conservatism; the other (the English) sought adjustment to the American scene. Consequently the seminary was attacked by its German constituency for its spirit of accommodation, and by its English District for its intolerance and conservatism.

The synod's initial constitution did not require confessional subscription on the part of its members. Beginning in 1836, however, minor revisions in a confessional direction were made. Despite these changes, large numbers of the German constituency were dissatisfied. Some of them withdrew in 1845 and later became partially responsible for the organization of the Missouri Synod. Finally, in 1854 the synod altered its constitution by adopting a new article:

This Synod shall be composed of representatives from all Ev. Luth. Synods, now united in the existing Synod of Ohio, and such other Synods as may from time to time adopt this constitution, and with us adhere to the doctrine of the word of God as set forth in all the Symbolical Books of the Evangelical Lutheran Church,

2.
Sources for the history of the Ohio Synod include Clarence V. Sheatsley, *History of the Evangelical Lutheran Joint Synod of Ohio and Other States* (Columbus, Ohio: Lutheran Book Concern, 1918), and Willard D. Allbeck, *A Century of Lutherans in Ohio* (Yellow Springs, Ohio: Antioch Press, 1966).

174

Table 2

**Lutheran Church Bodies
Organized
Between 1840 and 1875**

Note:
Abbreviations are used to
indicate the original
and/or later general church
relations.

GS	General Synod
GC	General Council
USS	United Synod South
SC	Synodical Conference
Ind.	Independent

1840				Ev. Luth. Synod of the West, (GS)
1840				English Ev. Luth. Synod of Ohio I, (GS)
1842				Southwestern Virginia Synod, (GS,USS)
1842				East Pennsylvania Synod, (GS)
1842				Allegheny Synod, (GS)
1844				Miami Synod, (GS)
1845				Buffalo Synod, (Ind.)
1845				Pittsburgh Synod of the Ev. Luth. Church, (GS)
1846				Southwest Synod, (GS)
1846				Eielsen Synod, (Ind.)
1846				Indianapolis Synod, (Ind.)
1846				Ev. Luth. Synod of Illinois, (GS)
1847				Missouri Synod, (SC)
1847				Central Virginia Synod, (Ind.)
1847				Wittenberg Synod of the Ev. Luth. Church of Ohio, (GS)
1848				Tuscawaras Synod, (Ind.)
1848				Olive Branch Ev. Luth. Synod of Indiana, (GS)
	1850			Wisconsin Synod, (SC)
	1851			Northern Illinois Synod, (GS)
	1851			First Ev. Luth. Synod of Texas, (GS,GC)
	1853			Norwegian Ev. Luth. Church of America (Norwegian Synod), (SC)
	1854			Ev. Luth. Synod of Iowa (and Other States), (Ind.)
	1854			Salem Ev. Luth. Synod of Ohio and Adjacent States, (Ind.)
	1854			Ev. Luth. Synod of Kentucky, (GS)
	1855			English Ev. Luth. Synod of Ohio and Adjacent States II, (GS,GC)
	1855			Ev. Luth. Synod of Central Pennsylvania, (GS)
	1855			Ev. Luth. Synod of Iowa, (GS)
	1855			Mississippi Synod, (USS)
	1855			Northern Indiana Synod, (GS)
	1856			Southern Illinois Synod, (GS)
	1857			Melanchthon Synod, (GS)
	1857			District Synod of Ohio, (GC)
	1859			Union Synod of the Ev. Luth. Church, (GS)
		1860		Augustana Synod, (GC)
		1860		Ev. Luth. Synod in the State of Georgia, (USS)
		1860		Holston Synod, (GS,GC,USS)
		1860		Ev. Luth. Synod of Minnesota, (SC)
		1860		Ev. Luth. Synod of Michigan, (SC)
		1861		Canada Synod, (GC)
		1861		Ev. Luth. Synod of New Jersey, (GS)
		1862		Concordia Synod of the West, (Ind.)
		1866		Steimle Synod (German Ev. Luth. Synod of New York and other States), (Ind.)
		1867		Central Illinois Synod, (GS)
		1867		Ev. Luth. Synod of Illinois and other States, (GC)
		1867		Ev. Luth. Synod of New York, (GS)
		1867		Susquehanna Synod of the Ev. Luth. Church in the U.S., (GS)
		1868		Concordia Synod of Virginia, (SC)
		1868		Kansas Synod, (GS)
			1870	Norwegian-Danish Augustana Synod in America, (Ind.)
			1870	Norwegian-Danish Conference, (Ind.)
			1871	Indiana Synod of the Ev. Luth. Church, (GC)
			1871	Ev. Luth. Synod of Nebraska, (GS)
			1872	Church Missionary Society (Danish Luth. Church, 1874), (Ind.)
			1872	Finnish Apostolic Luth. Congregation, (Ind.)
			1872	New York and New Jersey Synod, (GS)
			1874	Swedish Ev. Luth. Ansgarius Synod in the United States, (GS)
			1875	Immanuel Synod, (Ind.)
			1875	Wartburg Synod, (GS)

or who in their own Constitution confess and maintain the unaltered Augsburg Confession and Luther's smaller Catechism in the sense and spirit of the other symbols.[3]

Beginning in 1842, the synod published the *Lutheran Standard* as its English organ, and initiated a German publication, the *Lutherische Kirchenzeitung,* in 1860. Both publications served to strengthen the confessional character of the synod.

Largely influenced by the Pennsylvania Ministerium and the Tennessee Synod, the Ohio Synod did not join the General Synod when that body was formed in 1821. During the controversy over the *Definite Platform* in the 1850s (see chapter 11), Ohio gravitated toward Missouri, and through the "free conferences" of the late 1850s became a cofounder of the Synodical Conference in 1872. Although initially interested in the formation of the General Council, Ohio never joined. In 1930 the Joint Synod of Ohio became a part of the American Lutheran Church.

The Buffalo Synod[4]

Established in 1845 as "The Synod of the Lutheran Church Emigrated from Prussia" by J. A. A. Grabau in Milwaukee, Wisconsin, the Buffalo Synod attracted many who emigrated under persecution from Silesia and Prussia. It was organized by four clergymen and eighteen lay delegates. From the outset, it adopted all the historic Lutheran confessions and depended heavily upon the old "church orders" from Saxony.[5]

Originally, Grabau hoped to join hands with the Saxon immigrants in Missouri. However, when in 1840 he issued a "Pastoral Letter" to give instructions to congregations under his spiritual care which were without a pastor, he sent a copy to the Saxons to solicit their opinion and support. The document set forth a strong position on church and ministry, opposing vagabond ministers and lay preachers. Grabau emphasized the need for ordination and the practice of sacramental life, stressing the "regularly called" aspects of the pastoral ministry:

Therefore the point of discussion is the public administration of the Holy Sacraments, of which the Confession claims and instructs, that this is not to be done through one who has not been called or who has been improperly called. The Confession calls him "not called" or "improperly called" who is not called *rite,* i.e., called in accordance with the old church polity.[6]

In the "regular call" of the pastor, Grabau included proper training, the necessary spiritual gifts, and provision for the ordinand's examination and ordination before the congregation or its delegates; the laying-on of hands was regarded as an essential part of the act. Grabau held that only in emergencies might a lay Christian dispense a valid and efficacious sacrament.

The "Pastoral Letter" was one of the first documents among immigrants to address the doctrine of the church and the ministry. Most of the immigrants, accustomed to a state church, were now forced to think through the problem of the ministry

3.
Joint Synod of Ohio, *Minutes of the Eighth Session* (New York: H. Ludwig, 1854), pp. 6–7.

4.
Sources for the history of the Buffalo Synod include Paul H. Buehring, *The Spirit of the American Lutheran Church* (Columbus, Ohio: Lutheran Book Concern, 1940), pp. 15–33; Johann A. Grabau, *Lebenslauf des ehrwürdigen J. An. A. Grabau* (Buffalo, N.Y.: Reinecke & Zesch, 1879); *Wachende Kirche,* 63 vols. (1866–1929); and *Kirchliches Informatorium,* 14 vols. (1853–67).

5.
These "church orders," often of territorial or provincial origin, provided legislative and constitutional regulations and procedures for church life and practice. For further study see Emil Sehling, ed., *Die Evangelischen Kirchenordnungen des XVI. Jahrhunderts,* 5 vols. (Leipzig: O. R. Riesland, 1902–13).

6.
Der Hirtenbrief des Herrn Pastors Grabau zu Buffalo vom Jahre 1840 (New York: H. Ludwig, 1849), p. 12, quoted in Roy A. Suelflow, "The Relations of the Missouri Synod with the Buffalo Synod up to 1866," *Concordia Historical Institute Quarterly* 27 (April 1954): 5.

in and for a church free of civil control. Grabau's pastoral letter raised issues that became the cause for future controversy.

The Saxons in Missouri, who had just rebounded from their Stephanite difficulties (see chapter 9 and below) and were caught in an anticlerical atmosphere, were not immediately in a position to reply to the pastoral letter. Almost three years later Gotthold Heinrich Loeber responded for the Saxon clergy:

If we are to give a general opinion of the *Hirtenbrief* [pastoral letter] we will say that in one part, in view of the great emphasis on the old church polity, the essentials are confused with the non-essentials, and the divine with the human. Thus Christian freedom is curtailed. In the other part more is ascribed to the office of the ministry than is proper, so that the spiritual priesthood of the congregations is put last.[7]

The Saxons contended that neither ordination nor installation were divinely commanded but were human arrangements—and thus not absolutely necessary. Grabau held that the congregation owed obedience to its pastors in all things not contrary to God's Word. The Saxons, on the other hand, held to the principle that matters not demanded by Scripture belonged to the realm of Christian liberty and thus should be decided by majority vote.

The battle was on. Not until a colloquy was held between representatives of the two synods in late November and early December 1866 were some issues resolved. The consultation was made possible by an internal rupture in the Buffalo Synod dividing the compact group into two factions, each claiming to be the original synod. The majority, led by Christian Hochstetter and Heinrich von Rohr, found Grabau guilty of error and deposed him as the synod's head. Refusing to accept the decision, Grabau and three other pastors maintained that they constituted the original organization. In the meantime the colloquy between the Buffalo and Missouri synods was held and agreement on the controversial issues was reached. This led the Buffalo majority into the Missouri Synod. Von Rohr, however, refused to accept Missouri's position on the office of the keys, and thus he became the leader of a third Buffalo Synod which, however, was dissolved by 1877 when its members individually joined the Wisconsin Synod.

The original Buffalo Synod (the minority under Grabau) did not officially adopt a constitution until 1886, when considerable modifications in its polity and practices were provided. Its confessional position, however, was demonstrated from the very beginning in pertinent resolutions adopted from time to time at its conventions. Like the Joint Synod of Ohio, this synod became a part of the American Lutheran Church in 1930.

In 1840, five years before the synod was organized, Grabau had established the Martin Luther Seminary in Buffalo, New York. He remained head of the institution until his death in 1879. The institution was closed at the time of the 1930 merger. Publications of the synod included the *Kirchliches Informatorium*

7.
Hirtenbrief, p. 22, quoted in Suelflow, "Relations," p. 10.

177

begun in 1851, and *Wachende Kirche* in 1866. Its English organ, *Forward* was begun in 1914.

The Missouri Synod[8]

The seven hundred immigrants from Saxony, Germany, who settled in Perry County and St. Louis, Missouri, in 1839, began the arduous task of establishing a planned spiritual and secular community. But even before they completed their crude log shelters, their leader, Martin Stephan, was accused of mismanaging accounts and of adultery. After a hasty investigation, Stephan was excluded from the community, and the colonies stood at the brink of collapse. Laymen and clergymen both engaged in soul-searching questions centering on the nature of the church. Were they merely a mob or sect? If so, they had but one alternative, namely, to return to the church of their homeland. On the other hand, if they constituted a church, then order could be created out of chaos. During the immigration they had invested their leader with all the authority of a European bishop. The "Confirmation of Stephan's Investiture" revealed complete submission:

And the more we have come to know of your doctrine, your method, your intention, your faith, your long-suffering, your love, your patience, your persecution, and your tribulations, the more we cannot but give thanks that the gracious and merciful God has kept you for His Church until now, and that your paternal, faithful care for the reflorescence of this dear Church did not permit you to refuse at this perilous time the episcopal office offered to you. . . . Therefore . . . we . . . herewith promise solemnly and before God that we will at all times and with unqualified confidence follow your further paternal leadership, for which we plead, as well as comply with childlike, willing obedience with your episcopal ordinances in all things.[9]

After the expulsion of its leader, a member of the immigrant group and a lawyer by profession, Franz Adolph Marbach, challenged the clergymen to debate the issues regarding the nature of the church. C. F. W. Walther emerged as his opponent, and in April 1841 the two men publicly discussed the doctrines of the church and ministry in the Altenburg Debate. An excerpt from Walther's thesis may help clarify what later was to become a fundamental principle of the polity in the Missouri Synod.

The true Church, in the most perfect sense, is the totality of all true believers, who from the beginning to the end of the world, from among all peoples and tongues, have been called and sanctified by the Spirit through the Word. And since God alone knows these true believers (II Timothy 2:19) the Church is also called invisible. No one belongs to this true Church who is not spiritually united with Christ, for it is the spiritual body of Christ.
The name of the true Church also belongs to all those

8.
Sources for the history of the Missouri Synod include Christian Hochstetter, *Die Geschichte der Evangelisch-lutherischen Missouri-Synode in Nord-Amerika* (Dresden: Verlag von H. J. Naumann, 1885); Walter O. Forster, *Zion on the Mississippi* (St. Louis: Concordia Publishing House, 1953); Carl S. Mundinger, *Government in the Missouri Synod* (St. Louis: Concordia Publishing House, 1947); and Carl S. Meyer, ed., *Moving Frontiers: Readings in the History of the Lutheran Church—Missouri Synod* (St. Louis: Concordia Publishing House, 1964).
9.
Forster, *Zion*, pp. 299–300. The document was adopted on January 14, 1839.

visible societies in whose midst the Word of God is purely taught and the Holy Sacraments are administered according to the institution of Christ. True, in this Church there are also godless men, hypocrites, and heretics, but they are not true members of the Church, nor do they constitute the Church. . . .

Even heterodox societies are not to be dissolved, but reformed. . . . The orthodox church is said to be judged principally by the common, orthodox, and public confession to which the members acknowledge themselves to have been pledged and which they profess.[10]

Shortly after the arrival of the Saxons, the Pennsylvania Ministerium had expressed words of welcome to the immigrants and requested its president, Karl R. Demme, to communicate with them.[11] The extant records do not reveal how the Ministerium's resolutions were carried out. Perhaps because of the chaotic conditions in the Saxon colonies not much happened. However, approximately a year later, one of the Saxon clergymen, Georg Albert Schieferdecker, requested membership in the Ministerium. After a lengthy introduction, he concluded his communication:

In order now, to take all the necessary steps which are required according to God's order, I am herewith applying for placement through the Lutheran Pennsylvania Synod as a candidate for the Holy Ministry or for a teaching position in an elementary or higher institution. . . . I would naturally, gladly subject myself to examination of your honorable Synod.[12]

Although Demme's reply has not been preserved, his report to the Ministerium of Pennsylvania the following year stated: "He renders a most interesting account of his spiritual experiences and development. In my answer, I informed him that, in order to accede to his wishes, it would be necessary for him to appear personally before this body, and encouraged him that he join one of the western synods of our church."[13]

The door was now left open for an affiliation with a "western synod." But contrary to popular opinion the prime mover in the formation of the Missouri Synod was not Walther but Loehe missionaries who had joined the Joint Synod of Ohio. Dissatisfied with their organization, these men met on September 18, 1845, at Cleveland to discuss their concerns. Their criticisms were threefold: the lack of an acceptable confessional standard, the ascendance of English at the seminary in Columbus, Ohio, and the process of Americanization. After discussing these issues the group adopted a formal document of separation. Subscribing unequivocally to all the symbols of the Lutheran church, they declared:

Accordingly, it is a matter of the heart and conscience for us to separate from our former synodical associations in view of the recent decisive results . . . in which the majority decidedly ignored the original constitution of the seminary. In addition—and this, of

10.
For the complete text see *Lutheran Cyclopedia* (St. Louis: Concordia Publishing House, 1954), p. 21.

11.
Pennsylvania Ministerium, "Report of the Executive Committee of the Missionary Society of the Synod of Pennsylvania, Containing Brother Wyneken's Report," *Proceedings of the Missionary Society of the Evangelical Lutheran Synod of Pennsylvania*, appended to *Minutes . . .* (Easton, Pa.: A. H. Senseman, 1839), pp. 5–14, reprinted in *Concordia Historical Institute Quarterly* 20 (October 1947): 124–35.

12.
Letter of Georg A. Schieferdecker to "The honorable Dr. Demme," postmarked August 13, 1840, Krauth Memorial Library Archives, Lutheran Theological Seminary, Philadelphia.

13.
Pennsylvania Ministerium, *Verhandlungen . . . 1841*, p. 7.

course is the chief reason for our separation—it has taken the crying need of our church and its oppression by false union so little to heart that it will not grant even the most legitimate request for aid to the most urgent need; finally, too, it has neither ear nor eye for the oral and written explanations of these requests.[14]

Their subsequent query of the Saxons in St. Louis ascertaining interest in forming a new church body was met with enthusiasm. As a result the separated Ohioans and the Saxon Missourians met in St. Louis in May 1846 to draft a constitution. The confessional paragraph presented its position on Scripture and the confessions:

Acceptance of Holy Scripture, both the Old and the New Testament, as the written Word of God and as the only rule and norm of faith and life.

Acceptance of all the symbolical books of the Evangelical Lutheran Church (these are the three Ecumenical Symbols, the Unaltered Augsburg Confession, the Apology, the Smalcald Articles, the Large and the Small Catechism of Luther, and the Formula of Concord) as the pure and unadulterated explanation and presentation of the Word of God.[15]

A third group of German immigrants consisting chiefly of the Loehe settlements in the Saginaw Valley, Michigan, joined the discussions when a third meeting was held in Fort Wayne in July 1846. Thus, numerically augmented, the constituting convention was held in Chicago in April 1847. Twenty-five congregations were represented through twelve voting and ten advisory pastors. Only four lay delegates were present. Because of its earlier "episcopal" experiences under Stephan, the new synod developed a distinctive congregational polity. Its constitution emphasized:

Synod is in respect to the self-government of individual congregations only an advisory body. Therefore no resolution of the former, when it imposes anything upon the individual congregation as a synodical resolution, has binding force for the latter.—Such a synodical resolution has binding force only when the individual congregation through a formal congregational resolution has voluntarily adopted and confirmed it.—Should a congregation find a synodical resolution not in conformity with the Word of God or unsuited for its circumstances, it has the right to disregard, that is, to reject it.[16]

The road from episcopacy to congregationalism was treacherous and difficult. The spiritual distress, self-accusations, and soul-searching molded the synod indelibly.

At the time of its organization the synod adopted as its official organ *Der Lutheraner,* which first had made its appearance in 1844 under Walther's editorship. An English periodical, *Lutheran Witness,* was started in 1882. In 1855 a theological journal, *Lehre und Wehre,* was added to the synod's list of publications. After Wilhelm Loehe transferred his Indian mission enterprises

14.
Kirchliche Mitteilungen 4, no. 2 (1846): col. 8, trans. in August R. Suelflow, "The Missouri Synod Organized," in Meyer, *Moving Frontiers,* p. 146.
15.
"Synodalverfassung," *Der Lutheraner,* September 5, 1846, p. 2, trans. Roy A. Suelflow in *Concordia Historical Institute Quarterly* 16 (April 1943): 3.
16.
"Die neue Verfassung oder Constitution der deutschen ev. luth. Synode von Missouri, Ohio u. a. Staaten," *Der Lutheraner,* June 21, 1853, p. 146, quoted in A. R. Suelflow, "Missouri Synod Organized," p. 151.

17.
Carl S. Meyer, *Log Cabin to Luther Tower: Concordia Seminary . . . 1839-1964* (St. Louis: Concordia Publishing House, 1965).
18.
Walter A. Baepler, *A Century of Blessing* (Springfield, Ill., 1946).
19.
Sources for the history of the Iowa Synod include Gerhard S. Ottersberg, "The Evangelical Lutheran Synod of Iowa and Other States, 1854-1904" (Ph.D. diss., University of Nebraska, 1949); Johannes Deindoerfer, *Geschichte der Evangel.-Luth. Synode von Iowa* (Chicago: Wartburg Publishing House, 1897); Karl Eichner, *Wilhelm Loehe*, 2d ed. (Chicago: Wartburg Publishing House, 1908); and George J. Zeilinger, *A Missionary Synod with a Mission* (Chicago: Wartburg Publishing House, 1929).
20.
Kirchliche Mittheilungen, no. 6 (1848), col. 44.

in Michigan and his Fort Wayne seminary to the synod, it was challenged to continue extensive programs. In 1854 the synod divided itself in four geographical districts (western, northern, eastern, and central) because of its expanding home mission work.

The log-cabin seminary which had been established by the Saxons in Perry County, Missouri, in 1839 became the clergy-training institution of the synod at the time of its founding in 1847. The institution was permanently transferred to St. Louis, Missouri, in 1849, the year when its first president, C. F. W. Walther, began his long career there. Other instructors during this period were Friedrich A. Craemer and Ernst A. Brauer.[17]

Closely allied with the St. Louis school is Concordia Theological Seminary of Springfield, Illinois. It traces its history to 1844 when Friedrich C. D. Wyneken began the instruction of two missionaries in his parsonage at Fort Wayne, Indiana. With the assistance of Loehe, the seminary was formally established in 1846 under the direction of Wilhelm Sihler. The institution remained in Fort Wayne until 1861 when it was joined to the St. Louis seminary. However, in 1875 it was moved to Springfield, Illinois, where it occupied the buildings formerly used by Illinois State University (Synod of Northern Illinois) and where it remains today.[18]

The Iowa Synod[19]

Shortly after the Loehe-sponsored agencies in America had been transferred to the new Missouri Synod, Wilhelm Loehe (1808-72), who had sent hundreds of "missioners" to the scattered and orphaned settlements in America and had organized Lutheran Indian missions, found himself in disagreement with the Missouri Synod's democratic, congregational church polity. Even though both Wyneken and Walther visited him in Neuendettelsau in 1851 to discuss the differences, Loehe's leanings remained closer to the position of Grabau. To Loehe, Missouri's polity was nothing more than "American mob-rule." He opposed Walther's formulation of the "transference theory," according to which the congregation, as participating in the universal priesthood of believers, held all the rights and powers of the ministry and transferred the public exercise of these functions to a pastor through its call. As early as 1847, Loehe commented on the Missouri Synod's constitution: "We fear certainly with a perfect right, that the fundamental strong mixing of democratic, independent, congregationalistic principles in your constitution will cause great harm, just as the mixing in of princes and secular authorities in our land has done."[20]

When no resolution of the difficulties between Loehe and Missouri was achieved, it was agreed that Loehe's adherents would leave the state of Michigan and migrate to Iowa. George Grossmann (1823-97) and Johannes Deindoerfer (1828-1907) led this exodus of some twenty persons in September 1853. When the small party arrived at Dubuque they were virtually destitute. Some of the party moved some sixty miles farther west and founded the small community of St. Sebald in Clayton

181

County. Abject poverty prevailed everywhere. In spite of this, Grossmann reestablished the teacher's seminary in Dubuque, the institution which had formerly been located in Saginaw, Michigan. That same year (1853) the school developed into a full theological seminary. After brief periods of location in St. Sebald, Iowa, and Mendota, Illinois, Wartburg Seminary was permanently located in Dubuque in 1889. Since 1930, it has been maintained by the American Lutheran Church. The Fritschel brothers, Sigmund (1833-1900) and Gottfried (1836-89), served as the mainstays of its faculty during the nineteenth century.

21.
Deindoerfer, *Geschichte*, p. 41, trans. in Fred W. Meuser, *The Formation of the American Lutheran Church* (Columbus, Ohio: Wartburg Press, 1958), pp. 24-25.

The German Evangelical Lutheran Synod of Iowa was organized at St. Sebald, Iowa, by four clergymen—George Grossmann, Johannes Deindoerfer, Sigmund Fritschel, and Michael Schueller—who met in the uncompleted local parsonage. Grossman was elected president and Fritschel secretary. A treasurer was unnecessary because there were no funds. No formal constitution had been prepared, and since the number of the organizers was so small (there were no lay delegates present) only a brief confessional statement was adopted:

The synod subscribes to all the symbolical books of the Evangelical Lutheran Church because it recognizes all the symbolical decisions on controverted questions before or during the time of the Reformation as corresponding to the divine Word. But because within the Lutheran Church there are different tendencies, the Synod espouses that one which strives for greater completeness by means of the confessions and on the basis of the Word of God. In the founding of congregations the synod is not content with mere acceptance of its principles of doctrine and life, but requires probation and therefore re-establishes the catechumenate of the ancient church. The goal to be sought in its congregations is the apostolic life; to attain this, official and fraternal discipline is to be practiced.[21]

Thus another German Midwestern synod came into being. Although the Iowa Synod received wholehearted support from Loehe, its doctrinal stand was attacked by more conservative Lutherans. The confessional paragraph, it was argued, lacked precision and definiteness and was open to subjective interpretation. In defense the synod adopted a series of theses in 1856, hoping thereby to elaborate its confessional position. This explanation, however, was not acceptable to Buffalo, Ohio, and Missouri. In the meantime, the relationships between Missouri and Iowa deteriorated still further when two pastors of the Missouri Synod, accused of chiliastic views, were received by Iowa in 1858. Thus, beside the attitude toward the confessions and the doctrine of church and ministry, chiliasm was added to the points of difference.

The synod in 1858 began the publication of its *Kirchenblatt*, and under the editorship of the Fritschel brothers, its theological journal, *Kirchliche Zeitschrift*, in January 1876. Loehe's mission zeal was carried forth through the synod's abortive attempts to bring the gospel to the Crow, Cheyenne, and Arapahoe Indians in Montana and Wyoming between 1859 and 1867. When the General Council was formed in 1867 Iowa participated in the discussions but preferred advisory to voting membership. It maintained its separate existence until 1930 when it became a part of the American Lutheran Church.

The Wisconsin Synod[22]

The Wisconsin Synod drew its membership from the scattered German immigration which arrived in Wisconsin in the late 1830s and 1840s. Unlike the founding of the Missouri, Buffalo, and Iowa synods, there was no planned Lutheran immigration to Wisconsin which served as the nucleus for its formation. Some of the early Wisconsin settlers had been a part of the 1839 Grabau immigration and held membership in the Buffalo Synod.

Three immigrant clergymen hold the distinction of being the founders of the Wisconsin Synod: John Muehlhaeuser, John Weinmann, and Wilhelm Wrede. All three were commissioned by the Langenberg Mission Society, a European agency supported both by the Reformed and Lutheran churches, established for the purpose of supporting German Protestants in America. Muehlhaeuser, a former baker, received his theological training at the mission school at Barmen. In October 1837 he arrived in New York, where he was ordained by the New York Ministerium. Shortly thereafter he served a parish in Rochester, New York, a member of the General Synod.

Weinmann and Wrede arrived in America in July 1846. Both had been sent to serve the Germans in Milwaukee and neighboring settlements. Thus Weinmann served Town Oakwood, near Milwaukee, while Wrede was stationed at Granville, Wisconsin. Upon the urging of Weinmann, Muehlhaeuser joined the two in 1848 to serve the Germans in Milwaukee. Not particularly attracted to the Old Lutherans who had already established congregations in the area, Muehlhaeuser found himself in a dilemma. He was determined to be a Lutheran, but, because of his associations, harbored an aversion to Old Lutheranism. This accounts for the fact that Muehlhaeuser organized a separate synod, even though the Missouri and Buffalo synods were both represented in Wisconsin.

With the support of Weinmann and Wrede, Muehlhaeuser conducted a preliminary meeting in Milwaukee in December 1849. Realistically, the group chose the name "First Evangelical Lutheran Synod of Wisconsin" for the new synod. Muehlhaeuser was elected president, Weinmann secretary, and Wrede treasurer. A constitution was drafted and presented to a second meeting held in Granville, Wisconsin, in May 1850. By that time two additional clergymen joined the group for a total of five pastors serving eighteen congregations. Patterned after the constitution of the New York Ministerium, the young synod reflected the ministerium type of government. The first paragraph stated: "We . . . call this our gathering 'the German Evangelical Ministerium of Wisconsin,' and our meeting 'a

22.
Sources for the history of the Wisconsin Synod include John P. Koehler, *Geschichte der Allgemeinen Evangelisch-Lutherischen Synode von Wisconsin und anderen Staaten* (Milwaukee: Northwestern Publishing House, 1925); and Martin Lehninger et al., *Continuing in His Word* (Milwaukee: Northwestern Publishing House, 1951), prepared by the Centennial Committee of the Wisconsin Synod. The Koehler volume has been published in English, edited and with an introduction by Leigh D. Jordahl as *The History of the Wisconsin Synod* (St. Cloud, Minn.: Sentinel Publishing Co., 1970).

183

Ministerial Assembly,' and our gathering with the delegates of the congregations assembled 'a synodical assembly.' "[23] In practice, candidates for the ministry were examined only by the clergy members of the synod. The decision whether a pastor was to be included or excluded from synodical membership was confined to the clergy. Candidates were licensed for a two-year period prior to their ordination.

The constitution for the new synod lacked a confessional paragraph. However, in its provisions for ordination the ministerial candidates were pledged to the confessions: "At the time of his ordination, each candidate shall be pledged to the Augsburg Confession and to the other confessions of the Evangelical Lutheran Church."[24] Gradually, and in keeping with the times, the synod became increasingly more confessional. In a large degree this was due to the influence of John Bading (1824-93), also an emissary of the Langenberg Society, who arrived in Wisconsin in 1853. Probably under the influence of Ludwig Harms (1808-65) of Hermannsburg, Germany, a foe of German rationalism, Bading gained a renewed interest in the confessions. The clerical membership of the synod was further augmented in 1861 by the arrival of Edward F. Moldehnke (1835-1904) and in 1862 by Adolph Hoenecke (1835-1908).

When Bading succeeded Muehlhaeuser as the Wisconsin Synod's president in 1860 he took aggressive steps in developing a greater confessional consciousness. Through his presidential address in 1862, Bading encouraged the synod to reformulate its theological platform. The following year, the church adopted a new confessional statement: "This body acknowledges all the canonical books of the Old and New Testaments as the sole standard of faith, and all the Symbolical Books of the Evangelical Lutheran Church as the proper interpretation of the Word of God."[25] The same confessional adherence was required of any prospective congregation joining the synod.[26] The pattern was now set for a new theological direction.

Prior to the opening of its own seminary in Watertown, Wisconsin, in June 1863, many of the synod clergy had been sent by German mission societies. A few had been trained at the seminary in Gettysburg, Pennsylvania. To obtain funds for the newly created institution, Bading was sent on a fund-raising tour of Germany. Although theological instruction began immediately when Moldehnke started to train two seminarians, the school, known today as Northwestern College, was not formally opened until 1865. Despite the original purpose to conduct a seminary, the synod entered an agreement with the Missouri Synod in 1869 to use Concordia Seminary, St. Louis, as its theological seminary. This left Northwestern College as primarily a pre-seminary preparatory school for its students in Wisconsin. With a faculty of three (Hoenecke succeeded Moldehnke in 1869) the school maintained the arrangement until 1878 when the seminary was once more reopened in Milwaukee, Wisconsin. From 1917 to 1929 it found its home in Wauwatosa, Wisconsin, and since 1929 has occupied its spacious grounds in Mequon, Wisconsin.

23.
Koehler, *Geschichte*, p. 189.
24.
Ibid., p. 191.
25.
Constitution der deutsch-evangel.-lutherischen Synode von Wisconsin (Watertown, Wisc.: Weltbuerger Office, 1863), p. 3.
26.
Ibid., pp. 6-7.

The theological transition, initiated by Bading and Hoenecke, offended the supporting churches and missionary societies in Germany. As a result, the Wisconsin Synod sought closer relationships with other American Lutherans. Thus, in the mid-1860s, Wisconsin began to exchange fraternal delegates with the Iowa Synod. Subsequently, however, Iowa's position on "open questions," which anticipated further theological formulations where differences existed, became distasteful to Wisconsin and the relationship was terminated. Wisconsin also had expressed itself favorably on the formation of the General Council and joined it in 1867. Two years later, however, it withdrew in order to develop closer relationships with the two neighboring synods, namely Minnesota and Michigan, and consequently, in 1872, together with Missouri and Ohio, formed the Synodical Conference.

185

Scandinavian Organizations

The Scandinavians, like the Germans, gravitated into numerous bodies instead of into one general synod. Their theological emphases and personal tendencies also produced several independent synodical organizations.

The Eielsen Synod[27]

The Eielsen Synod was organized in April 1846 by the followers of the Norwegian itinerant lay preacher, Elling Eielsen (1804–83). With the spirit of a crusader he introduced the Haugean lay movement to America and together with his friends established the Evangelical Lutheran Church in America, popularly known as the Eielsen Synod. Born in the midst of the Norwegian awakening, Eielsen stressed the importance of repentance, conversion, and lay preaching. As a result, the new body was based primarily on loose, individualistic ties. Eielsen opposed the ritualism and formalism which he associated with the Norwegian state church. Typical is the reply he gave when someone asked whether minutes of a meeting should be kept: "I have never read that Christ kept any minutes when he went about holding meetings among the people."[28]

Eielsen's associates in organizing the Eielsen Synod in Jefferson Prairie, Wisconsin, in April 1846 were Paul Andersen and Ole Andrewson. Andersen, who had arrived in Wisconsin in 1843, was the most Americanized of the group, a fact partially explained by his training under a Presbyterian pastor in Beloit, Wisconsin. Andrewson, who like Andersen had been associated with the Franckean Synod and the Synod of Northern Illinois, was eager to see the Lutheran church adjust to American ways and culture.

This triumvirate adopted a constitution typifying their faith and action. In the first and second articles of the constitution, they declared that their organization was built "in conformity with the genuine Lutheran faith and doctrine, and built upon God's Word in the Holy Scriptures in conjunction with the Apostolic and Augsburg Articles of Faith."[29] The second article

27.
For information on the Eielsen Synod and other Norwegian synods see E. Clifford Nelson and Eugene L. Fevold, *The Lutheran Church Among Norwegian-Americans*, 2 vols. (Minneapolis: Augsburg Publishing House, 1960).

28.
Quoted by T. J. Bothne, *Kort Udsigt over det Lutherske Kirkearbeide blandt Normaendene i Amerika*, supplement to H. G. Heggtveit, *Illustreret Kirkehistorie* (Chicago: Knut Taklas Forlag, 1898), p. 834. Cited by Nelson and Fevold, *Lutheran Church Among Norwegian-Americans*, 1:127.

29.
Nelson and Fevold, *Lutheran Church Among Norwegian-Americans*, 1:129.

subjectively restricted membership in the synod: ". . . No one ought to be accepted as a member of our body, except he has passed through a genuine conversion or is on the way to conversion."[30] Congregations, moreover, were directed to call converted pastors. Because of its brevity and indefiniteness, the new constitution was criticized by unsympathetic Norwegians. Primary criticism was leveled against its requirement of conversion as a condition of membership, and its failure properly to define the synod's administration and its relationship to the member congregations.

From its beginning the synod led a precarious existence. Two years after its formation, Andrewson and Andersen separated from it. Undaunted, Eielsen called a second meeting in 1850 and attracted another clergyman, Peter Andreas Rasmussen, also a Haugean, who had arrived from Norway that year.

The earliest seminary established among the Norwegian immigrants came into being at Lisbon, Illinois, in October 1855. Rasmussen, its only teacher, taught the three students until May 1856, when the school was closed and Rasmussen accused Eielsen of false doctrine. Once more the small synod was divided with half of its membership supporting Rasmussen. Once more a seminary was opened at Deerfield, Wisconsin, between 1865 and 1867 with Andreas P. Aaserod as instructor. When he resigned the doors were once more closed since a successor could not be found. A final effort in establishing a seminary came when a new institution opened in Chicago in 1871. This, too, ended in failure.[31]

The struggling synod published *Kirkelige Tidende* from 1856 to 1861, and from 1857 to 1862 Eielsen edited *Organ*. The final crisis which the small synod faced came in 1875/76 when two of its five clergymen repudiated Eielsen and organized Hauge's Synod. This rupture grew out of the inadequacies of the earlier constitution and increasing dissatisfaction with both the leadership and theological emphases of Eielsen. When the break occurred the synod numbered 24 pastors, 59 congregations, and approximately 7,500 members. Hauge's Synod, though retaining the pietistic characteristics of the older body and considering itself the legitimate continuation of the original body (1846), found it necessary to give greater attention to constitutional and formal matters. Neither of the two church bodies are in existence today. The Eielsen Synod had virtually disappeared by the late 1960s and the Hauge Synod had become a part of the merger of 1917, the Norwegian Lutheran Church of America.

The Norwegian Synod[32]

The Norwegian Evangelical Lutheran Church in America, the second church to be formed by Norwegians, was organized at Luther Valley, Wisconsin, October 3-7, 1853. In its initial stages it bore some of the characteristics of the Church of Norway both in theology and tradition. This was due in part to J. W. C. Dietrichson, who contributed significantly to its development even prior to its formal organization. Before Dietrichson

30.
Ibid., p. 130.
31.
Ibid., p. 143.
32.
The history of the Norwegian Synod during this period is also treated in S. C. Ylvisaker, ed., *Grace for Grace: Brief History of the Norwegian Synod* (Mankato, Minn.: Lutheran Synod Book Co., 1943); and Johann C. K. Preus et al., eds., *Norsemen Found a Church* (Minneapolis: Augsburg Publishing House, 1953). The most extensive treatment of the Norwegian Synod is Gerhard Belgum's "The Old Norwegian Synod . . . " (Ph.D. diss., Yale University, 1957). The most recent work on Dietrichson is E. Clifford Nelson, ed., *A Pioneer Churchman: J.W.C. Dietrichson in Wisconsin 1844-1850* (New York: Twayne Publishers, Inc., 1973).

returned to Norway in 1850 he had laid the groundwork for a synod on the basis of a constitutional draft which included a doctrinal, liturgical, and disciplinary platform.

Several preliminary meetings prior to the organization were required. The first, held in January 1851 at Luther Valley, Wisconsin, elected Adolph Carl Preus chairman. The matter which provoked the greatest discussion was the name of the new body. A tentative constitution provided for a superintendent, to which the Dane Claus L. Clausen was elected. The position would enable the synod to function until a second meeting could be held. In the meantime prospective members were to seek approval of their congregations for the proposed constitution and to submit their reaction. Formal organization, however, was not to develop immediately. With the arrival of new clerical manpower from Norway, opposition began to develop against Dietrichson's draft of the constitution because of its Grundtvigian paragraph which tended to place the baptismal confession (Apostles' Creed) above Scripture as the criterion of Christian teaching:

The doctrine of the Church is that which is revealed through God's Holy Word in our baptismal covenant and also in the canonical books of the Old and New Testaments, interpreted in agreement with the Symbolical Writings of the Church of Norway, which are: 1) the Apostolic Creed, 2) the Nicene Creed, 3) the Athanasian Creed, 4) the Unaltered Articles of the Augsburg Confession which was delivered to Emperor Charles V at Augsburg 1530, 5) Luther's Small Catechism.[33]

The new clergymen who arrived in America rejected Grundtvigianism as did the majority of Lutherans in Norway. Thus, the criticisms of the phrase "in our baptismal covenant" in the proposed constitution were thoroughly aired at the second meeting held at Muskego, Wisconsin, in February 1852. In addition to the theological criticism, there was also a growing fear of clerical domination with the result that when the February 1852 meeting convened, only six congregations sent delegates. For the new arrivals, led by Herman Amberg Preus, only a dissolution of the 1851 organization proved acceptable. When this was granted, several additional clergy and lay delegates were received, bringing the total to six pastors and thirty-seven delegates representing twenty-one congregations.

In February 1853 the group adopted the constitution, and in October of the same year the Norwegian Evangelical Lutheran Church in America was formally organized at Luther Valley, Wisconsin. Adolph C. Preus was elected president by the six pastors and delegates representing seventeen congregations located in Illinois, Iowa, and Wisconsin. Clausen, who had played a prominent part in the preliminary meetings, was absent, having accepted a call to St. Ansgar, Iowa. The new church adopted the confessional paragraph excising the last vestige of Grundtvigianism by eliminating the phrase "in our baptismal covenant."

33.
C. Anderson, "Historical Sketch of the Beginnings, Growth and Development of the Norwegian Synod," in Ylvisaker, *Grace*, pp. 35–36.

The polity of the church, described as "synodical-presbyterial," placed the highest authority in the synod. The synod reserved for itself disciplinary supervision over its pastors, responsibility in making initial judgments in religious-ecclesiastical matters, and the authority to call extraordinary sessions.[34] This contrasted with the congregational polity of the newly organized Missouri Synod. The new synod grew rapidly as it was augmented by large numbers of immigrants from Norway.

A few years after its organization, the synod established close ties with the Missouri Synod by means of a joint theological seminary program. In 1855 the synod sent Nils Brandt and Jacob A. Ottesen to investigate the seminaries of the Ohio Synod in Columbus, Ohio, the Buffalo Synod in Buffalo, New York, and the Missouri Synod in St. Louis, Missouri, with a view toward utilizing one or more of them to educate its students. When the synod met again in 1857 the committee recommended Concordia, St. Louis. Unanimously the convention resolved to make the necessary arrangements to establish a professorship. As a result, Lauritz Larsen was called to fill this position in 1859. He remained until 1861 when antithetical attitudes on the Civil War and the slavery issue caused a disruption of the relationship. Simultaneously, the seven Norwegian students at Concordia returned to the North. When Luther College was established at Half Way Creek, Wisconsin, in October 1861, Larsen became its president. The Concordia professorship for Norwegians remained vacant until Friedrich August Schmidt, the second teacher at Luther College, was called to Concordia in 1872. He remained until 1876 when the Norwegian Synod established Luther Seminary at Madison, Wisconsin. In 1888 the institution was transferred to Minneapolis, Minnesota. Finally, in 1899 it was moved to St. Paul, Minnesota. In 1917 it and the Hauge's seminary were merged with the United Church Seminary in St. Paul, the present Luther Theological Seminary.

The synod published *Kirklige Maanedstidende* beginning in 1856 and changed its name in 1874 to the *Evangelisk Luthersk Kirketidende*. An English periodical, the *Lutheran Watchman*, appeared briefly from 1866 to 1868. The university-trained clergymen of the synod emphasized the theological and liturgical tradition of the Norwegian state church. One can better understand the frontier anticlericalism of low-church Ellingians and Haugeans when it is realized that the latter saw the high view of the ministry and the general authoritarianism of the Church of Norway reflected in the Norwegian Synod. Moreover, when this synod established fellowship with the Missouri Synod in the Synodical Conference (1872), it only served to heighten the growing conviction that two widely different religious ideologies were separating Norwegian Lutherans in America.

The Norwegian-Danish Augustana Synod
Formed in 1870, the Norwegian-Danish Augustana Synod traced its roots back to the Synod of Northern Illinois organized in 1851. This latter synod drew its membership from American

34.
Nelson and Fevold, *Lutheran Church Among Norwegian-Americans*, 1:159–60.

Lutherans, as well as from German, Swedish, and Norwegian Lutheran immigrants. It held membership in the General Synod. Its ethnic heterogeneity, however, was short-lived. In the throes of the theological tensions precipitated by the circulation of the "American Lutheran" *Definite Synodical Platform* in 1855, the Scandinavians, as noted earlier, withdrew from the Northern Illinois Synod to form the Scandinavian Augustana Synod in 1860.

The Norwegians in the new Scandinavian synod held to a mediating position between the Eielsen Synod and the Norwegian Synod. The latter criticized the Augustanans as being theologically ambivalent, whereas the Eielsen group considered them "spiritually" deficient. Ten years later, in 1870, the Norwegians and the Swedes in the Augustana Synod separated peacefully to form separate national groups. Unfortunately, the Norwegians who left Augustana could not agree among themselves, and instead of forming a single body, as did the Swedes, they established two additional Norwegian bodies. One adopted the name "Norwegian-Danish Augustana Synod," and the other the name "Conference for the Norwegian-Danish Evangelical Lutheran Church in America," usually referred to as "the Conference." Thus by 1875 there were five separate Norwegian church organizations in America: Eielsen's Synod, Hauge's Synod, the Norwegian Synod, the Norwegian-Danish Conference, and the Norwegian-Danish Augustana Synod. Of these, the Norwegian Synod was by far the strongest, while the Norwegian-Danish Augustana Synod was the smallest.

The Norwegian-Danish Augustana Synod, consisting of approximately thirteen pastors and several small congregations, elected Ole J. Hatlestad (1823–92) as its president. This small group labored valiantly to perpetuate both its Haugean and its American spirit. Most of its clergymen had no formal theological training, but had been significantly imbued with Haugeanism in Norway. In spirit and practice, it frequently found itself in opposition to the larger Norwegian Synod. At the time of its founding in 1870, it patterned its constitution after its forerunner, the Scandinavian Augustana Synod. In contrast to other Norwegian Lutherans, the synod subscribed to the entire Book of Concord. Even though most of its clergymen came out of the lay-preaching background, the Norwegian Augustana Synod, like the Norwegian Synod, held a high view of the pastoral office and endowed it with more authority than some other Norwegian Lutherans. The fact that ordination of ministerial candidates was approved and conducted by the synod is worthy of note because it was in contrast to the congregational orientation of the Haugeans and the Conference.

Swedish and Norwegian immigrants had also collaborated with the Synod of Northern Illinois in establishing a Scandinavian professorship at Illinois State University in Springfield in the 1850s. Later this was continued in Chicago and Paxton, Illinois, until an amicable separation between the Swedes and Norwegians led the Norwegians to found Augsburg Seminary at Marshall, Wisconsin, in 1869. The Norwegian-Danish Conference, also organized in 1870, moved this seminary to Minneapolis, Minnesota, in 1872. In the meantime, the Norwegian Augustanans began a seminary in Springfield, near Decorah, Iowa, in 1874. In 1881 it was moved to Beloit, Iowa, where it remained until 1890 when it was merged with Augsburg Seminary, Minneapolis, as a result of the formation of the United Norwegian Lutheran Church. The synod published *Ebenezer* from 1869 to 1873 and thereafter *Lutherske Kirketidende* from 1874 to 1890. Although the Augustanans were cordial to the General Council, they never officially affiliated with the larger group. Rather, in 1890, they united with the Conference and the Anti-Missourian Brotherhood to form the United Norwegian Lutheran Church.

The Norwegian-Danish Conference

The second church emerging from the Scandinavian Augustana Synod in 1870, the Norwegian-Danish Conference, had an interesting and turbulent history. Claus L. Clausen, who had originally participated in the formation of the Norwegian Synod only to be excluded for his antislavery views, was virtually called out of retirement to be elected its first president. Painfully aware of the criticisms by Haugean-inclined Augustanans and the Norwegian Missourians (Norwegian Synod), the Conference determined to occupy a mediating position between the latter and the low-church pietists. Theological differences were bound to emerge. Clausen had endeavored, in the new constitution, to provide greater freedom in polity than the Norwegian Synod by making no provision for an executive synodical council and by designating the new group as simply a conference of congregations. Clausen, in his first presidential address, ridiculed the Norwegian Synod's blind adulation of Missourianism by observing that all Walther had to do was to wiggle his little finger and the entire Norwegian Synod would come running.[35]

The Norwegian-Danish Conference found its main center in Augsburg Seminary and published its views in its organ, *Lutheraneren* (1871). Besides Clausen, August Weenaas, who had come to America in 1868, exercised the chief theological leadership in the Conference. Prior to the separation of the Norwegians and Swedes, he served on the faculty of Augustana Seminary when it was located at Paxton, Illinois. At the new Augsburg Seminary of the Norwegians in Marshall, Wisconsin, Weenaas soon aligned himself with the younger Norwegian clergymen who had but recently arrived from Norway and moved toward the formation of the Conference. Thus the Conference inherited Augsburg Seminary at the time of its founding.

Weenaas, a natural leader, caused the Conference to walk the tightrope between the lay orientation and loose federation of some of the synods and the dogmatic stance and tight organization of the Norwegian Synod. As president and sole teacher at Augsburg, Weenaas soon found support in the addition of three professors, Georg Sverdrup, Sven Oftedal, and Sven R. Gunnersen. This triumvirate was to add stature to one segment of

35.
Ibid., p. 220.

Norwegian Lutheranism in the decades to follow. The Conference became a part of the United Norwegian Lutheran Church in 1890.

The Augustana Synod[36]

The Swedes comprised the third major linguistic group of Lutherans to migrate to America during this period. Initially, the Swedish Lutherans arriving in America in the 1840s generally joined the Synod of Northern Illinois, which included the United Scandinavian Conference comprised of two parts, the Chicago (Norwegian) Conference and the Mississippi (Swedish) Conference. Temporarily this affiliation provided the Swedes with both a theological seminary and a working church structure.

Like the Norwegians, the Swedish Conference of the Synod of Northern Illinois in 1854 formally encouraged its students to prepare for the ministry at Illinois State University. Originally founded in Hillsboro, Illinois, in 1849, the institution was moved to Springfield in 1852. The synod, responding favorably to urging by the Swedes, created a separate Scandinavian professorship. But funds to endow the new chair were lacking. Lars P. Esbjorn, the leader among the Swedes and a member of the university's board of trustees, was given the task to gather the needed monies. In spite of months of sacrificial solicitation, he had gathered only $2,147.50. His health impaired, he resigned from the task and accepted a call to Princeton, Illinois. When the new chair finally was created in 1856, Esbjorn was called.

The Scandinavians required that Esbjorn teach "according to the Word of God and the Augsburg Confession."[37] Basically, the Swedish Conference and Esbjorn found themselves in strong opposition to the school's administration, which espoused the theological position of the *Definite Platform* and its "Americanization" proposals. Thus the polarization which occurred in Lutheranism elsewhere arose in miniature in the Synod of Northern Illinois. After several unsuccessful attempts to iron out the differences, Esbjorn concluded that his position was untenable and in 1860 he abruptly resigned. He reminded the administration that he had been pledged to the Augsburg Confession and that because of the modifications suggested by the *Definite Platform* in the confessional formulation, he was unable to continue. When the United Scandinavian Conference met in April 1860 it concurred with Esbjorn's conclusions. In addition, it also resolved to move its portion of the seminary to Chicago and establish a separate church body.

Within less than two months, in June 1860, the Scandinavian Evangelical Lutheran Augustana Synod of North America was organized at Jefferson Prairie, Wisconsin, the same location where the Eielsen Synod had been formed fourteen years earlier. Host pastor was Ole Andrewson, a Norwegian, who had originally been associated with the Eielsen Synod and subsequently helped form the Norwegian-Danish Augustana Synod. The twenty-six pastors and fifteen lay delegates present repre-

36.
Sources for the history of the Augustana Synod include G. Everett Arden, *Augustana Heritage: A History of the Augustana Lutheran Church* (Rock Island, Ill.: Augustana Press, 1963), and Oscar N. Olson, *The Augustana Lutheran Church in America: Pioneer Period, 1846 to 1860* (Rock Island, Ill.: Augustana Book Concern, 1950).

37.
Arden, *Augustana Heritage*, p. 60. The American "nativist" sentiment, usually directed against Roman Catholics, may have been present among some "American" Lutherans who saw the Scandinavian Lutherans through "nativist" spectacles. This attitude perhaps contributed to the lack of cordiality between "American" and immigrant Lutherans, hastening the split in the synod.

sented forty-nine congregations with a combined membership of 4,967. Tuve Nilsson Hasselquist (1816–91) became the first president, and as such he was to exert a strong and lasting influence on the Augustana Synod.

When the delegates met, they had before them a preliminary draft of a constitution. Largely based upon the constitution of the Synod of Northern Illinois, it provided a congregational polity, giving primary authority to the member congregations.

The synod was comprised of clergy and lay teachers from member congregations and granted membership only to those congregations who subscribed to its constitution. It added a novel provision in that it rested continuing membership on annual financial contributions to the synodical treasury. The new constitution was theologically dependent upon the confessional paragraph which the United Scandinavian Conference had adopted in 1857. Article II committed the Scandinavians to the *Confessio Augustana* (the unaltered Augsburg Confession) at a time when strict confessional subscription was devalued in some Lutheran quarters. The article testified:

As a Christian body in general, and particularly as Evangelical Lutheran, this synod acknowledges that the holy Scriptures, the revealed Word of God, are the only sufficient and infallible rule and standard of faith and practice, and also retains and confesses not only the three oldest symbols (the Apostolic, the Nicene and the Athanasian), but also the unaltered Augsburg Confession as a short and correct summary of the principal Christian doctrines, understood as developed and explained in the other Symbolical books of the Lutheran Church. This article shall never be altered.[38]

The seminary of the newly formed Augustana Synod included both a preparatory and a theological department. Esbjorn continued to serve as its professor. However, when he returned to Sweden in 1863 the institution was moved to Paxton, Illinois, where Hasselquist became Esbjorn's successor and served the institution as president until 1891. Augustana Seminary found a permanent home in Rock Island, Illinois, in 1875, where it remained until the seminary realignments accompanying the formation of the Lutheran Church in America (1962). Several seminaries, including Augustana, were merged then in the new Lutheran School of Theology in Chicago.

Among the newspapers and periodicals produced under the aegis of the Augustana Synod was *Hemlandet,* begun in 1855. However, the official church periodical which appeared in 1868 assumed the name of the synod and its seminary, namely *Augustana.* An English publication, the *Lutheran Companion,* appeared in 1892, making it a pioneer in the anglicization of Midwestern Lutheran church periodicals.

The Augustana Synod combined its confessional theological position with an evangelical piety. Under Hasselquist's leadership, the synod participated in the formation of the General Council and remained in close fellowship with it. The peaceful

38.
Ibid., p. 86.

separation in 1870 between the synod's Norwegian and Swedish constituents resulted in a church body which was distinctively Swedish, while maintaining a lively interest in English work.

The Danish Church[39]

Danish Lutheran immigration to America, a trickle in the 1840s, was numerous enough to form a separate church organization in 1872. The immigrants who had arrived earlier gravitated toward Norwegian and Swedish churches. Not until the Church Mission Society was founded at Neenah, Wisconsin, in 1872 did Danish Lutheranism receive its first official structure. The society was organized by Adam Dan (1848–1931), Rasmus Andersen (1847–1930), Anders Sixtus Nielsen (1832–1909), and Niels Thomsen (1842–92). A former missionary to the Holy Land, Adam Dan was elected president of the society and editor of its periodical, *Kirkelig Sammler,* which made its appearance in October 1872.

The confessional standard and the statement of purpose formulated by the society placed it squarely within the context of Grundtvigianism, which later was to cause a separation among the Danish Lutherans. Dan declared in the first issue of the periodical:

The Church Mission Society is founded on the holy catholic church's baptismal covenant and the Holy Scriptures as God's word to the church, and intends to stand in full agreement with the confessions of our Danish Lutheran Mother Church. Its aim is to gather our compatriots who sense the loss of, but yearn for, the preaching of the Word of God into congregations and serve them with the Word and the sacraments. The mission society will seek through the preaching of the gospel to awaken in those who sleep in sin an awareness of the kingdom of God, and will, by the grace God gives, with all its might combat disbelief, sects, and fanatics, and, if possible, bring those who have strayed back to the Fatherhouse whence they have come.[40]

The Mission Society was restructured into the Danish Evangelical Lutheran Church in America in 1874. In 1962 this body became a part of the Lutheran Church in America.[41]

Immigrant Churches Reach Out

The population of the United States more than doubled between 1840 and 1870, from 17,069,453 to 39,818,449.[42] During this period it has been estimated that the German, Norwegian, Swedish, and Danish immigration exceeded 1,200,000, indicating that one out of every thirty to forty American residents had arrived from one of these four countries. Small wonder that both the American-born and immigrant churches were painfully aware of the need to bring the Word and sacraments to their countrymen. Far too often, however, the churches lacked the necessary funds and manpower to engage in aggressive mission work in their new homeland.

193

39.
The history of Danish Lutheranism in America is treated by John M. Jensen, *The United Evangelical Lutheran Church: An Interpretation* (Minneapolis: Augsburg Publishing House, 1964), and Enok Mortensen, *The Danish Lutheran Church in America* (Philadelphia: Board of Publication, LCA, 1967).

40.
Mortensen, *The Danish Church*, p. 47.

41.
For the histories of other synodical organizations established between 1840 and 1875 see *The Encyclopedia of the Lutheran Church*, ed. Julius Bodensieck, 3 vols. (Minneapolis: Augsburg Publishing House, 1965), 2:1379–1407. See also Robert C. Wiederaenders and Walter G. Tillmanns, *The Synods of American Lutheranism* (St. Louis: Concordia Print Shop, 1968).

42.
Historical Statistics of the United States (Washington, D.C.: U.S. Government Printing Office, 1960), p. 8.

The "awakening" in Europe had sparked renewed interest in missions and social service. Originally, German Lutherans understood inner missions as a combined effort to reclaim fellow Lutherans spiritually and to rehabilitate them physically. In contrast, foreign missions was considered work among heathen in distant countries. The majority of the churches did not distinguish between inner (home) missions and social ministry. These went hand in hand.

Feelings of frustration arose at the lack of necessary funds and manpower. Frustration was intensified by the scarcity of itinerant missionaries, who sought out the new colonies of settlers and consistently found the number of people and the distances between settlements overwhelming. One such itinerant, F. C. D. Wyneken, was prompted to issue an urgent appeal for help to meet the enormous need.[43]

Wave upon wave of immigrants spread over the Midwest. Subsequent decades saw them move into the Far West and into Canada. Primitive means of transportation and inadequate communication systems isolated communities and the lonely frontier missionaries. Wyneken decried the fact that there were countless communities which had not seen a Lutheran pastor for as long as from five to ten years. The problem was further compounded by the continuing waves of immigrants pouring into new territories. In emergency situations, laymen were frequently called upon to provide a limited ministry. Support from European state churches and various mission societies was sorely needed. The American Home Missionary Society granted aid and assistance wherever it could. Methodists were particularly effective in their work among the Swedish immigrants.

If his church membership in the homeland had been nominal prior to his emigration, the Lutheran immigrant was not inclined to probe theological differences. Some of the immigrants were open and unabashed in their hostility to the religious beliefs and practices of their homeland and welcomed the ministrations of Anglo-American evangelicals; some even fell prey to the proselytizing of such groups as the Mormons. Radicals arrived in America from Germany, Sweden, and other countries, only too happy to shake the religious and ethnic dust off their feet. Just as Wyneken had astonished those in his homeland by pointing to the possibility that "German heathen" could develop in America unless help were soon to arrive, Hasselquist addressed the 1869 Augustana Synod convention with alarm:

Think of it, brethren! Out of the fifty or sixty thousand Swedish nationals who have emigrated, only about twenty thousand are connected with us, and a few other thousand united with other churches which leaves a formidable remainder of some twenty to thirty thousand countrymen who are being lost in worldliness, sin, and unbelief. . . . Can anyone do for them what we can, we who speak their language and who have been fed with the same spiritual food, and therefore understand more

43.
See chapter 9, pp. 157-58.

intimately than others what they have lost and what they need? No! Let us in God's name redouble our zeal, our sacrifices, and above all else our prayers, that the Lord of the harvest will send faithful laborers into His harvest. The night is at hand. Woe unto us if our work is half done.[44]

In most cases the task was even greater than such observers believed. On the other hand, however, many of the immigrants were attracted to their fellow countrymen by language if not by religion. How happy and grateful they were when they found their mother tongue and the customs of their homeland.[45]

195

American synods, such as the Pennsylvania Ministerium and the federated General Synod, established separate missionary societies in the 1830s and 1840s in order to meet the challenges of the immigrants. When these societies, often patterned after their counterparts in Europe and based upon voluntary support, could not meet the needs, the General Synod as an organization encouraged the use of "explorers" on a temporary basis to visit new settlements, often during the summer months. During the absence of the pastor who served as explorer, congregations received temporary student help.

The first real breakthrough in the complicated situation was made by the Pittsburgh Synod in 1846. Its committee on missions presented a series of far-reaching resolutions, emphasizing that the entire synod was a missionary agency. This approach effectively challenged the earlier concept that mission programs were to be carried on by auxiliaries. Secondly, the resolution also provided for geographical division, with each division responsible for the work in its area. Because of its significance, the report is quoted extensively:

. . . The church has lost its primitive character. It has ceased to be what it originally was: *a missionary church!*

This obvious defect of the pastoral system is acknowledged by all its friends, and to remedy its inefficiency and supply a lack of service, various expedients have been tried. Hence the different missionary organizations *without* the pale of the church and wholly separate from it,—all based on the admitted inefficiency of the church, and doing the work which its divine founder designed it to do. It was to the church *as such,* and not to a society independent and distinct from it, that Christ hath given the great commission . . . assuring them of His gracious presence even to the end of the world.

What then do we plead for? Not for the formation of a missionary association, not for a society within a society—but simply for a return to the primitive form. That was perfect and entirely lacking nothing. It continued in itself the principles of preservation and *propagation.* It was both aggressive and progressive. It was in its very constitution as much a missionary society as a society for worship and discipline. . . .

44.
Protokoll, Augustana Synod, 1869, p. 8, cited in Arden, *Augustana Heritage*, p. 129.
45.
Marcus Lee Hansen, *The Immigrant in American History* (Cambridge, Mass.: Harper & Row, 1940), pp. 136–37.

**That the Synod has full power to incorporate the
missionary feature into its own organization, and make
every necessary amendment for the prosecution of this
part of our work may be seen by a reference to the
second section of article first of our Constitution, in
which a prominent object in the formation of the Synod
is stated to be "to devise and carry out such a system of
missionary operations as will enable us, so far as lies in
our power, to preach the gospel to every creature."[46]
[Italics in original]**

46.
Lutheran Observer, July 3, 1846, pp. 177–78.

Enthusiastically the Pittsburgh Synod launched out "into the
deep," relieved some of the needs of the non-English immigrants
in the Midwest, and moved all the way into Canada.

Primary concerns, however, for the new arrivals from northern Europe rested with their countrymen who had arrived earlier and had organized churches. In addition, the more recently
established Midwestern synods, with headquarters located in
closer proximity to the new settlements, ministered more readily
and less expensively to the spiritual needs of the immigrant than
the Eastern churches which sometimes were separated from him
by more than a thousand miles.

The younger Midwestern synods used explorers and colporteurs extensively. The Missouri Synod established a separate
office of colporteur in 1852, as did the Swedish Mississippi
Conference in 1856. According to the plan, several men visited
the German and Scandinavian settlements and encouraged
them to organize parishes. In addition, the Scandinavians, who
had extensively experienced the lay evangelistic movements
prior to immigration, used lay preachers more readily than their
German brethren. But all were concerned with issues relating to
the function and authority of such lay preachers. The Norwegians divided structurally in large measure over the issue. Grabau in his "Pastoral Letter" warned against an unordained
clergy, while the Missouri Synod debated the doctrine of the
call, the office of the ministry, and the rights of the local church.
Early in their history, the Swedes emphasized that their synod
had the right to issue a call and send missionaries to distant
settlements.

The Norwegians and the Missouri Synod, adhering to the
position that only a congregation could rightly issue a call to a
clergyman, induced their frontier congregations, with synodical
financial support, to call assistant pastors for large territories.
Such assistants often served a parish with a radius of fifty to one
hundred miles. But whether the workers were lay colporteurs,
clergy explorers, assistant pastors sent by an organized church,
or free itinerants, the immigrant churches were missionary
churches.

Among the outstanding home missionaries, both native-born
and immigrant, were William Alfred Passavant, John Christian
Frederick Heyer, F. C. D. Wyneken, Eric Norelius, and a host
of Loehe's "emergency men." Mission boards, as arms of officially established church bodies, began with the Norwegian

47.
Nelson and Fevold, *Lutheran Church Among Norwegian-Americans*, 1:277–78.
48.
Arden, *Augustana Heritage*, p. 131.
49.
J. Nicum, *Geschichte des Evangelisch-Lutherischen Ministeriums vom Staate New York* (Reading, Pa.: T. Wischan, 1888), p. 361.
50.
Missouri Synod, *Siebenter Synodal-Bericht* (St. Louis: Moritz Niedner, 1853), p. 39.

Synod's restructure in 1864.[47] Other Norwegian churches followed suit. The Augustana Synod in 1870 provided for an all-out effort to reach the new immigrants through a centralized board. It, too, designated each of its conferences as a mission district, and the presidents of the conferences, together with additional representatives, comprised the mission board.[48] The General Council had provided a similar structure in 1867.

But even the structured boards did not adequately meet the needs. Several of the synods established an immigrant ministry at the port of debarkation. The concept was nothing new; Olaf Hedstrom, a Swedish Methodist, had rendered such services, though independently, at the port of New York in the 1840s. Both the Pennsylvania Ministerium and the Missouri Synod initiated an "immigrant ministry" in the 1850s. Christian K. A. Brandt served the Ministerium,[49] while Theodore J. Brohm, followed by Stephanus Keyl, served the Missouri Synod in New York.[50] The work of these men and their successors remained an important factor in the life of the immigrant, primarily because of the contact made with the church at a crucial time.

Concern for Social Welfare

The nineteenth century witnessed an upsurge of organized Christian social concern and welfare in Europe. Through the efforts of Theodore Fliedner an institution for the education of deaconesses was begun in Kaiserswerth, Germany, in 1833. The same year, Johann H. Wichern established "Das Rauhe Haus" (a rescue home) outside of Hamburg as a village for delinquent boys. By the late 1840s inner mission societies, offering opportunities for works of love motivated by faith, sprang up in many localities. Orphanages, homes for the aged, hospitals, and resettlement missions were established. From Germany the work spread into the Scandinavian countries and to America.

The foremost American Lutheran "inner missionary" was William Alfred Passavant (1821–94). He has the distinction of establishing the largest number of orphanages, hospitals, homes for the aged, and other institutions of mercy among Lutherans in America. This remarkable man, in addition to all his labors and extensive travel, served as editor of several periodicals and as a founder of the Pittsburgh Synod in 1845 and the General Council in 1867. His definition of "inner missions," written in 1848, embraced virtually every church activity except foreign missions:

These are missions within the church, such as Scriptural revivals of religion; the instruction of the children of the church, comprehending Sunday-schools, infant schools, catechetical classes, Bible classes, etc.; the education of our people, comprehending Church schools, academies, colleges, theological seminaries and education societies; the relief of the temporal need of the members, including the Institution of Protestant Deaconesses, together with the various funds, societies, and

institutions for the indigent, the aged and infirm, for disabled ministers, for the widows and orphans of the clergymen, etc.; the improvement of church architecture, of congregational singing, of the liturgical service, of the better observance of the order and worship of God's house.[51]

This unusual man, without financial support and permanent quarters, established the first Protestant hospital in America in Pittsburgh in 1849. When a boatload of discharged soldiers (from the Mexican War) arrived in Pittsburgh, Passavant went to the dock to meet the sick and the wounded. Finding two, he transported them to his empty hospital, even though the quarters had not been completed.[52] In rapid succession he established two additional hospitals in Milwaukee in 1863 and in Chicago in 1865.

The German spiritual father of the deaconess movement, Theodore Fliedner, arrived in America on July 14, 1849, accompanied by Elizabeth Hubberts, Pauline Ludewig, Louise Henrichsen, and Elizabeth Hess.[53] The credit for establishing the oldest Protestant orphanage in America with a continuous existence is also due Passavant through the institution he founded in Pittsburgh in 1852. Two years later it was moved to Zelienople, Pennsylvania. Thereafter he established similar homes at Germantown, Pennsylvania (1859); Mt. Vernon, New York (1869); and Jacksonville, Illinois (1870).

The arrival of orphan children filled Passavant with emotion. His biographer noted that Passavant expected to find clean and happy children.

Instead of this he found them begrimed with dust of travel and bestained with tears. When he told them who he was, one of the larger girls ran up to him, threw her arms about his neck and sobbed: "So you are Mr. Passavant, and you will be our father." Then and there, he told us, he received a new and needed lesson on what it means to be director of an Orphanage.[54]

Similarly motivated by love and service, Johann F. Buenger of St. Louis was instrumental in establishing the Lutheran Hospital in that city in 1858, and ten years later he founded a home for orphans and the aged at Des Peres, Missouri.[55] The Swedes were encouraged by Passavant to begin orphanages of their own. The first was opened by 1868 near Andover, Illinois. Another was begun in Vasa, Minnesota, about the same time. Other orphanages and hospitals soon followed.

These institutions served as the pattern for a large number of welfare organizations all over the country. Sometimes mutual-aid societies were established among Lutherans in a community which rendered both personal and financial support when needed. In the Missouri Synod an agency for the support of professional workers and their families was formed in the early 1850s.[56] The fact that there was not an even greater need for welfare institutions was largely due to the immigrant's individualism and exceptional self-reliance. Not typical, but neverthe-

51.
George H. Gerberding, *Life and Letters of W. A. Passavant* (Greenville, Pa.: Young Lutheran Co., 1906), pp. 195–96.
52.
Ibid., p. 184.
53.
Frederick S. Weiser, *Love's Response* (Philadelphia: Board of Publication, ULCA, 1962), p. 54.
54.
Gerberding, *Passavant*, pp. 224–25.
55.
August R. Suelflow, *Heart of Missouri* (St. Louis: Concordia Publishing House, 1954), pp. 134–35.
56.
Ernst M. Buerger and Adam Ernst, "Vorlagen von Statuten für eine Prediger-und Schullehrer-Wittwen-und Waisen-Gesellschaft," *Der Lutheraner*, February 5, 1850, pp. 92–93.

less illustrative of the settler's ingenuity, is the account about Lars D. Reque at Koshkonong, Wisconsin:

This ambitious pioneer had come to America in 1839, but it was not until the spring of 1842 that he began farming. In the meantime he had worked on the Illinois Canal and as a fireman on a Great Lakes steamboat; he had been a lumber jack in the pine woods of Michigan and Wisconsin, floated logs on the Muskegon River, and held a job in a sawmill. Even after beginning his career as a farmer, he worked winters in the Wisconsin lead mines. He became very prosperous, lived four years in the first log cabin that he built—its roof made of planks that he had shaped with a broad axe—then put up a larger cabin, and by the 1850s had a frame house,— "one of the finest places in the community." His farm grew to nearly three hundred acres and boasted an orchard of more than seven hundred apple trees.[57]

57.
Theodore C. Blegen, *Norwegian Migration to America: The American Transition* (Northfield, Minn.: Norwegian-American Historical Assoc., 1940), p. 38.

American Indian Missions

In the tradition of John Campanius and John C. Hartwick, Lutherans in the nineteenth century did not overlook work among the American Indians. One of the first to alert the church to these missionary needs was Friedrich Schmid, founder and first president of the first Michigan Synod in 1840. With the support of the Pennsylvania Ministerium he began his career as missionary to the Germans and Indians in Michigan in 1833. In 1845, as Loehe began his support of German immigrants, he also became intrigued with work among the Indians. Loehe's method was noteworthy in that it (1) provided direct material and spiritual assistance to the settlers as they began life in their adopted country; (2) utilized the colonists, under the leadership of a missionary, in demonstrating practical aspects of Christian life and hope to the Indians living around them; and (3) established a church extension fund available to the colonists and their mission endeavors to be repaid and thereafter reused by another group.

Friedrich August Craemer (1812–91), equally proficient in English and German, headed the first settlement in Frankenmuth, Michigan (1845), to carry out these principles, and he established a school for children which reached a peak enrollment of thirty children. He baptized his first Chippewa youngsters on the third day of Christmas 1846, naming them Abraham, Magdaline, and Anna. When the work became too taxing, the Leipzig Evangelical Lutheran Mission Society lent Eduard R. Baierlein, who arrived in April 1847.

By that time three stations were in existence, Frankenmuth, Sebewaing, and Shebahyonk, all in Michigan. After Baierlein's arrival, the Indians were withdrawn from the Frankenmuth area to St. Louis, Michigan, where a flourishing mission, Bethany, was established in 1848. Again a school was begun with the enrollment reaching nineteen a year later. Ernst Gustav Herman Miessler came from Leipzig in 1851 to assist Baierlein.

When the latter was reassigned in 1853 for work in India, Miessler became the director. Not long afterward a decline in the work set in when the government transferred the Indians to new areas to make room for the constantly encroaching white settlers. The Indians, frequently influenced by the immoralities of the white men, especially the unprincipled peddlers of whiskey and purveyors of "religion," concluded that all white men were deceitful and untrustworthy.

Hopeful that Christian work could be expanded into Minnesota, the Missouri Synod sent Ottomar Cloeter to that state in 1857. His work, especially after the Indian uprising of 1862, was no more fruitful than the earlier efforts in Michigan. Faced with continual reverses, the synod, which had been responsible for the Indian missions since 1847, terminated the work in 1868.[58]

The Iowa Synod, with Loehe's support and encouragement, attempted to initiate new work among the Indians with the arrival of Johann J. Schmidt in 1856. After conducting several exploratory trips as far as the Bay of Grand Portage in Canada in 1857 and to the mouth of the Yellowstone River in Montana in 1858, work was finally established in the spring of 1860 on the Powder River in Montana. Schmidt, accompanied by Moritz Braeuninger, established a mission among the Crows. After Braeuninger's murder a few months later, the work was abandoned. A new attempt to serve the Cheyenne in the spring of 1861 was made when a station was established about a hundred miles west of Fort Laramie, Wyoming. Christian Kessler, supported by Karl Krebs and Georg Flachenecker, initiated the work. During the Indian uprising in 1862 the work was disrupted once more. With a second uprising in 1864 the missionaries finally abandoned their station and the work was terminated in 1867.

Neither zeal nor sacrifice were lacking in the Indian mission enterprise. Rather, the mobility of the Indians resulting from governmental policies, the demoralizing association with unprincipled white people, and unrealistic mission methods all interacted to thwart and finally to end the work.

Into Foreign Countries

The spiritual awakening among all Protestants in Europe and in America contributed to making the nineteenth century the "great century" for missionary outreach. America's Lutherans joined hands with some of the European and American societies in order to bring the gospel to distant countries. Numerous German and Scandinavian missionary societies were organized during the first half of the nineteenth century and proved to be influential as the century unfolded. Originally, most of them were equally concerned with inner and foreign missions. A few of these were Basel, 1815; Danish, 1821; Berlin, 1824; Rhenish, 1828; Norwegian, 1842; Swedish, 1835; North German, 1836; Gossner, 1836; Leipzig, 1836; the Foreign Mission Society of the Evangelical German Churches in the United States, 1837; Hermannsburg, 1849; Neuendettelsau, 1849; and Finnish, 1859.[59]

58.
Walter P. Schoenfuhs, "Edward Raimund Baierlein," *Concordia Historical Institute Quarterly* 27 (October 1954): 133–41; ibid. 27 (January 1955): 145–62; ibid. 28 (Spring 1955): 1–26. See also idem, "O Tebeningeion—O Dearest Jesus," ibid. 37 (October 1964): 95–114, for an account of the Bethany mission and why it failed.
59.
James A. Scherer, *Mission and Unity in Lutheranism* (Philadelphia: Fortress Press, 1969), pp. 26–40.

60.
George Drach and Calvin F. Kuder, *The Telugu Mission* (Philadelphia: General Council Pub. House, 1914), pp. 13-21.

Lutherans in America were intimately interrelated with these societies. The Foreign Mission Society of the Evangelical German Churches in the United States, formed in 1837, was the first American society following in the wake of the new mission interest. It joined Moravians, Reformed, and Lutherans, especially members of the General Synod. Prior to this time Lutherans occasionally supported the work of the American Board of Commissioners for Foreign Missions organized in 1810. Through the work of Karl F. A. Guetzlaff (1803–51), the first Lutheran missionary to China commissioned by the Berlin Society, American Lutherans developed a greater mission consciousness. As a result, they established several separate societies, the first of which was the Central Missionary Society formed by the Pennsylvania Ministerium in 1836. It concerned itself with both a home and a foreign program. In the meantime, the General Synod concluded that efforts in support of foreign missions across denominational lines were unproductive and in 1841 it transformed the foreign Mission Society into the Foreign Missionary Society of the Evangelical Lutheran Church in the United States. In response to the appeals of Carl Rhenius who served in India under the support of the Berlin Society, the new General Synod society directed its attention to India.

In decisive action in 1841 the society of the Pennsylvania Ministerium commissioned John Christian Frederick Heyer (1793–1873) for work in India. At age forty-eight he became the first American missionary in a foreign field sent by American Lutherans.[60] Five months later he arrived at Colombo, Ceylon. Between 1842 and 1857 he enjoyed but a single furlough. Upon his retirement in 1857, at the age of sixty-four, this inveterate missionary accepted a call from the East Pennsylvania Synod to work in Minnesota. Dramatic events in 1869 led this veteran, already seventy-seven years old, back to Rajahmundry, India. Serving as one of the four special mission-speakers at the sessions of the Pennsylvania Ministerium that year, he addressed the hushed audience:

I appeal to you, the Ministerium of Pennsylvania, to intervene and prevent the transfer of the Rajahmundry station to the Church Missionary Society of the Anglicans. You, as the Ministerium under whose auspices I was sent out to India in 1842, should again assume the responsibility of supporting some foreign missionaries. It is not *too* late. If this venerable body consents, I shall plead with the General Synod's Board to rescind its decision to abandon Rajahmundry; and I shall communicate with the Church Missionary Society in England to reconsider the grounds on which it would be accepting this station. More than that, Brethren. Although I am nearly seventy-seven now, I am willing to go to India myself and reorganize that work! Twelve thousand miles lie between us and our objective. But let not distance alarm us. If there is someone else who would be more capable of restoring order in our

Events developed quickly and the Ministerium, with the concurrence of the General Council, sent out the rugged and mentally alert missionary in August 1869. Heyer arrived at Rajahmundry on December 1, 1869. After restoring order in less than two years, he returned to America and died in retirement on November 7, 1873. Thus a dramatic chapter in the history of American Lutheran foreign missions came to a close.

The General Synod began work in Liberia in 1860 when it established its Muhlenberg Mission in the newly formed country. Missionary Morris Officer initiated the work, but ill health forced him to return afterward only for a year and a half. Within the next thirty-six years eighteen additional missionaries were commissioned. Outstanding among them was David A. Day, who was commissioned in 1874 and served for the next twenty-three years.

The demands of gathering Lutheran immigrants in America prevented many of the newer, Midwestern synods from undertaking their own foreign missions until later in the century. However, they gave financial and moral support to existing missionary societies both in America and in their former homelands.

Into Canada

As noted earlier, Lutheranism existed in Canada during the colonial period only on a small scale, and, lacking adequate support, was assumed by other denominations. Shortly after the revolutionary war, Lutheran immigrants relocated in widely scattered areas in the midwestern provinces of Canada, especially in Ontario. As the nineteenth century dawned, several German Lutheran settlements existed without pastoral services and synodical connections. Vagabond preachers often operated in these areas, causing spiritual confusion. The need for permanent resident pastors was pressing. In Ontario, the earliest settlements were made in the southeastern tip of Dundas County. Herman Hayunga, formerly of the Hartwick College faculty, was sent by the New York Ministerium in 1826 to serve the Lutherans in that county.

Prolonged vacancies intensified by primitive communication and transportation systems often created intense hardships. Yet the concern to obtain pastors resulted in almost unbelievable feats. The account of Adam Keffer, delegated by the Vaughan congregation in Dundas County to obtain a pastor at the end of a lengthy vacancy, may illustrate. In the spring of 1849 the sixty-year-old Keffer hiked the distance of more than 250 miles from Vaughan to Saegerstown, Pennsylvania, to plead his cause. Full of determination, he called upon Pastor John Nunemacher at that place. Since the Pittsburgh Synod was in session at nearby Klecknerville, Pennsylvania, Nunemacher encouraged Keffer to attend the sessions. Passavant, at the end of the day, found Keffer barefoot on his way to the meeting.

202

61.
E. Theodore Bachmann, *They Called Him Father* (Philadelphia: Muhlenberg Press, 1942), pp. 303–4.

62.
Gerberding, *Passavant*, pp. 142–43.
63.
Ernest G. Heissenbuttel and Roy H. Johnson, *Pittsburgh Synod History* (Warren, Ohio: Studio of Printcraft, 1963), pp. 49–50.
64.
Erich R. W. Schultz, "Tragedy and Triumph in Canadian Lutheranism," *Concordia Historical Institute Quarterly* 38 (July 1965): 68.

With Keffer's emphatic plea underscored by his appearance and obvious personal sacrifice, the Pittsburgh Synod delegated Gottlieb Bassler to conduct a survey of the area in September of the same year. Unfortunately, however, the synod lacked the necessary manpower to implement this beginning. To the amazement of all, Keffer reappeared in the synod's midst the following year. The sixteen-year vacancy at the Markham and Vaughan parishes compelled action. Such pleas could not remain unanswered, and the synod sent Charles F. Diehl, a graduate of the Gettysburg Seminary, in October 1850.

Farther west, in Waterloo County, Ontario, German Lutheran immigrants established parishes in Waterloo, Kitchener, and elsewhere. The Pennsylvania Ministerium commissioned John H. Bernheim to survey and explore these areas in 1835. In the wake of this survey the Pennsylvania Ministerium, the New York Ministerium, the Franckean Synod, and the Tennessee Synod rendered financial support, commissioned pastors, and in ever widening circles established congregations.

On the eastern tip of Canada, at Halifax, Nova Scotia, Passavant stumbled upon Lutheran needs in an unusual way. Delegated by the Pittsburgh Synod to attend the meeting of the Evangelical Alliance in London in 1846, he debarked from his ship, which required repairs. During the free time he explored the city and chanced upon deteriorating St. George's Church, formerly German Lutheran but now Episcopalian. Passavant was unable to shake the recollection of this experience from his mind. After he returned from Europe, he initiated correspondence with Carl E. Cossman, who, since 1835, had served in Lunenburg County, Nova Scotia.[62] Several years later, in 1855, the congregation was occupied by William W. Bowers, who had attended Gettysburg Seminary.

In 1873 the Pittsburgh Synod commissioned Henry W. Roth of Thiel College to conduct a mission survey in the far southeastern portion of Canada. Receiving favorable reports, the synod sent several additional men to reinforce the Canadian Lutherans. Cumulatively, this work resulted in the formation of the Nova Scotia Conference in 1876.

Through the continued support of the Pittsburgh Synod in eastern Canada, the Canada Conference, the first in all Canada, was organized as early as 1853. The Synod of Canada was formed in 1861 after the Pittsburgh Synod had supplied all seven pastors in the field.[63] Its first president was Carl F. W. Rechenberg. Relationships between Canadian Lutherans and the Pittsburgh Synod were cemented through a visit of Passavant to all the parishes in September 1867.

The Missouri Synod entered Ontario through the work of Johann Adam Ernst, a Loehe missioner stationed at Eden, New York. In 1854 he began serving the congregations at Rhineland and Fisherville, Ontario. Subsequently, in 1863, he transferred to the Flordale-Elmira parish, where he remained for eighteen years. When the Ontario District of the Missouri Synod was organized in 1879, he became its first president.[64]

Danish Lutherans formed St. Peter's Lutheran Church in Salmanhurst in 1872. Icelanders began arriving in the Quebec area during the same year. Earliest traces of Norwegian settlements on the Gaspé Peninsula in Quebec had become noticeable after 1859. The majority of the Norwegian immigrants, however, were not to arrive until after 1875.

Although eastern Canada was beginning to show signs of Lutheran activities, the work in western Canada was not begun until several decades later. The church's challenges and opportunities were overwhelming, particularly in comparison with its financial resources and personnel. It is amazing that such vast territories, both in North America and in foreign countries, could be covered successfully, securely planting the church for subsequent generations.

65.
For details on the history of this institution see Abdel Ross Wentz, *Gettysburg Lutheran Theological Seminary . . . 1826–1965* (Gettysburg, Pa.: Lutheran Theological Seminary, 1965).

Theological Training and Education

In contrast to the colonial Swedish Lutheran settlers on the Delaware River, subsequent Lutherans devoted extensive effort to the establishment of theological seminaries and colleges. Their efforts frequently were closely connected with the unrelenting demands for pastors in the North American missionary situation.

Although the German and Scandinavian immigrant churches were initially dependent upon the European supply of clergymen, they soon realized that a native ministry would be the only answer to the growing need for pastors. Grateful for the many "emergency men," often tradesmen hastily trained for pastoral work in America, and countless lay-workers who kept the gospel alive in communities, the churches felt the need for education and training of a native American Lutheran ministry more urgently as time went on.

The earlier period witnessed the establishment of Hartwick Seminary in Oneonta, New York, in 1797, the Lutheran Theological Seminary in Gettysburg, Pennsylvania, in 1826,[65] and the Lutheran Theological Southern Seminary, originally at Pomaria, South Carolina, in 1830. This latter institution was forced to discontinue during the Civil War, but in 1867 the General Synod, South reestablished it at Walhalla, South Carolina. After being temporarily located at Salem, Virginia, the institution was finally moved in 1911 to Columbia, South Carolina, where it has remained since. Another seminary, also founded in 1830, was begun in the Joint Synod of Ohio at Canton. In 1831 it was moved to its present site in Columbus, Ohio.

While most of the theological seminaries established during the period were founded by the Midwestern German and Scandinavian synods, we need to take cognizance of Wittenberg College and Seminary, established in 1845 at Springfield, Ohio. Today this seminary has developed into Wittenberg University including the Hamma School of Theology under the auspices of the Lutheran Church in America. Originally it was founded by the English Synod of Ohio and was served by Ezra Keller as its first president. Subsequently, Samuel Sprecher and John H. W. Stuckenberg served on its faculty.

Another major institution established during the period was the Lutheran Theological Seminary at Philadelphia. Although it had been the original dream of Henry M. Muhlenberg to establish a seminary in Philadelphia, it was not until the confessional controversy among the constituent synods of the General Synod that concrete steps were taken by the Pennsylvania Ministerium to establish it. Rejecting the "American Lutheranism" among leaders of the General Synod, and more accustomed to the use of the German language than the seminary in Gettysburg, the Philadelphia school opened its doors on October 4, 1864, with five professors and eleven students. Charles Porterfield Krauth became the foremost theologian of a faculty that included Charles F. Schaeffer, William J. Mann, Charles W. Schaeffer, and Gottlob F. Krotel. The institution became the theological stronghold of the General Council after its organization in 1867. In 1889 the institution was moved to suburban Mt. Airy where it has remained.[66]

The majority of the seminaries founded during this period were established either by individual synods or a combination of synods. Among the several causes for the establishment of separate institutions were theological emphases, regionalism, ethnic interests, and, at times, personalities. Under such circumstances, financial support was often meager and some of the institutions were operated on a shoestring. Fund-raising efforts conducted among Lutherans in Europe often augmented the limited support which the seminaries received in America.

Colleges, academies, and high schools were also founded. A mere listing must suffice: Hartwick College, Oneonta, New York, founded in 1797, originally as a theological seminary; Newberry College, Newberry, South Carolina, 1831; Gettysburg College, Gettysburg, Pennsylvania, 1832; Wittenberg College, Springfield, Ohio, 1845; Muhlenberg College, Allentown, Pennsylvania, 1848; Susquehanna University, Selinsgrove, Pennsylvania, originally in 1858 as a Missionary Institute; Augustana College, Rock Island, Illinois, 1860; Augustana College, Sioux Falls, South Dakota, 1860; Luther College, Decorah, Iowa, 1861; Gustavus Adolphus, St. Peter, Minnesota, 1862; Concordia Teachers College, River Forest, Illinois, 1864; Northwestern College, Watertown, Wisconsin, 1865; Thiel College, Greenville, Pennsylvania, 1866; Carthage College, Kenosha, Wisconsin, originally emerged from Illinois State University, Springfield, Illinois, 1869; Augsburg College, Minneapolis, Minnesota, 1869; and St. Olaf College, Northfield, Minnesota, 1874. Beginning with Concordia College, Fort Wayne, Indiana, in 1846, the Missouri Synod established a network of preparatory schools. The academy system developed among the Norwegians chiefly after 1875, producing a host of separate institutions on the high-school level. One of the earliest of these was the academy in Holden, Minnesota, established in 1869 by Bernt J.

66.
Theodore G. Tappert, *History of the Lutheran Theological Seminary at Philadelphia, 1864-1964* (Philadelphia: Lutheran Theological Seminary, 1964).

Muus. Others followed in rapid succession.[67] While the Norwegians established academies, the Danes provided "folk schools"—intermediate, short-term institutions with a strong cultural emphasis chiefly after 1875.[68]

Worship

Precious to the immigrants were their church books—Bibles, hymnals, catechisms, orders of worship, and prayer books. Coming from various European backgrounds, the immigrants introduced a wide variety of liturgical literature to America. It has been estimated that in Saxony alone seventy-five different hymnbooks were in use, accounting for the wide hymnological variety in the crude churches.

At the same time the Americanized Lutherans had been influenced to some extent by "American Evangelicalism," an amalgam of denatured Calvinism, revivalism, and liturgical Zwinglianism. Moreover, immigrant conditions and an anti-Catholic spirit led some of the churches to employ little formal ritual in public worship. This observation, however, must be qualified by the fact that the Lutheranism imported from Germany in the late eighteenth and early nineteenth century already gave evidence of a non-Lutheran ethos. The frontier conditions served in many instances only to accentuate what were already "low" liturgical practices in the old country. In the absence of organs, the song leader or cantor became an important worship leader.[69] Without him, congregational singing often became unenthusiastic and ponderous.

One of the lowest liturgical levels among Lutherans in America was reached when Frederick H. Quitman prepared a new English liturgy for the New York Ministerium in 1814.[70] Accepted by the General Synod in 1837, it confined its rubrics primarily to the ministerial acts. Apart from the hymns, the congregation rarely participated in the service. A German service recommended in 1843 was equally devoid of responsive elements.

By 1847 a change was in the offing. The General Synod adopted a new liturgy, revised in 1856, which took greater cognizance of Lutheran liturgical practices associated with an earlier era in Europe. With the adoption of the Washington Service in 1869, which derived its name from the fact that the General Synod first used this liturgy at its convention in Washington, D.C., traditional liturgical standards were gradually introduced during the next decades.[71] The new service was based extensively on Beale M. Schmucker's "Provisional Liturgy" of 1862 with such additions as the "Gloria Patri," the "Kyrie," and the "Gloria in Excelsis." It became a significant link in the somewhat romantic revival of Lutheran liturgical worship. Revisions in the German services, in 1855 and 1860, gave impetus to the American Lutheran liturgical movement.

One of the first German-American hymnals to be published by an immigrant group in America was produced in 1842 by J. A. A. Grabau, founder of the Buffalo Synod. Extensively based upon the formulas in use in Saxony and Pomerania,

67.
Bert H. Narveson, "The Norwegian Lutheran Academies," *Norwegian-American Studies and Records* 14 (1944): 187.
68.
Mortensen, *The Danish Church*, pp. 84ff.
69.
Paul M. Glasoe, "A Singing Church," *Norwegian-American Studies and Records* 13 (1943): 92-107.
70.
Luther D. Reed, *The Lutheran Liturgy* (Philadelphia: Muhlenberg Press, 1947), p. 170. For further background see Reginald W. Deitz, "The Lord's Supper in American Lutheranism," in *The Meaning and Practice of the Lord's Supper*, ed. Helmut T. Lehmann (Philadelphia: Muhlenberg Press, 1961), pp. 135-65; and J. F. Ohl, "The Liturgical Deterioration of the 17th and 18th Centuries," *Memoirs of the Lutheran Liturgical Association* 4 (1902): 67-78.
71.
The entire service appears in General Synod, *Proceedings of the Twenty-Fourth Convention* (Lancaster, Pa.: Pearsol & Geist, 1869), pp. 35-38.

72.
Ev. Luth. Kirchen-Gesangbuch (Buffalo, N.Y.: George Zahm, 1842).

73.
Wilhelm Loehe, *Agenda für christliche Gemeinden des lutherischen Bekenntnisses* (Noerdlingen, 1844).

74.
Kirchen-Agenda für Evangelisch-Lutherische Gemeinden (St. Louis, 1856).

75.
Kirchen-Gesang-Buch für Evangelisch-Lutherische Gemeinden (New York: H. Ludwig, 1847).

76.
Church Book (Philadelphia: Lutheran Book Store, 1868).

77.
Book of Worship (Columbia, S.C.: Duffie & Chapman, 1867).

78.
R. Morris Smith et al., "Liturgical Development Within the Evangelical Lutheran Church in the United States," *Lutheran Church Review* 36 (October 1917): 469–519. Cf. *Encyclopedia of the Lutheran Church*, 2:1052.

79.
Oscar N. Olson, *The Augustana Lutheran Church in America, 1860–1910* (Davenport, Iowa: Arcade Office and Letter Service, 1956), pp. 69–74.

Grabau considered Luther's *"Deutsche Messe"* as his standard. Liturgical practices came highly recommended. In fact, Grabau's interest in ancient forms motivated him to publish some hymns in the original Latin.[72]

The emissaries of Wilhelm Loehe used the 1844 *Agenda* (book of worship) which the author had dedicated to Friedrich Wyneken.[73] Since several of the Midwestern German immigrant congregations were unaffected by it, the Missouri Synod, nine years after its founding, published its *Kirchen-Agenda*.[74] Prior to this time, in 1847, in efforts to develop greater uniformity of worship among its churches, it had prepared a new German hymnal.[75]

The General Council established a special committee to prepare new church books at its preliminary meeting in 1866. The following year the committee outlined the proposed liturgical changes. When the delegates responded favorably, the convention instructed the committee to continue its revisions and plan its publication. The new hymnal was published in 1868.[76] It was supplemented in 1871 with an edition containing orders of service. A German edition (*Kirchenbuch*) appeared under council auspices in 1877.

Liturgical renewal also became noticeable in the southern part of the country after the Civil War. The General Synod of the South published its first book of worship in 1867.[77] Prior to that time some southern Lutherans used Paul Henkel's "English Liturgy" of 1817. Most of the southern synods, however, were chiefly dependent upon the materials produced in the north until the war. John Bachman, in 1870, recommended that a new uniform order of service be produced. After painstaking labors and several revisions, the Common Service was adopted by the General Council, the General Synod, and the General Synod of the South in 1887.[78]

Among the Swedish immigrants the "Church Book," first published in Sweden in 1614, served as the standard immigrant edition. Individual pastors and congregations often made minor changes, depending upon their own predilections. The first hymnal published in this country appeared in 1865 produced by the Swedish Evangelical Lutheran Publication Society and was called the *Psalmbok*. It chiefly represented a reprint of the Swedish hymnal of 1811. Revisions both in the liturgy and in the hymnal were slight until the end of the century.[79]

Danish and Norwegian immigrants arrived with their "Ritual of the Church of Denmark and Norway of 1685." Based upon liturgical revisions dating back to the Reformation period, the volume consisted of both liturgy and church law. The forms had been modified somewhat under the influence of pietism and rationalism. Attempts to develop a renewed interest in liturgical forms were usually met with diverse reactions. The Haugean movement, popular among the common people, recaptured some of the devotional literature and hymns of a former age. In spite of such additions, the Norwegian church did not make any major revisions until the late 1880s. Danish liturgical development and hymnology followed a similar pattern with major revisions occurring just prior to the turn of the century.

The immigrant was often deeply touched in heart and mind by the hymnody and the forms of worship with which he grew up. Small wonder, therefore, that he was extremely reluctant to accept change in liturgical practices or to adopt those of other Lutherans. Modification in worship sometimes required a minimum of two or three generations.

Publishers and Printing

The immigrants' books of course eventually wore out. Since foreign languages were involved, the church bodies at times made efforts to have certain books reprinted in Europe. Ultimately, such factors as long delays in filling orders and the increasing accessibility and development of local presses led to ecclesiastically controlled printing programs. At first, publishing interests were primarily directed to meeting practical needs; scholarly journals and technical works were to come later.

Bible societies (the first was established in America in Philadelphia in 1808) such as the American Bible Society (1816) supplied complete Bibles and New Testaments in the language of the immigrants. Separate societies, such as the German Evangelical Lutheran Bible Society for Missouri, Illinois, and Iowa (1853), were organized later with the membership limited to the supporting denomination. Branches were frequently established.[80]

Church bodies as such seemed reluctant to engage in publishing ventures and preferred the establishment of publication associations or societies. The Henkel Press was established at New Market, Virginia, in 1806, and became one of the aggressive publishers of English Lutheran confessional literature. The Tennessee Synod unanimously resolved in 1845 to translate and publish the entire Book of Concord containing all the confessional writings of the Lutheran church. The volume, an ambitious venture for so small a group, appeared in 1851.[81]

Lutherans in America perhaps never witnessed such personal sacrifice and effort in publication as that rendered by the indomitable Elling Eielsen in 1841. In order to have Luther's Small Catechism published in English he trudged from Illinois to New York, accompanied only by his rucksack and walking stick.[82] Not satisfied with this accomplishment, the Norwegian evangelist made a second, similar trip to New York a year later in order to publish Pontoppidan's explanation of the catechism, *Truth Unto Godliness,* into Norwegian. Interestingly, "Henry Ludvig," the publisher of the edition, became "Heinrich Ludwig" as the German publisher of the Missouri Synod's hymnal.

Although a large amount of the publishing was by private printers, pioneer leaders such as Tuve N. Hasselquist established printing presses in their own homes. In January 1855 Hasselquist produced the first issue of *Hemlandet det Gamla och det Nya.*[83] From Hasselquist's small beginning emerged the Swedish Lutheran Publication Society in the United States. When stock in the society was sold, its work was placed on a firm basis. Indirectly this developed into the Augustana Book Concern in 1889.[84]

80.
A. R. Suelflow, "Missouri Synod Organized," p. 180.
81.
Socrates Henkel, *History of the Evangelical Lutheran Tennessee Synod* (New Market, Va.: Henkel & Co., 1890), pp. 111–12.
82.
Nelson and Fevold, *Lutheran Church Among Norwegian-Americans,* 1:77.
83.
Olson, *Augustana Church,* p. 349.
84.
Arden, *Augustana Heritage,* p. 113.

A similar development took place within the Missouri Synod. A short-lived publication society, also formed as a stock company, had its beginning in 1849. After its demise in the 1850s, private publishers were designated as "synodical printers" and carried on projects under the supervision of the synodical committee. From this Publication Committee, formed in 1857, developed Concordia Publishing House, St. Louis, Missouri, in 1869.

With a constant demand for catechisms, hymnals, and Bibles **209** on the part of the member congregations of the General Synod, the Lutheran Publication Society was formed as an auxiliary association of the synod in 1855.[85] It received recognition by the synod two years later[86] and became its board of publication. In contrast to the General Synod, the General Council immediately established a separate board of publication at its constituting convention in 1867. Its initial purpose was to produce a new hymnal. Subsequently, however, the board developed into the General Council Publication House in 1899.[87] Other publication houses of various synods were established during the latter part of the century.

The first popular edition of Luther's selected writings appeared through the efforts of the American Luther Society organized in 1859. Within a year the society numbered more than 1,660 members. It produced the popular laymen's edition known as Luther's *Volksbibliothek* in thirty volumes between 1859 and 1876.

Martin Luther had made extensive use of the printing press to proclaim and defend the gospel during the Reformation. Ever since, Lutherans have been concerned with the production and publication of literature addressing itself to contemporary needs. The number of books, tracts, and periodicals is impressive. Through many of them significant contributions to the life and thought of both the American church and society were made.

85.
General Synod, *Proceedings of the Seventeenth Convention* (Baltimore: T. Newton Kurtz, 1855), p. 25.
86.
General Synod, *Proceedings of the Eighteenth Convention* (Gettysburg, Pa.: Neinstedt, 1857), pp. 72–79.
87.
Documentary History of the General Council . . . (Philadelphia: General Council Pub. House, 1912), pp. 489–94.

11 Sectionalism, Conflict, and Synthesis

The nineteenth century dawned upon an era of good feeling and interdenominational goodwill. Religious revivals flourished, cooperative agencies for the distribution of Bibles, tracts, and other church literature were being established, and missionary societies followed aggressively in the wake of westward movements. The Congregational and the Presbyterian churches implemented their cooperative endeavors through their "Plan of Union" in 1801, and neighborliness typified the frontiersman. Would the nineteenth century usher in a golden age?

Hardly had the 1830s come to a close when the country and its churches became involved in bitterness and strife. A few ruptures among some of the churches had already occurred during the first two decades of the new century, but these seem minor in comparison to the events of the period 1840–75. Changes in economic life were hastened by the Industrial Revolution. The floodgates of immigration had been opened and a host of people speaking strange languages were crowding the eastern seaports and filtering toward the Midwest. During the course of the years, too, the common man, depending upon his frontier resourcefulness, had developed an individualism and an independence, which, in religious and ecclesiastical matters, often led to divisiveness.

Discord and disunity soon became apparent both within and among the churches. Tensions between Protestants and Roman Catholics were heightening, and even within the Protestant churches strife and schism developed rapidly. The Presbyterians were embroiled with their "New School" and "Old School" controversies. The Episcopalians, affected in America by the Oxford Movement, had already been introduced to the "high-churchism" of John H. Hobart (1775–1830). William A. Muhlenberg (1796–1877), a grandson of the patriarch of the Lutheran Church in America, paved the way for the differences within the Episcopal Church to exist side by side by his urging an "evangelical catholic" attitude. Antagonisms and finally violent persecution against Mormonism ended in skirmishes, violent deaths, and expulsions. Both the Methodist and Baptist denominations suffered internal dissensions that were to be institutionalized, especially as the churches became involved in the controversy over slavery (see below). Moreover, as this period dawned, William Miller, a Baptist farmer-preacher, predicted the end of the world in March 1843. This gave rise to the Adventist movement. The Fox sisters developed spiritualism in New York. Formerly flourishing interdenominational Sunday school unions were replaced by denominational ones. The Evangelical Alliance, in which Lutheran leader Samuel S.

Schmucker played a leading role, had convened in London in 1846 with high enthusiasm, only to see its ecumenical hopes fade away. Thus the 1830s and 1840s witnessed much religious turbulence.

In addition to the trouble in the churches, the clouds of violent controversy gathered on the political horizon. Tensions between geographical areas of the country increased as the 1860s approached. America seemed to be turned in upon itself with the South pitted against the North and the West being contested by both. The melting-pot of nations seemed to realize that individual, geographical, economic, and cultural differences could not be easily overcome. It was in this period of tension that Lutheranism, too, became engaged in one of its most serious struggles for self-identification and reinterpretation in the new homeland.

211

Philip Schaff (1819–93), a professor at the Reformed seminary in Mercersburg, Pennsylvania, foresaw the internal Lutheran tensions with clarity. In an address to the "Evangelischer Verein für innere Mission" in Berlin in 1854, the knowledgeable church historian observed:

In general one may speak of three general tendencies in the American Lutheran church, excluding insignificant and local divisions. For brevity's sake, we shall call them the "Neo-Lutheran," the "Old Lutheran," and "Moderate Lutheran," or Melanchthonian.

The "Neo-Lutheran" party originated out of a conflict and an amalgamation of Lutheranism with American Puritanism and Methodistic elements. It consists mostly of American-born Germans and proudly calls itself, in an emphatic way, the American Lutheran Church. This group is probably the largest, undoubtedly the most active, the most practical and progressive, and is best acquainted with the English spirit. It is to a large extent English and un-German, not only in language, but also in all its sympathies and antipathies.

Theological training and thorough education is not found among them, but instead mostly superficial American routine sophistication, gift of eloquence, knowledge of parliamentary order, and business-manship. To this group nominally belong the Lutheran institutions of Gettysburg, Pa. (where in the last few years at least a partial reaction and modification of these aspects and more favorable Lutheran and German tendencies have entered in), Springfield, Ohio, and Springfield, Ill. Up till now it has carried the most weight in the General Synod. One can best learn to know them through their organ, THE LUTHERAN OBSERVER, edited by Dr. [Benjamin] Kurtz, and out of the numerous writings of Dr. [Samuel S.] Schmucker of Gettysburg, especially in his POPULAR THEOLOGY.

The Old Lutheran division has just recently immigrated to America from Germany, chiefly from

Saxony (the Stephanites), from Prussia (Grabau . . .), and from Bavaria (Loehe's missioners). They are still totally German and have not blended in the least with the English and the American spirit. Even though outwardly they are progressing quite well, they are still strangers and foreigners in a new world. With the second generation things will probably look quite different. . . .

212 The pastors of the Old Lutheran group are for the most well indoctrinated, faithful, conscientious, and self-sacrificing. At the same time . . . they could hardly consider the most pious Reformed as a Christian and would not at any price partake of the Lord's Holy Supper with him.

. . . They are not even in agreement among themselves. Concerning the doctrine of the ministry, . . . they are divided into two enemy camps and are vying with each other in their weekly church papers with an antipathy and bitterness which certainly is not an honor to Lutheranism and Christianity and does not in the least command respect from the Anglo-American concerning this portion of German Christianity in case he should by chance hear of it.

The Synod of Missouri, which was organized in 1847 and since then has grown rapidly, represents in this controversy, especially through the LUTHERANER, edited by Professor [C. F. W.] Walther, the usual Protestant point of view, which considers the ministerial office as the mouthpiece of the universal priesthood and bases its belief on the published documents of the Lutheran Church and the private writings of their outstanding theologians. The Synod of Lutherans immigrated from Prussia presents the catholicizing doctrine. This is set forth in THE INFORMATORIUM, edited by Pastor [J. A. A.] Grabau in Buffalo, New York. It bases its stand especially on the doctrine of ordination and the universal priesthood of the baptized members, which have a very specific priestly office, on the basis of important proofs from Scripture and tradition. . . .

The moderate Lutheran tendency standing in the center of these two extremes . . . has the oldest American Lutheran tradition on its side, because the first missioners came chiefly from the Halle Orphanage and from the Spener and Francke schools of Pietism. . . . This group is represented by the oldest and largest synod, the Pennsylvania, and in some degrees also by the Joint Synod of Ohio, which a few years ago has announced that the Symbolical Books, including the Formula of Concord, are obligatory. It does not sympathize with the exclusive spirit of the Old Lutherans, since its leaders are too Americanized already and know the English Reformed Church better than to accuse them of heresy unhesitatingly. THE LUTHERAN STANDARD, which appears in Columbus, may in a manner be considered its organ. A goodly number of their preachers, especially among the older men, have few firm convictions, are poorly educated, stagnant, and are much more concerned about building programs and politics than theology and church affairs. . . .

A deeper spiritual life and a church consciousness developed within recent years in the Pennsylvania Synod. The most influential man in this movement in the last two decades was without a doubt Dr. R. Demme of Philadelphia, who was born in Altenburg. He is an outstanding pulpit orator and a man with a noteworthy solid, strong, and a true German personality, the author of the liturgy and new hymnbook in use in this synod. One of the most outstanding among the younger spiritual leaders is a colleague of his, the Rev. W. J. Mann of Philadelphia, who had studied theology in Wuerttemberg. He is endowed with extraordinary gifts, a lively spirit, a wide scope of knowledge, and an amiable character; he belongs to the school of the new Evangelical theology of Germany, which will probably come to the fore more and more in this body, since it would be very unnatural for the Lutheran church to shut itself out from the evolution and progress in the theology of the mother country.

To this group are also added many promising young theologians, some who were trained in America and some who have emigrated from Europe, who generally follow the same tendencies. The true task of the old Pennsylvania Synod lies herein, not only to be a conciliatory force between the ecclesiastical Old-Lutheranism and the Puritanic Neo-Lutheranism, but also at the same time to mediate between the European-German and the American interests and thereby effect a drawing together and consolidation of the different elements in the Lutheran church of America. This task it can rightly fulfill now for the first time, since its more progressive members have effected the passage of two important measures, the union with Gettysburg and with the General Synod.

This synod has, after numerous unsuccessful attempts to establish their own theological school, set up a German professorship at the Gettysburg institution. No one, however, is filling this chair yet. The spirit of the institution has changed during that time and approached their views. Through the establishment of the professorship it has a legitimate permanent influence on the institution and on the next generation of pastors. Accordingly it has joined the General Synod and at its last session in 1853 sent 6 delegates, who used their voices in behalf of a stronger Lutheran and ecclesiastical influence.

213

Schaff continues his description of the three parties within American Lutheranism by pointing out that they differed theologically, constitutionally, and liturgically.

The Old Lutherans (largely the Missouri and Buffalo synods) adhered strictly to "pure doctrine" which was set forth in the Book of Concord (1580). The latter had binding authority. The Moderates, typified by the Ministerium of Pennsylvania, affirmed two of the documents in the Book of Concord, the Augsburg Confession and Luther's Small Catechism, as the primary confessional statements of Lutheranism. The Neo-Lutherans, however, had "really given up all specific characteristics of Lutheran doctrine. . . ." They were, in fact, much more closely identified with "American Evangelicalism," exhibiting a strong "Arminianism" and an exaggerated anti-Romanism. The leader of this group, Samuel S. Schmucker, according to Schaff, had his own dogmatic position which could be stated as follows: (1) rejection of the binding authority of all Lutheran confessions except the Augsburg Confession; (2) the acceptance of the latter "insofar as" (*quatenus*) it agreed with the Bible (the Augsburg Confession was "substantially correct" as an expression of biblical doctrine); (3) the rejection of such Lutheran teachings and practices as exorcism, original sin and guilt, private confession, baptismal regeneration, the "real presence" in the Lord's Supper, and non-Puritanical observance of the Sabbath—all of which were judged unbiblical.

Schaff is at pains to point out that the Neo-Lutheran view of the Lord's Supper was essentially Zwinglian. When Schaff's colleague, John W. Nevin, defended Calvin's doctrine of the spiritual real presence and true eating of the body and blood by faith, Benjamin Kurtz, one of Schmucker's co-workers, attacked Nevin's views as romanizing and ridiculous. However, the Neo-Lutheran platform was in no sense liberalism—Schmucker stoutly affirmed the deity of Christ and the verbal inspiration of Scripture—but it was American Zwinglian Puritanism on Lutheran soil.

Against these Anglo-American Neo-Lutherans the Moderates within the General Synod, led by such men as William J. Mann, John G. Morris, and especially Charles Philip Krauth raised the banner of evangelical Lutheran confessionalism, taking a theological position between the extremes of Old Lutheranism and Neo-Lutheranism. Unfortunately, Schaff continues, the three camps were constitutionally as well as theologically disunited. This led to a bewildering confusion, an overlapping of jurisdictions, and unregulated practices.

Finally, the differences mentioned above led to a variety of liturgical attitudes. The Old Lutherans adhered generally to traditional Lutheran forms of worship. The Neo-Lutherans, fearful of liturgical formalism, found the ways of "American Evangelicalism" attractive, even to the extent of accepting in part revivalistic patterns, including "new measures" and the "anxious bench." The Moderates, though rejecting the theological rigidities of Old Lutheranism, found the Neo-Lutheran neglect of traditional Lutheran liturgical piety quite as repugnant. Consequently, they urged what Schaff calls a "healthy tendency, active between two extremes . . . ," a tendency that "urged the reviving and furthering of a solid, churchly, religious life. . . ."[1]

From this lucid description of Lutheranism in America, the reader might anticipate that sectionalism and controversy would erupt shortly. The situation was conducive to conflict. Suspicion and irritability marked relationships. Although the adoption of a constitution for a General Synod in 1820 had seemed to usher in a new unity and optimism, only three district synods (the Ministerium of Pennsylvania, the North Carolina Synod, and the Maryland-Virginia Synod) constituted the first convention of the General Synod in 1821.

215

Before the century was a little more than half over violent controversy, separation, and realignments became commonplace. The process of Americanization and acclimatization which the second- and third-generation Lutherans had already undergone would cause conflicts with the arrival of new immigrants from the Lutheran countries in Europe. Language barriers further affected inter-Lutheran relationships because dialogue and communication were not easy. The Lutheran confessions and Lutheran literature were largely inaccessible to a sizeable segment of American Lutherans. In contrast, however, a wealth of general Anglo-American Protestant and Reformed literature was readily available in English.

Revivalism

In addition to the language difficulties there was the controversial issue of revivalism. When, in the wake of the revolutionary war and the subsequent westward movements, individuals and groups frequently became detached from their churches, revivalism offered a means to renew and reawaken spiritual life. Protracted meetings and enthusiastic and emotional outbursts were often employed in attempting renewal. Some Lutherans were not immune to such methods and considered them spiritually vitalizing. In fact, sometimes Lutherans rivaled the Methodists, Baptists, and Finneyites in employing the techniques of the revivalistic system. Benjamin Kurtz, editor of the *Lutheran Observer* for many years, defended revivalism's "new measures." In a lengthy series of articles Kurtz carried on a running battle with Reformed theologian John W. Nevin (1803–86), who had written a severe criticism of the "anxious bench." Kurtz said:

If the great object of the anxious bench can be accomplished in some other way, less obnoxious but equally efficient—be it so. But we greatly doubt this. We consider it necessary in many cases, and we believe there are circumstances when no measures equally good can be substituted. Hence we are free to confess that we go for this measure *with all our heart*.[2] [Italics in original]

1.
For the English text of Schaff's address see August R. Suelflow, "Nietzsche and Schaff on American Lutheranism," *Concordia Historical Institute Quarterly* 23 (January 1951): 149–57. The reader may wish to compare the English edition of *America*, ed. Perry Miller (Cambridge: Harvard University Press, 1961), esp. pp. 150–59. By far the best treatment of the theological issues in nineteenth-century Lutheranism in America is Theodore G. Tappert, ed., *Lutheran Confessional Theology in America, 1840–1880* (New York: Oxford University Press, 1972).

2.
Benjamin Kurtz, "Notes on the 'Anxious Bench,'" *Lutheran Observer*, December 1, 1843, p. 3.

Further, a dichotomy appeared between "head" and "heart" Christians, as it had on the Continent. Kurtz observed:

. . . The Catechism, highly as we prize it, can never supersede the anxious bench, but only, when faithfully used, renders it more necessary. During the whole time that the church was declining in Germany, and even in its most languishing state, it was gorged with catechetical instructions, and so continued to be until nearly the whole church had fallen into neology and lifeless formality.[3]

As a prelude to the controversy of the 1850s, Kurtz came to grips with Nevin in another article:

Has the Doctor [Nevin] forgotten that we [Lutherans] have no "creed" or "catechism" which requires *uniformity of belief* in non-essentials? That we allow our members to believe what they think the Bible teaches provided they agree in *fundamental* points; in a word, that we have adopted the Melanchthonian maxim: *in certis unitas, in dubiis libertas, in omnibus caritas.* [In essentials unity, in non-essentials liberty, in all things charity.] Hence, we bear and forebear; agree in some points and differ in others; but are we therefore "split into different divisions?"[4] [Italics in original]

Where revivalistic techniques were employed consistently, the central doctrine of justification by faith in Christ was endangered and the theological complexion often became Arminian. The denial of original sin followed and the sinner was granted the ability to cooperate with God in the act of justification. Luther's catechism fell into disuse. Half a century later David H. Bauslin evaluated the "new measures" as follows:

That it was an abnormal and unhistorical importation from extra-Lutheran sources, that it was an alien in our midst, will at this day hardly be denied. The phrase "New Measures" stood for a type and as representing a system of religious activity which in some sections of the church largely supplanted an antagonized method which had been from the very beginning of its life associated with the genius and development of the Evangelical Lutheran Church. In the 4th and 5th decades of the last century what was technically denominated the "New Measure movement" did not stand for a revival of religion in the best use of that word, but rather for certain extravagances which seem to be inseparable from the introduction of certain revivalistic machinery. . . . It was associated with solemn tricks for the sake of effect, decision displays at the bidding of the preacher, genuflections and prostrations in the aisle or around the altar, noise and disorder, extravagance and rant, mechanical conversions, justification by feeling rather than by faith, and encouragement to all sorts of fanatical impressions . . . many of our people were swept along with the current until they found the Catechism and all other historical belongings of the Church supplanted by

216

3.
Ibid., November 24, 1843, p. 2.

4.
Ibid., December 29, 1843, p. 3. It should be pointed out that the author of the maxim was not Melanchthon. The famous phrase is more commonly ascribed to the German Lutheran pastor from Augsburg, Peter Meiderlin (*nom de plume*: "Rupert Meldenius") (1582–1651). See *Religion in Geschichte und Gegenwart*, ed. Kurt Galling et al., 3d ed. (Tübingen: J. C. B. Mohr, 1960), 4:846; *The New Schaff-Herzog Encyclopedia of Religious Knowledge*, ed. Samuel Macauley Jackson (New York: Funk & Wagnalls, 1910), 7:287; and *Real-Encyclopedie für Protestantische Theologie und Kirche*, ed. J. J. Herzog et al. (Leipzig: J. C. Hinrich'sche Buchhandlung, 1881), 9:528–30.

the "anxious bench" and other human and mechanical revivalistic appliances.[5]

5.
"The Genesis of the 'New Measure' Movement in the Lutheran Church in This Country," *Lutheran Quarterly* 40 (July 1910): 360–91.
6.
Abdel Ross Wentz, *Pioneer in Christian Unity: Samuel Simon Schmucker* (Philadelphia: Fortress Press, 1967), p. 132.

Confessional Struggle

The General Synod experienced some of its most severe struggles for survival during this period. In its conscientious efforts to reinterpret Lutheranism on the American scene it responded with an openness of character and structure (federal) which ultimately weakened its Lutheran witness. It is ironic that the General Synod—which in the 1820s had rallied Lutheran synods to a greater consciousness of Lutheranism, had banded almost two-thirds of all independent synods together in a single federated organization, and had reintroduced the Augsburg Confession into the life and thought of the church—was to become the potential nadir of Lutheranism in the middle of the century. At the outbreak of the Civil War that general body was on the verge of experiencing serious theological conflicts and organizational disruptions.

217

The foremost leader in the General Synod was Samuel S. Schmucker. His primary work centered at the Gettysburg Seminary where he became its first and most distinguished professor for forty years. The history of the General Synod and Schmucker are so intimately intertwined that it is often difficult to distinguish them (see chapters 7 and 8). Even as some others in the General Synod, Schmucker expended efforts to reintroduce the Augsburg Confession into the Lutheran church. He deemed this necessary lest the church lose its confessional character and become simply another ingredient in what became "American Evangelicalism." The inaugural oath, which Schmucker himself had written in 1826, reveals his position:

I solemnly declare in the presence of God and the Directors of this Seminary, that I do *ex animo,* believe the Scriptures of the Old and New Testament to be the inspired Word of God, and the only perfect rule of faith and practice. I believe the Augsburg Confession and the Catechisms of Luther to be a summary and just exhibition of the fundamental doctrines of the Word of God. . . . And I do solemnly promise not to teach anything either directly or by insinuation, which shall appear to me to contradict, or to be in any degree more or less remote, inconsistent with the doctrines or principles avowed in this declaration. On the contrary, I promise, by the aid of God, to vindicate and inculcate these doctrines or principles . . . while I remain a professor in this Seminary.[6]

An interesting question with which historians have toyed for many decades is whether Schmucker changed his theological-confessional position over the course of years or whether Lutheranism in America changed during that period of time, or both. Schmucker's chief biographer, Abdel Ross Wentz, maintains: "The student of Schmucker's thought should observe that these theological positions, particularly his views on the Lord's Supper and his attitude toward creeds and confessions, were set down in writing as early as 1833 and remained essentially the same through the rest of his life."[7] Luther Weigle also points to the changes which Lutheranism underwent, and which consequently left Schmucker behind:

You do not know that Dr. Schmucker advocated what was known in his day as "American Lutheranism," that he lost out, and that "American Lutheranism" passed with him . . . the man who did more than any other to establish and strengthen the General Synod . . . , who for many years drafted its most important documents and was its acknowledged leader, who founded the Seminary and College at Gettysburg and gave his life to the service of the first of these institutions, toward the end of his days lost his leadership. He was no longer Lutheran enough. His position had not changed; but all about him had. "He had fallen behind," the historian puts it, "in the progress of conservative Lutheranism."[8]

It is difficult to say whether Schmucker was totally aware of the changes that were occurring in the theological and confessional position of America's Lutherans. In his *Portraiture of Lutheranism,* published in 1840,[9] he demonstrated precisely that cleavages would occur between him on the one hand and the new confessionalists among the "native" Lutherans and the later immigrants on the other hand. Opposing positions on confessional subscription, the real presence of Christ in the sacrament, private confession, exorcism, and the authority of the church fathers were already apparent. What caused the two positions to be even more completely separated was the fact that the new immigrants had experienced religious persecution in their homelands and were determined in a free America to adhere to the doctrines taught in the confessions. A conflict could not be avoided.

Concurrently with the arrival of the Old Lutherans, there was developing among some synods of the General Synod a greater confessional consciousness which, in a practical way, manifested itself by the insertion of confessional commitments into synodical constitutions. This tendency had become noticeable even before the arrival of the Lutherans from Scandinavia and Germany in the 1840s. The European neo-confessionalism had come to America ahead of the immigrants in the form of German theological literature which reflected an awakened Lutheran self-consciousness.

An examination of the confessional statements which had been adopted or were modified by the synods is illuminating. In order to show the contrasting range, we shall compare the confessional paragraph of the Frankean Synod (founded in western New York in 1837) with two Midwestern synods. It should be recalled that the Frankean Synod had been organized as a protest against the Hartwick Synod because the latter was not, in the former's opinion, moving rapidly enough in a direction of revivalism and in its opposition to slavery. The Frankeans, however, remained bland with respect to confessional position. Its

7.
Ibid., p. 162. The apparent contradiction between this statement and the inaugural oath (1826) seems to be explained in the oath's words "which shall appear to me."
8.
Luther A. Weigle, "Foreword" in Vergilius Ferm, *The Crisis in American Lutheran Theology* (New York: Century Co., 1927), pp. vii–viii. Weigle's "historian" in this quote is Abdel Ross Wentz.
9.
Portraiture of Lutheranism (Baltimore: Publication Rooms, 1840).

constitution merely acknowledged ". . . the Lord Jesus Christ as the supreme Head of the church, and the Word of God as the sufficient and infallible rule of faith and practice. . . ."[10] Contrast this minimal statement, which omitted all references to the Augsburg Confession and to Luther's Catechism, with the paragraph adopted by the Norwegian Synod at its constituting convention in 1853:

10.
Ferm, *Crisis*, p. 150.
11.
E. Clifford Nelson and Eugene L. Fevold, *The Lutheran Church Among Norwegian-Americans*, 2 vols. (Minneapolis: Augsburg Publishing House, 1960), 1:344.
12.
Joint Synod of Ohio, *Proceedings . . . 1854*, pp. 6–7.

219

The doctrine of the Church is that which is revealed through God's holy Word in the canonical writings of the Old and New Testaments, interpreted in accord with the symbols or confessional writings of the Church of Norway, namely: 1) the Apostles' Creed; 2) the Nicene Creed; 3) the Athanasian Creed; 4) the Unaltered Augsburg Confession, delivered to Emperor Charles V at Augsburg, 1530; 5) Luther's Small Catechism.[11]

The Joint Ohio Synod in 1854 amended its constitution even more explicitly:

This synod shall be composed of representatives from all Ev. Lut. [*sic*] Synods, now united in the existing Synod of Ohio and such other Synods as may from time to time adopt this Constitution, and with us adhere to the doctrines of the word of God as set forth in all the Symbolical Books of the Evangelical Lutheran Church, or who in their own Constitution confess and maintain the unaltered Augsburg Confession and Luther's smaller Catechism in the sense and spirit of the other symbols.[12]

Schmucker's pledge to the Augsburg Confession, freely given at the time of his installation as the first professor at Gettysburg, was already demonstrative of the new tendency developing among Eastern Lutherans. The Henkel Press (New Market, Va.) contributed significantly to this confessional renaissance by a translation and publication program which made many of the Lutheran confessional writings available in English. A confessional renewal, therefore, was apparent in America.

As further evidence of this transition, we cite the work of William A. Passavant who began publishing *The Missionary* as a conservative voice in 1848. In Gettysburg itself, Charles Philip Krauth (1797–1867) (father of Charles Porterfield Krauth), president of Gettysburg College, and, after 1850, president of Gettysburg Seminary, began a new theological journal in 1850, the *Evangelical Review*. Though not specifically expressed, the new journal was intended to counterbalance the influence of Kurtz's *Lutheran Observer* which, as has been noted, had taken up the cudgels for revivalistic measures and was still defending Schmucker's position. The relationships between Krauth and Schmucker, serving on the same faculty, became strained.

In spite of these indications of a renewed interest in the Lutheran confessions, Schmucker and his friends (Benjamin Kurtz, Henry N. Pohlman, John G. Morris, and Henry I. Schmidt) addressed a revealing letter to the united Lutheran-Reformed church of Germany in 1845. Adolf von Harless, of the Leipzig faculty and a leader of the confessional party in Germany, published the letter. In his introduction, von Harless stated that the contents were sufficiently characteristic to elucidate church conditions in America. The letter stated in part:

Now as to our doctrinal views, we confess without disguise, indeed confess it loudly and openly, that the greatest majority of us are not old Lutherans, in the sense in which a small party exists in Germany under that name. We are convinced that, if the great Luther were still living, he would not be a member of it either. We believe that the three last centuries have also produced men who were capable of independent thought, research and growth equal to the 16th. Yea, as insignificant as we consider ourselves, we are nevertheless emboldened, particularly through our feeling of duty, to investigate and explore Scripture, and to draw our doctrinal views from this heavenly source. But, nevertheless, we are Evangelical Lutheran. Committed to Luther's fundamental principle that God's Word is without error, we have proved that Luther's doctrinal construction is essentially correct. In most of our church principles we stand on common ground with the union or merged church of Germany. The distinctive views which separate the old Lutherans and the Reformed Church we do not consider essential; and the tendency of the so called old Lutheran party seems to us to be behind our time. . . . With all fundamental [sic] principles of the Christian faith we agree with Luther and the Symbols of the Lutheran church. . . .

The doctrine of the absolute predestination none of our pastors accepts. The peculiar view of Luther on the bodily presence of the Lord in the Lord's Supper has been abandoned long ago by the great majority of our preachers. . . . Concerning the art and meaning of the presence of the Lord in the Lord's Supper we allow freedom, as does also the Evangelical Church of Germany.[13]

A few years later, in 1851, Schmucker wrote in the *Evangelical Review* indicating precisely where he felt modifications ought to be made:

For them [the Gettysburg faculty] to inculcate on their students the obsolete views of the old Lutherans, contained in the former symbols of the church in some parts of Germany, such as exorcism, the real presence of the body and blood of Christ in the Eucharist, private confession, baptismal regeneration, immersion in baptism, as taught in Luther's Larger Catechism, etc., would be to betray the confidence of those who elected them to office, and to defeat the design of the Institution, not one dollar of whose funds was contributed by Synods or Individuals professing these views.[14]

How radical the transition actually had become may best be demonstrated by the observation which John G. Morris (1803–95), a student of Schmucker's and a member of the Gen-

220

13.
"Aus Amerika," *Zeitschrift für Protestantismus und Kirche* 11 (1846): 263-64.
14.
"Vocation of the American Lutheran Church," *Evangelical Review* 2 (April 1851): 509.

eral Synod, made toward the end of his long career when he commented on the 1845 letter:

Never was a more senseless blunder committed. Whilst the Appeal [to the church in Germany] may have been in conformity to the theological opinions of some in the United Church of Prussia, yet there were thousands of Lutherans who would not sanction it theologically. The United could not understand how men professing such doctrines or denying the fundamental principles of Lutheranism, could honestly call themselves Lutherans, for they have high notions of consistency abroad, and the Old Lutherans could not recognize men as such who had given up the distinctive points. The result was, to my personal knowledge, that when Drs. Schmucker and Kurtz went to Europe in 1846, not one of them was invited to preach in any pulpit on the Continent! This *I know* [*sic*] to be true for I was with them.[15]

What actually had happened was that in the 1820s Schmucker was far more confessional than many of his contemporaries. Two or three decades later quite a number of his influential contemporaries had moved significantly into the confessional orbit, while he remained static. In the meantime he participated in the London meeting of the Evangelical Alliance (1846) and continued his concerns for greater rapprochement among America's Protestants. In this context, though really not unexpectedly, Schmucker together with Kurtz and Samuel Sprecher (1810–1906), Schmucker's brother-in-law and president of Wittenberg College as well as the General Synod, issued the *Definite Synodical Platform* in 1855.

The stage was set for a violent controversy. The *Definite Platform* appeared somewhat mysteriously and anonymously in the mail. The only clue to its origin was the note contained in the introduction:

THIS PLATFORM is sent to some brethren who had no opportunity to order it, as it was thought they would desire to have this. Such are requested to peruse it, and if they wish to retain it, to send 25¢ in silver, or post-office stamps by mail, post-paid, to Messrs. Miller and Burlock, Philadelphia. Should any not desire to retain it, they will please enclose it carefully in paper, and send it, postpaid, to the same address.[16]

The only contact, therefore, was with the publisher. Further, the introductory note revealed:

N.B.—This Platform was prepared and published by consultation and co-operation of Ministers of different Eastern and Western Synods, connected with the General Synod, at the special request of some Western brethren, whose churches desire a more specific expression of the General Synod's doctrinal basis, being surrounded by German churches, which profess the entire mass of the former symbols.[17]

The *Definite Platform,* consisting of several parts, contained the "American Recension of the Augsburg Confession," which it

15.
John G. Morris, *Fifty Years in the Lutheran Ministry* (Baltimore: James Young, 1878), p. 123.
16.
Definite Platform, Doctrinal and Disciplinarian, for Evangelical Lutheran District Synods: Constructed in Accordance with the Principles of the General Synod (Philadelphia: Miller & Burlock, 1855).
17.
Ibid., p. 2.

221

heartily recommended for adoption, as a replacement for the original confession of 1530. A comparison of several paragraphs drawn from the two texts will demonstrate the differences:

Augsburg Confession 1530	The American Recension 1855
II. Original Sin	**II. Of Natural Depravity**
Our churches also teach that since the fall of Adam all men who are propagated according to nature are born in sin. That is to say, they are without fear of God, are without trust in God, and are concupiscent. And this disease or vice or origin is truly sin, which even now damns and brings eternal death on those who are not born again through baptism and the Holy Spirit.	Our churches likewise teach that since the fall of Adam, all men who are naturally engendered, are born with sin, that is, without the fear of God or confidence towards Him, and with sinful propensities; and that this disease, or natural depravity, is really sin, and still causes eternal death to those who are not born again. And they reject the opinion of those, who, in order that they may detract from the glory of the merits and benefits of Christ, alleged that man may be justified before God by the powers of his own reason.
Our churches condemn the Pelagians and others who deny that the vice of origin is sin and who obscure the glory of Christ's merit and benefits by contending that man can be justified before God by his own strength and reason.	
VIII. What Is the Church?	**VIII. What Is the Church?**
Properly speaking, the church is the assembly of saints and true believers. However, since in this life many hypocrites and evil persons are mingled with believers, it is allowable to use the sacraments even when they are administered by evil men, according to the saying of Christ, "the scribes and Pharisees sit on Moses' seat," etc. (Matt. 23:2). Both the sacraments and the Word are effectual by reason of the institution and commandment of Christ even if they are administered by evil men.	Although the church is properly a congregation of saints and true believers yet in the present life, many hypocrites and wicked men are mingled with them.
Our churches condemn the Donatists and others like them who have denied that	

the ministering of evil men may be used in the church and who have taught the ministry of evil men to be unprofitable and without effect.

IX. Baptism

Our churches teach that Baptism is necessary for salvation, that the grace of God is offered through Baptism, and that children should be baptized, for being offered to God through Baptism they are received into His grace.

Our churches condemn the Anabaptists who reject the Baptism of children and declare that children are saved without Baptism.

IX. Baptism

Concerning Baptism, our churches teach, that it is "a necessary ordinance," that is a means of grace, and ought to be administered also to children, who are thereby dedicated to God, and received into His favor.

223

X. Lord's Supper

Our churches teach that the body and blood of Christ are truly present and are distributed to those who eat in the Supper of the Lord. They disapprove of those who teach otherwise.

X. Lord's Supper

In regard to the Lord's Supper they teach that Christ is present with the communicants in the Lord's Supper, under the emblems of Bread and wine.

XI. Confession

Our churches teach that private absolution should be retained in the churches. However, in confession an enumeration of all sins is not necessary, for this is not possible according to the Psalm, "who can discern his errors?" (Ps. 19:12).

XI. Confession

A Private Confession and Absolution, which are inculcated in this Article, though in a modified form, have been universally rejected by the American Lutheran Church, the omission of this Article is demanded by the principle on which the American Recension of the Augsburg Confession is constructed; namely, to omit the several portions, which are rejected by the great mass of our churches in this country, and to add nothing in their stead.

The die was cast. Not since the days of Melanchthon, who had looked upon the Augsburg Confession as somewhat of a private possession (he was its author), had anyone tampered with its text so radically as this. The reaction was explosive. The introduction of the *Definite Platform* stated that the Augsburg Confession contained five errors:

1. the approval of the ceremonies of the mass
2. the approval of private confession and absolution
3. the denial of the divine obligation of the Christian Sabbath
4. the affirmation of baptismal regeneration
5. the affirmation of the real presence of the body and blood of the Savior in the Holy Communion[18]

The vast majority of the constituent synods of the General Synod refused to accept the *Definite Platform*. Some expressed strenuous opposition to it, reaffirming their subscription to the unaltered Augsburg Confession. Still others ignored it. Only three small synods, East Ohio (founded in 1830), Wittenberg (organized 1847), and the Olive Branch (founded in 1848) adopted it "heartily."

Among the first to sound the alarm was the Synod of East Pennsylvania (organized on the territory of the Ministerium of Pennsylvania in 1842) which met in September 1855. This synod immediately expressed its "most unqualified disapprobation of this most dangerous attempt to change the doctrinal basis, and revolutionize the existing character of the Lutheran churches . . . and . . . most solemnly warn our sister Synod against this dangerous proposition. . . ."[19] As was to be expected, Benjamin Kurtz came to the *Definite Platform*'s defense in the *Lutheran Observer*. Sprecher, one of the co-authors, defended it in the Wittenberg Synod convention where the Recension was unanimously adopted.

The most vigorous discussion was conducted by the West Pennsylvania Synod held at Gettysburg toward the end of September and early October 1855. Schmucker, Charles Philip Krauth, and others were present. For them it was not merely a single document which was at stake. Profound issues of two opposing theological positions within Lutheranism were to be decided. After heated debate, the synod decisively rejected the *Definite Platform* and thereby repudiated Schmucker's leadership.[20]

The inevitable tractarian and pamphlet war broke out shortly. Comments first appeared in the Lutheran press, followed by a host of pamphlets. The most devastating blow against the *Definite Platform*, however, was rendered by William J. Mann of the Ministerium of Pennsylvania and later professor at the Philadelphia Seminary in his *A Plea for the Augsburg Confession*. . . .[21]

Several of the opponents met in February 1856. It seemed the church was ready for an armistice. The "Pacific Overture" suggested the route often customary in controversy. Signed by sixty-four clergymen and laymen, including representatives of both sides of the issue, it promised to desist from further controversy and to abide by the doctrinal basis of the General Synod which required ". . . absolute assent to the Word of God, as the only infallible rule of faith and practice, and fundamental

18.
Richard C. Wolf, *Documents of Lutheran Unity in America* (Philadelphia: Fortress Press, 1966), p. 103.
19.
Synod of East Pennsylvania, *Proceedings . . . 1855*, pp. 13-14, as quoted by Ferm, *Crisis*, p. 237. It should be noted that the Synod of East Pennsylvania (1842) was formed by congregations of the Pennsylvania Ministerium, largely to foster the use of English. See E. J. Wolf, *The Lutherans of America* (New York: J. A. Hill, 1890), p. 361.
20.
Ferm, *Crisis*, pp. 242-43.
21.
A Plea for the Augsburg Confession, in Answer to the Objections of the Definite Platform . . . (Philadelphia: Lutheran Board of Publication, 1856).

22.
Lutheran Observer, March 7, 1856, p. 3, as quoted by Ferm, *Crisis*, p. 296.
23.
Baltimore: T. Newton Kurtz, 1856.
24.
Definite Platform, 2d ed. (1856), p. 25.
25.
Lehre und Wehre 2 (June 1856): 178. (Translation composite)

agreement with the Augsburg Confession. . . ."[22] Even though Schmucker signed the document, he nevertheless reserved the right to answer any further criticisms that might arise. When, however, the debate would not be quieted (there was lively response to Mann's *Plea*), Schmucker answered with an almost 200-page volume entitled *American Lutheranism Vindicated.*[23]

After continued pamphleteering and discussion, James A. Brown (1821–82) in 1857 made formal representations to the Gettysburg Seminary board of directors charging Schmucker with a violation of his professorial oath and asking for his recall. In answer, the board ordered the seminary professors to subscribe to the constitutional oath of office.

225

Although the controversy involved the Lutherans in the East primarily, Scandinavian and German Lutherans in the Midwest were indirectly affected. The Swedes had joined with the Germans, Norwegians, and Eastern Lutherans in the Synod of Northern Illinois where they felt the effects of the *Definite Platform*. Since the Swedes were highly dissatisfied with the *Definite Platform*'s type of Lutheranism, they, together with the Norwegians, withdrew to form the Scandinavian Augustana Synod in 1860. Several factors were involved in the withdrawal but the primary factor, as indicated by the word "Augustana," was theological. The Norwegian Synod, which had been in existence for only two years when the *Definite Platform* appeared, apparently let the issue pass without much comment. There was, however, little doubt as to where this synod stood theologically because it had already committed itself to confessional subscription.

The Missouri Synod, which had pledged itself to all Lutheran symbols, immediately saw the implications of the *Definite Platform,* although the first article appearing in its theological journal referred to the incident without comment. Subsequently, several articles analyzed the proposals contained in the *Definite Platform* from a theological point of view, particularly on the real presence of Christ in the sacrament. The *Definite Platform* had singled out Missouri as upholding the practice of private confession, stating:

As the Sacred Volume contains not a single command, that laymen should confess their sins to ministers, anymore than ministers to laymen; and as not a single such example of confession and absolution is contained in the Word of God, our American Church has universally repudiated the practice. By the old Lutheran Synod of Missouri, consisting entirely of Europeans, this rite is still observed.[24]

To this, August Hoyer, the author of the articles revealing Missouri's response, answered that his synod retained the practice of private confession "not because it may have derived from ancient church usage, but because it is not contrary to Scripture and affords a wonderful opportunity for evangelical pastoral care."[25] His review concluded critically:

With deep sorrow and anxious misgivings, we declare: that theology—which expresses itself in such

mishandling of the doctrines of Holy Communion and of Confession and Absolution or the Office of the Ministry—is not merely the theology of the three articles here adduced in the *Observer,* but the same which is continually praised by the *Lutheran Observer* as the genuine theology of the American Lutheran Church . . . brought forth by professors and doctors of theology with appeal to scholarly Germans whose rationalistic bent and thinking are not recognized here. . . . [It interprets] Scripture not with Scripture but with common sense, thereby depriving itself of the sole means by which it could attain to a recognition of its own defects and to a blessed reformation of itself. Yet unnoticed—so much the more irresistible because of their hiddenness—two tyrants divide between themselves the lordship over these United States, both derived from a common mother, namely disdain of Word and Sacrament—two tyrants, more terrible than Antiochus Epiphanes and Herod: rationalism and Roman Catholicism. Is it not now their very hour?[26]

Thus Missouri dismissed the *Definite Platform* as consisting of a mixture of rationalism, enthusiasm, and Roman Catholicism, and maintained that it was neither American nor Lutheran.

A contemporary, Joseph A. Seiss (1823–1904), later a president of the General Council, reflected on the entire issue:

A happy thing would it have been for our Church, its usefulness and success in this country if their successors and descendants [colonial Lutheran leaders] had all and always remained steadfast to the true confessional basis on which the Lutheran Church in this new world was started. But a long period of defection came—a period of rationalistic and then Methodistic innovations—a period of neglect of the confessions and of the doctrines of the church as Luther and Muhlenberg taught them—a period of self-destructive assimilation to the unsound and unchurchly spirit of surrounding sects, by which the life and vigor of our churches were largely frittered away—a period from which the Lutheran Church in America is only now beginning effectually to emerge.[27]

Even Samuel Sprecher, one of the co-authors of the document, wrote in 1891, a few years prior to his death:

It is true that I did once think the Definite Synodical Platform—that modification of Lutheranism which perhaps has been properly called the culmination of Melanchthonianism—desirable and practical, and that I now regard all such modification of our creed as hopeless. . . . In the meantime an increased knowledge of the spirit, methods and literature of the Missouri Synod has convinced me that . . . the elements of true Pietism—that a sense of the . . . importance of personal assurance of salvation—can be maintained in

26.
Ibid., pp. 182–83. (Translation composite)
27.
Joseph A. Seiss, *Ecclesia Lutherana: A Brief Survey of the Evangelical Lutheran Church,* 4th ed. (Philadelphia: Lutheran Book Store, 1871), pp. 223–24.

connection with a Lutheranism unmodified by the
Puritan element.[28]

Abdel Ross Wentz comments on the situation in his biography
of Schmucker:

The issue was settled. "American Lutheranism" was
definitely defeated. The leading advocates of the
modified Lutheranism or Melanchthonianism, with all
their great personal influence, were in a hopeless
minority. After the incident of the *Definite Synodical
Platform* their influence waned rapidly. It was the
registered conviction of the great host of Lutherans in
America that Lutheranism can live and flourish in this
country without giving away its own spirit or adulterating
its own original life and character.[29]

227

Struggle for Unity

During the time that the *Definite Synodical Platform* and its recension of the Augsburg Confession caused extensive shock waves
among America's Lutherans, other movements were making
themselves felt. For example, the Midwestern, younger immigrant churches were involved in efforts to establish theological
understanding and unity. The union movement faced such obstacles as differing European backgrounds, immigrant motiva-
tions, and theological emphases which in many instances had
been transplanted to American soil and now suddenly took on
great significance in the attempt to bring unity to Lutherans in
the New World. In fact, one of the major factors in the defeat
of the *Definite Platform* was the desire for Lutheran unity. Among
the doctrinal controversies that affected the Midwestern synods
were those involving questions about church and ministry, and
attitudes toward confessional subscription, chiliasm, and the
Antichrist.

The issue of church and ministry affected the relationships
between the Buffalo and Missouri synods and, to a lesser degree,
the Iowa Synod. It will be remembered that the Saxons in
Missouri had wrestled with the need for a formulation on
church and ministry, having moved in a short period of time
from episcopacy to congregationalism. It should also be recalled
that J. A. A. Grabau's "Pastoral Letter" and overall position
maintained that the office of the ministry had been committed
to the entire church, and more specifically to the Ministerium.
The Missourian emphasis on a congregational ecclesiology was
in a large measure a reaction to the episcopal pretentions of the
deposed Stephan. In contrast to this, Grabau, believing that the
Missourians had gone too far, taught that ordination existed by
divine command, that the ministry gave validity to the sacraments, and that the office of the keys can be exercised by the
ministry alone.[30] Buffalo compounded the differences by adding
a unique feature that the congregation owes obedience to its
pastor in all things *not* contrary to God's Word. This position was
based on Buffalo's interpretation of Article 28 of the Augsburg
Confession.[31] In fact, when Grabau noted the congregational

28.
Lutheran Evangelist, May 1, 1891, p. 1.
29.
Wentz, *Pioneer*, p. 229.
30.
Buffalo Synod, *Synodical Letter* (1848), pp.
9–10, 15, 16.
31.
Ibid., p. 14.

polity which the Missouri Synod adopted at its organizational meeting, he termed it "anabaptistic, democratic stupidity."

Despite the fact that the Buffalo and Missouri synods possessed a common confessional base, a bitter debate went on for years. Finally, younger men emerged to positions of leadership in the Buffalo Synod and, recognizing the destructive nature of the conflict, requested a conference with Missouri. As a result, a colloquy was held in late November and early December 1866 in Buffalo. The leader of the young Buffalo men, Christian Hochstetter, and eleven other clergymen joined the Missouri Synod in 1866, while Heinrich von Rohr and six other ministers continued a second Buffalo Synod until 1877 when they joined the Wisconsin Synod. Grabau, along with three pastors, claimed to continue the original Buffalo Synod.

The issue of church and ministry also strained the relationship between Loehe and Missouri. Loehe, and later the Iowa Synod (founded 1854), objected particularly to Walther's theory that the congregation transferred its ministry to an individual member of the priesthood of believers by calling him to be its pastor. Missouri, on the other hand, objected to what it alleged were hierarchical tendencies in the Iowa Synod's teaching on church and ministry. Adding to the difficulty was the expulsion from the Missouri Synod of one of its district presidents, Georg Albert Schieferdecker, on the charge of chiliasm. The fact that he was then accepted into the Iowa Synod quite understandably did not lessen the tension between the two bodies. In the meantime, Iowa and Buffalo had established friendly relationships and an exchange of pastors and congregations. After a few years, however, this relationship was abrogated despite the fact that both churches shared somewhat similar views of church and ministry.

Another obstacle to Lutheran unity was the differing interpretations of the meaning of confessional subscription. Both Iowa and Missouri required subscription to the Lutheran confessions. Yet the former maintained that the confessions could be properly understood and interpreted only in their historical context. This meant that the confessions were not the final word in all the theological matters. In fact, a distinction must be made between essential and nonessential items. Certain matters must be considered "open questions," thus allowing for growth and development in the apprehension of Christian truth. In sharp contrast to this, C. F. W. Walther and the Missouri Synod demanded unconditional subscription because the confessions were completely in harmony with Holy Scripture. Consequently, no differences about the Antichrist, Sunday observance, and chiliasm were to be tolerated. There could be no "open questions." The Iowa Synod, however, felt that valid differences could exist between Lutheran churches without disrupting fellowship.

In 1867 Iowa, in an attempt to improve relationships with Missouri, minimized the distinction Iowa had made between exegetical, confessional, and explanatory statements in the confessions and pledged itself to all articles of faith. This action led to a conference between Iowa and Missouri in Milwaukee in November. Both sides agreed that there were certain "theological or exegetical problems" which were not clearly set forth in Scripture, and some not touched upon at all. Therefore, such problems ought not to be considered divisive in the church. The discussions, however, were abortive because the Iowa delegates had to proceed on to the convention of the General Council and no plans were made for a second meeting.

229

32.
"Vorwort zu Jahrgang 1856," *Lehre und Wehre* 2 (January 1856): 4. Translation and further account given by Ervin L. Lueker, "Walther and the Free Lutheran Conferences," *Concordia Theological Monthly* 15 (August 1944): 529–63.

Free Conferences

Two entirely different solutions were offered in response to the confessional upheaval in the mid-1850s. Both were committed to seeking unity and fellowship among Lutherans. The first comprised a series of "free conferences" which were conducted between 1856 and 1859. The second would base fellowship and unity on an acceptance of the unaltered Augsburg Confession. The Missouri Synod favored the first approach; the General Council (1867), the second.

Only a few months after the *Definite Platform* had been circulated, C. F. W. Walther issued an open invitation to "free conferences" and outlined the purposes and objectives:

So we venture openly to inquire: would not meetings, held at intervals, by such members of churches as call themselves Lutheran and acknowledge and confess without reservation that the unaltered Augsburg Confession of 1530 is the pure and true statement of the doctrine of sacred Scripture, and is also their own belief, promote and advance the efforts towards the final establishment of one single Evangelical Lutheran Church of America? We for our part would be ready with all our heart to take part in such a conference of truly believing Lutherans whenever and wherever such a conference would be held, pursuant to the wishes of the majority of the participants; at the same time we can promise in advance the support of numerous theologians and laymen to whom the welfare of our precious Evangelical Lutheran Church in this new fatherland is equally a matter of deepest heartfelt yearning and with whom we have discussed the thought here expressed.[32]

The concept of the "free conferences" required that the participants pledge unconditional subscription to the Augsburg Confession, especially in light of the confessional "indefiniteness" of the *Definite Synodical Platform*. In addition, none of the participants was to appear as an official "delegate" or "representative" of any synod. The conferences were to be "free."

In all, four conferences were held between 1856 and 1859. Attendance varied at each of the conferences. The first, held at Columbus, Ohio, attracted fifty-four pastors and nineteen laymen. Members of the Ohio, Pennsylvania, New York, and Missouri synods were in attendance. Three additional synods, Tennessee, Wisconsin, and Iowa, indicated interest but expressed regrets over their inability to attend. Attendance at subsequent meetings (Pittsburgh, 1857; Cleveland, 1858; and Fort Wayne, 1859) averaged about forty. In these later meetings, the Pittsburgh, Tennessee, and Norwegian synods also participated.[33] Because the Augsburg Confession had been so seriously challenged by the proponents of the *Definite Platform*, it was only natural that the substance of the confession should form the exclusive basis of discussion at these sessions. A large degree of unanimity was found to exist among the participants.

Although the conferences had begun with enthusiasm, by 1859 interest had waned. It is difficult to ascertain precisely what caused the demise of the conferences, but the fact that both Walther and the conference chairman, William F. Lehmann, were absent in 1859 may have contributed to the disappearance of enthusiasm. Moreover, the English-speaking Lutherans were at a disadvantage in German-dominated conferences. William A. Passavant favored the purpose of the meetings, but he had pointed out that they were premature because of the language barrier. Although a fifth conference had been planned for 1860, it was not held. The above-mentioned factors plus mounting tensions between the Ohio and Missouri synods all contributed to the end of the free conferences.[34] Despite their short life they nevertheless paved the way for the consolidation of confessionalistic Lutheran groups in the decade after the Civil War. Before that goal was achieved, a second series of conferences were held in the late 1860s between various Midwestern, predominantly German, synods. It was these meetings that proved to be the prelude to the emergence of the Synodical Conference in 1872.

The General Council

A more frontal attack on the problem of uniting the Lutheran church was provided by the Ministerium of Pennsylvania when it issued its "Fraternal Address" to all Lutheran synods in North America, inviting them to join in a new effort for union. The only prerequisite was acceptance of the unaltered Augsburg Confession. However, before we can pursue this development in greater detail, it is necessary briefly to look at the sequence of events transpiring between the Ministerium of Pennsylvania and the General Synod after the former rejoined the latter in 1853.

The Ministerium of Pennsylvania itself had experienced a change of heart in the second quarter of the nineteenth century. Though initially (until 1823) a member of the General Synod, it had abandoned its membership in order to explore a closer fellowship with the German Reformed. Subsequently, however, the Ministerium had experienced a marked renewal of confessional interest, and because of it, rejoined the General Synod in 1853. It did so with some reservations. Its uneasiness over its new membership in the General Synod stemmed from a twofold fear. It lacked confidence in the General Synod's theological stance, and it was concerned over its tendencies toward centralization of church government. In view of this, the Ministerium

33.
"Auszug aus den Verhandlungen der freien Ev. Lutherischen Konferenz" (New York: H. Ludwig, 1858).
34.
Fred W. Meuser, *The Formation of the American Lutheran Church* (Columbus, Ohio: Wartburg Press, 1958), pp. 49–50.

of Pennsylvania adopted the following paragraph as a condition of its membership:

That we neither intend nor ever suspect that the principles which have hitherto governed our Synod in respect to church doctrine and church life shall suffer any change whatever, by our connection with the General Synod; but that, should the General Synod violate its constitution and require of our Synod or of any Synod, as a condition of admission or of continuation of membership, assent to anything conflicting with the old and long established faith of the Evangelical Lutheran church, then our delegates are hereby required *to protest against* such action, to withdraw from its sessions, and to report to this body.[35]

This resolution was to cause serious problems in the next eleven years.

Although the issuance of the *Definite Platform* (1855) had not caused the Ministerium to secede from the General Synod, a series of events, beginning in 1859 when the Melanchthon Synod was admitted to membership, led to an increased wariness. Moreover, the withdrawal of the Scandinavians from the Synod of Northern Illinois in 1860 together with the secession of the southern synods in the Civil War were signs of impending rupture. The final straw was the application in 1864 of the Franckean Synod for membership in the General Synod. The Franckeans had never subscribed to the Augsburg Confession; they had merely adopted a "declaration of faith" devoid of references to Lutheranism's distinctive doctrines. Although the application for membership was at first declined, it was subsequently accepted when the Franckean delegates explained that they had assumed adoption on their part of the General Synod's confession of faith through their membership in it. A spirited and long debate followed, and by a vote of ninety-seven to forty the Franckean Synod was admitted. The resolution of membership instructed it to adopt the confessional position of the General Synod officially at its next meeting. Representatives of the Pennsylvania Ministerium and others vigorously protested the admission of this new synod. They maintained that by accepting the new member the General Synod was guilty of violating its own constitution. When they were not heeded, the Ministerium delegates pointed to the conditions of membership in the General Synod of 1853, and having registered their protest they withdrew to report to the parent body.[36]

In their protest the Ministerium's delegates had averred:

The whole history of the Franckean Synod presents it as having no relation nor connection whatever with the Augsburg Confession; and upon diligent examination of its official documents we have failed to discover any evidence that it has ever accepted said Confession. It is not therefore a regularly constituted Lutheran Synod, and by admitting it as an integral part of the General Synod, the General Synod has violated its Constitution

35.
Wolf, *Documents*, p. 92.
36.
General Synod, *Minutes . . . 1864*, pp. 12, 17, 19.

. . . we cannot refrain from solemnly declaring that our consciences are burdened by holding Synodical connection with a body, the declaration of whose faith is that of the Franckean Synod, which declaration remains in force to this day.[37]

A major technicality arose in the procedures. The Ministerium delegation assumed that they had withdrawn temporarily; the General Synod, on the other hand, interpreted the withdrawal as a permanent action. Although the General Synod at that same 1864 convention adopted a resolution strengthening its affirmation of the Augsburg Confession, this action, taken after the departure of the Ministerium delegates, did not ameliorate the situation. The General Synod statement declared:

All regularly constituted Lutheran Synods, not now in connection with the General Synod, receiving and holding with the Evangelical Lutheran Church of our fathers the Word of God, as contained in the Canonical Scriptures of the Old and New Testaments, as the only infallible rule of faith and practice, and the Augsburg Confession, as a correct exhibition of the fundamental doctrines of the Divine Word, and of the faith of our Church founded upon that Word, may at any time, become associated with the General Synod, by complying with the requisitions of the Constitution, and sending delegates to its Convention according to the ratio specified in Article II.[38]

Further contributing to the cleavages which already existed were problems associated with the management and control of the Gettysburg Seminary and the establishment of the Philadelphia Seminary. When Schmucker submitted his resignation as president of the seminary in February 1864, the Ministerium of Pennsylvania wanted Charles Porterfield Krauth to succeed him. Instead, another of Schmucker's most severe critics, James A. Brown, was elected. Animosities were multiplied, and, in the opinion of the Pennsylvania Ministerium, the situation demanded the establishment of a new seminary. Therefore, at its convention in July 1864, the Ministerium took action to set up its own seminary in Philadelphia. It called Charles Porterfield Krauth, Charles F. Schaeffer, the German professor at Gettysburg, and William J. Mann, a friend of Philip Schaff and an open opponent of the *Definite Platform*. With this decisive action, two seminaries—one moderately conservative and "American," the other, strictly conservative and "German"—existed on the territory of the General Synod.

As the Fort Wayne, Indiana, 1866 convention of the General Synod approached, churches and delegates were filled with trepidation and foreboding. Discussions of the complex situation were carried on in periodicals and pamphlets. There was no longer any question where the participants stood. Even those with mediating positions were inclined, by this time, to take sides. Strategies were formulated and became crystallized. Rumors circulated that an element within the Pennsylvania Ministerium was planning secession from the General Synod. Sam-

232

37.
Ibid., pp. 23–24.
38.
Ibid., p. 39.

uel Sprecher, president of the General Synod, planned his strategy carefully and decided to reject the credentials of the Ministerium's delegates. In his opinion, their parent body had already seceded in 1864. Consequently, if its delegates were to appear the General Synod convention would first have to organize itself. Thereafter, one of its committees would examine the Ministerium's application for readmission. The stage for parliamentary procedure now seemed to be set.

President Sprecher made an announcement to the delegates at the opening of the fateful convention:

The Chair regards the act of delegates of the Pennsylvania Synod, by which they severed their practical relations with the General Synod, and withdrew from the partnership of the Synods in the governing functions of the General Synod, as the act of the Synod of Pennsylvania, and that consequently that Synod was out of practical union with the General Synod up to the adjournment of the last convention, and as we cannot know officially what the action of that Synod has been since, she must be considered as in that state of practical withdrawal from the governing functions of the General Synod, until the General Synod can receive a report of an act restoring her practical relations to the General Synod; and as no such report can be received until said Synod is organized, the Chair cannot know any paper offered at this stage of the proceedings of the Synod as a certificate of delegation to this body.[39]

After the convention constituted itself, the case was presented to a special committee headed by Schmucker. In its report back to the convention the committee stated that the conditional clauses under which the Pennsylvania Ministerium had rejoined in 1853 were contrary to the rights and privileges granted to other members. It suggested further that these reservations could no longer be honored, recommending that in spite of this the Ministerium ought to be received with the understanding that the conditional clause be rescinded. The report was adopted.

Although an appeal had been made from Sprecher's decision, the synods already seated sustained the exclusion of the delegation from the Ministerium of Pennsylvania from the election of officers. In the election James A. Brown, a conservative, was elected president. This action gave hope that the unity of the synod would thereby be preserved.

The convention now took up the matter of the 1853 reservations. After three days of debate, the Pennsylvania Ministerium was asked to "waive what might seem to them an irregular organization of this body and acquiesce in the present organization. . . ."[40] The Ministerium delegates were willing to do this, provided the General Synod would admit their constitutional right to have been recognized prior to the election of officers and to have participated in the elections. A majority vote of seventy-seven to thirty-two refused to accede to this request. The withdrawal two years earlier was interpreted as secession.

39.
Ibid. *1866*, p. 4.
40.
Ibid., p. 25.

On the Sunday between the sessions the Ministerium delegation worshiped and received Holy Communion at the Missouri Synod's St. Paul's Lutheran Church where Wilhelm Sihler was pastor. The fervent hope was expressed that the day would soon come when America's Lutherans would be one.[41]

With the action of the General Synod the rupture between it and the Pennsylvania Ministerium was complete. The door was now open for the establishment of a new federation. Shortly thereafter, the Ministerium, in convention assembled, approved the action of its delegates, formally severed its connection with the General Synod[42] and simultaneously issued a call to all Lutheran synods in the United States and Canada "which confessed the Unaltered Augsburg Confession, inviting them to unite with us in a Convention, for the purpose of forming a Union of Lutheran Synods."[43]

A preliminary meeting was called for Reading, Pennsylvania, December 12-14, 1866. Charles Porterfield Krauth of the Philadelphia Seminary had emerged as the leader of the conservative forces and presented a set of theses entitled "The Fundamental Principles of Faith and Church Polity" at the meeting. Thirteen bodies responded favorably to the invitation: the Pennsylvania Ministerium, the New York Ministerium, the Pittsburgh Synod, the Minnesota Synod, the English Synod of Ohio, the Joint Synod of Ohio, the English District Synod of Ohio, the Wisconsin, Michigan, Iowa, Canada, Norwegian, and Missouri synods. The Augustana Synod had replied by letter. As the delegates arrived in Reading the future seemed to be promising.

Krauth had prepared a paper, the "Fraternal Address," in which he emphasized subscription to the unaltered Augsburg Confession. The main paragraphs were as follows:

The unaltered Augsburg Confession is by pre-eminence the confession of that faith. The acceptance of its doctrines and the avowal of them without equivocation or mental reservation make, mark and identify that Church which alone in the true, original, historical and honest sense is the Evangelical Lutheran Church.

The only churches, therefore, in any land which are properly in the Unity of the Communion, and by conscience entitled to its name, Evangelical Lutheran, are those which sincerely hold and truthfully confess the doctrines of the unaltered Augsburg Confession. . . .

In thus formally accepting and acknowledging the unaltered Augsburg Confession, we declare our conviction that the other Confessions of the Evangelical Lutheran Church, in as much as they set forth none other than its system of doctrines and articles of faith, are of necessity pure and scriptural. Pre-eminent among such accordant, pure and scriptural statements of doctrine, by their intrinsic excellence, by the great and necessary ends for which they were prepared, by their historical position, and by the general judgment of the Church, are these: The Apology of the Augsburg

41.
Theodore G. Tappert, "Intercommunion in 1866," *Concordia Historical Institute Quarterly* 40 (April 1967): 42.
42.
Wolf, *Documents*, p. 140.
43.
Ibid., p. 141.

234

Confession, the Smalcald Articles, the Catechisms of Luther and the Formula of Concord, all of which are, with the unaltered Augsburg Confession, in the perfect harmony of one and the same scriptural faith.[44]

The polity proposed for the new organization by Krauth allowed the individual synods complete freedom in regulating their own affairs. This provision was of special importance because the individual synods were jealous of their own autonomy and fearful of the centralization of jurisdiction in some "higher" body or synod of synods.

With these items before it, the Reading meeting got under way. Matthias Loy of the Joint Synod of Ohio preached the opening sermon, and Gottlob F. Krotel of the Pennsylvania Ministerium conducted the liturgy. Temporary officers were elected and included William F. Lehmann of the Joint Synod of Ohio as president, with Henry W. Roth of the Pittsburgh Synod as English secretary and Adam Martin of the Wisconsin Synod as German secretary. Forty-eight delegates (thirty-three pastors and fifteen laymen) and fifty guests were present. Both the German and English languages were used, depending upon the choice of the speaker. The chief discussion centered on Krauth's "Fundamental Principles," which were discussed paragraph by paragraph. After careful consideration they were unanimously adopted.

A special committee was named to prepare the text of a proposed constitution which would be sent to the presidents of the synods for their concurrence. Permanent officers elected were: Gottlieb Bassler (Pittsburgh Synod), president; Wilhelm Streisguth (Wisconsin Synod), German secretary; and Henry W. Roth (Pittsburgh Synod), English secretary. The Joint Synod of Ohio, the Iowa Synod, and the Missouri Synod, though represented by delegates, expressed themselves as unwilling to join a new body because they believed that theological unanimity had not been reached.

The constituting convention of the General Council, as the new federation was to be called, was held in Fort Wayne, Indiana, November 20–26, 1867. Thirteen synods again were represented, including the Scandinavian Augustana Synod, which affiliated officially with the council in 1870. The Missouri and Norwegian synods, however, were not present, and Ohio withdrew after the convention. The Iowa Synod assumed an informal relationship to the new council; its delegates would have the right of debate but not of vote. The Illinois Synod joined subsequently.

The new body addressed itself to the preparation of a liturgy and church book, a model constitution for congregational use, and to charitable services. Although the General Council's constitution followed the terminology of the "Fundamental Principles" in its subscription to the confessions and acknowledged God's Word as the only rule of life and allowed for theological colloquia with nonmember bodies, the Missouri, Ohio, and Iowa synods felt that the constitution did not sufficiently guarantee a Lutheran doctrinal stance. The Missouri Synod partic-

44.
Ibid., p. 145.

ularly was anxious to conduct additional free conferences prior to the formation of a new federation and it considered the Reading and Fort Wayne actions premature. The newly organized council, on the other hand, felt that it had left the door sufficiently open so that it was not an either/or but a both/and proposition. The General Council could sponsor such free conferences, but Missouri countered that if the council did so they would no longer be free. Its reply to the council's invitation to send representatives with the privilege of debate stated its position:

We are, by no means, unmindful of the value of the privilege herein accorded to us by said Rev. body, and the good intention which prompted this cordial invitation, but after having considered what position our Delegates would occupy at the sessions . . . we have arrived at the conviction that we dare not avail ourselves of so honorable a proposal. In view of the relation we sustain toward different members of the Church Council, in reference to doctrine and churchly practice, we must be apprehensive that the consideration and discussion of differences still existing in the Convention . . . might give rise to the reflection that we intended to interrupt the bringing about of a unity, and are therefore fearful lest our participation, instead of leading to an agreement, might be productive of greater alienation.

Even at the risk of appearing capricious . . . and diligent in our efforts for churchly unity, we . . . declare it again, as our conviction, that Free Conferences . . . are the only proper means for an exchange of such convictions, as are still divergent, and which, by the Grace of God, may lead to a unity on the basis of our beloved Confession.[45]

The General Council, of course, already organized, could not dissolve itself and revert to free conferences. Instead, it expressed its appreciation to Missouri and declared its willingness at one of the future sessions to meet "them simply as a Free Conference." But this was precisely what Missouri did not want, namely, meeting officially with another church organization, regardless of name. When neither side was willing to abandon its position, communications were discontinued.

Like Missouri, Ohio had sent delegates to the preliminary meeting in 1866 but cautiously remained apart. In 1867 it requested from the General Council a position paper with respect to chiliasm, altar fellowship, pulpit fellowship, and secret or "unchurchly societies." These issues became known as the Four Points. The Iowa Synod, too, desired clarification on three of the issues, but excluded chiliasm, undoubtedly because it was wrestling with that issue itself at the time. The General Council's reply, formulated in 1867, did not prove to be satisfactory. It stated, among other matters, that it did not see an immediate problem which could not be answered on the basis of its "Fundamental Principles" and offered to render a specific reply when "official evidence" of need would be presented to it.[46]

45.
Ibid., p. 155.
46.
General Council, *Minutes . . . 1867*, p. 13.

It is understandable that the General Council, having just been formed, could not allow itself to take any hasty action on issues where there might well be divided opinion within its constituency. Instead of answering the queries raised, the council encouraged the synods to join and then to resume the discussion on these issues. For the questioning synods, on the other hand, the replies seemed like simple evasion, confirming their suspicion that the General Council was not ready to come to grips with these issues. In view of the council's actions in 1867, therefore, both Missouri and Ohio remained apart.

The issues were again taken up when the General Council met in 1868. It was now ready to adopt statements or definitions on the Four Points.[47] The council's positions on all four issues proved unsatisfactory to the questioners. Now the Wisconsin (1869) and Minnesota (1870) synods also expressed their dissatisfaction with the formulations. The council now had to contend not with three but with five synods.

When the General Council met in Chicago in 1869, it had hopes that understandings could be worked out, but Missouri had presented a communication to the convention which reiterated its preference for free conferences.[48] Consequently the General Council felt it had no alternative but to repeat its "readiness to receive and entertain any proposals . . . looking to the much to be desired organic union of all true Lutherans in this country."[49]

Dissatisfaction mounted over what was considered the General Council's sidestepping of issues. The Wisconsin Synod expressed disapproval, and the Illinois Synod in 1869 resolved to seek closer ties with the Missouri Synod. Nevertheless, the Illinois and the Minnesota synods appealed to the General Council to reformulate its position on the Four Points. But when the council's replies were deemed unacceptable, secessions developed. Wisconsin withdrew in 1869, Illinois in 1870, and Minnesota in 1871. The General Council continued to struggle with the issues raised by the Four Points, and in 1872 it adopted the Akron Rule which stated the council's principles on altar and pulpit fellowship:

I. The rule is: Lutheran pulpits are for Lutheran ministers only. Lutheran altars are for Lutheran communicants only. II. The exceptions to the rule belong to the sphere of privilege, not of right. III. The determination of the exceptions is to be made in consonance with these principles, by the conscientious judgment of pastors, as the cases arise.[50]

Reaffirmed as the Galesburg Rule in 1875, its issues continued under debate in several subsequent sessions into the twentieth century.

Meanwhile, some of the growing Midwestern synods, such as Ohio and Missouri, began to conduct a series of free conferences or colloquies, looking toward the establishment of ecclesiastical fellowship. These conferences opened the way shortly for the formation of the Synodical Conference (1872). This meant that American Lutherans with pronounced or indistinct German

47.
Ibid. *1868*, pp. 36–39.
48.
Wolf, *Documents*, p. 158.
49.
Ibid., pp. 69–70.
50.
Ibid., p. 170.

backgrounds were divided into three major federations: the General Synod (1820), the General Council (1867), and the Synodical Conference (1872).

Civil War

While these severe conflicts were going on within the Lutheran church, the country itself was torn apart by the slavery issue and the Civil War. Differences of opinion had existed on slavery almost since the first boatload of slaves arrived in the West Indies in 1562. Prior to the revolutionary war, most of the American churches saw opposition to the slave trade as a Christian virtue. Some hoped that by the dawn of the nineteenth century the blight would be abolished. But several factors intervened so that the slavery issue became aggravated, particularly among Protestants. For Lutherans, too, the issue was to become one of grave concern.

Some Lutherans spoke out on the evils of slavery as the nation became more deeply affected by the antagonisms between the North and the South. Historically, they had ministered to the blacks with only scant distinction as to race. Different circumstances and environments, however, produced different and at times opposing answers to the problems of sectionalism and slavery. Thus, for example, the Franckean Synod was organized in 1837 because its parent, the Hartwick Synod, had declined to make bold antislavery pronouncements. The Franckean Synod, formed by radical abolitionists, demanded concrete and decisive action. At its second convention, its president lashed out against slavery, and the synod itself adopted a resolution "against this great national and heinous sin."[51] In 1845 the Franckean Synod declared that it would not practice fellowship with any other body tolerating slavery.

As the tensions continued to mount over the Fugitive Slave Law, which granted the right to the slaveholder or his agent to return slaves to their masters and to prosecute those who aided the fugitives, the national situation became polarized. When this law was augmented by the Kansas-Nebraska Bill in 1854, it had the effect of negating the Missouri Compromise of 1820; political tempers flared even more pronouncedly. Many of the clergy protested vigorously. In spite of furious opposition the bill was adopted. Kansas became a battleground as the proslavery and antislavery forces attempted, by any means at their disposal, to capture the votes of the state for their position.

In the face of such events the Whig party endeavored to provide a compromise and straddle the issues which increasingly divided the country. Out of the opposition to compromises such as the Kansas-Nebraska Act and a pronounced opposition to the extension of slavery the Republican party was formed. The new party captured the imagination of people through its emphasis on popular sovereignty. Because of its platform, a host of recent immigrants, especially laymen, supported the new party which elected Abraham Lincoln to the presidency in 1860. Not all Lutherans, however, supported Lincoln and his party. One such was C. F. W. Walther, who termed the infant

51.
Franckean Synod, *Proceedings . . . 1838*, p. 30. For a history of this synod see Douglas C. Stange, *Radicalism for Humanity: A Study of Lutheran Abolitionism* (St. Louis: Oliver Slave, 1970).

party a "revolutionary mob." Despite Walther, however, the majority of Lutherans were increasingly sympathetic to the Republican party.

As the 1860s approached, the immigrant press, including the Norwegian, Swedish, and German, became more strongly opposed to slavery. Tuve N. Hasselquist exerted a wide influence over the Swedish Lutheran immigrants through his antislavery editorials in *Hemlandet*. Cautiously he approached the Republican party and wrote: "It [slavery] is ungodly in its very foundation and cannot stand the test of Christianity or be defended by a clean conscience, which has been cleansed in the blood that was shed for the people regardless of race."[52] Speaking almost as an orthodox abolitionist, he presented the usual arguments that slavery was degrading, cruel, immoral, and tyrannical. It will be noted that the Augustana Synod was founded in the midst of the political upheavals in the country. Fortunately, its parishes, like those of the Norwegian Synod (see below), were not located in the primary areas of conflict. Thus Augustana, spared the practical problem of slavery, found it relatively easy to assume an antislavery line in contrast to other Lutheran groups whose membership extended into the southland.[53]

One of the most outspoken Lutheran opponents of slavery was William A. Passavant. The Pittsburgh Synod, which he had been instrumental in organizing, labeled slavery as a moral and national evil. It even declined to join the General Synod in 1851 because it did not want to associate with that body's delegates, some of whom were slaveholders from the South. The General Synod, extending both into the North and the South, attempted to avoid the issue. Many of the older Americanized state synods had taken earlier decisive action by adopting antislavery resolutions.

Various shades of opinion began to emerge. Some churchmen did not condemn slavery as a sin but only as a moral evil. As has been noted, the Franckean Synod considered slavery an outright sin against God. The Wittenberg Synod, a small synod in Ohio, in 1852 termed slavery a national evil and an abomination before God. Several other synods took similar positions.

The Missouri Synod, headquartered in a border state, conducted a series of pastoral conferences to discuss the vexing problem as a theological issue. Basically, the synod had an aversion to making public social pronouncements. However, a citizen's relationship to the government was a frequent topic. For the most part, discussion was confined to the theological journals. The position of the Missouri Synod, not unlike the attitude of southern churches, held that according to Scripture slavery in itself was not sinful. It was considered a judgment of God as a punishment for sin. Although God permits slavery, the synod held, it is his desire that through the gospel both master and slave come to faith in Christ, and thereafter their relationship be motivated by Christian love. In effect, it justified the existence of slavery.

Lauritz Larsen, who served as the Norwegian professor at Concordia Seminary from 1859 to 1861, attempted to introduce

---

52.
Hemlandet, June 2, 1855, as cited in Oscar F. Ander, *T. N. Hasselquist* (Rock Island, Ill.: Augustana Historical Society, 1931), p. 153.
53.
G. Everett Arden, *Augustana Heritage: A History of the Augustana Lutheran Church* (Rock Island, Ill.: Augustana Press, 1963), pp. 91–92.

this position among his fellow Norwegian immigrants. Severe opposition arose. The majority of the Norwegians, as well as many of the German and other Scandinavian immigrants, were unambiguously opposed to slavery and volunteered in large numbers to fight for the Union. In a highly charged atmosphere, made so by the slavery debate, the Norwegian Synod in 1861 resolved to establish its own seminary at Halfway Creek, Wisconsin (opened in October 1862) and to break its ties with Concordia.

The main issue among the Norwegians was the laymen's attitude that slavery with all of its social, political, and historical implications was absolutely wrong. The majority of the Norwegian Synod clergymen, following Missouri's principles, held that "slavery in itself" could not be termed a sin. A Norwegian pastoral conference resolved:

Although according to the Word of God, it is not in and by itself a sin to keep slaves, nevertheless it is in itself an evil and a punishment from God. We condemn all abuses and sins connected therewith, and furthermore, when official duties require it and when Christian love and wisdom demand it, we will work for its abolition.[54]

Long after the Civil War was ended, in fact until 1868, the synod was debating the slavery issue. Manifestly the conflict was no longer slavery but rather a hermeneutical conflict regarding the definition of the Word of God and the authority of the Bible.

Young men of various immigrant groups fought valiantly in the war, especially on the side of the North. One estimate indicates that there were more than twenty regiments in the Northern army constituted primarily of Americans of German descent. It has been estimated that the German-born volunteers exceeded the Irish by more than 30,000 for a total of 176,817.[55]

Hans Christian Heg symbolizes the patriotism of the vast number of Norwegian immigrants during the war. Enthusiastically responding to Lincoln's call for volunteers, Heg was commissioned a colonel of the Fifteenth Wisconsin, a predominantly Norwegian regiment of the Federal Army. He died during the battle of Chickamauga, Tennessee, in September 1863.[56]

Not all Scandinavian and German volunteers in the war were Lutherans. Nevertheless, since several of the regiments were predominantly Lutheran, chaplains from the denomination volunteered for service. Claus L. Clausen accepted Heg's invitation to become the chaplain of his regiment. A Missouri Synod chaplain, Frederick W. Richmann, served for several months with the Fifty-eighth Regiment of Ohio volunteers and saw battle in Mississippi. In 1862 the Missouri Synod issued a special prayerbook for soldiers which could be used by both the Northern and Southern forces. The prayers were based extensively upon those which had been prepared in Germany for those engaged in the Thirty Years' War.

Passavant was called by the Pennsylvania Ministerium to serve as a missionary chaplain. He had undoubtedly been selected because he had offered the services of his deaconesses and his hospital in the interest of the Northern cause.[57] Passavant

54.
Nelson and Fevold, *Lutheran Church Among Norwegian-Americans*, 1:175. See especially the account of the post-Civil War extension of the conflict within the Norwegian Synod.
55.
Albert B. Faust, *The German Element in the United States*, 2 vols. (New York: Steuben Society, 1927), p. 525.
56.
Arlow W. Andersen, "Lincoln and the Union: A Study of the Editorials of *Emigranten* and *Faedrelandet*," *Norwegian-American Study and Records* 15 (1949): 85–121.
57.
George H. Gerberding, *Life and Letters of W. A. Passavant* (Greenville, Pa.: Young Lutheran Co., 1906), pp. 307–25.

accepted the challenges offered him and reported on his ministry:

The pulpit was a camp chest with the heavens for a sounding board, while the many soldiers, not yet recovered from the prostration of the hurried march on Monday last, were stretched out on the ground before me. At the close of the service a large number came forward and gladly accepted some tracts but the stock on hand was exhausted before half of the soldiers were supplied. Not knowing of any Germans in the regiment, no provision was made for an entire company of honest fellows who would have been most thankful for some German reading.[58]

Another chaplain, John H. W. Stuckenberg, was attached to Company K and was especially active between 1862 and 1863 at Antietam, Sharpsburg, Fredericksburg, and Gettysburg.[59]

In addition to such chaplains there were parish pastors who served their people and the war effort in every possible way. If they could not serve in a personal, direct way they attempted to maintain contact with the soldiers by providing literature and corresponding with them. Lutheran parishes in the North gave support to the United States Christian Commission, organized in November 1861. A host of women volunteered their services as nurses. Laymen, including seminary students, visited the camps, hospitals, and battlefields, assisting the chaplains and doctors where they could. After hostilities ceased, the churches supported relief and rehabilitation programs in the South.

In a special way, the battle of Gettysburg brought the war right to the doorstep of the General Synod Lutherans. Of all the difficulties the Gettysburg Seminary had experienced, this one was perhaps the most severe. President Schmucker's home was invaded and damaged by the Confederate soldiers who destroyed part of his library. The seminary building was severely damaged by cannon fire; even so it was used as a hospital. The seminarians volunteered and established their own company under the direction of a student, Frederick Klinefelter. This regiment participated in some of the early skirmishes in the prelude to the battle at Gettysburg. During the afternoon of the first day, the Northern forces lost their control of Seminary Ridge, including access to the building, the cupola of which had been used as a lookout tower. The entire campus, including professors' homes, was occupied by the Confederate forces. The Schmucker and Krauth families sought shelter elsewhere. Schmucker later reported:

The injury done to the property of the institution is considerable. The house I occupy was most damaged. The rebels, having driven the occupants out on the first day of the battle, took possession of it themselves and their batteries being also planted in the immediate vicinity, it was unavoidably shattered by the Federal artillery from Cemetery Hill. . . . The seminary edifice was perforated by several [cannon] balls, and large portions knocked out of the north east gable corner.

58.
Ibid., p. 314.
59.
John O. Evjen, *The Life of J. H. W. Stuckenberg* (Minneapolis: Lutheran Free Church Publishing Co., 1938), pp. 105–36.

There being also a crack in the wall extending over two stories. . . . Dr. Krauth's dwelling also received some injury, though not of the very serious nature.[60]

The Lutheran seminary in St. Louis was likewise affected by the war. A number of skirmishes were fought in St. Louis. The city itself, as well as the whole state, had shown considerable pro-Southern sympathies. When Lincoln called for 75,000 volunteers, the governor of Missouri refused to send a single man, but ordered the militia to seize the federal arsenal in St. Louis. Street skirmishes took place in the city between Northern and Southern sympathizers, so that Concordia Seminary was closed and the students were sent to their homes. As in Gettysburg, the students volunteered their services and elected a captain and a second lieutenant to support the North. The Norwegian student Styrk S. Reque, who had seen previous military service, was chosen captain. Daily drills were conducted. When the pressures of street fighting diminished, the group was dissolved.

It was said that during the war the seminary flew the Confederate flag on its cupola, influenced perhaps by Walther's defense of slavery and criticism of Lincoln. The account related that Northern cannons were leveled against the seminary, finally offering sufficient persuasive powers to have the flag withdrawn.[61] The story apparently had originated with John D. Severinghaus in *Der Lutherische Kirchenfreund* of the General Synod. But in 1870 Walther vehemently denied the account and referred to the "myth of the rebel flag" as a pipe dream, adding, "The truth is that during the war the rebel flag not once flew over our college . . . but the union flag repeatedly did."[62]

The work of the Lutheran church in the North, and particularly its colleges and seminaries, was severely handicapped or disrupted during the war. Young men who could have assisted measurably in the establishment and extension of the local church were called into military service, many never to return. But the sufferings of the Northern Lutherans could in no way be compared to those in the South.

Southern Lutherans Organize

The internal schism caused by the slavery issue and the Civil War did not affect the Lutherans as extensively as it did some other Protestants. One reason for this was the fact that the majority of the Lutherans lived in the northern areas of the country and thus were not as intimately and directly involved with the existential problem of slavery and emancipation. The General Synod, however, had constituent synods in the South and their loyalties were unquestionably tied to the Southern cause, but an outright break was avoided until 1862.

The General Synod, scheduled to meet in Lancaster, Pennsylvania, at the end of May 1861, postponed its convention, hoping that it might thereby avert an open rupture within its ranks. When, however, a permanent Confederate government was set up on February 17, 1862, and the battles became more bloody and more frequent, the synod decided it was essential to meet. The convention was held in Lancaster in May 1862. The

242

60.
Abdel Ross Wentz, *History of the Gettysburg Theology Seminary . . . 1826-1926* (Philadelphia: United Lutheran Publication House, 1926), p. 201.
61.
Georg J. Fritschel, *Geschichte der Lutherischen Kirche in Amerika*, 2 vols. (Gütersloh: Bertelsmann, 1896-97), 1:195. Cf. Ludwig E. Fuerbringer, *Eighty Eventful Years* (St. Louis: Concordia Publishing House, 1944), pp. 222-29.
62.
Der Lutheraner, August 15, 1870, pp. 186-87.

die had now been cast. Just as the southern states had seceded from the Union, five of the southern synods withdrew from the General Synod. They were North Carolina, South Carolina, Virginia, Western Virginia, and Georgia. The presidential "State of the Church" address at Lancaster took no notice of the defections. Rather, a separate committee on the "State of the Country" took cognizance of the "fiery trials" through which the country was passing, cherishing the hope that "a purer nation and a holier, more spiritual, consecrated and zealous church" would emerge.[63] The report condemned the revolt on the part of the Southerners in the strongest terminology:

That it is the deliberate judgment of this Synod, that the rebellion against the constitutional Government of this land is most wicked in its inception, unjustified in its cause, unnatural in its character, inhuman in its prosecution, oppressive in its aims, and destructive in its results to the highest interests of morality and religion.

That in the supression of this rebellion and in the maintenance of the Constitution and the Union by the sword, we recognize an unavoidable necessity and a sacred duty, which the Government owes to the nation and to the world, and that therefore we call upon all our people to lift up holy hands in prayer to the God of battles, without personal wrath against the evildoers on the one hand, and without doubting the righteousness of our cause on the other, that He would give wisdom to the President and his counsellors, and success to the army and navy, that our beloved land may speedily be delivered from treason and anarchy.[64]

The Lutherans south of the Mason-Dixon Line supported their government as faithfully as did their northern counterparts. They had anticipated an early victory and consequently felt that a new nation would emerge in the South. It is therefore not at all surprising that some of the southern synods did not consider it necessary to adopt formal resolutions breaking away from the General Synod. Such action was considered a natural consequence. In contrast, the synods of the North, preceding and following the convention of the General Synod in 1862, pledged their support and loyalty to the federal government.

One of the first southern synods to take official action was the Virginia Synod which met in October 1861. Its resolution reveals the thought of the southern Lutherans:

Whereas it is manifest to us, in view of the final disruption of the former United States, the hostile attitude of those yet adhering to the remaining unscrupulous despotism at Washington and the uncharitable and intolerant spirit and bearing of many of those whom we once esteemed as brethren in the same faith, and the interest of our Church, loyalty to our government, as well as promptings of self respect, imperatively demand that we should at once dissolve all ecclesiastical alliance with them. Therefore,
***Resolved:* that we do hereby withdraw our connection**

63.
General Synod, *Minutes . . . 1862*, p. 39.
64.
Ibid., p. 30.

243

**with the General Synod of the United States, and
earnestly favor the organization of a General Synod of
the Confederate States.**[65]

South Carolina concurred in its January 1862 convention, a meeting which had originally been scheduled the year before. In his presidential address Elias B. Hort stated:

**Through the mercy of God we are permitted once more
to assemble as a Synod, and although not as anticipated
in regard to time and place, or circumstances, our lives
have been spared, and we have much to be truly
thankful for.**

**Merged in a war of self-defense, the preservation of
our religious, social and political liberties, our cause is
in the hands of Infinite Justice, and if faithful to God and
to our country, we can not fear for the result.**[66]

Hort further encouraged the synod to send delegates to Salisbury, North Carolina, to consider the possibility of forming a southern General Synod and urged support of the *Southern Lutheran* as a periodical for the South. The convention responded with a formal resolution:

**Whereas, in the distracted condition of our once happy
country we deem it impracticable to send our delegates
to the next meeting of the General Synod about to
convene at Lancaster, Pennsylvania; and, feeling that
other Synods South are in a similar situation with this
body, therefore**

**Resolved, that we recommend a convention of all
Southern delegates to the General Synod to meet at
Salisbury, North Carolina, on Thursday preceding the
third Sabbath in May, 1862, for the purpose of endorsing
the proceedings of the next meeting of the General
Synod if practicable; otherwise to take such steps as
may best promote the future harmony and prosperity of
that portion of the church represented by the absent
delegates.**

**Resolved, that we hereby commission our present
delegates to the General Synod to attend the said
convention.**[67]

In its meeting of May 1861 the North Carolina Synod deemed it "impracticable to send" delegates to the General Synod convention scheduled for that year. Instead, the synod resolved that its delegates meet with other southern synods in Salisbury for the formation of a southern federation. The following year, meeting at the Organ Church in Rowan County, North Carolina, the synod president commented:

**The past year begun with clouds of doubts and
apprehensions, then followed a brilliant succession of
victories which swept every cloud from the horizon, and
then a sky darker and stormier than ever before. . . .
Many of our parishioners, who at the commencement of
the present ecclesiastical year, stood at our altars, and
whom we followed with our prayers, and to whom we
imparted our affectionate counsel, have fallen in defense**

244

65.
Virginia Synod, *Minutes . . . 1861*, p. 10.
66.
South Carolina Synod, *Minutes . . . 1862*, p. 5.
67.
Ibid., pp. 22-23.

of our homes, our lives, and our earthy all, while we have mourned the departure of so many loved ones at home.[68]

The formal resolution adopted by the synod in 1862 supplies additional insights:

Whereas, the duty of rendering obedience to rulers and magistrates, as those ordained by God for the exercise of justice and the maintenance of order, is enjoined in the Word of God: *and whereas,* . . . these states seceded and formed a government under the name of the Confederate States of America, therefore,

Resolved, that we recognize the hand of God in the wisdom of those councils and the heroism of our brave defenders, which have enabled us to form a government of our choice.

Resolved, that we recognize the right of these States in having seceded and formed an independent government, to which our undivided allegiance is due.

Whereas, this Synod was formerly connected with the General Synod of the United States of America, in which we are represented by delegates, we have now arrived at the solemn conviction that it is essential to the good of our church and the glory of God, that the Evangelical Lutheran Churches of these Confederate States withdraw all connection with the Northern General Synod, and by this solemn and unanimous act declare our connection as a Synod dissolved.

Resolved, that we are in favor of forming a General Synod of the Confederate states on the basis of the Augsburg Confession, and that our delegates elected to the Convention, to be held in Salisbury, North Carolina, in this month, be empowered to vote for such an organization.[69]

With surprising rapidity a preliminary meeting was held at Salisbury, North Carolina, on May 15, 1862, to consider the possibilities of forming a General Synod in the South. Because of the limited attendance, however, little more was accomplished than the naming of a special committee to prepare a constitution and present the ground rules for a constituting convention. Nicodemus Aldrich of Charlestown, South Carolina, was elected the temporary chairman.

When the constituting convention met in Concord, North Carolina, May 20, 1863, only weeks before the battle at Gettysburg, John Bachman (1790–1874) of Charleston, South Carolina, was elected the first president. Thus the "General Synod of the Evangelical Lutheran Church in the Confederate States of America" came into being. The new synod declared its position by summarizing grievances against the General Synod:

That ecclesiastical body, composed of the most influential Lutherans of the North, acknowledged and endorsed the unconstitutional acts of the Federal government; called and denounced secession as a crime, proclaimed through the Church that the defenders

68.
North Carolina Synod, *Minutes . . . 1862,* p. 4.
69.
Ibid., p. 17.

245

of liberty were rebels, insurgents and solemnly declared and branded our southern brethren as traitors to man, to their government, and to God. Hence we can never expect from them mercy or pardon, much less equal rights and privileges, unless we bow in submission to their opinions and denounce as wicked what we conscientiously believe to be just and right.[70]

A second major resolution, defining the synod's position on slavery, noted the body's concern over the moral relations existing between master and slave. The resolution, however, reiterated that slavery, as an institution, was not sinful. In addition, the *Southern Lutheran*, which began publication in 1861 at Charleston, South Carolina, became the official publication of the new body.

In the context of the confessional upheaval, Article II, adopted by the delegates at Salisbury, pointed significantly to the fact that more than the issue of slavery and the war compelled the southern Lutherans to withdraw from the General Synod. The new federation pledged itself to a scriptural and confessional formula:

We received and hold that the Old and New Testaments are the Word of God, and the only infallible rule of faith and practice.

We likewise hold that the Apostles' Creed, the Nicene Creed, and the Augsburg Confession, contain the fundamental doctrines of the Sacred Scriptures, and we receive and adopt them as the exponents of our faith.

In as much as there has always been, and still is, a difference of construction among us with regard to several articles of the Augsburg Confession; therefore we, acting in conformity with the spirit and time-honored usage of our Church, hereby affirm that we allow the full and free exercise of private judgment in regard to those articles.[71]

The ravages of war were to work exceptional hardships upon Lutherans in the South. Farm animals and equipment were appropriated by the government, the economy virtually collapsed, and the barest essentials became luxuries. Conditions were further aggravated as Federal troops moved into Southern territory and personal violence was exercised upon people and property. For example, Old Ebenezer Lutheran Church, near Savannah, founded by the persecuted Salzburgers more than a century earlier, was converted into a horse barn and warehouse by Sherman's army marching through Georgia. Roanoke College in Virginia suffered.[72]

Lincoln's Emancipation Proclamation, issued on January 1, 1863, was observed as a national day of prayer in the North. In the South it spurred on the war effort. Electrifying was the news of President Lincoln's assassination on April 14, 1865. Just five days prior, Generals Grant and Lee had met in the Appomattox courthouse and arranged for the surrender. In rapid succession other Southern generals surrendered and the Civil War was over. But the antagonisms and ill will that had been generated

246

70.
General Synod, Confederate States of America, *Minutes . . . 1863*, appendix.
71.
Ibid.
72.
For details see William Edward Eisenberg, *The First Hundred Years, Roanoke College, 1842-1942* (Salem, Va.: Roanoke College, 1942), pp. 92-113.

were slow to disappear. The southern Lutherans did not find reunion with their northern brethren a live option in 1865. Slavery had been abolished, the South had been defeated, and the task of reunifying the nation was undertaken. Meeting in 1866, the General Synod in the Confederate States of America modified its name (The Evangelical Lutheran General Synod, South) and declared that for theological and confessional reasons the Lutherans in the South determined to remain distinct. Later, in 1886, the synod again altered its name; henceforth, it was known as "The United Synod, South." Hard days of reconstruction continued. Only time and patience would heal the wounds. It was not until fifty years later that a reunion took place, when the three bodies (the General Council, the General Synod, and the United Synod, South) formed the United Lutheran Church in America (1918).

The Synodical Conference

In the aftermath of the *Definite Platform* (1855) two methods for furthering Lutheran unity were proposed. As noted above, the first consisted of a series of free conferences begun the year after the *Definite Platform* was issued and ending in 1859. These efforts finally culminated in the formation of the Synodical Conference in 1872. In the meantime, the founders of the General Council worked out a second way, the organization of a federation with the promise that subsequent colloquia for unity could be held. In this context the General Council was organized in 1867.

For two reasons the Missouri Synod expressed its preference for free conferences. The first pointed to the lack of doctrinal unity which it detected among the constituent synods of the General Council. The second reason emphasized that the General Council seemed to tolerate practices which to the Missouri Synod were inconsistent with the Lutheran confessions.[73] Representatives of the Norwegian Synod, fearing that theological differences would be glossed over, assumed a similar position.

As noted earlier, the General Council was immediately agitated by the question of the Four Points. This had resulted in the defection of several synods. To some degree these synods had been in communication with the Missouri Synod even prior to the formation of the General Council in the free conferences. It was thus a natural development, as they expressed their dissatisfaction with the council's position, that they move toward the Missouri Synod.

Ironically, concrete action was taken not in the form of free conferences but in "colloquies" or conferences held specifically between official commissioners of synods to explore the possibilities of altar and pulpit fellowship. The first of these, conducted between the Missouri and Buffalo synods, was held in December 1866. A newer element had come to the fore in the Buffalo Synod and had requested a "colloquy." The vexing and disrupting differences between the two synods with respect to church and ministry were now thoroughly discussed. It will be remembered that Buffalo had adopted the position that the ministerium (clergy) made virtually all decisions in the synod

73.
W. Sihler, "Sollte die alsbaldige . . . Bildung . . . Generalsynode . . . rathsam und heilsam sein?" *Lehre und Wehre* 12 (September 1866): 264.

and in the parish. Missouri's congregationalism, on the other hand, had been labeled "anabaptistic, democratic stupidity." Agreement between the two synods was not to come immediately, but a major portion of the pastors and congregations of Buffalo in due course joined Missouri. The remaining pastors and congregations subsequently divided into two factions, each claiming to represent the original Buffalo Synod.

The Iowa Synod had asked the General Council for clarification on several points. When this did not materialize, Iowa, reluctant to break relations with the new federation, became an advisory member. At the same time, this action opened the way to a colloquy with Missouri. Consequently, in November 1867 representatives of the two synods met and discussed those issues which had traditionally separated them, namely, confessional subscription, "open questions" (Antichrist, Sunday observance, chiliasm, etc.), and church and ministry. While considerable progress was made, the Iowa Synod was not drawn into Missouri's orbit.

The relationships between the Missouri Synod and the Joint Synod of Ohio can be described as "on again, off again," for several decades. Yet, there was a mutual attraction theologically, linguistically, and ethnically. This they had learned by the method of free conferences. Ohio, like Missouri, did not join the General Council, and hence both bodies were casting about for new affiliations. Ohio felt that the General Council had not gone far enough with its formulations on the Four Points. Thus Ohio and Missouri, geographically proximate and theologically compatible, met at the invitation of the former in a colloquy in March 1868.[74] After only a few days of discussions, the commissioners announced complete theological agreement.

Several additional colloquies were held. In 1868 Missouri met with Wisconsin also. This was a year before the Wisconsin Synod withdrew its membership from the General Council. Wisconsin was at the point of becoming disillusioned and even suspicious of the council and its position on the Four Points. Since its founding, Wisconsin had moved from a moderate to a strict confessional position. This was evident particularly in its constitutional revisions of 1863. Thus when Missouri and Wisconsin met in Milwaukee in October 1868 they discovered that their attitudes toward Scripture and the confessions were virtually identical. After two days of deliberation the representatives reported that doctrinal unity had been achieved.[75] Wisconsin withdrew from the General Council in 1869.

The Illinois Synod, with its varied history, also voiced its dissatisfaction over the General Council's position on the Four Points. Between 1868 and 1870, Illinois sought a closer fellowship with Missouri. A conference in 1869 showed that the time was not ripe for immediate fellowship between Illinois and Missouri[76] but served to increase disaffection with the General Council. This led to the withdrawal of the Illinois Synod in 1871. After a second meeting was conducted between Illinois and Missouri in 1872, theological agreement was achieved.[77]

74.
Ohio Synod, *Proceedings . . . 1867*, pp. 7, 10–11.
75.
C. F. W. Walther, "Wieder eine Friedensbotschaft," *Der Lutheraner*, November 1, 1868, pp. 37–38; and Missouri Synod, *Proceedings . . . 1869*, pp. 87–92.
76.
Illinois Synod, *Minutes . . . 1870*, pp. 16–17.
77.
Missouri Synod, *Proceedings . . . 1872*, pp. 26–27.

78.
General Council, *Minutes . . . 1869*, pp. 20–28, 39–40.
79.
Minnesota Synod, *Minutes . . . 1870*, pp. 43–44.
80.
Missouri Synod, *Proceedings . . . 1872*, pp. 94–95.
81.
Nelson and Fevold, *Lutheran Church Among Norwegian-Americans*, 1:162; Missouri Synod, *Proceedings . . . 1857*, pp. 53–54.
82.
O. F. Duus, *Frontier Parsonage* (Northfield, Minn.: Norwegian-American Historical Association, 1947), pp. 103, 107–8.

The Minnesota Synod virtually owed its existence to the Pennsylvania Ministerium, and consequently, when the General Council was founded, it joined the ranks. But once again dissatisfaction emerged over that knotty issue of full fellowship. In 1869 Minnesota requested doctrinal clarification from the General Council but received a tabled action in response.[78] After president Johann H. Sieker reported this to the convention, Minnesota agreed to remain in the council only as long as the latter protested un-Lutheran practices.[79] In the meantime, a growing warmth between Minnesota and Wisconsin was evident. Thus, when Wisconsin withdrew from the General Council in 1869 Minnesota followed suit two years later. This led to several conferences between Minnesota and Missouri beginning in January 1871. The result was a declaration of theological unity.[80]

Southern Lutherans from the eastern seaboard had migrated into parts of Missouri as early as the 1820s and 1830s. These Lutherans formed the "English Conference of Missouri" in 1872 and in August of that year met with representatives of the Missouri Synod to explore theological questions. Agreement was discovered. The conference subsequently developed into the English Synod, which in 1911 joined the Missouri Synod as its English District.

The relationships between the Norwegian Synod and the Missouri Synod had been cordial and intimate virtually since the founding of both. The difference in language did not seem to form an effective barrier. This close relationship had begun when the Norwegian Synod authorized in 1857 the use of Concordia Seminary, St. Louis, as the theological training institution for Norwegian students.[81] In addition, the two synods also learned to know each other through the free conferences and other smaller meetings held during 1858. Undoubtedly much credit for the new relationships was due to Olaus F. Duus, who investigated St. Louis Lutheranism in depth in 1858.[82]

Lauritz Larsen, who had been called to serve as the Norwegian Synod's professor on the St. Louis Seminary faculty to train Norwegian students for the ministry, arrived in St. Louis on November 1, 1859. He continued to serve until 1861. During the early days of the Civil War, rumblings of disagreement became apparent between the Norwegian and Missouri synods on the issue of slavery. Larsen, who had espoused Walther's position, found it difficult to persuade his constituency to accept the Missourian view. After an interval, which permitted the strong feelings about the war and slavery to die down, Friedrich A. Schmidt served as Larsen's successor on Concordia's faculty from 1872 to 1876. Thus, happy relationships existed between these two synods when an overture from Ohio led to the founding of the Synodical Conference. The details of this development are spelled out below.

The first concrete resolution looking to the formation of a third federation among Lutherans came from the Eastern District of the Ohio Synod when it met in Youngstown, Ohio, in

249

June 1870. Declaring itself to be in full theological agreement with the Missouri Synod, it urged its parent, the Joint Synod of Ohio, to concur. The resolution suggested that the Ohio and the Missouri synods establish cooperative activities, particularly in their educational institutions.[83] Moreover, a year earlier, in 1869, president John Bading of the Wisconsin Synod had recommended that the Wisconsin, Missouri, and Norwegian synods work cooperatively in a ministerial training program with Missouri. This proposal had been accepted by the Wisconsin Synod.[84]

Thus, when the Joint Synod of Ohio met in 1870 President Matthias Loy reported the action of the Eastern District and encouraged favorable response. The synod adopted the proposals and appointed a committee to confer with Missouri and other synods on these matters. The committee was authorized to call a special session of the synod for further implementation.[85] What hastened this action was the precarious status of theological education in Joint Ohio at the time.

Everything was propitious. The Joint Synod of Ohio extended an invitation to the Missouri, Wisconsin, Illinois, and Norwegian synods to send representatives to a meeting in Chicago. All responded favorably and the commissioners met January 11–13, 1871. President Robert Knoll of the Illinois Synod, though in attendance, did not officially participate in the deliberations since his synod still held membership in the General Council. He reacted enthusiastically to the discussions and subsequently encouraged his synod to join the new conference.

Though no special agenda had been prepared for the three-day sessions, discussions were carried on in a friendly atmosphere. The commissioners adopted the goal of forming a union or federation, rather than merely declaring intersynodical fellowship. A committee, comprised of one representative of each of the participating synods, drafted a constitution. After its adoption by the commissioners, it was recommended for ratification. C. F. W. Walther (Missouri) was elected chairman and Friedrich A. Herzberger (Joint Ohio), secretary.[86]

One of the chief purposes of the meeting had been to explore the possibility of conducting a joint theological seminary. The conferees discussed merging Joint Ohio's Columbus Seminary with Missouri's St. Louis Seminary. Wisconsin, too, was interested. Under the plan, Joint Ohio would appoint a theological professor for the St. Louis institution and move its preparatory school from Columbus to Pittsburgh, where it would receive Missouri's support. A tentative framework for concrete action had thus been laid.

A second meeting of the same commissioners was held in Fort Wayne, Indiana, November 14–16 of the same year, 1871. The program of the group was arranged along the lines of a free conference, allowing anyone to participate. In addition to the synods previously represented, Minnesota joined the sessions. Two important items of business appeared before the group. One was the proposed constitution, and the second was a comprehensive essay produced by Friedrich A. Schmidt in which he

83.
Ohio Synod, Eastern District, *Proceedings . . . 1870*, p. 22.

84.
Wisconsin Synod, *Proceedings . . . 1869*, pp. 6, 22–23.

85.
Ohio Synod, *Proceedings . . . 1870*, pp. 24–25.

86.
"The Chicago Conference," *Lutheran Standard*, February 1, 1871, pp. 20–21.

discussed the reasons for the formation of the new conference. Schmidt thoroughly and systematically discussed the confessional attitudes of the General Synod, the General Synod, South, and the General Council, concluding that none of the three presented the kind of confessional, theological, and practical platform acceptable to the participants at this meeting.

Discussion of the preliminary draft of a constitution formed the second major subject before the group. After some changes were made it was adopted. In view of the earlier controversies on confessional subscription, the confessional paragraph of the constitution may seem unusually brief. It affirmed: "The Synodical Conference acknowledges its adherence to the canonical Scriptures of the Old and New Testaments as God's Word, and to the symbolical books of the Evangelical Lutheran Church constituting the Book of Concord of 1580 as its own."[87]

One of the chief objectives of the new federation was the "union of all Lutheran Synods in America in one orthodox American Lutheran church." The autonomy of the member synods was carefully preserved. The relationship of the Synodical Conference to the synods was defined as being advisory. Only upon the unanimous approval of each of the synods could new members be accepted into the conference. The same principle was to apply to the participation of the constituent synods in other federations or agencies. Finally, the delegates accepted the ultimate goal of establishing state synods and joint seminaries.

The machinery had now been put together for the Synodical Conference. At its first regular convention in July 1872, the conference accepted two new members: the Illinois Synod and the Minnesota Synod. The first permanent officers elected were C. F. W. Walther, president; William Lehmann, vice-president; Friedrich A. Schmidt, secretary; and John Schmidt, treasurer.[88] Thus the Synodical Conference began an existence that was to last almost a century.

During its first decade the Synodical Conference exhibited a spirit of optimism, vigor, and zeal that made it a potentially powerful force for strict confessionalism in America. The prospects for theological uniformity and ecclesiastical peace permeated the new structure. However, by the early 1880s the Synodical Conference was to experience the most convulsive and divisive conflict since the debate over the *Definite Synodical Platform* (1855), namely, the predestination or election controversy. The account of this fracture will appear in the next section.

251

87.
Denkschrift (Columbus, Ohio: Schulze & Gassmann, 1871), p. 5.
88.
Synodical Conference, *Proceedings . . . 1872*, p. 75.

Eugene L. Fevold

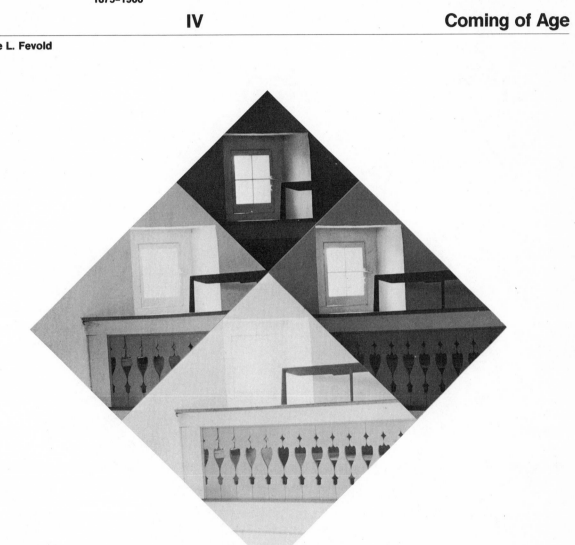

12 Reaching the Immigrant: Home Missions

1.
Helen F. Eckerson, "Immigration and National Origins," in *The New Immigration,* ed. Edward P. Hutchinson (Philadelphia: American Academy of Political and Social Science, 1966), p. 5. Maldwyn A. Jones, *American Immigration* (Chicago: University of Chicago Press, 1960), pp. 179-80.
2.
Arthur M. Schlesinger, *New Viewpoints in American History* (New York: Macmillan, 1937), p. 13. In the decade 1881-90 northern and western Europe provided 72 percent, with only 18.3 percent of the immigrants coming from southern and eastern Europe. During 1891-1900 the comparative percentages were 44.6 and 51.9 percent, and for 1901-10 the proportion had reached 21.7 and 70.8 percent respectively (Eckerson, "Immigration," p. 6).
3.
Jones, *American Immigration,* p. 195.
4.
Albert B. Faust, *The German Element in the United States* (Boston: Houghton Mifflin Co., 1909), 1:586. For example, Theodore C. Blegen, *Norwegian Migration to America, 1825-1860* (Northfield, Minn.: Norwegian-American Historical Assoc., 1931), 1:18.

The majestic Statue of Liberty in New York Harbor was dedicated in the autumn of 1886. A gift from the people of France to commemorate friendship between the American and French nations, it also was a symbol of the magnetic appeal of the United States as the hope and haven of immigrants. The words of Emma Lazarus inscribed on its base suggested the promise of America: "Give me your tired, your poor,/Your huddled masses yearning to breathe free. . . ." The monumental statue was erected at the height of the immigrant flood to America, midway in the period now to be considered.

The Immigration of the Late Nineteenth Century

The "immigrant century" spanned the period from around 1820 to World War I. The first great wave of immigration to America had crested on the eve of the Civil War; a second wave covered the post-Civil War period to 1890; and a third the 1890s to World War I. Lutherans and those from predominantly Lutheran lands were involved in all three immigrant waves. From the beginning of the movement and through the 1880s, northern and western Europe was the chief source of American immigration with British, Irish, German, and Scandinavian elements predominating. In the course of the 1880s a shift in the geographical origins of immigrants occurred. The "old" immigration from northern and western Europe was superseded in numbers by a "new" immigration from southern and eastern Europe. During the 1890s and following the chief sources of immigrants were Italy, Austria-Hungary, and Russia.[1] The changing trend as to national origins became quite apparent about 1885, but not until 1896 did the immigration from the last-named states exceed in volume that from the British Isles, Germany, and Scandinavia. In the first decade of the twentieth century the "new" immigration was three-and-a-half times greater than the "old."[2]

A peak year for immigration from heavily Lutheran lands was 1882, which was a prosperous year for the American economy. More Germans and more Scandinavians crossed the Atlantic to America in 1882 than in any prior or subsequent year, there being a total of 250,000 Germans and 105,000 Scandinavians who came in that single year.[3] In the 1890s German immigration declined sharply, but Scandinavians continued to arrive in large numbers until World War I.[4] Among Scandinavians, the Danes, Finns, and Icelanders began to migrate in sizable numbers at a later date than the Norwegians and Swedes. Before the Civil War they constituted only a trickle, but in the postwar period and particularly in the last decade of the nineteenth century they came in large numbers.[5] Since they never became as numerous in America as Swedes and Norwegians, the other Scandinavian groups did not see their church bodies achieve the size of those of their Swedish and Norwegian brethren. In addition, a smaller percentage of the later immigration from Lutheran lands was retained for the Lutheran church than was the case earlier. The "new" immigration from southern and eastern Europe brought comparatively few Lutherans. Amongst them the Slovaks were the most numerous.

The forces which set in motion the immigration of the late nineteenth and early twentieth centuries were essentially the same as those which had been at work in the earlier period. The desire for economic betterment was primary, frequently combined with the expectation of greater personal freedom than that experienced in Europe. Religious motivation in migrating was an important factor for some but, generally speaking, religious considerations were not prominent in accounting for the later immigration.[6] Economic and social change in northern and western Europe in the nineteenth century had an unsettling effect. Changes in rural society with resultant crises in agriculture accompanied growing industrialization, the development of factories, and the growth of cities. At the same time, because of a great increase in population, Europe experienced labor surpluses and heavy population pressures.[7] Worsening agricultural conditions sent tens of thousands of farmers and agricultural workers to America.[8] Fewer and fewer of the rural population were willing to put up with the traditionally hard lot of agricultural renters, day-laborers, and servants.[9] The immigrant was usually poor, a laborer, and often motivated by a great hunger for land.

Post-Civil War America continued to be a land of economic opportunity. Cheap land was still to be had in the plains states under provisions of the Homestead Act. And there was a great need for labor—to build continent-spanning railroads; to harvest the rich natural resources of forest and mine; to build, operate, and maintain America's great industrial machine. At a time when there was a population surplus in Europe, burgeoning industrial America still needed and wanted workers. Furthermore, there appeared to be greater personal freedom in America. Society was more fluid and democratic; social conventions and restrictions were fewer.

The many catalysts which had long been at work in furthering immigration were still operative: "America letters," publicity brochures and books, tickets or travel money sent by friends or relatives, returned immigrants, the activity of immigrant agents of states or transportation companies, and the like. George Stephenson illustrates the response of many restless Scandinavians to the "pull" of America in the following words: "Their small parcels of land seemed even smaller when they read in an 'America letter' that Ole Olson, formerly a humble cotter, was the owner of a 160-acre Minnesota farm. To make matters still worse, perhaps Ole had returned for a visit, wearing

5.
Paul C. Nyholm, *A Study in Immigrant History: The Americanization of the Danish Lutheran Church in America* (Copenhagen: Institute for Danish Church History, 1963), p. 67; A. William Hoglund, *Finnish Immigrants in America, 1880-1920* (Madison, Wisc.: University of Wisconsin Press, 1960), pp. 7-8; K. K. Olafson, *The Icelandic Lutheran Synod* (n.p., 1935), pp. 7-8.
6.
Jones, *American Immigration*, p. 192; Schlesinger, *New Viewpoints*, p. 3; Ingrid Semmingsen, *Veien mot Vest* (Oslo: Aschehoug, 1950), 2:511.
7.
For a brief discussion of the great increase in world population, particularly in Europe, see R. R. Palmer and Joel Colton, *A History of the Modern World*, 3d ed. (New York: Alfred A. Knopf, 1965), pp. 559-63.
8.
Jones, *American Immigration*, pp. 192-95.
9.
Ingrid Semmingsen, *Utvandringen og det utflyttede Norge* (Oslo: Aschehoug, 1952), pp. 74-76.

American clothes and with American money jingling in his pockets at every step."[10]

An important new factor in the later immigration was the improvement in transportation which made the long trip overseas much less arduous. Most notable was the supplanting of sailing vessels by steamships. The latter became dominant in immigrant traffic from the late 1860s and by the mid-1870s were used exclusively.[11] Coupled with this improvement in sea transportation was the growing network of railroad lines which made travel from the port of debarkation to the inland destination so much easier than earlier. The first of the transcontinental railway lines, the Union Pacific, was completed in 1869, and it soon was followed by others. Likewise, the development of railroads in Europe facilitated travel to ports of embarkation.

Fluctuations in the rate of immigration were determined by conditions in both Europe and America. When German immigration sharply declined in the 1890s, changed conditions in Germany were being reflected. In Faust's words, "Germany's great rise as an industrial nation, her development of colonies in Africa and elsewhere for her surplus population, her exemplary laws insuring the laboring class against accident, disability, etc., have made her population far less eager to emigrate to foreign parts."[12] Conditions were changing in America, too—the virtual disappearance of the geographic frontier (1890), a greatly reduced supply of cheap land, economic depression in the 1890s (the Panic of 1893), and the strong competition in the labor market of the many immigrants from southern and eastern Europe. Similar deterrents to a continued high level of immigration were present in Scandinavia as well as Germany, but at a somewhat later date. After 1900, because of growing industrialization and the onset of a decline in the birthrate, northwestern Europe did not have the manpower available for export that it had earlier.[13]

The destination of the largest number of German and Scandinavian immigrants of the post-Civil War period was the Upper Mississippi River Valley, the plains states of mid-America, and the Pacific Northwest. Older areas of settlement farther east received many, and enclaves of settlement were to be found in New England, in the south, particularly in Texas, in the mountain states, and in California. The majority who came were tillers of the soil, but a greater variety of vocational interests was represented in the later immigration, and proportionately larger numbers settled in the cities than was the case earlier.[14]

The religious interest of many late-nineteenth-century immigrants continued to be strong. The impact of powerful nineteenth-century religious awakenings, particularly in the Scandinavian lands, continued to influence the religious loyalties of the immigrants. However, other currents which were indifferent and sometimes hostile to Christianity and the church were running strongly in the late nineteenth century. Socialist and Marxist thinking was effectively alienating the working classes

257

10.
George Stephenson, *A History of American Immigration, 1820-1924* (Boston: Ginn & Co., 1926), p. 33.
11.
Semmingsen, *Veien mot Vest,* 2:140.
12.
The reference is to pioneering social legislation under Bismarck. Faust, *The German Element,* 1:587.
13.
Jones, *American Immigration,* p. 196.
14.
Ibid., p. 194.

from the church in both Germany and Scandinavia. Contributing to the alienation of laborers was the generally conservative social and political attitude of the church in those lands. Cultural and intellectual circles, under the influence of positivistic and rationalistic modes of thought, were likewise taking a critical stance over against the church.[15] The immigrants of the late nineteenth century more frequently than earlier were indifferent to the church, occasionally even hostile, considering it a bulwark of conservatism and the enemy of enlightened progress.[16] This attitude was more common among workers in the cities than among rural dwellers. This was not a new phenomenon, of course, but it was more apparent among late-nineteenth-century immigrants than it had been earlier.[17] On the other hand, the reactions of immigrant church people toward new anti-Christian influences were often strong as well. Illustrative of their attitude was the hostile reception given by Norwegian-American Lutherans to Bjornstjerne Bjornson, famous Norwegian poet and patriot, who on a lecture tour in America in 1880–81 espoused in a superficial way the findings of biblical critics and challenged traditional Christian beliefs.[18] Among German immigrants after 1870, the year of German victory in the Franco-Prussian War, there frequently was to be found a spirit of anti-intellectualism, marked by suspicion of the German universities, together with a strong spirit of German nationalism.[19]

Historian Oscar Handlin has eloquently and convincingly demonstrated the difficult and traumatic side of the immigrant's experience in America.[20] The immigrant's church and his religious faith were among the most important stabilizing and supportive social factors in his unsettled world. In matters of religious belief and practice the immigrant tended to be very conservative. Naturally, Scandinavian and German immigrants were attracted to a Lutheran church in which their native tongue was used, for nationalistic and cultural reasons as well as for religious ones. On the other hand, some immigrants were so impressed with the freedom and newness of America that they discarded old religious affiliations and entered into new ones. Thus some readily severed old religious ties, which probably were rather tenuous in the first place, and joined a variety of non-Lutheran denominations or religious communities.[21]

The Growth and Expansion of the Lutheran Church

During the last quarter of the nineteenth century, home mission activity took priority over all other forms of church work for Lutherans in America. It was a time when enormous energies were expended in meeting and locating immigrants, in providing them with pastors, and forming them into congregations. Even the vigorous efforts devoted to college and seminary education, for example, were strongly influenced by the necessity of providing pastors for the multiplying congregations.

It was not only the Lutheran synods of the Midwest that reaped a bountiful harvest in the wake of the immigrant flood

15.
The rapidity with which changes of attitude toward the church occurred in some places is illustrated by the extensive influence of Georg Brandes, who represented the new skepticism, in Denmark and Norway. See Nyholm, *Immigrant History*, p. 64; Einar Molland, *Fra Hans Nielsen Hauge til Eivind Berggrav* (Oslo: Gyldendal, 1951), pp. 66–68.
16.
Of immigrant groups from Lutheran lands during the later period of immigration the Finns included some of the most politically radical elements. Especially after the turn of the century many socialist clubs were organized by the Finns. See Hoglund, *Finnish Immigrants*, pp. 44–45.
17.
John Jensen, *The United Evangelical Lutheran Church: An Interpretation* (Minneapolis: Augsburg Publishing House, 1964), pp. 14–15, 155–56; Douglas J. Ollila, "The Formative Period of the Finnish Evangelical Lutheran Church in America or Suomi Synod" (ThD. diss., Boston University School of Theology, 1963), pp. 37–39, 318; Sigvard Sondresen, *Norsk-Amerikanerne* (Bergen: A. S. Lunde, 1938), p. 97.
18.
Arthur C. Paulson, "Bjornson and the Norwegian-Americans, 1880–81," *Norwegian-American Studies and Records* 5 (1930): 84–89.
19.
Arthur C. Repp, "Concordia Historical Institute and Its Educational Role in the Church," *Concordia Historical Institute Quarterly* 37 (1964): 39. F. Pfotenhauer pointed out that in the 1880s German immigration was especially heavy from the peasant classes. W. H. T. Dau, ed., *Ebenezer* (St. Louis: Concordia Publishing House, 1922), p. 338.
20.
Particularly in *The Uprooted* (Boston: Little, Brown & Co., 1951).
21.
Marcus L. Hansen, *The Problem of the Third Generation Immigrant* (Rock Island, Ill.: Augustana Historical Society, 1938), p. 16; Frederick C. Luebke, "The Immigrant Condition as a Factor Contributing

to the Conservatism of the Lutheran Church—Missouri Synod," *Concordia Historical Institute Quarterly* 38 (1965): 20.

22.
William E. Hubbert, "The Lutheran Church Between the Potomac and the Rio Grande," *Lutheran Quarterly* 9 (1879): 249, 252. Gilbert P. Voigt, "Documentary History of the United Synod of the Evangelical Lutheran Church in the South," mimeographed (Beaufort, S.C., 1955), pp. 6–7; W. L. Seabrook, "Our Home Mission Field—South," *The Second General Conference of Lutherans in America . . . 1902* (Newbury, S.C.: Lutheran Publication Board, 1904), pp. 183, 188–89.

23.
Henry Eyster Jacobs, *A History of the Evangelical Lutheran Church in the United States* (New York: Christian Literature Co., 1893), p. 446.

24.
Charles R. Keiter, "Immigration in the Nineteenth Century in Its Relation to the Lutheran Church in the United States," *Lutheran Church Review* 31 (1912): 279.

25.
David L. Scheidt, "The Ministerium of Pennsylvania and Its Linguistic Constituencies, 1865–1916," unpublished paper, p. 7.

26.
Ibid., pp. 4–6.

27.
Ibid., pp. 19–22.

28.
See the discussion of the Pittsburgh Synod and Passavant in chapter 10.

29.
As the result of correspondence between a Nova Scotia congregation and Passavant, Henry W. Roth, then president of the synod, during the summer of 1873 visited Lutheran congregations in Nova Scotia. See Ellis B. Burgess, *Memorial History of the Pittsburgh Synod . . .* (Greenville, Pa.: Beaver, 1925), p. 129.

30.
Ibid., pp. 157, 164, 132.

of the late nineteenth century. Eastern Lutheranism experienced notable growth as well. Lutheran expansion in the eastern United States occurred chiefly in the east central states, particularly in New York and Pennsylvania, where Lutherans were already numerous. There was also a limited expansion into the New England states. Lutheran growth in the southern section of the nation was minimal. Comparatively small numbers of immigrants from the northern states and from Europe benefited a few congregations in the cities and larger towns.[22]

The oldest synods of the East, the Ministerium of Pennsylvania and the New York Ministerium, both of which were members of the General Council, received many immigrants and were extensively involved in home mission activity. Most of them settled in the cities and towns; rural areas did not benefit as much.[23] As a result of the influx of immigrants the New York Ministerium underwent a process of Germanization, becoming more German in the late nineteenth century than it had been earlier. By the early twentieth century approximately one-third of the New York constituency of the three largest Lutheran bodies—the General Synod, the General Council, and the Missouri Synod—were of German foreign-born parentage.[24]

Since large numbers of the new immigrants settled in Pennsylvania, the experience of the Ministerium of Pennsylvania may be regarded as illustrative. Many immigrants joined existing congregations, but frequently new congregations were formed because of the influx of new inhabitants. A German Missions Committee was chosen to supervise this work.[25] Pastors of the Ministerium were ordinarily able to use both German and English because it had been bilingual since about mid-century. In 1882 it was reported that the majority of the synod's congregations used both languages and that few congregations used one language exclusively.[26] The natural trend in the direction of Americanization was retarded by the influx of German immigrants. In the 1870s and 1880s there was a vocal German nationalistic group which resisted the growing use of English. This group was strengthened and supported by the new immigration. When German immigration declined sharply from 1890 on there was also a decline in German influence and the strong nationalistic spirit associated with it.[27]

The Pittsburgh Synod (General Council) was one of the most mission-minded Lutheran bodies in the country. It achieved its reputation as "the missionary synod" primarily because of the leadership of William A. Passavant.[28] Although the focus of its activity was western Pennsylvania and the frontier farther west, one of its more interesting home mission fields was located in Nova Scotia, Canada. A small group of Nova Scotia congregations affiliated with the Pittsburgh Synod and in 1903 organized the Nova Scotia Synod.[29] The western Pennsylvania area was also occupied by the smaller Pittsburgh Synod of the General Synod, which became very active in home mission work, especially from the late 1880s on. This created a competitive situation between the General Synod and General Council in that region, a situation duplicated in other places as well.[30]

Of the two large eastern-based church bodies the General Council was in the best position to work among recent immigrants inasmuch as linguistically it was about one-third English, one-third German, and one-third Swedish.[31] The Swedish element was represented by the Augustana Synod, which had been affiliated with the General Council since 1870. The General Synod, on the other hand, was predominantly English. Devoting comparatively slight attention to reaching foreign-language-speaking groups, it concentrated on outreach to those speaking English. After the formation of the General Council (1867), the number of German-speaking members of the General Synod was small. By 1875 the English language was used exclusively in its seminaries, which were no longer preparing bilingual pastors. It should be noted, however, that two small German synods which affiliated with the General Synod were organized in the Midwest, namely the Wartburg Synod (1875) and the German Nebraska Synod (1890).[32]

The Midwest-based synods picked up some strength in the eastern states at this time also. Of the strongly confessionalistic Midwestern German synods, the Missouri Synod made the most headway. Included in its membership were Eastern congregations, whose origins went back to the beginnings of the synod—in Buffalo, New York City, and Baltimore, for example. These pioneer congregations mothered other churches in their respective areas. Not infrequently an older congregation in the East would change its synodical affiliation for a variety of reasons, including linguistic and doctrinal considerations. The Missouri Synod gained several congregations in this way. An outstanding illustration of this was St. Matthew's congregation in New York City, which joined the Missouri Synod in 1886. Particularly in the 1860s there were several accessions to Missouri from the Buffalo Synod.[33]

The Scandinavian immigration of the late nineteenth century resulted in the establishment of many Lutheran congregations in the East. A relatively small number were Norwegian, Danish, or Finnish, although there were a few heavy concentrations of these groups, the Norwegian settlement in Brooklyn being an example. It was the Augustana Synod that reaped the greatest Scandinavian harvest in the East because the Swedes were particularly numerous in certain areas in New York State (Jamestown, for example) and in New England, particularly in Massachusetts and Connecticut.

The "new" immigration from southern and eastern Europe included comparatively few Lutherans. Attempts were made by Lutheran synods to reach them, but on a small scale and with only limited success. Of these the Slovaks were the most numerous, settling chiefly in Pennsylvania, Illinois, and Minnesota. As will be noted later they eventually organized their own national synod (1902). In the early period of their settlement in this country, Slovak Lutherans had contacts with several church bodies. The General Council was the first to show interest in them. Karol Horak came to America in 1882 in response to the call of its mission board. The next year he was ordained by the

31.
C. E. Sparks, "The Development of the General Synod Lutheran Church in America," *Lutheran Quarterly* 36 (1906): 584.

32.
Willard D. Allbeck, "Christian Jensen and the Germans of the General Synod," *Lutheran Church Quarterly* 12 (1940): 269–70.

33.
H. B. Hemmeter, "The Missouri Synod in the East and Southeast," in Dau, *Ebenezer,* pp. 173–208.

34.
Scheidt, "The Ministerium of Pennsylvania," p. 9; George Dolak, *A History of the Slovak Evangelical Lutheran Church . . . 1902-1927* (St. Louis: Concordia Publishing House, 1955), p. 16.
35.
Burgess, *Memorial History*, p. 129.
36.
Willard D. Allbeck, *A Century of Lutherans in Ohio* (Yellow Springs, Ohio: Antioch Press, 1966), p. 261.
37.
Dolak, *History*, p. 17.
38.
Dean Lueking, *Mission in the Making* (St. Louis: Concordia Publishing House, 1964), pp. 190-91.
39.
Scheidt, "The Ministerium of Pennsylvania," pp. 15-17.
40.
Lueking, *Mission*, p. 192.
41.
Scheidt, "The Ministerium of Pennsylvania," p. 14; Burgess, *Memorial History*, p. 162.
42.
Allbeck, *Century*, p. 259.
43.
Ibid., p. 263.

Ministerium of Pennsylvania to work among his countrymen, and soon there were several Slovak congregations in Ministerium territory.[34] The Pittsburgh Synod carried on Slovak work in the coal and iron regions of western Pennsylvania beginning in 1890.[35] In 1905 the General Council established a Slovak-Hungarian Mission Board. The Joint Synod of Ohio supported work on a small scale among the Slovaks in the state of Ohio, their first congregation in that state being organized in Cleveland in 1892.[36] The Missouri Synod also manifested interest in the spiritual welfare of the Slovaks, with whom several contacts were made, including the provision of theological training for Slovak students at its seminaries.[37]

261

Immigrants from the Baltics were ministered to by the Missouri Synod and the General Council. Hans Rebane, ordained by the Missouri Synod in Boston in 1896, ministered to Latvians and Estonians distributed over a vast area, including Canada and the Midwest. In 1902 he was joined by another Latvian ministerial colleague. Meanwhile, the Missouri Synod had designated its Lativan-Estonian work as part of the "foreign-language" mission of the church. In the early twentieth century two districts of the Missouri Synod initiated work among Lithuanian immigrants in Brooklyn and Baltimore.[38] The Ministerium of Pennsylvania carried on work among Latvians in Boston, Philadelphia, and New York through the activity of the brothers John and Peter Steik, beginning early in the twentieth century.[39] A mission to Poles scattered in several cities in the East was begun in 1904 by the Missouri Synod.[40] An Italian congregation was organized by the Ministerium of Pennsylvania in Philadelphia just prior to World War I, and another by the Pittsburgh Synod of the General Synod in 1918 in western Pennsylvania.[41]

Brief reference is made to these modest efforts to reach Lutheran immigrants from eastern and southern Europe as a partial corrective to the impression that all Lutheran congregations formed by immigrants were German or Scandinavian.

During the last quarter of the nineteenth century the greatest concentration of home mission energy was on reaching the immigrant hordes that flooded the Midwest and the Pacific Northwest. By 1875 most of the land east of the Mississippi River had been occupied. Nevertheless, large numbers of Lutheran immigrants continued to come to states which had been carved out of the old Northwest Territory—Ohio, Indiana, Illinois, Michigan, and Wisconsin. What transpired in Ohio may serve to illustrate developments in that region. From 1880 to 1910 the number of foreign-born in the state increased from 400,000 to nearly 600,000, but the number coming from Lutheran lands in Europe decreased slightly. In 1880 the German-born numbered 192,000 and in 1910, 175,000. The number of Scandinavians increased from about 2,000 to 12,000, of which one-third were Finns.[42] In Ohio German immigrants of the conservative Old Lutheran persuasion usually joined the Joint Synod of Ohio, the Iowa Synod, or the Missouri Synod, all of which experienced membership growth in the state during the period.[43] General

Council and General Synod work in Ohio was chiefly in the English language, but their synods grew rapidly, too. Growth was chiefly in the cities, however.[44] By the late nineteenth century, although the German influx contributed to significant growth, the English element in the Joint Synod of Ohio was strong.

The story of Lutheran involvement in "the winning of the West" includes the vigorous home mission endeavors of every major Lutheran synod in America except the United Synod, South. Since the areas of mission activity were primarily determined by the pattern of immigration, for the period under consideration middle America was the primary arena for mission work. Already possessing many Lutheran settlers, the states immediately west of the Mississippi River, such as Iowa and Minnesota, continued to be the scene of heavy home mission activity, especially in their western sections. However, the frontier of settlement had by this time penetrated to the next tier of states or territories westward, located in the Great Plains area drained by the Red River of the north and the Missouri River. This region included the Dakotas, Nebraska, and Kansas. Although these states never became as populous as their neighbors immediately to the east, the Lutheran element in their population was high, making the Great Plains one of the most staunchly Lutheran regions in the entire nation. Texas, whose Lutheran population dated back to mid-century, continued to receive both German and Scandinavian immigrants, particularly the former. It was the only southern state that received a sizable number of Lutheran settlers during the last quarter of the nineteenth century.

It was natural that the Midwest-based synods should be most active in middle America—the Norwegian and Danish bodies, the Augustana Synod, the Missouri Synod, the Iowa Synod, the Joint Synod of Ohio, and the several German bodies which united to form the Wisconsin Synod. Each synod worked vigorously to reach people of its own national background, and because the Missouri Synod was the largest its activity was most extensive. German and Scandinavian communities in the heartland of America during the latter part of the nineteenth century became a veritable bastion of American Lutheranism. The two large Lutheran bodies of the East, the General Synod and the General Council, also were involved in the effort to extend Lutheranism in the West. They led the way in English work. The General Synod was most active in central mid-America, in Kansas and Nebraska, continuing westward from those states to California. The General Council assumed a special responsibility for the Upper Midwest and the Pacific Northwest.

The completion of the railroads was important everywhere for the extension of settlement, particularly in the plains states, where the railroad lines sometimes preceded rather than followed settlement. Such lines as the Union Pacific, the Northern Pacific, the Great Northern, and the Canadian Pacific were crucial in the settlement of the territory and in the extension of the church. Lutherans were never to be strongly represented in

262

44.
Ibid., pp. 271-72.

45.
Carl S. Meyer, "Early Growth of the Missouri Synod," in *Moving Frontiers: Readings in the History of the Lutheran Church—Missouri Synod,* ed. Carl S. Meyer (St. Louis: Concordia Publishing House, 1964), pp. 198–99.

46.
In 1887 the California and Oregon District of the Missouri Synod was organized and in 1891 the California Synod of the General Synod and also its Rocky Mountain Synod.

47.
On Hvistendahl see Kenneth Bjork, "Hvistendahl's Mission to San Francisco, 1870–75," *Norwegian-American Studies and Records* 16 (1950): 1–63.

48.
The General Council's English Synod of the Northwest (1891) embraced the vast territory from Wisconsin to the Pacific until its Pacific Synod was formed (1901).

49.
Carl R. Cronmiller, *A History of the Lutheran Church in Canada* (Toronto: Synod of Canada, 1961), p. 10.

50.
George M. Stephenson, *The Religious Aspects of Swedish Immigration* (Minneapolis: University of Minnesota Press, 1932), p. 307.

the Rocky Mountain states, although scattered congregations were found throughout. In the 1880s Lutheran congregations began to appear in Montana and neighboring states. Although the largest number of Lutherans on the West Coast were attracted to Washington, Lutheran work in the Far West began in the San Francisco area. A pioneer missionary to the German Lutherans was Jacob M. Buehler, a pastor of the Missouri Synod, who came to San Francisco in 1860.[45] It was nearly two decades later that he was joined by a ministerial colleague of his synod in that field. Before the end of the century both the Missouri Synod and the General Synod had organized district synods in the Southwest, which was evidence of the growth, albeit limited as yet, of both German and English-speaking Lutheranism.[46] A pioneer missionary to Scandinavians was Ole Hvistendahl of the Norwegian Synod, who began work in San Francisco in 1870, organizing a Scandinavian congregation in that year. However, it was not long before Swedes, Danes, and Norwegians organized their own congregations along national lines.[47]

Lutheranism was extended northward from California into Oregon and Washington in the late 1870s and 1880s by a coterie of pioneer home missionaries. As earlier noted, however, the main line of movement and mission activity was from the Upper Midwest to the Pacific Northwest via the railroad lines. The heaviest concentration of Lutherans on the West Coast was in the Puget Sound area of Washington, to which thousands of immigrants, especially Scandinavians, came during the latter part of the nineteenth century. By the turn of the century many of the major Lutheran church bodies had organized one or more synods, districts, or conferences to unify and promote their work in the West.[48]

The pace of Lutheran settlement in Canada picked up markedly in the latter part of the nineteenth century, although the greatest growth of Lutheranism in Canada occurred in the early years of the twentieth century. The number of Lutherans in Canada increased from 37,900 in 1871 to 92,500 in 1901, but only ten years later the figure had nearly reached 230,000. Many of the settlers had moved into Canada from the United States. During the first decade of the new century the German population increased by 26 percent and the Scandinavian element by 246 percent.[49] The greatest growth was in the Midwest provinces of Manitoba and Saskatchewan where Lutherans were first ministered to by home mission pastors from synods located in adjacent Minnesota and Dakota Territory. In the 1870s pastors of the Missouri and Norwegian synods made trips across the border into Canada, inaugurating the work of those two groups. The General Council, the Iowa Synod, and the Joint Synod of Ohio did likewise at a later date. In time, the efforts of the German Home Mission Committee of the General Council were chiefly concentrated on Canada. Augustana's mission work among the Swedes in western Canada began in 1883.[50] The original center of Icelandic Lutheran work in North America was in Canada, as will be noted later. The city of

Winnipeg developed into an important reception center for immigrants and a center for western Canadian Lutheranism as did Edmonton and Saskatoon later. Initially the Lutheran congregations and pastors in Canada belonged to districts, conferences, and synods headquartered in the United States, but in the twentieth century several western Canadian districts and synods were organized, continuing, however, as members of American church bodies. Earlier (1861), Lutherans of eastern Canada had organized their own synod, the Evangelical Lutheran Synod of Canada, which became a charter member of the General Council.

The Approach to Home Missions

The basic approach of America's Lutherans to the home mission task—whether by pastors, congregations, or synods—was to search out and reach with the gospel fellow Lutherans of the same national background as themselves. Fortunately there were exceptions to this approach, especially on the part of those Lutherans who had been in America longer and who were thus more Americanized. A statement of an Augustana Synod leader is representative when he describes home missions as the ingathering of "our scattered countrymen throughout the land."[51] By "scattered countrymen" he meant Swedes. A Norwegian, Danish, or Finnish clergyman would just as readily and naturally have made the same statement. The same idea was expressed, for example, in the articles of union of the United Danish Lutheran Church (1896) and in its constitution, where the synod's purpose was stated to be "the upbuilding and strengthening of God's kingdom among our people in America."[52] Likewise, the German circuit rider on the frontier exhibited similar sentiments with his standard inquiry upon arrival in a community, "Do any Germans live around here?"[53]

There was logic in this primary concern for their own countrymen. The pioneer missionaries were better prepared by virtue of language, culture, and geographical proximity to reach and minister to their own people than to someone else. Tuve N. Hasselquist, Augustana's able president, gave expression to this fact in an impassioned appeal to his church body's annual convention (1869).[54] Overwhelmed by the home mission task confronting them on the frontier, all the synods tried to engender in their pastors a sense of personal responsibility for reaching the unchurched. The Norwegian Synod, for example, in 1873 characterized home missions as "a sacred duty" for all pastors serving in frontier situations.[55]

An important first contact with many immigrants was made through the immigrant missions established in eastern seaports by several of the Lutheran bodies. Immigrant missionaries in the port cities assisted in conserving newcomers for the Lutheran church by providing information concerning congregations in the areas in which they planned to settle. They also served as a source of information and advice regarding work opportunities and suitable destinations. They provided temporary housing in a hostel or "emigrant house" when such facilities were available,

51.
G. Everett Arden, *Augustana Heritage: A History of the Augustana Lutheran Church* (Rock Island, Ill.: Augustana Press, 1963), p. 127.
52.
Nyholm, *Immigrant History*, p. 115.
53.
William J. Danker, "Into All the World," in Meyer, *Moving Frontiers*, p. 294.
54.
See *Protokoll*, Augustana Synod, 1869, in Arden, *Augustana Heritage*, p. 129.
55.
Norwegian Synod, *Beretning . . . 1873*, p. 70.

56.
Lueking, *Mission,* p. 59.
57.
E. Clifford Nelson and Eugene L. Fevold,
The Lutheran Church Among Norwegian-Americans, 2 vols. (Minneapolis: Augsburg Publishing House, 1960), 1:281.
58.
Arden, *Augustana Heritage,* p. 22.
59.
Enok Mortensen, *The Danish Lutheran Church in America* (Philadelphia: Board of Publication, LCA, 1967), p. 43.
60.
Adolph Spaeth, *The General Council of the Evangelical Lutheran Church in North America* (Philadelphia, 1885), pp. 40–41.
61.
Adam Stump and Henry Anstadt, *Centennial History of the Evangelical Lutheran Synod of West Pennsylvania* (Chambersburg, Pa.: J. R. Kerr & Bro., 1925), p. 96.
62.
Spaeth, *The General Council,* pp. 37–38.

received mail and wrote letters for immigrants, distributed tracts and other Lutheran literature, held religious services, and provided many types of ministerial service.[56] The Missouri Synod's mission in New York was for many years served by the influential Stephanus Keyl, son-in-law of C. F. W. Walther. A succession of immigrant missionaries of the Norwegian Synod found Keyl most cooperative, including his granting permission for Norwegian use of Missouri's "Pilgrim House" until the Norwegians had their own facilities.[57] Swedes debarking in New York found an Augustana missionary ready to serve them, although for years the "Bethel Ship" harbor mission conducted by Methodist Olof Hedstrom had successfully diverted many immigrants from Lutheranism to Methodism.[58] Rasmus Andersen over a long period of time served as Danish seamen's missionary and immigrant pastor in Brooklyn.[59] Shortly prior to the formation of the General Council (1867), the Ministerium of New York and the Ministerium of Pennsylvania cooperatively supported an immigrant missionary in New York City. Responsibility for this mission was taken over by the General Council in 1869, and an emigrant house was later established.[60] Other cities in which Lutheran immigrant missionaries were stationed for varied periods of time included Baltimore, Boston, and Philadelphia.

Structures and procedures for the promotion, supervision, and support of home mission endeavors varied from synod to synod, some preferring a strongly centralized system, others opting for a more decentralized approach. Perhaps the most centralized administrative approach to home missions was that of the General Synod whose Board of Home Missions supervised home mission work for the entire general body.[61] At this point there was a difference between the General Synod and the General Council. The General Council's dissatisfaction with a centralized approach resulted in its changing in 1882 to a more decentralized operation when separate English, German, and Swedish committees were set up. District synods of the General Council, such as the Ministerium of Pennsylvania, continued to carry on their own home mission programs. The Central Mission Committee of the Augustana Synod served as the General Council's Swedish committee. The home mission operation of the Augustana Synod provided example and stimulus for both the German and English home mission work of the General Council.[62] In most of the synods, especially the larger ones, primary responsibility for initiating and sponsoring home mission work was left to districts and conferences, which meant that synodical boards exercised coordinating or general supervisory functions. This was the case with the Augustana, Missouri, Ohio, and Norwegian synods. In some of the smaller synods supervision was in the hands of the synod rather than its subdivisions; illustrative of this approach were the United Norwegian Lutheran Church (a relatively large body), the Lutheran Free Church, and the Danish and Finnish bodies.

The pluralism of American society created a situation quite different from that in the European immigrants' homelands. As a result pastors and leaders of foreign-language-speaking Lutheran groups were constantly on the watch for competition from other denominations and were extremely sensitive to proselytizing activity. Frequently their judgments on the other church bodies were unduly severe. The synods of the East, more Americanized than their more recently formed counterparts farther west, were less inclined to make sweeping condemnations of other churches. A pioneer German missionary in Wisconsin, for example, characterized those whom he was seeking to reach as "so weak in knowledge that they are unable to distinguish between our love, whereby we seek to keep them with Christ through wholesome Lutheran doctrine, and the love of fanatics, who behind a pious front lead them from Christ and His Word to their own sects."[63] The immigrant who was the object of concern of the Lutheran pastor and missionary was in that context considered to be "a lost sheep threatened with spiritual destruction at the hands of non-Lutheran and secular wolves."[64]

As long as the home mission enterprise was geared to reach "our countrymen" or "our own people" it was carried on in the appropriate foreign language. As noted earlier, some segments of the Lutheran church were prepared to use English, particularly the General Synod and the United Synod, South, although the latter's home mission activity was geographically restricted. Also, the General Council, through its English Home Mission Committee and through the more Americanized of its constituent synods, pushed the cause of English. Representative of the latter was the activity of the Synod of the Northwest in an area in which foreign-language-speaking Lutherans predominated. The Synod of the Northwest concentrated on establishing congregations in strategic cities such as Milwaukee, Minneapolis, St. Paul, Fargo, Tacoma, Seattle, and Portland.[65] Many Lutherans who moved from the East to the Midwest found no English Lutheran congregations and united with other denominations.[66] A veteran General Council missionary pointed out that even when English congregations were formed in the cities growth usually was quite slow for a variety of reasons: the Lutheran church's "foreign" image; the religious disinterest of many migrants from the East; a lack of Lutheran consciousness on the part of many who had grown up in the environment of western cities; the hostility of some Lutheran pastors to English work; and successful recruiting by other denominations.[67] General Council activity in some of the larger cities stimulated other synods to begin English work, too—the Synodical Conference in St. Paul, for example.

Indicative of the difficulty experienced in trying to break the linguistic barrier in some of the conservative synods of the Midwest was the experience of those who in 1872 organized the English Evangelical Lutheran Conference of Missouri. They were refused admission to the Synodical Conference and also to the Missouri Synod because Missouri regarded itself as "purely German."[68] They organized a separate English Synod in 1890, together with others formerly of the Joint Synod of Ohio who

63.
Quoted from *Der Lutheraner* in Lueking, *Mission,* p. 55.
64.
Ibid., p. 57.
65.
William K. Frick, "Lutheranism in the Great Northwest," *Lutheran Church Review* 14:135.
66.
George H. Trabert, *English Lutheranism in the Northwest* (Philadelphia: General Council Pub. House, 1914), pp. 22-23.
67.
Ibid., pp. 65-71.
68.
Everette Meier and Herbert T. Mayer, "The Process of Americanization," in Meyer, *Moving Frontiers,* p. 361.

had formed the Concordia Synod in Pennsylvania. It was not until 1911 that this English Synod was admitted into the Missouri Synod as a nongeographical English district. At the heart of the difficulty was the fact that most Missourians indentified the use of the English language with doctrinally lax, unionistic Lutheranism.[69] This point of view was expressed as follows in a sermon in 1887:

When we consider that we live in a land where English prevails; when we consider that the pure doctrine is preached by so few in English; when we consider that God has graciously given us pure doctrine, not without reason placed us in this land; when we consider that we are duty-bound to transmit the heritage of the pure doctrine to our descendants who will perhaps use English—should all this not move us to pray earnestly: "Dear God, grant that the Word may also be preached pure and unadulterated also "among those who speak English, as it is among us."[70]

Formation of Additional National Synods

As a result of the late-nineteenth-century immigration, several new Lutheran church bodies were organized on the basis of national backgrounds. These included Danish, Finnish, Icelandic, and Slovak synods. It must always be borne in mind, of course, that many immigrants of the national groups named affiliated with already established Lutheran synods. By way of illustration, since Danes got a comparatively late start in organizing a church body of their own, they were often found in Norwegian congregations inasmuch as the two nationalities had much in common in terms of language, culture, and history. Two predominantly Norwegian synods included the word "Danish" in their official names for brief periods of time, indicating their desire to reach their fellow Scandinavians, namely the Norwegian-Danish Conference and the Norwegian-Danish Augustana Synod.[71]

The Danish Synods

In 1872 a small Danish Lutheran organization was brought into being as a result of the efforts of the Committee for the Propagation of the Gospel Among the Danes in America. The purpose of this committee, formed in Denmark in 1867, was to provide religious leaders, both lay and clerical, for the Danes in America. The new organization was initially called a mission society, underscoring the fact that its members regarded themselves as a part of the Church of Denmark with the task of doing mission work among their countrymen. Two years later the mission society was reorganized as a church and in 1878 it officially adopted the name, "The Danish Evangelical Lutheran Church in America" (commonly known as the Danish Church).[72]

Two influential movements within the Church of Denmark—Grundtvigianism and the Inner Mission—were represented within the newly organized synod. It was not long before tensions built up between them in America, as was the case in

69.
Roy A. Suelflow, "The History of the Missouri Synod . . . 1872–1897" (Th.D. diss., Concordia Seminary, St. Louis, 1946), pp. 384–95.
70.
Quoted in Lueking, *Mission*, p. 139.
71.
See chapter 10.
72.
Jensen, *The United Evangelical Lutheran Church*, pp. 49–51; Mortensen, *The Danish Church*, pp. 45–48, 63–67. The four pioneer leaders of the new church body were Adam Dan, Niels Thomsen (both of whom had had brief experiences as foreign missionaries), a Dane who had served Norwegian congregations in America, was an important point of contact between the committee in Denmark and the American situation.

Denmark, culminating in a clash that produced a parallel church body.

Nicolai F. S. Grundtvig (1783-1872)—pastor, historian, patriot, and hymn-writer—was the source of the movement known as Grundtvigianism. He early gained fame as an outspoken critic of the rationalism prevalent in Denmark in the early nineteenth century and as an advocate of traditional Christian teaching. Then in 1825 he experienced a "matchless discovery" which led him to stress the priority of the church over the Bible and the priority of "the living word," particularly as contained in the Apostles' Creed as confessed at baptism, over "the dead word" of the written Scriptures. He reacted negatively to the doctrinal emphasis of Lutheran orthodoxy, and he alienated the pietists who earlier had hailed him as a champion of evangelical Christianity by his Christian humanism with its positive emphasis on man's life and experience in this world. His deep love for all things Danish—the language, culture, and nation—expressed itself in a strongly nationalistic spirit and in his contributions to a renaissance of Danish culture. An important educational contribution was the Danish folk-school movement, which sought to enrich the total life and experience of the ordinary Dane. Grundtvig was a highly controversial personality, and the only thing about which nearly all Danish church people could agree concerning him was the excellence of his many hymns, which were beloved by Danish Christians of all shades of belief.[73]

The second type of emphasis brought from Denmark was known as the Inner Mission movement.[74] An association for Inner Mission was first organized in Denmark in 1853 by laymen of pietistic leanings who nurtured small-group devotional meetings and advocated lay preaching. In 1861 the association was reorganized as the Church Society for Inner Mission, and thereafter Vilhelm Beck (1829-1901) was its dominant leader.[75] Its goal was to effect spiritual renewal within the framework of the Church of Denmark. The emphasis in this movement was on repentance, conversion, and a personal experience of faith. Extensive use was made of lay preachers, and their preaching, as well as that of the pastors associated with the movement, resulted in revivals. The doctrinal position of the Inner Mission was conservative and opposed to distinctive Grundtvigian emphases. Strict standards of conduct, such as abstinence from common amusements, underscored the difference in behavior between believers and the unrepentant. The Inner Mission stressed lay as well as clerical responsibility for the work of the church and stimulated interest in youth activities, charitable work, and foreign missions.

Strong tensions developed between Grundtvigians and Inner Mission people, but within the roomy folk church of Denmark they coexisted. Inner Mission adherents regarded Grundtvigians as doctrinally unsound, worldly, and generally defective in spirituality. Grundtvigians, on the other hand, believed that those associated with the Inner Mission were narrow, self-righteous, and sectarian.

73.
Helpful works about Grundtvig in English include Hal Koch, *Grundtvig* (Yellow Springs, Ohio: Antioch Press, 1952); Johannes Knudsen, *Danish Rebel* (Philadelphia: Muhlenberg Press, 1955); Ernest D. Nielsen, *N. F. S. Grundtvig: An American Study* (Rock Island, Ill.: Augustana Press, 1955).
74.
As used in Scandinavia, the term *"Indre Mission"* designated the church's activity in the homeland, particularly its efforts at evangelization, as contrasted with "foreign" missions.
75.
For helpful information about Beck and the Danish Inner Mission see Vilhelm Beck, *Memoirs,* ed. with an introduction by Paul C. Nyholm (Philadelphia: Fortress Press, 1965).

76.
Mortensen, *The Danish Church*, pp. 99–103.
77.
Ibid., p. 105.
78.
Jensen, *The United Evangelical Lutheran Church*, pp. 113–14.

In its early years the Danish Church in America was representative of the various currents found in the Church of Denmark. Although the two divergent views were present almost from the start, a polarization did not occur until the 1880s. This polarization was hastened by external criticism from Norwegian-American churches and from Danish Lutherans not in the Danish Church and by the forceful advocacy of Grundtvigian views by such men as Frederik L. Grundtvig, son of the Danish patriarch and leader in the organization in 1887 of the Danish Folk Society (*Dansk Folkesamfund*), a nonreligious society with broadly cultural interests. The conflict between Grundtvigian and Inner Mission views came to a head at the synod's small theological seminary located at West Denmark in eastern Wisconsin in 1887. The principal contestants were the two professors of the school, Thorvald Helveg, a Grundtvigian, and Peter S. Vig of the Inner Mission group. Helveg, who was president of the school, had sought a colleague with Inner Mission orientation in order that that element of the synod's constituency might be represented at the seminary.

There were three main areas of disagreement between American Grundtvigians and Inner Mission people at that time: the question of conversion after death; the relation of the church to Danish cultural organizations and activities, particularly the Danish Folk Society; and differing positions regarding the Bible.[76] The possibility of conversion after death was maintained by the Grundtvigians but rejected by their opponents as a dangerous invitation to careless living. The conflict over culture revealed divergent attitudes toward the world—the openness of the Grundtvigians to everything human and the concern of the Inner Mission lest secular interests and activities be substituted for Christian faith and experience. At the seminary the dispute centered particularly on the doctrine of the Word. Vig adhered to the traditional Lutheran view that the Bible is the inspired Word of God and the only source and norm of faith and life. Helveg identified himself with the Grundtvigian distinction between the dead word of the written Scriptures and the living word of the Apostles' Creed, with priority given the latter. The strained relationship between the two professors, particularly regarding views of the Bible, led to the disruption of the seminary and its discontinuance in 1892.[77]

The obvious differences in spirit, emphasis, and doctrine represented by the two groups within the Danish Church led to the withdrawal in 1894 of an Inner Mission minority. The withdrawal took the form of a refusal by pastors and congregations to sign a new synodical constitution adopted by the Danish Church at its convention in the autumn of 1893. The deadline for compliance was February 15, 1894. Constitutional revision was not the issue at stake, however, as the dissenters had not opposed its adoption at the synodical convention.[78] Of fifty-six pastors in the Danish Church forty-one appended their signatures, and of these a few later reconsidered, and only 40 of 119 congregations signed. A number of congregations that had never formally been members of the Danish Church continued to be loosely affiliated with it. The break also involved splits in congregations and unseemly lawsuits over property ownership. The ultimate effect of the contention was the secession of approximately one-third of the Danish Church's congregations and pastors.[79]

In the fall of 1894 a new church body was organized by the Inner Mission element that had withdrawn. It adopted as its name the "Danish Evangelical Lutheran Church of North America," differentiating itself from the parent body by the insertion of the word "North" (commonly called the North Church). Only two years later the North Church merged with another Danish body to form the United Danish Evangelical Lutheran Church in America.

The group with which the North Church united in 1896 also had an Inner Mission orientation. Its roots were in the Norwegian-Danish Conference, which had been formed in 1870.[80] Although predominantly Norwegian, the conference ministered to a number of Danish congregations and attracted many pietistically inclined Danes. The conference took a critical stance over against the Danish Church because of the latter's Grundtvigian leanings. Several Danish theological students studied at Augsburg Seminary in Minneapolis, the divinity school of the conference. There were ten Danish graduates in the period from 1872 to 1884. They were ordained by the conference for work primarily among Danes, and it was anticipated that when the Danish element became strong enough a separate organization would be formed. The Danish pastors of the conference worked through their own home mission committee and published their own church periodical. They reached the conclusion that in the face of the increased immigration of the early 1880s they could more effectively reach Danish immigrants by organizing an independent Danish church. To transfer to the Danish Church was not a live option for them.

Early in 1884 a small group of Danish pastors and congregations, members of the Norwegian-Danish Conference, decided to withdraw in order to form their own organization. They hoped to establish close relations with the Inner Mission organization in Denmark, and it appears that they began to function as a separate church body almost immediately following the decision.[81] Their separation from the conference occurred in a spirit of goodwill on both sides, and they left with the blessing of the parent body. In September 1884 the Danish Lutheran Church Association in America was organized. It was called "the Association" by its own members, but it was generally referred to by others as the Blair Church because its educational institutions and its publishing house were located in Blair, Nebraska. In the fall of 1884 the Blair Church's Trinity Seminary was established, to which Dana College was later added. A. M. Andersen was the first theological professor, followed by Gottlieb B. Christensen.

The Blair Church and the North Church had so much in common, including their Inner Mission orientation and their

79.
Ibid., p. 116; Mortensen, *The Danish Church,* pp. 117, 133.
80.
See chapter 10.
81.
Jensen, *The United Evangelical Lutheran Church,* pp. 80–81.

anti-Grundtvigian position, that it was almost inevitable that they should unite. The 1896 merger was effected without difficulty. At the time of its organization the United Danish Evangelical Lutheran Church numbered 63 pastors, 127 congregations, and a baptized membership of nearly 14,000.[82] Gottlieb B. Christensen served the new body as president for a quarter-century (1896–1921). Peter S. Vig joined the seminary faculty at Blair and was its dominant personality for a generation, except for short intervals when he was not at the school. Close ties were maintained with the Inner Mission in Denmark rather than with the Church of Denmark.[83] The emphasis of the United Church was on evangelism, personal Christianity, and missions. While United Church congregations were found in widely scattered areas from coast to coast, its strength was concentrated in Wisconsin, Iowa, Minnesota, and Nebraska.[84] In 1946 with the elimination of the word "Danish" the official name of the synod was changed to the United Evangelical Lutheran Church in America (UELC).

After the withdrawal of the Inner Mission minority in 1894, the Danish Church rallied around the project of establishing a new school to supplant the dissolved seminary. Grand View College began operation in Des Moines, Iowa, in the fall of 1896, Helveg returned to Denmark after his conflict with Vig, and R. R. Vestergaard arrived from Denmark to assume the presidency of the school in 1897. The establishment of Grand View College and Seminary was an important milestone in the history of the Danish Church because it became the center of that church's life and activity.[85]

The Danish Church continued to maintain its Grundtvigian character. Its congregations established several folk schools on the Grundtvigian pattern. Placing little emphasis on repentance and conversion, it stressed baptismal grace, Christian nurture, and fellowship. The desire to perpetuate its Danish heritage—linguistic, cultural, and religious—resulted in the retention of its Danish character longer than its sister synod and delayed Americanization. Many of its pastors returned permanently to Denmark and this contributed to its slower growth, as did the comparatively little attention paid to missions and evangelism. The membership of the Danish Church opposed any tendency toward centralization of organization and leadership.[86] Like the UELC, although it had widely dispersed congregations, its strength was in the Midwest, where 80 percent of its membership was found on the eve of World War I.[87] In 1953 the name of the Danish Church was changed to the American Evangelical Lutheran Church (AELC).

Relations between the two Danish synods continued to be cool and strained throughout most of their history. Probably only a fraction of Danish immigrants were avowedly Grundtvigians or Inner Mission people, and they did not always have an opportunity to select their synod. If they moved, they often joined a congregation of "the other synod" since no change of language, hymnbook, or liturgy was involved. Differences between the two synods were stressed by the pastors, but in the

271

82.
Ibid., p. 128.
83.
Ibid., pp. 128–31.
84.
Ibid., p. 132.
85.
Mortensen, *The Danish Church,* p. 137.
86.
Ibid., pp. 278–89; J. Knudsen, "The Danish Lutheran Church in America," in J. Knudsen and Enok Mortensen, *The Danish-American Immigrant* (Des Moines, Iowa, 1950), pp. 20–21.
87.
Mortensen, *The Danish Church,* p. 155.

context of bitter controversies some lay members felt even more strongly than their pastors about the differences which separated the two groups.[88] In 1960 the United Evangelical Lutheran Church participated in the formation of the American Lutheran Church, and in 1962 the American Evangelical Lutheran Church merged with three other synods to form the Lutheran Church in America.

Finnish Church Bodies

The vanguard of nineteenth-century Finnish immigration arrived during the Civil War when workers were solicited for the copper-mining country of Upper Michigan, which became the first Finnish center in America. Earlier in the century a few Finnish seamen had come to the United States. The mines of Michigan, northern Minnesota, and the mountain states; the docks and steel mills of Ohio and Pennsylvania; the factories of Massachusetts and New York; and logging camps all across the northern part of the United States attracted the Finns, many of whom later turned to farming. Finnish immigration reached its peak in the late 1890s and the following decade. While motives for migrating were often varied and complex, including in the early-twentieth-century political restraints by the Russian government to which Finland was subject, most of those who came to America did so for economic reasons. An agrarian and industrial revolution was effecting far-reaching changes in Finland, as elsewhere, and the largest number who sought their fortunes in America were landless migrants from the rural provinces.[89] Between 1865 and 1905, 231,000 immigrants arrived.[90] The later stages of Finnish immigration included many socialists who were hostile to Christianity and with whom the church had almost entirely negative relationships. Since the Finnish immigration was relatively late, the Finnish Lutheran churches established in America were among the last of the Lutheran groups to be Americanized.

During the nineteenth century several revival movements which were pietistic in character developed within the Church of Finland. Several expressions of the religious awakening affected Finnish Lutheranism in America, as well as in the homeland. The most influential of these movements was known as the Later Awakening, and its leading early representative was Paavo Ruotsalainen (1777–1852), a layman. It represented a churchly pietism, with which many clergymen identified themselves, and thus it became a powerful force in Finland. The Later-Awakeningists stressed the struggle of repentance, justification by faith, small-group meetings (conventicles), and large yearly gatherings. The basic concern of this group was with subjective Christian experience.

The Evangelical Movement was a second expression of the Finnish religious awakenings. Its lineage went back to Herrnhutism (Moravianism), which was fathered by the pietistic German Count Zinzendorf and was characterized by a deep con-

88.
Nyholm, *Immigrant History*, pp. 79–80.
89.
Hoglund, *Finnish Immigrants*, pp. 7–15, 60–61.
90.
Armas Holmio, "The Suomi Synod," *Augustana Annual, 1960*, p. 94.

cern for the objective nature of Christ's atonement. Frederick G. Hedberg (1811-93) was its chief leader and his name was sometimes applied to the movement (Hedbergianism). A Gospel Society was formed by representatives of the Evangelical Movement. There was controversy between the Later-Awakeningists and the Evangelicals concerning the relative emphasis to be placed on the subjective and objective elements in Christianity, but both groups were pietistic.

A third Finnish revival movement was called Laestadianism, taking its name from Lars Laestadius (1800-1861), a pastor to Lapps and Finns in northern Sweden, who after his own conversion became a particularly effective revival preacher. Laestadian meetings were often accompanied by much emotional excitement. Juhani Raattama (1811-99), a lay preacher, gave to the Laestadian Movement a definite lay orientation characterized by lay preaching. A distinctive feature of Laestadianism was its practice of individual absolution with laying-on of hands, performed by any fellow believer.[91]

In the late nineteenth century significant changes occurred in the status of the Church of Finland. Increased religious freedom was granted by law to individuals and congregations. The church lost heavily among the educated classes, its experience being parallel to that of neighboring Scandinavian lands in this regard, and it became more dependent upon the peasant population than formerly. Although the influence of the revival movements was pervasive, many active and faithful church people were not touched by them. In the face of increasing secularism in the nation, the Church of Finland pursued a policy of comprehensiveness, making place within itself as a roomy folk church for a variety of religious emphases. The theology of Finland was strongly influenced by the conservative biblicism of the German theologian Johann Tobias Beck, whose theology was represented at the University of Helsinki during the years 1875 to 1884 by Gustaf Johansson, later bishop and archbishop.[92]

In America, Finnish Lutherans formed three organizations whose orientations were the Laestadian Movement, the Church of Finland, and the Evangelical Movement.

In 1867 a Scandinavian Lutheran congregation, served by a Norwegian-American pastor, was organized in Hancock, Michigan. It included Norwegians, Swedes, and Finns. When the Laestadian element was excommunicated by the pastor for what he considered un-Lutheran beliefs and practices, the group in 1872 organized their own congregation under the leadership of Salomon Korteniemi, a lay preacher. A few years later it adopted the name "Finnish Apostolic Lutheran Congregation." The constitution of this congregation, which set forth a strictly congregational polity, was the pattern for other Laestadian congregations which were organized as independent congregations unaffiliated with any larger organization.[93] It was not until 1928 that the Laestadians organized a national church body, the Apostolic Lutheran Church, which was a fellowship of

91.
The above material on the revival movements is based on Ollila, "The Formative Period," pp. 10-36; and Walter J. Kukkonen, "The Suomi Synod's Stream of Living Tradition," *Lutheran Quarterly* 10 (1958): 10-14.
92.
Ollila, "The Formative Period," pp. 37-44.
93.
Ibid., pp. 65-70, 75-82.

independent congregations rather than a synod. The Laestadian, or Apostolic Lutheran, movement in America has been characterized by several factions or divisions.[94] The Apostolic Lutherans have functioned essentially as a lay-led revival movement. Their congregations have relied mainly on lay preachers or on ordained ministers trained in seminaries of other churches.[95]

The first Finnish congregation representing the more churchly element was organized in Calumet, Michigan, in 1876. It was served by Alfred E. Backman, the first pastor to come from Finland since colonial times. His successor was Juho K. Nikander who arrived in 1885 to serve congregations in Michigan's Upper Peninsula. Nikander became the patriarch of Finnish Lutherans in America. He represented the cultural and religious heritage of Finland. Not identified with any specific revival movement, he espoused in America the comprehensive spirit of the Church of Finland. In 1890 the Finnish Evangelical Lutheran Church or Suomi Synod was organized by four pastors and sixteen laymen representing nine Michigan congregations. Nikander was elected president, an office which he held almost continuously until his death.[96]

The Suomi Synod's constitution and the centralized polity for which it provided were the occasion for bitter disagreement. Congregational rights were limited and much authority was placed in the hands of the president and the consistory (the executive board of the synod). Critics charged that the constitution provided for an undemocratic and clergy-dominated organization. During the next few years it was made clear that the annual convention, in which lay delegates outnumbered clergy, was the governing authority of the synod, rather than the consistory, and that congregational rights (regarding property ownership, for example) were safeguarded. The consistory which was elected by the annual convention continued, however, to have important responsibilities and extensive authority. Questions raised about the Suomi Synod, particularly its polity, divided congregations, and toward the close of the decade a rival synod, the Finnish National Church, was finally organized.[97]

The Suomi Synod wanted to be a "true daughter" of the Church of Finland and sought to include all Finnish Lutheran parties and movements. It was unable to achieve this goal because the Laestadians and the Evangelicals refused to be included, although representatives of both emphases were to be found within Suomi.[98]

An academy and theological seminary was established in 1896 at Hancock, Michigan, later to become Suomi College and Seminary. The school was coeducational from the start but its most important contribution in the early years was the preparation of men for the ministry. As the president, Nikander was in the position of exercising influence and leadership both as synodical executive and theological professor. The congregations of the Suomi Synod were widely dispersed, being found on both coasts and in the Midwest. Geographical dispersion, to-

94.
U. Saarnivaara, *The History of the Laestadian or Apostolic Lutheran Movement in America* (Ironwood, Mich.: National Publishing Co., 1947), pp. 64–66. Saarnivaara characterizes five different groups of Apostolic Lutherans.
95.
Ibid., p. 88; Kukkonen, "The Suomi Synod's Stream of Living Tradition," p. 15.
96.
Ollila, "The Formative Period," pp. 7, 83–95, 180–81, 258.
97.
Ibid., pp. 145–231. J. W. Eloheimo, one of the organizers of Suomi, promoted the idea of an episcopal church body. Under his leadership an Episcopal Fenno-American Church was organized in 1892, but it did not thrive and it passed out of existence in a few years (ibid., pp. 208–10).
98.
Ibid., pp. 267–69. Kukkonen stresses the pietistic character of the Suomi Synod, writing that it was "largely pietistic" ("The Suomi Synod's Stream of Living Tradition," p. 15). Ollila, on the other hand, while acknowledging the influence of pietism on Suomi, stresses its inclusiveness, similar to the folk-church comprehensiveness of the Church of Finland. ("The Formative Period," pp. 2–3). Armas Holmio agrees with the latter ("The Suomi Synod," p. 96).

99.
Ollila, "The Formative Period," pp. 230–31.
100.
Ibid., pp. 295–315; Hoglund, *Finnish Immigrants,* pp. 44–45, 74.
101.
Holmio, "The Suomi Synod," p. 95.
102.
Beginning in 1919 the United Lutheran Church in America (ULCA) provided a subsidy for home mission work among Finns (Ollila, "The Formative Period," p. 246). In 1930 Finnish congregations in Canada joined the Canada Synod of the ULCA (Holmio, "The Suomi Synod," p. 95).
103.
In 1946 it was renamed the National Evangelical Lutheran Church (NELC). J. E. Nopola, "National Evangelical Lutheran Church," *The Encyclopedia of the Lutheran Church,* ed. Julius Bodensieck, 3 vols. (Minneapolis: Augsburg Publishing House, 1965).
104.
Ollila, "The Formative Period," pp. 172–79. If there were theological differences, as National Church spokesmen later were to insist, Ollila believes that they were latent rather than apparent (ibid., p. 178). Also see Kukkonen, "The Suomi Synod's Stream of Living Tradition," p. 16.
105.
Ollila, "The Formative Period," pp. 276–77, 317–18.
106.
Walter J. Kukkonen, "The Evangelical Movement of Finland in America," *Concordia Historical Institute Quarterly* 42 (1969): 122–24.
107.
Nopola, "National Evangelical Lutheran Church."

gether with a shortage of pastors, encouraged lay leadership in its congregations, but there was little lay preaching in the Sumoi Synod.[99] A formidable deterrent to growth was the strength of socialism among American Finns. Socialist societies were found in many Finnish communities. Not only were they hostile to Lutheran congregations, but they constituted direct competition because of their sometimes elaborate educational, recreational, and social activities. Many Finns who migrated after 1905 became deeply involved in labor unions and strikes and it was difficult for the church to communicate with them. Pastors of the Suomi Synod were conservative and generally agrarian in attitude and thus were strongly critical of the radical labor movement and the violent strikes which took place in mining communities in the early twentieth century, but after World War I some pastors began to sympathize with workers and the labor movement.[100] Another type of organization common in Finnish communities was the temperance society. These societies were numerous and usually worked harmoniously with the churches.

To illustrate the relative recentness of Finnish Americanization, it was not until 1958 that the circulation of the English language publication of the Suomi Synod exceeded that of its Finnish paper.[101] In 1962 the Suomi Synod became a part of the Lutheran Church in America.[102] On the eve of the merger Suomi's baptized membership was slightly over 36,000.

In 1898 the Finnish-American National Evangelical Lutheran Church was organized as an alternative to the Suomi Synod.[103] Its origins went back to the controversy over the centralized polity of the Suomi Synod. The first National Lutheran congregation was organized when the Calumet congregation split over the issue of joining the Suomi Synod. Those who objected represented a democratic concern for congregational polity, and during the early years of Suomi's history this people's movement grew. Theological differences appear not to have been a factor at the time.[104] Early in its career the National Church identified itself with the Evangelicals and the Gospel Society in Finland. It shared a similar concern for such doctrines as universal grace, forensic justification, and the objective atonement.[105] This body also showed its affinity with the Evangelicals by its obvious concern for revival preaching. During its first two decades nearly all the clergymen of the National Church began their ministries as lay preachers, several of whom had been converted in Finland and had gained experience with the Gospel Society.[106]

Beginning in the early 1920s the National Church was drawn into the orbit of the Missouri Synod, with whom fellowship was established. Both synods shared a common concern for doctrinal uniformity. National Church pastors were trained in Missouri Synod schools. Also during the 1920s connections with the Gospel Society and the Evangelical Movement in Finland were severed.[107] Several attempts to unite the National Church and the Suomi Synod failed. In 1964 the National Church merged with the Missouri Synod. At that time it was about one-third the size Suomi had been when it merged with the Lutheran Church in America.

The Icelandic Synod

Immigration from Iceland was largely confined to the period from 1870 to 1900. During that generation about 16,000 Icelanders migrated to the United States and Canada, a remarkably high percentage of the population inasmuch as Iceland's total population in 1890 was about 70,000.[108] Although Icelanders became widely scattered in both countries, major areas of settlement were in Manitoba (the New Iceland settlement on the west shore of Lake Winnipeg), northeastern North Dakota (Pembina County), and to a lesser extent Minnesota. Winnipeg became the center of the Icelandic population in North America.

Two early religious and immigrant leaders were pastors Jon Bjarnason and Pall Thorlaksson. Both made early contacts with the Norwegian Synod and with Norwegian settlers, which were particularly close and meaningful for Thorlaksson. Bjarnason, an ordained minister when he migrated, became the outstanding religious and cultural leader of the Icelanders in America. Thorlaksson, a young college graduate when he arrived, received his theological education at Concordia Seminary, St. Louis, from where he graduated in 1875.[109] It was he, then serving as a minister of the Norwegian Synod, who organized the first Icelandic Lutheran congregation in America in Shawano County, Wisconsin, the site of a temporary Icelandic settlement. In 1877 both Bjarnason, at the time editor of a Norwegian paper, and Thorlaksson were called as pastors to the Lake Winnipeg settlement. Religious differences in the settlement crystallized around the two pastors, some favoring a relationship with the doctrinally strict Norwegian Synod, others preferring a less rigorous stance typical of the Icelandic tradition. Thorlaksson led a migration from Manitoba into the northeastern corner of Dakota Territory, where several congregations were established and where he died in 1882 at an early age. Thorlaksson's successor was Hans B. Thorgrimson, a graduate of Luther College (Iowa) and Concordia Seminary, St. Louis.[110]

The Icelandic Evangelical Lutheran Synod of America was organized in 1885 through the initiative of Hans Thorgrimson. Jon Bjarnason, then pastor in Winnipeg, was chosen president, an office he held until 1908. It is interesting to note that the Icelandic Synod pioneered in giving women the right to vote and to hold office in the church, including the privilege of serving as synodical delegate.[111] With no seminary of its own, the Icelandic Synod was dependent on other church bodies for theological training. In 1913 it established its only school, the Jon Bjarnason Academy in Winnipeg, but it was discontinued during the depression of the 1930s. A nontypical form of competition in Lutheran communities appeared in the American Unitarian Association, which conducted church work in some Icelandic communities. The Unitarians won some adherents,

108.
Thorstina Walters, *Modern Sagas: The Story of Icelanders in North America* (Fargo, N.D.: Institute for Regional Studies, 1953), pp. v, 31–32. On Icelandic immigration also see Knut Gjerset, *History of Iceland* (New York: Macmillan, 1924), pp. 458–71.
109.
Olafson, *Icelandic Synod,* pp. 9–10. Bjarnason, who arrived in 1873, was briefly assistant to U. V. Koren (Norwegian Synod) at Decorah, Iowa, and for a few months in 1874 taught at Luther College (Gjerset, *History of Iceland,* p. 460). Thorlaksson went to Concordia Seminary upon the advice of N. F. Wiese, who had befriended him in Milwaukee shortly after his arrival in America (Walters, *Modern Sagas,* p. 36).
110.
Olafson, *Icelandic Synod,* pp. 9–12.
111.
Ibid., p. 13.

particularly in Winnipeg, and the Icelandic Synod lost a few congregations to them.[112]

During its history the Icelandic Synod, especially through its pastors, had a wide range of Lutheran synodical contacts and in 1940 joined the United Lutheran Church in America as a nongeographical synod.[113] With the formation of the Lutheran Church in America (LCA) in 1962, the Icelandic Synod was discontinued and its congregations became members of various district synods. The Icelandic Synod's relatively small size is indicated by the fact that in 1960 it had 7,300 baptized members.[114]

Slovak Synods

The mass migration of Slovak immigrants to America began about 1880. By 1899 there were between 160,000 and 200,000 Slovaks in the United States, and the immigrant wave continued to be heavy until World War I. They settled mainly in the eastern seaboard states—Pennsylvania, New York, New Jersey, and Connecticut—but also in Ohio, Illinois, and Minnesota.[115] The Slovaks came from the dual monarchy of Austria-Hungary in order to improve their generally depressed economic status and because the Hungarian government pursued a policy of oppressing and discriminating against its Slovak population at the same time that all things Hungarian (Magyar) were being favored and promoted.[116] The first Slovak immigrants came without pastors, and frequently there was a considerable time lag between the settlement of Slovaks in a community and the establishment of a congregation. The efforts of several American Lutherans to minister to Slovak immigrants has been briefly referred to earlier.[117] In the early years, in addition to contacts with various Lutheran bodies, Slovaks joined several non-Lutheran denominations, and in a few instances union congregations with the Reformed were established. By the end of the century twenty-two Slovak Lutheran congregations had been organized, the oldest of which dated from 1883.[118]

After an abortive attempt at uniting Slovak congregations in the mid-1890s, the Slovak Evangelical Lutheran Church was organized in 1902 at Connellsville, Pennsylvania, by ten pastors and four laymen who represented fifteen congregations.[119] Of the ties established with several American Lutheran synods the strongest were with Missouri. In fact, there was an element among the Slovak pastors that favored uniting Slovak congregations with the Missouri Synod or the Synodical Conference rather than forming a separate national synod, but their sentiments did not prevail. At the constituting convention a resolution was passed stating that the Slovak Synod was of one mind with the "orthodox Missouri Synod."[120] This indicated the nature of the synod's future relationships. Efforts of the General Council to establish close relations were rejected, and in 1908 the Slovak Synod was received into the Synodical Conference.[121] Over the years its theological students have been trained in the colleges and seminaries of the Missouri Synod. In 1959 the synod's name was changed to "The Synod of Evangeli-

277

112.
Ibid., p. 17. Among prominent Icelandic Unitarian leaders were Bjorn Pjetursson, who was influenced by the Norwegian Unitarian pastor in Minneapolis, Kristofer Janson, and Rognvaldur Petursson (Walters, *Modern Sagas*, pp. 97–98).
113.
In the 1890s there was some agitation for joining the General Council, but the majority regarded it as inadvisable at that time (Olafson, *Icelandic Synod*, p. 33). F. J. Bergmann was a graduate of Philadelphia Seminary (1886) and was ordained by the Ministerium of Pennsylvania. An influential and controversial pastor, he eventually left the Icelandic Synod (ibid., pp. 15, 20–21).
114.
K. K. Olafson, "Icelandic Synod," in "Lutheran Church in America," *Encyclopedia of the Lutheran Church*.
115.
Dolak, *History*, pp. 11–13, 16. By 1906 there were 400,000 Slovaks in the U.S. Immigrant statistics are not accurate because many Slovaks were listed as Hungarians in census reports.
116.
Ibid., pp. 3–9.
117.
See pp. 260–61.
118.
Dolak, *History*, pp. 18–19, 26.
119.
Ibid., pp. 42–45. The full name, according to the constitution, was the Slovak Evangelical Church of the Augsburg Confession in the United States of America.
120.
Ibid., p. 45.
121.
Ibid., pp. 54, 72.

cal Lutheran Churches" (SELC), eliminating "Slovak." In 1971 the Slovak Synod merged with the Missouri Synod.

Approximately one-half of all Slovak Lutheran congregations did not join the Slovak Synod for a variety of reasons, some of which stemmed from early controversies in the synod and its pro-Missouri orientation. In 1919 the Slovak Zion Synod was organized to gather these congregations into a church body, and the next year it joined the United Lutheran Church in America.[122] Even after the formation of the Lutheran Church in America (1962) the Slovak Zion Synod continued as a bilingual nongeographical synod, the only one in the new church body.[123]

122.
Ibid., p. 92; John Zornan, "Slovak Zion Synod," in "Lutheran Church in America," *Encyclopedia of the Lutheran Church.*
123.
Baptized membership of the Slovak Zion Synod in 1968 was 14,507 compared with 20,556 for the Synod of Evangelical Lutheran Churches (*Yearbook, 1970,* Lutheran Church in America, p. 344; *1970 Lutheran Annual,* Lutheran Church—Missouri Synod, p. 59).

13 The Broadening Work of the Church

1.
Among the European mission societies were the following: the Hermannsburg, Leipzig, and Neuendettelsau societies, all of Germany; the Norwegian Mission Society, the Schreuder Mission of South Africa (Norwegian); the Swedish Mission Society, the Evangelical Missionary Society (Swedish); the Finnish Missionary Society; Santal Mission in India (Scandinavian).

The last quarter of the nineteenth century was a period of rapid growth and expansion for the Lutheran church in America. Although the home mission enterprise continued to receive top priority among its endeavors, the scope of the church's activity was considerably broadened on many fronts. World missions was an activity that gripped the imagination and marshaled the resources of Western Christendom in the nineteenth century, and America's Lutherans gave increasing attention to that cause as the century drew to a close. Several American Lutheran church bodies began overseas work, and at the same time a larger concept of missions led to increased, although still limited, efforts to evangelize such minority groups at home as Blacks, Indians, and Jews. As in the preceding period much effort was devoted to the establishment of educational institutions and activities, not only to provide clergymen for an expanding church but also to give educational opportunities for the laity. The closing decades of the century witnessed the proliferation of Lutheran seminaries, colleges, and academies, particularly in the Midwest where numerical growth was greatest. The establishment of charitable institutions, such as hospitals, orphanages, and homes for the aged, was also given more attention than hitherto. Thereby, the Lutherans of America entered more fully into the tradition of institutional social ministry made famous in Lutheran Germany and Scandinavia. Small beginnings were also made in the development of synodical organizations for women and youth, at least partially in response to examples and stimuli from the American Protestant environment.

Foreign and Special Missions

As noted earlier, by 1875 America's English-speaking Lutherans had assumed responsibility for overseas missions of their own: the Rajahmundry mission in India of the General Council and the Liberia mission of the General Synod. The synods composed of more recent immigrants continued to send financial contributions earmarked for foreign missions chiefly to various European mission societies and fields—German, Swedish, Danish, Norwegian, and Finnish.[1] The heavy concentration of effort on home missions by all the American bodies delayed direct foreign mission activity. During the last two decades of the century popular sentiment for the establishment of their own foreign fields began to build up in some quarters, and by the turn of the century responsibility for overseas missions was assumed by church bodies that previously had no fields of their own. They were quickly joined by many others early in the twentieth century.

Because the Augustana Synod joined the General Council it was natural that its mission interest and support would be directed to the Rajahmundry field in India. August B. Carlson, a Philadelphia Seminary graduate, and his wife were the first Augustana missionaries to serve on that field. They went to India in 1878, and other Augustanans eventually followed their example. Although his service was terminated by his untimely death a few years later, Carlson made an important contribution to the awakening of mission interest in the Augustana Synod.[2]

India was also the location of the Missouri Synod's first overseas mission. This came about because of contacts between the synod and missionaries of the Leipzig Mission Society. In the mid-1870s a group of the society's missionaries left their field in India. Two of them came to America at Walther's invitation and became pastors of the Missouri Synod.[3] In 1894 Theodor Naether and Franz Mohn, who were serving on the Leipzig field in India, clashed with the leadership of the mission society in a repetition of the earlier controversy. That same year they were invited to America by Missouri's Board of Missions, and after a colloquy they were commissioned as the synod's first foreign missionaries. By 1900, of the five missionaries on Missouri's field in India, four were formerly of the Leipzig Mission Society and one had been trained by the Saxon Free Church.[4]

Among Norwegian immigrants, mission interest was stimulated during the 1880s by the American visits of missionaries of the Norwegian Mission Society and by a series of intersynodical (intra-Norwegian) mission meetings. In the late 1880s the Norwegian Conference sent Johan P. Hogstad (1887) and Erik H. Tou (1889) to serve in Madagascar under the supervision of the Norwegian Mission Society. In 1892 the society turned over a portion of its Madagascar field to the recently formed United Norwegian Lutheran Church. In turn the latter body divided its field with the Lutheran Free Church. Despite the difficult conditions under which missionaries had to work, the gospel won a favorable hearing in Madagascar.[5]

China was also a favorite mission field for American churches. Of America's Lutherans the Norwegians were the first to participate in the many-pronged campaign to evangelize China, an enterprise which ended in frustration as the turbulence of the twentieth century ultimately denied them access to mainland China. In 1890 an independent Norwegian Lutheran China Mission Society was organized. Early missionaries were Daniel Nelson, Halvor N. Ronning, and his sister Thea, the pioneer vanguard of the many American Lutherans who served in China. In 1892 Hauge's Synod established its own China field, and in 1903 the China Mission Society's work was taken over by the United Norwegian Lutheran Church. In 1917 these two fields and that of the Norwegian Synod (1912) were united.[6]

The beginnings of American Lutheran mission work in Japan also go back to the late nineteenth century. In 1892 James A. B.

G. Everett Arden, *Augustana Heritage: A History of the Augustana Lutheran Church* (Rock Island, Ill.: Augustana Press, 1963), pp. 125–26; S. Hjalmar Swanson, *Foundations for Tomorrow* (Rock Island, Ill.: Augustana Book Concern, 1960), pp. 35–38; idem, *Three Pioneer Missionaries* (Rock Island, Ill.: Augustana Book Concern, 1945), pp. 7–36.
3.
Dean Lueking, *Mission in the Making* (St. Louis: Concordia Publishing House, 1964), pp. 67–78. Carl M. Zorn served as pastor in the Missouri Synod, 1876–1911, and John F. Zucker as pastor and college professor, 1876–1921. See William J. Danker, "Into All the World," *Moving Frontiers: Readings in the History of the Lutheran Church—Missouri Synod*, ed. Carl S. Meyer (St. Louis: Concordia Publishing House, 1964), pp. 300–301.
4.
Lueking, *Mission*, pp. 203–15. In 1893 the synod had decided to begin mission work in Japan with a Missouri-educated Japanese student as missionary. These plans did not materialize, and India replaced Japan as Missouri's first foreign field.
5.
E. Clifford Nelson and Eugene L. Fevold, *The Lutheran Church Among Norwegian-Americans*, 2 vols. (Minneapolis: Augsburg Publishing House, 1960), 1:282–83, 236–37.
6.
Ibid., pp. 288–89.

7.
Andrew S. Burgess, ed., *Lutheran World Missions* (Minneapolis: Augsburg Publishing House, 1954), pp. 160–62, 193–94; S. T. Hallman, ed., *History of the Evangelical Lutheran Synod of South Carolina, 1824–1924* (Columbia, S.C., 1924), p. 35.
8.
Documentary History of the General Council . . . (Philadelphia: General Council Pub. House, 1912), pp. 313, 469–70; Swanson, *Foundations*, pp. 22–24.
9.
Lueking, *Mission*, pp. 176–84.

Scherer and Robert B. Peery of the United Synod, South initiated the work to which the General Council also gave support. Six years later J. M. T. Winther, newly ordained by the United Danish Evangelical Lutheran Church, arrived in Japan. In 1903 that church body adopted Winther as its missionary and in subsequent years sent out additional workers. In 1919 the Japanese work of the United Danish Evangelical Lutheran Church and the United Lutheran Church in America was merged.[7]

At the very close of the nineteenth century limited American Lutheran efforts were directed toward Latin America. Following the Spanish-American War the island of Puerto Rico came under the jurisdiction of the United States. Early in 1899 G. Sigfrid Swensson, an Augustana theological student, began to hold services in San Juan. In response to his appeal the General Council in the autumn of that same year commissioned two workers for service in Puerto Rico. In the course of a decade five congregations were organized. Mission work was conducted in both the Spanish and English languages with the latter predominating. The Augustana Synod maintained a particular interest in the Puerto Rico work and contributed several workers to it. In 1918 the field came under the jurisdiction of the United Lutheran Church in America, eventually being placed under its Board of American Missions.[8]

A Latin American mission of the Missouri Synod begun at the end of the century more accurately comes under the category of "home missions abroad." Large numbers of Germans settled in South America in the nineteenth century. By 1890 there were 90,000 in Brazil, and church work was carried on among them by German state churches and societies. The Missouri Synod became involved when it sent Carl J. Broders to be its first missionary pastor to Brazil. He came in response to an appeal to the Missouri Synod from a Lutheran pastor already serving in Brazil as a member of the Rio Grande Synod. Missouri sent other workers who shared a field with the Saxon Free Church. Capitalizing on work that had already been carried on for several decades, the Missouri Synod in 1904 organized a Brazil District and three years later a seminary was begun at Porto Alegre. In 1905 Missouri's South American mission was extended into Argentina.[9]

Other instances of "home missions abroad," particularly as sponsored by the Missouri Synod, may be briefly mentioned. In the 1870s contact was made with C. F. W. Walther by one element of the small but divided German Lutheran community in Australia with the result that in 1881 Casper Dorsch, the first of a succession of Missouri-trained pastors and professors, went to the vast land "down under." About two decades later (1903) an appeal from German settlers in New Zealand led to the sending of Missouri men and financial support. On the other side of the world in the capital of the British Empire Missouri in 1896 provided a pastor to serve German laymen affiliated with the Saxon Free Church. In the fall of that year F. W. Schulze was ordained in London by a pastor of the Saxon body.

Four years later he was joined by a ministerial colleague, and in a short time the Missouri Synod had two small congregations and three small parochial schools in London. All activity was carried on in the German language.[10]

In each of these instances of home missions abroad—in Brazil, Argentina, Australia, New Zealand, England—the goal was to reach those already Lutheran and German-speaking and to preserve them for the type of Lutheranism represented by Missouri.

An interesting facet of the mission movement of the nineteenth century was a concern for the conversion of the Jews. There were several instances of European Jewish converts to Christianity who became prominent Christian scholars, including professors August Neander, Carl P. Caspari, and Franz Delitzsch. Immigration brought a flood of Jews to America, whose Jewish population was estimated at 250,000 in 1880, almost all of whom had come from German lands and were widely dispersed in America. Thereafter large numbers came from eastern European nations, a half million by 1900 and another million-and-a-quarter by World War I, locating chiefly in eastern cities.[11] Missions to the Jews were inaugurated by a variety of Christian organizations during the late nineteenth century.[12]

Several attempts to reach the Jews with the gospel were made by American Lutherans, who ordinarily regarded such efforts as "foreign" mission work. The endeavors were on a relatively small scale and success was limited. In 1878 the Zion Society for Israel was organized by members of the Norwegian-Danish Conference. Its membership was drawn from other Scandinavian synods as well. In its early years the Zion Society supported missionaries Theodor Meyersohn and Rudolph Gurland in Russia and Paul Werber in Baltimore, all of whom were Jewish converts. Later the society's work was expanded to Chicago, New York, and Minneapolis.[13]

The Missouri Synod's pioneer missionary to the Jews was Daniel Landsmann, who served in New York City from 1883 to 1896. A Russian Jew who had been converted to Christianity in the Middle East and had served as a Christian missionary in Constantinople under the auspices of the Scottish Society, Landsmann entered Missouri's service through contacts with immigrant misssionary Stephanus Keyl of New York. He engaged in a lay ministry, and those he reached were turned over to parish pastors for integration into Missouri congregations. The results of his arduous work were far from dramatic, but this was the typical experience of Lutheran missionaries to the Jews. Following Landsmann's death one of his converts, Nathaniel Friedmann, carried on his work.[14]

From 1893 to 1902 the Iowa Synod conducted a mission to the Jews of Chicago's West Side. The first missionary was Emanuel N. Heimann, later with the Zion Society. For a time the Joint Synod of Ohio sponsored a mission among the Jews of Pittsburgh with A. R. Kuldell as missionary (begun in 1896). The General Council in 1897 appointed a Committee on Cor-

10.
Ibid., pp. 187–88. During 1879–91 L. Carlsen, pastor of the Norwegian Synod, was responsible for serving Norwegian immigrants in Australia, but upon his permanent return no provision was made for a successor. Nelson and Fevold, *Lutheran Church Among Norwegian-Americans*, 1:286.
11.
Nathan Glazer, *American Judaism* (Chicago: University of Chicago Press, 1957), pp. 23, 60–62.
12.
A. E. Thompson, *A Century of Jewish Missions* (Chicago: Revell, 1902), chap. 21.
13.
C. K. Solberg, *A Brief History of the Zion Society for Israel* (Minneapolis, 1928); J. H. Blegen, *Zionsforeningens Historie* (Minneapolis: Frikirkens Boghandels Trykkeri, 1903).
14.
Lueking, *Mission*, pp. 159–73; Walter A. Baepler, *A Century of Grace* (St. Louis: Concordia Publishing House, 1947), pp. 182–83.

respondence Concerning Jewish Mission Work, which sought to keep council membership informed about Lutheran missions and urged cooperation in their work.[15]

In the latter part of the nineteenth century there was only limited Lutheran work among American Negroes. Prior to emancipation Blacks worshiped with their masters in Lutheran churches of the South. After the Civil War the South Carolina Synod, which had a larger proportion of Negroes than any other Lutheran synod at that time, encouraged continuation of the old system, but it was soon discontinued. A second approach, that of urging the organization of separate Negro churches, was the one followed but only to a limited degree. Although first suggested by the Tennessee Synod, only the North Carolina Synod carried on work among southern Negroes from 1868 to the early eighties when the Synodical Conference entered the field. The General Synod had discussed possible approaches for work among Negroes, but its interest did not get beyond the discussion stage. The North Carolina Synod licensed capable Negroes for pastoral work (by 1876 there were three), who worked under the supervision of white pastors, the first of whom was D. J. Koontz, who served all-Negro congregations. Difficulties resulting from inadequate financial support threatened the continuance of the synod's Negro work and led the Black pastors to obtain permission to organize a separate synod in 1889, the Alpha Synod of the Evangelical Lutheran Church of Freedom in America. Two years later the Alpha Synod appealed to and received help from the Synodical Conference.[16]

The Negro Missions of the Synodical Conference dated from 1877 when conference president Herman A. Preus asked "whether it was not time . . . to devote attention to heathen missions and bring into being a mission among the Negroes or Indians."[17] That same autumn John F. Doescher, frontier missionary of the Missouri Synod serving in Dakota Territory, was installed as the conference's missionary to the Negroes. He engaged in itinerant evangelism in several southern states, making New Orleans his headquarters. Doescher's freewheeling methods brought him into disfavor with his superiors, and his connections with the Missouri Synod were severed in the mid-1880s. Other pioneer missionaries were Friederich Berg, who served in Little Rock for a few years, and Nils Bakke, originally of the Norwegian Synod. It was Bakke who made the most important and permanent contribution to the cause of Negro missions in the course of his forty-year career (1880-1920) as missionary in the South, particularly in New Orleans and North Carolina.[18] In its mission to Blacks the Synodical Conference heavily accented educational work. In 1903 Emanuel Lutheran College, Greensboro, North Carolina, was established with three departments—high school, normal school, and seminary. The same year saw the beginnings of Luther College, New Orleans, on the same pattern.[19]

Lutheran mission work to the American Indian goes back as early as the mid-seventeenth century to the New Sweden colony on the Delaware River. Initial efforts by Lutherans in the mid-

15.
Johannes Deindoerfer, *Geschichte der Evangel.-Luth. Synode von Iowa* (Chicago: Wartburg Publishing House, 1897), pp. 272-76; George J. Zeilinger, *A Missionary Synod with a Mission* (Chicago: Wartburg Publishing House, 1929), pp. 69-71; Solberg, *Zion Society*, pp. 54-56; *The Lutheran* 3 (1898): 53, for brief notice about the Ohio Synod's mission; *Documentary History, General Council*, pp. 296, 302, 308.

16.
This paragraph is based on H. George Anderson, *Lutheranism in the Southeastern States, 1860-1886* (The Hague: Mouton, 1969), pp. 209-17. Also see Lueking, *Mission*, pp. 115-18.

17.
Lueking, *Mission*, p. 85.

18.
Ibid., pp. 83-118.

19.
Baepler, *Century of Grace*, p. 269.

nineteenth century came to an unhappy and unsatisfactory conclusion. These were the endeavors of the Loehe emissaries and the Missouri Synod among the Chippewas of Michigan and Minnesota, and of the Iowa Synod among the Crows of Montana and the Cheyennes of Wyoming.[20]

During the last quarter of the nineteenth century several Indian missions were begun, most of which met with some success. Work among American Indians was regarded as a "foreign" mission challenge and opportunity. Two Norwegian synods began work in the mid-1880s in the vicinity of Wittenberg, Wisconsin. The Bethany Mission of the Norwegian Synod, begun in 1884, centered its work in a school for children of the Winnebago tribe. The key leader in the early years was Axel Jacobson, a layman. The Bethany Mission was finally discontinued by the Evangelical Lutheran Church in 1955. The second Indian mission in the Wittenberg area was undertaken by the tiny Eielsen Synod among the Pottawatomies under the leadership of Erik O. Morstad, who began his career in the Norwegian Synod as its first missionary to the Indians.[21]

In the 1890s three additional Indian missions had their start. Niels L. Nielsen, a young Dane, began to preach the gospel to the Cherokee tribe in Oklahoma in 1892. It was six years before he performed his first baptism, but thereafter progress was more rapid. An important feature of this mission was a boarding school. With the division of the Danes into two synods shortly after Nielsen began his work, the Cherokee mission went with the United Danish Evangelical Lutheran Church.[22] At about the same time as the Danes began their mission, the Wisconsin Synod was contemplating an Indian mission in the American Southwest. In 1893 it sent two young missionaries to work among the Apaches of Arizona. Of the two, John Plocher was chiefly responsible for establishing the work since the other young man left after only a year. Again it was six years before the first baptism occurred. Among the Apaches, as with other Indian missions, much effort was devoted to schools.[23] The Missouri Synod in 1899 began mission work among the Stockbridge tribe in Shawano County, Wisconsin, at the request of a delegation from the tribe. Originally from Massachusetts, the Stockbridge Indians had been served by Presbyterians, but for some time they had been without ministerial services.[24]

The Eskimos of Alaska were the concern of the Norwegian Synod beginning in 1894 when Tollef L. Brevig went to Teller as a governmental school teacher. His missionary career, although broken by several rather long absences, continued until 1917, when the Alaskan Mission was taken over by the Norwegian Lutheran Church in America.[25]

Theological Education

An acute shortage of pastors in the face of rapidly increasing numbers of immigrants led to the high priority given theological education by Lutheran church bodies. Although some men who had received their theological training in Europe continued to come to America and helped alleviate the need for pastors, it

20.
See chapter 10.
21.
Albert Keiser, *Lutheran Mission Work Among the American Indians* (Minneapolis: Augsburg Publishing House, 1922), pp. 168–86.
22.
Ibid., pp. 115–20; John Jensen, *The United Evangelical Lutheran Church: An Interpretation* (Minneapolis: Augsburg Publishing House, 1964), pp. 200–202.
23.
Keiser, *Lutheran Mission Work*, pp. 121–51.
24.
Ibid., pp. 152–68; Baepler, *Century of Grace*, p. 240.
25.
Nelson, *Lutheran Church Among Norwegian-Americans*, 2:95; J. Walter Johnshoy, *Apaurak in Alaska* (Philadelphia: Dorrance & Co., 1944).

was clear that the American churches would have to provide for the training of the bulk of their pastors. Reflecting their European heritage, the Lutheran churches in America were dedicated to the ideal of an educated ministry. Because of the pressing need, men with inadequate academic training or with an abbreviated exposure to theological education were sometimes ordained. Such procedures were justified as emergency measures, but the ideal of a thoroughly trained ministry was never forgotten.[26]

Special relations with certain schools in Europe, but not the universities, were developed in an effort to increase the number of theological candidates. Friedrich Brunn, at the encouragement of Walther and with some financial support from the Missouri Synod, conducted a school at Steeden, Nassau, Germany, from 1861 to 1878 for the preliminary training of ministerial candidates who planned to serve in America. Upon arrival in America they were to receive a year or two of final training. Brunn was mission-minded, concerned about the spiritual welfare of German immigrants, and strongly confessional. His students imbibed his strict confessionalism, which was congenial to the spirit of Missouri. He sent about 235 students to America, some of whom received training at Missouri's Addison, Illinois, normal school as teachers in parish schools, but the majority of them attended the "practical" seminary of the Missouri Synod and became pastors.[27] Theodor Harms was another German confessionalist who recruited workers for America and gave them some training in his institution at Hermannsburg.[28]

During the late nineteenth century the General Council, confronted by a large number of German immigrants, found itself in need of additional German-speaking pastors. Since this need was not being met by Philadelphia Seminary, which was being criticized in some quarters for having become too Americanized, the General Council established informal relations with Ebenezer Lutheran Seminary in Kropp, Schleswig-Holstein, Germany. This school had been founded in 1882 by Johannes Paulsen for the specific purpose of educating ministers for America. In contrast to Brunn's school at Steeden, which operated on the preseminary level, the Kropp seminary prepared men deemed ready for the ministry. Not surprisingly, an agreement entered into by Philadelphia Seminary and Paulsen to the effect that his graduates should spend a year at Philadelphia in order to become acquainted with the American situation was an unfortunate source of resentment and misunderstanding on the part of the Kropp men. In addition, they were militant representatives of German nationalism. The "Kropp Controversy" which followed lasted for more than twenty years. By 1930 when the Kropp institution was discontinued more than 200 ministers had come from it to serve German language congregations in America.[29]

The English-speaking General Synod also found it desirable to establish relations with a seminary in Germany, located in this instance at Breklum, Schleswig-Holstein. Although the German element in the General Synod was relatively small, it

26.
For a discussion of the problem see G. Everett Arden, *The School of the Prophets: History of Augustana Theological Seminary* (Rock Island, Ill.: Augustana Theological Seminary, 1960), pp. 154–56.

27.
Carl S. Meyer, *Log Cabin to Luther Tower: Concordia Seminary . . . 1839–1964* (St. Louis: Concordia Publishing House, 1965), pp. 46–48; Carl S. Meyer, "Early Growth of the Missouri Synod," in *Moving Frontiers,* pp. 221–24.

28.
Meyer, *Log Cabin,* p. 48.

29.
Theodore G. Tappert, *History of the Lutheran Theological Seminary at Philadelphia, 1864–1964* (Philadelphia: Lutheran Theological Seminary, 1964), pp. 64–65. In the midst of the disunity in the Ministerium of Pennsylvania over the Kropp school, Synod President Krotel reported in 1888 that one pastor would say, "I am of Philadelphia," and another, "I am of Kropp" (Helen E. Pfatteicher, *The Ministerium of Pennsylvania* [Philadelphia: Ministerium Press, 1938], p. 104).

was strong enough to form two small Midwestern district synods—the Wartburg Synod (out of the Central Illinois Synod), 1875, and the German Nebraska Synod, 1890. Because the seminaries of the General Synod by 1875 were using English exclusively, John D. Severinghaus, leader of the German segment, made provision for the training of German-speaking pastors. In 1882 Christian Jensen of Breklum made a trip to America to view firsthand the spiritual needs of Midwestern Germans and made contact with Severinghaus. The next year Jensen opened a practical seminary to train pastors for service in America. His emphases were practical, pietistic, and mildly confessional. The Breklum men usually received additional training at the German Seminary which Severinghaus operated in Chicago from 1885 to 1898. It was reported in 1908 that about 140 Breklum men were occupying positions in America, chiefly but not only in the General Synod, and others came after that time. In 1907 official relations were established between the General Synod and Breklum. Following the disruptions caused by World War I the Breklum and Kropp schools were merged, and the United Lutheran Church in America maintained official relations with the merged school until 1930. By that time an Americanized church was no longer in need of the products of Breklum-Kropp.[30]

Nonuniversity sources of pastors in Scandinavia included the Askov Folk High School in Denmark, with its department for training pastors for America; the small school conducted by Johan C. H. Storjohann in Oslo, Norway, for a short time in the 1880s; and the preparatory schools conducted by Peter Fjellstedt and P. A. Ahlberg in Sweden.[31]

A dozen new theological seminaries were established by the Lutherans of America during the last quarter of the nineteenth century, all of them in the Midwest. To its seminaries in Pennsylvania (Gettysburg) and Ohio (Springfield) the General Synod added two schools, both of which remained small in size. Reference has been made to its German Seminary in Chicago, begun in 1885. Its second new theological school was Western Theological Seminary, begun in 1893 under modest circumstances in connection with Midland College, Atchinson, Kansas. When Severinghaus's German Seminary was discontinued in 1898, a German department was created at Western with Juergen L. Neve as dean, to which Breklum students were drawn. Some years later (1919) both college and seminary were moved to Fremont, Nebraska, and the seminary was eventually renamed Central Lutheran Theological Seminary.[32]

The establishment of the General Council's seminary in Chicago in 1891 marked the fruition of long-cherished plans. Probably more than any other easterner William A. Passavant perceived the importance of the West for the future of Lutheranism in America. Consequently he was an early advocate of building a seminary in the West. As early as 1869 the General Council had adopted a series of resolutions looking to the establishment of such a school in or near Chicago, in which pastors would be trained for English, German, or Scandinavian churches.[33] It was

30.
Willard D. Allbeck, "Christian Jensen and the Germans of the General Synod," *Lutheran Church Quarterly* 13 (1940): 268–78.
31.
Jensen, *The United Evangelical Lutheran Church*, pp. 51–52; Andreas Brandrud, "Lutherseminariet," *Norsk Teologisk Tidsskrift* 46 (1945): 282–89; Arden, *School of the Prophets*, p. 155; George M. Stephenson, *The Religious Aspects of Swedish Immigration* (Minneapolis: University of Minnesota Press, 1932), pp. 36–38.
32.
H. A. Ott, *A History of the Evangelical Lutheran Synod of Kansas* (Topeka, Kans.: Kansas Synod, 1907), pp. 246–54; Harold C. Skillrud, *LSTC, Decade of Decision* (Chicago: Lutheran School of Theology at Chicago, 1969), pp. 119–20.
33.
Documentary History, General Council, p. 229.

planned that the new seminary should be patterned after Philadelphia Seminary.[34] Efforts to unite Augustana Seminary with
the proposed institution foundered because of formidable opposition in the Augustana Synod, including that of Tuve N. Hasselquist, the venerable president of the Rock Island school.[35]

When Chicago Theological Seminary finally opened as a
General Council school, although managed by an independent
corporation, it was a tribute to the persistence of Passavant in
particular. Its first theological professor and president was Revere F. Weidner, who had been a professor at Augustana College and Seminary since 1882. A graduate of Philadelphia
Seminary and a member of the Ministerium of Pennsylvania,
he was a forceful exponent in teaching and writing the conservative theology of the General Council and was the dominant
figure in the early history of the new school.[36] English was the
language of the classroom in the Chicago Seminary, and it had
an appeal to theological students from the Midwest who were
interested in both conservative theology and the English language. In 1910 the seminary was relocated in Maywood, a
Chicago suburb, and thereafter was commonly known as Maywood Seminary.

At the time when the Synodical Conference was formed
(1872) under Missourian leadership, two of its member synods
were already sending their young men to Concordia Seminary,
St. Louis, for theological training. The Norwegian Synod had
been doing so since the late 1850s, also providing a professor of
theology for two brief stints: Lauritz Larsen, 1859-61, and
Friedrich A. Schmidt, 1872-76. The Wisconsin Synod closed its
struggling seminary in Watertown, Wisconsin, in 1870 and sent
its students to St. Louis; among them were three young men
who later became influential theologians—Franz Pieper, August Pieper, and John P. Koehler—but the synod was never
able to provide a professor.[37] Shortly after the birth of the Synodical Conference a project was promoted which profoundly
affected the future of theological education in its constituent
synods. A proposal, which had the support of Walther along
with other prominent Missourians, was made that a joint Synodical Conference theological seminary be established to serve
all the member churches. A parallel proposal involved the formation of geographical district synods, which would have meant
extensive realignment of synodical boundaries. Neither proposal gained the required support. There were varying degrees
of interest in and enthusiasm for the joint seminary, with the
dominant sentiment in the synods other than Missouri being
that the time was not yet ripe for such a step.

In the context of the discussion about the proposed joint
seminary, the Norwegian Synod in 1876 established Luther
Theological Seminary in Madison, Wisconsin, thus ending its
dependence upon Missouri for theological education. Friedrich
A. Schmidt left Concordia, St. Louis, to be professor of theology
and he was soon joined by Hans Gerhard Stub and Johannes
Ylvisaker. The young seminary, badly rent by the predestination controversy, remained in Madison for a dozen years, find-

287

34.
Ibid., p. 12.
35.
Arden, *School of the Prophets*, p. 205.
36.
Skillrud, *LSTC*, pp. 16-18.
37.
Martin Lehninger et al., *Continuing in His
Word* (Milwaukee: Northwestern Publish-
ing House, 1951), pp. 141-42.

ing its permanent home in St. Paul in 1899 after intermediate stops in Minneapolis and suburban Robbinsdale.[38]

The Wisconsin Synod resisted the idea of a joint seminary, too, and in 1878 reopened its own seminary in Milwaukee with August Hoenecke as president. Any Missourian resentment of Wisconsin's action was soon forgotten when the seminary faculty and practically the entire Wisconsin Synod strongly supported Walther during the predestination controversy. Hoenecke was a strongly confessional theologian who had a profound impact on his synod's theological position and whose long career was marked by a policy of tightening Wisconsin's bonds with Missouri.[39] The story of theological education in the Wisconsin Synod at that time includes two additional small seminaries. In 1892 three conservative synods—Wisconsin, Minnesota, and Michigan—formed a closely knit federation in which the cooperating bodies retained their identities, the Joint Synod of Wisconsin, Minnesota, and Other States. Organic union of the three, together with the Nebraska Synod, took place in 1917.[40] The Minnesota Synod conducted a theological department in connection with its Dr. Martin Luther College, New Ulm, Minnesota, from 1886 until the formation of the federation. The Michigan Synod opened Michigan Seminary at Saginaw, Michigan, in 1887. It functioned for two decades, weathering a difficult period of controversy and bickering, and was later reopened as a high school. As a result of federation the Joint Synod moved its seminary to Wauwatosa, a Milwaukee suburb, at which time the theological department of Dr. Martin Luther College was discontinued. The additions of John P. Koehler (1900) and August Pieper (1902) as professors of the Wauwatosa school gave the Wisconsin Synod a distinguished faculty which, under Hoenecke's leadership, adhered to a strict confessional position but with strong historical and exegetical, as well as dogmatic, interests.[41]

One by-product of the disruption of the Synodical Conference which accompanied the predestination controversy was the establishment of a second seminary by the Joint Synod of Ohio (in addition to its Columbus school). German immigrants were coming to the Upper Midwest in large numbers in the seventies and eighties, and after its withdrawal from the Synodical Conference in 1881 Ohio was not disposed to leave that fertile mission field to such rivals as the Missouri, Minnesota, and Wisconsin synods. Joint Ohio's Luther Seminary was opened in Afton, Minnesota, in 1885 in a vacant academy building, but eight years later it was relocated in the Phalen Park section of St. Paul. It was a "practical" seminary which produced many pastors who served frontier parishes in the Midwest, Northwest, and Canada.[42] In 1932 Ohio's Luther Seminary was united with Wartburg Seminary, Dubuque, Iowa.

The fragmented situation among Norwegian Lutherans was reflected in the several theological schools maintained by them. Augsburg Seminary (1869), Minneapolis, was the school of the rapidly growing Norwegian-Danish Conference. Under professors Georg Sverdrup and Sven Oftedal it developed an inte-

38.
Nelson and Fevold, *Lutheran Church Among Norwegian-Americans,* 1:186–87.
39.
Lehninger et al., *Continuing in His Word,* pp. 142–44.
40.
Ibid., p. 34.
41.
Ibid., pp. 146-47, 176–77, 185–90. Leigh D. Jordahl, "Introduction," in John P. Koehler, *The History of the Wisconsin Synod* (St. Cloud, Minn.: Sentinel Publishing Co., 1970), pp. viii-xxix.
42.
Clarence V. Sheatsley, *History of the Evangelical Lutheran Joint Synod of Ohio and Other States* (Columbus, Ohio: Lutheran Book Concern, 1918), pp. 206–8. It should be noted that three theological schools in St. Paul were known as Luther Seminary: in the Phalen Park area (Joint Synod of Ohio); in the Hamline area (Norwegian Synod, to 1917); in the St. Anthony Park area (Norwegian Lutheran Church of America, from 1917—at the site of the United Norwegian Lutheran Church's seminary).

grated theological educational program, including academy, college, and seminary departments. The conference took pride in the fact that it had established its own seminary when its larger and stronger rival, the Norwegian Synod, was relying on Missouri to train its pastors. Reference has just been made to the beginnings of the Norwegian Synod's Luther Seminary (1876). Hauge's Synod, the most pietistic and lay-oriented of the Norwegian groups, in 1879 opened a theological school with preparatory departments at Red Wing, Minnesota, known simply as Red Wing Seminary. The Norwegian Augustana Synod, quite similar to Hauge's Synod in many respects and sharing a common origin with the Norwegian-Danish Conference, also deemed it necessary to have its own seminary. It was begun in 1874 in the parsonage of David Lysnes, near Decorah, Iowa, and then was for a short time in Marshall, Wisconsin, where it was given the name Augustana Seminary. From 1881 until 1890 it was located in the village of Beloit on Iowa's western border, whereupon it became a part of the seminary of the United Norwegian Lutheran Church.[43]

When the latter church body was formed in 1890 through a three-way merger (Norwegian Augustana Synod, the Norwegian-Danish Conference, and the Anti-Missourian Brotherhood), Augsburg Seminary was designated the seminary of the new church. However, shortly after merger a controversy involving the ownership of Augsburg Seminary and the nature of theological education disrupted the new church body and led to the formation of the United Church Seminary (1895), first located in Minneapolis and after 1902 in St. Paul. Its key professors in the early years were Friedrich A. Schmidt and Markus O. Bockman. Augsburg Seminary thereafter was the school of the Lutheran Free Church, a comparatively small church body. In 1917 the seminaries of the Norwegian Synod, Hauge's Synod, and the United Church were united in St. Paul, taking the name Luther Theological Seminary. Finally, in 1963, Luther Seminary and Augsburg Seminary were merged.

Danish Lutheran theological institutions have been dealt with in the preceding chapter, namely, Trinity, Blair, Nebraska (1884); the short-lived seminary at West Denmark, Wisconsin (1887–92); and Grand View, Des Moines, Iowa (1896).[44] The Finns' Suomi College and Theological Seminary, Hancock, Michigan, was founded in 1896, but it was not until eight years later that the theological department began to function.

The dominant interest in Lutheran seminaries was to provide the type of training that would prepare their graduates for the practical tasks of the parish ministry. The confessional movement was in full swing in American Lutheranism, and the theological climate supported a conservative and traditional point of view. In nearly all the seminaries there was a marked concern, obviously with varying degrees of commitment, for faithfully transmitting inherited Lutheran theology as expressed in the confessions of the Lutheran church and by the theologians of the Age of Orthodoxy (seventeenth century).

43.
Nelson and Fevold, *Lutheran Church Among Norwegian-Americans*, 1:214–16.
44.
See pp. 269–71.

The impact of the confessional movement was also evident in the General Synod, as represented at Gettysburg, its major seminary, although it was less marked there than in the seminaries of the other bodies. The growth in a more confessional direction was seen in James A. Brown, Schmucker's successor as seminary president, and in Milton Valentine, professor of systematic theology, 1884–1903, who was one of the distinguished Lutheran theologians of the era. Brown and Valentine championed basically conservative doctrinal views, but their confessionalism was milder and more tolerant than that represented by the bulk of America's Lutherans at that time, and their views regarding the controverted question of pulpit and altar fellowship were much more liberal.[45]

Meanwhile, Charles Porterfield Krauth and his colleagues of Philadelphia Seminary were in the vanguard of the confessional movement in Eastern Lutheranism and in the English-speaking portions of the Lutheran church generally. When Krauth died in 1883, having exhausted himself through the extent and variety of his professorial and ecclesiastical responsibilities, he was acknowledged by all as his generation's "leading interpreter of Lutheranism in the English language."[46] His successor was Henry Eyster Jacobs, who continued to teach at Philadelphia Seminary until 1930. A scholarly man of the same conservative cast of mind as Krauth and an effective exponent of traditional orthodox theology, he made important contributions through his writings in both the systematic and historical fields.[47] In characterizing the emphasis of Philadelphia Seminary in the late nineteenth and early twentieth centuries, its historian has written that its professors

were intent on restoring a theology and a practice of the past. No matter in what discipline of theology they were teaching, their attention was concentrated on a tradition. . . . Since there was a tendency to be content with the discovery of historical precedents and to be rather uncritical in the adoption of them, there was actually more of a spirit of romantic repristination at work than there was of disciplined historical inquiry.[48]

This characterization could fairly be applied to the efforts of nearly all Lutheran theological faculties during the era described.

During the post-Civil War period the one Lutheran seminary in the South barely limped along. Comparatively more attention was given to college education. The seminary was conducted in several locations at various times, including Newberry and Columbia, South Carolina, and Salem, Virginia, before finally finding a permanent home in Columbia in 1911. The General Synod, South in 1872 voted to support the seminary as a general institution of the southern synods. The men who taught theology in the South represented both General Synod and General Council points of view, with leanings toward the theological position of Philadelphia Seminary. Theologically the South experienced a deepened appreciation of the Lutheran heritage, as was also evident in the realm of worship and the

45.
Abdel Ross Wentz, *Gettysburg Lutheran Theological Seminary,* 2 vols. (Gettysburg, Pa.: Lutheran Theological Seminary, 1965), 1:243, 245–46, 396–403.
46.
Tappert, *History,* p. 48.
47.
Ibid., pp. 71–72.
48.
Ibid., p. 74.

liturgy. At the same time progress was made in the direction of requiring full seminary training for the ministry and in the virtual abandonment of licensure and home-study courses, which had been common in the South.[49] George A. Voigt, a moderate conservative, was the theologian most responsible for strengthening the South's identification with traditional Lutheranism. A graduate of Philadelphia Seminary, he served as theological professor of Southern Theological Seminary during the years 1891 to 1898 and 1903 to 1933. His biographer suggests that he exemplified Henry M. Muhlenberg's legacy to American Lutheranism, "a combination of orthodoxy, inward piety, and practical sense."[50]

291

The strictest and most uncompromising type of confessionalism was found in Synodical Conference schools under the leadership of Concordia Seminary, St. Louis. Upon Walther's death in 1887 Franz Pieper, a young colleague, succeeded as president of the seminary and exercised theological leadership in the Missouri Synod until his death (1931). Pieper and his contemporaries were particularly motivated by the desire to conserve what they had received from the past, and they were staunchly loyal to the understanding of the tradition as explicated by Walther and those of his generation. This trait has prompted the historian of Concordia Seminary to designate the post-Walther era in the Missouri Synod as "the period of conservation."[51] Missouri's theologians of Pieper's generation manifested less breadth in their scholarship and greater defensiveness than did those of Walther's generation. The chief exponents of strict orthodoxy in other seminaries associated with the Synodical Conference for longer or shorter periods during the seventies and eighties were the Wisconsin Synod's August Hoenecke, Ohio's William F. Lehmann and Matthias Loy, and the Norwegian Synod's Friedrich A. Schmidt and Hans G. Stub. Members of the theological faculties of Synodical Conference seminaries were the major contestants in the predestination controversy of the eighties, and much of their time and energy was channeled into that conflict.

The brothers Fritschel, Gottfried and Sigmund, of Wartburg Seminary, Dubuque, were the theological leaders of the Iowa Synod. They espoused a conservative and confessional theology more moderate in nature than that of the Synodical Conference because more historically oriented, which led them into a number of theological controversies, particularly with Missouri. Having much in common with the General Council, they nevertheless had their reservations about it because its stance on the issues of lodge membership and pulpit-altar fellowship was less strict than theirs.

The seminaries of the Scandinavian bodies, with the exception of the school of the Grundtvigian Danes, reflected the same heightened confessional consciousness which we have been considering. A significant difference between them and the bodies of German background was the fact that pietism was more strongly represented among the Scandinavians, primarily because of the powerful impact of religious revivals in their Euro-

49.
Anderson, *Lutheranism,* pp. 172–86.
50.
Gilbert P. Voigt, *G. A. Voigt: Molder of Southern Lutheranism* (Columbia: Farrell Printing Co., n.d.), p. 51.
51.
Meyer, *Log Cabin,* pp. 89–91.

pean homelands. This was also true of the Norwegian Synod which shared the confessional stance of the Synodical Conference, as noted above. In the Scandinavian synods orthodoxy and pietism were wedded. Theological professors who exemplified the pan-Scandinavian pietistic confessional spirit in the late nineteenth century were Augustana's Tuve N. Hasselquist and Olof Olsson, the Danes' Peter S. Vig, the Norwegians' Georg Sverdrup and Markus O. Bockman, and the Finns' Juho K. Nikander.

Colleges, Academies, and Parochial Schools

During the years between the Civil War and World War I institutions of higher education proliferated in the United States at an almost unbelievable rate. Perhaps as many as two thousand were begun, of which over eight hundred are still in operation. A substantial number were founded under religious auspices.[52] Lutherans were among the many denominations actively engaged in the founding of schools. In the forty-year period between 1870 and 1910 Lutherans established twenty-eight colleges compared with seventeen in the preceding forty years (1830–70) and eight in the subsequent fifty years.[53] When the term "college" or even "university" was applied to a new school, the word was often used in a broad and imprecise sense, indicating aspiration rather than actuality. Many of these institutions began as academies which later developed into junior colleges or full-fledged four-year colleges.

The Lutheran church was motivated in the founding of many of its colleges by the desire to provide students for its theological schools. In time this goal was widened to include general education for lay vocations as well, although some colleges established as "feeders" for seminaries did not become coeducational until the twentieth century. Several colleges were coeducational from the start. In 1877 Milton Valentine, at that time president of Gettysburg College, acknowledged that the Lutheran college's role in preparing for theological study was "a feature of perhaps more worth than any other," but that its task included preparation "under Christian auspices, for *all* the callings of life."[54] In the Synodical Conference, particularly in the Missouri Synod, the colleges were established as feeders for the seminaries. The European immigrants who provided the interest and support which made these schools possible had in most instances been denied the opportunity of higher education for themselves. They frequently demonstrated an amazing willingness to sacrifice for schools in order that pastors and teachers might be provided the church and that their children might benefit from the education that had been denied them.

The church colleges provided leadership in the preservation of the European cultural heritage, along with their more specifically church-related goals. Moreover, they led the way in the Americanization process for their constituencies, effecting the language transition more quickly than congregations or theological seminaries.

52.
Manning M. Patillo, Jr., and Donald M. Mackenzie, *Church-Sponsored Higher Education in the United States* (Washington, D.C.: American Council on Education, 1966), p. 15.

53.
J. Gould Wickey, *The Lutheran Venture in Higher Education* (Philadelphia: Muhlenberg Press, 1962), p. 52.

54.
Henry Eyster Jacobs, ed., *First Free Lutheran Diet in America* (Philadelphia: J. F. Smith, 1878), p. 154.

Table 3

**Lutheran Colleges
Established 1875–1900
Still in Existence**

Name	Location	Date of Origin	Church Auspices
Concordia	Bronxville, N.Y.	1881	Missouri Synod
Bethany	Lindsborg, Kans.	1881	Augustana Synod
Concordia	Milwaukee, Wis.	1881	Missouri Synod
Wagner	Staten Island, N.Y.	1883	General Council
Dr. Martin Luther	New Ulm, Minn.	1883	Minnesota Synod
St. Paul's	Concordia, Mo.	1884	Missouri Synod
Dana	Blair, Nebr.	1884	United Danish
Midland	Fremont, Nebr.	1887	General Synod
Lenoir Rhyne	Hickory, N.C.	1891	North Carolina Synod
Concordia	Moorhead, Minn.	1891	United Norwegian
Texas Lutheran	Seguin, Tex.	1891	Texas Synod
Upsala	East Orange, N.J.	1893	Augustana Synod
Concordia	St. Paul, Minn.	1893	Missouri Synod
St. John's	Winfield, Kans.	1893	Missouri Synod
Concordia Teachers	Seward, Nebr.	1894	Missouri Synod
Pacific Lutheran	Tacoma, Wash.	1894	Norwegian Synod
Grand View	Des Moines, Iowa	1896	Danish Church
Suomi	Hancock, Mich.	1896	Suomi Synod

Based on information in J. Gould
Wickey, *The Lutherans Venture in
Higher Education* (Philadelphia:
Muhlenberg Press, 1962), pp. 140–42.

Present-day Lutheran colleges whose origins go back to the last quarter of the nineteenth century were chiefly located in the Midwest, reflecting the pattern of the church's expansion and growth. The list of schools in table 3 includes only those still in operation. Some include mergers with other institutions in their histories. Several began as academies and later developed into colleges. A number of teacher-training institutions, also known as normal schools, were started in the late nineteenth century by several synods, to provide teachers for parochial and/or public schools. Except for those of the Synodical Conference (Seward, Neb., and New Ulm, Minn., from this period) the normal schools were casualties of later developments.[55]

Perhaps too many higher educational institutions were established, overtaxing the ability or willingness of their constituencies to support them adequately. A prominent Lutheran educator of the time contended that Lutheran colleges were increasing in numbers at the expense of quality.[56] Augustana Synod historians refer to the "school mania" of the 1880s and subsequent years when establishment of schools was an expression of regionalism in opposition to centralizing tendencies in the synod.[57] Each of the several Norwegian synods felt it necessary to have its own academies, college, and seminary. Many were small, all struggled, and although most evoked remarkable support there were many casualties along the way. The colleges that have continued to the present, however, represent a virile segment of the private liberal arts segment of American higher education. The educational endeavors of the Lutheran churches of the late nineteenth century must be numbered with their important contributions. In 1899 a Lutheran leader expressed a sentiment shared by many others: "Our colleges and seminaries are the fountains of our church's prosperity."[58]

The church-related academy was a common phenomenon of the Lutheran educational scene in the late nineteenth and early twentieth centuries. The Scandinavians, particularly the Norwegians, were most zealous in starting academies. A study of Norwegian Lutheran academies in the United States and Canada lists a total of seventy-five over a period of not quite a century (from the 1850s to the 1940s).[59] Of that total only a couple survive today. Vigorous in the 1880s and 1890s, the academy movement reached its peak around the turn of the century. Many of the academies were short-lived, some of them victims of the financial depression of the 1890s. A number of new ones, however, were begun in the early twentieth century.

Academies were part of the larger educational system created to provide training for pastors and teachers. This was particularly true of the Midwestern German bodies. "All junior colleges and academies established under the auspices of the Lutheran Synodical Conference, or its constituent bodies, or bodies closely related, had as their purpose the preparation of men for the ministry and teachers for parochial schools."[60] After the Civil War Walther promoted secondary education for the laity, and schools were begun in St. Louis and Milwaukee. They were short-lived, however, except for one academy in St. Louis which

55.
Included among the normal schools were the Ohio Synod's Woodville Normal, the Iowa Synod's Wartburg, and under Norwegian auspices schools at Wittenberg, Wisc., Sioux Falls, S.D., and Madison, Minn.
56.
Milton Valentine in Jacobs, *First Free Lutheran Diet*, p. 154.
57.
Stephenson, *Religious Aspects*, p. 334.
58.
G. F. Spieker in *The Lutheran*, April 6, 1899, p. 323.
59.
Bert H. Narveson, "The Norwegian Lutheran Academies," *Norwegian-American Studies and Records* 14 (1944): 217-21.
60.
Wickey, *Venture in Higher Education*, p. 66.

continued into the twentieth century.[61] Most of the academies had the larger goal of providing secondary education for immigrants and their children to enable them to become useful and informed citizens. Along with academic or college preparatory courses many academies provided a variety of practical subjects such as business courses. They rendered an important service in assisting the process of Americanization. A speaker at a cornerstone-laying for a southern Minnesota academy in 1890 spoke regarding the purpose of the school:

The advantages . . . that we expect from the establishment and maintenance of this school are the advantages of Christian education. It is the fond hope and the fervent prayer of those whose sacrifices are rearing this noble edifice, that it shall afford . . . an opportunity for acquiring that education which, while it prepares for the arduous duties of this life, is not forgetful of the life to come, and that it shall be the means of preserving and transmitting to posterity, pure and undefiled, those divine truths which have become the inheritance of our Church through that God-chosen instrument Dr. Martin Luther.[62]

In considering reasons for the decline and eventual demise of the academy movement among Swedish Lutherans, one authority suggests a variety of factors: far-reaching socioeconomic changes which accompanied the immigrants' merging with the main stream of American life and an end to nationalistic isolation; the growth and improvement of the public school system; insufficient financial support; reluctance or inability to develop a philosophy of education justifying continuance of academies over against public schools.[63] These reasons, with some variation in emphasis and importance, account for the decline of Christian academies among other Lutheran groups as well. While the academy movement waned, Lutheran colleges developed in the twentieth century into vigorous and effective institutions.

An aspect of the educational enterprise which engaged much attention from Synodical Conference bodies was the parochial, or congregational, school. Other synods advocated and established congregational schools, but not to the same extent nor with the same degree of commitment as those in the Synodical Conference. These included the Norwegian Synod and the Joint Synod of Ohio (both members of the Synodical Conference for a decade), the Iowa Synod, and to a limited degree the General Council.[64]

The Missouri Synod promoted parochial schools as essential to the preservation and inculcation of sound doctrine. In the course of a discussion about schools at the 1872 meeting of the Missouri Synod it was said that "next to the pure doctrine our schools are the greatest treasure we have."[65] Walther's conviction regarding their importance was frequently expressed: "May God preserve for our German Lutheran Church the gem of parochial schools! for upon it, humanly speaking, primarily depends the future of our Church in America."[66] In the late nineteenth century Missouri promoted parochial schools vigor-

61.
Meyer, "Early Growth of the Missouri Synod," in *Moving Frontiers,* pp. 224–26.
62.
Lars S. Reque was the speaker. Bert H. Narveson, *Luther Academy* (Northfield, Minn.: St. Olaf College Press, 1951), p. 106.
63.
Paul M. Lindberg, "The Academies of the Augustana Lutheran Church," in *The Swedish Immigrant Community in Transition,* ed. J. Dowie and Ernest M. Espelie (Rock Island, Ill.: Augustana Historical Society, 1963), pp. 102–3.
64.
See statistical table for 1895 in Walter H. Beck, *Lutheran Elementary Schools in the United States . . .* (St. Louis: Concordia Publishing House, 1965), p. 224. The Ministerium of Pennsylvania and the Ministerium of New York together had 62 schools, with the latter synod having a much higher percentage in relation to the total number of its congregations. Augustana had only summer and part-time schools. Approximately one-half of the large number of schools listed for Ohio (265) and Iowa (370) were summer and part-time schools.
65.
A. C. Stellhorn, *Schools of the Lutheran Church—Missouri Synod* (St. Louis: Concordia Publishing House, 1963), p. 176.
66.
Ibid., p. 172.

ously in response to indifference within the synod and to hostility from without.[67] In advocating congregational schools the chief argument continued to be that they were superior to public schools because all instruction could center in the Word of God whereas public schools could not include religious instruction. The alleged superior instruction and discipline of the parochial schools was made much of, but this contention was not so convincing as it may have been earlier in view of the significant improvement that had taken place in public education. In fact, synod officials were sensitive to the fact that the argument regarding superior instruction and discipline was frequently being made on behalf of the public school.[68] The proparochial school stance of Missouri did not include a completely antipublic school attitude since it was conceded that the state had both the right and duty to provide public education. Nevertheless, the Missouri Synod followed a policy of maintaining a parallel school system to make it unnecessary for its members to use public schools.

The use of the German language as the medium of instruction was a strong factor in immigrant support of congregational schools. When the immigrant and his children no longer spoke German, interest in parochial schools lessened. It was more difficult to get English congregations to organize parish schools than German ones.[69] In the late nineteenth century the parochial school was ordinarily a German school and a powerful factor in preserving Missouri's doctrinal conservatism and cultural isolation. The battle over the transition from the German language to English was waged with particular vigor at the parish school level.[70]

Among the Scandinavians there was a limited interest in congregational schools as alternatives to public schools. The summer parochial school, held when the public school was not in session, was common in Scandinavian Lutheran communities. Of the several Scandinavian church bodies only the Norwegian Synod promoted parochial schools as an alternative to the public school, but unsuccessfully so. The reasons the Norwegian Synod espoused a parish school system were essentially the same as those earlier noted: criticism of the public school, doctrinal conservatism, and cultural nationalism. Through the influence of its clerical leadership it officially endorsed a parochial school system, and during the mid-seventies launched several ambitious parochial schools, which were short-lived. Effective lay defense of the public school and its support by the large majority of laymen, for financial reasons and because of a general belief in the value of public education, prevented the parochial-school system from being a success in the Norwegian Synod. The short-term summer parochial school was common in the Norwegian Synod, as in the other Norwegian bodies.[71] Among Augustana Synod congregations parochial schools patterned after the Christian folk schools of the homeland were promoted in the early years. However, this movement did not take hold, and it was the summer "Swede school" in which religion and Swedish were taught that became widespread. In 1890 Augustana offi-

67.
Everette Meier and Herbert T. Mayer, "The Process of Americanization," in Meyer, *Moving Frontiers,* pp. 344–45.
68.
Ibid., pp. 369–71.
69.
Stellhorn, *Schools,* pp. 191–93.
70.
Meier and Mayer, "Process of Americanization," p. 361.
71.
A helpful discussion of the "common school controversy" among Norwegian-Americans is found in T. C. Blegen, *Norwegian Migration to America* (Northfield, Minn.: Norwegian-American Historical Assoc., 1940), 2:241–76. One of the outspoken advocates of the public school system among Norwegian-American theologians was Georg Sverdrup of Augsburg Seminary. See *The Heritage of Faith: Selections from the Writings of Georg Sverdrup,* trans. M. A. Helland (Minneapolis: Augsburg Publishing House, 1969), pp. 87–99.

cially went on record in support of public schools, while affirming at the same time the right of the church to establish parochial schools.[72]

In the 1880s and early 1890s a public campaign was carried on against parochial schools. The spirit of nativism was powerfully represented at that time by the American Protective Association and similar groups. Parochial schools were attacked as hindrances to Americanization. Under the guidance of the Boston Committee of 100 efforts were made to get state legislatures to pass laws containing provisions which parochial-school supporters deemed unfair and dangerous. Examples of such laws, which were of special concern to Lutherans because of large constituencies in the states involved, were the Bennett Law in Wisconsin and the Edwards Law in Illinois, both passed in 1889.

The Bennett Law provided for compulsory attendance in either a public or private school, but it also stipulated that the local board of education should supervise enforcement and further required that the English language be used in teaching certain subjects. The Wisconsin Synod labeled the law "tyrannical and unjust" and provided leadership in a vigorous campaign against it, to which several synods gave their support, including Missouri, Michigan, Minnesota (all of the Synodical Conference), the Joint Synod of Ohio, Iowa, and the Norwegian Synod. The law was opposed on the basis that it violated natural parental rights, infringed on liberty of conscience, and interfered with religious liberty and separation of church and state.[73] It was viewed as an attack which not only questioned the patriotism of supporters of parish schools but also endangered the very existence of the schools because of civil interference.

A crucial factor in the repeal of the Bennett Law in 1891 in the wake of the defeat of the Republican party, which had supported the law, was the united campaign against it on the part of concerned Lutherans of the state of Wisconsin. This issue was regarded as so important that many Lutheran voters, at least temporarily, defected from the Republican party. The battle in Illinois over the Edwards Law, of the same character as the Bennett Law but with slightly different provisions, was similar but with the Missouri Synod leading the Lutheran opposition. The basic issues and arguments were the same with minor variations, and the outcome was the repeal of the law.[74]

Bills similar to the Bennett and Edwards laws were introduced into the legislatures of several states, both in the East and the Midwest in the 1890s. Among those active in opposing them were the Iowa Synod in South Dakota, the Minnesota and Missouri synods in Minnesota, and the New York Ministerium in New York.[75] In the many discussions and conflicts about parochial schools, their Lutheran defenders repeatedly stressed that church and state must be separate, and thus public funds ought not be used for the erection and maintenance of parochial schools.[76] The controversies of the time did not help the public image of parochial schools and they also revealed the presence of much popular misunderstanding, but another more positive

297

72.
Emmett E. Eklund, "Faith and Education," in *Centennial Essays* (Rock Island, Ill.: Augustana Press, 1960), pp. 76–77. Eklund mentions several reasons for the failure of the "Swedish school" movement: readiness of Swedish immigrants to be Americanized, the wide dispersion of the Swedes, lack of competent parish school teachers, and a friendly attitude toward the public school system (Stephenson, *Religious Aspects,* pp. 409–12).
73.
Beck, *Lutheran Elementary Schools,* pp. 229–42. He includes the text of the Bennett Law, pp. 227–29.
74.
Portions of a pamphlet opposing the Edwards Law, including several arguments against it, are found in Meyer, *Moving Frontiers,* pp. 372–73.
75.
Beck, *Lutheran Elementary Schools,* pp. 248–50.
76.
An official statement of the Missouri Synod in 1890 concerning parochial schools sets forth this position.

result was the strengthening of resolution and effort to improve them on the part of sponsoring congregations and synods.

The Sunday school was becoming increasingly important as a part of the Lutheran educational picture. For a long time ambivalent attitudes toward it could be found in large segments of American Lutheranism. The Sunday school was introduced into English-speaking Lutheran congregations in the early nineteenth century when the Sunday school movement took root in American Protestantism, and by mid-nineteenth century it had become a fixed institution.[77] Sunday schools were most commonly found in the General Synod. However, the historian of Ohio Lutheranism points out they they were "part of the program of most of the congregations in Ohio from early days," German as well as English.[78] Of the foreign-language Lutheran churches particularly the Scandinavians readily adopted the Sunday school from the American environment.[79]

A careful study of the Sunday school movement among Lutherans in the southeastern states reveals its great growth in that region during the two decades following the Civil War.[80] Important aspects of Sunday school work, in addition to its usefulness for instruction, were the greatly enhanced opportunities for lay work which it provided, its effectiveness as an instrument of mission outreach, and its contribution to the developing sense of responsibility for foreign missions.[81] At a time when revivalism was a powerful and pervasive movement in American Protestantism Lutherans chose the catechetical or instructional approach rather than revivalism. Nevertheless, some English-speaking Lutherans, especially in mid-century, adopted the methods of revivalism and regarded the Sunday school primarily as an instrument of conversion. Since the Sunday school movement originated in non-Lutheran circles and was characterized by interdenominational cooperation, English-speaking congregations often used non-Lutheran instructional materials, particularly those of the American Sunday School Union. With the developing confessional consciousness of English-speaking Lutherans in the later nineteenth century, there was an increased concern for providing distinctively Lutheran instructional materials and for withdrawing from union Sunday schools and from other interdenominational cooperative efforts. The General Council took the lead in developing Lutheran Sunday school materials.[82]

Into the twentieth century Sunday schools were opposed, or at least regarded with suspicion, by the most conservative elements of American Lutheranism. This was especially true of Synodical Conference churches. Sunday schools were considered an element in the non-Lutheran environment that naturally went along with the public school system and unionistic religious practices. They were looked upon as a threatening but totally inadequate substitute for parochial schools and were deemed unnecessary where parochial schools were in operation.[83] When some urban congregations introduced English, a more favorable attitude toward Sunday schools began to appear, and by the late 1880s a few voices were being raised in

77.
Lutheran Church Review 15 (October 1896): 417. This issue contains a lengthy symposium on the Sunday school which provides valuable historical information.
78.
Willard D. Allbeck, *A Century of Lutheranism in Ohio* (Yellow Springs, Ohio: Antioch Press, 1966), p. 180.
79.
Paul Andersen as early as 1848 began a Sunday school in Chicago in which English as well as Norwegian was used; as did Hans A. Stub at Muskego, near Milwaukee, in 1849. Lydia B. Sundby, "Holding High the Torch—Christian Education," *Norsemen Found a Church,* ed. Johann C. K. Preus et al. (Minneapolis: Augsburg Publishing House, 1953), pp. 295, 299-304. Lars Esbjorn, pioneer Augustana pastor, began Sunday schools in Andover and Galesburg, Ill., as early as 1850 (Eklund, "Faith and Education," p. 77).
80.
Anderson, *Lutheranism,* pp. 126-27.
81.
Ibid., pp. 128-31.
82.
Ibid., pp. 132-37. Theodore E. Schmauk, "The Graded Lessons for the General Council Sunday Schools," *Lutheran Church Review* 16 (1897): 463ff.
83.
Stellhorn, *Schools,* p. 175; Meier and Mayer, "Process of Americanization," pp. 354-55.

their defense within Missouri.[84] In the course of the twentieth century all segments of American Lutheranism accepted and utilized the Sunday school as a valuable means of Christian instruction.

Ministry of Mercy

The remarkable William A. Passavant, more than anyone else, provided guidance and inspiration for a "ministry of mercy" by America's Lutherans in the nineteenth century. He wanted his church to be an aggressive force in America, to be a working as well as a worshiping and witnessing community. His reputation as a pioneer in Lutheran social service, together with his being a Lutheran leader of broad interests, is based on several tangible achievements: the establishment of four hospitals, including the Pittsburgh Infirmary, the first Protestant hospital in America (the others: Milwaukee, Chicago, Jacksonville, Illinois); the introduction of deaconess work in America on the pattern developed by Fliedner in Germany; the founding of several orphanages; the beginning of a college (Thiel) and a seminary (Chicago Lutheran).[85] The various charitable institutions arose out of and were sponsored by the Institution of Protestant Deaconesses, which was legally incorporated at Pittsburgh by Passavant.[86] His influence upon a number of Lutheran leaders, particularly Norwegians and Swedes, was important. Through his leadership and example his church body, the General Council, achieved a certain degree of eminence in the area of social service in the same way that the Pittsburgh Synod, chiefly through his leadership, had been a pioneer leader in home missions.

The Lutheran diaconate did not flourish in America in the way that Passavant had expected. The slowness with which it took root in American Lutheranism is evident in the fact that only a dozen consecrated deaconesses served in his Institution from 1849 to 1891. Passavant himself was partially to blame in that he did not provide the external organization necessary for the diaconate to thrive, and his energies were so widely dispersed that he did not concentrate on the problem. The basic difficulty, however, seems to have been that of transplanting a European institution into a dynamic American environment in which social conditions were different from those in the German homeland.[87] In the mid-eighties the diaconate received a new lease on life and the establishment of several deaconess motherhouses followed, inaugurating a period of modest growth and development. The beginning of this new phase was the coming in 1884 to German Hospital (later Lankenau Hospital), Philadelphia, of seven deaconesses from Germany through the efforts of prosperous financier John D. Lankenau and the prominent General Council pastor Adolph Spaeth.[88] Shortly thereafter the Philadelphia Motherhouse of Deaconesses was established, closely related to but not officially owned by the Ministerium of Pennsylvania. Its first deaconess was consecrated early in 1887, and a large new building was dedicated the next year. The pattern of life, work, and organization for the Philadelphia

84.
Meier and Mayer, "Process of Americanization," p. 367.
85.
Robert H. Fischer, "New Light on Passavant and His Era," in *The Lutheran Historical Conference: Essays and Reports* (St. Louis: Lutheran Historical Conference, 1968), 2:18–29.
86.
Frederick S. Weiser, *Love's Response* (Philadelphia: Board of Publication, ULCA, 1962), pp. 54–55.
87.
Ibid., pp. 56–57.
88.
The significance of Lankenau's philanthropy and leadership for the hospital, motherhouse, and related institutions is made evident in E. Theodore Bachmann, *The Story of the Philadelphia Motherhouse, 1884–1959* (Philadelphia: Philadelphia Deaconess Assoc., n.d.).

motherhouse was the great Lutheran inner mission institutions of Germany. A cluster of institutions was created at the one location in Philadelphia—a hospital, home for the aged, children's hospital, girls' school, kindergarten, and motherhouse.[89]

Deaconess work among Norwegians in America dates from the arrival from Norway of Sister Elizabeth Fedde in Brooklyn in 1883. In the course of a decade-and-a-half three Norwegian Lutheran deaconess homes and hospitals were established—in Brooklyn (1883), Minneapolis (1888), and Chicago (1896).[90] In each case the diaconate developed slowly and the home (motherhouse) was closely connected with the hospital. Erik A. Fogelstrom was the pioneer in the introduction of hospital and deaconess work in the Augustana Synod, setting in motion in 1889 the activity that developed into the impressive Immanuel Deaconess Institute of Omaha, Nebraska.[91] Through the Omaha institution's contacts with Bethesda Hospital in St. Paul, a deaconess motherhouse was established in the latter city in 1902.[92] New life stirring in Passavant's Institution of Protestant Deaconesses resulted in the establishment of a deaconess motherhouse (1892) in conjunction with its Milwaukee hospital, an institution which eventually came under the supervision of the American Lutheran Church. At last provision had been made for the training and supervision of the diaconate, which had been so notably lacking in Passavant's pioneering work. In 1895 the General Synod, under the leadership of the Board of Deaconess Work which had been created a few years earlier, opened a motherhouse in Baltimore to be the center of its deaconess work, which developed into a more parish-centered service than was the case of its sister institution in Philadelphia.

All of this activity connected with the development of deaconess institutions and activities was the prelude to a time of relative growth during the first four decades of the twentieth century.[93] In 1899 there were 197 Lutheran deaconesses in America; by 1938, the year of the largest total, there were 487.[94] In the twentieth century additional institutions were established: by the Danes at Brush, Colorado (1903); by Augustana at Axtell, Nebraska (1917); and by the Synodical Conference at Fort Wayne, Indiana (1919).[95] At Brush and Axtell both male and female deaconesses served. The diaconate, however, never effectively took root in American Lutheranism except in a very limited way. It was to experience so serious a decline in the mid-twentieth century that its very continuance would be called into question despite serious attempts to effect the changes necessary to make it appealing to young women as a field of service.

During the late nineteenth century and even more so in the early twentieth, numerous Lutheran hospitals were established under local auspices in many communities where Lutherans were strongly represented. Although some were discontinued and others lost their Lutheran identity, many such hospitals continue to serve their communities today.

Orphanages and homes for the aged were established in relatively large numbers in the period under consideration, with the former receiving the most attention initially. In many instances

89.
Ibid., pp. 10-15; Weiser, *Love's Response,* pp. 57-60.
90.
Dates indicate beginnings rather than incorporation of institutions. See Nelson and Fevold, *Lutheran Church Among Norwegian-Americans,* 1:293-94.
91.
Arden, *Augustana Heritage,* p. 119.
92.
Weiser, *Love's Response,* p. 64.
93.
Ibid., p. 67.
94.
Ibid., p. 70.
95.
Ibid., pp. 68-69.

homes for children and the aged were located at the same site and were under the same administration. Although the inspiring example of Passavant was an important factor in the founding of such institutions, even more compelling was the plight of orphan children, which evoked a response of Christian compassion by both individuals and congregations. While charitable institutions were sometimes owned and operated by synods, more commonly they were owned and supported by subdivisions of a church body or by individuals from within its constituency.

The multiplication of institutions of mercy may be illustrated by a few representative facts. The first orphanage of the Augustana Synod was started in 1865; by 1917 there were seventeen institutions for children in the synod. Its first home for the aged was organized in 1896, but several more were begun in the next couple of decades.[96] Although the first Norwegian charitable institution did not appear before 1882, a home in which both children and the aged were cared for, by 1914 there were twelve children's homes and seven homes for the aged under Norwegian Lutheran auspices.[97] By the end of the nineteenth century eight orphanages had been established within Missouri Synod circles, the earliest dating from 1868, and the number remained at that figure for many years. Its first home for the aged was established in 1875, with a total of five by the end of the century and eight prior to World War I.[98] The pattern in the other synods was similar to that indicated by these few examples.

Another pioneer venture in Lutheran social missions was a school for the deaf (Evangelical Lutheran Institute for the Deaf) at Detroit, established in 1874 by Missouri Lutherans. Two decades later another Missouri pastor, August Reinke of Chicago, began conducting services for Lutheran deaf-mutes, a ministry which was extended to several midwestern cities. In 1896 the Missouri Synod assumed responsibility for the work and a year later had three missionaries working with the deaf.[99] J. F. Ohl of the General Council (Ministerium of Pennsylvania) was a pioneer Lutheran city missionary, serving in that capacity in Philadelphia from 1899 to 1930.

Women's and Youth Organizations

During the last quarter of the nineteenth century Lutheran women's and youth organizations made their appearance on the national and synodical level. Societies for women and for youth were found in many Lutheran congregations much earlier. What was new was the successful attempt to organize on a broader basis.

It is difficult to say to what extent the participation of women in various movements on the American sociopolitical scene—women's suffrage or temperance (WCTU, 1874), for example—influenced the emergence of Lutheran women's organizations. Discussing the place of women in the Augustana Synod, one writer observes that "directly or indirectly, these social and political issues influenced the Augustana Church and its members."[100] The comment would apply, in varying degrees, to some

96.
First orphanage begun by Eric Norelius, Vasa, Minn. See Arden, *Augustana Heritage,* pp. 118–19.
97.
First home founded by E. J. Homme, Wittenberg, Wisc. See Nelson and Fevold, *Lutheran Church Among Norwegian-Americans,* 1:293.
98.
W. H. T. Dau, ed., *Ebenezer* (St. Louis: Concordia Publishing House, 1922), pp. 453–55.
99.
An historical review of Missouri's ministry to the deaf is provided by August R. Suelflow, "Away from the Crowd: The Deaf Mission of the Lutheran Church—Missouri Synod," *Concordia Historical Institute Quarterly* 42 (1969): 3–26. See also, Baepler, *Century of Grace,* pp. 185–86; and Lueking, *Mission,* pp. 188–90.
100.
Burnice Fjellman, "Women in the Church," in *Centennial Essays,* p. 208.

301

other Lutheran church bodies, particularly the more American-ized ones. In others, the general women's movement made no apparent impact at the time. Women's organizations were formed on the synodical level for the purpose of promoting and supporting financially the church's mission task, both at home and abroad. Illustrative of what occurred in many synods was the formation of the Women's Foreign Missionary Society of the General Synod (1879), the earliest of Lutheran women's synodi-cal mission organizations, and the Women's Home and Foreign Missionary Society of the Augustana Synod (1892), the first such organization among the Scandinavians. Emmy Carlson Evald of Chicago, Augustana's pioneer leader in women's work, represented the effective leadership that was emerging in many of the synods. [101]

The synods that longest retained the use of the German lan-guage were generally most cautious in permitting or encourag-ing their women to form synod-wide societies. The women's missionary societies formed at this time and later compiled outstanding records of financial support of the missionary enter-prise. Women's societies, both local and synodical, became an important vehicle for lay involvement in a church that was led and managed by men. The development of the diaconate, as discussed earlier, was a possibility for full-time church service for women, but had only a limited appeal. A few single women missionaries, among them deaconesses, had gone to foreign fields by the end of the century, including Anna S. Kugler, a medical doctor, who went to India in 1883 under General Synod auspices and developed its medical mission. [102]

The growing youth movement in American Protestantism resulted in the formation of such well-known organizations as Christian Endeavor (1881, interdenominational), the Epworth League (1889, Methodist), and the Baptist Young People's Union (1891). They had in turn been influenced by the earlier organization of the Young Men's Christian Association (1844), and the Young Women's Christian Association (1866). Parallel to them and partly in response to their stimulus, two Lutheran youth organizations made their appearance, the Walther League (Synodical Conference) and the Luther League of America (intersynodical). [103] The advocacy of organized youth work by Lutheran pastors and lay leaders was a primary factor in the emergence of the Lutheran youth movement, but an important precipitating factor was the success of other Protes-tant youth programs, particularly Christian Endeavor, which some Lutheran parish youth societies joined. [104]

The organization of the Walther League in 1893 followed the earlier interest and promotion of young men's societies in Buf-falo, New York, and Detroit, Michigan, whose members favored creating a league of youth societies having common interests and goals. When it was formed, the stated aims of the Walther League included the inculcation of loyalty to the church, the promotion of local societies, their preservation from affiliation with heterodox societies, and the promotion of sociability within and among societies. [105] It was in 1894 that the name "Walther

101.
Arden, *Augustana Heritage,* p. 212; Juergen L. Neve, *History of the Lutheran Church in America,* 3d ed., rev. (Burlington, Iowa: Lutheran Literary Board, 1934), p. 128.
102.
Neve, *History,* p. 128.
103.
Two helpful studies of Lutheran youth work are Gerald Jenny's *The Young People's Movement in the American Lutheran Church* (Minneapolis: Augsburg Publishing House, 1928); and Clarence Peters, "De-velopment of the Youth Programs of the Lutheran Churches in America" (D.Th. diss., Concordia Seminary, St. Louis, 1951). Peters relies heavily on Jenny for his historical surveys.
104.
Jenny, *Young People's Movement,* pp. 12, 42, 67, 139. Henry Eyster Jacobs observes that in some places the development of the Lutheran youth movement was stimu-lated by pressure on pastors and congre-gations to join Christian Endeavor (*A His-tory of the Evangelical Lutheran Church in the United States*) [New York: Christian Litera-ture Co., 1893], p. 515.
105.
Jenny, *Young People's Movement,* p. 22.

League" was adopted in honor of the Missouri Synod's leader, who had been the first to organize a congregational youth society within his church body and had advocated a united youth association. The Walther League grew slowly, for despite its firm support by a few pastors and laymen, many others looked on the youth movement with skepticism. There was a marked reluctance in the Missouri Synod to promote youth work on the national level.[106] In fact, the Walther League experienced much uncertainty and neglect through the first decade of the twentieth century, but after the upturn in its fortunes which dated from 1910 it developed into a thriving and effective organization.[107]

303

Although the Luther League of America was formed two years later than the Walther League, its antecedents preceded those of the Synodical Conference organization. There was more widespread support of a youth program among the Luther League's constituency, although opposition was not lacking there either. Junius B. Remensnyder of Lewiston, Pennsylvania, a General Synod pastor, was the pioneer leader who laid the groundwork for the Luther League. Through his advocacy and leadership youth societies were organized in eastern Pennsylvania and New York on the pattern of the successful society formed in his own congregation in 1875. Under his leadership the Luther Alliance of the Susquehanna Synod was formed in 1889, the first permanent synodical league of youth societies. Five years later it became part of a state-wide association of Luther Leagues.

Another important locus of Lutheran youth activity in the eighties was the New York metropolitan area, where the celebration of the Luther quadricentennial (1883) had made a significant impact on Lutheran young people.[108] In 1888 the Central Association of Lutheran Young People's Associations of the City of New York was formed. The Central Association was avowedly intersynodical and strongly committed to the extension and organization of Lutheran youth work. In the matter of a few years several regional and state youth federations were formed, first in the eastern states but soon extending as far west as Kansas. The New York state organization adopted the name "Luther League."

The formation of the Luther League of America in Pittsburgh in 1895 was the logical outgrowth of these earlier developments. The invitation to the organizational meeting urged the attendance of representatives of youth societies "of whatever name and however synodically related, who would sustain the endeavor of a national Luther League to quicken, by churchly methods, especially among the youth, a clearer consciousness of Christian faith, and to promote among them a practical Christian life."[109]

Although the Luther League was intersynodical in scope and discouraged the formation of synodical youth groups, the future development of Lutheran youth work was with the latter. In the early years, before formation of synodical organizations, local societies of many synods were represented in the Luther League, including Norwegian and Swedish societies, for example. The

106.
Meier and Mayer, "Process of Americanization," pp. 366–67.
107.
Jenny, *Young People's Movement,* pp. 24–27.
108.
George U. Wenner, *The Lutherans of New York* (New York: Petersfield Press, 1918), p. 49.
109.
Quoted in Jenny, *Young People's Movement,* p. 46.

majority of member societies were from General Synod and General Council congregations. After the formation of the United Lutheran Church in America (ULCA) the Luther League became the official youth organization of that body (1920). Besides providing opportunity for youth involvement in the life of the church and serving as an important vehicle of instruction, inspiration, and fellowship, the Luther League assisted in the development of intersynodical friendships and in promoting the merger that produced the ULCA.[110]

110.
Ibid., pp. 48, 58–59.

14   The Theological Scene

During the post-Civil War era an aggressive and vital American Christianity was engaged in trying to evangelize and educate an entire nation which was rapidly expanding westward and experiencing unprecedented growth through immigration. The goal was to Christianize every aspect of its life and culture.[1] In the same period a new intellectual climate was emerging in America which appeared to have threatening implications for traditional theology. Among the powerful forces or factors contributing to the new situation were the following: Darwin's theory of biological evolution, "social Darwinism" and its application of the principle of development to nearly every learned discipline, the application of rigorous historical analysis to the Bible (higher criticism), the comparative study of world religions, and the growing importance of sociology and psychology.[2] The response of the churches and their members to the new science ranged all the way from a total rejection or a complete ignoring of its religious implications to a virtual substitution of a scientific world-view for Christian faith. Many sought an intermediate position between the two extremes. At this time a liberal theological movement, espousing a "new theology," made headway in American Protestantism as it sought to adjust traditional Christian belief to the findings of modern science. The tensions created in American Protestantism by the new theological situation climaxed in the 1920s in the modernist-fundamentalist controversy.

The American church experienced a challenge not only to its theology but also to its entire program of activity in the late nineteenth century. This was brought on by the rapid development of an industrial and urban society and the multitudinous social problems that followed in its wake.[3] One important and controversial response to the new social situation was an emphasis on "social Christianity" and the emergence of the social gospel movement, which envisioned the realization of the kingdom of God on earth through the creation of a Christian society. This chapter, however, focuses on theological issues confronting the Lutheran churches in America; chapter 15 will note its response to social developments.

Lutherans and the New Intellectual Climate

The issues raised by evolution, biblical criticism, and social change were not seriously confronted by American Lutherans in the nineteenth century. On the grass-roots level they had made practically no impact by the end of the century. A few theological and intellectual leaders, particularly in the Eastern part of

1.
Robert T. Handy, "The Protestant Quest for a Christian America," *Church History* 12 (1953): 10. According to Handy, American Roman Catholics shared with Protestants in pursuit of the same goal.
2.
Winthrop S. Hudson, *Religion in America* (New York: Scribner's, 1965), pp. 263–65.
3.
Arthur M. Schlesinger, Sr., *A Critical Period in American Religion, 1875–1900* (Philadelphia: Fortress Press, 1967), pp. 1–2.

the church, were beginning to react and respond to the new developments. The Lutheran church was primarily preoccupied with the practical tasks of missions, evangelism, and education. Moreover, large segments of it were isolated by language from many facets of the environment. Basic problems for Lutherans continued to be their confessional indentity and their adjustment to their environment (Americanization), but the latter development had not as yet involved the new scientific views being accepted by many Americans.[4] It was within the General Synod that there was most openness to considering the problems posed by evolution and higher criticism, which is not surprising since of the Lutheran bodies it was best acquainted with developments in English-speaking Protestantism.[5]

In all segments of American Lutheranism, Darwinism, if dealt with at all, was viewed in a fundamentally negative way. It was regarded as a serious threat to Christianity because of the skeptical, agnostic, and materialistic viewpoint with which Darwinism was identified.[6] This was also true of those leaders of Eastern Lutheranism who cautiously acknowledged the need to come to terms with the new science.[7] The General Synod's Milton Valentine was one who expressed this position, believing in the possibility of a reconciliation of Christianity and evolution in some form, but maintaining at the same time a basically conservative stance which was highly critical of evolution. Alert to American currents and convinced that the problem could not be ignored, Valentine was more liberal than most of his Lutheran contemporaries.[8] Henry E. Jacobs, Valentine's General Council counterpart, had comparatively little to say about evolution. His primary interest was with the tradition and heritage of Lutheranism, but he believed that science and religion need not conflict if each would stick to its own field. In their emphases these two theologians represented the attitudes of their church bodies—the greater awareness in the General Synod of the new science and the need for taking it into account, and the General Council's concern for the Lutheran tradition and its lesser interest in issues such as evolution.[9] Although a few leaders in the Eastern branch of Lutheranism were making a cautious adjustment to Darwinism by the end of the century, the characteristic response in American Lutheranism was that of emphatic rejection or an ignoring of its implications.

As with evolution, the discussion of biblical criticism, insofar as it occurred, remained on the academic level where it was carried on by and for theologians and ministers. In all of American Lutheranism the initial response to biblical criticism was hostile, and it continued to be so in nearly all quarters far into the twentieth century. There was general agreement that the new biblical studies were negative and destructive in nature. The developmental assumptions of the historical approach to the Bible were highly suspect. Higher criticism was deemed an especially dangerous threat to the authority, inspiration, and infallibility of the Bible at a time when there was virtually

4.
A helpful study of the Lutheran church in America in relation to Darwinism, biblical criticism, and the social gospel is Reginald W. Deitz's "Eastern Lutheranism in American Society and American Christianity, 1870–1914" (Ph.D. diss., University of Pennsylvania, 1958).
5.
Biblical criticism as represented by English scholars was generally more conservative than German criticism which was frequently quite extreme, and with the latter the theologians of the General Council and the Midwestern synods were better acquainted than was the General Synod.
6.
An unpublished investigation of ten Norwegian-American Lutheran periodicals for the period 1860–80 made by Lawrence E. Brynestad reveals no articles dealing with Darwinism. Typical of the critical attitude expressed in subsequent years is Hans G. Stub's "Darwinism Weighed and Found Wanting," *Evangelisk Lutherske Kirketidende* 19 (1872): 293. An extensive critical evaluation of evolution was undertaken in a series of articles in Missouri's *Lehre und Wehre* during 1900 (vol. 46).
7.
Deitz, "Eastern Lutheranism," chaps. 2 and 3.
8.
Ibid., pp. 97–103.
9.
Ibid., pp. 103–5.

unanimous agreement on those matters among American Lutherans. Theodore E. Schmauk, prominent General Council pastor, editor, theological professor, and during 1902-18 its forceful president, was the leading critic in English-speaking Lutheranism of biblical criticism, and he sought to alert the church to its dangers.[10] When higher criticism first began to make its impact on American Protestantism, Lutheran conservatives did not regard it as a problem for their church. Around the turn of the century, however, it was becoming clear that American Lutheranism would be influenced by the new biblical scholarship to some degree, inasmuch as a few influential men in Eastern Lutheranism, in both the General Synod and the General Council, were modifying their positions regarding inerrancy and verbal inspiration, but in a cautious and conservative manner.[11] In the course of the twentieth century questions concerning the validity of biblical criticism and the inspiration and infallibility of the Bible were much discussed among Lutherans, and positions regarding them were important for inter-Lutheran relationships, but until the end of the nineteenth century they had created little excitement in American Lutheran circles.

Only minimally affected as yet by the issues confronting American theology in general, Lutherans in the late nineteenth century centered their theological interest on two issues particularly: (1) the Lutheran confessions and some practical problems related to their subscription, and (2) the doctrine of predestination and related doctrines. Through most of the century there was a marked development of a Lutheran confessional and historical consciousness which manifested a greater appropriation and appreciation of the Lutheran doctrinal heritage. The confessional spirit of most Midwestern synods was quite strong from the time of their founding, reflecting the revival of confessional Lutheranism in Europe, but it was further strengthened by the influence and example of the Missouri Synod. The development of a stronger confessionalism was particularly noticeable in Eastern Lutheranism, both through indigenous forces and the impact of the later immigration. In the early nineteenth century Eastern Lutheranism had been plagued by doctrinal looseness and at mid-century had been rent by a bitter conflict over "American Lutheranism," in which the place and authority of the Lutheran confessions, specifically the Augsburg Confession, were at stake.[12] The chief theological interest of Eastern Lutheranism during the last quarter of the nineteenth century continued to be the confessions—a continuing growth in appreciation of them (particularly in the General Synod and the United Synod, South) and practical problems resulting from a confessional spirit, particularly relating to church fellowship (General Council). The predestination controversy was largely a Midwestern phenomenon, and it had a determinative influence in shaping subsequent ecclesiastical relations among the synods involved. That controversy also re-

10.
Theodore E. Schmauk, in his *The Negative Criticism and the Old Testament* (Lebanon, Pa.: Aldus Co., 1894), voices his conviction that the new biblical studies were defective in method and destructive in their effects.

11.
In an interesting evaluation of book reviews in the *Lutheran Quarterly* (General Synod) and the *Lutheran Church Review* (General Council) in the period 1870-1914, Deitz shows that books setting forth a conservative position on higher criticism were discussed sympathetically in both quarterlies. Books espousing critical views were often treated sympathetically in the General Synod quarterly but almost always were evaluated negatively in the General Council periodical (Deitz, "Eastern Lutheranism," pp. 170-78).

12.
See chapter 11.

vealed the typical American Lutheran preoccupation with the confessions.

Growing Confessionalism in Eastern Lutheranism

The formation of the General Council in 1867 was a traumatic experience for the General Synod. It resulted in the loss of about one-half of its membership, its most conservative and confessional elements, and left a residue of hard feeling that persisted even beyond the generation of those directly involved in the events of the 1860s. [13] Originally the General Synod as such had no official confessional basis, leaving the matter of doctrinal affirmation to its member synods. Not until 1864, in the midst of internal controversy, was its constitutional article on membership altered so that all synods uniting with the General Synod were required to "receive and hold, with the Evangelical Lutheran Church of our Fathers, the Word of God as contained in the Canonical Scriptures of the Old and New Testaments, as the only infallible rule of faith and practice, and the Augsburg Confession as a correct exhibition of the fundamental doctrines of the divine Word, and of the faith of our Church as founded upon that Word."[14] By this action the General Synod explicitly affirmed its allegiance to the Augsburg Confession. It was apparent that the Schmucker-Kurtz wing of the General Synod, the leading advocates of "American Lutheranism," was on the wane. In 1895 the position of the General Synod was made still more explicit when it was specified that it was to the unaltered Augsburg Confession that it was committed as being "throughout in perfect consistence" with the word of God.[15]

In 1864 James A. Brown succeeded Schmucker as president of Gettysburg Seminary, and under his leadership the moderate party of the General Synod was greatly strengthened. This party, rather than the liberal wing, shaped the position of the General Synod after the withdrawal of the conservatives. More appreciative of the Lutheran doctrinal heritage than the "American Lutherans" but critical of the strong confessionalism of the General Council, especially as it was represented by Charles Porterfield Krauth, Brown influenced several generations of theological students toward a positive appreciation of the Augsburg Confession and its theology.[16]

Another significant leader in the General Synod's gradual but perceptible swing to a more confessional position was Milton Valentine, president first of Gettysburg College and then of Gettysburg Seminary, a more accomplished and sophisticated theologian than Brown. Valentine identified the General Synod's doctrinal positon with "the Catholic Lutheranism of the Augsburg Confession."[17] He insisted that subscription to the Augsburg Confession alone is enough to identify a church body as genuinely Lutheran, contending that those American synods subscribing to the entire Book of Concord were the ones having most difficulty reaching complete doctrinal agreement (notably the conservative Midwestern synods struggling over predestination and conversion).[18] That the General Synod's position played down the importance of the remaining Lutheran sym-

308

13.
See Adolph Spaeth's brief history of the General Council, "The General Council," *Lutheran Church Review* 4 (1885): 81–126; and Milton Valentine's critical reaction to its interpretation of historical events in "The Effort to Reconstruct History in the Interest of the General Council," *Lutheran Quarterly* 16 (1886): 571–93. Valentine particularly resented Spaeth's contention that the formation of the General Council was a doctrinal necessity because the General Synod had not been faithfully Lutheran.
14.
Quoted by Milton Valentine, "The General Synod," in *The Distinctive Doctrines and Usages of the General Bodies of the . . . Lutheran Church . . .* (Philadelphia: Lutheran Publication Society, 1893), p. 39.
15.
Abdel Ross Wentz, *A Basic History of Lutheranism in America* (Philadelphia: Muhlenberg Press, 1955), p. 239.
16.
Brown was a vigorous leader but not an accomplished theologian. Coming out of a non-Lutheran background, he became a convinced Lutheran with a constantly developing appreciation of Lutheran doctrine, but he continued to appreciate theologies other than his own. See C. A. Stork's tribute and assessment in *Lutheran Quarterly* 13 (1883): 415–49.
17.
Ibid. 14 (1884): 598.
18.
Distinctive Doctrines, p. 43.

bols is clear, but that it did not involve a rejection of them is evident in the subsequent action of the General Synod (1913) in adopting all the Lutheran symbols, although those other than the Augsburg Confession were designated "secondary symbols," which were characterized as "expositions of Lutheran doctrine of great historical and interpretative value."[19] Gettysburg Seminary's annual Holman Lectureship on the Augsburg Confession inaugurated in 1866 was both indicative of the growing confessional spirit of the General Synod and a positive force in creating a higher appreciation of that confession and of Lutheran doctrine.[20]

The theological stance of the General Synod, although increasingly confessional, continued to be more relaxed and inclusive than that of the General Council. The General Synod was little interested in doctrinal pronouncements, desiring liberty within the bounds of the Augsburg Confession and believing that essential doctrinal agreement did in fact exist among American Lutherans on that basis. Its confessional and doctrinal position was the broadest and most lenient of all the major American Lutheran bodies, a fact which subjected it to frequent criticism from many quarters.

The theological position of the General Council was made evident at the outset of its existence when it affirmed its purpose to be "the development of the Lutheran Church in this country, in accordance with the principles of Confessional and Historical Lutheranism," and in its "Fundamental Principles of Faith and Church Polity" pledged itself to the unaltered Augsburg Confession, "by preeminence" the confession of the Lutheran faith, and the remaining symbols of the Book of Concord. The confessions are called "articles of agreement" and "contracts" which "must be accepted in every statement of doctrine, in their own true, native, original, and only sense."[21] In contrast to what has been called the General Synod's "common law" type of confessionalism, the General Council, in its "Fundamental Principles," set forth an explicit "constitutionalism," involving a legalistic and rigid interpretation of what subscription to the confessions involves.[22] In the light of the ultimate rapprochement of the General Synod and the General Council, it should be noted that the "Fundamental Principles" asserted that a church which sincerely subscribed to the unaltered Augsburg Confession is a true Lutheran church and that the remaining symbols do not add to the Augsburg Confession but serve to guard it from ambiguity. Moreover, while all the symbols of the Book of Concord are intended for the ministry, only the Augsburg Confession and the Small Catechism are doctrinal standards for the laity.[23] While applauding the evidence of growing confessionalism in the General Synod, the General Council did not regard the other body's doctrinal basis as adequate "and thus sought to have the General Synod arrive at a higher appreciation of the full body of our Lutheran confessions."[24]

During the last portion of the nineteenth century the confessional position of the General Synod gradually approached that of the General Council, and at the same time the latter inter-

19.
Richard C. Wolf, *Documents of Lutheran Unity in America* (Philadelphia: Fortress Press, 1966), pp. 266–67.
20.
See Henry Eyster Jacobs in *Lutheran Church Review* 8 (1889): 210–11.
21.
Wolf, *Documents*, pp. 144–46; Henry Eyster Jacobs, "The General Council," in *Distinctive Doctrines*, pp. 87–118, is a commentary on the General Council's "Fundamental Principles."
22.
Robert H. Fischer, "The Confessionalism of American Lutheran Church Bodies of German Background," in *The Church and the Confessions*, ed. Vilmos Vajta and Hans Weissgerber (Philadelphia: Fortress Press, 1963), p. 77.
23.
Jacobs, "The General Council," pp. 96–100, 107.
24.
Documentary History of the General Council . . . (Philadelphia: General Council Pub. House, 1912), p. 408. See theses prepared by Henry Eyster Jacobs (1907) on "The Relation of the General Council to the General Synod," in ibid., pp. 405–9.

preted its "Fundamental Principles" in a flexible manner and manifested more of an historical approach to the confessions than the literalism of its principles implied. These two large bodies which in the past had been one were in the process of growing together again. The development can be gauged by a comparison of the spirit which permeated the free Lutheran diet of 1877 and that of the first general conference of 1898, both held in Philadelphia. These were intersynodical gatherings for the purpose of discussing mutual concerns, but the participants were predominantly from the General Council and the General Synod. At the 1877 meeting the old animosities and suspicions were conspicuous, particularly in the discussion periods which followed formal addresses; in 1898 synodical differences were hardly apparent.[25]

Essentially the same confessional development occurred in southern Lutheranism as in the General Synod, except at a more rapid pace. The South was influenced by the increased appreciation of Lutheran history, doctrine, and practice which characterized American Lutheranism generally. When during the Civil War (1863) the southern synods withdrew from the General Synod and organized the General Synod, South, the latter reflected the doctrinal basis of the mother body. In 1872 a resolution committed it to the Augsburg Confession "in its true, native and original sense." By the early 1880s interest in Lutheran unity had grown to the point where the General Synod, South was ready to merge with others on "an unequivocal Lutheran basis." The traditionally conservative Tennessee Synod, with which merger was contemplated, in 1866 had revised its constitution to include subscription to the entire Book of Concord. When in 1886 the United Synod, South was formed through the merger of the General Synod, South, the Tennessee Synod, and the Holston Synod, its confessional basis included all the Lutheran symbols, with the explanation that the Augsburg Confession has preeminence as a Lutheran symbol.[26] The confessionalism of the southern churches was moderate in nature, manifesting influences from both the General Synod and the General Council, but the explicit confessional position adopted in connection with the 1886 merger reflected the influence of the Tennessee Synod.[27]

The Church-Fellowship Issue in Eastern Lutheranism

The practical implications of the confessional position of the General Council prompted discussion within that body for a couple of decades. The debate initially centered on the Four Points: chiliasm, lodge membership, pulpit fellowship, and altar fellowship. Although the position adopted by the General Council regarding these four issues was too restrictive for the General Synod, it was considered too lax by most of the conservative synods of the Midwest. The Missouri Synod and the Norwegian Synod had no inclination to participate in the formation of the General Council, and both the Iowa Synod and the Joint Synod of Ohio, who were more inclined to do so, held

25.
Henry Eyster Jacobs, ed., *First Free Lutheran Diet in America, 1877* (Philadelphia: J. F. Smith, 1878); idem, *The First General Conference of Lutherans in America . . . 1898* (Philadelphia: General Council Board of Publication, 1899). An interesting comparison of the two gatherings is made by George C. F. Haas, *Lutheran Church Review* 18 (1899): 293–300.

26.
Edward T. Horn, "The United Synod in the South," in *Distinctive Doctrines,* pp. 172–83.

27.
Andrew G. Voigt, "The United Synod in the South," in *Distinctive Doctrines* (4th ed., 1914), pp. 186–89.

back from joining. Others withdrew shortly after its formation: Wisconsin (1869), Minnesota (1871), and Illinois (1871).[28]

The basic complaint of the Midwestern synods was that the practice of the General Council did not conform to its commendable confessional position as set forth in its "Fundamental Principles." Obviously, the problems of the Eastern synods regarding lodge membership or pulpit and altar fellowship were more complex than those of the Midwestern synods, inasmuch as the former had been in America for a much longer period of time, had passed through periods of doctrinal indifference and confessional laxity, and had been influenced by American practices and attitudes. Lodge members had been permitted to join Lutheran congregations in the East. It had been the occasional practice to permit ministers of other evangelical denominations to preach in Lutheran pulpits, and Lutheran pastors had preached in churches of other denominations. A general invitation to the Lord's Supper was also in use in some Eastern congregations with the result that non-Lutherans communed in Lutheran churches.[29] With the development of a more confessional spirit in the East, such practices were deplored by the more conservative members of the General Council, who thought they ought to be eliminated, but others, especially of the English-speaking constituency, disagreed. In any case, the remedy chosen by the General Council for bringing practice in line with principle was education and persuasion rather than legalistic discipline. During the 1870s and 1880s it was particularly the issue of pulpit and altar fellowship that received much attention in the General Council.

The General Synod continued its earlier practices regarding church fellowship. It cultivated fraternal relations with other evangelical denominations, not only as a privilege but also as a duty and a responsibility.[30] Consequently it enacted no prohibitions against pulpit and altar fellowship with non-Lutherans and permitted both ministers and laymen "the freedom of conscience and love in this matter."[31] The General Synod's practice regarding pulpit and altar fellowship was viewed by many in the General Council as evidence that the General Synod's confessionalism was still deficient. However, there was lack of uniformity in the General Council on the fellowship question, and those inclined to a more liberal policy were not particularly agitated by General Synod practice.

The discussion of the fellowship question in the General Council usually centered on the Galesburg Rule.[32] Its earliest version dated from the Akron convention (1872) of the General Council, at which Charles Porterfield Krauth, its president, reduced to writing statements earlier made by him in explanation of the General Council's position:

1.

The Rule is: Lutheran pulpits are for Lutheran ministers only. Lutheran altars are for Lutheran communicants only.

311

28.
See chapter 11, concerning the Four Points controversy.
29.
Wentz, *Basic History,* p. 242.
30.
In the words of C. E. Sparks, the General Synod "holds that membership in secret societies is not a question for ecclesiastical legislation and that fellowship with evangelical Christians is a duty" ("The Development of the General Synod Lutheran Church in America," *Lutheran Quarterly* 36 [1906]: 582).
31.
Valentine, "The General Synod," p. 60. The same author indicates that not all in the General Synod shared this liberal attitude (*Lutheran Quarterly* 17 [1887]: 526).
32.
For a thorough discussion of the fellowship question consult Donald L. Huber, "The Controversy over Pulpit and Altar Fellowship in the General Council of the Evangelical Lutheran Church, 1866–1889" (Ph.D. diss., Duke University, 1971). Also see Dorris A. Flesner, "The Galesburg Rule: A Study of Lutheran Exclusivism" (M.A. thesis, Divinity School, University of Chicago, 1953).

2.

The *Exceptions* to the rule belong to the sphere of *privilege*, not of right.

3.

The *Determination* of the *exceptions* is to be made in consonance with these principles by the conscientious judgment of pastors as the cases arise.[33]

After a protracted discussion of the problem of pulpit and altar fellowship at the 1875 convention at Galesburg, Illinois, a resolution was passed which included the statement: ". . . the rule, which accords with the Word of God and with the confessions of our Church, is: 'Lutheran communicants only.'"[34] When a question was asked as to the relation of this statement to the Akron declaration, Krauth's official ruling was that the Galesburg resolution was an amendment to paragraph one of the earlier declaration for the purpose of underscoring the *source* of the Rule, and that paragraphs two and three, dealing with exceptions, remained in effect.[35] This meant that, according to Krauth's interpretation, the Galesburg Rule was the full Akron declaration plus the explanatory clause inserted in paragraph one.

The action of the Galesburg convention was variously interpreted within the General Council. The staunch conservatives, opposed to permitting exceptions, thought that the explanatory clause annulled paragraphs two and three. Others insisted that the paragraphs permitting exceptions were still in effect. A long controversy resulted concerning the General Council's intention in devising the Galesburg Rule, the meaning of terms, and the internal consistency of the three paragraphs. At the General Council's request Krauth drew up 105 theses on pulpit and altar fellowship, which provided the basis for discussion of the subject at several conventions beginning in 1877. According to Krauth it was not intended that the Galesburg Rule be applied in a legislative or disciplinary manner, but rather it set forth a "general principle" for guidance and had an "educational" function.[36] He gave expression to the General Council's approach to all of the controverted Four Points for which it was criticized by the Midwestern synods and by some in its own membership who wanted the Galesburg Rule to be applied legalistically. Although Krauth defended the principle of allowing exceptions to the basic rule, he interpreted permissible exceptions in a narrow and restricted manner. Opposition to so strict an interpretation of the Galesburg Rule was expressed by several prominent General Council pastors, including Gottlob F. Krotel of New York and Joseph A. Seiss of Philadelphia.[37] Thus, while the General Council's practice regarding pulpit and altar fellowship was tighter than that of the General Synod, there was internal disagreement regarding the issue, with the result that the Galesburg Rule was interpreted and applied strictly by some and flexibly by others. Uniformity could not be expected under such circumstances, particularly since the General Council's approach was educational and persuasive rather than disciplinary.

33.
Documentary History, General Council, p. 216.
34.
Ibid., pp. 216–17.
35.
Ibid., pp. 340–41.
36.
Ibid., p. 345.
37.
Adolph Spaeth, *Charles Porterfield Krauth* (Philadelphia: General Council Pub. House, 1909), 2:206. Robert H. Fischer points out that the extent and the dynamics of opposition within the General Council to a strict interpretation of the Galesburg Rule have not yet been accurately assessed. The legendary home mission pastor Michael Schweigert illustrates grass-roots opposition to such an interpretation ("This Unassuming Servant of the Master: Michael Schweigert," in *The Maturing of American Lutheranism*, ed. H. T. Neve and B. A. Johnson [Minneapolis: Augsburg Publishing House, 1968], pp. 159–61).

38.
Huber, "The Controversy," pp. 219-23.
39.
Documentary History, General Council, pp. 219-20.
40.
Huber points out that differing views within the General Council concerning the doctrine of the church remained unresolved—the contrast between the traditional Old Lutheran view and that prevalent in the dominant revivalistic Protestantism of that day ("The Controversy," pp. 274-76).

The discussion concerning pulpit and altar fellowship continued in the General Council into the 1800s but with less intensity than earlier. A consensus was developing that variance in practice would be tolerated. The emergence of the predestination controversy diverted attention from the fellowship issue even though the General Council was not directly involved. After Krauth's death early in 1883 no one was disposed to promote his position, the most rigorous in the General Council, in an aggressive manner.[38] In response to a request from the New York Ministerium, the General Council in 1889 made it unambiguously clear that the Galesburg Rule included both the original declaration made at Akron (1872), including provision for exceptions, and the amendment made at Galesburg (1875), which was in the form of an explanation concerning the source of the Rule. The most accurate designation would be to term it the Akron-Galesburg Rule.[39] The 1889 decision which ended the fellowship controversy in the General Council meant that the council was satisfied to approve the discriminate practice of fellowship without insisting on uniformity in practice.[40] Dissatisfaction with the General Council's handling of the pulpit-altar fellowship question led the Michigan Synod to withdraw in 1888. A short time later it affiliated with the Wisconsin Synod in a joint synod and became a member of the Synodical Conference.

The Galesburg Rule played an important role in the twentieth century because it was adopted by a group of Midwestern synods occupying a position as to theology and practice between the Synodical Conference on the right and the United Lutheran Church in America on the left. Five church bodies—the Augustana Synod, the American Lutheran Church (1930), the Norwegian Lutheran Church in America, the Lutheran Free Church, and the United Danish Evangelical Lutheran Church—formed the American Lutheran Conference in 1930. The basis for this organization was the Minneapolis Theses (1925), which included the designation of the Galesburg Rule (only part one, however) as regulative of relations with non-Lutherans. In this way the Galesburg Rule continued to have significance in Midwestern Lutheranism long after its importance for Eastern Lutheranism had passed.

The Predestination Controversy

Divisiveness and controversy were obvious facts of life in American Lutheranism during the late nineteenth century. (Fortunately, however, some progress was also made on the merger front during that period, as chapter 15 will show.) The most abrasive of the conflicts was the predestination, or election, controversy. The terms "predestination" and "election" ("election of grace," according to German or Scandinavian terminology) were used interchangeably. This controversy developed within the Synodical Conference late in the 1870s and reached its climax in the next decade, during which it agitated much of Midwestern Lutheranism. No resolution of the conflict occurred at that time, and issues raised by the election controversy con-

313

tinued to plague American Lutheranism far into the twentieth century. Some of its consequences in terms of synodical relationships and alignments are still in evidence.

It is somewhat unexpected that the Lutheran church should have been so thoroughly disturbed by a conflict over a doctrine that is not central in Lutheran teaching. The Formula of Concord, the last of the Lutheran confessional writings of the sixteenth century, includes an article on election (Article XI) not because it had been controversial within Lutheran circles but because it was acknowledged to be a doctrine about which Lutherans and Calvinists disagreed. The authors of the Formula hoped that the article's inclusion would prevent dissension, disunity, and schism among their posterity.[41]

The starting point for Lutheran theology is the love of God. Emphasizing God's gracious redemption of all men and his desire that all should be saved, Lutheranism speaks of an election of grace: "The eternal election of God or God's predestination to salvation does not extend over both the godly and the ungodly but only over the children of God, who have been elected and predestined to eternal life. . . ."[42] Classical Calvinism, by way of contrast, taught a double predestination both to salvation and to damnation. According to Lutheran teaching, if a person is not among the saved it is because he in his sinfulness has rejected the grace of God, not because God has predestined him. The cause of man's unbelief, in the words of the Formula of Concord, is his own "perverse will, which rejects or perverts the means and instrument of the Holy Spirit which God offers to him through the call and resists the Holy Spirit who wills to be efficaciously active through the Word. . . ."[43] The Lutheran understanding of election "gives God his glory entirely and completely, because he out of pure grace alone, without any merit of ours, saves us 'according to the purpose' of his will."[44] Intimately involved in the Lutheran doctrine of election are the universality of God's grace, the particularity of the experience of salvation (not all are saved), and human responsibility for unbelief. Although election per se is not a central Lutheran doctrine, its relation to salvation by grace alone, justification by faith, man's sinful nature, and other important teachings accounted for the intensity of the controversy which agitated many of America's Lutherans in the late nineteenth century.

At the beginning of the controversy efforts were made to confine it to pastoral circles, but in vain. Many pastors were not well-versed in their church's position regarding predestination.[45] The subject is difficult and the Lutheran consensus concerning the doctrine was more negative in nature than positive.[46] That is, all knew that they were opposed to Calvinistic predestinarianism, but there was not the same understanding as to the content of the Lutheran position. The dispute drove many theologians and pastors to the Scriptures, the Lutheran confessions, and Lutheran theologians of the past.

The highly polemical theological climate of the period contributed to the vehemence of the debate. Several of the Midwestern synods involved in the controversy had been engaged in

314

41.
Theodore G. Tappert, ed., *The Book of Concord* (Philadelphia: Muhlenberg Press, 1959), pp. 494, 616. Article XI, Epitome, par. 1; Article XI, Solid Declaration, par. 1.
42.
Ibid., p. 617.
43.
Ibid., p. 623.
44.
Ibid., p. 496.
45.
Lutheran Witness, June 21, 1882, p. 4.
46.
Fred W. Meuser, *The Formation of the American Lutheran Church* (Columbus, Ohio: Wartburg Press, 1958), p. 64.

earlier theological disputes, sometimes with one another. Antagonisms had resulted, personal prejudices had developed, and the positions of various synods had been stereotyped by their opponents. The Midwestern synods were conservative in character, composed for the most part of those who had recently migrated from Europe, some of them for confessional reasons. In the American environment of separation of church and state and religious freedom it was possible for them to adhere tenaciously to distinctive teachings and practices without external interference. Disagreements could easily be overemphasized and differences accentuated. The differences among the participants in the election controversy were rooted in strongly held religious convictions, but the character of the controversy was also determined in part by pioneer individualism and the American environment of religious freedom. The parties to the conflict were convinced that they were in basic theological disagreement and at the same time shared the conviction that complete doctrinal unity is prerequisite for church fellowship. The degree to which personality conflicts were a factor in the controversy is impossible to measure, but they were important. Varying judgments have been made as to the motivation of Friedrich A. Schmidt, for example, who was so important in the development of the controversy. Intensity of feeling was heightened by the involvement of ex-Missourians and ex-Ohioans as they combatted erstwhile colleagues and associates. Obviously those involved also were in agreement that defense of the truth as they understood it was to be preferred to the peace of the church.

The occasion for the beginning of the election controversy was the 1877 meeting of the Western District of the Missouri Synod, at which the doctrine of election was discussed at length under the leadership of C. F. W. Walther. For several years the general theme, *soli deo gloria,* had been discussed at these district meetings, and election was one in a series of topics related to the general theme.[47] Among the points stressed in the discussion were the following: There is a predestination of individual persons which is the cause of their salvation and which insures that the elect ones will not lose their faith; the election of individuals is not based on divine foreknowledge; man's faith is not a cause of his election; God does not cause man's condemnation; the sinner himself is responsible.[48] Some of Walther's statements had a Calvinistic sound to a few men who began to express themselves critically about them—particularly Friedrich A. Schmidt of the Norwegian Synod, and Henry A. Allwardt and Frederick W. Stellhorn, both of the Missouri Synod. These men believed that they detected a deterministic view of grace and an absolute predestination in statements such as the following:

God has even from eternity chosen a certain number of persons unto salvation; He has determined that these shall and must be saved, and surely as God is God, so surely will they also be saved, and besides them none others.[49]

47.
The full theme was: "That only through the teaching of the Lutheran Church God alone is given all honor; this is an irrefutable proof that the teaching of the Lutheran Church is the only true one" (*Synodal-bericht,* Western District, Missouri Synod, 1877, p. 20).
48.
Hans R. Haug, "The Predestination Controversy in the Lutheran Church in North America" (Ph.D. diss., Temple University, 1968), pp. 272-85. This thesis is a thorough discussion of the predestination controversy among America's German Lutherans through the 1880s. The present writer acknowledges his indebtedness to it.
49.
Synodal-Bericht, Western District, Missouri Synod, 1877, p. 24.

**God *foresaw nothing,* absolutely nothing, *in those
whom he resolved to save,* which might be worthy of
salvation, and even if it be admitted that He foresaw
some good in them, this, nevertheless, could not have
determined Him to elect them for that reason; for as the
Scriptures teach, all good in man originates with Him.[50]
(Italics added)**

The views expressed by Walther had been set forth by him in
an article as early as 1863, by John A. Huegli in 1868 at a
meeting of the Northern District of the Missouri Synod, and in
an extensive literary controversy involving chiefly Walther and
Gottfried Fritschel of the Iowa Synod during the years 1871–73.
In the Walther-Fritschel debate nearly all of the basic issues and
points of view discussed in the controversy of the 1880s were set
forth.[51]

Following the 1877 Western District meeting a discussion of
predestination was begun in Missouri's theological journal, and
the critics of Walther's views expressed themselves at pastoral
conferences and to individuals. At the 1879 meeting of the same
district the doctrinal discussion again centered on predestination, at which time Walther strongly criticized his opponents,
although not by name. Schmidt's response was to begin publication in January 1880 of a journal entitled *Altes und Neues* ("the
old and the new"), the appearance of which has been described
as a "theological bombshell" because it contended that it was
necessary to counteract what was considered to be Missouri's
antiscriptural, anticonfessional, and crypto-Calvinistic view of
election.[52] From that point and on the dispute became a public
controversy. It was somewhat ironical that Schmidt, hitherto an
ardent Missourian with a reputation for unquestionable orthodoxy, should have been one of the chief leaders of the opposition
to Walther. A product of the Missouri Synod and of Concordia
Seminary (St. Louis), he had since 1861 been a professor in the
Norwegian Synod—at Luther College, Decorah, Iowa; at Concordia Seminary as faculty representative of the Norwegian
Synod; and since 1876 at Luther Seminary, Madison, Wisconsin. He had been a vigorous theological opponent of the Iowa
Synod, and when Norwegian Synod professor Ole Asperheim
early in 1878 publicly voiced criticism of Missouri and of his
synod's close ties with Missouri, Schmidt had criticized him
sharply. Early in the controversy both Allwardt and Stellhorn,
Schmidt's associates, left the Missouri Synod and joined the
Joint Synod of Ohio, continuing as hitherto to advocate the
anti-Missourian position on election and related subjects.

The major controversy, particularly during the early 1880s,
was carried on between the Joint Synod of Ohio and the Missouri Synod. The Norwegian Synod also became deeply involved and experienced a traumatic split, which the other two
bodies were spared. Crucial to the relations between Ohio and
Missouri was the fact that Matthias Loy, long-time professor at
Columbus Seminary and president of the Joint Synod of Ohio,
a warm friend of Missouri and an admirer of Walther, came out
against the latter on the issue of election.[53] Since the late 1860s

50.
Ibid., p. 51; trans. J. T. Mueller, "The
Predestinarian Controversy," in *Ebenezer,*
ed. W. H. T. Dau (St. Louis: Concordia
Publishing House, 1922), p. 408.
51.
Haug, "Predestination Controversy," pp.
82–235. The chief vehicle for the Walther-Fritschel discussion was Brobst's *Theologische Monatshefte,* published in Allentown, Pa., until its discontinuance at the
end of 1873.
52.
Ibid., p. 311.
53.
Meuser, *American Lutheran Church,* p. 66. In
1878 Loy received the call to the chair of
English Theology at Concordia Seminary,
St. Louis, which he declined.

their two synods had been enjoying increasingly friendly relations; Joint Ohio was a charter member of the Synodical Conference.[54] With the emergence of the predestination issue relations between the two rapidly deteriorated, particularly after a colloquium of Synodical Conference theological professors and district presidents held at Milwaukee in January 1881. That meeting witnessed a virtual declaration of war between Walther and Schmidt, and Ohio sided with the latter. Once begun, the estrangement between Missouri and Ohio developed rapidly. Contributing to the intensity of subsequent Missouri-Ohio differences was the fact that ex-Missourians like Allwardt and Stellhorn were leading critics of Walther. Among Walther's most active allies in his own synod were Huegli, earlier mentioned, and St. Louis professors George Stoeckhardt and Franz Pieper.

It has been noted that Walther was charged by his opponents with Calvinism (or crypto-Calvinism). His opponents, Schmidt and the Ohioans, in turn were accused of synergism (or semi-Pelagianism). Such terms, of course, were emotionally charged expressions when applied to fellow Lutherans, and great offense was taken by both sides at being labeled in such a way that one's Lutheranism was called into question. The aversion to both Calvinism and Roman Catholicism was strong among American Lutherans at the time. The use of such labels as "Calvinistic" and "synergistic" indicates in a negative way basic concerns of both parties. Walther stressed God's grace and glory (grace alone) in everything related to man's salvation. Schmidt and others were basically concerned with the centrality of faith in man's experience of salvation (justification by faith). Both sides insisted that they were teaching salvation by God's grace alone and man's justification by faith alone.

The Missourians stressed that the individual believer is predestined *unto* faith, solely on the basis of God's grace and the merit of Christ. Their opponents insisted that when speaking of God's predestination of the individual believer one must understand that predestination takes place *in view of* his faith which has been foreseen by God. The Latin term *intuitu fidei*, "in view of faith," which had been used extensively by Lutheran dogmaticians of the seventeenth century, figured prominently in the discussion. The Missourians were accused of espousing the absolute predestination and irresistible grace of Calvinism, jeopardizing the universality of God's grace which makes it possible for all to believe. Their opponents, according to the Missourians, opened the door to synergism because they made salvation dependent on something in man (his decision, nonresistance, faith) and thereby seriously compromised the teaching of salvation by grace alone.

It will be helpful to note the way in which major participants in the controversy viewed the issues. In a tract published in 1881 Walther defined what was at stake:

It consists simply in the following twofold question: 1st, whether God from eternity, before the foundations of the world were laid, out of pure mercy and only for the sake

54.
Ibid., pp. 52–53.

317

of the most holy merit of Christ, elected and ordained the chosen children of God to salvation and whatever pertains to it, consequently also to faith, repentance, and conversion;—or 2nd, whether in His election God took into consideration anything good in man, namely the foreseen conduct of man, the foreseen non-resistance, and the foreseen persevering faith, and thus elected certain persons to salvation in consideration of, with respect to, on account of, or in consequence of their conduct, their non-resistance, and their faith. The *first* of these questions *we affirm,* while our *opponents deny* it, but the second question we deny, while our *opponents affirm* it.[55]

According to Loy what was at stake in "the burning question" of predestination was the universality of God's grace and justification by faith.[56] It is "believers who are elected to sonship and salvation, and as God knew from eternity who would be believers, He from eternity elected them in foresight of their faith. . . ." But neither foreknowledge nor faith is a cause of election, for "the divine election takes place on account of the mercy of God and the merits of Christ."[57] It was Loy's contention that because Missouri's doctrine of election did not take faith into account it "endangers the great central doctrine of justification by faith," which it makes subordinate to election.[58]

The term "election" was used in a narrow sense by Missouri; that is, election is *particular,* applying to those individuals who are saved and will be preserved in their faith unto the end. Missouri's opponents preferred to speak of a *general* election, God's determination that all who believe in Christ will be saved; if the term "election" is applied to an individual, it is necessary to speak of his election in view of foreseen faith. Each side claimed the support of the Formula of Concord (Article XI) for its position, the Missourians insisting that it discussed election in the narrow sense, while the anti-Missourians insisted as firmly that the Formula described a general election of grace or used the term in both senses.[59] Much heat was generated over the proper interpretation of the Formula, and despite the strong confessionalism of both parties they could not agree on the matter.

In the subtitle of his 1881 tract Walther stated that he was providing advice (guidance) for those desiring to know "whose doctrine in the present controversy concerning predestination is Lutheran, and whose is not." All participants operated from within the framework of Lutheran orthodoxy and sought to show that their positions were in harmony with traditional Lutheran teaching. They went to great lengths to demonstrate that they were genuinely and loyally Lutheran, marshaling citations and references from Luther, the Lutheran confessions, and the theologians of the Age of Orthodoxy (seventeenth century). The ultimate authority, of course, was the Bible, but as interpreted by the normative Lutheran authorities. Of the scriptural passages cited, the interpretation of Romans 8:28–30 was most frequently under dispute.[60] Nineteenth-century Lutheran theo-

318

55.
C. F. W. Walther, *The Controversy Concerning Predestination,* trans. A. Crull (St. Louis: Concordia Publishing House, 1881), p. 5.
56.
Matthias Loy, "The Burning Question," *Columbus Theological Magazine* 1 (February 1881): 1–28.
57.
Ibid., pp. 6–7.
58.
Ibid., pp. 18, 21–22.
59.
Haug, "Predestination Controversy," p. 685. Stellhorn contended that pars. 15–22 of Article XI describe election in a broad sense, par. 23 in a narrow sense.
60.
"And we know that all things work together for good to them that love God, to them who are the called according to his purpose. For whom he did foreknow, he also did predestinate to be conformed to the image of his Son, that he might be the firstborn among many brethren. Moreover whom he did predestinate, them he also called: and whom he called, them he also justified: and whom he justified, them he also glorified" (Rom. 8:28–30, K.J.V.).

logians were only infrequently cited, and nearly always in a negative way by the Missourians, but occasionally with approbation by the anti-Missourians, Iowa's Gottfried Fritschel being a case in point for the latter.[61] There was a tendency on both sides to draw extreme conclusions from the statements of the opposition, conclusions which usually were emphatically rejected. There was constant concern about what appeared to be dangerous tendencies of an opposing position.

In the course of the election controversy the Synodical Conference lost two of its strongest synods—the Joint Synod of Ohio and the Norwegian Synod. The Missouri Synod's influence was as dominant in the Synodical Conference as Walther's was among the theologians. It was Missouri's consistent position that within the Synodical Conference there must be complete agreement concerning the doctrine of election.[62] Earlier reference has been made to the Milwaukee Colloquium of early 1881, which intensified the conflict rather than contributing to its solution. The Missouri Synod's meeting at Fort Wayne the following May had far-reaching consequences for the Synodical Conference. At that time the Missouri Synod adopted as expressing its official position Walther's Thirteen Theses on election, which were also adopted by the Synodical Conference the next year. It was decided that any of their members who were convinced that Calvinism was being espoused by the Missouri Synod should sever ties with the synod; otherwise district presidents were to begin disciplinary action against them. As to relations with anti-Missourians in other Synodical Conference synods, the synod instructed its delegates to the next Synodical Conference meeting to refuse to deliberate with those who had publicly charged Missouri with Calvinism. In effect this decision severed fellowship with all of Missouri's opponents in the Synodical Conference.

Missouri's action at Fort Wayne precipitated a sharp and prompt response from the Joint Synod of Ohio. A special synodical meeting was convened at Wheeling, West Virginia, in September 1881, at which time the Joint Synod withdrew from the Synodical Conference by action taken in direct response to Missouri's Fort Wayne resolutions.[63] Joint Ohio's official teaching concerning election was made explicit in four theses adopted at that time. It was stated that those who disagreed with Ohio's doctrine and felt compelled to oppose it could not remain in the synod, an indication that Ohio was as firmly committed to the necessity of internal doctrinal unity as was Missouri. Contributing to the swiftness of Joint Ohio's reaction to Missouri's decisions was the expulsion or withdrawal during the summer of 1881 of several pastors from the Missouri Synod who sought membership in Joint Ohio. At the same time, Ohio experienced the withdrawal of several pro-Missourians. Accompanying these developments was the unsavory spectacle of congregational fights, splits, and court cases.[64] The ex-Missourians formed their own district synod within the Joint Synod of Ohio and a group of anti-Ohioans organized the Concordia Synod, which merged with Missouri.[65] The withdrawal of the Joint

---

61.
Haug, "Predestination Controversy," pp. 141, 147, 182–89.

62.
A general pastoral conference of the Missouri Synod was held in Chicago in September of 1880. Discussed were Article XI of the Formula of Concord and the concept *intuitu fidei*. By decision of the conference public writing against the synod was forbidden. According to Haug, "this conference proved that Walther's word was considered the final authority in the Missouri Synod. He had completely dominated the theological discussions . . ." (ibid., p. 699). For an informative discussion of *intuitu fidei* see Robert Preus, "The Doctrine of Election as Taught by the Seventeenth Century Lutheran Dogmaticians," *Quartalschrift—Theological Quarterly* 55 (October 1958): 229–61.

63.
For the text of Ohio's decision see Wolf, *Documents*, pp. 204–6.

64.
A study by Stephen J. Carter of the period 1880–85 indicates that 27 pastors left Missouri and joined Ohio, and 20 withdrew from Ohio, 19 of them eventually joining Missouri (Haug, "Predestination Controversy," pp. 744–45).

65.
Regarding the formation of the Concordia Synod see *Lutheran Witness*, September 7, 1882, p. 60.

Synod of Ohio from the Synodical Conference was of great importance in determining the synod's future course, making possible in time the establishment of fellowship with the Iowa Synod and the ultimate formation of the American Lutheran Church (1930).

A brief comparison of the two sets of theses adopted in 1881 will reveal differences in the teachings of the two synods. The Thirteen Theses were considered a moderate statement of the Missourian position. The first portion of the document set forth views held by all Lutherans: God wills the salvation of all men, Christ redeemed all, the means of grace are efficacious for all, and men are lost because of their unbelief and resistance to the Holy Spirit. Proceeding to election, it is stated that the elect include only persevering believers and that each elect person will assuredly be saved. Speaking directly to the controverted question, it is affirmed (Thesis IX):

1st, that the election of grace does not consist in a *mere divine foreknowing* of which men are saved; 2nd, that election of grace is also *not the mere purpose of God* to redeem and save men, so as to be a *universal* one and to pertain to *all men* in common; 3d, that election of grace does not concern those *believing for a time only* (Luke 8:13); 4th, that election of grace is not a *mere decree of God* to save all those who would believe unto the end. . . .

The cause of election is God's grace and the merit of Christ, "not anything *good* foreseen by God in the elect, not even *faith foreseen* by God in them" (Thesis X). The election of grace, therefore, is a *cause* of the salvation of the elect and whatever pertains to it (Thesis XI).[66]

Joint Ohio's Four Theses, briefer and more restricted in content, immediately addressed themselves to questions under consideration;

If by election we understand, as is done in the Formula of Concord, the entire "purpose, counsel, will, and ordination of God pertaining to our redemption, vocation, justification, and salvation," we believe, teach, and confess that election is *the cause* of our salvation and of everything that in any way pertains to it. . . . (Thesis I)

It was Joint Ohio's conviction that the Formula of Concord teaches election in a broad sense, that is, an election in Christ, faith in whom was made possible by God's provision of everything needful for man's salvation. In the second thesis the implications of a narrower understanding of election were set forth:

But if by election, as the dogmaticians generally do, we understand merely this, that from eternity God elected and infallibly ordained to salvation certain individuals in preference to others, and this according to the universal way of salvation, we believe, teach, and confess that election took place *in view of Christ's merit apprehended by faith,* or, more briefly stated but with the same sense, *in view of faith.* According to this understanding faith

66.
Wolf, *Documents,* pp. 199-203.

**precedes election in the mind of God . . . and thus
election properly speaking, is not the cause of faith.**

It was Joint Ohio's contention that if election is taken in a
narrow and particular sense (Missouri's position) it is necessary
to say that election takes place "in view of faith" and is not the
cause of faith. In this position the synod identified itself with the
dogmaticians of the Age of Orthodoxy. The mystery in election,
according to Joint Ohio, is rooted in the limitations of man's
knowledge and comprehension (Thesis III); in other words, it is
an anthropological mystery. For Missouri the mystery of election is a divine mystery into which man ought not to inquire or
try to reconcile with reason (Missouri's Thesis XII). The individual's certainty of his election is a conditional certainty, according to Joint Ohio (Thesis IV). In the early stages of the
controversy much attention was given to assurance of salvation,
and Missouri stressed that the mysterious doctrine of election is
both necessary and salutary (Missouri's Thesis XIII).[67]

321

After Joint Ohio's withdrawal from the Synodical Conference
and the defection of pastors from Missouri to Ohio, and vice
versa, relative peace was restored within each of the two synods.
The debate continued, but it was carried on from entrenched
positions with little or no effect on the views of the participants.
The question of internal doctrinal unity was no longer at stake.

As to the involvement of other German-background groups in
the Synodical Conference, both the Wisconsin and Minnesota
synods rallied around Walther's banner in a remarkable show
of unity. In 1882 the two synods met jointly in LaCrosse, Wisconsin, and under the leadership of Adolph Hoenecke and August L. Graebner formally approved the Missourian doctrine of
election and conversion. Defections of pastors and congregational schisms were held to a bare minimum.[68] An interesting
aspect of the Wisconsin Synod's participation in the election
controversy was the debate carried on between its theologians
and the theological faculty of Rostock University in Germany.
In response to a request from a congregation of the synod, the
Rostock faculty rendered a highly critical opinion of the official
teaching of the Wisconsin Synod. Chief participants in the discussion that followed were Graebner and August W. Dieckhoff
of Rostock.[69]

The Norwegian Synod, in addition to the Joint Synod of
Ohio, withdrew from the Synodical Conference as a result of its
involvement in the predestination controversy. The withdrawal
was precipitated by the refusal of the Synodical Conference to
seat Friedrich A. Schmidt, an official delegate of the Norwegian
Synod, at its Chicago convention in October 1882, and without
giving him an opportunity to defend himself against charges of
accusing Missouri of Calvinism and of creating dissension in
congregations. This action was consistent with the policy spelled
out by the Missouri Synod at its Fort Wayne meeting a year
earlier. Whatever the provocation for which he was responsible
because of his polemical style, many in his own synod felt that
Schmidt had been unfairly treated. The disunity which pre-

67.
Ibid., pp. 203-4.
68.
Haug, "Predestination Controversy," pp.
802-12.
69.
Ibid., pp. 857-69.

vailed within the Norwegian Synod was evident in the varying attitudes of its delegates toward the Schmidt case.[70] Peter A. Rasmussen, a prominent supporter of Schmidt, crystallized support within the Norwegian Synod for withdrawal from the Synodical Conference.[71] At the grass-roots level there was not much enthusiasm for the Norwegian alliance with the Germans in any case. Even the pro-Missouri leaders of the Norwegian Synod advocated withdrawal in the hope that it would lead to the restoration of peace and unity to the synod. In 1883 the Norwegian Synod severed its connections with the Synodical Conference. As was true of Joint Ohio's withdrawal, this one was fraught with important consequences for the future. The Norwegian Synod's break with the Missourians in 1883 paved the way for the eventual unification of the great majority of Norwegian-American Lutherans in 1917 (Norwegian Lutheran Church of America).[72]

Election and related issues were discussed as intensively in the Norwegian Synod as among the German Lutherans of the Synodical Conference. A voluminous literary production in the Norwegian language was the result. Essentially the same doctrinal ground was covered as by the Germans, with some slight variations in emphasis.[73] In contrast to the situation in the Joint Synod of Ohio, about two-thirds of the pastors and congregations of the Norwegian Synod sided with Walther in the dispute. The strength of Norwegian Missourianism is accounted for by the fact that many pastors in the synod had been trained for the ministry under Walther, most of its officials including synodical president Herman A. Preus supported him, and the leading exponents of Walther's teaching included such able and persuasive men as pastors Ulrik V. Koren and Jacob A. Ottesen, Luther College president Lauritz Larsen, and Schmidt's professorial colleagues Hans G. Stub and Johannes Ylvisaker. Among the leading advocates of the anti-Missourian position, in addition to Schmidt, were Bernt J. Muus, John N. Kildahl, Markus O. Bockman, and Thorbjorn N. Mohn, president of St. Olaf College.[74]

There is no need to repeat issues already touched upon, but two aspects of the Norwegian controversy may be noted. The first has to do with the two "forms" of election which have been taught in the Lutheran church, the second with the prominence given to the doctrine of conversion. The "first form" of election was that set forth by Walther and the Missourians—election unto faith. The "second form" was that espoused by their opponents—election in view of foreseen faith. Complicating the situation among Norwegians was the fact that the Formula of Concord was not well-known inasmuch as the Church of Norway had never officially subscribed to it. Moreover, Bishop Pontoppidan's *Explanation* of Luther's Small Catechism, beloved by clergy and laity alike and used as a basis of instruction for confirmation, specifically taught the second form of election.[75] Most Norwegian Missourians were more tolerant of the second form of teaching than their German counterparts. As early as 1881 Stub had conceded that while the second form was inferior

70.
E. Clifford Nelson and Eugene L. Fevold, *The Lutheran Church Among Norwegian-Americans,* 2 vols. (Minneapolis: Augsburg Publishing House, 1960), 1:264–65; Haug, "Predestination Controversy," pp. 751–77.
71.
Evangelisk Luthersk Kirketidende 10 (1883): 20–25.
72.
Nelson and Fevold, *Lutheran Church Among Norwegian-Americans,* 1:264–65.
73.
Leading participants kept informed as to what was happening and being written in both arenas of the dispute.
74.
During 1886–90 the anti-Missourians operated a theological seminary at St. Olaf College with Schmidt and Bockman as professors.
75.
Both the Church of Norway and the Church of Denmark subscribed to the three ecumenical creeds, the Augsburg Confession, and Luther's Small Catechism.

to the first because synergistic error could more easily hide behind it, it represented a Lutheran position that could be maintained without falling into doctrinal error. Stub personally was committed to the first form.[76] This position regarding the two forms of teaching was of much future importance inasmuch as the 1917 merger, which united about 90 percent of Norwegian-American Lutherans, was made possible by the Madison Agreement (1912), which acknowledged the legitimacy of both forms of teaching concerning election. The Madison Agreement was a practical rather than a theological resolution of the controversy among Norwegians. The 1917 merger of Norwegians was sharply criticized by the Missouri Synod as resting on a doctrinal compromise, and a small minority of the Norwegian Synod refused to participate in the merger for that reason. The minority effected a separate organization now known as the Evangelical Lutheran Synod.

The doctrine of conversion was the focus of much debate among the Norwegians. This issue, as earlier noted, was also to the fore in the discussion among the Germans. Walther regarded the question of conversion as central to the entire debate.[77] Perhaps because of the powerful influence of the Haugean Revival in Norway the question was a particularly sensitive one for Norwegian-Americans. A prominent Norwegian Missourian formulated the issue as follows:

In the last analysis is God's gift of faith through the Word contingent upon something in man, or is it received by grace alone for Christ's sake? Is the ultimate decision for salvation in God's hands or in man's? In his opinion the anti-Missourians were guilty of synergism because, as he believed, they made man's choice, or decision, or refraining from resistance ultimately decisive, despite their ascribing salvation to God's grace and Christ's merit. What is at stake is the sovereignty of grace.[78]

A Norwegian anti-Missourian retorted that the stated position jeopardized faith, for man thereby is regarded as a totally passive object upon whom grace works irresistibly in the Calvinistic manner.[79] Although he contended that the central issue was justification by faith, in fact the discussion focused increasingly on conversion.[80] With conversion under consideration, the anti-Missourian formulation of the issue could be expressed in a question such as: Are all men whom God calls through the Word able to respond in faith, or are only those individuals whom God has elected able to do so? The anti-Missourians affirmed that God's offer of grace extended to all and that anyone who came within the Holy Spirit's influence was, through God's empowering grace, able to respond in faith. Much attention was given to the nature of man's resistance to grace and the operation of grace upon his will.[81]

The discussion of this topic was difficult, and positions adopted required frequent clarification, restatement, and modification. While the Missourians stressed man's total passivity and conversion as the occurrence of an instant, the other side contended for the possibility of man's response through prevenient grace and regarded conversion more broadly, as begin-

76.
Om Naadevalget: Guds Ord og den lutherske Bekjendelses Laere derom (Decorah, Iowa: Den norske Synodes Bogtrykkeri, 1881), pp. 17–32.
77.
Haug, "Predestination Controversy," p. 468.
78.
Jakob A. Ottesen, "Det egentlige Stridspunkt," *Evangelisk Luthersk Kirketidende* 9 (1882): 733–40, 749–58.
79.
Friedrich A. Schmidt, "Hvad der i Virkeligheden strides om," *Lutherske Vidnesbyrd* 2 (1883): 5–15.
80.
Bernt J. Muus acknowledged that inasmuch as the Missourians insisted on discussing conversion rather than election, the former was the basic issue. See *Lutherske Vidnesbyrd* 3 (1884): 545.
81.
The question of man's resistance to grace (whether willful or natural) and how it is overcome was much discussed among the theologians of Missouri, Ohio, and Iowa.

ning with the sinner's awakening and culminating in regeneration. Both sides frequently claimed that they had been misrepresented or misunderstood by their opponents. Undeniably both sides were endeavoring to be faithful to the classic Lutheran position that salvation is by grace alone through faith alone and that failure to believe in Christ is entirely man's responsibility.

The final split in the Norwegian Synod was adumbrated by a number of practical problems that intensified hard feelings and polarized the church body—depositions of pastors by congregations, squabbles over ordinations, editorial policies of periodicals, disputed elections of district officers, and the like. The anti-Missourians began to function as an identifiable fellowship within the synod, collecting funds for activities parallel to those of the synod proper, including the establishment in 1886 of a private seminary in conjunction with St. Olaf College. Many of the anti-Missourian pastors were younger men who were rejecting synodical leadership.[82] The withdrawal during 1887–88 of anti-Missourian pastors and congregations, comprising about one-third of the Norwegian Synod's membership, provided the occasion for a merger movement which quickly gained momentum and culminated in the formation in 1890 of the United Norwegian Lutheran Church in America, about which more will be said later.

Although Lutheran church bodies outside the orbit of the Synodical Conference generally pursued a "hands-off" policy (the Iowa Synod being a notable exception), their sympathies were mainly with the opponents of Walther and the Missourians. One significant formal evaluation of the issues of the controversy from an outside source was the scholarly *Opinion* of the conservative and confessional faculty of Philadelphia Seminary.[83] It was given in response to a request from the General Council's New York Ministerium, which had been affected directly by the predestination controversy and had lost a few pastors because of it. The *Opinion*, which included a valuable historical introduction, was restrained and cautious in tone. Although it opposed the use of the expression "in view of faith," it was on the whole more favorable to Missouri's opponents than to the Missourians.[84] Insofar as contemporary Lutheran theologians of Europe expressed themselves on the subject of election, they were generally critical of Missouri, but notable exceptions were the strongly pro-Missouri theologians of the small Lutheran Free churches of Europe.[85] Undoubtedly, the predestination controversy was an important factor in increasing the isolation of the synods of the Synodical Conference from the remainder of American Lutheranism and from much of European Lutheranism as well.

That the election controversy of the 1880s was of great importance for the future of American Lutheranism is an incontrovertible fact. In retrospect one may discern both positive and negative features, with the influence of the latter outweighing the former. The participants were earnest and zealous contestants for the truth as they understood it. Their concern for the

82.
Evangelisk Luthersk Kirketidende 13 (1886): 114.

83.
Text in *Lutheran Church Review* 3 (1884): 223–36.

84.
Haug, "Predestination Controversy," p. 852.

85.
Ibid., pp. 813–30.

86.
Sydney E. Ahlstrom, "Facing the New World: Augustana and the American Challenge," in *Centennial Essays* (Rock Island, Ill.: Augustana Press, 1960), pp. 16–17.

Lutheran doctrinal heritage led them to a serious study of the confessions of the church and its theologians, a study, however, that was often rather limited as to purpose. The controversy also stimulated interest in theology in lay circles, for whom a number of pamphlets and tracts were written. Theological writing was stimulated, but preoccupation with the election issue probably delayed the entrance of Lutheran theologians into the broader arena of American scholarship. It can be said that the disputants had basic Lutheran concerns—God's glory and grace, justification by faith, and human responsibility—and assisted many laymen to a greater concern for them as well.

At the same time, valid insights tenaciously held, combined with insistence on complete unity in teaching and little charity for the point of view of one's opponent, produced negative consequences with which American Lutherans were to live for a long time. Immediately obvious was the adverse affect on support given such synodical enterprises as education and missions. In the wake of the controversy there were many instances of fractured personal relationships, congregational splits, a synodical schism, the destruction of fellowship among synods, and even a number of lawsuits to determine ownership of disputed church property. Such aspects of the predestinarian conflict left long-lasting scars on the body of American Lutheranism. Barriers to fellowship between the Synodical Conference synods and the rest of America's Lutherans were hardened and heightened, and the ultimate goal of the union of all the Lutheran bodies was made much more difficult of achievement. The ongoing discussion far into the twentieth century of the same theological issues which were the preoccupation of the eighties is evidence of that consequence.

While one is aware of the divisive nature of the predestination controversy, it should be noted also that it had the effect of strengthening ties between certain groups of Lutherans—between the Missouri and Wisconsin synods, between the Iowa Synod and the Joint Synod of Ohio, and among the three Norwegian groups which formed a new church body in 1890.

Crucial Issues Confronting Augustana: Church Polity, Waldenstrom

Throughout its history the Augustana Synod was relatively free of theological controversy. Its remarkably smooth history was disturbed by only one schism and that a relatively small one which occurred during the period now being considered when a group of pastors and congregations influenced by the Mission Friends Movement in Sweden withdrew from Augustana and participated in the formation of the Evangelical Mission Covenant Church.[86] During the same period of time an extended discussion about church polity took place, which was the most controversial issue faced by Augustana during the late nineteenth century and potentially the most divisive. The latter problem will be considered briefly first.

In the polity dispute the conflict was between proponents of a centralized synodical organization and those advocating decentralization. The supporters of decentralization stressed the importance and authority of the individual conferences of which the synod was composed, whereas the centralists stressed the authority of the synod. The question was whether there should be strong conferences and a weak synod or vice versa. The two points of view corresponded approximately to states' rights and federalist positions on the political scene. Tuve N. Hasselquist was the most influential advocate of a strong synod. The Minnesota Conference led in the promotion of regionalism, for which Peter Sjoblom was chief spokesman. It was of crucial significance that Eric Norelius, the pioneer Minnesota leader who initially favored a weak synod, became more synodically-minded in the course of time and did not support the anticentralist forces during the seventies when he was synodical president (1874–81) and thereafter. Also involved in the polity discussion was a difference of opinion regarding the composition of the synod. Did it consist of pastors and lay delegates, of congregations, of conferences, or of pastors and congregations? Uncertainties regarding polity were finally resolved in 1893 with the adoption of a new synodical constitution. It provided for a strong synod with conferences as lesser and subordinate units. It defined the synod as consisting of pastors and congregations, thus supporting a relatively high view of the ministerial office, and it also clarified relations between the synod, conferences, and congregations. Therewith the conflict over polity came to an end, although sectionalist sentiments continued to have advocates.[87]

The Waldenstrom controversy, which led to the withdrawal of Mission Friends elements from the Augustana Synod, originated in Sweden within the influential revival movement of the time. The outstanding leader of the Swedish revival was Carl Olof Rosenius (1816–68), lay preacher and devotional writer, who nurtured a fellowship of converted people within the Church of Sweden, seeking to renew and revitalize religion within the established church. Distinctive of the Rosenian emphasis was the holding of small-group meetings (conventicles) for edification and a stress on religious experience (conversion), combined with a doctrinally orthodox theological position and a friendly attitude toward non-Lutheran evangelicals.[88] Rosenius exerted a strong influence on early leaders of the Augustana Synod. The Swedish revival embraced diverse elements, including some who tended in a separatist direction, being highly critical of the Lutheran Church of Sweden, particularly its inclusive folk-church concept of membership, ministerial authority, and confessional theology. In some parishes in Sweden groups who were committed to the idea of regenerate church membership formed societies (sometimes called St. Ansgar societies) in which lay celebration of the Lord's Supper occurred. They were known as "Mission Friends" because of their concern for "soul-winning."[89]

The most prominent leader of the more liberal wing of the revival was Paul P. Waldenstrom, a Church of Sweden pastor and a disciple of Rosenius, although he later parted company

87.
G. Everett Arden, *Augustana Heritage* (Rock Island, Ill.: Augustana Press, 1963), pp. 192–97; A. D. Mattson, *Polity of the Augustana Synod* (Rock Island, Ill.: Augustana Book Concern, 1941), pp. 93–95; Oscar F. Ander, *T. N. Hasselquist* (Rock Island, Ill.: Augustana Historical Society, 1931), pp. 129–51.
88.
Karl A. Olsson, *By One Spirit* (Chicago: Covenant Press, 1962), pp. 47–58. This volume is a comprehensive history of the Evangelical Covenant Church of America and has a helpful discussion of the nineteenth-century revival movements in Sweden.
89.
Arden, *Augustana Heritage,* pp. 160–61.

90.
Olsson, *By One Spirit*, pp. 105–15; and idem, "Paul Peter Waldenstrom and Augustana," in *The Swedish Immigrant Community in Transition*, ed. J. Dowie and Ernest M. Espelie (Rock Island, Ill.: Augustana Historical Society, 1963), pp. 110–16.
91.
On the early mission societies and their relation to Augustana see Arden, *Augustana Heritage*, pp. 162–74; and Olsson, *By One Spirit*, pp. 197–212, 237–62.
92.
Arden, *Augustana Heritage*, pp. 182–86. The branch of the Mission Friends movement led by Princell, the Mission Free Church, advocated a congregational form of polity and in 1908 was incorporated as the Swedish Evangelical Free Church.
93.
Ibid., p. 186; Karl A. Olsson, "Waldenstrom and Augustana," p. 115. Karl Olsson contends that Olof Olsson's charge that Waldenstrom set forth a Socinian (Unitarian) position was "inaccurate," but he acknowledges that his Christology raises "a suspicion as to its ultimate implications" (*By One Spirit*, p. 113).

with his theological mentor on crucial points of doctrine. He was not an advocate of separation from the Church of Sweden, but by his severe criticism of the institutional church he gave much encouragement to separatist tendencies. He attacked confessional theology, advocated simple biblical teaching, minimized the ministerial office, encouraged lay activity and leadership, and manifested perfectionist tendencies in his teaching about the fellowship of believers and in his disparagement of state church membership practices. The most controversial feature of Waldenstrom's teaching was his rejection of the traditional objective view of Christ's atonement taught by orthodox Lutherans, including Rosenius, in favor of a subjective view which restricted the significance of Christ's atonement to the impact that it makes on man. His position on the atonement evoked the major Lutheran criticism of Waldenstrom.[90]

327

When those who were influenced by the revival movement migrated to America, they ordinarily associated with congregations of the Augustana Synod. An early leader of the Mission Friends in America was lay preacher Carl A. Bjork, who came to Swede Bend, Iowa, in 1864 and provided leadership in the formation of a mission society. From there the movement to form mission societies spread. Other centers were Galesburg, Illinois, and Chicago, the latter city being the site of an independent congregation organized in 1870. In the early years the Mission Friends sometimes had the support and cooperation of Augustana pastors. Although Bjork and others like him were critical of the Augustana Synod, which they regarded as an extension of the Church of Sweden, their purpose was to be a leaven to reform and spiritualize it. However, their basically perfectionist view of the church and their persistent criticism aroused the animosity of Augustana leaders, many of whom looked with favor on the Swedish revival, having been positively influenced by it themselves.[91]

Both Augustana clergy and laity took an increasingly negative attitude toward the Mission Friends for both practical and theological reasons, considering them to be a disruptive element in the synod and questionably Lutheran on such important doctrines as those of the atonement and the church. This attitude strengthened tendencies toward separatism, and when the Mission Friends proceeded to organize themselves, three separate church bodies came into being in the first half of the 1870s.

When Waldenstrom's "new theology" was promoted in America by Augustana Synod pastor Johann G. Princell beginning in 1876, relations between the Mission Friends and Augustana further deteriorated. Princell's activities led to his suspension from the Augustana Synod in 1878.[92] Hasselquist and Olof Olsson were the leading Augustana critics of Waldenstrom's theology, particularly his view of the atonement.[93]

In 1885 the Swedish Evangelical Mission Covenant in America was formed, patterned after the organization of the Waldenstromian movement in Sweden seven years earlier. The Mission Covenant represented a merger of two Mission Friends organizations, both of which had been in existence for slightly over a decade and had borne the Lutheran name. Most of the Mission Covenant's forty-nine congregations had come out of the Augustana Synod, but the new church body did not consider itself to be Lutheran.[94]

The most obvious effect of the Waldenstrom controversy on the Augustana Synod was the removal of dissident elements and the emergence of another denominational competitor for the allegiance of Swedish immigrants. The controversy also contributed to a further strengthening of its conservative theological position as a result of being confronted by Waldenstrom's nonconfessional biblicism.[95] With the passage of time the tensions between Augustana Synod and Mission Covenant churches and people moderated, but differences in emphasis, particularly regarding the nature of the church, persisted.[96]

Several theological issues were under discussion among Norwegian and Danish branches of American Lutheranism during the last quarter of the nineteenth century. They are considered elsewhere in this section. Among the Danes there was a confrontation between pietism and Grundtvigianism, involving differences regarding the Bible, the confessions, and Christianity's relation to culture. The Norwegian Synod was involved in the predestination controversy, as this chapter has indicated, and another predominantly Norwegian church body, the Norwegian-Danish Conference, debated such questions as the nature of the congregation in relation to the church body, lay activity and the ministerial office, the significance of doctrinal declarations, and the character of theological education. Brief attention will be given to these matters in chapter 15 in connection with the discussion of a church merger.

94.
Olsson, *By One Spirit,* pp. 119–20, 313–21.
95.
Arden, *Augustana Heritage,* pp. 187–88.
96.
Olsson, "Waldenstrom and Augustana," pp. 119–20.

15   Merger Developments—
         Americanization

1.
Richard C. Wolf, *Documents of Lutheran Unity in America* (Philadelphia: Fortress Press, 1966), p. xxv.
2.
For an historical study of the three approaches to merger, together with an analysis of their significance for the twentieth century, see John H. Tietjen, *Which Way to Lutheran Unity?* (St. Louis: Concordia Publishing House, 1966).

The quarter-century from the early 1860s to the late 1880s was marked by intense controversy and increased divisions within the Lutheran family in America.[1] The decade of the sixties saw the fragmentation of Eastern Lutheranism with the withdrawal from the General Synod of its southern synods to form the General Synod, South, and the organization of the confessionally-minded General Council. The decade of the eighties witnessed the withdrawal from the Synodical Conference of the Joint Synod of Ohio and the Norwegian Synod as a result of the predestination controversy. The latter synod in turn experienced a major schism during 1887 and 1888. In addition, particularly because of the predestination controversy, attitudes and positions were polarized in such a way that the road to future Lutheran unity was made much more difficult.

Nevertheless, each of the three major general bodies included the union of American Lutheranism among its goals, but each was identified with a distinctive approach to the achievement of that goal. The General Synod advocated a policy of "inclusive confederation," desiring to include all shades and types of Lutheran emphasis and favoring a minimum of doctrinal or other tests for either fellowship or merger. The General Council favored the road of "confessional subscription," stressing earnest and unqualified acceptance of the Lutheran confessions as a requisite but demonstrating a willingness to tolerate differences in the interpretation and application of the confessions, which it expected could be overcome through a process of education and discussion. The Synodical Conference's approach was most strict and rigorous, requiring complete unity in doctrine and practice on the part of those contemplating merger or fellowship. Several conservative Midwestern synods, not members of the three bodies named, were closest to the Synodical Conference's position on merger, although the principle of unity in both doctrine and practice was applied by them in a less rigorous manner.[2]

At the same time that America's Lutherans appeared hopelessly divided and the situation seemed to be worsening rather than improving, there were forces at work in some sectors of the church which were effecting better relations and promoting union. The closing years of the nineteenth century and the early years of the twentieth saw unitive forces grow in strength and influence. Several mergers occurred in the late nineteenth century: the United Synod, South (1886), the United Norwegian Lutheran Church in America (1890), the Joint Synod of Wisconsin (1892), and the United Danish Evangelical Lutheran Church (1896). In addition, important progress was made in improved relations among the Eastern synods of the Muhlenberg tradition—General Synod, General Council, and United Synod, South—leading to their eventual reunion in 1918. Likewise, a beginning was made in the development of fellowship between the Iowa Synod and the Joint Synod of Ohio, which ultimately led to the formation of the American Lutheran Church in 1930.

Unification of Southern Lutheranism: United Synod, South

In the years following the Civil War the General Synod, South was composed of six synods—Virginia, Southwestern Virginia, North Carolina, South Carolina, Georgia, and Holston (eastern Tennessee). The Tennessee Synod, the most conservative synod in the South, did not belong. The General Synod, South was comparatively ineffective as a general church body and had not succeeded in evoking any significant loyalty from its members. Its one practical achievement was the preparation of a *Book of Worship* (1867). Other practical enterprises, missionary or educational in nature, were carried on by individual synods.

During the early seventies (1870–72) the General Synod, South experienced a crisis which threatened its continued existence. In 1871 the North Carolina Synod withdrew following disputes about a synodical paper and the location of the seminary which was to be reopened. North Carolina found itself outvoted on both issues by a Virginia–South Carolina alliance and decided to pull out. This action left the General Synod, South in two geographically separated segments. Having moved in a more confessional direction since the Civil War, the North Carolina Synod seriously explored merger possibilities with the Tennessee Synod, but without results at that time. Another blow to the General Synod, South was the withdrawal in 1872 of the Holston Synod, a daughter of the Tennessee Synod.[3] The Holston Synod joined the General Council in 1874. The General Synod, South was weakened by these withdrawals, but it survived the crisis and in 1872 resolved the seminary issue by deciding to locate it at Salem, Virginia. At the same synodical session the tiny Mississippi Synod joined its ranks. During the next decade the General Synod, South continued to be relatively dormant although it now operated a seminary, but it did serve the important function of holding the majority of the southern synods together until a more effective general body could be organized.[4]

In the early seventies, when the survival of the General Synod, South appeared uncertain, both the General Council and the General Synod explored the possibility of merger with the southern body but without success. The Civil War was still too fresh in mind and postwar reconstruction policies were too much resented in the South.[5] Again, in the early eighties, with somewhat improved North-South relations following the end of the era of Reconstruction, the possibility of merger with Lutherans in the north was promoted in some quarters, but such a move was obviously premature.[6]

3.
Socrates Henkel, *History of the Evangelical Lutheran Tennessee Synod* (New Market, Va.: Henkel & Co., 1890), pp. 153–56.
4.
The chief source for this paragraph is H. George Anderson's *Lutheranism in the Southeastern States, 1860–1886* (The Hague: Mouton, 1969), pp. 223–42.
5.
For an expression of opinion in 1872 regarding the importance of Lutheran union by a Southern leader see Wolf, *Documents,* pp. 261–62.
6.
Anderson, *Lutheranism,* pp. 251–53.

7.
Ibid., pp. 254–56.
8.
Andrew G. Voigt, "The United Synod in the South," in *The Distinctive Doctrines and Usages of the General Bodies of the . . . Lutheran Church . . .* , 4th ed. (1914), pp. 187–88.
9.
The Tennessee Synod, somewhat fearful that its independence and purity of doctrine would be jeopardized, had advocated a federation similar in structure to the Synodical Conference. The General Council granted permission for the withdrawal of the Holston Synod so that it might join the new general body.
10.
Article 1 of the constitution; Wolf, *Documents,* p. 133.
11.
Voigt, in *Distinctive Doctrines,* pp. 203–4.
12.
Ibid., pp. 194–95.
13.
Ibid., p. 184. In 1888 a resolution of non-cooperation in protest against the United Synod's position was passed by the Tennessee Synod (Henkel, *History,* pp. 245–46).
14.
Anderson, *Lutheranism,* pp. 246–48.

The groundwork for a more inclusive union of southern Lutherans was prepared when the North Carolina Synod resumed membership in the General Synod, South, particularly as a result of lay influence, and the traditionally aloof Tennessee Synod altered its stance toward merger.[7] Tensions between Tennessee and the synods with whom it was competitive in Virginia and the Carolinas had gradually diminished. A basic factor in Tennessee's changed posture was the growth of confessionalism which occurred in southern Lutheranism following the Civil War. Initially it was most evident in North Carolina, which in the past had a reputation for a relatively weak confessional position. However, as described by one of the men who contributed to the molding of the southern churches in a more traditional fashion, the spirit of southern Lutheranism was marked by a moderate conservatism, an aversion to theological controversy, and impatience with efforts to enforce uniformity in belief or practice through constraint.[8]

331

The merger effected in 1886 brought together the General Synod, South, the Tennessee Synod, and the Holston Synod into the United Synod of the Evangelical Lutheran Church in the South.[9] Its doctrinal basis was the entire Book of Concord, that is, the unaltered Augsburg Confession and the remaining Lutheran symbols "as true and Scriptural developments of the doctrines taught in the Augsburg Confession, and in the perfect harmony of one and the same pure, Scriptural faith."[10] Total baptized membership in 1886 was about 30,000, which meant that in size it was greatly overshadowed by its two northern sisters. As to polity, the function of the united synod was almost entirely advisory. The individual synods had comparatively greater authority, being responsible for ordination, the discipline of pastors, and appeals from congregations.[11] The United Synod, South maintained a theological seminary and several of the district synods operated small colleges. It assumed responsibility for its own foreign mission field in Japan, and established home mission congregations in some of the larger cities of the South while district synods concentrated their home mission efforts in the smaller towns and rural districts.[12]

It took several years for the 1886 merger to coalesce, particularly as far as the Tennessee Synod was concerned. Because the United Synod refused to take an official stand on the Four Points, which had agitated many northern bodies, and concerning which the Tennessee Synod had adopted a conservative position prior to the merger, the latter felt unable to cooperate in the United Synod's missionary and educational activities.[13] The Tennessee Synod opposed lodge membership and chiliasm, as did the Holston Synod which had been a member of the General Council, and disapproved of pulpit and altar fellowship with non-Lutherans (the Galesburg Rule). The Holston Synod approved the interpretation of the Galesburg Rule which permitted exceptions to the general rule regulating fellowship, and thus was more liberal than Tennessee on that issue.[14] Not until 1900 were the scruples of the Tennessee Synod overcome. At that time a resolution of the United Synod affirmed that its synods were obligated to maintain practices which accorded with the Word of God and the confessions. Thereafter, the Tennessee Synod actively cooperated in the work of the United Synod.[15] In general, the southern churches lacked enthusiasm for the Galesburg Rule, not for theological reasons primarily but because it was stricter than traditional southern practice regarding relations with non-Lutherans.[16]

The formation of the United Synod, South had significance for the larger picture of Lutheran unity. It provided an example for other synods to follow in effecting union. Sharing the same origins as the General Synod and General Council, it functioned as a mediator between the two large northern organizations, serving as an effective catalyst in the improvement of relations between them. It played an important role in the final merger of the three bodies.

Rapprochement in Eastern Lutheranism

The gradually improving relations among Eastern Lutherans was one of the significant late-nineteenth-century phenomena relating to Lutheran unity. Not that the course of intersynodical relations was marked by uninterrupted progress or improvement. There were periodic sharp clashes between leaders of the General Synod and General Council—between James A. Brown (GS) and Charles Porterfield Krauth (GC) in the seventies, between Milton Valentine (GS) and Adolph Spaeth (GC) in the eighties, and between James Richard (GS) and Theodore E. Schmauk (GC) in the early twentieth century. Such confrontations were evidence of continuing rivalry in the midst of the process of rapprochement.[17]

In the early seventies an effort was made to establish communication among the separated Eastern synods when the General Synod proposed an exchange of delegates with other Lutheran bodies.[18] The General Council replied that it was not ready for such an interchange because the two bodies "do not sustain the same relation to the Confession of the Church" and an exchange of delegates "would involve not only an evasion and ignoring of the important points upon which we differ, but a formal and distinct recognition by each body, of the position of the other, while in reality each body at heart condemns the position of the other." Instead, the General Council proposed the holding of a colloquium or free conference of Lutherans who subscribed to the Augsburg Confession.[19] Such an assembly, called a "free diet," was convened in 1877 through the initiative of concerned individuals, and a second one in the following year. The purpose as expressed in the invitation to the first diet was "to discuss living subjects of general worth and importance to all Lutherans."[20] Although open to all Lutherans, the diets were attended chiefly by members of the General Synod and the General Council, with a much smaller number from the General Synod, South. Sharp differences of opinion were evident, but there was also much friendly discussion, and the two diets served the important function of bringing together men who had been

15.
Voigt, in *Distinctive Doctrines,* pp. 184–85.
16.
Anderson, *Lutheranism,* p. 247.
17.
Robert H. Fischer, "The Healing of the Schism Between the General Synod and the General Council: Sources for a Reevaluation," *Gettysburg Seminary Bulletin,* Fall 1968, pp. 34–35.
18.
Wolf, *Documents,* p. 247.
19.
Ibid., pp. 248–49.
20.
Ibid., p. 251.

separated for over a decade and of reestablishing lines of communication. Years later Henry Eyster Jacobs described the great service the two diets had rendered "in moulding opinion and cultivating mutual esteem."[21]

By the mid-seventies the General Synod, South was ready to establish fraternal relations with both general bodies in the East, sending an official delegate to the convention of the General Synod in 1877 and to the General Council in 1878.[22] This practice was continued and both of the large bodies responded by sending delegates to the conventions of the General Synod, South. It was not until 1895, however, that the General Synod and the General Council were ready to exchange fraternal delegates. Further evidence of the interest of the General Synod, South in nurturing closer intersynodical relations was the decision of its 1880 meeting to channel funds received for foreign missions to the appropriate board of either northern body.[23]

The most significant endeavor in which the three general bodies cooperated was the preparation of an English liturgical service known as the Common Service. Since about mid-century, leadership in liturgical matters in American Lutheranism had been provided by the Ministerium of Pennsylvania and the General Council. This was particularly because of the interest and expertise of Beale M. Schmucker, the confessionally-minded son of Samuel S. Schmucker, with the cooperation of such leaders as Charles Porterfield Krauth and Joseph A. Seiss. It was their desire to restore in America the liturgical tradition of the Lutheran church in worship, hymnology, and services for ministerial acts. They focused attention on providing this heritage in the English language, but an important impact was also made on German language worship forms. The *Church Book* of the General Council appeared in 1868, containing a liturgy and hymnal, to which a series of orders for ministerial acts was later added. The influence of Beale Schmucker and others of similar liturgical interests was to be seen in the *Book of Worship* (1867) of the General Synod, South, an improved service of the General Synod (the Washington Service, 1869), and the Tennessee Synod's adoption of the *Church Book*.[24]

The joint project to produce a common service was initiated by the General Synod, South, which in 1876 proposed that "with the view to promote uniformity in worship and strengthening the bonds of unity throughout all our churches" the three general bodies confer concerning "the feasibility of adopting but one Book containing the same hymns and the same order of services and Liturgic forms to be used in the public Worship of God in all the English speaking Evang. Lutheran Churches of the United States."[25] The General Council made its participation contingent upon acceptance of the following rule for determining liturgical questions: "The common consent of the pure Lutheran liturgies of the sixteenth century, and when there is not an entire agreement among them the consent of the largest number of greatest weight."[26] That the other two bodies agreed to the rule was a reflection of the spirit of confessionalism and traditionalism which had become dominant in American Lu-

21.
The First General Conference of Lutherans in America . . . 1898 (Philadelphia: General Council Board of Publication, 1899), p. 31.
22.
Anderson, *Lutheranism,* p. 249.
23.
Ibid., pp. 251–52.
24.
Luther D. Reed, *The Lutheran Liturgy* (Philadelphia: Muhlenberg Press, 1947; rev. ed., 1960), chap. 8.
25.
Wolf, *Documents,* p. 253.
26.
Ibid., pp. 253–54.

theranism. A joint committee produced the Common Service which appeared in 1888. Key figures in the committee's work were Beale M. Schmucker (General Council), Edward T. Horn (United Synod, South), and George U. Wenner (General Synod), particularly the first two.

The Common Service was incorporated into the respective combined service books and hymnals of the three bodies and made an important contribution toward drawing their members closer together. Some congregations and synods were more open to its introduction than others, and in some quarters (particularly within the General Synod) there was bitter opposition to it. In the course of time several synods which did not belong to any of the three bodies, including the English Synod of Missouri, received permission for its use in their English-speaking congregations.[27] After having produced the Common Service the joint committee, which continued to function for several years, prepared a new English translation of the Augsburg Confession and of Luther's Small Catechism and worked at the preparation of a common hymnal and forms for occasional services.

By the end of the century the three Eastern bodies were cooperating in foreign missions, deaconess work, and the exchange of official visitors. A beginning had been made in the effort to avoid competition and friction in the establishment of home missions, but rivalry between the General Synod and the General Council continued in that area of work.[28] Both lay and ministerial contacts leading to increased understanding and friendship resulted from such activities as celebrations of the 400th anniversary of Luther's birth in 1883, various associations for youth work culminating in the formation of the Luther League in 1895, and local organizations such as the Lutheran Social Union of Philadelphia. A consciousness of kinship with Lutherans of other synods was promoted through influential books such as histories of American Lutheranism by Edmund J. Wolf (1889) and Henry Eyster Jacobs (1893), professors of the Gettysburg and Philadelphia seminaries respectively, the informative *Distinctive Doctrines and Usages of the General Bodies of the Evangelical Lutheran Church in the United States* (1893), and various Lutheran handbooks and almanacs.[29] Moreover, many members of the three bodies knew the ties of kinship, a common congregational membership in the past, and similar educational experiences, having attended the same institutions and studied under the same professors.[30]

In 1898 a "general conference" of members of the General Council, General Synod, and United Synod, South was held in Philadelphia, the purpose of which was "to prepare the way for a better understanding and a more harmonious co-operation among the Lutherans in the bodies named."[31] The conference was planned and officially recognized by the three church bodies, whereas the diets held two decades earlier had been arranged by interested individuals. Both doctrine and the practical work of the church were discussed. The tenor of the conference was congenial and the differences which appeared

27.
Reed, *Lutheran Liturgy,* pp. 183-97.
28.
First General Conference, p. 34.
29.
Abdel Ross Wentz, *A Basic History of Lutheranism in America* (Philadelphia: Muhlenberg Press, 1955), pp. 280-81.
30.
The Second General Conference of Lutherans in America . . . 1902 (Newberry, S.C.: Lutheran Publication Board, 1904), p. 26.
31.
First General Conference, p. 16.

cut across synodical lines. Two additional general conferences of similar composition and character followed in 1902 and 1904. It was understood that the purpose of the general conferences was to promote understanding and not to plan for merger, which nearly all who were involved would have regarded as premature. Henry Eyster Jacobs concluded his opening address to the 1898 conference by saying: "We have come together . . . in the fear of God to meet the issues that our calling demands; and to learn, by a comparison of judgments, where we are and whither Providence directs us."[32] The general conferences at the turn of the century represented an important step in developing the understanding and confidence which made merger possible less than two decades in the future.

The United Norwegian Lutheran Church in America (1890)

The period from 1870 to the end of the century was a turbulent one for Norwegian Lutherans in America. More fragmented than their sister Scandinavians, they were divided into four church bodies as of 1870.[33] The largest by far of the Norwegian-American bodies was the Norwegian Synod (1853). Well organized and ably led, it represented the traditional worship and practice of the Church of Norway combined with zeal for doctrinal orthodoxy. Through its leadership it had established close ties with the Missouri Synod, in whose seminary its theological students were trained, and with whom it joined in the establishment of the Synodical Conference in 1872. If the Norwegian Synod represented the right wing of Norwegian-American Lutheranism, the group popularly known as Eielsen's Synod (1846), identified by the name of its pioneer leader Elling Eielsen, represented the left wing. Its roots were in the Haugean Awakening in Norway,[34] and it promoted lay preaching, "living" Christianity, a "low-church" skepticism regarding formal worship and clerical vestments, and suspicion of clerical authority and ecclesiastical organization. The Eielsen Synod early discovered that in the American free church environment it could not simply be a spiritual movement comparable to the Haugeanism of Norway which presupposed the existence of an established church. A growing concern for churchliness, church order, and ministerial education developed in the group. This resulted in 1876 in a reorganization of Eielsen's Synod under the leadership of Osten Hanson and the adoption of a new name, "Hauge's Synod." Increased organizational efficiency and churchliness meant no abatement of concern for Christian experience and lay activity. The organizational changes displeased the venerable Eielsen, who resisted them and continued Eielsen's Synod on the old basis with a tiny following of pastors and congregations. Henceforth Eielsen's Synod was on the periphery of Norwegian-American Lutheran developments, but it continued an isolated existence until in the 1960s when it faded away as a synodical organization.

In 1870 the number of Norwegian Lutheran synods was increased from two to four with the formation of the Norwegian-Danish Augustana Synod in America and the Conference for

32.
Ibid., p. 34.
33.
By the end of 1870 there were four Norwegian-American Lutheran church bodies: Norwegian Synod, Eielsen's Synod, Norwegian-Danish Augustana Synod, and the Norwegian-Danish Conference.
34.
See chapter 10.

the Norwegian-Danish Evangelical Lutheran Church in America.[35] The latter group was usually identified simply as "the Conference." Those who formed the two new bodies had a common origin, having since 1860 been members of the Scandinavian Augustana Synod, in which the Swedish element was dominant. Prior to that they had been part of the Synod of Northern Illinois, in which they had associations with English-speaking Lutherans of the General Synod. Differences within the Norwegian portion of the Scandinavian Augustana Synod became evident in the course of the 1860s. The older element was composed of men strongly stamped by Haugean pietism. They were lay-oriented, more concerned with experience than doctrine, and "low church" in worship attitudes, but they were also Americanized to a degree. The latter was evident in their encouragement of the English language and in their openness to the religious practice and polity of American Protestantism, which was combined with a dislike for some traditional Norwegian rites and ceremonies. Even prior to membership in the Synod of Northern Illinois a couple of pastors of this group, Paul Andersen and Ole Andrewson, had been in the liberal and Americanized Franckean Synod. Another of their leaders was Ole J. Hatlestad.

Among more recent immigrants who found their way into the Scandinavian Augustana Synod was a more churchly element which, while Haugean in spirit, was devoted to the traditional worship, ceremonies, and ecclesiastical garb of the Church of Norway. Critical of Americanizing tendencies, it identified with the nationalistic Dano-Norwegian tradition. This second group was led by pastors who migrated in the 1860s: Botolf Gjeldaker, Johan Olsen, Johannes Muller-Eggen, and August Weenaas. There were no doctrinal differences between the two groups, both being unequivocally committed to the Augsburg Confession, which had given its name to their synod (Augustana). The difficulties within the Norwegian segment of the Scandinavian Augustana Synod were partially an expression of the tensions between loyalty to a heritage and Americanization.

The process of separating from the Swedes for nationalistic reasons in 1870 provided the occasion for the two Norwegian groups to organize separately. The Norwegian Augustana Synod, formed under the leadership of Ole J. Hatlestad by those representing the older element in the Scandinavian Augustana Synod, remained a small, struggling synod during its twenty-year existence, seemingly never quite able to surmount its problems. Its strongly Haugean cast meant that it was quite similar to Hauge's Synod, from whom it was chiefly differentiated by its greater association with Americans and its cultivation of the English language. Although maintaining contact with the General Council, it never joined. The synod operated Augustana Academy and Theological Seminary, which was initially located in Marshall, Wisconsin. It was then moved to Beloit in northwestern Iowa, where seminary and preparatory departments were separated, with the latter being moved across the state line to Canton, South Dakota. When merger was proposed

336

35.
The word "Danish" was eliminated from the name of the Augustana group in 1878. Several Danish pastors and congregations left the conference in 1884 to form the Danish Evangelical Church Association (the Blair Church). For a discussion of the Norwegian-Danish Augustana Synod and the conference see E. Clifford Nelson and Eugene L. Fevold, *The Lutheran Church Among Norwegian-Americans,* 2 vols. (Minneapolis: Augsburg Publishing House, 1960), 1:191–238.

in the late 1880s the Norwegian Augustana Synod responded enthusiastically.

The Conference rapidly developed into a large and vigorous church body. Its goal was to occupy a position between the Norwegian Synod on one side and extreme Haugeanism on the other. The term "conference" suggested the decentralized and congregation-centered polity of the church body. During its first years its most influential leaders were August Weenaas and Claus L. Clausen, formerly of the Norwegian Synod. Weenaas was president of Augsburg Seminary, begun in Marshall, Wisconsin, in 1869, the year before the separation from the Swedes, and moved to Minneapolis in 1872. Between 1870 and 1890 the major stream of events among Norwegian Lutherans outside the Norwegian Synod flowed in Conference channels.[36]

The faculty of Augsburg Seminary played a decisive role in shaping the character and spirit of the Conference. To begin with, the sole professor was Weenaas, a typical product of the Johnsonian Awakening in Norway, combining the characteristic concerns of both pietism and a moderate confessionalism. He was joined by three young colleagues in 1873-74: Sven Oftedal, George Sverdrup, and Sven R. Gunnersen. Both Weenaas and Gunnersen returned to Norway in the 1880s (Weenaas left Augsburg and returned to Norway for the first time in 1876), leaving Sverdrup and Oftedal as the shaping influences at Augsburg. Shaped by the growing democratic social-political movement in Norway, as well as by the religious awakenings of the time, the young professors were dedicated to living Christianity, lay activity, democratically organized and led congregations, free from domination by the state (Norway) or by the clergy (Norway and America). Their views were sometimes expressed in such slogans as "a free church in a free state," or "living Christianity in free congregations."[37] Under the Augsburg professors an integrated educational program for training ministers was developed, comprising academy, college, and theological departments, with the theological professors involved on all three levels of teaching.

The determining factor in the Conference's external relationships, particularly during its first decade, was its conflict and competition with the Norwegian Synod. Its theological position was frequently expressed as over against that of the Norwegian Synod. Beginning in the sixties and continuing to about 1880, acrimonious debates were carried on between leaders of the synod and the Conference (Scandinavian Augustanans in the sixties) over absolution, the gospel, and justification.[38] In each case one observes a clash between the synod's concern for that which is objective, the given-ness of God's redemption and grace, on the one hand, and the Haugean and "orthodox pietistic" concern for the subjective, personal appropriation of grace, on the other. Thus, for the Conference the gospel or absolution (the personal application of the gospel) was God's offer of forgiveness; for the synod it was the declaration or, more strongly put, the impartation of forgiveness. In regard to justification the Conference insisted that no one is justified before he has faith,

36.
Ibid., p. 216.
37.
Although Weenaas clashed with Sverdrup and Oftedal, he shared fundamental viewpoints with them. For a characterization of the Augsburg professors see Eugene L. Fevold, *The Lutheran Free Church* (Minneapolis: Augsburg Publishing House, 1969), pp. 30-33.
38.
These theological disputes are discussed in Nelson and Fevold, *Lutheran Church Among Norwegian-Americans,* 1:241-53.

337

whereas the synod stressed that all men were justified through Christ's atonement (justification of the world).[39] The same two concerns, for the objective and the subjective, were involved in the predestination controversy in which the Norwegian Missourians taught God's election as the cause of faith (objective) and the Anti-Missourians held to election in view of faith (subjective). Although the Conference was not involved in the predestination controversy, its position was consistently Anti-Missourian.

At the same time that its rapid growth was evidence that the Conference was thriving, its internal development was hindered by the emergence of two parties, the Old School and the New School.[40] It is necessary to compare the two briefly in order to understand the problems which emerged in the United Norwegian Lutheran Church following the 1890 merger. The two groups emerged in the mid-1870s, although the terms "Old School" and "New School" were not applied to them until several years later. The New School leaders were Sverdrup and Oftedal. The Old School included such original founders of the Conference as Claus L. Clausen, Johan Olsen, and Botolf Gjeldaker, who claimed that an alien spirit had been introduced by the new Augsburg professors.

There were differences in spirit, emphasis, and temperament between the two groups, but they were somewhat intangible. Doctrinal issues were not at stake. Differences about practical matters such as the operation of Augsburg Seminary and personality conflicts were involved. Two areas of difference seem to have been most important: the concept of a "free church" and the significance of doctrinal statements. The New School championed free congregations and opposed ministerial authoritarianism, which it believed existed in the Norwegian Synod. For them freedom included congregational self-government, a democratic ministry, and unrestricted lay activity. The Old School believed that the threat to congregational freedom was not as great as pictured by the opposition, felt that the New School failed to appreciate the proper relation between the pastoral office and the priesthood of believers, and favored supervised lay activity. The entire Conference was critical of Missourian, or Norwegian Synod, orthodoxy and the spirit of exclusivism it engendered over against those with whom there was not full doctrinal agreement. The New School was especially fearful of what it viewed as doctrinal despotism, and it took a negative attitude toward conferences for doctrinal discussion and toward extraconfessional doctrinal statements as a basis for church fellowship, insisting that the doctrinal beliefs of the congregation expressed in Luther's Small Catechism and the commonly used explanation of the same by Pontoppidan was sufficient. The Old School believed that New School men undervalued doctrine, minimized the importance of doctrinal discussion, and by their attitude invited fuzziness in doctrinal teaching. Another related aggravation for the Old School was the New School's initial lack of enthusiasm for merger with

39.
During the eighties it was agreed to discontinue use of the term "justification of the world" because of the possibilities of misunderstanding, but the substance of the teaching was unchanged. Lauritz Larsen and J. A. Bergh, *Referat af Forhandlinger i en Frikonference i St. Ansgar, Iowa . . . 1881* (Decorah, Iowa: Den Norske Synodes Trykkeri, 1881), pp. 23, 25.
40.
The Norwegian terms were "*den nye Retning*" and "*den gamle Retning*," the noun meaning "tendency."

other synods, since the latter believed that each of the church bodies had a legitimate vocation and that cooperation in practical church work was more important than merger.[41]

The tensions between the two schools were formally resolved as a result of the annual meeting of 1883, and the last half-dozen years of the Conference's history were marked by internal harmony and external development, but the old antipathies remained below the surface, erupting in the Augsburg Controversy of the 1890s.

The fragmented condition of Norwegian-American Lutheranism provided a fertile field for merger agitation, particularly since those who were separated shared a common religious heritage and since the spiritual needs of tens of thousands of Norwegian immigrants cried out for a united outreach. All of the synods except Eielsen's tiny group were interested in union. Through the leadership of Peter A. Rasmussen, a Norwegian Synod pastor who had originally been associated with Eielsen, a union movement got underway in 1880. Rasmussen proposed the merger of all Norwegian-American Lutherans on the basis of their common heritage, beliefs, and practices. Numerous meetings during the 1880s brought together members of the various Norwegian groups, including foreign mission meetings promoted by Rasmussen; a series of unofficial free conferences (1881–83), particularly for doctrinal discussion; and three synodically approved joint meetings (1885–87), for the discussion of both doctrinal and practical matters. The doctrines discussed were those that had been in dispute among Norwegian Lutherans, and the practical issues considered included possible areas of cooperation in church work. In the course of these meetings men of different synods became convinced of their kinship as they tended to stress their points of agreement. Particularly significant was the rapport established between the Anti-Missourians of the Norwegian Synod and the Old School of the Conference, especially in view of the earlier hostilities between the Conference and the Norwegian Synod. It was also significant that after abstaining from the first two free conferences, New School leaders became prominent participants in the meetings, with Sverdrup playing a most important role in shaping the form of the merger.

It has been noted earlier that the divisive predestination controversy in the Norwegian Synod actually served to hasten the union movement among Norwegians. This followed from a decision of the Anti-Missourians who left the Norwegian Synod during 1887–88. They decided to promote a merger movement rather than constitute themselves another synod inasmuch as their participation in the conferences and meetings of recent years had convinced them that they were essentially at one in both doctrine and practice with the Conference, the Norwegian Augustana Synod, and Hauge's Synod. They disliked the name "Anti-Missourian" because of its negative connotation but used it of themselves in their 1889 minutes. They were commonly identified as the "Anti-Missourian Brotherhood."[42] The deci-

339

41.
A comparison of the two schools, together with references to the literature of the controversy, will be found in Nelson and Fevold, *Lutheran Church Among Norwegian-Americans,* 1:225–38.

42.
Beretning om Det andet aarlige Møde af det Antimissourisk Broderskap . . . 1889 (Northfield, Minn.: Northfield Publishing Co., 1889).

sion to work for merger made, events moved rapidly from the meeting of the joint union committee in August 1888 to the consummation of the union in June 1890.[43]

Three documents prepared the way for merger: a doctrinal settlement, a proposed constitution, and articles of union. The doctrinal settlement stated that acceptance of the Scriptures, the confessions of the Norwegian Lutheran Church (the Church of Norway), and the catechism in common use within the conferring synods and congregations (Pontoppidan's *Explanation*) constituted a sufficient basis for union. Such reference to the catechism was tantamount to elevating it to confessional status, but the synodical constitution did not list it in its confessional paragraph, which included the ecumenical creeds, the Augsburg Confession, and Luther's Small Catechism. Statements presenting a consensus of teaching regarding controverted doctrines of the recent past, especially involving the Conference and the Norwegian Synod, were drawn up, covering the atonement and justification, the gospel, absolution, Sunday observance, and predestination. The doctrinal statements, however, were not to be voted on by the conferring church bodies inasmuch as there was strong feeling against what was termed the "thesis approach" of the Missourians.[44] The constitution provided for a church structure similar to that of the Conference, having a strong congregational orientation (the church body was composed of congregations) and reflecting the desire to avoid centralized control.[45] Two provisions of the articles of union were particularly controversial in subsequent years. One designated Augsburg Seminary as the theological seminary of the new church; the other provided that immediately upon the incorporation of the new church body the boards of trustees of the merging bodies should transfer all property to the new corporation.[46]

Of the conferring groups Hauge's Synod was least enthusiastic about merger, having misgivings that its views concerning living Christianity, lay activity, and nonliturgical worship would not be properly emphasized in a merged church. Efforts to reassure on these points were unavailing, and Hauge's Synod withdrew from the merger negotiations.[47]

The United Norwegian Lutheran Church in America was formed in 1890 by the Conference, the Norwegian Augustana Synod, and the Anti-Missourian Brotherhood. Its baptized membership of approximately 152,200 made it larger than the combined membership of the Norwegian Synod (94,166) and Hauge's Synod (22,279).[48] The United Church bridged the gap between the other two, and a quarter-century later (1917) the three would be ready to unite. The United Church was committed to the principle of inclusivism within the limits of Norwegian Lutheranism and to a moderate confessionalism, requiring subscription to the basic Lutheran symbols, but in the latter regard it was not entirely consistent, as noted above. Included within it were those who prized both doctrine and piety, both churchliness and lay activity, both order and freedom. This meant that

43.
A helpful survey by a contemporary and participant is that of J. A. Bergh, "Historisk Indledning," in N. C. Brun, ed., *Fra Ungdomsaar* (Minneapolis: Augsburg Publishing House, 1915), pp. 9–40.

44.
For a discussion of merger preparations see Nelson, *Lutheran Church Among Norwegian-Americans,* 2:4–21.

45.
See the English text of the constitution, ibid., pp. 333–38.

46.
Articles of Union, ibid., pp. 338–41 (pars. 2, 22).

47.
For example, to accommodate Hauge's Synod the statement in the constitution setting forth the church's objectives was enlarged to include the statement that it "promotes Christian lay activity" (ibid., pp. 13–14).

48.
Brun, *Fra Ungdomsaar,* pp. 45–46; Hauge's Synod, *Beretning . . . 1891,* pp. 8–9. Norwegian Synod statistics for 1890 are in separate district reports for 1891: *Beretning . . . 1891;* Eastern District, pp. 74–77; Iowa District, pp. 118–21; Minnesota District, pp. 98–101.

its emphases were not as sharply delineated as those of either the Norwegian Synod or Hauge's Synod.

For over a decade the United Church was led by Gjermund Hoyme, its vigorous first president, but much of its great potential for growth and church work was inhibited by internal dissension. During most of the 1890s it was rent by a controversy centering on Augsburg Seminary. A decision of the constituting convention which designated St. Olaf College, Northfield, Minnesota, as the college of the United Church, in response to the offer of the school's board of trustees, set off a chain of events which led to the disruption of the church body. St. Olaf had not figured in the premerger negotiations because it was not owned by any of the merging groups but was a private corporation under the control of an Anti-Missourian Brotherhood constituency. This decision was regarded by Sverdrup and Oftedal and other supporters of Augsburg Seminary as a threat to the continuance of Augsburg's college department and to its whole program of integrated theological education. Latent New School suspicion of the Norwegian Synod (albeit in Anti-Missourian form) came to life. Compounding the problem was the emergence of an unanticipated legal difficulty. The Conference could not legally transfer Augsburg Seminary to the new church body because it did not actually own it. The Augsburg board, under the chairmanship of Oftedal, which legally owned the school, refused to transfer ownership because of its fears for the future of Augsburg and its educational program should the United Church gain possession of it. The Augsburg Controversy was finally resolved by a ruling of the Minnesota Supreme Court in 1898, but by that time the Lutheran Free Church had come into being.[49]

341

The Lutheran Free Church (1897)

The Friends of Augsburg, an organization formed in 1893 within the constituency of the United Church, was the forerunner of the Lutheran Free Church. Under the leadership of Sverdrup and Oftedal it drew its membership from what had been the New School of the Conference, although the two groups were not identical. Believing that the future of Augsburg Seminary was at stake, the Friends of Augsburg were primarily concerned about providing for its support. When the Augsburg board continued to refuse to transfer title to the United Church, even after the latter formally severed its connections with St. Olaf College, the church body decided to establish another theological school and no longer give support to Augsburg Seminary. The United Church Seminary began operation in the fall of 1893 at a Minneapolis location, moving in 1902 to St. Paul at the present site of Luther Theological Seminary. Its leading professors were Markus O. Bockman and Friedrich A. Schmidt.

Involved in the Augsburg Controversy, in addition to the problem of the ownership of the seminary and the nature of a theological school, was the question of the relationship of a dissenting minority to the majority of the church body of which

49.
The Augsburg Controversy is discussed in Nelson, *Lutheran Church Among Norwegian-Americans*, 2:38–81; and Fevold, *Lutheran Free Church*, pp. 61–79.

it was a part.[50] Augsburg supporters were often referred to as "the Minority," and they believed that they were being dictated to in a tyrannical manner by "the Majority." The latter believed that the decisions reached by the conventions of the church body should be accepted by all and that Augsburg Seminary should be transferred to the United Church inasmuch as a legally valid method for effecting the transfer had been worked out by lawyers. There was a clash between principles of congregational freedom and church order.

The Friends of Augsburg, while still members of the United Church, carried on a program of church work parallel to that of the church body, including support not only of Augsburg but also of home mission and foreign mission programs. In addition it began to ordain its own theological candidates. Between 1893 and 1896 relations between the Minority and Majority steadily deteriorated, with provocation and blame on both sides. In 1897 the Friends of Augsburg separated from the United Church and formed the Lutheran Free Church. The previous year the United Church had initiated court action to resolve the ownership problem. The case reached the Minnesota Supreme Court which in 1898 ruled that the Augsburg board and corporation, and not the United Church, were the legal owners of Augsburg Seminary. The unincorporated Conference had never legally owned the school and thus had no right to agree to transfer it to the United Church. The court was not ruling on an ethical question and suggested that since the United Church possessed whatever rights the old Conference had had in relation to Augsburg Seminary it could pursue the matter in a court of equity. Fortunately at this point an out-of-court settlement was reached which provided for a division of Augsburg's assets, the Augsburg Seminary corporation retaining the campus and school property and the United Church the endowment fund and a portion of the library's book collection.[51] The Augsburg Controversy left deep wounds, which were a long time in healing. Relations between the Lutheran Free Church and the United Church continued to be strained until the latter's participation in the merger of 1917. The division produced by the conflict was finally healed as recently as 1963 when the Lutheran Free Church merged with the new American Lutheran Church.

The basic document upon which the Lutheran Free Church was founded was "Fundamental Principles and Rules for Work," which had been prepared by Sverdrup. The first section of the document, consisting of twelve short articles, deals with the congregation (the local church) and sets forth the Lutheran Free Church ideal of free and living congregations.[52] The key principle is the first, which states: "According to the Word of God, the congregation is the right form of the Kingdom of God on earth." "Fundamental Principles" treats of the basic principles of congregational polity and their practical implications. From the beginning the primary interests of the Lutheran Free Church were twofold: concern for the independence of the congregation and stress on personal religious experience. Its members believed that their dedication to the latter justified their

342

50.
The Friends of Augsburg in 1894 adopted an eight-point "Program of the Minority" (Friends of Augsburg, *Beretning . . . 1894*, pp. 78–80).
51.
The text of the final settlement may be found in Lutheran Free Church, *Beretning . . . 1899*, pp. 30–33; and in Brun, *Fra Ungdomsaar*, pp. 118ff.
52.
Texts in Norwegian and English may be found in Fevold, *Lutheran Free Church*, apps. A, B.

separate existence fully as much as their congregational principles.[53] Its Haugean piety stressed lay preaching (lay witnessing) and expressed itself in a preference for free and informal worship services.

"Rules for Work," the second section of the basic document, functioned as a constitution although it was not designated as such. The "Rules" did not provide for a synodical organization or a church body. The Lutheran Free Church was not a synod but an association or fellowship of independent congregations through which common goals could be promoted and common endeavors and joint activities could be carried out. The goals were the development of spiritual life and freedom together with cooperation in practical church work. The requirement for membership in the Lutheran Free Church was subscription to the ecumenical creeds, Luther's Small Catechism, and the unaltered Augsburg Confession (the symbols of Norwegian Lutheranism) and acceptance of "Fundamental Principles and Rules for Work."[54] To insure the autonomy of the congregation the annual meeting was given no authority, and no limitations were placed on the number who could attend. Any member of a Lutheran Free Church congregation and anyone else who accepted "Fundamental Principles and Rules for Work" could participate. Elected officials were granted no real authority. The president was elected for one year, could succeed himself but once, and had his responsibilities restricted chiefly to serving as moderator of the annual meeting, even the ordination of pastors being made the responsibility of a specially chosen ordainer. The activities of the organization were carried on by independent boards and corporations, to which the annual meeting nominated candidates and from which it received reports. That is, a separate corporation and board owned and operated Augsburg Seminary, another supervised home mission work, still another foreign mission work, and so on. An Organization Committee (eventually named the Board of Administration) originally had a very ambiguous status, but in time came to function as a quasi-executive committee, eventually being incorporated so that it could legally hold property on behalf of the Lutheran Free Church.

Since its polity was so decentralized, the Lutheran Free Church had difficulty in marshaling its resources for cooperative work and in providing unified or integrated leadership for its activities. In the course of the twentieth century many changes were made in the "Rules for Work" and strong leadership emerged, which resulted in the Lutheran Free Church's functioning more and more like other Lutheran synods. However, the distinctive feature of carrying on various phases of church work through separate and independent corporations and boards continued throughout the life of the church body.

There are no accurate membership statistics for the first years of the Lutheran Free Church's existence. It has been estimated that at the time of its formation it included less than 125 congregations, most of them very small, with a baptized membership of about 6,250.[55] The first year for which reasonably reli-

343

53.
For a discussion of the relation between the two interests precipitated by John Evjen in 1918, see ibid., pp. 137–41.

54.
Par. 4, "Rules for Work," ibid., pp. 305, 309.

55.
Clarence Carlsen, *The Years of Our Church* (Minneapolis: Lutheran Free Church Publishing Co., 1942), p. 167.

able statistics were compiled was 1907, and they revealed a membership of 283 congregations and 26,442 baptized members.[56] This meant that the Lutheran Free Church was slightly smaller than Hauge's Synod, which it resembled in many ways (but not in polity), and with which it had amicable cooperative relations.

Just at the turn of the century the United Norwegian Lutheran Church experienced a second small schism. In 1900 a very small group of pastors and congregations, under the leadership of Knut O. Lundeberg, most of whom were from the United Church, formed the Church of the Lutheran Brethren.[57] Its primary concern was the establishment of "pure" congregations and the maintenance of regenerate membership through the exercise of church discipline.[58] The Lutheran Brethren represented a strict Haugean pietism but differed from other Norwegian Haugeans in its view of the congregation. It established a Bible school and became actively engaged in foreign mission work. The Lutheran Brethren has remained a very small but active church to the present day, in 1969 numbering 9,255 baptized members.[59]

Another development on the Scandinavian merger front in the nineties was the formation in 1896 of the United Danish Evangelical Lutheran Church through the union of two Danish groups popularly designated the Blair Church and the North Church. This merger has been discussed earlier.[60]

The Joint Synod of Wisconsin (1892)

In 1892 three Upper Midwest synods of German background formed a loose federation for cooperation in church work, particularly in home missions and education. All three synods had been organized in mid-century: Wisconsin (1850), Minnesota (1860), and Michigan (1860). The action bringing the three together was not a merger inasmuch as each retained its sovereignty, having the status of a district synod in the federation.[61] The original name chosen was the General Evangelical Lutheran Synod of Wisconsin, Minnesota, Michigan and Other States, which underscores the fact that it was a general church body. When in 1904 the Nebraska Synod, formerly a conference of the Wisconsin Synod, joined the federation, the name was altered to Joint Synod of Wisconsin, Minnesota, Michigan, and Nebraska. The popular designation was the Joint Synod of Wisconsin, which reflected the actuality that Wisconsin was the largest and most influential of the affiliating synods.

Besides a common language, common antecedents, and geographical propinquity, the federating synods experienced a similar theological development and established the same ecclesiastical relationships.[62] Among the leaders of all three synods were pastors trained by unionistic mission societies in Germany, including the Langenberg, Barmen, Basel, and Berlin societies. These societies represented Lutheran, Reformed, and United churches in Europe and sought to assist mission work in North America with little regard for confessional distinctions.[63] All three synods moved in a more confessional direction, affiliating

56.
Lutheran Free Church, *Beretning . . . 1908,* pp. 28–31.
57.
Lundeberg rejoined the United Norwegian Lutheran Church in 1911.
58.
For an historical sketch see the golden anniversary publication, *The Church of the Lutheran Brethren in America . . . 1900-1950* (Fergus Falls, Minn.: Board of Publication, Church of the Lutheran Brethren, 1950).
59.
Yearbook, Lutheran Church in America, 1971 (Philadelphia, 1970), p. 394.
60.
See chapter 12, pp. 270-71.
61.
Wolf, *Documents,* p. 283.
62.
Ibid., p. 282.
63.
Martin Lehninger et al., *Continuing in His Word* (Milwaukee: Northwestern Publishing House, 1951), pp. 11-12.

first with the General Council and then with the Synodical Conference. Wisconsin and Minnesota were in the General Council for short periods, two and four years respectively, but Michigan remained for twenty-one years. Wisconsin and Minnesota participated in the organization of the Synodical Conference (1872), whereas Michigan joined twenty years later.

In its early years during the presidency of its patriarch John Muehlhaeuser, the Wisconsin Synod was sharply criticized by both the Missouri and Iowa synods for its relaxed theological position and for its relations with unionistic mission societies and with the Ministerium of Pennsylvania from whom it had received some financial support.[64] A more conservative spirit began to develop with the coming of confessionally-minded pastors. Through the leadership of men like John Bading and August Hoenecke, Wisconsin's ties with the German mission societies, which hitherto had provided both workers and financial assistance, were severed, and at the same time pulpit and altar fellowship was established with the Missouri Synod (1868).[65] Coming within the orbit of Missouri's influence, Wisconsin withdrew from the General Council, protesting its position regarding the Four Points, and became a bulwark of the Synodical Conference. Joint Wisconsin also loyally supported Walther in the predestination controversy. However, a certain independence as over against Missouri has always characterized Wisconsin, which was evidenced by its unwillingness in the mid-seventies to support the idea of a united Synodical Conference seminary and realignment of synodical boundaries to form state synods, both projects being promoted by Missouri.[66] This led Wisconsin to reestablish its theological seminary in 1878 under the leadership of Hoenecke. It was located in Milwaukee until 1893 when it was moved to neighboring Wauwatosa. The wrangle over state synods also threatened Missouri-Wisconsin friendship, but these differences were forgotten during the predestination controversy.[67]

The founder of the Minnesota Synod was the colorful John C. F. Heyer, pioneer foreign and home missionary of the Ministerium of Pennsylvania and the General Synod. He spent six years in Minnesota (1857–63) with St. Paul as his headquarters.[68] The synod's makeup was diverse, and for a brief period it belonged to the General Synod and then to the General Council.[69] Contacts between the Wisconsin and Minnesota synods were established early. In the sixties pastors of the Wisconsin Synod serving in Minnesota developed close ties between the two. Among the most influential of these was Johann H. Sieker, a rigorous confessionalist. As early as 1868–69 a proposal for merger was considered but it foundered on the question of General Council relationships. For many years the two synods had an arrangement whereby the Minnesota Synod sent students to Wisconsin's educational institutions, particularly to Northwestern College, and assisted in the publication of *Gemeindeblatt*, the official periodical of the Wisconsin Synod.[70] By the mid-eighties the Minnesota Synod was strong enough to establish Dr. Martin Luther College at New Ulm, which was much

64.
John P. Koehler, *The History of the Wisconsin Synod*, ed. with intro. by Leigh D. Jordahl (St. Cloud, Minn.: Sentinel Publishing Co., 1970), pp. 79–86.
65.
Lehninger et al., *Continuing in His Word*, pp. 16–24.
66.
Ibid., pp. 27–28, 77.
67.
Koehler, *History*, p. 142.
68.
For his biography see E. Theodore Bachmann, *They Called Him Father* (Philadelphia: Muhlenberg Press, 1942).
69.
Heyer went with the Ministerium of Pennsylvania into the General Council.
70.
Lehninger et al., *Continuing in His Word*, pp. 104–6; Koehler, *History*, pp. 132–33, 173–74.

more conveniently located for its constituency and made it less dependent on its sister synod.

The Michigan Synod was organized under the leadership of Frederick Schmid, the first Lutheran pastor in Michigan and the organizer of an earlier Michigan synod which had a short life in the 1840s. He and other founders were products of the Basel Society.[71] In the early years the spirit of the Michigan Synod was much like that of Wisconsin—a relatively weak confessionalism accompanied by leniency in church fellowship practices. During the presidencies of Stephen Klingman (1867–81) and Christoph Eberhardt (1881–90) there was a marked development in a more confessional direction, although not to the same degree as in the Minnesota and Wisconsin synods. When the Michigan Synod joined the General Council in 1867, an important factor in its decision was its desire to gain additional pastors, but in this expectation it was largely disappointed.[72] Favoring a strict interpretation of the Galesburg Rule, it eventually withdrew (1888) from the General Council because the latter's practice seemed too tolerant regarding pulpit and altar fellowship. The Michigan Synod was particularly offended by the fact that during the 1884 convention of the General Council held in Monroe, Michigan, two of its pastors preached in a Presbyterian church, and the objections of the Michigan Synod went unheeded.[73] During the late nineteenth century until his death in 1893, Eberhardt was Michigan's most influential leader. He was an aggressive home missionary, a moderate confessionalist, and the father of Michigan Lutheran Seminary, begun in 1885 and located at Saginaw two years later.[74] The Michigan Synod had unusual home mission opportunities but continued to be plagued by a shortage of pastors, depending on various sources, both German and American, for its supply. Having experienced many disappointments after obtaining pastors with a wide variety of interests and emphases, it finally decided to train its own.

In 1891 the presidents of the Minnesota and Michigan synods conferred concerning the possibility of Michigan's joining with Wisconsin and Minnesota in the formation of a new general church body.[75] The Michigan Synod was attracted by the prospect because it would open up a home mission field farther west and would strengthen its efforts in other areas of church activity as well, particularly education. Moreover the common convictions and similar developments of the three synods were recognized.[76] At its 1892 convention the Michigan Synod applied for membership in the Synodical Conference and approved the proposed affiliation with the Wisconsin and Minnesota synods.

The formation of the Joint Synod was followed by internal turbulence for the Michigan Synod. There had not been the preparatory mutual acquaintance and cooperation between Michigan and the other two synods that had marked the relations between Wisconsin and Minnesota, and strong support for membership in the Joint Synod was lacking within its constituency. The specific occasion for the tension was the agreement which called for the closing of the theological department at

71.
Later the chief German sources for Michigan Synod pastors were Hermannsburg and Kropp (Koehler, *History,* p. 175).
72.
Ibid., pp. 176–77; Lehninger et al., *Continuing in His Word,* pp. 88–91.
73.
Koehler, *History,* p. 177.
74.
Ibid.
75.
Ibid., p. 179.
76.
Lehninger et al., *Continuing in His Word,* p. 95.

Saginaw and the continuance of the institution as a preparatory school. Refusal to close the seminary led to a split in the Michigan Synod, with one element (the minority) continuing in the Joint Synod as the Michigan District Synod and the other element, the Michigan Synod, withdrawing during the period 1896–1907. Reunion was made possible by the discontinuance of the seminary in the latter year. The school was reopened as an academy in 1910.

A more tightly knit organization of the Joint Synod of Wisconsin was effected in 1919 when a genuine amalgamation of the four synods into one occurred. It was then subdivided into geographical districts. In accordance with the merger agreement all institutions and other property of the individual synods were transferred to the Joint Synod.[77]

Some of the Wisconsin Synod's present-day characteristics which locate it on the most conservative side of right-wing Lutheranism were not fully developed until well into the twentieth century. The history of Wisconsin from the beginning has been marked by a steady movement to the right.[78]

Iowa-Ohio Relationships

To complete the picture of important developments affecting unity in the German-background sector of American Lutheranism, note should be taken of the growing understanding that developed between two staunchly confessional Midwestern church bodies, the Joint Synod of Ohio and the Iowa Synod. This occurred in the wake of the controversy over predestination inasmuch as both found themselves opposing Missouri's doctrinal position. Their agreement on the issue of election made them conscious of their many similarities: nearly identical approaches to the problems of pulpit-altar fellowship and membership in secret societies, their predominantly German membership, contiguous and overlapping synodical boundaries, and for both nonaffiliation with general bodies since Ohio's withdrawal from the Synodical Conference.[79]

Two significant colloquies were held between leaders of the two synods, an unofficial meeting at Richmond, Indiana, in 1883 and an official one at Michigan City, the same state, ten years later. Contemporary doctrinal issues were discussed at the conferences, with special attention to those that had disturbed Iowa-Missouri relations in the past: the church, the ministry, the confessions, "open questions," chiliasm and the Antichrist, and predestination. Sets of theses dealing with these subjects were discussed at both colloquies.[80] The participants in the Michigan City meeting recommended that the synods declare pulpit and altar fellowship and begin cooperation in church work. It turned out that neither synod was willing in the mid-nineties to take that step because minority factions in each synod were not convinced as yet that the doctrinal differences between Iowa and Ohio, which had been apparent in the earlier Missouri-Iowa debates, had been overcome. The minority in the Joint Synod of Ohio, most vigorously represented by Allwardt and other ex-Missourians, was pro-Missourian in its

77.
Ibid., p. 37.
78.
Leigh D. Jordahl, "Introduction," in Koehler, *History,* p. viii.
79.
Fred W. Meuser, *The Formation of the American Lutheran Church* (Columbus, Ohio: Wartburg Press, 1958), pp. 71–72.
80.
Ibid., pp. 73–76, 85–95.

position on all doctrines except predestination and was particularly skeptical of Iowa's position on "open questions" because it would permit church fellowship even though complete doctrinal agreement was not present. A minority in the Iowa Synod believed that the Michigan City theses were pro-Missourian in content and that there was too much Missourian sentiment in Ohio, especially as revealed in the latter's reservations about Iowa's position on "open questions" and its implications for church fellowship. Because Iowa's attitude toward fellowship was somewhat more liberal than Ohio's, the Iowa minority did not oppose fellowship with Ohio but it did disapprove of the Michigan City theses.[81]

Despite the inability of the synods to establish church fellowship, the meetings and the vehement discussion which they provoked contributed positively to the development of Ohio-Iowa understanding and friendship. It became clear that a remarkable degree of agreement existed regarding the Scriptures, the confessions, and even the prerequisites for church fellowship, in addition to their earlier evident agreement about predestination and conversion.[82] At the same time there was a somewhat different approach toward doctrine in the two synods. Ohio's approach was systematic and dogmatic, Iowa's more historical and less insistent on a unified doctrinal system.[83] The majority in both synods, convinced that there was doctrinal consensus, desired fellowship and union but not at the price of the disruption of their own synod. More time was required for the establishment of fellowship but important progress had been made toward that goal.[84]

In 1896 the Iowa Synod entered into a close affiliation with the much smaller Texas Synod, whose beginnings went back to 1851. The Texas Synod belonged to the General Synod for several years and during 1868 to 1894 to the General Council. Over the years it had established a number of contacts with the Iowa Synod. The Texans desired the affiliation with Iowa because they believed that it would assist them in obtaining additional men and means with which to meet the home mission challenge confronting them. No doctrinal issues had to be resolved, but Iowa insisted that the Texas Synod give up its long-standing connection with the nonconfessional St. Chrischona institute in Switzerland, from which many of its pastors had come. While desirous of organizational ties with Iowa, Texas was unwilling to enter into an organic union. After 1896 it was a district synod within the Iowa Synod while retaining its legal autonomy and identity. The relationship effected between the two was a close affiliation but not a merger.[85] When the American Lutheran Church was formed in 1930, the Texas Synod was one of the participants along with the Iowa, Ohio, and Buffalo synods.

Lutherans and Their Environment

At the same time that America's Lutherans were both struggling with one another over theological issues and seeking to overcome differences in order to form mergers and establish

348

81.
Ibid., pp. 95–102.
82.
Ibid., p. 106.
83.
Ibid., pp. 93–94.
84.
Ibid., pp. 107–8.
85.
Ibid., pp. 108–11.

church fellowship, the process of Americanization was going on. The process might be delayed by efforts at religious and cultural isolation but it was inevitable. Adaptation to the American environment was an ongoing development for a church which was continuously receiving recruits from abroad. Successive generations of Lutheran immigrants experienced the tensions of adjusting to a new social environment at the same time that they tried to preserve their religious and cultural heritage.

During the late nineteenth century America's Lutherans **349** were at various stages in the Americanization process. As would be expected, the churches in the East whose roots went back to the colonial period included many who were fully Americanized in speech, thought, and attitude. Since of all the Lutheran bodies the United Synod, South was least affected by the immigration of the nineteenth century it was probably the most completely Americanized of all the Lutheran groups. By the end of the century the transition to the use of English in the churches of the United Synod was virtually complete although there were still a few German congregations in some cities, products of the later immigration.[86] The Americanization of the General Synod likewise was nearly completed in the East, but immigration had brought it a number of German-speaking adherents, particularly in the Midwest, resulting in the formation of the Wartburg and German Nebraska synods.[87]

Of the Eastern bodies the General Council benefited most from the later immigration, and it continued to experience the problems of Americanization and language transition to a much greater degree and for a longer period of time than either the General Synod or the United Synod, South. Illustrative of this situation is the case of the New York Ministerium, which at the time of the formation of the General Council (1867) had again been transformed into a German synod although English continued to be used, and a generation later (1897) its synodical convention evidenced an overwhelmingly German character.[88] Elsewhere in the General Council, despite a strong infusion of German immigrants, the transition to English continued at a steady pace. For several years, continuing into the early twentieth century, the General Council was plagued by controversy over the issue of language, precipitated particularly by the addition of ministers trained at Kropp Seminary in Germany and imbued with a strong nationalistic spirit.[89] Since it included the Augustana Synod the General Council was actually a trilingual synod, as is indicated by the comment of Henry Eyster Jacobs (1893) that at General Council meetings "the Germans have preponderated in numbers; the English have very largely shaped its legislation and led in its debates, while the Swedes have held the balance of power." It was at Swedish insistence that English was made the official language of the General Council.[90] It has been estimated that by the turn of the century the council's German element was about 20 percent of its membership.[91]

During the last quarter of the nineteenth century Midwestern Lutheranism was still characterized by a high degree of

86.
Distinctive Doctrines (1893 ed.), p. 170.
87.
On differences between the German and English element in the General Synod in the 1870s see E. F. Giese, "Misdevelopment of the Lutheran Church in America in Consequence of Its Division," *Lutheran Quarterly* 7 (1877): 517–41.
88.
David L. Scheidt, "The Role of Linguistic Transition in the Muhlenberg Tradition of American Lutheranism" (S.T.D. diss., Temple University, 1963), p. 30.
89.
Ibid., pp. 32–40.
90.
Distinctive Doctrines (1893 ed.), p. 112.
91.
Scheidt utilizes the estimate of George W. Sandt, *Theodore Emanuel Schmauk* (Philadelphia: United Lutheran Publication House, 1921), p. 147.

isolation from the American environment, particularly through the maintenance of linguistic barriers. This did not apply to General Synod or General Council district synods. Of Midwestern synods not affiliated with the General Council or the General Synod, the Joint Synod of Ohio was most Americanized, tracing as it did its origins back to the Ministerium of Pennsylvania. Ohio, like the General Council, profited greatly from German immigration and by 1900 its English and German elements were of about equal strength. Most of the Midwestern synods were still overwhelmingly foreign-language bodies—Iowa, Wisconsin, Missouri, Augustana, the Norwegian, Danish, Finnish, Icelandic groups. Some of their oldest congregations, especially those in cities, had made headway in making the transition to English. Heavy immigration was still in progress, particularly from the Scandinavian lands, at the turn of the century, and all these bodies were preoccupied with reaching immigrants. A few individuals and small minorities were agitating for the formation of English congregations and the holding of English services. Of the church's activities and institutions it was the colleges and academies which were in the vanguard of the linguistic transition. Not until the twentieth century would the movement to English make significant headway in the Midwestern synods mentioned.[92]

Opposition to the use of English, or extreme caution regarding it, was rooted in the belief of many that its introduction would result in an erosion of the Lutheran doctrinal position and adoption of non-Lutheran practices. The use of English was associated with doctrinally indifferent Lutheranism, with which conservatives identified the General Synod in particular. In the course of discussing the language problem in 1890, Heinrich C. Schwan, president of the Missouri Synod, commented: "It is not the English language in itself which contains the danger. The danger rests in something . . . very apt . . . to appear in the train of the English language. It is the American spirit. . . ."[93] Resistance to Americanization and maintenance of linguistic walls as long as possible was nourished by fear of "the American spirit," with which was identified materialism, doctrinal indifference, emotionalism, and moralism. This attitude was not confined to any particular synod. It was present in many of the Lutheran bodies to some degree, usually combined with a nationalistic loyalty to traditional beliefs and practices, but the attitude was most explicit in the strongly confessional bodies of German background. In the General Council, for example, the advocates of German usage identified whatever was German with genuine Lutheranism and the English language with a diluted Lutheranism.[94]

Those who advocated the English language acknowledged the lack of an adequate Lutheran literature in English, stressing the need of dogmatic, exegetical, catechetical, Sunday school, devotional, and worship materials.[95] During the late nineteenth century scholars of the General Council, more so than leaders of any other American Lutheran group, were concerned about meeting those needs. A leader of the General Council expressed

92.
George M. Stephenson, *The Religious Aspects of Swedish Immigration* (Minneapolis: University of Minnesota Press, 1932), pp. 459–60; Paul C. Nyholm, *A Study in Immigrant History: The Americanization of the Danish Lutheran Church in America* (Copenhagen: Institute for Danish Church History, 1963), pp. 211–12; O. M. Norlie, *History of the Norwegian People in America* (Minneapolis: Augsburg Publishing House, 1925), p. 357. Norlie estimates that in 1905 only 5 percent of the services in Norwegian Lutheran churches were in English and 17 percent of the Sunday school pupils received instruction in English.
93.
Everette Meier and Herbert T. Mayer, "The Process of Americanization," in *Moving Frontiers: Readings in the History of the Lutheran Church—Missouri Synod*, ed. Carl S. Meyer (St. Louis: Concordia Publishing House, 1964), p. 356.
94.
Scheidt, "Role of Linguistic Transition," p. 88.
95.
Meier and Mayer, "Process of Americanization," p. 358.

that concern as follows: "The General Council was called from the beginning to prove that the change of language need not interfere with the unity and purity of the faith, and that our Church is bound and is able to preserve her own spirit, also in the garb of the English language."[96] Particularly important contributions to making the Lutheran heritage available in English were made by theologians Charles Porterfield Krauth and Henry Eyster Jacobs. The following works are illustrative: Krauth's *The Conservative Reformation and Its Theology* (1872), and veritably a small library edited, translated (in collaboration with others) and written by Jacobs—Hutter's *Compend of Lutheran Theology* (1868); *The Book of Concord* (1882, supplanting the English edition of the Henkels); Schmid's *Doctrinal Theology of the Evangelical Lutheran Church* (1875); *Martin Luther: Hero of the Reformation* (1898); *The Lutheran Commentary* (several volumes, 1895–98); and *Lutheran Cyclopedia* (1899). Such a listing ought not obscure the significant writings of such General Synod men as Milton Valentine, but it does underscore the concern for providing a conservative historical and doctrinal Lutheran literature in English.

351

From the time of its early history in this country the Lutheran church was influenced by its environment in many significant areas of its doctrine, life, and practice. The strongly confessional spirit which became dominant following the mid-nineteenth century was in part a reaction to the doctrinal accommodations to American evangelical Protestantism made by the "American Lutherans." Pietistic attitudes toward life and conduct brought by many Lutherans from Europe—attitudes toward Sunday observance, alcoholic beverages, and such amusements as dancing, card-playing, and the theater—were reinforced by the dominant Puritanical-Methodistic environment and in reaction to tendencies toward moral laxity and lawlessness under frontier conditions. It is important to note that Lutherans were not in agreement on these matters, there often being a difference between Scandinavian and German attitudes, with the former usually manifesting a more pietistic spirit. Permanent influences upon Lutherans from the American Protestant environment were particularly evident in forms of church polity and in the practical affairs connected with the carrying on of church work in an environment of complete religious freedom and separation of church and state. Specific areas of influence were congregational-synodical polity, the Sunday school, youth and women's organizations, devotional literature, worship and hymnody, and church architecture.[97] It is difficult to generalize about these influences because their extent varied greatly depending upon the church body being considered. Moreover, such influences were variously evaluated. For example, although originally suspect in many Lutheran quarters because of its Reformed origin, the Sunday school was in time regarded positively by nearly everyone. On the other hand, judgments varied concerning the non-Lutheran devotional literature and hymns and songs which had become common in English-speaking circles in the early nineteenth century. Later in the century

96.
Adolph Spaeth, *The General Council of the Evangelical Lutheran Church in North America* (Philadelphia, 1885), p. 32.

97.
By way of illustration, Gilbert P. Voigt points out that southern Lutherans had been strongly influenced in worship and church practices by their larger Protestant neighbors, especially the Methodists and Baptists. *A. G. Voigt: Molder of Southern Lutheranism* (Columbia, S.C.: Farrell Printing Co., n.d.), p. 30.

an evident aspect of the growing appreciation of the Lutheran heritage was the desire to return to Lutheran sources for the devotional and worship life.

The growth of a spirit of conservatism and traditionalism in areas of doctrine, worship, and practice to a position of dominance in American Lutheranism has been frequently noted in preceding pages. The qualifying comment of an American historian in this connection helps to keep developments in perspective: "Historic Lutheran doctrine was asserted in official constitutions, and it was expounded in seminaries. But in Lutheran congregations across the land the attitudes and the practices of American Evangelical Protestantism maintained a lively existence. Much that one could see and hear reflected the fact: church design, vestments, hymnody, worship, preaching, and ethical advocacy."[98]

A specific problem arising out of the American environment which would long hamper inter-Lutheran relationships was that of membership in secret societies (lodges). Freemasonry was of dominant concern, but questions also extended to such organizations as the Odd Fellows, and to complicate the picture further there was also difference of opinion about various farm and labor organizations, the Grange and the Knights of Labor being examples. It will be recalled that the lodge issue was one of the Four Points which figured so prominently at the time of the General Council's organization and in subsequent years. Historical circumstances accounted for the more tolerant attitude toward the lodge which was found in the Eastern Lutheran bodies. For example, the founding of congregations in the East antedated the establishment of lodges. That is, the arrival of the church preceded the arrival of the lodge; thus, the latter was not generally considered as occupying the primary loyalty in people's lives. Among the Midwestern Germans a century later the situation was reversed: secularist, anticlerical, deistic immigrants arrived first and organized lodges.[99] When the churchly immigrants came, they saw the lodge as endangering the religious, and particularly the evangelical, commitment of church members; hence it was an enemy to be fought. It was therefore common for Eastern Lutheran churches to have lodge members in the early nineteenth century. When the conservative Midwestern synods were organized their attitude toward the lodge was understandably uniformly hostile and it was easier to exclude lodge members from the start than it was to get rid of them once they had become members of the congregation. The secretism of the lodge was criticized, as was the character of its charitable programs or activities, but opposition was basically doctrinal in nature.[100] The fundamental criticism was that the lodge substituted a religion of moralism and rationalism for evangelical Christianity.[101]

The General Synod adopted no official position regarding the lodge, leaving the matter to the conscience of the individual or to the decisions of district synods. Of the American Lutheran church bodies it was the most permissive regarding lodge membership, but in some sections of the General Synod there was

98.
Sydney A. Ahlstrom, "Facing the New World: Augustana and the American Challenge," in *Centennial Essays* (Rock Island, Ill.: Augustana Press, 1960), p. 15.
99.
John W. Constable, "Lodge Practice Within the Missouri Synod," *Concordia Theological Monthly* 39 (1968): 477–81.
100.
For discussion of the Missouri Synod's opposition to mutual-aid societies, especially as set forth by Huegli, see Roy A. Suelflow, "The History of the Missouri Synod . . . 1872–1897" (Th.D. diss., Concordia Seminary, St. Louis, 1946), pp. 214–18. For presentation of the position that the lodge's emphasis on charity is "bait" to get members, see *Lutheran Witness,* January 7, 1888, p. 15.
101.
Constable, "Lodge Practice," pp. 477–81.

102.
C. E. Sparks, "The Development of the General Synod Lutheran Church in America," *Lutheran Quarterly* 36 (1906): 582; *Distinctive Doctrines* (1914 ed.), p. 64.
103.
Distinctive Doctrines (1893 ed.), p. 192.
104.
Ibid. (1914 ed.), pp. 188–89.
105.
Documentary History of the General Council (Philadelphia: General Council Pub. House, 1912), pp. 161, 164.
106.
Distinctive Doctrines (1893 ed.), p. 108; Oscar F. Ander, *T. N. Hasselquist* (Rock Island, Ill.: Augustana Historical Society, 1931), p. 204.
107.
Distinctive Doctrines (1893 ed.), pp. 18–20, 67.
108.
Ibid. (1914 ed.), pp. 272–73; for information about the Danish Folk Society (*Dansk Folkesamfund*) and its strength among Grundtvigian Danes see Enok Mortensen, *The Danish Lutheran Church in America* (Philadelphia: Board of Publication, LCA, 1967), pp. 90–91, 109–12.
109.
The Knights of Kaleva (1898) and the Ladies of Kaleva (1904) included church members. A. William Hoglund, *Finnish Immigrants in America, 1880–1920* (Madison: University of Wisconsin Press, 1960), p. 124.
110.
Thesis 9 of the set of theses on church fellowship approved by the Synodical Conference in 1875 (*Verhandlungen*, Synodical Conference, 1875, pp. 26–29).
111.
Distinctive Doctrines (1893 ed.), p. 130. A helpful historical survey is contained in George F. Lobien, "A Systematic-Historical Study of the Policy of the Lutheran Church—Missouri Synod with Respect to Fraternal Organizations in the Past Fifty Years" (Th.D. diss., Concordia Seminary, St. Louis, 1971).

antilodge sentiment.[102] In the United Synod, South differences of opinion existed and formal action regarding the lodge was avoided.[103] The scruples of the Tennessee Synod, which had rules against lodge membership as well as against altar and pulpit fellowship with non-Lutherans, led the United Synod to take a position forbidding any of its officials to promote the lodge or unionistic fellowship.[104] The General Council officially opposed the lodge, but its approach to the problem of lodge membership among its own congregations was educational rather than disciplinary.[105] Among the General Council's constituency, the Augustana Synod adopted the strictest line against the lodge but did not usually refuse a person admission to its congregations because of lodge membership.[106] The General Council's stand was not strict or consistent enough for the Joint Synod of Ohio, the Iowa Synod, and other Midwestern synods and was a factor, along with its position on the remaining three of the Four Points, in their refusal to become members. The Ohio and Iowa synods sought to enforce strict discipline by forbidding admission of lodge members to their congregations, but Ohio, especially in some congregations in the eastern portion of its territory, confronted a problem of long standing and advocated a policy of continuing witness and patient counseling in dealing with lodge members who belonged to their congregations.[107] Among the Midwestern Norwegian groups an antilodge position was consistently adopted, but strict discipline in enforcement of the policy was not ordinarily invoked. The pietistic Danes opposed secret societies, but did not forbid membership in their congregations to lodge members, whereas the Grundtvigian Danes were not opposed.[108] Finnish Lutherans were frequently members of national lodges.[109]

The Synodical Conference, with the Missouri Synod in the lead, was the severest critic of the lodge and was also critical of many Lutheran synods for laxity in handling the lodge problem. It was considered serious enough to make differences in practice concerning lodge membership divisive of church fellowship.[110] In contrast to an educational approach toward those who were lodge members, such as that followed by the General Council, the Synodical Conference advocated a disciplinary approach. In 1893 Missouri's theologian Franz Pieper wrote:

Secret societies, such as Odd Fellows, Free Masons, etc. are incompatible with the Christian Church. . . . A Christian can not enter into membership with secret societies without professing a false way to heaven and participating in a false worship, and thus denying Christ, man's only hope for salvation. It is the sacred duty of the Christian Church to raise her voice against secret societies for a public testimony, and especially for the purpose of regaining such of her members as are already led astray by the Lodges.[111]

As Pieper's statement and also periodic synodical discussions of the matter indicate, even the Missouri Synod could not achieve complete consistency in practice, but the development was in the direction of greater strictness and increasing use of discipline. Walther, in a now famous letter (1864) which revealed some diversity of practice had advocated an evangelical (educational) approach in dealing with lodge members who were members of a congregation, as did some other leaders, viewing the issue as one of pastoral counseling and thus permitting some variance in practice. However, indefinite procrastination in dealing with congregational members who were also lodge members was forbidden.[112] Although the general trend in Missouri was toward a stricter position regarding the lodges, it was not until the 1920s that the Missouri Synod officially adopted a position that permitted no deviation in practice and insisted upon a policy more legalistic than that which had been espoused in an earlier era.[113]

The lodge issue continued to be a factor in inter-Lutheran relations in the twentieth century, particularly between the synods of the Synodical Conference and the rest of American Lutheranism, although the middle-of-the-road synods, while not consistent in their own practice, believed that the United Lutheran Church in America (having inherited General Synod and United Synod, South as well as General Council attitudes) was too lax regarding this matter.

The rapid progress of industrialization and urbanization in the late nineteenth century produced the important phenomenon in American Protestantism known as the social gospel movement.[114] Underlying this movement was an awareness of many social problems in our national life and a conviction that Christianity had something to contribute to the solution of the social crises of the time. Leaders of the social gospel movement included such prominent Protestant pastors as Washington Gladden and Walter Rauschenbusch, who sought to apply the teachings of Christ and the New Testament to the whole gamut of social, economic, and political problems in order to create a Christian society. Its goal was the transformation of the American social order by attacking the basic causes of its failings and disorders rather than ministering to its victims, as was the approach of traditional Christian charity. The approach of the social gospel contrasted sharply with the characteristic individualism of evangelical Protestantism which focused on the salvation of the individual. Large numbers of American Protestants were critical of the new emphasis on "social Christianity" or were indifferent to it. Those who were concerned about social issues ranged from those who continued to adhere to a basically individualistic orientation to those of such a radical posture that they rejected the American socio-economic system. In between were those who are usually identified with the social gospel movement, for whom Christian involvement in social issues was of primary concern.[115]

The Lutheran church was little influenced by the social gospel movement. Although by the end of the nineteenth century there was evidence of a growing awareness of the problems arising from an industrialized society, there were few Lutheran advocates of a social Christianity. A number of factors account for this situation. The great majority of America's Lutherans

354

112.
R. A. Suelflow, "History of the Missouri Synod," p. 125; Constable, "Lodge Practice," pp. 478–81. Synodical discussions, resolutions, and teachings of Missouri leaders regarding the lodge are contained in the pamphlet *The Lodge Practice of the Missouri Synod* (1932?).
113.
Constable, "Lodge Practice," p. 486.
114.
There are a number of studies of the social gospel movement. A brief discussion of the movement in its historical context will be found in Winthrop S. Hudson, *Religion in America* (New York: Scribner's, 1965), chap. 12. Also see the introductory section in Robert T. Handy, ed., *The Social Gospel in America, 1870-1920* (New York: Oxford University Press, 1966).
115.
Henry F. May differentiates among three types of social Christianity: conservative, progressive (the social gospel), and radical. See his *Protestant Churches and Industrial America* (New York: Harper & Bros., 1949).

spoke a foreign language and were located in rural America, where they had no direct contact with urban social problems. There was greater social sensitivity, although still limited, in the English-speaking segments of the church where eastern urban problems were close at hand. Everywhere in Lutheranism, as was generally true of American Protestantism in the late nineteenth century, the socio-economic status quo was defended and such a new phenomenon as the growing labor movement was viewed with skepticism if not outright hostility, particularly when it resorted to strikes. The large numbers of recent immigrants in the Lutheran churches were a force in support of traditional institutions and in opposition to radical social change.[116] The majority of immigrants of that period were conservative in their political and social views.[117] Consequently, Scandinavian and German Lutherans, despite their predominantly rural orientation, opposed the liberal social-political programs of the Midwestern Populists of the 1890s, whose views seemed too unconventional. The next generation, the children of the immigrants, included many who favored more liberal views.[118]

With such a large number of immigrants to minister to, it was to be expected that the Lutheran church bodies would concentrate their energies on such activities as home missions, evangelistic outreach, and education.[119] They had neither energy nor resources to devote to social issues, even had they been so inclined, which they were not. It was a matter of fundamental importance, entirely apart from other considerations, that Lutherans considered it to be the church's primary responsibility to proclaim the gospel to the individual for his salvation. Since man's sin is the cause of both personal and social evils, the latter is to be combatted and remedied through the action of redeemed individuals, whose influence could be expected to penetrate and leaven the social order. Individual regeneration was the primary thrust of the Lutheran message, and that emphasis continued into the twentieth century.

Traditionally the Lutheran church has manifested social concern in its inner mission activity, concentrating on the alleviation of distress and the care of the ill, the poor, orphans, the aged, and the like. The initial impetus for its endeavors and institutions was provided by August H. Francke and the German pietists of the early eighteenth century. The inner mission movement experienced a powerful resurgence and expansion during the nineteenth century in the Lutheran churches of Germany and Scandinavia. William A. Passavant, whose importance in American Lutheranism has been discussed earlier, was the pioneer leader of this type of Lutheran social service in America. In the closing years of the nineteenth century a few individuals, mainly in the General Synod and the General Council, began to express themselves concerning the seriousness of social issues and the importance of a Christian response to problems resulting from the American economic and social system. They showed sympathetic awareness of the problems and needs of labor at a time when there was widespread criticism of

116.
Reginald W. Deitz, "Eastern Lutheranism in American Society and American Christianity, 1870-1914" (Ph.D. diss., University of Pennsylvania, 1958), pp. 256ff.
117.
Oscar Handlin in David F. Bowers, ed., *Foreign Influences in American Life* (Princeton: Princeton University Press, 1944), p. 91; Maldwyn A. Jones, *American Immigration* (Chicago: University of Chicago Press, 1960), p. 230.
118.
Marcus L. Hansen, *The Immigrant in American History* (New York: Harper & Row, Harper Torchbook, 1964), pp. 91-92. That the generalization concerning the political conservatism of immigrants requires qualification is demonstrated by Jon Wefald, *A Voice of Protest: Norwegians in American Politics, 1890-1917* (Northfield, Minn.: Norwegian-American Historical Assoc., 1971).
119.
See chapters 12 and 13.

355

labor unions.[120] There were similar voices in other synods as well but they were few in number.[121]

John H. W. Stuckenberg was the one Lutheran of his generation who wrote significantly in the area of Christianity's relation to society, appealing for greater Lutheran awareness of the need for social Christianity.[122] A pastor and college professor (Wittenberg) of the General Synod, he spent periods of study in German universities and for a decade-and-a-half was pastor of the American Church in Berlin. As a pietist he was deeply interested in movements devoted to the reform of the individual, such as the temperance movement, but his particular concern was that Christianity should be a force in the transformation of society. He believed that the teachings of Christ and of the New Testament had application to social evils and provided resources for the creation of a Christian society. He was a pioneer author in the field of sociology, beginning with *Christian Sociology* (1880) and concluding with *Sociology, the Science of Human Society* (1903). His writings became progressively less theological and increasingly sociological in their orientation as he grew older. During his latter years his connections with the Lutheran church were more tenuous than earlier. He was primarily a theorist rather than a social activist, and his influence within Lutheranism as an advocate of progressive social Christianity was limited.[123]

The focus of Lutheran interest was on personal rather than social ethics. An evil that received much attention from the more pietistically oriented Lutherans was drunkenness. General Synod, United Synod, South, and Scandinavian Lutherans provided much support to American temperance and prohibition movements. Many synodical resolutions were passed condemning abuses in the use of alcohol and supporting legal prohibition. To a lesser degree the same groups and individuals supported efforts to maintain strict Sunday observance. Such efforts were influenced by American evangelical Protestant movements but also had their source in the pietistic heritage carried with them from Europe. The temperance movement, for example, was very strong among Lutheran pietists in Scandinavia. Generally speaking, German-background Lutherans who migrated in the nineteenth century were opposed to the prohibition movement and to "puritanical" Sunday observance. Descendants of German immigrants of an earlier time (eighteenth century) were frequently found in prohibitionist ranks.[124] Whatever their differences about the specifics of Lutheran conduct, American Lutherans were in agreement that their church should concern itself with the salvation of the individual and the transformation of his life. It was expected that social reform would result from the leavening effect in society of transformed individuals.

120.
Samuel Wagenthals, Charles Albert, Revere F. Weidner, Edmund J. Wolf, Theodore E. Schmauk, and Edwin H. Delk are mentioned by Deitz, "Eastern Lutheranism," pp. 206-7.
121.
J. C. Wambsganz and H. Katt of the Missouri Synod showed a sympathetic attitude toward labor (Ralph L. Moellering, "The Missouri Synod and Social Problems: A Theological and Sociological Analysis of the Reaction to Industrial Tensions, War, and Race Relations from 1917 to 1941" [Ph.D. diss., Harvard University, 1964], pp. 99-101).
122.
John O. Evjen, *The Life of J. H. W. Stuckenberg* (Minneapolis: Lutheran Free Church Publishing Co., 1938).
123.
Deitz, "Eastern Lutheranism," pp. 212ff.
124.
Albert B. Faust, *The German Element in the United States* (Boston: Houghton Mifflin Co., 1909), 2:146-50.

V   **Facing the Twentieth Century**

Fred W. Meuser

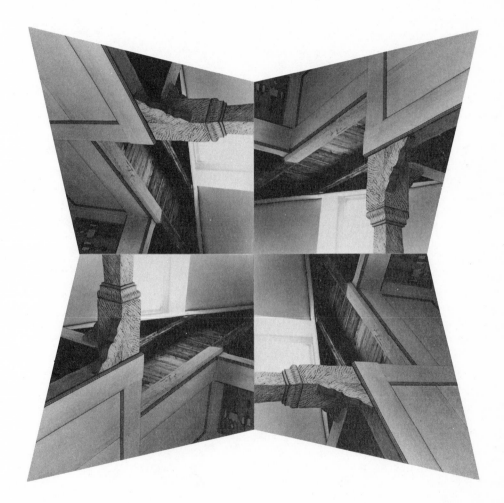

1.
See the address delivered by Roosevelt on January 29, 1905, at the rededication of Luther Place Memorial Church, Washington, D.C., in *Presidential Addresses and State Papers, April 1, 1904, to May 4, 1905,* vol. 3.
2.
A literacy test law was passed by Congress but vetoed by President Cleveland in 1896.
3.
Estimates range from about one-fifth to almost one-third in the decade between 1900 and 1910.

Exhortations to repentance and reminders of the undeserved mercies of God were typical Lutheran responses to the start of a new century. While society celebrated the calendar change and Protestant churchmen hailed the start of the "Christian century," for Lutherans as a whole it was "business as usual." A change in calendar meant no essential change in the church's task or in its attitude toward a sinful society and a fragmented Christendom. Only an occasional Lutheran optimist saw a "mighty stream sweep[ing] toward the throne" of God, or shared the vision of America as a "promised land for Christ, and the best vantage point for saving the world." In 1905 Theodore E. Schmauk reminded the General Council that if Christians would only "convert America the world will have a second Pentecost."

Gathering in the Flock

America's Lutherans, however, were more oriented toward immediate reality—finding and drawing into Lutheran congregations the more than ten million Americans who by birth or baptism were related to their church but were in danger of drifting into other Protestant churches or into practical paganism. So great was this challenge, in spite of the heroic efforts of the 1800s, that it overshadowed every other responsibility. Only if Lutherans meant business could President Theodore Roosevelt's prediction which they loved to quote, that the Lutheran church could become one of America's greatest, be realized.[1]

In the United States

The task seemed endless. Efforts to restrict immigration were being blocked by either Congress or the President.[2] The Scandinavian wave which had ebbed in the 1890s was cresting again and would not decrease significantly until the Great War. German immigration was diminishing, to be sure, but the slack was being taken up by new groups of Lutherans from Central Europe and Russia. And like all immigrant groups, the Lutherans, from whatever country, were in no danger of forgetting how to reproduce. On the maps the frontier was no more, but vast unoccupied lands in the Upper Midwest and Canada could still be had for the asking, and the traditionally attractive rural and urban areas had room for many more people. By 1910 over a million Scandinavians were living in Minnesota alone. In spite of a relatively high percentage of returnees to the homeland,[3] the enormous task of gathering in fellow Lutherans left almost no time or energy to be concerned about others. Efforts of other churches, especially the Methodist and Baptist which regarded

Lutheran immigrants as unconverted, made quick action all the more urgent. The Sunday school board of the Methodist Episcopal Church, referring in 1915 to the wave of Scandinavian immigrants, asked, "Who will make them Christians and Americans?"[4] Lutherans reacted to such proselytizing with indignation and missionary determination.[5]

For all synods home mission work was primary. Least oriented to the immigrants were the General Synod, only 10 percent of whose clergy could speak German, and the even more Americanized United Synod, South. In spite of a continuing trickle of German-speaking pastors from the Breklum Seminary in Germany and the Martin Luther Seminary at Lincoln, Nebraska, the German element in the General Synod felt that synodical interest was far from adequate. For years a few traveling missionaries organized congregational nuclei in the Nebraska and Wartburg synods where settled pastors were always in short supply. The general shortage of pastors throughout the General Synod kept home mission work, especially among Germans, in a constant mild crisis.[6] Rapid growth of industrial areas brought calls for a greater urban effort and reminders that to neglect the cities in favor of the frontier was to jeopardize the Christian character of the nation. Boasting that the Lutheran rate of growth in northern cities was greater than that of any other Protestant church, one General Synod optimist claimed, that "if Lutherans but furnish a well-equipped and enthusiastic minister for any eligible quarter of our large cities" the masses of laboring people will "flock to the Lutheran banner."[7] Efforts were made to establish city churches, but seldom did they reach out beyond transplanted Lutherans and rarely did even these flock in without hard pastoral work.

In contrast to the General Synod, the General Council and the Ohio, Iowa, and Missouri synods did extensive work in the German language, especially in the so-called new fields of the Pacific Northwest and Canada. Traditional areas of strength in the eastern and central Midwest also required constant attention. The Missouri Synod, thanks to a very adequate supply of pastors from its own comprehensive school system, augmented by a training school in Steeden, Germany, founded the largest number of new congregations. New graduates and pastors without call could always, at very small salary, be sent into "German" areas to gather congregations. Few synods and pastors could resist the temptation to capitalize on malcontents in congregations of other synods, with the result that many smaller settlements soon had several brands of German Lutherans. Though great in number, the Missouri missions often grew slowly because of the principle that daily parochial-school instruction of the young was more vital to the future life of the church than door-knocking to find more adults. Yet, between 1890 and 1916 Missouri's membership increased by almost 120 percent. Missouri also outdid all others in what were called its foreign-language missions, by which it meant mission work in languages other than English and German. By 1915, the Missouri Synod had missionaries at work among Estonians, Latvi-

4.
Quoted by Otto H. Pannkoke, *A Great Church Finds Itself* (Quitman, Ga., 1966), p. 16.
5.
See E. Clifford Nelson and Eugene L. Fevold, *The Lutheran Church Among Norwegian-Americans,* 2 vols. (Minneapolis: Augsburg Publishing House, 1960), 2:28, n. 20, on Lutheran reaction to Congregationalist efforts.
6.
Reasons given for the shortage in regular synodical reports on the subject were decline of the rural church, low salaries, worldly spirit, no pension fund, secular education, unsure faith due to biblical criticism, and the decadence of family religion (General Synod, *Minutes . . . 1905,* pp. 83–85).
7.
Ibid. *1901,* p. 88.

ans, Lithuanians, Poles, Finns, Slovaks, and Persians in their native languages. Missouri and several other synods had missions to the Jews. In 1915 Missouri had nine congregations and fifty-five preaching places for deaf-mutes.

The Joint Synod of Ohio's work in the Upper Midwest and the Northwest grew rapidly thanks to the manpower from its practical seminary, St. Paul-Luther, in St. Paul, Minnesota. The General Council's constant problem of finding enough German-speaking pastors was alleviated somewhat by reestablishing a working agreement with the Kropp Seminary in Germany, and by the German training of pastors at Waterloo Seminary in Ontario (established 1913), and Saskatoon Seminary in Saskatchewan (1915). In 1912, 116 of the council's 330 subsidized missionaries worked mainly in the German language. By 1917, however, the shortage of German-speaking pastors in the General Council had become critical. Yet the council also had Slovak, Magyar, Transylvanian, Latvian, and Slovenian missions.

Unique among the various kinds of mission work was Missouri's "home mission abroad" (*Innere Mission im Ausland*), so named because it gathered German immigrants in various lands into German-speaking congregations. In the early twentieth century, Missouri Synod pastors began such mission work in Brazil, Cuba, Argentina, London, and New Zealand. Requests to start similar work in other lands were frequently presented to synodical conventions. In Denmark and Germany the Missouri Synod encouraged the formation of "free church" congregations as a protest against Lutheran-Reformed cooperation and the doctrinal laxity of the territorial churches.[8] By 1914 the Missouri Synod was in fellowship with thirty-six such congregations in Saxony, Prussia, and Denmark.

Because of continued heavy immigration from Scandinavia, the Swedes, Norwegians, and Danes confronted a challenge at least as great as that of the German synods, and their degree of success was similar—probably about 25 percent of the immigrants affiliated with the Lutheran church.[9] Danish immigrants continued to prefer Nebraska, Iowa, and Michigan. The new Norwegian Lutheran missions were concentrated largely in northwestern Minnesota and the eastern Dakotas (the heaviest concentration of Norwegians in the United States), especially along the route of the Great Northern railroad across the prairies into Montana. The effort to establish the church among them was not nearly so difficult as their heroic struggle to fashion a new life in the face of extreme climate, stubborn soil, and the lonely, windy vastness of the treeless plains.[10] Between 1890 and 1916, over four thousand new Norwegian Lutheran congregations and preaching places were established in the United States and Canada, some as far north as Alaska. But by World War I, 50 percent of these had either dissolved or merged with other congregations.

Equally active were the Swedish Lutherans who tried to establish congregations wherever there was a cluster of Swedes. Because the Augustana Synod's geographical jurisdictional

8.
On the "free church" movement see W. Wöhling, *Geschichte der Ev. Luth. Freikirche in Sachsen u.a. St.* (Zwickau: Verlag des Schriftenvereins E. Klärner, 1925).
9.
See Paul C. Nyholm, *A Study in Immigrant History: The Americanization of the Danish Lutheran Churches in America* (Copenhagen: Institute for Danish Church History, 1963), p. 286.
10.
See Ole E. Rolvaag's *Giants in the Earth: A Saga of the Prairie* (New York: Harper, 1927), and the recollections of a frontier pastor in Thaddaeus F. Gullixson's *In the Face of the West Wind* (Minneapolis: Augsburg Publishing House, 1963).

units (called conferences), rather than the general body, were responsible for missionary work, the Swedes could respond quickly when new opportunities arose. To a higher degree than Germans and Norwegians, Swedish immigrants preferred the cities and the areas where earlier Swedes had settled along the eastern seaboard and in the cities of the Upper Midwest. The wide spread and relatively slow growth of many Swedish congregations is reflected in the fact that in 1912, 491 of Augustana's congregations were receiving financial assistance from the general synodical treasury.

All Lutheran synods followed much the same approach to mission work. A man would be sent to any area where Lutherans wanted or needed a pastor. His task was to contact all Lutherans in his community and to be alert to other areas where preaching places might be established. A small salary would be subsidized by his synod but he would be left largely on his own financially. After "church extension funds" began to be established just before and after 1900, small interest-free loans were sometimes available. Under this system many congregations were given some help, but the system hardly encouraged repayment of loans or growth toward self-support. Both the immigrant self-consciousness and a stepsisterly relationship between congregations and church bodies contributed toward the "side-street" mentality of most Lutherans. Sheer economics often dictated purchase of the cheapest ground and erection of the humblest kind of structure with donated materials and labor. The casual planning and operation of many missions made a relatively high rate of attrition inevitable, especially in areas where intersynodical competition produced too many congregations, or where immigrant groups remained small.[11]

With the exception of the Lutheran Free Church (LFC), the goal of mission work was to gather Lutherans into congregations by appealing to their baptized and confirmed status or to the religious needs of their children. The assumption was that they knew the Lutheran faith and, therefore, ought to be members of a Lutheran congregation. Deficiencies in Christian knowledge or commitment could be rectified as they worshiped and communed. Lutheran Free Church pastors, on the other hand, were trained to think of their task primarily as leading men to Christ and only secondarily as enrolling people in congregations. LFC missionaries were instructed not to establish congregations unless they had a nucleus of really "converted" Christians among whom the gifts of grace were evident. In the absence of such assurance, pastors were to conduct evangelistic meetings for the "so-called Lutherans" and others who might come, rather than to rush into organizing a congregation. Such rigorous standards resulted in many small congregations with a high percentage dependent on the larger ones for financial help. The competitive disadvantage of LFC pastors in the statistical race is obvious.[12]

Frictions between synods multiplied as the desire for English-speaking services and congregations grew. So long as some synods were unable to recognize certain others as genuinely Lu-

11.
In the United Danish Church between 1901 and 1910, fifty-two congregations were established, fourteen closed; between 1911 and 1920 thirty-nine were established, twenty-one closed (Nyholm, *Immigrant History,* p. 148).
12.
Eugene L. Fevold, *The Lutheran Free Church* (Minneapolis: Augsburg Publishing House, 1969), p. 126.

theran, comity in mission planning was an impossibility. After 1900 the General Synod, and especially the General Council, started new churches in areas where the foreign-language groups delayed too long in the move to English. In the Twin Cities, Chicago, Detroit, and San Francisco, for example, German and Scandinavian groups protested the General Council's "intrusion" into areas which they felt perfectly able to serve. The situation was particularly sensitive in Minnesota, where the Synod of the Northwest (a member of the General Council) established many English-speaking congregations on territory which Swedish and Norwegian Lutherans thought of as their own.[13] Naturally they resented losing the cream of their English-speaking members to other synods. They took even greater offense, however, at the relative unconcern shown by General Synod and General Council pastors toward membership of Lutherans in secret societies. People who had been refused membership in one of the stricter foreign-language synods were often welcomed by the others with no questions asked—or even worse, drawn in with the assurance that membership in secret societies was of no concern to the church. Occasionally the difficulties were settled amicably, but more frequently each synod was convinced of its own rectitude and refused to yield.

Even the General Synod and the General Council came into conflict in their mission work as both frequently moved missionaries into areas where the other had congregations. In an effort to avoid friction, committees of the two bodies proposed that specific states and territories be assigned to each but the General Synod was not ready to accept such fixed boundary lines.[14] It proposed instead that no synod being new work in a parish or community which was being "adequately" served by another. Not surprisingly, the church body already on the scene seldom admitted the need for help from other groups.

In Canada

One area, Canada, remained frontier territory par excellence well into the twentieth century, especially the western provinces of Manitoba, Saskatchewan, Alberta, and British Columbia. Late in the nineteenth century this vast area from the Red River to the Pacific Coast, long regarded as agriculturally inferior, began to open up to settlement. The hardiest, most adventuresome settlers came first, trying out the land on the 800-mile stretch of prairie between Winnipeg and Calgary, living in isolated sod huts or cabins, with a few clusters of homes in villages and towns. Then the Canadian Pacific railroad pushed its way westward from Winnipeg with occasional spurs to the north and the south, followed by waves of settlers from the Canadian east and from the states to the south, a great many of them Germans from Russia fleeing poverty and enforced military service imposed under Alexander III. Others in sizable numbers came from Austria, Hungary, Poland, Bessarabia, Yugoslavia, Romania, and Germany.[15]

The Canadian government, aware that homogeneous ethnic settlements would appeal to newcomers and draw additional

13.
See George H. Trabert, *English Lutheranism in the Northwest* (Philadelphia: General Council Pub. House, 1914), pp. 65-77; and George H. Gerberding, *Reminiscent Reflections of a Youthful Octogenarian* (Minneapolis: Augsburg Publishing House, 1928), pp. 144-231.
14.
General Synod, *Minutes . . . 1913*, pp. 19-22; W. D. C. Keiter, "The Question of Arbitration Between the General Synod and the General Council," *Lutheran Church Review* 32 (October 1913): 687-98.
15.
Literature on the Russia-Germans in America is scarce. An informative essay is S. Joachim's "Toward an Understanding of the Russia Germans," Concordia College Occasional Papers, no. 1 (Moorhead, Minn.: Concordia College, 1939).

363

immigrants, offered land free or at very nominal cost—ten dollars per homestead upon the "fulfillment of certain conditions."[16] The railroads—Canadian Pacific, Canadian Northern, Grand Trunk Pacific—sold their lands reasonably on long-term payments and attracted churches by offering forty-acre church and parsonage lots free. Although farming was difficult and the growing season short, the Canadian prairie held promise of becoming one of the richest granaries of the world. Winnipeg, the gateway, soon became the largest city in Western Canada. Calgary, Saskatoon, and Edmonton grew rapidly. In the first decade of the century Manitoba's population almost doubled, and Saskatchewan and Alberta increased over 500 percent, with the German population of these territories increasing in almost the same proportion.

Mission work done much earlier far to the east in Ontario by the Pittsburgh Synod had resulted in organization of the Canada Synod in 1861, but it could not begin to meet the needs of all the immigrants to the west. In the 1880s Missouri, Augustana, and Norwegian synod pastors from Minnesota and General Council pastors of the Canada Synod began to make missionary trips into the western provinces and to attract other pastors to the area.[17] Every difficulty of home mission work in the United States was accentuated in the Canadian setting, especially the problem of pastoral supply. The Kropp Seminary in Schleswig, Germany, Missouri's Concordia in St. Louis, the Norwegian seminaries of the Upper Midwest, and the Joint Ohio Synod's St. Paul-Luther (after 1905) tried to provide men, but the supply never came close to meeting the demand. Because of the shortages seven- to fifteen-point parishes were not at all uncommon for province missionaries.

The disunity and animosities of Lutherans in the United States appeared all too soon in Canada. The General Council's German Synod of Manitoba and the Northwest Territories was organized in 1897; its Synod of Central Canada in 1908; the Joint Synod of Ohio's Canada District in 1909; far to the east, the Nova Scotia Synod (General Council) in 1903; Augustana's Canada Conference in 1913. Missouri's Canadian work was under the aegis of its districts in the Upper Midwest until the Alberta and British Columbia districts were organized in 1921. The Joint Synod of Ohio sent no pastors until 1905, but for the next two decades it enjoyed more rapid growth than any of the other German groups. The Norwegians, however, outstripped them all, with the United Norwegian Lutheran Church setting the pace. Between 1890 and 1916, 430 Norwegian Lutheran congregations and 120 preaching places were established, of which 340 were still in existence in 1917—over half of the total being in Saskatchewan. The Icelandic, Finnish, and Danish synods also tried to provide spiritual care for their fellow countrymen to the north. In all synods, the rate of congregational dissolutions was high, sometimes up to 95 percent.

In spite of sacrificial labors and exemplary service by some pastors in all synods, the growth of the Lutheran churches in Canada was slow. Among the reasons were: (1) Intersynodical

16.
Ernst George Goos, *Pioneering for Christ in Western Canada: The Story of the Evangelical Lutheran Synod of Manitoba and Other Provinces* (n.p., 1947), pp. 5–7.

17.
Typical is the report of Friedrich Pfotenhauer, later president of the Missouri Synod, that in one month he traveled 900 miles by rail, 130 by wagon and on foot; a total of 7,000 miles in eight months ("The Opening up of the Great Northwest," in *Ebenezer*, ed. W. H. T. Dau [St. Louis: Concordia Publishing House, 1922], pp. 344-45). Similar information on other synods is in Valdimar Jonsson Eylands, *Lutherans in Canada* (Winnipeg: Icelandic Ev. Luth. Synod, 1945); Holger N. Madsen, "A History of the West Canada District of the United Evangelical Lutheran Church in America" (B.D. thesis, Saskatoon Lutheran College, 1964); Harold O. P. Engen, "A History of the Evangelical Lutheran Church of Canada" (B.D. thesis, Luther Theological Seminary, Saskatoon, Can., 1955). Also Carl R. Cronmiller, *A History of the Lutheran Church in Canada* (Toronto: Synod of Canada, 1961); John A. Herzer, *Homesteading with God: A Story of the Lutheran Church (Missouri Synod) in Alberta and British Columbia* (Edmonton, Alberta: Commercial Printers, 1946).

hostility and competition imported from the United States, which caused confusion among the people, heartache and frustration for the young missionaries.[18] (2) The shortage of pastors. The General Council started Waterloo Seminary in 1913 and Saskatoon in 1915, but survival was difficult in the early years. The other synods started academies and colleges but none established a seminary in Canada. (3) The attitude of American pastors who regarded Canada as no more than a temporary call and seldom declined calls back to the United States. (4) Lack of enthusiasm in the sponsoring synods for investing much money or manpower in Canada because other places seemed to promise greater returns. (5) Poverty of the settlers. Sod or log huts, small harvests, very low prices were their perennial lot.[19] (6) Scattered small settlements which made congregational growth, catechetical instruction, and parochial school education difficult.[20] (7) Lack of understanding of the voluntary or free-church situation. The Russia-Germans, especially, felt that the government should pay the pastors and that congregations ought to receive money from church bodies instead of giving to their benevolence work.[21] (8) Competition from evangelists and missionaries of other churches. (9) The tenacity with which some of the pastors clung to foreign languages. Some intensely Norwegian and German pastors in the United States welcomed calls to Canada in the face of wartime pressures to preach in English and so deterred "Canadianization" of the church.

Christian education in Canada was limited largely to the congregational level before World War I. Missouri pastors tried to establish parochial schools, but obstacles to thriving schools were much greater than in the United States. One outstanding exception was the school at Stony Plain, Alberta. The natural desire for higher education brought forth many plans and numerous abortive attempts, successful exceptions before the war being the General Council's seminaries at Waterloo and Saskatoon, the Norwegians' Saskatoon Lutheran College at Outlook (1911), and Camrose Lutheran College at Camrose, Alberta (1911), both of which were secondary-level schools, the Joint Synod of Ohio's Luther College at Melville, Saskatchewan (1913), the Danish high school at Calgary, and the folk school at Dalum, Alberta (1921). Church papers, orphans' and homes for the aged, and an occasional hospice for young people were also attempted by men of faith, vision, and compassion in all synods, usually with the most meager of resources and at considerable personal cost.

Language

In 1900 the identification of "Lutheran" with "foreign" would not have pleased all Lutherans, especially not those who had long thought of themselves as fully Americanized, but it was close to the truth. The language struggle had faced Lutherans ever since the first immigrants had had children, but each church body had to go through the process for itself, living through the same tensions and marshaling the same arguments, eventually to come out at the same place. Although some prog-

18.
Alfred M. Rehwinkel, "Laying the Foundation of a New Church in Western Canada," *Concordia Historical Institute Quarterly* 38 (April 1965): 9. Recalling his own Canadian ministry, Rehwinkel says that when trouble broke out in a congregation the troublemakers promptly appealed to an opposing synod which usually saw nothing unchristian about establishing a competing congregation.
19.
Sometimes the price they received for butter was so low that they lubricated their axles with it instead of selling it to buy grease (Goos, *Pioneering,* p. 15).
20.
In 1907 in all of British Columbia and Alberta the Missouri Synod had only 5 pastors. By 1910 it had 12 pastors, 47 congregations and preaching places, of which only 2 were normal-sized congregations. Forty-two of the 47 had less than 100 members, 18 had less than 25 (Rehwinkel, "Laying the Foundation," p. 7). On occasion, confirmands even lived at the parsonage all winter because of the difficulty of getting from their homes to the church (Goos, *Pioneering,* p. 60).
21.
In 1917, when the Missouri Synod appealed for $3 million to establish a pension fund, a Russia-German who was pro-German in his wartime loyalty claimed that the money would be used to save the U.S. from bankruptcy which its role in the war had caused (Rehwinkel, "Laying the Foundation," pp. 11–12).

ress had been made in the previous century, 80 percent of all Lutherans still used one or another of twenty-nine different foreign languages in worship. The strength of the mother-tongue ties is indicated by the percentage of congregations which used a foreign language to some degree in 1900:

5 % United Synod of the South
20 % General Synod
87 % Joint Synod of Ohio
92 % General Council
97 % Synodical Conference
99 % Norwegian Synod
99.5% United Norwegian Lutheran Church

In some bilingual situations, for example, in the General Council, attendance at foreign-language services might be very low, while in others it would be very high. The statistics are not surprising, however, in view of the fact that in 1910 there were nine million German-speaking people in the United States, more than at any other time.[22] Undoubtedly this was also true of the Scandinavians. Before 1900 all but three pastors of the Danish Lutherans had been born in Denmark. In 1910, of the 625 Augustana Synod pastors only 110 were American-born. In 1908 the same synod permitted English-speaking congregations to organize an unofficial "association" but refused to give them the full status of an official "conference."

In spite of the fact that in 1905, 376 Missouri Synod congregations and preaching stations had some or all services in English, the synod that year resolved to always remain German. Even in 1909 it was still optional whether pastors would report their English work to the synod. For a time all English-speaking congregations were to affiliate with the English Evangelical Lutheran Synod of Missouri and Other States, but many preferred to belong to the (German) Missouri Synod. In 1911, the request of the English synod to become a nongeographical district of the Missouri Synod was granted. The new district's organ, the *Lutheran Witness*, became the official English paper of the synod.

In most synods the debates over language were not about whether English should be introduced but about when and to what degree. As was the case a century earlier, pastors and lay people feared that those who knew religious language only in their mother-tongue would be deprived of meaningful worship or that non-Lutheran religious ideas were inevitable consequences of English instruction and worship. Seldom was the argument used that the German or Scandinavian languages were inherently superior as a vehicle for divine truth.[23] Whereas catechetical instruction in English was the rare exception in the immigrant synods before 1900, nearly half the confirmations were in English by 1917. Frequently, as in the case of Norwegians and Swedes in the Twin Cities, aggressive mission work by English-speaking Lutherans caused foreign-language congrega-

22.
Heinz Kloss, "German-American Language Maintenance Efforts," in *Language Loyalty in the United States,* ed. Joshua A. Fishman (New York: Humanities Press, 1968), p. 213.

23.
In all synods there were a few who argued that preservation of their language was a "God-given task from the heavenly Father who had bestowed upon His favorite children the precious gift of the [particular] language through which the Holy Spirit could speak as in no other tongue" (Nyholm, *Immigrant History,* pp. 225–26).

24.
Trabert, *English Lutheranism*, pp. 65–77, and Gerberding, *Reminiscent Reflections*, pp. 144–231, indicate how the English Evangelical Lutheran Synod of the Northwest exerted that kind of stimulus in the Upper Midwest.
25.
English church papers were established by the Norwegian Synod in 1905, the United Norwegian Church in 1907, the Hauge Synod in 1910, the Lutheran Free Church in 1911, and the Missouri Synod in 1911. Of the 33 titles published by Concordia Publishing House between 1908 and 1911, only 8 were English. Of the 54 reported in 1917, 27 were English. See Missouri Synod, *Synodal-bericht . . . 1914*, pp. 146–47; ibid. *1917*, pp. 96–97. On the language problem in the Missouri Synod see R. D. Biedermann, "Die 'englische' Frage oder die Pflichten einer deutchen christlichen Ortsgemeinde gegen ihre sich anglisierenden Glieder," in Missouri Synod (Mittlere Distrikt), *Verhandlungen . . . 1903*, pp. 10–48; and August L. Graebner, "A Lesson on the Language Question," *Theological Quarterly* 5 (1901): 238.
26.
Emmett E. Eklund, "Faith and Education," in *Centennial Essays* (Rock Island, Ill.: Augustana Press, 1960), p. 85. On the other hand, in the Missouri Synod preparatory schools the use of English was very restricted until after 1917 (Kloss, "German-American Language Maintenance," p. 236).

tions and church bodies to move more quickly to English than they would have if left to themselves.[24]

After 1900 speeches and articles advocating more English became more frequent. English secretaries began to be appointed by synods and congregations. The speaking of English was permitted in conventions. Between 1900 and 1917 most of the foreign-language synods established or adopted English-language church papers, published some kind of English hymnal and catechism, and tried to provide at least a few devotional books and tracts in English.[25] Of all the synods, the Danish Lutheran Church in America probably clung most tenaciously to the foreign language, for the reason that religion and Danish culture were so intimately intertwined in its Grundtvigian heritage. In all synods, however, officials who pushed too hard for English were still subject to vigorous criticism. Missouri's widely used *Homiletisches Magazin* introduced a separate English section in 1903, but not until 1929 did the English content outweigh the German. Most seminaries would have agreed with Franz Pieper's comment in 1907 that the church could not use pastors who did not know English, but seminary instruction in Missouri, Iowa, and the Norwegian synods was mainly in the foreign tongue until some time after World War I. By way of contrast, the General Council's Philadelphia Seminary had dropped the last remnant of instruction in German in 1910. Quite understandably the church colleges were far ahead of congregations, officials, and seminaries in relating themselves aggressively to American society. When Carl Swensson, president of Bethany College, died in 1904, every message from congregations, church officials, and the seminary was in Swedish, every one from college faculties, students, and officials in English.[26]

In the Missouri Synod at least, misgivings about English were related closely to the parochial-school question on both cultural and confessional grounds. The minority who favored the schools as the best preservers of German culture opposed all inroads of English into the congregations as a matter of course. In addition, they were quick to notice that English congregations, even in the Missouri Synod, seemed to favor the Sunday school pattern of religious education over the parochial school. Here, they felt, was a confessional issue because from its very founding Missouri had insisted that confession of the pure faith implied opposition to the education of Christian children by a heterogeneous body of teachers in schools operated by the secular community. The synod's leaders tried to insist on the confessional aspect of the question without playing into the hands of those whose primary interest was cultural. For some, the conclusive argument was that both the schools and the German language must remain strong because of the dearth of good Lutheran literature in English. As was the case with earlier immigrant groups and non-Lutheran bodies, the frictions, factions, and intransigence related to language issues comprise one of the more sorry chapters of church history. Even the most ardent advocates of the Ameri-

367

canization of the church assumed that the process of anglicization would stretch out over many decades.

Finances

Financially, Lutheranism had a hard time entering the twentieth century. It was assumed that the pastor need not mention
money in any setting other than church announcements. Lutheran theology held that instruction in detailed obligations of
Christian living was risky because of the danger of emphasizing
human works over the grace of God, and unnecessary because
faith would naturally express itself in grateful and willing dedication of the whole of life. The average pastor was not taught to
translate such theological assumptions into concepts of the stewardship of money, nor did the synods have a tightly knit administrative structure to exert financial pressures on the congregation.

It is only a slight overstatement to say that Lutheranism's
evolution before 1900 was from the passed hat, to the *Klingel-
beutel* (a cloth sack on the end of a long pole), to special quarterly
appeals plus a Sunday offering of small coins. Modern church
administrative structures and the financial system which they
require are post-1900 and, in Lutheranism, largely post-World
War I phenomena. Most synods had no set budgets, each particular treasury being independent of the others and all of them
totally dependent on whatever offerings happened to come in.
Quarterly offerings for missions, orphans, general treasuries,
and pastors' salaries were the rule, augmented by "occasional"
special emergency appeals (for causes such as institutions, repairs, and new buggy sheds) which soon became the rule rather
than the exception. One could have applied almost equally to
all Lutherans the comment of one editor that, judging by the
level of giving, "you would think that [the whole synod] was
made up of poor widows whose only sons are employed as
freight handlers and drain diggers."[27]

In 1905 the Missouri Synod authorized "visitors" to contact
congregations giving little to the work of the synod, and in 1911
encouraged annual benevolence goals for congregations. Such
actions reflected a budding concern in all synods, as did occasional and usually unsuccessful gimmicks such as the General
Synod's Penny-a-Day Fund for seminaries and the General
Council's and United Synod's One-Day Income Plan. Two
unusually successful appeals were the General Synod's million-
dollar appeal for education which, despite a national depression
in 1903, raised more in gifts and pledges in the five years between 1903 and 1908 than in any previous twenty-five, and the
Iowa Synod's appeal to build a new Wartburg Seminary in
observance of the Reformation's 400th anniversary. A few jurisdictional bodies were far in advance of the majority. The Synod
of the Northwest (ULCA), for example, which had adopted a
congregational apportionment system early in the century,
abandoned it in 1918 as an inadequate stewardship device
before some of the other bodies had advanced far enough to
consider it seriously.

27.
Lehre und Wehre 63 (January 6, 1917): 27.

A systematic approach to stewardship education and promotion came into Lutheranism through the nondenominational Laymen's Missionary Movement. In 1908 the General Synod, in urging all congregations to adopt some financial system and recommending the movement's publicity methods, duplex envelope system, and every-member visitation, sent field secretaries into the congregations to teach the system.[28] Shortly thereafter the United Synod, South and the General Council followed suit. Both reported a high proportion of acceptance and greatly increased offerings. Although individual pastors and congregations in other synods experimented with similar methods, systematic synodical promotion of stewardship principles was the exception in the foreign-language synods before 1917. During these years most synods became concerned about pensions for aged pastors and their dependents, and they appointed study committees but found no way to solve the financial problem of establishing pension funds. Retired pastors or those who were ill had no recourse except to rely on meager savings, care by their children, help of friends, or an occasional synodical dole.

In all synods inner mission work of the nineteenth-century type continued to expand, with more and larger hospitals, and homes for orphans, the aged, and the handicapped. Seamen's and immigrant missions of the General Synod, General Council, United Norwegian Church, and the Missouri and Augustana synods prospered until the start of World War I.[29] Then, for a time, they concentrated on assisting Germans stranded in New York en route to Germany from South and Central America. Expecting that the Panama Canal would bring direct ship service from Germany to the West Coast, the Missouri Synod made plans for an immigrant mission in San Francisco, but war intervened. The only significant new development in the inner mission field was the organization of synodical inner mission boards to bring unified planning to the many disconnected ventures and to try to enlist "the entire Christian congregation and all its individual members" in Christian service.[30]

Foreign Missions

Preoccupation with the need of their immigrant brethren limited foreign missionary interest of most Lutherans prior to 1900.[31] In theory, American Lutherans were in favor of the evangelization of all men. In practice, before 1900 only scattered missionary efforts in India, China, Madagascar, and Africa gave any evidence of the desire. The turn of the century, however, marked a turning point. Suddenly, Lutheran bodies without a foreign mission were determined to "have our own field." Denominational pride was no doubt a factor. More important, however, was the general surge in Protestant missionary interest and the growing awareness on the part of all Americans of the open world and the great role which America could play in its civilization/Christianization, all of which affected even foreign-language Lutherans. Synods which had foreign fields began to give them better support: the General Synod in

28.
General Synod, *Minutes . . . 1913,* pp. 78–80. In 1918 the United Synod, South reported that about 85 percent of its congregations were using the duplex system and that contributions had increased more than 100 percent since its introduction (United Synod, South, *Minutes . . . 1918,* p. 54).
29.
Between 1900 and 1902 the Missouri Synod immigrant mission in New York had almost 10,000 "guests" (Missouri Synod, *Synodal-bericht . . . 1902,* pp. 87–89).
30.
General Synod, *Minutes . . . 1917,* p. 259.
31.
Dean Lueking's *Mission in the Making* (St. Louis: Concordia Publishing House, 1964) is an unusually incisive study of the Missouri Synod's missionary spirit and policies. See also Andrew S. Burgess, ed., *Lutheran World Missions* (Minneapolis: Augsburg Publishing House, 1954); and *Our Church Abroad: The Foreign Missions of the Lutheran Church in America,* ed. George Drach (Columbus, Ohio: Lutheran Book Concern, 1926).

Africa and India; the General Council in India; the United Synod in Japan; the United Norwegian Church in China and Madagascar; Hauge's Synod in China; the Danes to the Santal Mission in India; the Lutheran Free Church in Madagascar; Missouri to its very young mission (1894) in India; the Iowa, Hauge, and Joint Ohio synods and the Norwegian Synod gave generous support to the work of European societies. Among the new ventures were Augustana's mission in China in 1906; Ohio's purchase of part of the Hermannsburg Society's India field in 1912; the Norwegian Synod's China field in 1913; the Lutheran Free Church, China, 1913; the Lutheran Brethren in China in 1902 and French Cameroon in 1916; the Missouri Synod, China, in 1917 (by adopting the work of Elmer L. Arndt which it had declined to sponsor in 1912); the Lutheran Orient Mission Society (intersynodical in membership) in Persia in 1910; and the General Synod in British Guiana in 1915. Of all the synods, the United Norwegian Lutheran Church sent out the most volunteers, many of whom were recruited by Michael J. Stolee, a former missionary to Madagascar. In 1911 Stolee became professor of missions at the United Church (Norwegian) seminary in St. Paul, the first such professorship among American Lutherans.

Healing Old Rifts

Although at the start of the century Lutherans were still divided into several dozen fragments, efforts to overcome the divisions quickly began to alter the picture. Resolution of old theological issues among the Norwegian Lutherans and among the so-called Eastern synods made possible the first of the Protestant church mergers of the twentieth century. New but unsuccessful attempts at unity were also made by the Midwestern German synods as they continued to try to persuade each other on doctrinal questions related to the predestination dispute. A few visionaries even dreamed of all-Lutheran merger, but language differences, ecclesiastical and cultural traditions, and real or imagined theological differences—especially disagreement on the basic character of Lutheranism—made even conversation across some synodical lines impossible. Yet the hope that Lutherans would someday live in harmony and cooperate in the church's mission kept a few men working at it even when the cause seemed hopeless.

Norwegian Lutherans Find a Way

The merger of 1890 was Norwegian Lutheranism's continental divide. Difficult problems remained; some divisions were yet to come; but in principle fragmentation was over, greater unity on the way. To be sure, the Hauge Synod had declined to enter the United Norwegian Lutheran Church because of differences on the proper role of the laity, and the Norwegian Synod because of unresolved details in defining election and conversion. Emphasis on total congregational autonomy and a certain system of ministerial education had caused the Lutheran Free Church split from the United Church in 1897. Stress on personal experience of salvation and on a pure church composed of truly "converted" believers led to organization of the tiny Lutheran Brethren group in 1900. But in spite of these divisions and the collapse of the free conferences of the 1890s between the United Church and the Norwegian Synod, hope for a general unification was strong in all the Norwegian Lutheran synods.[32]

Part of the reason, as most historians of Norwegian Lutheranism have pointed out, was the common cultural heritage which they shared. Not only did they speak the same language and live in the same general region (the Upper Midwest), but Norwegians belonging to different synods had occasion for friendly contact with each other in the prevalent Norwegian musical, literary, historical, reform, athletic, or welfare societies. Especially important were the Norwegian Society of America, for the preservation of Norwegian culture, and the *bygdelag* groups which brought together immigrants from the same *"bygd"* or section of Norway. Although nonreligious, these cultural associations fostered a general sense of Norwegian solidarity, provided a setting for friendly contact between officials, pastors, and members of the various synods, and occasionally even exerted pressure for Norwegian church union. The cultural factors in the unification process, however, always augmented traditional religious bonds—the common heritage of hymnody, religious education via Pontoppidan's explanation of Luther's Small Catechism, and a state church situation in Norway which allowed for various group emphases within the Lutheran church structure. This combination of religious and cultural bonds kept Lutherans of Norwegian background from forgetting their kinship with each other.

In 1905 the unity discussions which had stalled on the question of election in the late nineties were revived at the initiative of the Hauge Synod. Agreement on absolution and the proper role (and control) of laymen in the work and worship of the church was achieved during 1906 in a series of meetings by representatives of the three major synods. Then came the touchy question, still unresolved, of the relationship between God's grace and man's will in conversion, and the relationship of both to election. Differences of theological emphasis, with the Norwegian Synod sharing the Missouri Synod's position complicated by some personal frictions in the intersynodical committee, led to a breakdown of discussion in 1910 and a brief exchange of literary salvos between Hans G. Stub, president of the Norwegian Synod, and John N. Kildahl, president of St. Olaf College and a leader of the United Church.[33] At the initiative of the United Church the discussions were resumed the next year with the Hauge Synod on the sidelines of what it considered a two-way battle. Because the theologians and officials had been unable to solve the question, both synods made the unusual move of appointing only parish pastors to the new committees.

The breakthrough came in 1912 with a "settlement" (*Opgjoer*) which tried to conserve what each side was contending for. The Norwegian Synod's emphasis on God's electing will as the cause

32.
The definitive account of the Norwegian merger of 1917 is E. Clifford Nelson's *The Lutheran Church Among Norwegian-Americans* (Minneapolis: Augsburg Publishing House, 1960), vol. 2.
33.
Ibid., 2:144-61.

of the individual's salvation and the United Church's emphasis on God's foreknowledge of man's response to the gospel are called the "two forms" of the doctrine of election. Each is recognized as a legitimate way of expressing the doctrine so long as the corresponding dangers of Calvinism and synergism are avoided.[34] Neither side was forced to accept for itself the preferred form of the other. What the "settlement" really says is that the two different approaches to this doctrine, so long as they remain within certain bounds, do not need to divide Lutheran Christians. The settlement was a compromise which the former committee of theologians would never have proposed, and challenges to its legitimacy from a Norwegian Synod minority plus the whole Synodical Conference have never ceased.[35] The membership of the United Church which, like the Joint Ohio and Iowa synods, had been contending mainly for its right as Lutherans to teach the "second form," was the more easily satisfied by the compromise. In the Norwegian Synod, however, many found it difficult to grant the legitimacy of a teaching which they had been accustomed to regard as heretical. Approval of the "settlement" by a special Norwegian Synod convention of 1913 came only after explicit assurance that the two forms do not mask two different doctrines. The strength of the negative vote in the convention (396 aye, 106 nay) plus the great number of congregations which did not vote in the congregational referendum[36] raised the specter of possible schism should the merger actually take place.

Bridging of the troublesome doctrinal barrier guaranteed the merger which occurred in the year of the Reformation's 400th anniversary. In a huge, enthusiastic convention in St. Paul, which combined Norwegian religious and cultural elements in a way not always easily distinguishable, over 92 percent of Norwegian Lutherans, comprising over 30 percent of all Norwegians in America, combined to form the Norwegian Lutheran Church of America.[37] Its official documents predictably gave it a traditionally Lutheran stance on Scripture, on Lutheran doctrine, and on relationships with other churches.[38] Alarmed at the restriction on fraternal relationships with other Christians, the Hauge Synod, whose congregations were used to participating in general evangelistic and reform ventures, demanded and received assurance that the constitution did not mean to prohibit such activities. The strong Haugean lay tradition is also reflected in recognition of the layman's right and duty of witnessing to his faith privately and in congregational gatherings.[39] A strongly confessional emphasis and a cautious spirit toward other Lutherans were guaranteed by the merger convention's choice for president, Hans G. Stub of the Norwegian Synod.

Unsuccessful efforts were made to draw all Norwegian Lutherans into the merger. The tiny Eielsen Synod declined. The Lutheran Brethren were willing to cooperate in evangelistic work but, because of their antipathy to the "lax standards" of Christian life of other Lutherans, had no interest in merger. The Lutheran Free Church, still agitated about the frictions of the

34.
For all the Norwegian Union Documents, including the "settlement," see ibid., vol. 2, app. C, pp. 344–58.

35.
Missouri and Wisconsin synod journals attacked the "settlement" both before and after the merger. The Synodical Conference devoted its 1912 program to its discussion. Franz Pieper's *Zur Einigung der amerikanisch-lutherischen Kirche in der Lehre von der Bekehrung und Gnadenwahl* (St. Louis: Concordia Publishing House, 1913) was a response to the Norwegian settlement which elicited further proposals from Ohio, Iowa, and General Council theologians and led indirectly to official negotiations between Missouri and its opponents after 1917.

36.
Three hundred fifty-nine congregations were for the "settlement," 27 against, and 231 did not report a decision. In accordance with a constitutional provision, those not reporting were counted as "for." See Nelson, *Lutheran Church Among Norwegian-Americans,* 2:192.

37.
At the time of merger there were 1,031 pastors, 3,009 congregations, 474,715 members.

38.
Scripture: "The revealed Word of God and therefore the only source and rule of faith, doctrine and life" (Constitution I, 2). Confessional writings: "The unaltered Augsburg Confession and Luther's Small Catechism" (Constitution I, 3). Other churches: "The three bodies promise one another in all seriousness to observe the rule not to carry on churchly cooperation with the Reformed and others who do not share the faith and confession of these bodies" (Articles of Union, 3). The Articles of Union refer to the Scriptures as "the inerrant Word of God" (Articles of Union, 1).

39.
Articles of Union, 2.

nineties, demanded retractions which the United Church refused to make.

Fears of some and hopes of others that the Norwegian Synod would suffer a major schism at the last moment also proved to be unfounded. In 1918 a small group (thirteen pastors), convinced that the "settlement" was doctrinally unsound and that culture and nationalism had triumphed over truth, organized a new Norwegian Synod of the American Evangelical Lutheran Church which claimed to be the faithful continuation of the original Norwegian Synod.[40] It joined the Synodical Conference in 1920. No other protest movement resulted, nor did the immediate postmerger years produce any great problems of adjustment. The Norwegians were convinced that they belonged together.

373

For Lutheranism as a whole the Norwegian Lutheran Church of America was a significant milestone. It marked the overcoming by one Lutheran family of doctrinal divisions which had seemed to be insurmountable. As the first large-scale merger of Lutherans it served as a stimulus and a sign of hope to many other Lutherans. By combining synods whose style of life and doctrinal emphasis varied considerably, it claimed to reflect the essential breadth of Lutheranism. The twenties were to test whether this church could find a way of accepting the diversities of Lutherans who were not Norwegian.

Eastern Lutheranism Reunites

A second family of Lutherans entered the twentieth century in a process of growing friendship and similarity. Unlike the Norwegians, their strongest common bond was not nationalistic even though most of them had some German ancestry. Most member synods of the General Synod, the General Council, and the United Synod, South traced their origins back to the first general organization of Lutherans, the General Synod of 1820. The causes of its fragmentation—partly linguistic, partly sectional, partly doctrinal—have been elaborated in earlier chapters. Animosities accompanying the schism precluded cordial relationships for several years, but from the late 1870s onward friendly contacts increased (for details see section 4). The Lutheran diets of 1877 and 1878 discussed questions of Lutheran faith and the Lutheran stance toward other churches.[41] In the 1880s the three synods cooperated in the compilation and publication of a new order of worship, the Common Service, which gradually replaced the variety of liturgies then in use. The intersynodical cooperation behind the Common Service and the common liturgical consciousness which it produced were important factors behind the eventual merger of the three synods. Later cooperative work produced a common hymnal (1917), a standard version of the Small Catechism (1899), and a book of ministerial acts (1918). By 1900 at least limited cooperation was going on in youth, women's and men's work, in home and foreign missions, in ministerial associations, and in a variety of special-interest groups, such as the Luther Society of New York

40.
Without mentioning the coming Norwegian merger by name, W. Broecker, "The Missouri Synod and Church Union," *Lutheran Witness,* August 22, 1916, pp. 256-57, said that all unions born of expediency, sentiment, or maudlin sympathy are immoral, hypocritical, and "characteristic of spiritual degenerates."

41.
First Free Lutheran Diet, 1877, ed. Henry Eyster Jacobs (Philadelphia: J. F. Smith, 1878); *Second Free Lutheran Diet, 1878* (Philadelphia: Lutheran Publication Society, 1879).

and the Lutheran Social Union of Philadelphia. In 1895 the three synods began to send fraternal visitors to each other's conventions. In 1898, 1902, and 1904 free conferences similar to those of the 1870s were held to foster understanding and cooperation.[42]

All these cordial relationships assumed a large measure of unity in principle. But the troublesome question of the proper doctrinal standards of genuine Lutheranism that had led to the split of 1867 still remained. Both the General Council and the United Synod, South were not completely assured that the General Synod had outgrown the doctrinal heritage of Samuel Simon Schmucker and his "American Lutheranism." They were considerably reassured by the General Synod's explicit designation of the unaltered Augsburg Confession as its doctrinal standard in 1895 and by its decision in 1901 to drop the traditional distinction between the fundamental and the nonfundamental doctrines of that confession. These resolutions had not, however, been incorporated into its constitution, nor had the General Synod ever modified an 1866 statement which spoke of "the Word of God as contained in the canonical Scriptures." Moreover, the General Council wanted the General Synod to recognize the whole Book of Concord as basic to sound Lutheranism, a position which was rapidly gaining ground in the General Synod but which two of the synod's leading theologians (Milton Valentine and James W. Richard, both of Gettysburg Seminary) fought publicly. Greater confessional consciousness was promoted especially through the pages of the *Lutheran World,* edited by the faculty members of Wittenberg Seminary, while Richard and Valentine sought to check the growing confessionalism in their teaching and writing. Especially distasteful to them was the insistence of the more conservative Lutherans that one could not be a truly Lutheran theologian without affirming the fine theological distinctions of the Formula of Concord of 1577. Such refinements and the argumentation behind them, according to the Gettysburg theologians, were in no way essential to Lutheran doctrine. The Augsburg Confession is basic. Within and beyond its affirmations variety is possible among Lutherans. The later confessional writings, though not without value, by their extended definitions pressed "disputed points one-sidedly into narrowest particularity, or unnecessary prominence" and are therefore not suited to produce unity among Lutherans. The Formula to them was not true Lutheranism but an exaggerated Lutheranism born out of the desire to destroy Melanchthon's influence and forever fostering internecine strife instead of unity.[43] Some of the eastern synods feared, with good reason, that the more German synods (Wartburg and Nebraska) were jeopardizing the General Synod's historic freedom regarding the Lutheran confessional statements, Communion practices, and membership in secret societies.[44]

The issue came to a head in 1907 when Henry E. Jacobs, the General Council's fraternal delegate to the General Synod, laid the council's misgivings before the Synod with unmistakable

42.
The First General Conference of Lutherans in America, 1898 (Philadelphia: General Council Board of Publication, 1898); *The Second General Conference of Lutherans in America, 1902* (Newberry, S.C.: Lutheran Publication Board, 1904).

43.
Milton Valentine, "The General Synod," in *The Distinctive Doctrines and Usages of the General Bodies of the . . . Lutheran Church . . .* , 3d ed. (Philadelphia: Lutheran Publication Society, 1902), pp. 41–46. A detailed analysis of Lutheran confessional history from this point of view is James W. Richard's *The Confessional History of the Lutheran Church* (Philadelphia: Lutheran Publication Society, 1909).

44.
General Synod, *Minutes . . . 1909,* pp. 125–27. Many articles on the subject appeared during these years in the *Lutheran Quarterly* and the *Lutheran Church Review.*

implications that closer relationships would depend on the Synod's favorable response.[45] In deference to the General Council and as evidence of a desire for greater unity, but with protestations of the adequacy of its traditional formulations, the General Synod in its conventions of 1909, 1911, and 1913 complied with all of the council's requests. It affirmed the Bible to *be* the Word of God and incorporated the pledge to the unaltered Augsburg Confession and acknowledgment of the other confessional writings into its constitution. That action not only paved the way for eventual merger but also placed all Lutherans in America, for the first time, on virtually the same confessional basis.[46]

Other differences between these two bodies remained to the moment of merger but seemed to cause no great difficulties. The General Council's official position barred non-Lutherans from communing or preaching in Lutheran services except in the most unusual circumstances; it officially disapproved of membership by pastors and laymen in secret societies with religious ceremonies; it discouraged participation in general Protestant cooperative ventures. The General Synod allowed freedom to the individual conscience on intercommunion and membership in secret societies, and was more ready to consult and cooperate with non-Lutherans.[47] But the General Council, assured of the General Synod's growing appreciation for the standards of historic Lutheranism, did not insist that the synod's position had to be identical with the council's on these questions. On most counts, the position of the United Synod, South was close to that of the General Council.

Although the General Council's official statements on doctrine and practice had always seemed closer to the conservative Midwestern German synods than to the General Synod, its ties to the General Synod were strengthened by the unsympathetic criticism of those Midwestern synods who demanded more rigorous discipline of fellowship infractions than the General Council could impose. By 1910 most of Eastern Lutheranism assumed that merger would be achieved some day. Fraternal delegates occasionally expressed hope for eventual merger, but no one seemed to be in a hurry about it. In 1914 when the suggestion to start planning for merger was made to a three-synod committee responsible for joint celebration of the Reformation quadricentennial, the committee took no action because it felt it had no such power. Presidents of the three synods gave the subject of merger occasional attention during the next several years, but the proposal which triggered serious merger planning came from the committee's lay members at its last meeting, April 18, 1917. This time the presidents supported the suggestion and began at once to draw up a merger plan. Within two months a constitution had been drafted. By November all three synodical conventions had approved. Of the forty-three district synods within the general bodies, all but one quickly approved the actions of the general conventions. The exception was the General Council's Augustana Synod. A national body rather than a geographical unit, and strongly Swedish in character, it had often felt less than at home within the General

45.
Schmauk's analysis of the problem is colorfully described in a letter to Leander S. Keyser of the General Synod, quoted by George S. Sandt, *Theodore Emanuel Schmauk* (Philadelphia: United Lutheran Publication House, 1921), pp. 176–78; cf. pp. 133–36.

46.
For the confessional development of the southern synods, see Abdel Ross Wentz, *A Basic History of Lutheranism in America*, rev. ed. (Philadelphia: Fortress Press, 1964), pp. 237ff.

47.
"The General Synod cultivates fraternal relations with other branches of orthodox Protestantism. . . . It enacts no restrictive law against fellowship at pulpit and altar, but allows to both ministers and members the freedom of conscience and love in this matter" (Valentine, "The General Synod," p. 59–60).

Council. Just before the merger Augustana withdrew, to the great disappointment of council president Theodore E. Schmauk who had influenced Augustana in several previous crises not to leave. He had always opposed the idea of "east coast Lutheranism uniting by itself and leaving the west out in the cold."[48] The determination to merge within the year of the Reformation quadricentennial explains at least in part the speed with which the merger was achieved, less than twenty months having elapsed between agreement of the presidents to proceed and the actual unification on November 14, 1918. The fact that it could be accomplished in so short a time is proof of how ready these synods were for amalgamation.

Doctrinally, the new United Lutheran Church in America stood precisely where its constituent synods had—the Scriptures as the inspired Word of God were accepted as the infallible rule of faith and practice; the three ecumenical creeds were affirmed; the unaltered Augsburg Confession was recognized as the basic doctrinal statement of Lutheranism, along with the other Lutheran confessions as elaborations of Lutheran doctrine. No reference was made in the constitution to the potentially troublesome matter of secret societies or relationships with non-Lutherans. An invitation in the constitution's preamble for all Lutheran synods in America to unite with the new church on this basis was regarded by its framers as a great contribution to further unity but by the more conservative synods as an arrogant affront.

For the future of the church, the choice of its first president was second in importance only to its doctrinal stand. Because of Schmauk's vigorous leadership of the General Council, his central role in the organizational planning of the new church, his reputation as conservative theologian, author, administrator, public figure, and the respect which he enjoyed in other synods, many assumed he was the logical choice. The General Synod had no candidate of equal reputation or versatility, partly because of its tradition of electing a new man to its presidency every two years. The merger convention's choice, however, was Frederick H. Knubel (1870–1945) of the General Synod, whose leadership in Lutheran wartime cooperation had given him considerable intersynodical visibility. Younger than Schmauk, he was not as attached to classical Lutheran theology nor as fearful of contact and cooperation with non-Lutheran churches. His election guaranteed that the new church would be less tied to a defensive Lutheran position in determining its course in doctrinal, ecclesiastical, and social questions.

In polity, both General Synod and General Council leaders had for years battled the individualistic and independent spirit of a self-sufficient congregationalism. Schmauk, especially, had insisted, against the general sentiment of Lutherans in America, that "the larger governmental unity of a general organization, which represents the local congregations . . . [as] a visible body of saints united in the same confession and for the fulfillment of a common mission" is also truly "church" with legitimate power and authority.[49] The ULCA's polity, from the outset, did not

48.
Sandt, *Schmauk,* pp. 164–74.

49.
Ibid., p. 143, paraphrase of a letter from Schmauk to Gottlob F. Krotel.

share the assumption of most other Lutherans that only the congregation was truly "church," or that each congregation must retain full independence over against supracongregational structures, or that the general body was merely "advisory" to the congregations. This merger gave to the general body and its boards and commissions powers greater than those of its own predecessor bodies or the other Lutheran synods.[50]

Midwestern Germans—Some Slow Progress

The Lutherans who tended to make doctrinal unanimity the one and only basis of intersynodical friendship entered the twentieth century in what seemed to be a hopeless impasse, in spite of their nearly identical positions on the confessions and the practical issues of church life. Their common German background did not exert the kind of cohesive influence which kept the Swedish Lutherans from serious schisms and which helped overcome the fragmentation of the Norwegians. Predestination, grace, and man's role in conversion were still the controversial issues. The decade of journalistic warfare in the 1890s, untempered by any personal contacts, had made each side (Synodical Conference on the one hand, the Iowa Synod and the Joint Synod of Ohio, on the other) more confident of its position and more suspicious of the other than ever.

Even more than the others, the Missouri Synod had boundless confidence that it represented the only real Lutheranism in America. Other Lutherans were charged either with unwillingness to separate themselves completely from erroneous teaching and church life, or with actual heresy in doctrine, or even with being no longer Christian. Other Lutherans were indicted as the troublemakers who tolerated the errors of non-Lutherans.[51] Behind the differences on individual points of doctrine (or theology) Missouri's theologians usually thought they detected an unwillingness to accept the doctrine of "grace *alone*" and an unwillingness to submit human opinions to the scriptural revelation. On that basis, they charged that other Lutherans did not even know what Christianity is, that "the Gospel was to them a deeply hidden mystery, yes, an offense and an aggravation," and that the real issue was simply "how man is saved. If we agree on that, that man is not saved by his own works but by faith in Christ, then the battle will have been won."[52] But in the meantime isolation from the others and vigorous witness against them was the only correct stance.[53] In defending their synod against attack, Missouri's theologians repeatedly affirmed that their synod was "in possession of the truth—the entire, unvarnished truth,"[54] and that "as certainly as Holy Scripture is God's Word—which it is—so certain is it that our doctrinal position is correct. . . . Whoever contests our doctrinal position contends against the divine truth."[55] "Never," wrote a Wisconsin Synod editor about the Missouri Synod, "has the pure doctrine of God's Word been in uninterrupted control of one and the same church body for so long a time."[56] Preservation, repetition, indoctrination of this truth, and its defense against all change was regarded as the church's primary task.

50.
Cf. Wentz, *Basic History,* pp. 274–75; and Juergen L. Neve, *History of the Lutheran Church in America,* 3d ed., rev. (Burlington, Iowa: Lutheran Literary Board, 1934), pp. 348–51.

51.
The classic statement of this position is Franz Pieper's "Ueber den Unterschied von rechtgläubigen und irrgläubigen Kirchen," Missouri Synod, Southern District, *Verhandlungen . . . 1889,* pp. 9–51.

52.
Lehre und Wehre 47 (1901): 233–34; and Pieper's presidential address of 1902, Missouri Synod, *Synodal-bericht . . . 1902,* pp. 18–19.

53.
See Georg Stoeckhardt, quoted by F. Richter, "Was ist zur Einigung nötig?" *Sprechsaal* 1 (1904): 7.

54.
From Stoeckhardt's sermon at C. F. W. Walther's funeral, quoted by Carl S. Meyer, *Log Cabin to Luther Tower: Concordia Seminary . . . 1839-1964* (St. Louis: Concordia Publishing House, 1965), p. 89.

55.
Franz Pieper, Missouri Synod, *Synodal-bericht . . . 1905,* p. 17.

56.
C. M. Zorn, "Unser Jubeljahr 1922 und Hohelied 5:2–6, 12," *Theological Monthly* 19 (August-September 1922): 263.

Friedrich Bente's editorial on the fiftieth anniversary of *Lehre und Wehre* illustrates this total confidence that Missourians had nothing to learn from Lutherans of other synods, which made the others less than anxious to discuss and debate the unresolved questions of the predestination controversy. Every issue of *Lehre und Wehre,* he wrote, represents every other. If you know one, you know them all. *Lehre und Wehre* has rejected the idea of doctrinal progress and has simply taken its stand on the theology of the sixteenth century. By God's grace it has been kept untarnished by false teaching. It knows that it has presented the divine truth in purity. In every case it has proceeded from the essence of the Christian faith. It is not immune to error. If it does not continue to hold to God's grace it might fall, as have some other Lutheran journals (for example, the *Lutheran Standard*). But in regard to what it has taught, it has no cause to repent. It does not ask God's forgiveness for what it has taught. "That would be to accuse God Himself, indeed, to mock God, who has commanded that these very doctrines be taught." And whoever hopes that *Lehre und Wehre* will do such penance at some future time, will be sorely disappointed.[57] Almost every issue of *Lehre und Wehre* and *Der Lutheraner* pointed out weaknesses and deviations from the truth on the part of other Lutherans. Theological books published by the other synods were given especially close scrutiny. Any suggestion that true Lutheranism does not have a perfect theology or that no one part of the church knows and understands all truth was taken as a sign of the relativizing influence of modern theology on Lutheranism.[58] Of course, each side charged that the other's unfair tactics and uncharitable interpretations were blatant violations of the eighth commandment.

Less inclined to be that harsh on each other, pastors took the initiative in reestablishing personal contacts between the theologians. Between 1903 and 1906 five large intersynodical conferences were held, primarily for the Midwestern German synods. At Watertown and Milwaukee in 1903, Detroit in 1904, Fort Wayne in 1905 and 1906, theologians of Missouri, Wisconsin, Ohio, and Iowa debated papers on various aspects of election, conversion, and scriptural interpretation. The polemics were not as harsh as on the printed page. Only "principles," not individuals, were occasionally consigned to hell, and a somewhat more objective attitude toward opponents' views seemed to emerge. No agreement, however, was reached on the doctrinal issues. Among the issues, as in the 1880s, were: (1) Why is one man converted while another is not? (2) Does a man's response to God's grace have anything to do with his conversion? (3) A question not previously debated, namely, how one interprets and uses Scripture passages which seem to conflict with one another, for example, that God wills the salvation of all but that he has elected some to salvation. Missouri and Wisconsin said that both must be affirmed without attempting any harmonization. Joint Ohio and Iowa said that the passages whose meaning is difficult must not be allowed in any way to becloud the clear central teachings of Scripture.[59] Both sides, as

57.
Lehre und Wehre 50 (January 1904): 1-20. Views such as Bente's were the reason some who lived through this period in the Missouri Synod felt that "intellectually, theologically, and in its ministerial education immigrant Lutheranism in America had reached intellectual stagnation in 1915." See Otto H. Pannkoke, *A Great Church,* pp. 14-15; chap. 1, "The Lutheran Church in America in 1915," is a critical description of immigrant Lutheran orthodoxy by a man who grew up in it.
58.
Theological Quarterly 11 (April 1908): 126-28; ibid. 15 (July 1911): 189; *Lehre und Wehre* 46 (March 1900): 85-87; ibid. 46 (May 1900): 153; ibid. 46 (July-August 1900): 242; ibid. 62 (November 1916): 508-16.
59.
Ohio's and Iowa's view was called "analogy of faith," Missouri's was called "analogy of Scripture." Accounts of the conferences were published in all church papers of the participating synods, and also in the General Synod's *Lutheran Observer* and the General Council's *Lutheran Church Review.* The best evaluation of the conferences is Neve's *History,* pp. 210-21. Theodore E. Schmauk's "The Lawful Method of Drawing the Church's Doctrine from Scripture," *Lutheran Church Review* 27 (October 1908): 539-45, contested the approach of Missouri.

in the case of the Norwegians, had a legitimate religious motivation. One wanted to exclude every shred of human merit from the doctrine of salvation. The other wanted to keep the reality of human responsibility from being stripped of all meaning.

After the Detroit conference of 1906, intersynodical discussion lapsed for almost ten years, not because of any truce such as the Norwegian settlement but because discussion by theologians seemed hopeless. In 1915, however, a small group of pastors of the Synodical Conference began meeting with Iowa and Joint Ohio synod pastors in Minnesota, agreeing to avoid all polemics and to concentrate instead on what they were teaching about the disputed doctrines in their pastoral work. Encouraged by the agreement which they discovered, they moved the conferences to St. Paul and opened them to pastors of the Synodical Conference and other German-background synods. Because professors had failed to bring the synods together via articles and debates all through the years, they were prohibited from participating in the discussions. The remarkable agreement of these pastors on election and conversion was given tangible form in the St. Paul Theses of 1916, which were circulated in all synods and eventually signed by 550 pastors.[60] Because the "experts" found the theses less than fully adequate, the hope of the pastors for a quick official recognition of doctrinal unity between the synods was frustrated. They were successful, however, through this kind of pressure from below in forcing the church administrators to find an official way to get the synods back into the search for peace. The German Lutherans would wrestle the issues to a conclusion, but not without many more decades of discussion.

At a number of other points slight progress toward Lutheran unity was made before World War I. The Joint Ohio and Iowa synods, which had tried to clear the barriers to church fellowship in the 1890s, again consulted officially in 1907 and 1912, slightly modifying their earlier theses of agreement and renaming them the Toledo Theses. In the intersynodical conferences with Missouri they had stood shoulder to shoulder. Why not recognize their doctrinal agreement officially? The barrier, not doctrinal, was Iowa's continuing cordial relationship with the General Council. Ohio still complained about lax observance of council principles regarding secret societies by several of the council's member synods, and council leaders criticized what they called Joint Ohio's Missouri-like "sharp and narrow" and "dictatorial and belligerent" spirit.[61] Not until Iowa severed fellowship with the General Council on the verge of the United Lutheran Church merger did the Joint Synod of Ohio declare formal fellowship with Iowa.

In 1908 the Synodical Conference gained a new member, the Slovak Evangelical Lutheran Synod of the U.S.A., which had been organized in 1902, not as a schism but as a natural coalescence of recent immigrants. Because of its small size, fifteen congregations at birth, its pastors were trained in Missouri Synod schools and its benevolent funds contributed to Missouri Synod agencies.[62]

60.
Zur Einigung: Leitsätze die auf der intersynodalen Konferenz . . . (n.p., 1916). The theses are evaluated by Joint Ohio's Frederick W. Stellhorn in "Die 'Leitsätze von St. Paul,'" *Theologische Zeitblätter—Theological Magazine* 6 (October 1916): 385–98; ibid. 6 (December 1916): 535–41; and by August F. Graebner, "Zu den Einigungssätzen in St. Paul," ibid. 7 (April 1917): 100–103.

61.
Theodore E. Schmauk, "The Five Theses of Ohio and Iowa," *Lutheran Church Review* 26 (October 1907): 808. On the Toledo colloquies, the Toledo Theses, and efforts toward fellowship, see Fred W. Meuser, *The Formation of the American Lutheran Church* (Columbus, Ohio: Wartburg Press, 1958), pp. 116–41.

62.
Stephen G. Mazak, "A Brief History of the Slovak Lutheran Synod of the United States," *Concordia Historical Institute Quarterly* 3 (October 1930): 80–86; ibid. 3 (January 1931): 105–12; George Dolak, *A History of the Slovak Evangelical Lutheran Church . . . 1902–1927* (St. Louis: Concordia Publishing House, 1955).

In the Joint Synod of Wisconsin, Minnesota, Michigan, and Other States, one defection of the previous decade was overcome and a drastic reorganization achieved. The defection had occurred in 1896 when the majority of the Michigan Synod left the Joint Synod which wanted to close Michigan's seminary in Saginaw. A minority of ten pastors, organized as the District Synod of Michigan, remained in the Joint Synod and the Synodical Conference. Passage of a few years cooled offended feelings and brought back perspective. Conferences in 1906 brought the reconciliation which led to reunification of the Michigan Synod with the District Synod of Michigan in 1910 and reaffiliation of the whole body with the Joint Synod and the Synodical Conference. The focal point of the difficulty, Michigan Lutheran Seminary, which had closed in 1907, was reopened in 1910 but only as a preparatory school.[63]

More significant for the Joint Synod was the reorganization of 1917–19. Heretofore the Joint Synod had been a loose federation with only an advisory function to the four state synods, Nebraska having become the fourth in 1904. The reorganization was really a merger in which the old synodical lines were demolished in favor of a new geographical alignment into eight territorial districts. Although the congregations were said to remain autonomous, the Joint Synod of Wisconsin and Other States ascribed actual "church" rights and privileges to every level of the church's structure, especially the rights of sacramental celebration and of excommunication. On this point the Wisconsin and Missouri synods were to have some frictions through the years.

In 1915 a committee of the whole Synodical Conference proposed a thorough reorganization of that body similar to the proposal of the 1870s. All individual synods were to be dissolved and the new Synodical Conference organized into districts which would eliminate geographical overlapping of the former synods. The conference was to be in charge of all benevolent and educational work. In 1916, however, Wisconsin failed to act on the plan due to its own reorganization problems. Missouri consequently postponed action and the plan died.[64]

As far as these Midwestern German synods were concerned, interest in unity was lively between 1900 and 1917, but in its pursuit they stressed agreement on details of doctrine and its expression in the church's practice much more than did the Norwegians or the ULCA synods. The fact that organizational unity was not achieved or the organizational lines of 1900 altered did not bother them. Organization was a tertiary concern. Doctrine (or theology) and practice dominated their thinking.

Unique in Synodical Conference history prior to World War II was the controversy of the 1920s centering around the Wisconsin Synod's seminary at Wauwatosa, Wisconsin. Concerned that overemphasis on dogmatical formulations was making real exegetical and historical research impossible, John P. Koehler tried in his teaching to break the stranglehold of dogmatics on theological study. In place of the doctrinal self-confidence of much orthodox Lutheranism, he and like-minded pastors under

63.
Martin Lehninger et al., *Continuing in His Word* (Milwaukee: Northwestern Publishing House, 1951), pp. 94–98. Wentz, *Basic History*, p. 267, mistakenly identifies the body with which the District Synod of Michigan affiliated as the Michigan District of the Joint Synod of Ohio; it was actually the Joint Synod of Wisconsin . . . and Other States.

64.
Missouri Synod, *Synodal-bericht . . . 1917*, pp. 129–30.

his influence stressed the need for a cautiously critical stance even over against their own synod's theological tradition. In spite of the fact that these "Wauwatosans" directed their criticism more against the prevalent dogmatic and polemical spirit than against the actual doctrine of their synod, they were suspended on charges of false doctrine and/or insubordination. The Protéstant Conference, organized in 1927 by the suspended group, has tried to preserve the spirit of Koehler's approach without actually becoming a new church body. No other similar effort to modify the rigidly dogmatic Lutheranism of the Synodical Conference occurred prior to World War II.[65]

Resisting the New

By one set of standards, at the start of the century the various Lutheran groups in America were dissimilar both culturally and theologically; by another set they were amazingly homogeneous. That homogeneity was most evident in their virtually unanimous resistance to new ideas and movements in theology, church life, and society. However unlike Lutherans were on some counts, as a denominational family they were unusually cautious about dropping inherited attitudes, almost unanimous in their suspicion of the new. Whatever they said to and about each other, they sounded much alike when confronted with the ideas of modern theologians or the dreams of ecumenical planners. In all synods there were exceptions, of course, and, as was to be expected, more in the General Synod than in any other. But as a whole Lutheranism was content with its inherited theology and its traditional view of the proper relationship between itself and society, itself and other churches. Yet gradual change was also under way.

Modern Theology

In all synods there was resistance to the idea that there could be development in doctrine. Seldom in all Lutheran literature of this period did one find sympathetic references to either contemporary European or contemporary American theologians. Not only the Synodical Conference but also General Synod spokesmen called for and sometimes rejoiced in the "unbroken front" of Lutherans against modern liberal theology. Warnings against acceptance of the idea of Christian self-consciousness or collective Christian experience as a source of theology abound in the literature of all the synods, as do repeated indictments of reliance on the standard of rationality in matters spiritual.[66] Only those who have given up the final authority of Scripture are attracted by such groundless theology. The Missourian August Graebner's review of Harnack's *What Is Christianity?* is less urbane than Victor G. A. Tressler's report to the General Synod on modern theology, but they share the same antipathy to its claims. Said Graebner, Harnack tries to answer questions about which he knows nothing. His religion is not even a distorted Christianity but "unmixed and unmitigated heathendom. . . . [His] Jesus was born in Harnack's brain. Harnack's Gospel, too, was 'made in Germany' . . . a gospel of damnation without

65.
Leigh D. Jordahl, "The Wauwatosa Theology, John Philip Koehler, and the Theological Tradition of Midwestern Lutheranism, 1900–1930" (Ann Arbor, Mich.: University of Michigan Microfilms, 1964); and John P. Koehler, *The History of the Wisconsin Synod,* ed. with intro. by Leigh D. Jordahl (St. Cloud, Minn.: Sentinel Publishing Co., 1970).
66.
Two examples are August L. Graebner's "What Is Theology?" *Theological Quarterly* 1 (July 1897): 359–75; and J. A. W. Haas's "Social Christianity," *Lutheran Church Review* 34 (July 1915): 331–40.

faith."[67] Tressler could have been speaking for all synods when he said that all dangers and changes in the church are "shoots from a common root, and that root is doubt as to whether God has ever had any communication with men. . . ."

There is a new theology . . . of those who accept as a basis of religious life and instruction the results of a radical negative criticism and evolutionary philosophy applied to Christ and the Christian life. Its plausible sophistries, scientific assumptions, presumptive assertions, assumed discoveries, rarefied exegesis, philological refinements, historical restorations and speculative vagaries have altogether broken with the Book which we hold as the very word of God. It denies the fundamental basis of theology expressed in the word "supernatural." . . . At one stroke, that Life of Incarnation, expiation, resurrection and ascension is dismissed, and with it the Church's hope of grace and crown of glory. . . . It talks of a God whom it does not know. It praises a Christ to whom it does not pray. . . . It makes of our God a mere immanent force, of our Christ a disabled Savior, of the Holy Spirit a becrippled Comforter. It maims the message it bears and muzzles the ministry that bears it. It numbs the heart of the Church's action in missions and on men. . . . It sends the Church forth to fight its battles . . . in the bunglesome armor of Saul . . . [and] she becomes inadequate, inefficient, inoperative. But this is not the Church which is to be and shall be the dynamic of the nation, the oak heart of the ages, which with the horizonless strength is to present and press upon the world—Jesus Christ.[68]

The Synodical Conference and the Joint Synod of Ohio rarely had anything favorable to say about any but the most traditionally confessional German theologians. Anyone who advocated new theological methods or emphases was rejected out of hand. Even the so-called positive theologians and the Erlangen school were said not only to have "pierced the hands and feet of Christianity, but to have stabbed it through the heart."[69] Friedrich A. Philippi's *Kirchliche Glaubenslehre* was one of the few new systematic theologies acceptable to them. Thomasius, Kliefoth, Luthardt, and Vilmar, along with von Hofmann, von Frank, and Loehe had all made too many concessions to modern thought.

Other Lutheran groups saw a little more value in attempts of the "positive" or mediating theologians to cut through the old scholastic formalism of Lutheran theology. More than any other of the newer approaches, the "Erlangen theology" of Johann C. K. von Hofmann gradually won some hearing from General Council and Iowa Synod theologians for its historical approach to the confessional writings and its careful reexamination of Lutheran scholasticism's definition of inspiration and biblical authority. Yet seminary instruction was little influenced by it before World War I. The General Synod's Committee on Ger-

67.
Theological Quarterly 6 (April 1902): 108–9.
68.
General Synod, *Minutes . . . 1913*, pp. 136–37.
69.
Friedrich Bente in *Lehre und Wehre* 50 (January 1904): 14.

man Correspondence early in the century reported somewhat favorably on the work of such men as Martin Kaehler and Adolf Schlatter, and maintained contact with Ludwig Ihmels, Albert Hauck of Leipzig, Theodore Kaftan, Wilhelm Walther of Rostock, and other theologians who had broken with a rigid confessionalism. Although reported on in synodical minutes, the influence of these theologians on the thinking of America's Lutheran theologians and pastors seems to have been minimal.

To most early-twentieth-century Lutherans, evolution was still the great enemy, along with critical study of the Bible. The idea of evolutionary theories seemed to lead inevitably to denial of God, Christ, salvation. Even the acceptance of evolution as "God's way of doing things" and a willingness to reinterpret Genesis to harmonize with such a view called forth grave warnings. All challenges to Darwinianism, whether in Lutheran or other writings, were recommended with enthusiasm.[70] Not only the occasional sermonic blasts but also the majority of theological treatises seldom betrayed any acquaintance with either the best or the most recent scientific literature. Save for a few exceptions in the General Synod and the General Council, the whole approach was a polemical a priori rejection which assumed that any concessions to evolution would lead eventually to relativizing all of Christian faith.

In the General Council and General Synod the greatest agitation about evolution had occurred in the 1870s and 1880s. As in other matters of cultural accommodation, the Eastern bodies were several decades ahead of the more strongly immigrant groups. Tempering of bitter opposition and the start of gradual accommodation, therefore, was already well under way in the East by 1900. Calls for evangelical faith to come to terms with science or to be ready to adjust to it if the new theories should be proved began with Milton Valentine's inaugural address at Gettysburg Seminary in 1884. Though always skeptical of the theory, he took seriously the problems raised by evolution and struggled to reconcile Christian faith with a theistic form of evolution.[71] Occasionally, such Lutheran writers as Henry Eyster Jacobs and John A. W. Haas assured their readers that Christianity had no quarrel with the possibility of evolutionary development or that, even if proven, it was no real threat to the Christian faith, but they made little effort to show how claims of the two could be reconciled.[72] Junius B. Remensnyder, an author and a leading pastor of the General Synod, made the first attempt within American Lutheranism to apply the idea of doctrinal development to Christian theology.[73] Among the Swedes, Carl J. Sodergren of Augustana Seminary could still shock his synod in 1914 by suggesting that "the time has arrived . . . for someone to say that the theory of evolution is not necessarily atheistic and that it might be quite consistent with the Bible and with a Christian belief in God as creator of heaven and earth."[74] It is obvious that no Lutheran made any major contribution to the theological discussion of evolution. Those who were influenced by evolutionary ideas were content to find reasonably satisfactory formulas of adjustment and to assume

70.
Benjamin B. Warfield's review of Vernon L. Kellogg's *Darwinianism Today* was reprinted in *Lutheran Church Review* 27 (January 1908): 68–81. Cf. also D. H. Geissinger, "A Symposium of Evolutionists," ibid. 32 (April 1913): 214–28. *Lehre und Wehre* of 1900 has five major articles against evolution, all entirely negative. The pattern is similar for the other foreign-language theological journals.
71.
Milton Valentine, "The Relations of Science and Philosophy to Theology," privately published for students, 1904; and *Christian Theology*, 2 vols. (Philadelphia: Lutheran Publication Society, 1906). Reginald W. Deitz, "Eastern Lutheranism in American Society and American Christianity, 1870–1914" (Ph.D. diss., University of Pennsylvania, 1958), is the only study of its kind on Lutheranism and it is limited to the General Synod and the General Council.
72.
Henry E. Jacobs, *A Summary of the Christian Faith* (Philadelphia: General Council Pub. House, 1905), pp. 104ff.; J. A. W. Haas in *Lutheran Church Review* 39 (July 1911): 487.
73.
The Atonement and Modern Thought (Philadelphia: Lutheran Publication Society, 1905).
74.
Lutheran Companion, December 12, 1914, quoted by G. Everett Arden, *Augustana Heritage: A History of the Augustana Lutheran Church* (Rock Island, Ill.: Augustana Press, 1963), p. 285.

that church life could go on as usual. To the Midwestern synods every attempt at reconciliation was just one more sign of laxity and decadence, further proof that fellowship with Eastern synods was out of the question.

In 1900 most Lutherans were also proud of their church's solid front against the claims of critical study of the Bible. Undoubtedly, the majority resisted critical studies intuitively rather than on the basis of careful investigation. The same synods which opposed evolution most vigorously also fought every modification of what they regarded as the only proper Lutheran view of Scripture, namely, total verbal inspiration and total verbal and conceptual inerrancy. Most professors in all synods still felt that any yielding on verbal inspiration and inerrancy would undercut all biblical authority. The most conservative bypassed the problem with the simple assertion that believers know a priori, apart from any critical investigation, that the Bible is inerrant. Biblical reliability on everything or on nothing was the only alternative they saw.[75] "German infidelity" was seen to be the source of higher criticism, and human pride its point of appeal. "There are many," wrote the editor of the *Theological Quarterly,* "who will take to popularized Higher Criticism, as boys in kneepants take to swearing and cigarettes, because it makes them feel big, while they are only bad boys."[76]

By 1900, however, some Lutherans had already lived through an initial shocked rejection and were beginning to study the issues more carefully. In the Norwegian unity discussions of the early 1890s, United Norwegian Lutheran Church representatives successfully opposed a proposal by the Norwegian Synod's president which would have made an anticritical definition of verbal inspiration into a condition of the union of the synods.[77] Some of the most influential men in both the General Synod and the General Council publicly challenged the dominant Lutheran view. One of the earliest was Frederick H. Knubel (General Synod) whose "Attitude of the Lutheran Church to Current Discussions Concerning the Holy Scriptures" insisted that Lutherans, in emphasizing the Bible as revelation, had done violence to its human aspects.[78] Even these men, however, remained basically very conservative. Their views caused little commotion in the church. Lutherans had no heresy trials. The *Lutheran Observer* and, to a lesser degree, the *Lutheran Quarterly* were the only publications which gave any regular favorable reaction to critical ideas.[79] All other Lutheran journals presented their readers with an unvaried diet of articles which stressed the dangers of critical ideas.

By mid-decade Theodore E. Schmauk, alarmed that some Lutherans were trying to hold both conservative and critical views at the same time, gave increasingly more attention to anticritical arguments. As editor of the *Lutheran Church Review,* president of the General Council, pastor of a large church, president (after 1908) of the board of the Lutheran Seminary at Philadelphia, and professor (after 1911) at the seminary, he tried to alert the clergy to the impossibility of combining a

75.
See George H. Schodde, "The Lutheran Church and Biblical Criticism," *Lutheran Church Review* 21 (1902): 327.
76.
Theodore Graebner, "Higher Criticism in the Pulpit," *Theological Quarterly* 7 (April 1903): 114.
77.
Nelson, *Lutheran Church Among Norwegian-Americans,* 2:133–35.
78.
The essay is included in *The Second General Conference,* pp. 222–30. At the next conference in 1904 both Jacobs and Haas delivered papers which denied that a doctrine of absolute verbal inspiration was either necessary or Lutheran. Deitz, "Eastern Lutheranism," p. 155, lists Henry Eyster Jacobs, John A. W. Haas, Milton Valentine, Edwin H. Delk, George U. Wenner, F. W. Conrad, Edmund J. Wolf, James W. Richard, and J. Stump as such "liberal conservatives."
79.
Deitz, "Eastern Lutheranism," examines much of this literature in detail in his chapter 4, "The Lutheran Church and Scientific Biblical Criticism."

"rationalistic method" with evangelical substance. None of those who were more open to critical studies or those who opposed them were any more thoroughly acquainted with the critical literature than he. From his pen came a long series of articles defending the credibility of Scripture against its attackers.[80]

Schmauk and the advocates of the traditional inerrancy doctrine in all synods were worried far less about the age of the earth and the specific authorship of certain books than they were about criticism's effect on what Scripture says of Christ. "If the Scriptures, in spite of many textual errors that have been and are being corrected, but which do not affect its substance, are not infallible, even to its very words—if we must be uncertain there—what guarantee have we that we know a real, historic Christ?"[81] Their aim was to defend the Bible's essential message; they saw no way of doing that other than by the doctrine of absolute inerrancy. Few saw the folly of obstructing objective study of the Bible or of attempting to dictate its conclusions.

As far as the church as a whole was concerned, modern theology, evolution, and biblical studies were not problems at all except in the sense that an enemy is a problem. The real problems were unchurched Lutherans, new mission fields, new communities, language problems, new culture. In such a setting they were satisfied with the old faith. In fact, they hardly took time to think about new theories. Among the English-speaking young people, especially those who attended college, there must have been some who sensed the problem, but their ideas were not yet being published.

The Social Gospel

In its social attitudes and its view of the church's role in social change, Lutheranism in the early twentieth century also changed little from the nineteenth. Interest in social questions, as before 1900, was strongest in the General Synod. Action, however, was rare even there. General Synod periodicals, especially the *Lutheran Observer,* began to give more attention after 1900 to the church's social mission, sensing the foolishness of preaching abstract righteousness while society was dominated by corruption. Editorial attitude toward labor became more friendly; Lutherans were reminded of their responsibility with regard to sweatshops, child labor, prison reform, and poor working conditions. Trusts and monopolies were indicted as evils dangerous to society. Although it spoke to social issues much less frequently, the attitude of even the General Council's *Lutheran* was obviously changing. Articles on the problems of industrial society and on the fallacies of socialism were not uncommon in these decades. The new concern seems to have been due, at least in part, to alarm over the growing interest of American workers in socialism. Instead of the old fearful hostility to strikes, the *Observer* asked that each be judged on its merits. Occasionally it even sympathized with the strikers. No such sympathy is to be found in journals of the Midwestern foreign-language synods.[82]

385

80.
For example, Theodore E. Schmauk, *The Negative Criticism and the Old Testament* (Lebanon, Pa.: Aldus Co., 1894); "Are There Two Genesis Narratives of Creation?" *Lutheran Church Review* 25 (October 1906): 780–809; "The Word of God and Criticism," ibid. 26 (January 1907): 65–79; "Not to Make Terms with It but to Fight It," ibid. 28 (October 1909): 668–75. Articles of the same type by Leander S. Keyser of the General Synod and George H. Schodde of the Joint Ohio Synod also appeared frequently in the *Lutheran Church Review.*
81.
Letter of Schmauk to Keyser, quoted in Sandt, *Schmauk,* p. 125. The Lutheran emphasis on total inerrancy in the seventeenth-century orthodox theologians and its reflection in theologians such as Schmauk disproves the claim that the inerrancy emphasis came into Lutheranism from fundamentalism.
82.
Categorically antilabor, to the point of making sympathy with labor a possible cause for excommunication, was August L. Graebner. See his "The Pastor and the Labor Question," *Theological Quarterly* 4 (January 1900): 107; ibid. 4 (April 1900): 221–29. Finnish Lutherans in the mining areas of Michigan and Minnesota were much more sympathetic to the rights of labor against management and to socialist ideas. See Douglas Ollila, "The Formative Period of the Finnish Evangelical Lutheran Church in America or Suomi Synod" (Th.D. diss., Boston University School of Theology, 1963), pp. 264–315.

More than any other Lutheran voice, the *Observer* reacted positively to the spate of early-twentieth-century books on the social teachings of Jesus, and even encouraged preachers to deal with social and economic reform from the pulpit.[83] The social concerns of Josiah Strong, Shailer Mathews, Walter Rauschenbusch, and Lyman Abbott were generally, though not always, approved. Within the General Synod the most modern social views were those of the Philadelphia pastor Edwin H. Delk, whose writings and actions gave editors of Missouri Synod's publications intersynodical ammunition for over two decades. Delk's *Three Vital Problems*[84] had some analyses of society similar to those of Rauschenbusch. He lamented that social justice, once part of the gospel, had been shunted aside by doctrine, organization, and individual salvation. He summoned Christians to support industrial justice, social and political reform, commercial integrity, and rectification of wrongs done to the working class.

Corporate decision or action, even within the General Synod, was another matter. Its social concern was largely limited to the views and publications of individuals. Seldom did the General Synod itself speak on these issues; occasionally there was a resolution, but usually no further action. Like most other Lutherans, the General Synod believed that social betterment should come through the efforts of individual citizens, Christians included, rather than by corporate pressure or action. The exception was the Pittsburgh Synod which, for several decades, took official positions on many social issues, especially the problems of labor, and cooperated heartily in the labor program of the Federal Council of Churches. The General Synod's most conspicuous corporate bow toward the general Protestant social emphasis was its participation in the Federal Council of the Churches of Christ. The most avid support for the Federal Council came from those who were most socially concerned, Delk, for example, who served for a time with Washington Gladden on the Federal Council of Churches' Commission on the Church and Social Service.

Nowhere in Lutheranism was there any inclination to substitute sociology for theology or to accept social progress in lieu of spiritual change. Lutherans recoiled instinctively from the secularization of Christianity by the more extreme advocates of social Christianity. Appeals for greater social *awareness* were frequent, but they usually pointed in the direction of the relief of suffering through various kinds of institutional inner mission work. They were usually also accompanied by reminders that human sin, the cause of all evil, could be remedied only by forgiveness and the new life in Christ. Most Lutherans, with their background of social and theological conservatism, seemed to assume that attempts by Christians to eliminate the social causes of suffering masked the idea that one could "cure the ills of the soul by satisfying the needs of the body."[85] Many, fearing for the integrity of the Christian faith, even doubted that social matters were a legitimate Christian concern. The vast majority of Lutherans would have agreed with a General Synod report

83.
On the social gospel in the General Synod see Harold Lentz, "History of the Social Gospel in the General Synod of the Lutheran Church in America, 1867–1918" (Ph.D. diss., Yale University, 1943). A more inclusive but less detailed treatment is in Deitz's "Eastern Lutheranism," chap. 5.

84.
Philadelphia: Lutheran Publication Society, 1909. This work is regarded by Lentz as Lutheranism's "outstanding contribution to the field of social gospel publications" ("History of the Social Gospel," p. 244).

85.
Lutheran Church Review 35 (January 1916): 39. One of the remarkable proposals on social problems is in "Theses on the 'Down-town' Problem," presented to the General Council in 1917: "The State should insist that slum conditions and all unhealthful environments are unnecessary and should forbid them" (General Council, *Minutes . . . 1917*, p. 300).

86.
General Synod, *Minutes . . . 1913*, pp. 150-51. One editor even insisted that it was scandalous for Lutherans to ask people outside the church how to win back the laboring classes because "the Lutheran Church has all it needs in the Word of God." See letter of Theodore Graebner to Otto H. Pannkoke, March 11, 1915, in the Theodore Graebner File, Concordia Historical Institute Archives, St. Louis.
87.
General Council, *Minutes . . . 1911*, p. 228.
88.
General Synod, *Minutes . . . 1907*, pp. 95, 109, 115.

"that the church can best contribute its great share to the solution of the various social problems . . . by holding itself strictly to the faithful preaching of the Gospel, and to the work of bringing individual members of society to a saving knowledge of Jesus Christ, and to a consecrated life of service in and for His kingdom";[86] and with a report to the General Council that "because Christ is the Savior of the soul, His relation to society is through the individual soul and through the community of saints . . . but He is not an abolisher of outworn forms of society, a reformer of its evils, or an adjuster of its economic distresses."[87]

Lutherans probably would have given more attention to social problems if the home missionary task had not been so great. There is no reason to believe, however, that the character of response would have been essentially different. Lutherans' pessimistic view of unconverted (and sometimes of converted) man, of society, and of history coupled with its fear of invading the domain of the state would still have determined how they responded. Failure to probe Luther's positive theology of "civil righteousness" (justice) only compounded the negative views of social action.

Ecumenical Experiments

The General Synod alone showed any sympathy for the Protestant cooperative movements which had their beginnings in the early twentieth century. Its traditional refusal to adopt any restrictive regulations on relationships with other Christians contrasted sharply with the convictions of all other Lutheran groups which felt that any cooperation with churches whose doctrine conflicts with the Lutheran implies approval of their teaching. The General Synod's only doctrinal concern about the Federal Council of Churches was whether all members have a "Scriptural doctrine of the Godhead" and affirm "principles of evangelical Christianity."[88] Assured on both counts by its delegates, it supported the Federal Council financially (never more than $500 per year), sent delegates to each convention, heard and adopted reports of its delegates, and had representation on some of the council's working committees. Membership expressed the General Synod's desire to be in touch with the "greater movements of our times" and to cooperate with other Christians in specific projects without controversy. General Synod representatives to the Federal Council praised its evangelical spirit and social concern but the synod took minimal part in its program. In 1913 the Federal Council's Social Creed was presented to the General Synod as part of the report of its delegates but, other than adoption of the report itself, no special attention was given to the creed.

One of the implications of the 1917 decision to merge with other Lutherans was termination of such interdenominational cooperation for the General Synod. Other Lutherans objected to the Federal Council on a variety of grounds: it claimed unity where there was none, mixed church and state, violated the church's true task by attempting political reform, underemphasized spiritual regeneration in favor of social regulation, stressed

387

statistical and social success, and had a materialistic conception of the mission of the church.[89]

The missionary aspect of interchurch cooperation elicited somewhat more Lutheran participation. The General Synod, the General Council, and the United Synod, South were represented at the 1900 Ecumenical Conference on Foreign Missions in New York. These three, and the Lutheran Free Church, were America's Lutheran contingent at the great Edinburgh conference of 1910. Most of the Midwestern synods shared Missouri's attitude that all joint meetings for inspiration and cooperation are syncretistic and unionistic unless they first aim to discover "pure doctrine."[90]

Of all the other early-twentieth-century church unity movements, only the proposal of Charles H. Brent and the Episcopal Church for a World Conference on Faith and Order elicited any favorable reaction from Lutherans, and Lutheran reaction followed closely the pattern of response to the Federal Council. The Norwegian Lutherans declined because of their own unity efforts, Augustana because union on the platform proposed by the Episcopalians would be "futile and no union at all," the General Council because essential unity of Christ's church already exists and because unity of faith, not of church government, must be the goal. Both Schmauk and Friedrich Bente, of the Missouri Synod, felt that Lutherans should not participate in any unity consultations unless they had prior assurance that the others would listen to and accept the Lutheran doctrine.[91] The General Synod's initial enthusiasm was quickly tempered by the emphasis on episcopacy and the favorable attitude toward the Roman Catholic Church of the Faith and Order conferences of 1913 and 1916. Displeasure over these trends, more than its own merger negotiations, caused the General Synod to withdraw from Faith and Order in 1917.[92] Other kinds of proposals for Protestant unity, such as the Association for Promotion of Christian Unity sponsored by Peter Ainsley and the Disciples of Christ and the Congregationalist commission for discussion of church unity, elicited no Lutheran support at all. Even the occasional exchange of fraternal visitors between the General Synod and some of the Reformed and Presbyterian churches had terminated by the time the General Synod went out of existence.

The intense doctrinal sensitivity and caution of even the Eastern Lutherans can be seen in one other significant area: Sunday school literature. Because of discontent with both the content and the teaching methods of the international Sunday school series, the General Council in 1895 began its own "graded" system of materials, the first such system anywhere. Objections to the child-centered method and un-Lutheran doctrinal interpretations of the international series also caused the General Synod to warn against the dangers of the materials and to encourage intra-Lutheran cooperation in the development of materials based on Lutheran doctrine and pedagogy.[93]

One area of interchurch relations on which Lutherans had no trouble agreeing was the Roman Catholic Church. Catholic

89.
Lehre und Wehre 62 (February 1916): 91–92; Theodore E. Schmauk, "The Federation of Churches," *Lutheran Church Review* 28 (January 1909): 131–46; George W. Sandt, "The Church and Social Service," ibid. 34 (July 1915): 491–98; ibid. 34 (October 1915): 511–20.
90.
Lehre und Wehre 46 (1900): 182–83.
91.
Theodore E. Schmauk, "The Reunion of Christendom," *Lutheran Church Review* 32 (April 1913): 169–86; Friedrich Bente in *Lehre und Wehre* 62 (April 1916): 183–84.
92.
A speech of Junius B. Remensnyder of the General Synod to the New York conference on Faith and Order in 1913 advocated Lutheran compromise on such issues as episcopacy and ceremonies; this may have sobered the rest of the General Synod. See Dorris A. Flesner, "The Role of the Lutheran Churches of America in the Formation of the World Council of Churches" (Ph.D. diss., Hartford Seminary Foundation, Hartford, Conn., 1956), p. 9. Flesner's dissertation is the only thorough review of Lutheran reaction to the early twentieth-century ecumenical ventures.
93.
Documentary History of the General Council . . . (Philadelphia: General Council Pub. House, 1912), pp. 498–508; General Synod, *Minutes . . . 1911,* pp. 57, 116; ibid. *1913,* pp. 114–17; Sandt, *Schmauk,* pp. 88ff.

aggressiveness and numerical success in the early twentieth century (due largely to the same cause, immigration, which had given Lutheranism much of its strength) accentuated Lutheranism's doctrinal opposition as well as its traditional fear of Catholicism's threat to American liberties. Anti-Catholic literature was prevalent especially at the death of Leo XIII and at the time of initial Lutheran planning for the 400th anniversary of the Reformation. Because the Missouri Synod identified the pope with the Antichrist, its polemic was most unrestrained.[94] The other synods, although they were more temperate, were no less opposed to Rome's doctrine, political principles, and growing strength.

The picture of Lutheranism before World War I as a quiet, almost totally foreign-language church, content to confine its activities to corporate worship, religious education, and private piety is only partly accurate. General Synod Lutherans, usually with an American heritage of several generations behind them, hardly fit the pattern at all. Because of the great difference between them and the immigrant-dominated synods, friction and mutual suspicion were natural. Lutherans of the foreign-language synods, in contrast to the General Synod and the United Synod, South, were only slightly incorporated into the life of their communities. In the case of the General Council, generalizations were particularly dangerous because of the vast differences between the individual synods. Scandinavians, with more of a religious-social community life than Lutherans of German background, were the most socially self-sufficient. The latter adhered with almost equal tenacity to their mother-tongue but did not seem to have as strong a tie to other nationalistic cultural customs as did the Scandinavians.

Did the Lutherans feel self-consciously inferior? Yes, to the same degree as other foreign-language groups. Their "Lutheran" character had far less to do with this cultural phenomenon than did a host of other cultural factors. In only one area did Lutherans think of themselves as superior: the area of doctrine. Whether they called themselves the true visible Christian church or not, Lutherans felt that other Christians, to the degree that they differed in belief from themselves, were wrong. Rather than seek close contact with other Christians in order to win them to their beliefs, most Lutherans chose the easier alternative of assuming that total organizational separation and refusal to commune members of other churches or allow other pastors to preach in Lutheran churches would get the message across. A message did come across, but it was not the message which Lutherans thought they were communicating.

Few Lutherans held political office. Those who did were usually in predominantly Scandinavian communities. One unusual attempt to bring the church into closer touch with American life was the journal *American Lutheran Survey*. Financed by the sale of stock and edited by a southern Lutheran, a Norwegian, and a pastor of the Joint Synod of Ohio, its general aim was "the advancement of Christian civilization" through articles on the

94.
Lehre und Wehre 47 (January 1901): 28: "If we are right in our doctrine that we are saved solely through Christ and not through our works, and that Christ is the only Lord and Master of the believers, then certainly the pope belongs to the devil. . . . Everything truly Lutheran condemns the pope and everything papistic we Lutherans condemn whole heartedly. . . . We have never seen the pope himself, but we have seen many pictures of him. If the pictures correspond even partly to the reality, the 'old man' . . . looks as if a whole flock of devils had taken possession of him. He smiles so antagonistically, so repulsively, so diabolically. . . ."

"most vital subjects of the day from the best thinkers in America and abroad."

Seldom did Lutheran congregations gain any converts of non-Lutheran background. The exceptions were usually through marriage with a Lutheran. As far as Christian influence through witness and service was concerned, Lutherans were beginning to be more aware of missionary responsibility outside their own country. At home, however, individual Christian living meant attendance at church, a minimal financial commitment, sending one's children to religious instruction, and living an ethical life. For about half the Lutherans the Christian life would include avoidance of all involvement in secret societies. Corporately, Christian witness meant affirmation of correct doctrine and support of some benevolent enterprises. Even the latter, however, in line with the European and, to a lesser degree, the American pattern, came from groups of individuals voluntarily organized for service rather than from church bodies officially.

Lutherans could hardly be called a ghetto community but most were hardly an integral part of American society. The differences among them on this score were great in a few areas of life. In complicated patterns the dynamic factors of age, language, length of time in America, theology, European experience, location in the United States, level of education, and character of the locality where they lived determined their rate of incorporation into society and their sense of belonging to this land. All of them seem to have anticipated acculturation someday, far in the future, after many more generations of slow adjustment.

17 Celebration, War, and the Great Change

To Lutherans, wary of the "new" and tied to their own traditions of belief and church life, change has come hard. Both practical advantages and solid theological rationale were regarded as prerequisites for any modifications in outlook and life. Because of this theological and institutional conservatism, the repeated shocks and explosions of twentieth-century society had traumatic repercussions for Lutherans, not because Lutherans had shared the American dream of an evolving utopia but because society's convulsions left little time for the deliberate action which was a Lutheran hallmark. Within the span of half a decade or less changes took place among the insular, defensive, and doctrinally-preoccupied Lutherans, changes which most Lutherans had assumed would require many decades. The combination of a great religious celebration and the wrenching experience of the Great War catapulted Lutherans into twentieth-century American society. In the process of reconciling conflicting national loyalties, confronting irrational hostility, reaffirming a spiritual heritage, and reacting to the new demands for quick response Lutherans began to see themselves, their inner bonds, their strengths and weaknesses, their great potential, in a new light. The years between 1915 and 1920, even between 1917 and 1920, constitute one of the most significant watersheds in Lutheran history in America. Theologically, there was little change, but the self-awareness and the spirit of the church has never been the same.

The 400th Anniversary of the Reformation

There was never a debate among America's Lutherans whether or not to celebrate the quadricentennial of the posting of the Ninety-five Theses in 1517. The only question was how and on how large a scale. The dreamers, building more on wishes than on sober reality, at first suggested cooperative celebration by all Protestants or by all Lutherans, or by all Lutherans except those in the Synodical Conference. What materialized were celebrations within each church body, cooperative projects by the natural coalitions, and a few surprise combinations that transcended the traditional taboos of synodical lines. In all synods, recollection of the event which triggered the Reformation was to emphasize the evangelical recoveries of Luther as a conscious witness against all "false Protestants" and an aggressive Catholicism. Lutherans across the land formed committees for local celebrations, implicitly agreeing to forget, at least for a time, their internal squabbles in order univocally to sing the praises of Luther and his doctrine. More was done in the East than anywhere else, very little in the communities where language (or language loyalty) was still a barrier, and practically nothing cooperatively by congregations of the Synodical Conference and other Lutherans. But everywhere there was enough joint Lutheran activity to make preparation for the 1917 observance a turning point for Lutherans in America.[1] All synods appointed special planning committees, encouraged special services, published special literature of some kind, provided study helps, announced special jubilee thank-offerings, and hoped that the world would hear the Reformation's message anew and, coincidentally, notice the importance of the Lutherans.

Of all the quadricentennial committees, three of national scope were especially important. One was the official planning agent for a number of synods. Another, completely unofficial, drew together Lutherans from across the synodical spectrum. The third was Missouri's Central Committee.

Initiative for the first, the Joint Lutheran Committee on Celebration of the Quadricentennial, came from the strongest advocate of an all-Lutheran celebration, the General Synod, which in 1909 invited all Lutherans to join in centennial planning. Missouri and the rest of the Synodical Conference, of course, declined; language factors and their own merger problems kept the Norwegians from taking part; the smaller synods ignored the invitation. Of the Midwestern Lutherans the Joint Ohio and Iowa synods showed some initial interest, but their early withdrawal left only the Eastern synods in the Philadelphia-based Joint Lutheran Committee.

From the first meeting of the Joint Committee in 1914 through the celebration's climax in 1917, the major interest was in cultivating a deeper appreciation of the Lutheran heritage among Lutherans and a better understanding of the Lutheran faith among others. In spirit it was completely nonpolemical. Articles by Lutheran scholars were distributed to church papers, books endorsed, newspaper publicity prepared and disseminated, a Luther medal struck and a Luther stamp issued, the composition of new Reformation music encouraged, over a million tracts and booklets distributed, and assistance to local rally committees provided through standard programs and publicity materials. Over 130 local Lutheran committees drew on the resources of the Joint Committee. Outlines of lecture series on Luther and the Reformation were also available, as was a special series of sermon topics for the whole jubilee year. "All-Lutheran" services, which not all Lutherans supported, gave many Lutherans their first intimate worship contact with their "strange" brethren. Efforts were even made to have all non-Catholic educational institutions include some kind of Reformation feature in their 1917 commencement programs.[2]

The climax of this committee's work, however, was not the celebration of October 31, 1917, but the 1918 merger of the General Synod, the General Council, and the United Synod, South, which the committee's proposal of April 1917 set into motion. To claim that the merger was due mainly to the Reformation quadricentennial would be to ignore the decades of rapprochement among the three synods, but to ignore the union

1.
Otto H. Pannkoke, *A Great Church Finds Itself* (Quitman, Ga., 1966), pp. 44–62, is the fullest account.
2.
See General Synod and General Council *Minutes* for 1913, 1915, 1917, esp. General Synod, *Minutes . . . 1913*, pp. 122–24; ibid. *1915*, p. 14; General Council, *Minutes . . . 1917*, pp. 62–63, 67–68. Also, Howard R. Gold, "Developing the Quadricentennial Commemoration," *Lutheran Church Review* 35 (October 1916): 527–31; this whole issue (no. 4) was on the centennial.

hopes emanating from the desire for a climactic celebration would be equally wrong. Merger would have come regardless; the centennial hurried it along, thanks to the Joint Committee's sense of the historical moment. The merger gave the movement for Lutheran unity a powerful forward thrust.

Without sponsoring a financial appeal of its own, but aware of the positive effect which successful financial appeals could have on the whole church, the Joint Lutheran Committee encouraged all synods to set unprecedented goals for their jubilee offerings. "Through magnanimous, voluminous, and universal giving," wrote President V. G. A. Tressler of the General Synod, "we shall close the molecular age and the atom era of our giving . . . , pass the milestone of mediocrity and meagerness," and quicken the whole process of Lutheran permanence in America.[3] In most synods the offerings fell far short of the goals, partly because the concurrent national Liberty Loan campaigns absorbed such great amounts, but, as a whole, they succeeded enough to be harbingers of a new esprit de corps in Lutheranism.

More unusual, and controversial, was the program of the New York Reformation Quadricentenary Committee, organized in 1915 by the Lutheran Society of New York, to "enlist the nation's intellectual, educational, religious, political leadership appropriately to recognize the great influence on civilization of the Lutheran Reformation."[4] The society, a social organization of laymen from the General Council, General Synod, Augustana, Ohio, Missouri, and Norwegian synods, with the leadership coming mainly from the Missouri Synod members, hoped to gain public recognition of the Lutheran church by fostering civic celebrations throughout the land and by providing great amounts of publicity material to newspapers and journals. From this committee's offices flowed a steady stream of tributes to the Reformation by notable Americans in all fields, articles by well-known scholars on the effects of the Reformation on economics, education, music, literature, and political freedom, and press releases on all important events related to the Reformation and the Lutheran church.[5] Behind this unusual public-relations program were two Missouri Synod pastors from the New York area, William S. Schoenfeld and Otto H. Pannkoke, the latter a German immigrant who visualized Lutheranism as a respected, dynamic, unified, English-speaking force in America and devoted his whole life to that dream. Idea brochures for speakers and instruction manuals for local publicity augmented the national publicity through church papers and dailies. Even Princeton, Yale, and Columbia universities appointed representatives to work on the committee. Never before had the Lutheran church enjoyed such visibility. Delighted by its success as a public-information agency the New York Committee decided late in 1917 to remain in existence after its anniversary task had been completed. Reorganized as the Lutheran Bureau, it continued to inform Lutherans about their own church and its work and to acquaint the world at large with Lutheran history, activities, and achievements. In the wartime

3.
The goals were of unprecedented size: Iowa $250,000, Ohio $300,000, Norwegian Synod $400,000, United Synod, South $750,000, United Norwegian Lutheran Church $800,000, General Synod $1,000,000, General Council $1,000,000, Missouri Synod $1,000,000 (Victor G. A. Tressler, "A Reformation Fund for Lutheran Permanence," *Lutheran Standard,* May 19, 1917, p. 312–13).

4.
Pannkoke, *A Great Church,* p. 50.

5.
Among the scholars who wrote such articles for the Quadricentenary Committee were Williston Walker, W. W. Rockwell, A. E. Harvey, Preserved Smith, Paul Monroe, D. C. Munro, E. C. Richardson. The *American Lutheran Survey* ran the full series of these articles during the jubilee year 1917–18. The New York Committee published fifteen numbers of *The New York Reformation Anniversary Bulletin* in 1917 and 1918 to publicize its Speakers Bureau service, lecture outlines, available literature, exhibits, bibliographies, pageants, and special events. It provided information on activities of other Protestants, pep-talks to Lutherans everywhere, and constant reminders of the Reformation's impact on all of society. The file of the *Bulletins* is in the Archives of Cooperative Lutheranism, Lutheran Council/U.S.A., New York.

cooperative associations of Lutherans, this bureau was to play a helpful role.

The third committee of national, though not intersynodical, scope was Missouri's Central Committee, representing Lutheranism's largest single synod (575,000 communicants) in 1917. Uninterested in general publicity and intersynodical services, it had only one purpose: to stress the "spiritual" meaning of the Reformation so clearly that erring Lutherans, other Christians, and unbelievers would be exposed to the "saving truths" which Luther recovered and which only the Synodical Conference had preserved faithfully in America. The true doctrine was to be contrasted with the false. Lutherans of the Synodical Conference were continually reminded that they dared not compromise the truth by any kind of worship or cooperation with other Lutherans. The New York Committee's social and civic emphasis and its publicity campaign, as well as the Joint Committee's nonpolemical stance, were scorned as efforts to gain recognition by diluting the truth of Lutheran doctrine. Any emphasis other than doctrinal was said to "destroy the spiritual effect which our celebration might otherwise have upon the American churches and the public at large."[6] Missouri's committee encouraged much of the same festive activity as the others, but always with the reminder that the walls of separation within Lutheranism dared not be breached even for this special occasion. In only a few localities such as New York did a few local Missouri Synod pastors and laymen violate the synod's official position.

Although not aimed at the world outside Missouri, publicity organizations oriented to the quadricentennial began to appear in the Missouri Synod at this time. The American Lutheran Publicity Bureau, organized in 1914, had been only moderately active until 1917 when the quadricentennial spurred it into action. Its National Lutheran Publicity Week, begun in 1917, and its journal, the *American Lutheran* (1918), brought fresh approaches to church work into the Missouri Synod. In a variety of cities "Lutheran Publicity Organizations," loosely related to the Publicity Bureau, came into being in 1915 and 1916 to stimulate Reformation observance. Some evidence of the less traditional approach can be seen in special well-publicized downtown Lenten services which the Lutheran publicity organizations sponsored. Begun in St. Louis in 1917, they quickly spread to all other cities where Missouri congregations were strong. Their downtown-theater setting and their well-known speakers who avoided polemical topics gave the Missouri Synod an entrée to non-Lutherans which it had seldom before enjoyed.[7]

The Good Friday declaration of war with Germany (April 6, 1917) shook Lutheranism to its roots, but in some ways it had a wholesome effect on the Reformation celebration. Although no one had planned to emphasize the Germanic aspects of the reform, German Lutherans (and Scandinavians to a large degree) had made little effort to underplay the Reformation's European setting. The outbreak of war dampened any tenden-

6.
"Shall It Be a Denatured Jubilee?" *Lutheran Witness,* November 14, 1916, pp. 350–51. The editor's criticism of the New York Reformation Committee was especially harsh because fellow Missourians were in charge: "Our people realize what they owe to Luther and the Reformation. Their enthusiasm needs no artificial stimulants. There is a well-defined line which marks the limits between healthy enthusiasm and hysteria." ("False Ideals of the Jubilee," ibid., May 1, 1917, p. 145.)

7.
Alan N. Graebner, "The Acculturation of an Immigrant Lutheran Church: The Lutheran Church—Missouri Synod, 1917-1929" (Ph.D. diss., Columbia University, 1965), p. 245.

cies toward glorification of the German dimension and caused Lutherans to concentrate on the content of the Reformation message rather than on its place of origin or the language it helped to shape. In general, whatever cultural effects were glorified were those which had found expression in America; others were bypassed. All large-scale celebrations except one (the National Lutheran Woman's Quadricentennial celebration scheduled for Chicago) survived the initial post-Good Friday temptation to postpone or cancel observance of the anniversary. Lutheran papers were unanimous in pointing out that the war, caused by man's sinfulness, made the church's message and celebration of its sixteenth-century purification more necessary than ever. "We are not going to hush up," wrote one editor, "but preach [our principles] more loudly and insistently than ever."[8]

Not nearly as much restudy of Luther accompanied the anniversary celebrations as might have been expected. Lutheranism's defensive posture over against Catholics and other Protestants expressed itself in an emphasis on the Lutheran church's distinctive teachings rather than the character and experience of Luther himself. Publications on Luther abounded, of course, most of them popular and inspirational rather than scholarly. Few Luther authors reflected any awareness of the Luther renascence of the day or contributed to it. Exceptions were J. Michael Reu's *Thirty-five Years of Luther Research,*[9] which introduced English-reading American Lutherans to recent European Luther studies, and the Holman Edition of *The Works of Martin Luther,* intended as a resource for theological discussions on Luther.[10]

Anti-Romanism was accentuated by the quadricentennial. Rome's religious and political principles seemed to all Protestants, and especially Lutherans, to be the most ominous threat to Christian faith and civil liberty. Lutheran editors naively cited the European "Los von Rom" movement as evidence that Rome's day would soon end.[11] Tracts, sermons, and church papers belabored Rome's apostasy. In response to the vigorous attack on Luther in O'Hare's *The Facts About Martin Luther*[12] (published as part of American Catholicism's "observance" of the Reformation), the New York Committee had Heinrich Boehmer's *Leben Luther's* translated and published in a twenty-five-cent edition which reached thousands of Lutheran families. Rome was one topic on which Lutherans could agree.

The results of the Reformation anniversary for Lutherans are not easy to assess because many of the benefits, such as new awareness of their basic oneness and potential strength, were interrelated with the wartime experience. Yet the Reformation anniversary did foster a new "Lutheran" awareness which made Lutherans more optimistic about their church's role in America and more aggressive in pursuing their goals. Psychologically, at least, the ghetto mentality had suffered a hard blow. Lutherans were beginning to assert themselves. Recollection of the past, inspiring services, large offerings, rededication to the

8.
"Luther: An Ideal for America," *Lutheran Standard,* September 22, 1917, p. 594.
9.
Chicago: Wartburg, 1917. Most of the materials had been published previously as articles in the *Lutheran Church Review.*
10.
The Works of Martin Luther, with introductions and notes, 2 vols. (Philadelphia: Holman, 1915). Six volumes had been planned but only two appeared in time for the anniversary. The remaining four were not published until 1930-32. This series served as the basic Luther source in English until publication of the fifty-five volume edition of *Luther's Works,* 1955- . In his introduction, Henry Eyster Jacobs says that the series was prepared with specific reference to the discussions of Luther which the anniversary was sure to bring. On popular works on Luther during this period see Helen M. Knubel, "The Quadricentennial Celebration of the Reformation, 1917: Summary of Facts on Activities and Publications as Found in the Library of the National Lutheran Council," an unpublished article by the librarian of the Department of Research and Statistics of the Lutheran Council/U.S.A.
11.
"Away from Rome" or "Free from Rome" movements developed in Europe during the nineteenth century, especially in Austria and Germany where they were as much political as religious, but also in France, Belgium, and even Spain and Portugal. A resurgence, especially in Austria, in the early twentieth century, coupled with the modernist movement, fed Lutheran hopes that the Roman church might soon fall. See John A. Bain, "Los von Rom," *The New Schaaf-Herzog Encyclopedia of Religious Knowledge* (1910), 7:42-44.
12.
New York: F. Pustet, 1916.

gospel of Christ, as they thought Luther had taught it, built up an expectant mood, perhaps even hope of a "kind of Pentecost era" just ahead.[13]

The War and Its Effects

The attitude of most Lutherans to the European conflict was predictably pro-German between 1914 and 1917. Not only those of German background but almost all Lutherans were products of inherited nationalistic preferences which regarded Great Britain with suspicion. So long as the United States claimed neutrality and remained officially a noncombatant, the pro-German loyalties cost little. With the declaration of war, however, many Lutherans were plunged into a dilemma and even those whose loyalty was not in doubt were made to pay for society's suspicions about their "foreign church." The war years shook foreign-oriented Lutherans loose from their assumption that adjustment to America could take generations and drastically reshaped much of the Lutheran spirit almost overnight.

The Lutheran Attitude Before 1917

Before America's entry into the war, the attitude of the Lutheran foreign-language press differed from the German-American press in general only in its greater moderation. Even the English Lutheran editors frequently challenged the pro-British interpretation of the conflict. "This war," wrote Theodore E. Schmauk in 1914, "is the result of the British plan of destroying Germany's foreign commerce and relations, and of doing away . . . with a rival whose influence on the world's markets was asserting itself more and more at the cost of British commerce."[14] Most German Lutherans would have agreed and, therefore, hoped for a German victory of which they were quite confident in the early days of the war. Occasionally, a synod even prayed publicly for Germany, as did the Wartburg Synod (of the General Synod) in 1914. After the prayer it sang "Deutschland über Alles" and "Die Wacht am Rhein." More typical were prayers for the protection and welfare of fellow believers in the homeland.[15] When American "neutrality" turned out to be in the Allies' favor, Lutherans began publicly to criticize the government in a fashion not at all typical of their church in the past. German church papers, especially, supported movements critical of the government's position, such as the American Neutrality League, the German-American National Conference, and the American Embargo Conference. Strange, in view of the Missouri's Synod's traditional social and political quietism, was the extent and vigor of its denunciations of the "atrocious trade in arms" and its charge that America's lust for profit had turned it into a hypocritical murderer.[16] Even more astounding was the theological justification for this new critical attitude voiced by Missouri's president, that "anything that touches moral issues is within the sphere of the church."[17] Attacks on both American and German manufacturers, favorable reviews of books which laid the blame for the war on England, defenses against the charge of hyphenism, and synodi-

13.
Lutheran Standard, October 13, 1917, p. 641.

14.
"The Great War of Germany Against Europe," *Lutheran Church Review* 33 (October 1914): 764. This is the most careful and comprehensive of the anti-British analyses in any Lutheran publication. Cf. a series by Theodore Graebner, "Moral Issues and Religious Aspects of the Great War," *Lutheran Witness,* February 22, 1916, pp. 50–53; March 21, 1916, pp. 80–83; May 2, 1916, pp. 126–28.

15.
General Synod, *Minutes . . . 1915,* p. 63.

16.
Friedrich Bente of Concordia Seminary, St. Louis, spoke frequently at neutrality conferences and editorialized regularly against American policy in *Der Lutheraner,* as did Theodore Graebner in the *Lutheran Witness.* Bente's appearance before the Foreign Relations Committee of the Senate in 1915 caused Henry Cabot Lodge to comment in a letter to Theodore Roosevelt in 1915 that Bente's accent was "so strong you could stumble over it . . . [as he] lectured us on Americanism, patriotism . . . [and] the opinions of George Washington. . . . Some of us are not hyphenates—we are just plain Americans—and the wrath of the members of the Committee, Democrats and Republicans, was pleasing to witness. I think they have overdone it." Quoted in Carl S. Meyer, ed., *Moving Frontiers: Readings in the History of the Lutheran Church—Missouri Synod* (St. Louis: Concordia Publishing House, 1964), p. 236.

17.
Der Lutheraner, February 15, 1916, p. 63. When the issues became emotional enough, Lutherans could appeal to the very same oversimplified principle which they had criticized repeatedly when used by other Protestants to justify concern and action on social or political issues.

cal resolutions against arms exports which were causing loss of American lives were other expressions of the German sympathies of Lutherans. Allied defeats were interpreted as punishment for its national sins, such as the opium trade in China; German suffering as divine retribution for its spiritual decline. Only the more extreme Germanophiles went so far as to praise the Kaiser and General von Hindenburg as Christians worthy of emulation.[18]

As the peace negotiations of early 1917 collapsed, church officials and editors called for renewed efforts toward peace while engaging in soul-searching for reasons why God was allowing America to be drawn into the war. With the declaration of war, pro-German expressions virtually disappeared, but reminders were frequent that America was entering the conflict with hands bloodstained by its trade in arms.[19]

The Storm Breaks Over the Lutherans

"Once lead this people into war and they'll forget there ever was such a thing as tolerance," said Woodrow Wilson prior to America's entry. Before the war was many months old, superpatriots and "100 percent Americans" seemed to be intent on proving how right the President had been. The Lutherans were not, of course, the only group to suffer intolerance, nor was the intolerance of America during and after the war essentially religious. During the war and the postwar scare years those fearful for their country struck out blindly against all advocates of cultures or ideas that seemed strange or foreign. Germans suffered most and among the Germans, the Lutherans more than any other religious group, because of national background and because of their hesitation to allow the church to become involved with affairs of state. Non-German-speaking Lutherans shared their lot through guilt-by-association. To carry on their church life as always now made them enemy-sympathizers and subjected them to the most extreme accusations and restrictions ever suffered by any Caucasian group in America. Obviously, the more "immigrant" a church body, the more despised it was. Lutherans in the East suffered least, those of the central Midwest most. Prejudice was worst during the critical spring offensive of 1918 when the Allied cause hung in the balance and American casualties rose alarmingly. But from April 1917 through much of 1919 the Midwestern Lutherans were scrutinized by those eager to find evidence of disloyalty. Determination to rid America of everything German led to the burning of German books by libraries, changing of German names on streets and menus, banning of German papers from bookstands, refusal of musical groups to perform works of German composers, and the boycotting of German artists.[20] No self-devised program could have hastened the divorce of Lutherans from their former cultural loyalties as rapidly as did this antagonism from the superpatriots.

Many of the charges were untrue; others had basis in fact. The head of the Lutheran church was said to be the Kaiser, to whom all Lutheran pastors were said to have sworn obedience.[21]

18.
Lutheran Witness, December 15, 1914, p. 207; August 10, 1915, p. 253.

19.
See Carl Wittke, *German-Americans and World War I* (Columbus, Ohio: Ohio State Archeological and Historical Society, 1936); Frederick Nohl, "The Lutheran Church Missouri Synod Reacts to United States Anti-Germanism During World War I," *Concordia Historical Institute Quarterly* 35 (July 1962): 49–66; Frederick C. Luebke, "Superpatriotism in World War I: The Experience of a Lutheran Pastor," ibid. 41 (February 1968): 3–11; Neil M. Johnson, "The Patriotism and Anti-Prussianism of the Lutheran Church—Missouri Synod, 1914–1918," ibid. 39 (October 1966): 99–118; Paul W. Roth, *Lutheran Loyalty to the American Idea* (Milwaukee, 1918). Also, "The Kaiser and the Kaiser's Church," *Literary Digest* 58 (1918): 28, 31; Charles Stewart, "Prussianizing Wisconsin," *Atlantic Monthly* 123 (January 1919): 99–105; John Higham, *Strangers in the Land: Patterns of American Nativism, 1860–1925* (New Brunswick, N.J.: Rutgers University Press, 1955), esp. chap. 9; C. J. Child, *The German-Americans in Politics, 1914–1917* (Madison: University of Wisconsin Press, 1939).

20.
A Baptist church in Oklahoma even refused to celebrate Easter because the congregation regarded it as "a German heathen custom" (*Lutheran Witness*, June 25, 1918, p. 204).

21.
The so-called oath to the Kaiser, widely publicized in the Midwest, to which all Lutheran pastors throughout the world were supposed to be bound, read: "I will be submissive, faithful, and obedient to his Royal Majesty . . . [and] cultivate in the minds of the people under my care a sense of reverence and fidelity toward the king, love for the fatherland, obedience to the laws [of Germany]. . . . In particular, I vow that I will not support any society or association . . . which might endanger the public security, and will inform his Majesty of any proposals made, either in my diocese or elsewhere, which might

Lutheran schools which used the German language were said to be hotbeds of treason, and pastors who preached in German were called enemy agents. Lutheran refusal to participate in joint Protestant rallies for the sale of war bonds was seen not as religious separation but as proof of subversive goals. Expressions of sympathy with the German cause prior to American involvement, especially when recalled in situations where Lutherans were unwilling to use their churches for governmental wartime programs, cost more than one pastor his parish. At best, foreign-language instruction was regarded as a barrier to Americanization, especially the inculcation of the ideals of democracy; at worst it seemed treasonous.

State and local councils of defense, starting with the Nebraska State Council in July 1917, took legal and illegal action against the suspects. Parochial schools were closed (hundreds in the Missouri Synod in 1918) and several burned. Services were disrupted and pastoral meetings broken up. Pastors were sometimes daubed with yellow paint, made to kiss the flag, to pledge allegiance, and to subscribe to war bonds. Altars were occasionally befouled and windows smashed. A few pastors and councilmen were tarred and feathered; some were flogged. Churches and schools were placarded.[22] German-speaking Lutherans were threatened with dire consequences if they used the forbidden tongue. Comments such as Billy Sunday's "If you turned hell upside down you'd find 'Made in Germany' stamped on the bottom of it," and Harry Lauder's charge that every Lutheran church in St. Louis sang a hymn of hate every Sunday fanned the popular hysteria.[23] Major newspapers were virtually unanimous in denouncing all use of German in the schools.[24] Proclamations prohibiting the use of any foreign language in elementary schools and in all public places (including on the telephone) and limiting the use of all foreign languages in worship to the home were made by several governors and proposed as laws in at least fifteen states.[25] Nebraska's Sedition Act (1918) required all preachers and teachers to be licensed by the district court and gave local defense councils the job of investigating the applicants. Lutherans were almost always given a hard time. Under Nebraska's Simian Act (1919) a Lutheran teacher, Robert T. Meyer, was convicted of teaching reading in the German language to a ten-year-old boy. However, a ruling of the United States Supreme Court that the law violated the Fourteenth Amendment eased this kind of pressure on the churches.[26]

Proven cases of disloyalty on the part of Lutheran pastors were few, although popular opinion assumed otherwise.[27] It is impossible to say how many Lutheran laymen were among the citizens convicted of disloyalty. No doubt many Germans, and some Lutherans among them, did speak carelessly about war issues as though the German cause were synonymous with the cause of Lutheranism or about their personal dislike of America and its ways.[28] Most of the suspicion of Lutherans, however, was due to their use of the German language, their unwillingness to give it up without a fight, mistaken identification of Lutheranism with the Church of Prussia, popular identification of all

prove injurious to the State. I will preach the Word as his Gracious Majesty dictates." (*Topeka Daily Capital,* April 7, 1918, quoted in *Lutheran Witness,* April 30, 1918, p. 131.) The Missouri Synod's official refutation was Frederick Brand's *The Lutheran Church versus Hohenzollernism: Testimony and Proof Bearing on the Relation of the American Lutheran Church to the German Emperor* (St. Louis: Concordia Publishing House, 1918).

22.
One such posted on a church door read: "God Almighty understands the English language. Hereafter use it. Don't tear this down. The Vigilantes." (*Lutheran Standard,* June 1, 1918, p. 329.)

23.
Ray H. Abrams, *Preachers Present Arms* (New York: Round Table Press, 1933), p. 16. The Abrams portrayal is challenged and corrected by John F. Piper, Jr., "The Social Policy of the Federal Council and the War: Churches of Christ in America During World War I" (Ph.D. diss., Duke University, 1964). Germans of today, said Newell D. Hills, "have no more relation to the civilization of 1918 than an orangutan, a gorilla, a Judas, a hyena, a thumbscrew, or a scalping-knife in the hands of a savage. These brutes must be cast out of society." Quoted by Clifton Olmstead, *History of Religion in the United States* (Englewood Cliffs, N.J.: Prentice-Hall, 1960), p. 511.

24.
Among them were the *New York Times, Philadelphia Ledger, Pittsburgh Times Gazette, St. Louis Star, St. Louis Globe-Democrat, Omaha Bee, Lincoln Star, Cleveland News, Milwaukee Journal, Nebraska State Journal, Ohio State Journal.*

25.
See the May 1918 proclamation of Governor W. L. Harding of Iowa in the *Lutheran Standard,* June 22, 1918, p. 378. The states were California, Illinois, Indiana, Iowa, Kansas, Michigan, Minnesota, Missouri, Montana, Nebraska, North Dakota, Ohio, Pennsylvania, South Dakota, and Wisconsin. (A. N. Graebner, "Acculturation," p. 31.)

Germans with the Lutheran church, and the refusal of some pastors, especially those of the Missouri Synod, to take part in patriotic services with other Protestants. On the other hand, some Lutherans were obviously using the principle of church-state separation to justify neutrality while their country was at war.

The Lutheran Response

The typical Lutheran reaction to active United States involvement in the war was for church conventions and papers to declare full support of their country. Exceptions were several strongly pro-German papers which preferred to say nothing. In general, the pattern was the more Americanized the group, the more unequivocal the pledge.[29] Evidences of misgivings about America's new role were more frequent in literature of the more conservative immigrant groups and usually advocated the traditional Lutheran line that citizens, even if they have doubts about their country's action, must be loyal because "it is the government's war and not the individual's" and the "state takes all the responsibility."[30] In all synods, support became less critical as the war proceeded. Earlier reminders about America's unclean hands gave way to assurances that America's unselfish motives justified prayers for America's victory. No synod, however, endorsed the popular view of a "holy war."[31]

Where Lutherans were attacked they quickly overcame fear and reticence and learned how to protest unjust accusations. In fact, defense against wartime prejudice was a powerful stimulus to the early experiments in Lutheran cooperation. It was the major reason behind the decision of the New York Reformation Committee to give its public relations activity permanent structure in the Lutheran Bureau, and one of the causes for the organization of the National Lutheran Council in 1918. Some of the first joint meetings of Lutherans across the broad synodical spectrum came from areas where councils of defense plagued Lutheran freedoms. For example, a protest meeting against the Nebraska Council of Defense produced a statement signed by representatives of the General Synod, General Council, Missouri, Augustana, and Ohio synods, the Norwegian Lutheran Church, and the two Danish Lutheran bodies.[32] The need to protest forced Lutherans to rely on each other as they engaged in what for them was novel activity—making the voice of their church heard in the legislative halls and committee chambers of the state, and in secular papers and magazines.

An even greater change was the growing awareness among all foreign-heritage Lutherans of the need to adjust church and individual life quickly to American ways. While language was undoubtedly the most drastic change for the average member of the immigrant synods, it was by no means the only one. At least as significant was the insight that in outlook and loyalty Lutheranism from now on would have to be American. Theologically, one editor after another saw that Lutherans were free to make any adjustment, put up with any inconvenience, yield to any of the needs of government and society so long as the Word of God

26.
For other school cases see Arthur L. Miller, *Educational Administration and Supervision of the Lutheran Schools of the Missouri Synod* (Chicago: University of Chicago Press, 1951), pp. 240-44. Also, Robert N. Manley, "Language, Loyalty, and Liberty: The Nebraska State Council of Defense and the Lutheran Churches, 1917-1918," *Concordia Historical Institute Quarterly* 37 (April 1964): 1-16.

27.
Reports of all Lutheran camp pastors to the Commission for Soldiers' and Sailors' Welfare were taken from the commission's files by officials of the U.S. Department of Intelligence for examination. A small percentage was taken to Washington and later "returned to us with a clean bill of health." (Files of the National Lutheran Commission for Soldiers' and Sailors' Welfare, Archives of Cooperative Lutheranism.)

28.
J. A. W. Haas, "Loyalty to Our Land," *Lutheran Church Review* 37 (January 1918): 103, deplores such attitudes. A. N. Graebner, "Acculturation," p. 74, quotes a Kansas Lutheran pastor to a fellow pastor: "I hate this country. I have been here for 25 years, still I hate this country."

29.
A collection of loyalty pledges is in the files of the National Lutheran Council (State and Society—Loyalty), Archives of Cooperative Lutheranism.

30.
"The Christian and War," *Lutheran Standard*, April 21, 1917, p. 241. Very similar is Frank H. Jordan's "Our Watchword of Today—Loyalty," in *Lutheran Church Year Book 1919*, pp. 46-47.

31.
Some individuals came close to it, e.g., Charles M. Jacobs: "When war is a clean-cut issue between two theories of the state, both of which cannot be right, and between two conceptions of national morality and obligations, one of which must be totally wrong, the voice of the church must be heard in defense of that conception which accords with the social teachings of Jesus" ("The Church and the

or the "free preaching of the Law and the Gospel and the administration of the sacraments" were not violated.[33] In carrying out this culturally liberating principle, the most difficult area of application was the governmental effort to enlist the aid of the churches in wartime programs. Early in the war most Lutherans had been hesitant about using worship services to publicize Liberty Bond drives, Red Cross appeals, food and coal conservation announcements, or even the Navy's appeal for binoculars, partly because the government's publicity for some of these programs frequently included outlines for sermons.[34] And on the content of sermons Lutherans would yield to no one. Even the appointment by the President of a day of national prayer was criticized by some as an intrusion on the sphere of the church. The trend, however, quickly swung away from the idea that "whatever is not religious, but merely social or political, does not concern the church" to ever greater church and clerical support of the war effort, including the reading of governmental announcements during the service (but not from the pulpit), honor rolls and service flags in the churches, enlistment of volunteers for the Red Cross, and other service functions.[35] Social pressure, because of Lutheran hesitation in the first and second Liberty Bond drives, stimulated an all-out Lutheran effort in the third. These adjustments in Lutheran attitude, plus a higher proportion of enlistments by Lutherans than by the population in general and a successful and well-publicized financial appeal for a ministry to Lutheran servicemen, eased much of the popular antipathy to Lutherans before the end of the war.

Cooperation on a Large Scale

Important as the societal tensions were for Lutherans, they were in a sense but backdrop for other challenges which pushed Lutherans into a new era—that of widespread and official cooperation.[36] Dreamers had hoped for it; optimists had predicted it; planners had suggested schemes; but it took the presence of thousands of young Lutherans in the armed services to convince their churches' leaders that the crisis left no time to argue old differences before uniting for action. Their young men needed spiritual care. They could not be served effectively if each little group acted independently. Inadvertently the government also gave Lutherans a nudge. It did not want to deal with the major denominations individually, preferring for a time that the ministry of all churches be handled through the Y.M.C.A. or the Federal Council of Churches. On two counts, the Lutherans demurred. Theologically, they felt responsible as Lutherans to minister to their own men. Practically, they felt the job was too big to be handled by one or two general agencies. Perhaps the new spirit of cooperation was "faith triumph[ing] over abstract theology,"[37] perhaps it was a case of the need for cooperation becoming so urgent that even conservative Lutherans could not find good reasons to hold back. Some did, of course, for reasons of conscience, but even the Missouri Synod's slight degree of cooperation with the other Lutherans was an advance upon the

War," *Lutheran Church Review* 37 [July 1918]: 235). This is mild compared to the views of many Protestant clergy as documented in Abrams, *Preachers Present Arms*, and Jess Yoder, "Preaching on Issues of War and Peace, 1915-1965," in *Preaching in American History*, ed. De Witte Holland (Nashville: Abingdon Press, 1969).
32.
Lutheran Standard, August 18, 1917, pp. 513-14. In Iowa, the Missouri Synod cooperated with the Iowa and Joint Ohio synods in fighting a pastor's conviction on the language law (Miller, *Educational Administration*, p. 242). Missouri's own committee to deal with unjust measures was called the Synodical Council of War.
33.
Theodore Graebner, "Stop, Look, and Listen!" *Lutheran Witness,* December 25, 1917, p. 406. A seminary colleague told Graebner that this editorial had brought more shame on Lutheranism than the unionists (A. N. Graebner, "Acculturation," p. 67). It meant a drastic change in spirit for the Missouri Synod. The aggressive and articulate Theodore Graebner became Missouri's champion of an actively pro-American spirit. He saw that the old neutral attitude as reflected in *Der Lutheraner*'s silence about the war had to be overcome. "When a new situation arises," he wrote, "the majority can almost absolutely be counted upon to be dead in the wrong" (letter to M. Graebner, March 4, 1919, Theodore Graebner File, Concordia Historical Institute, St. Louis). See also Johnson, "Patriotism and Anti-Prussianism," pp. 99-118.
34.
"So well recognized is the helplessness of preachers who have discarded the Gospel of Jesus Christ that the Federal Government is now stepping in and is supplying the preachers with text, topics, and a sermon outline" (*Lutheran Witness,* June 12, 1917, p. 182). "The less the people hear of war when they come to the sanctuary and the more they confess their sins and plead for peace, the nearer will the Church come to fulfilling the mission which Christ has charged her with. The newspapers are keeping hell before us

old isolation. For most Lutherans, the new situation demanded new answers; new needs had to be met by new kinds of action. Moreover, the sense of solidarity being created by the Reformation anniversary and the planning for two mergers liberated enough Lutherans from synodical isolation for the war years to become the first real sign of hope that the old cultural, sociological, and theological walls might soon be overcome.

The National Lutheran Commission for Soldiers' and Sailors' Welfare

As soon as mobilization began all Lutherans, whether or not they supported American entry into the war, became concerned about the spiritual care of Lutheran servicemen. The presence of a few Lutheran chaplains in the services was small comfort, for the military chaplaincy then was barely a shadow of what it later became. The few chaplains were really more recreational officers than spiritual shepherds. Missouri's 1917 convention, meeting two months after the declaration of war, authorized an Army and Navy Board. Smaller synods, not knowing just what to do, appointed committees. The sheer scope of the need made cooperation seem natural. Laymen from a number of synods in the state of Iowa, especially from the Norwegian Lutheran Church, sensing the need for quick action in behalf of Lutheran soldiers at Fort Dodge, established a loose organization and received permission to erect a building within the camp so long as the organization was not officially connected with any church body. Publicity for the novel plan soon enlisted the support of over 60,000 Lutheran laymen for building and equipping Lutheran centers in or near large military camps.[38] The Ministerium of Pennsylvania devised a plan to serve all military camps within its territory. Within three weeks of the start of war the Inner Mission Board of the General Synod invited similar boards of the General Council and the United Synod, South to work cooperatively in behalf of servicemen. This United Inner Mission, organized in May 1917 as a temporary agency, at once established contact with the Red Cross and the Federal Council's Wartime Commission through which the government consulted with the churches. Before the summer of 1917 was over it had planned an extensive program of suggestions to all pastors and congregations and much direct help to chaplains and congregations near the military camps.[39] From the beginning, more inclusive cooperation was visualized, first with Iowa, Ohio, and the Norwegians, but by September with all Lutheran bodies, partly because the military authorities were unwilling to accredit more than one Lutheran representative for any one military camp.

Seven Lutheran church bodies, including Missouri, were represented at an October 19, 1917, meeting called by the United Inner Mission to organize one central board for Lutheran wartime service. Six more quickly joined; but Missouri's representative could not commit his church to membership in the new National Lutheran Commission for Soldiers' and Sailors' Welfare. In view of the scathing attacks which Missouri Synod

seven days of the week: let the church speak of heaven on Sunday" (Theodore Graebner, "Lutheran Loyalty," ibid., August 7, 1917, p. 238).
35.
President Schmauk of the General Council was especially active in the Liberty Bond drives. See George S. Sandt, *Theodore Emanuel Schmauk* (Philadelphia: United Lutheran Publication House, 1921), pp. 104-5; and the files of the National Lutheran Council (Liberty Loans), Archives of Cooperative Lutheranism.
36.
See Fred W. Meuser, *The Formation of the American Lutheran Church* (Columbus, Ohio: Wartburg Press, 1958), pp. 137-41; and E. Clifford Nelson and Eugene L. Fevold, *The Lutheran Church Among Norwegian-Americans*, 2 vols. (Minneapolis: Augsburg Publishing House, 1960), 2:288, n. 9.
37.
Pannkoke, *A Great Church*, p. 79.
38.
The unusual story of the way in which a group of churchmen received permission to erect a building within Fort Dodge is in National Lutheran Commission for Soldiers' and Sailors' Welfare, *Reports . . . 1919* (New York: National Lutheran Commission, 1919), pp. 67-75.
39.
E. F. Bachmann and Frederick H. Knubel, "Our Church's Service in War Times," *Lutheran Standard*, September 29, 1917, pp. 616-18, describes the amazing scope of the young program.

papers were making on all planning for the United Lutheran Church merger of 1918, even the presence of a Missouri representative was surprising. Representatives of the others had no qualms about committing their churches to a well-defined program of cooperation. The commission was by far the most inclusive organization of Lutherans to this point in American history.[40] Even the Synodical Conference maintained a carefully delineated working agreement with it, especially in matters which required a single Lutheran approach to governmental or military units.[41] Full cooperation was established with the organization of laymen, the Lutheran Brotherhood of America, which continued to build and equip "Lutheran centers" for servicemen. President of the commission for its five-year life span was Frederick H. Knubel, a Manhattan pastor who had been chairman of the General Synod's Inner Mission Board and of the United Inner Mission. He was soon to be elected president of the United Lutheran Church from which position he would try in vain to lead fellow Lutherans into some form of cooperative work with other Protestants. His leadership, which combined spiritual depth and great executive ability, was a key factor in the success of the commission.

Through the program of the Commission for Soldiers' and Sailors' Welfare no area of wartime service to Lutherans was ignored. Chaplains were recruited and equipped; pastors of congregations near military installations were appointed as camp pastors; field secretaries were appointed to visit all bases so that every Lutheran young man had some opportunity for pastoral contact; churches near camps were given interest-free loans to provide proper facilities; workers were assigned to the centers built by the Lutheran Brotherhood; chaplain service was provided for military hospitals and camps for interned aliens;[42] a Washington office was established for united representation before the national government; Christian literature for servicemen was provided virtually free of charge; mail contact was maintained with all Lutheran servicemen whose addresses were provided; pastors were appointed to serve the Student Army Training Corps at church colleges; women were enlisted for volunteer work through a women's committee; representatives were even sent to France to augment what spiritual care chaplains could provide at and near the front and to assist the small and suffering Lutheran Church of France. Through the public-relations facilities of the Lutheran Bureau, almost daily articles were provided to the church and public press to keep the Lutheran constituency well-informed on what they were able to do together.

Would the new Lutheran spirit be strong enough to weather an assault on the traditionally well-guarded Lutheran pocketbook? To finance all the activities of the commission, funds were needed in unprecedented amounts. Resisting suggestions to cut its goal below basic needs, the commission set a goal of $750,000. Several weeks of concentrated publicity were to climax in a nationwide one-week every-member canvass. Under the leadership of Walton H. Greever, a southern Lutheran and editor of

40.
Member churches: Danish Lutheran, General Council, General Synod, Icelandic Synod, Iowa Synod, Lutheran Brethren, Lutheran Free Church, Norwegian Lutheran Church, Joint Synod of Ohio, Suomi Synod, United Danish Church, United Synod, South.
41.
For "Agreement with the Synodical Conference," and "Agreement with the Lutheran Brotherhood," see National Lutheran Commission for Soldiers' and Sailors' Welfare, *Reports . . . 1918*, pp. 19–21. On the work of the Brotherhood, see *Reports . . . 1919*, pp. 67–81; and *Lutheran World Almanac and Encyclopedia* (New York: National Lutheran Council, 1921), pp. 459–61. For a full report on Missouri's Church Board for Army and Navy, U.S.A., see Missouri Synod, *Synodal-bericht . . . 1920*, pp. 103–11.
42.
Work with aliens was assigned almost exclusively to the National Lutheran Commission by the Federal Council of Churches' Wartime Commission.

the *American Lutheran Survey,* and Otto H. Pannkoke of the Lutheran Bureau, the publicity was written and printed in spite of wartime restrictions and distributed in spite of an embargo on express in the East. Synodical and congregational leaders were trained in the novelties of the simultaneous campaign method. Even the most optimistic of the planners were amazed at the $1,350,000 which flowed in, a response which almost doubled the goal that had seemed unattainable to many. This appeal, like the Reformation anniversary, was another giant stride for a church emerging from its introspection and becoming aware of its potential.[43] More than one synodical leader interpreted the amazing success of the appeal as evidence that Lutherans had "entered the million-dollar class." The Missouri Synod, in a similar appeal, with all pledges to be made on September 29, 1918, raised $560,000 for its wartime work. A new dimension of church life was developing. The experience of the servicemen themselves in getting away from nationalistic enclaves and of the average church member in being exposed to a broader slice of life contributed significantly to the new mood.

403

The National Lutheran Council

Important as the Commission for Soldiers' and Sailors' Welfare was for giving Lutherans a way of doing together what they could not do separately, it had been in existence for only a short time when some of its inadequacies became obvious. Service to servicemen, which was the boundary of the commission authorization, was not the only need which had to be met cooperatively. War industries had resulted in many new communities which were without churches. The attacks on Lutherans because of the language hysteria made official and representative Lutheran presence in Washington desirable. The physical destruction and spiritual chaos attendant upon the war would leave countless European Lutherans in need and their mission work in Asia, Africa, and Oceana without support. Joint fundraising and publicity for service on a much broader scale than that of the commission would seen be imperative. To the pioneers in cooperation a new and more comprehensively authorized Lutheran agency was the logical answer. From several quarters came proposals in mid-1918 for such an agency. The National Lutheran Editors Association, one of the first pan-Lutheran cooperative groups, suggested that the presidents move to bring about such "concerted action." Pannkoke of the Lutheran Bureau pressed for immediate action and tried to convene the church presidents. Frederick H. Knubel saw the need clearly and urged presidents Theodore E. Schmauk (General Council), Morris G. G. Scherer (United Synod, South), V. G. A. Tressler (General Synod), and Hans G. Stub (Norwegian Lutheran Church) to take the lead in promoting a new agency.

In July and August 1918 preliminary meetings of presidents and others in Harrisburg and Pittsburgh laid plans for organization of a "Lutheran Federal Council" in Chicago on September 6. Once again church-body presidents were willing to take

43.
In chaps. 3 and 4 of *A Great Church,* Pannkoke tells the story from the perspective of almost half a century. His "Going Over the Top," *Lutheran Standard,* March 16, 1918, pp. 149ff., expresses all the excitement of the appeal. On the general Protestant response to wartime crises and other denominational campaigns see Samuel M. Cavert, *The American Churches in the Ecumenical Movement* (New York: Association Press, 1968), pp. 88-103.

immediate action without waiting for church bodies to approve. In addition to these four synods, Augustana, the Danish Lutheran Church, Iowa, the Lutheran Free Church, and Ohio attended the Chicago meeting and approved of the agency which was named the National Lutheran Council. The United Danish Lutheran Church, Buffalo Synod, and Icelandic Synod gave their support before the year's end. The Missouri Synod, although represented at the two preliminary meetings, again declined to take part. Its traditional criticism of other Lutherans on doctrinal and practical grounds, plus frictions between its Army and Navy Board and the National Lutheran Commission for Soldiers' and Sailors' Welfare, and unrestrained criticism of the coming United Lutheran Church made continued isolation inevitable.[44]

Awareness of the long-range possibilities for an agency such as the National Lutheran Council is obvious from the statement of purpose which the founders adopted: statistical information for all American Lutherans, publicity on matters affecting all Lutherans, representation of Lutherans to all other entities, joint action on problems arising out of the war, coordination of activities related to social, economic, and intellectual conditions affecting Christianity, fostering of loyalty to the nation, and maintaining proper relations between church and state.[45] Headquarters were to be in New York. Representation was one for every hundred thousand confirmed members or one-third fraction thereof. Hans G. Stub (Norwegian Lutheran Church) was elected president, John L. Zimmerman (General Synod layman) vice president, Lauritz Larsen (Norwegian Lutheran Church) secretary.

The striking contrast between the specific purpose of the Commission for Soldiers' and Sailors' Welfare and the more general mandate of the National Lutheran Council explains in part why some member bodies and some presidents were not convinced of the need for the new council. In committing their churches to membership some had exceeded their actual authority, and their second thoughts had to be put to the test during council's early years. Frederick K. Wentz, however, is correct in saying that "the Council came into being because of a sense of urgency shared by many Lutherans," that it "sprang into existence" and was "born running" with a full agenda from the start, and that it reflected a "real pioneering spirit" which was to become a trend in twentieth-century churchmanship.[46]

Every one of the purposes clamored for immediate attention. The Lutheran Bureau was adopted as the National Lutheran Council's publicity and research department, giving the Lutheran church news coverage as efficient as any Protestant church in the land, and a research and statistical arm whose accurate data on every aspect of Lutheran life was the first strong stimulus for Lutherans to take the church as a social institution seriously. Most influential of all the research and statistical services was the *Lutheran World Almanac and Annual Encyclopedia*. From its first volume in 1921 to the eighth and last

44.
All materials on NLC origins and activities are in the Archives of Cooperative Lutheranism. The best history is Frederick K. Wentz's *Lutherans in Concert* (Minneapolis: Augsburg Publishing House, 1968). Also useful is Osborne Hauge's *Lutherans Working Together: A History of the National Lutheran Council, 1918-1943* (New York: National Lutheran Council, 1945).
45.
Wentz, *Lutherans in Concert*, p. 19.
46.
Ibid.

in 1937, this work provided virtually all data on Lutheranism, including history, geography, doctrine, growth, activities, leaders, institutions, and comparative statistics. It brought to reality the dream of the New York Reformation Committee that the Lutheran church's light in America be brought out from under the bushel.

European needs also demanded action. Early in 1919 a team of five investigators left for Europe to check on conditions among Lutherans. Although authorized to give some on-the-spot aid, especially to keep Lutheran church life going, their chief task was to report on conditions to the home church. Reports of desperate need from France, Germany, Poland, the Baltic States, Finland, Russia, Austria, Hungary, Romania, Serbia, and Bulgaria were the basis on which the reconstruction and World Service appeals of the National Lutheran Council were based—a $500,000 special appeal early in 1919, a combined clothing and financial appeal later in 1919,[47] a $1,800,000 campaign in 1920. The very spontaneity of the program and the novelty of cooperative work made the repeated special appeals necessary. Synodical budgets themselves were so recent a development in many synods that no regular help could be expected from that quarter. By 1920, however, special-appeal funds were becoming harder to raise, not only because each goal was higher than the previous, but because Lutherans like Americans in general were losing their idealism in a wave of postwar weariness, disillusionment, and new isolationism. Lutherans were getting tired of giving.[48] The romance of being Europe's savior was fading. In addition, by this time, the council itself was in a kind of theological and practical quandary over what kind of agency it was to be.

405

Crisis in the National Lutheran Council

The implications of National Lutheran Council membership for relationships among the member churches, most of whom were not in official fellowship, was a major problem which the council had to confront almost from the start. The United Lutheran Church saw no impediment to full cooperation among Lutherans (or even merger) wherever this seemed advantageous, but no other synod shared this view. The Norwegian, Iowa, and Ohio synods were more cautious. Any activity which implied full unity of faith or full brotherly recognition of all other council members had to be avoided because, after all, not all the member churches were in full fellowship with each other. The United Lutheran Church was the stumbling block for the Midwestern synods. They, like the Missouri Synod, felt that the merger of 1918 had compromised true Lutheranism by failing to write into the constitution clear prohibitions against sharing pulpits with non-Lutherans, admitting non-Lutherans to Communion, and belonging to secret societies.[49] Like Missouri, they made these points tests of genuine Lutheranism. Unlike Missouri, they did not feel that every kind of cooperation with such a body was wrong but only those activities which implied that

47.
Mainly for the hundreds of thousands of Polish refugees. Some two million pounds of clothing were collected, plus almost $250,000. The wartime appeals team of Greever, Pannkoke, and G. L. Kieffer again directed the campaign. The NLC's published *Reports* and the unpublished "Proceedings" contain the full reports of the European commissioners. Almost every issue of every church paper in 1919 and 1920 carried a story of the experiences of the commissioners.

48.
One of the most powerful publicity posters was built on this theme. A pen-and-ink sketch of a mother with a small child sitting in the ruins of their home was captioned: "Tired of Giving? You don't know what it is to be tired" (Pannkoke, *A Great Church*, p. 103).

49.
Theodore Graebner, *The Merger: An Analysis* (St. Louis: Concordia Publishing House, 1918); and Meuser, *American Lutheran Church*, pp. 142-57.

all barriers were down, such as, worship, Christian education, full and free transfer of members, and complete cooperation in allocating home mission fields.

The occasions that brought these intracouncil differences into the open and "almost finished the Council"[50] were: (1) the help being given by the European commissioners to some Lutheran churches and institutions about whose orthodoxy the Midwestern synods were in doubt; and (2) the proposal that a coordinated program of home mission work be established. Both had to do with the nature of the National Lutheran Council as an agency for cooperative work in areas not requiring full church fellowship among the cooperating groups. Although the council survived, the confrontation produced by the crisis was to affect the whole future pattern of Lutheranism in America.

When the commissioners of the National Lutheran Council went to Europe in early 1919, they found desperate physical need wherever they were allowed to go as well as conditions within the Lutheran churches that called for immediate help. Wherever they went in both France and Poland (Germany still being off limits for them by action of the Allied powers) they tried to "strengthen the position of the Evangelical Lutheran Church in each country in the matter of orthodoxy"[51] while helping the Lutheran churches in their task of postwar recovery. Financial help was given to institutions of mercy, to aged pastors, and other victims of the postwar emergency. Some congregations in France were subsidized. Pastors' salaries were augmented in some places. Worship and educational materials were provided or subsidized. Efforts were made to help provide theological professorships. In a few places food and clothing were provided for the general population. Only rarely did the commissioners finance reconstruction of church buildings. Of the need for these kinds of assistance there could be no doubt.

But could Lutherans who were not in full fellowship with each other back in the States legitimately cooperate in such activities through the National Lutheran Council? Or did many of the services of the commissioners require prior full fellowship among the sponsors? From the moment of intra-Lutheran wartime cooperation the Missouri Synod had charged that only synods in fellowship could cooperate as the member churches of the National Lutheran Commission for Soldiers' and Sailors' Welfare and the National Lutheran Council were doing. Now from within the council the Iowa Synod raised a similar protest, namely, that in giving direct aid to churches for their specifically spiritual ministry the council was transgressing its own basic charter which confined cooperation to areas of church life not so intimately related to worship and proclamation. Beyond that, the Iowa Synod, and especially its leading theologian J. Michael Reu, protested vigorously against giving aid to churches and institutions which it considered liberal or at least not sufficiently orthodox.[52] Not only did this kind of aid imply fellowship among the donors, but giving it to such churches was tantamount to recognizing the recipients as legitimate Lutherans, that is, establishing fellowship with them. Complicating the

50.
Hauge, *Lutherans Working Together,* p. 47.
51.
Unpublished minutes of the European Commission of the National Lutheran Council, November 6, 1919, p. 9, in the Archives of Cooperative Lutheranism.
52.
The theological shorthand which some Lutherans found helpful in discussing these categories of church cooperation was (1) *res externae:* areas of church life "external" to its basic mission and proclamation and, therefore, not requiring full unity of doctrine as a prerequisite to cooperation; and (2) *res internae:* those areas integral to its mission and intimately involved with doctrine, which, therefore, did require full and explicit doctrinal unity. Examples of the former would be general relief of suffering or some kinds of joint publicity; of the latter, planning and carrying out of mission work, pastoral services, and theological education. Many activities did not fall neatly into either category. Reu's article, which touched off the crisis, was "Unmissverständliche Klarstellung in Sachen des National Lutheran Councils zur Nötigkeit geworden," *Kirchliche Zeitschrift* 43 (November-December 1919): 578-85.

situation was the feeling of Reu and other Lutherans of German descent that not enough of the council's funds were distributed in Germany. Richard C. H. Lenski, Joint Synod of Ohio theologian, professor, and editor, did his utmost to develop similar attitudes toward the council in his synod but gained only minimal support.[53]

Iowa proposed that the National Lutheran Council do no more than investigate needs and leave the actual work of relief and assistance to the synods themselves. Upon rejection of the proposal, Iowa established its own relief fund to be distributed as it saw fit. Its withdrawal from the council in 1920 on the grounds that the executive committee had eliminated confessional safeguards from the council constitution without authorization aroused widespread fears that the council's days might be numbered, not because Iowa was so important to the council's life but because its charges encouraged dissidents in the Ohio and Norwegian synods. Consultations between officials of Iowa and the council brought no agreement.[54] Iowa felt it could carry on a full relief ministry without the council's help, immune from the risk of becoming involved in cooperative causes of which it did not approve. The council made every effort to draw Iowa back in but refused to curtail its European assistance as Iowa demanded.

407

Although no other church body withdrew over this issue, the inner turmoil coinciding with American weariness with international involvements cost the National Lutheran Council dearly in public image and financial appeal. Such a challenge to the council's major area of service could not help but slow down in its pace and make the dominant mood one of caution rather than courageous response to need. Even though all other council members insisted that the agency was too valuable to drop or to restrict to an investigative role, the frictions generated during the crisis continued throughout the twenties. The debate over the relationship of the council to its constituent bodies did lead to one significant constitutional change, namely, the reinsertion in the constitution's Article II of a section proposed in 1918 but omitted because of different interpretations of its meaning:

In stating its objects and purposes, the National Lutheran Council declares That it will not interfere with the organization, the inner life, or the principles of fellowship of its constituent Bodies; That the execution of these purposes will be carried out without prejudice to the confessional basis of any participating Body (i.e., without dealing with matters which require confessional unity); That it is the right of the Bodies themselves to determine the extent of cooperation.[55]

The other aspect of the crisis was even more closely related to the implications of council membership for the historical barriers to fellowship among the member churches. During the war, so-called liberty churches for all Protestants had been established in some of the wartime industrial communities through a cooperative program of the Federal Council of Churches. Lutherans, represented in the program by Knubel, demurred at

53.
Among Norwegians of the former Norwegian Synod there were also strong critics of the NLC, especially the Preus and Ylvisaker families, who felt that many council activities required prior church fellowship among the cooperating churches. Most of Lenski's articles appeared in the Joint Ohio Synod's *Kirchenzeitung* of 1920. The crisis was serious enough for Charles M. Jacobs to write to Lauritz Larsen on November 29, 1919: "It is important that there should be no false steps just now. . . . The next two months are going to tell the story of the National Lutheran Council. . . . [We] must try to keep the Council's record very clear indeed, so that we may be in a position to make our real fight against the reactionaries with a prospect of success." (Letter in the files of the National Lutheran Council, Archives of Cooperative Lutheranism.)

54.
National Lutheran Council, *Report . . . 1920*, pp. 9–11; ibid. *1921*, p. 11. Also, "Minutes from the Joint Meeting of the Officers of the National Lutheran Council and the Officers of the Iowa Synod, Feb. 10, 1921," and Lauritz Larsen, "Silence More Agreeable, But Speech a Duty: A Reply to Professor Reu," in the files of the National Lutheran Council, Archives of Cooperative Lutheranism.

55.
The change is explained in "Report of the President," National Lutheran Council, *Report . . . 1921*, pp. 7–9.

the proposal of organizing nonconfessional community churches and insisted that Lutherans had the right to establish distinctively Lutheran ministries and congregations.[56] On the basis of extensive surveys by the Commission for Soldiers' and Sailors' Welfare, Lutheran missions were established in such paramilitary communities in eastern Pennsylvania, New Jersey, Delaware, Maryland, and in the Erie, Pennsylvania, area. As soon as possible the missions were turned over to the care of the strongest synod in the area. In any case, another wartime need had forced Lutherans to cooperate in work which they had always assumed required official mutual recognition. Could the Lutherans of the council now cooperate fully in home mission work with comity arrangements based on full acceptance of the legitimacy of each other's ministries? Were they ready for this degree of mutual recognition so that the acrimony frequently associated with church extension in the past could be avoided? The United Lutheran Church in America was ready. The Norwegians and the Midwestern Germans were not, at least not without further checking into the position of the United Lutheran Church on questions they considered crucial.

Out of this setting came several joint conferences on doctrine and practice of 1919 and 1920 which tried to bridge the historical chasm between the Midwestern synods and the synods which had just merged into the United Lutheran Church. As preparation for the first conference, Knubel was asked by the National Lutheran Council to prepare a statement defining "The Essentials of a Catholic Spirit" as viewed by the Lutheran church. Statements on the views of the various Lutheran churches were also to be prepared.

Lutherans outside the United Lutheran Church hoped that these conferences would persuade the United Lutheran Church to adopt their prohibition of all cooperation with other Protestants and their principles in regard to church fellowship among Lutherans. Only on these conditions would representatives of the Norwegian, Joint Ohio, and Iowa synods be able to report to their constituents that the United Lutheran Church was "sound." Understandably, the United Lutheran Church's representatives took offense at this approach but endured it in order to get their fellow Lutherans to think seriously, in the light of the great postwar problems, about the legitimacy of some cooperation with other Protestants.[57] Each side was equally convinced that its concerns were crucial for the welfare of Lutheranism. The first conference, March 11–13, 1919, revealed no basic disagreements on various points of doctrine and church practice presented in a paper by Hans G. Stub of the Norwegian Lutheran Church, as well as high hope for cooperation in mission work if the individual synods would approve the revised Stub paper, now known as the Chicago Theses.[58] The United Lutheran Church's concerns about catholicity were, however, not given adequate attention because of lack of time. Knubel's paper, "The Essentials of a Catholic Spirit," and that of Henry E. Jacobs on "Constructive Lutheranism" were read but not discussed. In order to give these important subjects proper consid-

408

56.
"Report on Industrial Centers," ibid. *1919*, pp. 13–15. On Liberty Churches see Cavert, *American Churches*, p. 98.
57.
The most complete analysis of these conferences and their significance is Nelson's *Lutheran Church Among Norwegian-Americans*, 2:289–302, which points out for the first time in Lutheran historiography that the results of the conferences would affect the future pattern of Lutheranism in America, extending even into the 1970s.
58.
See Richard C. Wolf, *Documents of Lutheran Unity in America* (Philadelphia: Fortress Press, 1966), pp. 298–301. The doctrinal points were (1) Christ, Redemption, and Reconciliation, (2) Gospel, (3) Absolution, (4) Holy Baptism and the Gospel, (5) Justification, (6) Faith, (7) Conversion, (8) Election. The record of the meeting, containing much of the discussion, is in National Lutheran Council, "Proceedings . . . 1919," pp. 11a–17, in Archives of Cooperative Lutheranism.

eration a committee composed of Knubel, Stub, and Theodore E. Schmauk was asked to bring definite proposals to a second meeting. As far as the Chicago Theses were concerned the Midwestern synods hoped they might become official statements of all the consulting bodies. However, because they knew that the United Lutheran Church was opposed in principle to making full cooperation dependent upon new statements of doctrinal agreement, they did not press for official adoption in their own churches. They received official status only when the Minneapolis Theses (1925), of which they became a part, were adopted by most of the Midwestern synods later in the decade.

409

At the 1920 conference, Knubel and Charles M. Jacobs presented a revised version of Knubel's 1919 paper on "The Essentials of a Catholic Spirit." It enunciated a doctrine of the church which affirmed classical Lutheran doctrine, opposed organic union with other Protestants, and insisted on Lutheranism's right and duty to witness to its understanding of the gospel in all contacts with other Protestants. In addition, it enunciated eight essential doctrinal points as a "basis for practical cooperation among the Protestant Churches." Whereas the attitude of many Lutherans toward other churches had been total separation, this statement affirmed as the proper Lutheran position

To approach others without hostility, jealousy, suspicion, or pride, in the sincere and humble desire to give and receive Christian service. To grant cordial recognition to all agreements which are discovered between its own interpretation of the Gospel and that which others hold. To cooperate with other Christians in works of serving love insofar as this can be done without surrender of its interpretation of the gospel, without denial of conviction, and without suppression of its testimony as to what it holds to be the truth.[59]

In regard to intra-Lutheran affairs the statement said that because there is no reason to doubt the sincerity of any synod's subscription to the confessional standards, all Lutherans are in unity of faith and "together do form one Church." A final section warned against anti-Christian ideas and organizations, without mentioning lodges by name, and encouraged Lutherans to be alert to all teachings and organizations that contradict the truth of Scripture.

Stub undoubtedly spoke for the majority at the conference in opposing the report of Knubel and Jacobs. Behind the details of his objections was the conviction that "if there is to be what we call cooperation in Church matters [with the non-Lutheran Protestant churches], then there must be unity of faith, not only in a general way but more especially in regard to doctrines that are characteristic of our Lutheran Church . . . [especially] the Lord's Supper." Moreover, said Stub, his own Chicago Theses were to be preferred not least because they had won the approval of the Missouri Synod. The Knubel-Jacobs paper, on the other hand, was dangerously inadequate because it did not mention the Bible as "the inerrant Word of God."[60] The very idea of cooperation with non-Lutheran American Protestants

59.
Minutes of the Joint Conference on Doctrine and Practice, January 27–28, 1920, in ibid. "1920," pp. 2–17. The papers were published in *Lutheran Church Review* 38 (April 1919): 198–212. "The Essentials of a Catholic Spirit" is also in Wolf, *Documents,* pp. 301–12.

60.
Letter of Stub to Lauritz Larsen, December 27, 1919, in Archives of Cooperative Lutheranism. In Article III of the Articles of Union of the Norwegian Lutheran Church the merging synods promised "to observe the rule not to carry on churchly cooperation with the Reformed and others who do not share the faith and confession of these bodies" (Gustav M. Bruce, ed., *The Union Documents of the Norwegian Lutheran Church of America* [Minneapolis: Augsburg Publishing House, 1948] p. 58). The verbatim of Stub's objections is in the minutes of the Joint Conference on Doctrine and Practice, January 27–28, 1920, pp. 18–27.

was inconceivable to the Midwesterners. When coupled in one document with a less blunt rejection of secret societies than they wanted and with the claim that they ought to have no misgivings about the United Lutheran Church, the combination was sure to be rejected. In spite of Knubel's and Jacobs's repeated pleas that their statement would be a great service to Lutheranism and would enhance its influence in the Christian world, the conference adjourned without any action. The door was left

open to further meetings of the conference, but the churches which had rejected the Knubel-Jacobs proposal were not sufficiently interested. The Knubel-Jacobs paper had confirmed their previous fears that the United Lutheran Church was un-Lutheran in its attitude toward other Christians, toward distinctive Lutheran doctrine, and toward secret religious societies.

In regard to problems of the past as outlined in Stub's Chicago Theses, agreement had not been difficult. On the newer issue of Lutheranism's stance toward the growing wave of ecumenical cooperation, agreement was impossible. Cooperation in home missions, which had triggered the discussions, became a forgotten casualty. And the possibility that the National Lutheran Council might play a positive role in achieving full fellowship among its participating churches was gone. In rejecting the Knubel-Jacobs proposal, Lutheranism within the council came to a parting of the ways. "Instead of a single-voiced and full-orbed Lutheran testimony within the NLC, there emerged two distinct parties each waving its own flag."[61] Yet cooperation in common tasks at home and abroad continued in spite of the failure to achieve fuller mutual recognition. Throughout the twenties and thirties the National Lutheran Council thus served as a symbol of enough unity to warrant limited cooperation, but the very limits of the cooperation testified to the unfulfilled desire for greater unity.

Two events of the twenties need to be seen as aftermaths of the joint conferences. Within a few years, the Norwegians and the Ohioans began to promote a new alignment of synods based on the full mutual recognition which the conferences did not achieve. This new cooperative body, the American Lutheran Conference of 1930, eventually included all National Lutheran Council bodies except the United Lutheran Church. The United Lutheran Church, meanwhile, adopted a revised version of "The Essentials of a Catholic Spirit" as its "Washington Declaration of Principles," thereby officially endorsing the very approach to other Lutherans and other Christians which the Midwestern synods had found objectionable. All subsequent intra-Lutheran tensions and efforts toward further unity can be understood only against the background of these events of 1919 and 1920.

The Role of the National Lutheran Council in the Twenties
Fortunately for suffering Lutherans in Europe, the crises over the National Lutheran Council's role in Europe, the debate about doctrine and practice at home, and the declining will of Lutherans to raise funds were not severe enough to terminate

61.
Nelson, *Lutheran Church Among Norwegian-Americans,* 2:299.

62.
Wentz, *Lutherans in Concert*, p. 45.
63.
For details of the relief work, including some confidential reports which were never published, see "Proceedings" of the National Lutheran Council in the 1920s, esp. "Confidential Report on Religious Conditions and Church Conditions in Russia" by Lauritz Larsen in "Proceedings . . . 1923," pp. 74–86. Richard Solberg, *As Between Brothers: The Story of Lutheran Response to World Need* (Minneapolis: Augsburg Publishing House, 1957), gives a good comprehensive picture.
64.
Minutes of the Lutheran Foreign Missions Conference, July 1, 1919, in "Proceedings . . . 1919," pp. 43–50; National Lutheran Council, *Report . . . 1919*, pp. 30–32; ibid. *1920*, pp. 30–33; ibid. *1921*, pp. 29–36.

the world service program of the council. By 1921 the council's assistance had materially improved the situation for the Lutheran churches in France, Czechoslovakia, Romania, Finland, and in parts of Germany, so that attention could be concentrated in Poland, Austria, the Baltic States, the large cities of Germany, and, in ever-increasing amounts, in Russia. In "one of the most dramatic episodes of the NLC's overseas program,"[62] the commissioners channeled assistance to starving Germans in the Volga Valley, the Ukraine, and southern Russia. Perhaps a million of the total Lutheran population of nearly four million received some form of assistance from American Lutherans. Avoiding any action or utterance that might be interpreted by the revolutionary government as politically motivated, the commissioners tried to encourage congregational life and synodical leadership. For years the Lutheran theological seminary in Leningrad received financial assistance. Plans were even made for a seminary in Moscow but they could not be carried out. Until the early thirties hope was strong that with outside help the Lutheran church might be able to survive in Russia. In purely financial terms, the total investment of American Lutherans in European relief reached almost $8 million by the time the council was ten years old.[63] Through the world service program an international dimension had been added to American Lutheranism which had been completely absent before the war.

Another expression of the growing international consciousness was the aid given to foreign missions of the European Lutheran churches. Largely supported by voluntary missionary societies on the Continent, they had been completely cut off from home support during the war and, in many cases, deprived of their leadership by the internship policies of various allied powers, especially Great Britain. Lest these missions be lost to the Lutheran church, the National Lutheran Council from the moment of its birth tried to aid the "orphaned missions" by convening mission authorities of the American bodies to plan emergency action and by channeling funds to the neediest fields. From this stimulus came the Lutheran Foreign Missions Conference of America, organized in 1920 by heads of the foreign mission boards of churches in the council. Together, the conference and the council helped save all the threatened missions, with the conference studying the problems, compiling budgets, and enlisting personnel, while the council raised funds in connection with its World Service Appeals and represented the churches' interests before governments, the Versailles Peace Conference, the International Missionary Council, and the European missionary societies. Through this cooperative effort substantial aid was given to four missions in China, two in Africa, one in Japan, and several in India, in addition to the support which individual synods were providing in India (Joint Synod of Ohio and the United Lutheran Church), New Guinea (Iowa Synod), and East Africa (Iowa Synod).[64] By 1925 over a half-million dollars had been given to preserve the Lutheran outreach in these areas. Through contacts with the World Alliance for International Friendship Through the Churches and with the organizational meeting of the International Missionary Council (at Lake Mohonk, N.Y., in 1921), American Lutherans joined other Protestants in protesting the exclusion of German missionaries from their fields and requesting the victorious powers to open the way for them to resume their work.

With so many new contacts between Lutherans of all lands it would have been strange if some structured expression of Lutheranism's new international self-awareness had not emerged in the twenties. Suggestions for some kind of international gathering of Lutherans from both sides of the Atlantic had been made before the war by the German General Evangelical Lutheran Conference as early as 1888 and periodically thereafter, possibly because other denominations (Anglicans, Baptists, Methodists, and Presbyterians) were forming worldwide organizations. In both the General Council and the General Synod interest was strong enough for the subject to have arisen in prewar conventions. With the end of the war and the extensive contacts of American commissioners in Europe, such an organization had new appeal to American Lutherans as a way to improve interchurch aid and to encourage conservative Lutheran theology.[65]

In 1919 and 1920, at the instigation of the European commissioners, the National Lutheran Council cautiously endorsed the idea of an international conference. Both the United Lutheran Church and the Augustana Synod advocated immediate arrangements which the council proceeded to make through contacts of its chief commissioner, John A. Morehead, with European leaders. In spite of numerous difficulties connected with the predominance of Germans in the Lutheran family and with the tense international situation to which ecclesiastical affairs were not immune, the National Lutheran Council joined the general organizations of Lutherans in Germany, the General Evangelical Lutheran Conference, and the Lutheran League in announcing a conference to be held in Eisenach, Germany, in August 1923. The growing strength of the Roman Catholic Church and of anti-Christian ideologies added to the sense of urgency of American and European leaders, but except for the United Lutheran Church, the Augustana Synod, and the Joint Synod of Ohio, American Lutherans were not enthusiastic. No one expected any support from within the Synodical Conference. The Norwegian Lutheran Church, despite the fact that two of its members (Lauritz Larsen and Michael J. Stolee) in National Lutheran Council staff positions had joined Morehead in the formal recommendation for the conference, was noncommittal at first. After its initial hesitation, the church finally appointed a delegate, as did the Iowa Synod. The smaller linguistic synods remained aloof.

The major purpose of the Eisenach assembly was not to form a permanent international organization but to build friendships among Lutherans from all over the world[66] and to foster awareness of the strength of Lutheranism by reaffirming its Reformation heritage and consulting on material assistance. Papers and discussions centered on the ecumenical character of Lutheran-

65.
The most complete American account of the origins and history of the convention is Willard D. Allbeck's "A Study of American Participation in Inter-Lutheran Cooperation Prior to the Formation of the Lutheran World Federation," unpublished manuscript, prepared at the request of the Department of Theology of the Lutheran World Federation, 1962, in Archives of Cooperative Lutheranism. An even fuller account is Bengt Wadensjö's *Toward a World Lutheran Communion: Developments in Lutheran Cooperation up to 1929* (Uppsala: Verbrun/Kyrklige Centralförlaget, 1970). Less detailed is E. Theodore Bachmann's *Epic of Faith: The Background of the 2nd Assembly of the Lutheran World Federation 1952* (New York: National Lutheran Council, 1952).

66.
Delegates came from 22 countries: Australia, Austria, Canada, China, Czechoslovakia, Denmark, Estonia, Finland, France, Germany, Holland, Hungary, India, Latvia, Norway, Poland, Roumania, Russia, South Africa, Sweden, United States, Yugoslavia. Abdel Ross Wentz and Fredrick K. Wentz gave the total as 151, Allbeck as 147. Eighty-one of the delegates were from Germany.

ism, the uniqueness of Lutheran doctrine, what Lutheranism could contribute toward church unity, and the missionary task. Hans G. Stub preached the opening sermon and Frederick Knubel delivered the lecture on Lutheranism and church unity. Other Americans participated in discussions and committee work, especially the doctrinal affirmation on Scripture and the confessions.[67] The value of the convention for the delegates was best attested by their decision to appoint committees to maintain contact between the various lands, to administer relief and reconstruction, and to plan for a subsequent convention later in the decade. By the time of the second convention at Copenhagen in 1929, the Lutheran Free Church, the United Danish Church, the Danish Church in America, and the Icelandic Synod had also decided to participate.

413

Momentous for American involvement was the election as chairman of the Lutheran World Convention's executive committee of John A. Morehead (1867-1936) who earlier in 1923 had been chosen executive director of the National Lutheran Council to succeed the deceased Lauritz Larsen. In the person of Morehead and under his leadership, the life of the two organizations was intertwined and the American contribution to world Lutheranism greatly enhanced. More than anyone else he personified "the growing consciousness among Lutherans that they constituted a world-wide fellowship."[68] His deep commitment to world Lutheranism and the critical needs of Lutherans outside of North America, in the context of the council's failure in 1920 to find a basis for full cooperation in domestic church work, gave to the National Lutheran Council's work throughout the remainder of the twenties a strong international emphasis. In fact, the overseas emergency appeals and a strong program of public relations comprised the whole of the National Lutheran Council's program in the late twenties.

Not only were no new programs established, but it became more and more difficult to raise funds for the worldwide cooperative program of the Lutheran World Convention, even as a greater world-consciousness developed. This anomaly had a twofold possible explanation: (1) the disillusioned isolation of Americans in the twenties and (2) the movement, referred to above, among a majority of the council's participating bodies to organize the American Lutheran Conference for full cooperation in all areas of church work.

Otto H. Pannkoke's sketch of Lutheranism between the wars is entitled *A Great Church Finds Itself.* To say that Lutheranism "found itself" between 1917 and 1920 is probably an overstatement. Obviously, however, Lutherans were beginning to discover their potential in a new way, to feel some of their heretofore obscured cohesiveness and corporate strength, to become aware of the possibility of new kinds of cooperation and unity. Lutherans experienced the trauma of persecution, the necessity of communicating a new kind of public image, the thrill of moving quickly in response to human need, the excitement of new kinds of cooperative service; and, for the Germans, the pain

67.
Considering the complex character of the assembly, the doctrinal resolution drafted by Charles M. Jacobs of the ULCA and Ludwig Ihmels, bishop of Saxony, is remarkably conservative but clearly not fundamentalistic: "The Lutheran World Convention acknowledges the Holy Scriptures . . . as the only source and infallible norm of all teaching and practice, and it sees in the Lutheran Confessions, especially in the Unaltered Augsburg Confession and Luther's Small Catechism, a pure exposition of the Word of God."
68.
F. K. Wentz, *Lutherans in Concert,* p. 59. See also Samuel Trexler, *John A. Morehead: A Biography* (New York: Putnam's, 1938).

of sloughing off the dearly loved mother tongue and of experiencing in four years a degree of acculturation greater than in the whole previous generation. Although the intensity of these experiences varied from church body to church body, Lutherans emerged from the war years with a new spirit of optimism for their church's place and future in America.

The years also had their chastening aspect. Those who had hoped that full cooperation or even union could come quickly discovered that old differences, such as the proper basis for full cooperation, had not disappeared; they were only temporarily submerged during the spontaneous cooperation in wartime service. The churches of the Synodical Conference retained their historic isolationist position, the Missouri Synod's guarded cooperation in a few aspects of service to military personnel being the only exception. Those churches which assumed the cautious but not isolationist posture were beginning to see that chances of bringing the United Lutheran Church to their position were not good. Yet greater unity was in the air and the atmosphere was heady. Lutheranism breathed new spirit even though the problem of Lutheran particularity vis-à-vis evangelical ecumenism had not been settled.

18 The Twenties— Continued Change, at a Slower Pace

1.
The Perils of Prosperity, 1914-1932 (Chicago: University of Chicago Press, 1958), p. 271.
2.
Ibid., p. 272.
3.
Under Attorney General A. Mitchell Palmer, individual constitutional rights were violated by the executive branch of government as never before in American history. The hysterical patriotism of the very early twenties, ignited by the "Red riots" of 1919, the suspicion, intolerance, suppressions, and bigotries, comprise a frightening chapter in American life which the later twentieth century has almost ignored and forgotten.

"In the twenties," wrote William E. Leuchtenberg, "the events of half a century finally caught up with America."[1] The nation's productive capacity exploded; it became the greatest of the world powers; the city overtook the country; and "all the institutions of American society buckled under the strain." Perhaps the world did not really break in two around 1922 as Willa Cather had claimed, but surely paradox characterized the American scene. It was a time of "conformity and liberation, of the persistence of strong rural values and the triumph of the city, of isolationism and new internationalist ventures, of laissez faire but also of government intervention, of competition and merger, of despair and of joyous abandon."[2] It was also a time when many Americans (including the Christians) sought ways to hold onto old values even while being torn loose from old moorings. To distinguish between cause and effect of the "vast dissolution of ancient habits" (Walter Lippmann) in the twenties is not the task of a church historian. His responsibility is rather to note how the dissolution affected the churches in the breakdown of religious sanctions, in the declining authority of the family, in the almost uncritical adoption of new methods and new ideas by some in the churches and in escape into the past by others.

Lutherans and Society

There is no doubt that Lutherans as citizens shared in the vast dissolution of the twenties. The exact degree of that involvement is, however, difficult to document. To be sure, liberation of Lutherans from old patterns had been accentuated greatly by wartime accusations, the rapid divorce from the old-world culture, and the great expansion of outlook which the whole war experience had produced. Yet Lutherans remained more rural than the population as a whole and more involved in some aspects of foreign cultures, all of which insulated them to a degree from the dissolution but made the shock of it more shattering once it came.

Manners and Morals

The United States in the twenties was weary of great causes and anxious for normalcy, rest, and pleasure. Anxious to make America safe for itself and ready to see dangerous radicalism behind the efforts of have-nots to share in the burgeoning prosperity, America began the decade with an outburst of fearful repression.[3] In its wake came a revolution in manners and morals which accelerated so rapidly that normalcy was not "doing what Americans had always done" but rather waiting for the newest fad. Women voted, demanded equal rights, used cosmetics, began to smoke, wore shorter dresses, drank in public, and competed in business with men as never before. The decade gloried in sex as if it had invented it and gave pseudoscientific imprimatur to self-indulgence. There may be some question whether the society was actually more hedonistic and materialistic than before, but it was surely more overtly so. Radio tied a nation of isolated sections into one mass culture; bootleg liquor loosed inhibitions, and the automobile (the key to America's skyrocketing prosperity) gave a totally new freedom of travel and behavior. It was the decade of Harding and Teapot Dome, a scandal which elicited even more condemnation by press and public of those who exposed corruption than of those who were guilty of it. It was the decade of precipitous economic ups and downs in an ascending seven-year pattern of prosperity climaxing in the "Everest of prosperity in 1929."[4] As never before success was measured in financial terms and worshiped as the goal of life. The great god business was supreme in the land and all aspects of life, even religion and the church, came to be measured by his attributes.[5] Because the future looked secure the nation as a whole was not disposed to take world and domestic problems seriously, preferring instead to concentrate on such distinctions as heavyweight boxing matches, new automobiles, the first solo transatlantic flight, Mah Jong, crossword puzzles, and bridge.

It was the decade when "science" became the shibboleth and the great judge of all things, including religion. The popular mind was surfeited with an outpouring of scientific and pseudo-scientific information from the public media. Psychology, the most recent of the sciences, seemed to hold all the secrets to curing man's problems and raising him to his potential. It was the decade of disillusionment of the intellectuals, of H. L. Mencken, of belief in freedom without knowing what freedom was for, of Walter Lippmann's attempts to lay new ethical foundations in *A Preface to Morals*. It was the decade of prohibition, on the one hand, and of more widespread social drinking than ever—much of its finances flowing directly into America's newest "industry," the omnipresent and almost omnipotent great urban crime organizations.

For the churches the twenties was a decade when they were losing ground without knowing it. Statistically they grew at least as fast as the population, even while the content of the faith became a debatable subject and spiritual dynamic began to fade. Religiously disruptive theological and scientific theories of previous decades filtered down to where the average church member lived. The battle of the fundamentalists against the modernists, already lost, became a public fight and spectacle. Public relations, management, business methods, new use of the media of communication—all these made possible wider spread of all kinds of information, including religious, than ever before. New members and new prosperity made possible bigger and more beautiful church buildings at the very moment when the churches' sense of purpose and its methods were being chal-

4.

Frederick Lewis Allen, *Only Yesterday: An Informal History of the Nineteen Twenties* (New York: Bantam, 1946), p. 183. Written at the very end of the decade, this is one of the best social histories of the twenties; it was first published in 1931. See also Paul Sann, *The Lawless Decade* (New York: Brown, 1957); and Lawrence Greene, *The Era of Wonderful Nonsense: A Casebook of the Twenties* (New York: Bobbs-Merrill, 1939).

5.

On the economy of the twenties see George Soule, *Prosperity Decade: From War to Depression, 1917-1929*, vol. 8 of *The Economic History of the United States* (New York: Holt, Rinehart, & Winston, 1947).

lenged and reviewed in the light of the claims of all other fields of knowledge.

Lutheran literature reflects little of the ferment which must have boiled within its members and its corporate life. Evidences of strong resistance to the new mood abound, but there is amazingly little gloom-peddling about the younger generation and almost no wholesale condemnation of the age. Perhaps this was due to the traditional Lutheran emphasis upon the spiritual or on the formal activities of worship and instruction to the neglect of the everyday world and its problems. Perhaps it was because Lutherans, as a whole, were more isolated from social currents than others. Could it have been that Lutheranism was too solid a faith or too closed an outlook to have been deeply affected by the twenties? Or could it be that church publications simply did not record the life-pulse of the people because they saw their task in other terms? Whatever the reason, one must assume that the tensions in Lutheranism between the old and the new were greater than appear in the sources with which the historian must deal and, therefore, greater than formal history can record.

Lutheran lack of attention to the specifics of conduct had its roots in the same theological assumptions as did the traditional hesitation about ethical rules. Lutherans assumed that the individual who is "right with God" would spontaneously know, love, and do what is right in his life. Emphasizing ethical rules, as Lutherans saw it, ran the risk of encouraging reliance on one's own performance rather than on the forgiving grace of God. Exceptions can be found in the Augustana Synod, many segments of the Norwegian church, and certain parts of the United Lutheran Church where "code morality" designated many sports, the theater, card-playing, dancing, liquor, and birth control as off limits for Lutherans.[6] Most Lutherans allowed considerable freedom of conduct and personal responsibility. In regard to the various issues of personal morality more attention was given to the emancipation of women and to prohibition than to other problems. To Lutherans, extension of the franchise to women involved no moral issue. No Lutheran body took official action pro or con. Of greater concern was the trend toward short dresses, which editors regarded as deliberate sensual provocation of men. The cocktail habit, the modern dance, other "flaunting indecencies," smoking, and the desire of women to work were seen as part of the general tendency to throw off all moral restraint.[7] There was concern about the loss of family stability and in the more conservative churches about women's desire for a voice in ecclesiastical affairs which Lutheran tradition had prohibited on the ground of Paul's command that women should keep silence in the churches.[8] The Lutheran woman was told that she could express her faith and her worth best by raising a Christian family, being submissive to her husband, perhaps teaching school or becoming a nurse or, if single, serving in the church as a deaconess.

As far as prohibition was concerned only Augustana, various

6.
See Emmer Engberg, "Augustana and Code Morality," in *Centennial Essays* (Rock Island, Ill.: Augustana Press, 1960), pp. 122–49.

7.
From an article by Frederick H. Knubel in *Lutheran Standard*, September 22, 1923, p. 600. See also Augustana Synod, *Minutes . . . 1922*, p. 18; and Harold Haas, "The Social Thinking of the United Lutheran Church in America, 1918–1948 (Ph.D. diss., Drew University, 1953).

8.
W. H. T. Dau, *Woman Suffrage in the Church* (St. Louis: Concordia Publishing House, 1916). Also C. L. Ramme, *Soll das Weib Schweigen?* (Chicago: Wartburg Press, 1919). At the turn of the century the General Synod's model constitution for congregations granted women the vote but not the right to hold church offices. In 1907 the Augustana Synod granted the right to vote in the congregation, and in 1930 to serve as conference and synod delegates. Congregations of other synods frequently extended the franchise without asking for synodical authorization and often without discussing the biblical and theological questions. See Christian O. Kraushaar, *Verfassungsformen der lutherischen Kirchen Amerikas* (Gütersloh: Bertelsmann, 1911), p. 87; and Burnice Fjellman, "Women in the Church," in *Centennial Essays*, pp. 219–21. The German bodies had tried to apply 1 Cor. 14:34, 35 literally, not even allowing women to ask questions in church meetings and objecting vigorously to a woman's addressing a Luther League convention (*Lehre und Wehre 46* [April 1900]: 121). In 1917 the General Council had debated whether a woman could serve on the home mission board of the church (General Council, *Minutes . . . 1919*, pp. 19, 197, 236).

Norwegian bodies, and the General Synod had supported the anti-liquor forces behind the Eighteenth Amendment. Following ratification of the amendment and passage of the Volstead Act, Augustana repeatedly called for resistance to those groups which propagandized for the legalization of alcoholic beverages, and it warned against the coalition of "wets" which claimed that prohibition was a failure. Augustana supported the Anti-Saloon League as the "mightiest force on the side of morals" in this matter, and commended Herbert Hoover's "fearless attempts" to enforce the law. "This cause," said the Augustana president in 1929, "is most assuredly of the Lord and if we are willing to do our duty, there can be no doubt as to the outcome in the end."[9] In the very year (1920) when the United Lutheran Church's Committee on Temperance hailed the Eighteenth Amendment as a great step for the nation and called for obedience on the part of all its people, the committee's name was changed to Commission on Moral and Spiritual Welfare and its assignment broadened accordingly. Although some individual synods were enthusiastically prohibitionist, officially the ULCA and most other Lutheran groups supported prohibition only in terms of obedience to the state. All rejoiced in elimination of the old-time saloon but none assumed that the problem could ever be settled by the constraint of law. From the Missouri Synod came the most outspoken criticism, not of the law as such but of the denominations which had made "this whole miserable business . . . a church issue" and which even appealed to the Ku Klux Klan and the pope for support. By getting involved in such political issues Protestants make fools of themselves; "the Church has greater tasks before it."[10] Such reactions were interpreted by "dry" Christians as proof of Lutheranism's reprobate character rather than as a theological conviction about the proper roles of church and government.

International Affairs

Like most Americans, Lutherans had considerable interest in America's international involvements immediately after the armistice. This interest quickly waned. That the scars of the war experience still smarted in the foreign-language groups can be seen in occasional scoffing references to the "pure motives" with which America entered the war and the skepticism toward any positive results of the war.[11] The results of the Washington Disarmament Conference of 1921 and 1922 were endorsed by both the National Lutheran Council and the United Lutheran Church, but with the observation that the real problem remains untouched so long as the sinful causes of war—national pride, fear, jealousy, hatred, suspicion and greed—remain uncorrected.[12] Individual Lutheran writers supported the League of Nations but no Lutheran body gave it support. Yet there is little indication in Lutheran literature of strong German-American opposition over the alleged betrayal of Germany to which secular historians refer.[13] The National Lutheran Council considered memorializing the Senate in support of the League of Nations but then dropped the item from its 1919 agenda and

9.
Augustana Synod, *Minutes . . . 1929,* p. 28. See also ibid. *1922,* p. 24; ibid. *1926,* p. 28; ibid. *1927,* pp. 28, 33; ibid. *1928,* p. 31; also, Kansas Synod (ULCA), *Minutes . . . 1918,* p. 5.

10.
W. H. T. Dau in *Theological Monthly* 6 (March 1926): 78–79. To most Lutherans the use of alcohol was not a moral issue. The only moral issue was obedience to a law of the state. Cf. *Lutheran Witness,* July 8, 1919, p. 220.

11.
See esp. the articles of Dau in *Theological Monthly* 1 (February 1921): 55–56; and ibid. 6 (March 1926): 82–83.

12.
National Lutheran Council, "Proceedings . . . 1922," pp. 110–11; ULCA, *Minutes . . . 1922,* p. 420. The basis of the ULCA decision was a paper by Jacob A. Clutz on "International Peace and Good Will." A number of ULCA synods favored the peace conferences, the court of justice, and the League of Nations. See Haas, "Social Thinking," pp. 209ff.

13.
For example, Samuel Eliot Morison, *Oxford History of the American People* (New York: Oxford University Press, 1965), p. 881.

dismissed the committee which had studied the question. The conclusion seems obvious that most Lutherans were either opposed or unconcerned or regarded the question as a strictly secular one on which Christian citizens should take a position but which was outside the sphere of the church.[14] Isolationist the Lutherans were, but this was a practical and not an ideological stance.

The surge of pacifism among a remorseful Protestant clergy in the twenties had little effect on Lutherans, partly because **419** they had shared so little in the crusade spirit of 1917 and 1918. Theologically, the traditional Lutheran doctrine of the state militated against pacifism as did its doctrine of man, which assumed that in any era occasions were bound to arise when evil power would have to be resisted by force. As was the case with the prohibition issue, only the United Lutheran Church and Augustana made pacifism a matter of convention debate, but in 1924 the United Lutheran Church refused to approve a resolution which would have declared flatly that "war is sin," adopting instead one which recognized the right of countries to fight in self-defense and the right and duty of Christians to "engage in just wars and act as soldiers."[15] Only a few geographical synods of the United Lutheran Church and the Augustana Synod approved pacifist resolutions, the latter in 1924 and again in 1927. On the basis of the deception behind America's entry into World War I, the advantage which war brings to the rich at the expense of the poor, the safeguarding of the rights of nations which had been achieved, the false arguments always advanced in behalf of military establishments, the threat that another war with advanced armaments might "lead to the ruin of the white race and the collapse of our boasted civilization," and the clear teaching of the "law of love" by Jesus, Augustana affirmed "that the time has now come for the whole Church of Christ to cut loose from the monstrous business of war as the complete negation of all that Christianity stands for." It called on all Christians to seek to win the world to Christ, and on the government to use all means to outlaw war, and pledged itself to demilitarize public opinion.[16] A strong pacifist influence was exerted through the *Lutheran Companion*, whose editor, Carl J. Bengston, was one of the synod's most outspoken opponents of war. On this emotional issue, Lutherans and their religious archenemies, the Roman Catholics, were least influenced by the general American religious mood.

Industry, Labor, Management, Social Responsibility

"For Christians the stomach is always secondary to the soul," said one of Lutheranism's more socially concerned educators in 1919.[17] Interest in the stomachs of their fellowmen had grown to some degree since the early years of the decade, but the stomach's relative importance had not. Lutherans were still as unanimous (officially) as ever that the church's essential task was to make individuals into new men through acquainting them with the saving love of God in the death and resurrection of Christ. Men made new in Christ could influence society for

14.
Cf. *Lutheran Witness,* May 13, 1919, p. 157. Positive articles are E. P. Pfatteicher's "Christian Internationalism," *Lutheran Church Review* 38 (October 1919): 356–61, which commends the idea of law in international affairs, and R. W. Mottern, "Blessings of the War," *Lutheran Church Work and Observer,* February 27, 1919, p. 6. One of the strangest reactions was that of the *Lutheran Standard* which scoffed at disarmament on the ground that if war were eliminated "the world would become so corrupt and rotten that respectable people would begin to pray for some intervention by the Almighty, it might be by war or some other catastrophe, to clean things up again. Human nature as such cannot stand peace for any great length of time" because material prosperity always causes men to forsake God. The past war was a "great purifying conflagration with which the good Lord sought to burn up some of the accumulated dross of the world." (*Lutheran Standard,* October 22, 1921, p. 678.)
15.
ULCA, *Minutes . . . 1924,* pp. 266–67. Thirty-six delegates registered their dissent, urging that "all reference to the right to war at this time" be avoided. See also Doniver A. Lund, "The Peace Movement Among the Major American Protestant Churches, 1919–1939" (Ph.D. diss., University of Nebraska, 1955), p. 137.
16.
Augustana Synod, *Minutes . . . 1924,* pp. 190–91. The reasons for Augustana's attitude is explored in F. H. Capps, "The Swedish-American Press and Isolationism," in *The Swedish Immigrant Community in Transition,* ed. J. Dowie and Ernest M. Espelie (Rock Island, Ill.: Augustana Historical Society, 1963).
17.
J. A. W. Haas, "Economic Theory and Christianity," *Lutheran Church Review* 38 (October 1919): 387.

the better by putting their faith into practice. But the church bodies continued to reject the idea of working for legislation on matters of social concern and they totally rejected all talk of a Christian social order except in terms of the personal redemption of all individuals in society.[18] Minimum wages, reduction of working hours, housing of the poor, protection of the worker against sudden fluctuations of the economy, regulation of movies, and a plethora of other humanitarian causes for which the Federal Council of Churches and its members labored and prayed had, for Lutherans, nothing to do with the kingdom of God, desirable as the fruit of such causes might be.

This is what the church has been called to do: convert the people, employers and employees alike; make good citizens; make good fathers and mothers, husbands and wives; honest merchants and dealers; god-fearing officials from the President down to the little town marshal; make the people good and then let them go out and settle the strikes, or rather, so deal with one another that there will be no strikes.[19]

In the light of a number of Supreme Court decisions in the early twenties, shackling almost every effort for social reforms by Congress, Lutherans would be all the less likely to crusade for social legislation.[20] Lutherans were among those skeptical of the investigation of the great steel strike of 1919 by a committee of the Federal Council of Churches and the Interchurch World Movement. Behind the Lutheran skepticism was the conviction that even when men know *what* is right they must be converted to *love* the right before they will be willing to do it. Occasionally some enthusiastic individual or committee talked in social-gospel terms or sought to deter Lutherans from identifying with reactionary forces, but as soon as they got to the theology of the church's mission the traditional Lutheran emphasis was obvious.[21]

Within the framework of the Lutheran approach the United Lutheran Church, through its Commission on Moral and Spiritual Welfare, wrestled more with the question of its proper social task than did the other Lutheran churches, most of whom spent their social energy in inner mission work or in criticizing the attitudes of other churches. Although the United Lutheran Church seldom took any action as a church, it did receive reports during the twenties on a variety of problems such as crime, housing, social legislative proposals, movies, sale of suggestive novelty items, prohibition, labor strife, Near East problems, law enforcement, problems of church and state, war and pacifism, marriage and divorce, and the 1924 Conference on Christian Politics, Economics, and Citizenship.[22] Lutheran action was largely confined to the inner mission institutions which continued to expand. Participation in this work by more Lutheran laymen and congregations did cause a developing social consciousness but also kept that consciousness within narrowly drawn limits enabling Lutherans "to stress, on the one hand that [they were] showing responsibility to society, but it was this same activity, on the other hand, which enabled the church[es]

18.
Even the more socially concerned Lutherans held firm on this point. Examples: Emil E. Fischer, *Social Problems: The Christian Solution* (Philadelphia: United Lutheran Publication House, 1927); idem, "The Church and Social Problems," *Lutheran Church Review* 43 (July 1924): 252–63; Franklin K. Fretz, "The Church and Its Approach to Social Problems," ibid. 41 (July 1922): 253–57; Henry Offerman, "Jesus and the Social Question," ibid. 44 (January 1924): 34–48.
19.
Lutheran Standard, August 12, 1922, p. 497.
20.
In 1915 the Supreme Court upheld the "yellow-dog contract." In 1918 it declared the Child Labor Act of 1916 unconstitutional. In 1922 it found invalid a new law which levied a prohibitive tax on products manufactured by children. In 1923 it declared a District of Columbia minimum-wage law for women unconstitutional. See Leuchtenberg's chapter, "The Politics of Normalcy," in *Perils of Prosperity,* pp. 84–103.
21.
By way of exception one can find a few references to the gospel which is "bound to regenerate society as well" as the individual, e.g., Henry Offerman, "Jesus and the Social Gospel," *Lutheran Church Review* 40 (January 1921): 22–35. A General Council committee in 1918 rejoiced that the "Christian principle of cooperation in place of the Christless principle of competition is being enthroned in all business and trade" and that the whole nation is ready to hear of Christ "whose mighty principles are uniting our strength and lifting us to nobler mankind!" (General Council, *Minutes . . . 1918,* p. 43.) ULCA, *Minutes . . . 1922,* pp. 25ff., has an analysis of the social gospel's emphasis in contrast to a "Lutheran" approach.
22.
See ULCA, *Minutes . . . 1920,* pp. 478–80; ibid. *1922,* pp. 413–17; ibid. *1924,* pp. 260–74; ibid. *1928,* pp. 582–95; ibid. *1930,* pp. 103–15.

to remain apart from the great social movements of the day without having an uneasy conscience."[23]

On specific social issues Lutheran views show a gradual change. More writers recognized the necessity for labor to organize. Violence on the part of labor was always deplored, but so was "union busting." Along with the injunction that all sides apply the Golden Rule there were some sound proposals for the development of a new business conscience. Responsibility of Christians to cry out against greed, injustice, and inhumanity received increasing emphasis, as did Christian responsibility to be concerned about the spirit behind any economic system in which the church finds itself. Seldom, however, was there any analysis from a Christian point of view of the prosperity and wild speculation of the twenties.[24]

421

On the most revolutionary piece of social legislation during the era, Lutherans had but little to say. After decades of study by federal commissions and repeated efforts of Congress, an immigration bill was finally enacted in 1921 and then modified in 1924. Ironically called "the second Declaration of Independence" by its advocates, this legislation substituted the idea of racial homogeneity for the old melting-pot philosophy and capitalized on fears of what would happen to America if immigrants from central and southeastern Europe were allowed to immigrate in uncontrolled numbers. The pre-World War I ideas of Madison Grant on the danger of mongrelization of the superior Nordic and Anglo-Saxon races bore fruit in Congress through the somewhat more refined arguments of Henry Cabot Lodge and Francis A. Walker. Until the 1924 Immigration Act was passed, Lutherans were silent, perhaps on the old grounds that the question was a purely secular one. Once the details of the national quotas were examined, however, protest came quickly—not because the act discriminated against the people who most needed a "land of opportunity" but because the act "would react inequitably against the immigrants to the United States coming from Northern Europe."[25] A leading Lutheran statistician's indictment of the whole "national origins" basis as unscientific, unfair, and unwise, as based on fiction and prejudice, not fact, climaxed in the charge that "it discriminates against the Germans and the Scandinavians" to the great advantage of the British.[26] Although the charge may have been true, neither this article nor other protests mentioned the even greater injustices against other national groups.

Congregational Life

The steady stream of population from the farms to the cities, underway since the close of the Civil War and accentuated sharply by the industrial needs of World War I, was one of the more important postwar factors to which Lutherans had to adjust. No exact statistics on the urban-rural ratio of Lutheran population before the war are available, but Lutherans were far more rural than urban. This was true even of the membership of the United Lutheran Church, the most urban of all the major Lutheran bodies in 1918. By the late twenties only 47.24 per-

23.
H. Haas, "Social Thinking," p. 50. What Haas says about the ULCA applies equally to all Lutheran groups. He also notes that inner missions gave Lutherans a sense of superiority over the efforts of other denominations.
24.
Ibid., pp. 332–57, has an analysis of the ULCA literature. Exceptions are Franklin K. Fretz's "The Newer Consciousness in Industry," *The Lutheran,* April 8, 1919, p. 30; and idem, "Will Business Have a New Conscience?" ibid., December 19, 1918, p. 10.
25.
Augustana Synod, *Minutes . . . 1926,* pp. 31, 163. On the history and details of the act see Robert A. Devine, *American Immigration Policy, 1924–1952* (New Haven: Yale University Press, 1957), pp. 3–25.
26.
O. M. Norlie, "National Origins," in *Lutheran World Almanac and Encyclopedia, 1927–1928,* comp. O. M. Norlie and G. L. Kieffer (New York: National Lutheran Council, 1927), pp. 280–82.

cent of Lutherans lived in small towns or open country, not significantly higher than the national figure of 44 percent. In the location of congregations, however, the former Lutheran rural strength could still be seen—only 30.7 percent of Lutheran congregations were located in cities in 1926, 69.3 percent in rural settings. Table 4 shows the great differences among the church bodies and the shrinking size of the individual rural congregations in 1926. After the early twenties, references to the rural church as a problem multiply in literature of the more urbanized bodies. Although few rural Lutheran congregations went out of existence in this decade, the trek of youth to the cities caused growing concern about the rural church's future. Moreover, the farmers' declining share in the national wealth added a serious financial dimension to the rural church's plight. The former trend was to be checked considerably during the thirties, the latter acutely accentuated.

The change from congregational use of a foreign tongue to English, accelerated during the war years, continued at a steady pace during the twenties.[27] In the United Lutheran Church and the Joint Synod of Ohio the change was relatively painless, but even there some pastors who could not handle English were faced with early retirement or sought calls to German congregations in Canada. Many of the Scandinavian Lutherans found the change even more painful than the Germans, perhaps because of stronger cultural ties with the homeland but also because only their "foreign-ness" and not their language itself had been under attack during the war.[28] Under pressure of war animosities the Norwegian Lutheran Church authorized a committee in 1918 to prepare a constitutional amendment for a change of name. By 1920, because of bitter feeling about the change and because peace had come, sentiment had changed and the convention voted to retain the name. With two-thirds of all sermons still in Norwegian the decision was not surprising. By 1930 the ratio had shifted to two-thirds English, and in every aspect of church life Norwegian had become embattled.[29] An index of the extent of change among the Swedish Lutherans was publication of their new English hymnal in 1925 and, even more significantly, the ordination of Augustana Seminary's 1924 graduation class in English. Among the Danish, the Sunday schools were predominantly English by the early twenties but change in the language of worship was slow even though their young people shared the view of many descendants of immigrants that one was not really American if one knew a foreign language.[30] Until long after 1930 virtually all pastors of the two Danish bodies in America were of Danish stock.

In the Missouri Synod, too, a language change was underway. Here also the change was relatively painless, although there was more misgiving about the dangerous influence of non-Lutheran, English religious literature than emotional attachment to the language. To supply the need for authentic Lutheran literature, Concordia Publishing House became an almost totally English concern. By the late twenties over 90 percent of Concordia's titles were English. Theodore Graebner's *Inductive*

27.
The *Lutheran World Almanac and Encyclopedia, 1930* lists thirty languages being used by Lutherans in America including Assyrian, Magyar, Yiddish, Persian, sign language, and "seven American languages" (p. 46).
28.
Nils Hasselma, "Language in Exile," in Dowie, *Swedish Immigrant Community,* pp. 121-46, gives a sympathetic picture of how difficult the change was for many Swedes.
29.
E. Clifford Nelson, *The Lutheran Church Among Norwegian-Americans,* 2 vols. (Minneapolis: Augsburg Publishing House, 1960), 2:249-52; *Lutheran World Almanac, 1921,* p. 213.
30.
Paul C. Nyholm, *A Study in Immigrant History: The Americanization of the Danish Lutheran Churches in America* (Copenhagen: Institute for Danish Church History, 1963), p. 302. Nyholm also recalls that youngsters often switched from English to Danish when they saw the pastor coming.

Table 4

**Urban-Rural Ratio
of Lutherans
in 1926**

Church Body	Congregations				Membership			
	Urban	Rural	% Urban	% Rural	Urban	Rural	% Urban	% Rural
ULCA	1,527	2,123	41.8	58.2	816,839	397,501	67.3	32.7
Augustana	486	694	41.2	58.8	188,711	122,714	60.6	39.4
Missouri	1,335	2,582	34.1	65.9	567,569	472,706	54.6	45.4
Wisconsin	152	557	21.4	78.6	109,956	119,286	48.0	52.0
Slovak	37	18	67.3	32.7	12,179	2,580	82.5	17.5
Norwegian Synod	13	58	18.3	81.7	2,603	5,741	31.2	68.8
Norwegian Lutheran Church	327	2,227	12.8	87.2	122,188	374,519	24.6	75.4
Joint Ohio	295	577	33.8	66.2	135,946	111,837	54.9	45.1
Iowa	142	731	16.3	83.7	62,871	155,002	28.9	71.1
Buffalo	16	25	39.0	61.0	4,949	4,318	53.4	46.6
United Danish	56	134	29.5	70.5	11,610	17,588	39.8	60.2
Lutheran Free	55	338	14.0	86.0	12,295	34,071	26.5	73.5
Danish Evangelical Lutheran	35	61	36.5	63.5	7,782	11,139	41.1	58.9
Suomi	63	122	34.1	65.9	17,809	14,262	55.5	44.5
Icelandic	1	13	7.1	92.9	120	2,066	5.5	94.5
Finnish Apostolic	38	100	27.5	72.5	5,518	18,498	23.0	77.0
Finnish Evangelical Lutheran	17	53	24.3	75.7	3,321	4,467	42.6	57.4
Lutheran Brethren	9	17	30.8	69.2	961	739	56.5	43.5
Eielsen	4	11			346	741	31.8	68.2
Jehovah	1	2	33.3	67.7	239	612	28.1	71.9
Independent	27	23	54.0	46.0	8,719	3,085	73.9	26.1
Total	4,636	10,466	30.7	69.3	2,092,591	1,873,472	52.76	47.24

Compiled from *Census of Religious
Bodies: 1926,* Vol. 2: *Separate
Denominations* (Washington, D.C.: U.S.
Government Printing Office, 1929), pp.
698–841 passim.

Homiletics of 1918 and Friedrich Bente's *American Lutheranism* of 1920 are examples of the new emphasis. That the change to English would not lead to neglect of the classical theological tradition was guaranteed by the publication in 1921 of the *Concordia Triglotta,* which contained the confessional writings of Lutheranism in English, German, and Latin along with detailed historical introductions, and by Franz Pieper's comprehensive three-volume *Christliche Dogmatik.* These were Missouri's most important publications of the twenties and each showed how strong the German classical Lutheran tradition remained. Somewhat surprisingly, as the synod became more English, the English church paper and theological journal became even more polemical than the German, perhaps to fill the need of reinforcing the Lutheran consciousness of their English-speaking constituency. The *Lutheran Witness,* especially, translated into English the "siege mentality" of Missouri's earlier period[31] and thereby effectively checked any possible "liberalizing" of Missouri's attitude toward English-speaking Lutherans. Frequently, warnings against dangers inherent in the use of English betrayed the writer's own inadequate "feel" for the language.[32]

In 1920 more than 60 percent of all sermons were still in German in the Missouri Synod, by 1925 50 percent, and from then on German lost ground rapidly.[33] Of the fifty-one varied periodicals begun within the synod after 1914 only eight were totally German (and of these five had English equivalents), twenty-seven were entirely English, and the remaining sixteen were basically in English but with some German. Another sign of the change was the reduction of the size of the German theological and homiletical journals in 1920 and the upgrading of the *Theological Quarterly* to a monthly. Yet at the point where the clergy could be most themselves, the district conventions, English gave way much more slowly, 70 percent of all essays presented still being in German in 1930. By the end of the twenties, seminary professors who still lectured in German had to repeat the essence of their lectures in English and by 1930 even the German theological journal *Lehre und Wehre* had become a casualty of Americanization as the Missouri Synod consolidated its theological journals into the all-English *Concordia Theological Monthly.* So rapidly had German faded in parochial and secondary schools that the convention of 1929 was warned that Lutheran pastors would be deprived of the treasures of the Lutheran classics in theology and hymnody unless educational institutions insisted on facility in German.[34]

Among the important side effects of the language transition was a decline in multicongregation parishes in all Lutheran church bodies. So long as people insisted on worshiping in their mother tongue they were content, if need be, to have pastoral services less frequently than weekly. Church officers could always conduct the liturgy and read a sermon from one of the German or Scandinavian "fathers." Once the services became English, however, the pastor could not spread himself so thin without losing members to congregations where the pastor was present every Sunday.[35] Both the pain of the change and Mis-

31.
See Alan N. Graebner, "The Acculturation of an Immigrant Lutheran Church: The Lutheran Church—Missouri Synod, 1917-1929" (Ph.D. diss., Columbia University, 1965), pp. 105-6. Theodore Graebner called the *Witness,* which he edited, "a Book of Chronicles of the war of a sound Lutheranism against the enemies that sought to encompass the ruin of our Western Zion" (*Lutheran Witness,* April 25, 1922, p. 129). On this phenomenon from a sociologist's point of view, see Heinrich H. Maurer, "The Fellowship Law of a Fundamentalistic Group: The Missouri Synod," *American Journal of Sociology* 31 (July 1925): 39-57.

32.
A classic example is "What Doctrinal Differences Must Be Ironed Out?" *Theologische Quartalschrift* 19 (July 1922): 221-22. The writer charges that the phrase "ironing out" applied to doctrinal questions proves how superficially English-speaking Christians approach doctrine. He warns against the tendency to externalize and superficialize, which is said to be inherent in a "business language" like English which deals only with external things.

33.
Paul T. Dietz, "The Transition from German to English in the Missouri Synod from 1910 to 1917," *Concordia Historical Institute Quarterly* 12 (October 1949): 97-127. Also G. Mezger, "Preaching in the Missouri Synod," in *Ebenezer,* ed. W. H. T. Dau (St. Louis: Concordia Publishing House, 1922), p. 287.

34.
Missouri Synod, *Proceedings . . . 1929,* p. 57. In 1929 only 3 percent of the parochial schools were all German, 67 percent all English. "The language question . . . has answered itself," said a Concordia Publishing House advertisement in 1929 (*Theological Monthly* [May 1929]: 160).

35.
Otto F. Hattstaedt, *History of the Southern Wisconsin District of the Evangelical Lutheran Synod of Missouri, Ohio, and Other States* (Madison, Wisc.: Wisconsin Historical Records Survey, 1941), p. 69.

36.
David H. Bauslin, "The Lost Note in Much of Present Day Preaching," *Lutheran Church Review* 39 (October 1920): 417–35; W. Henkel, "Missbrauch der Kanzel in den Sektenkirchen," *Theologische Quartalschrift* 19 (January 1922): 58–59. Missouri's *Homiletical Magazine* and Ohio's *Pastor's Monthly* tried to guide preachers away from these temptations. The former was used so widely, even in the pulpit, that it came to be known as the "Yellow Bible."

37.
No good history of Lutheran preaching in the United States and Canada has been written. On the Missouri Synod, see Lester A. Zeitler, "Preaching Christ to the Glory of God for the Salvation of the Hearer: An Analysis of the Preaching Proposed in the *Magazin für Ev.-Luth. Homiletik und Pastoraltheologie, 1877–1929*" (Th.D. diss., Concordia Seminary, St. Louis, 1968).

38.
The Precious and Sacred Writings of Martin Luther, ed. John Nicholas Lenker, 13 vols. (Minneapolis: Lutherans in All Lands Co., 1903–10).

39.
William Arndt's review of the first volume of *The American Pulpit* regretted that no Lutheran preacher had been included, but rejoiced that the Lutheran church had no Fosdicks or Hillises. "Preaching the Gospel of the crucified Savior, we shall rarely become popular, but the work we do will count for eternity" (*Homiletical Magazine* 59 [April 1926]: 154).

40.
An example of vigorous opposition is "The Individual Communion Cup," *Lutheran Standard*, November 24, 1923, pp. 744–46.

souri's hope of finding an English identity are expressed in the comment of one Missouri pastor that God had forcibly driven the synod into English work, perhaps so that it could become a refuge for those who "will leave the disintegrating modernistic sects."[36]

Whether in German or in English, preaching in Lutheran churches showed little change from earlier times. Dumbfounded and offended by what passed for preaching in much of Protestantism around them, seminaries laid heavy stress on expository preaching on the basis of the church's pericopes, and with a heavy doctrinal emphasis. Because some Lutheran pastors were attracted to the "free text" approach and to the sensational themes of the more popular American preachers, warnings abound in Lutheran literature against imitating the preaching style of the sects.[37] The recurring emphases in most sermons of the time were man's natural lost condition, Christ's saving work, salvation by grace alone, the worthlessness of human works in God's sight, the necessity of faith. The emphasis on "the truth" and on personal salvation virtually overshadowed all awareness of the church as the redeemed fellowship, the loving and serving community, or the worshiping family. Where baptism and the Lord's Supper were dealt with in sermons the emphasis was invariably upon the sin-forgiveness theme or upon the errors of other churches. Martin Luther was still recommended as an excellent model for preaching and the Lenker edition[38] of his sermons continued to sell well. During the twenties each synod began publishing sermons of its pastors, partly to thwart the influence of more liberal Protestant publications, such as the *American Pulpit* and the *Best Sermons* series which began in the mid-twenties.[39] Few non-Lutheran preachers rated very high, at least among the theologians, but Charles Haddon Spurgeon and Alexander MacLaren, both Baptists, were the outstanding exceptions.

Lutheran worship changed only slightly in the twenties. Mostly the old liturgical patterns continued, but with little appreciation of the corporate nature of worship. The people gathered together to hear the Word read and preached; everything else was secondary. Holy Communion was interpreted as assurance of forgiveness. It was a solemn and even sad occasion, with preparation limited to self-examination and personal repentance. In the more conservative groups private announcement to the pastor of one's intention to commune remained the pattern even when the pastoral care which such an announcement presupposed had become the exception. Substitution of individual Communion glasses for the traditional common cup by a growing number of city churches caused frequent controversy, but by 1930 the trend was already irreversible.[40]

Although the increased use of English brought more liturgical similarity, most of the German and Scandinavian groups preferred translations of their own familiar liturgies to the Common Service, whose universal use would have been a great unifying factor among the synods. To the Lutheran Free Church, the Eielsen Synod, the Lutheran Brethren, and Hauge elements in the Norwegian Lutheran Church, worship according to set forms was still regarded as the greatest cause of spiritual torpor in the church. Informal services seemed to be more suited to their goal of personal conversion and emotional religious expression. Clerical vestments were also taboo to them, as they were in some of the congregations of the former General Synod. Among the rest vestments remained simple. German-background congregations preferred the black robe with white tabs, Scandinavians the black robe with white fluted collar and perhaps a satin-covered black stole. On special occasions the Scandinavians, especially the Swedes, might also wear a white surplice. Robed choirs were still the exception but, along with acolytes, were becoming increasingly popular in the cities as Lutheran congregations sought ways of appealing to people of non-Lutheran background. The old custom of separating men and women, and even boys and girls, during the service began to give way to "mingling of the sexes" in worship, an innovation which the opponents of change saw as unseemly female self-assertion which might easily foster the desire to have an equal voice with men in the affairs of the church.

Before World War I a typical church building had a small niche for a chancel, lacking in depth to avoid any suspicion of high-churchism. The altar was ornate, with a tiny brass crucifix, Renaissance candlesticks, and a covering of velvet or velour. The ceiling was umbrellalike, painted blue with five-pronged stars, the chancel floor covered by a red carpet with a design of large roses, the windows translucent or of inexpensive colored glass.[41] Many of the buildings were distinctly unattractive in appearance and location.

In the twenties Luther D. Reed of the United Lutheran Church and Frederick R. Webber of the Missouri Synod led a movement for liturgical and architectural appreciation. As the prosperity of the decade made possible more expensive buildings in better locations, a number of synods appointed committees which recommended architects, made building suggestions, reviewed plans, and emphasized both honesty and quality in materials and craftsmanship. Webber, as head of the architectural committee of Missouri's English District, became the champion of the English Gothic style, which soon became a status symbol even though some congregations continued to prefer the more functional Akron Plan and others had to settle for the less expensive rectangular box. Through the monthly bulletin *Lutheran Church Art* and then through his *Church Symbolism*,[42] Webber exerted a significant influence in behalf of architectural beauty and form far beyond his own synod. Inevitably, in the flush of enthusiasm of the mid-twenties many congregations built beyond their means, a folly for which they would pay dearly in the early thirties after the economic bubble burst.

Financially, the more businesslike methods which had begun before the war and which had proved their effectiveness in the wartime campaigns gained wide acceptance. Regular weekly offerings, the duplex envelope system, every-member visitations, and congregational budgets were pushed everywhere as

41.
The description is less accurate for the Norwegian and Swedish church bodies than for the others.
42.
Frederick Roth Webber, *Church Symbolism* (Cleveland: Jansen Co., 1927).

"the scriptural plan of giving." As a result of concerted educational programs and "field-secretary" assistance to pastors and congregations, Lutheran per capita giving for all causes rose from $13.32 in 1920 to over $24.50 in 1929, which more than kept pace with the general economic growth of the nation.[43]

For the Missouri Synod, Christian education was the great question of the twenties. From its beginning Missouri had insisted that religious education could not be isolated from education in general. Because no aspect of life or learning is untouched by the insights of faith, conservative Lutherans (especially those of the Synodical Conference) felt that if religious education were separated from education as a whole both would be perverted. To allow "godless" teachers or those who belonged to erring churches to train one's children and to be satisfied with the Sunday-school smattering of religious knowledge cast doubts on one's own commitment to Lutheran doctrine and to the welfare of one's children. Until 1914 the St. Louis Seminary faculty even opposed the publication of Sunday school literature by Concordia Publishing House on the ground that Sunday schools undermine the day schools.[44] Adoption of English as the language of worship and instruction brought no lessening of emphasis on the parochial school. "More than ever we are unanimous in requiring, in maintaining, and in elevating the congregational school," said Missouri's 1923 convention.[45] Regarded by their advocates as the key to a doctrinal stable church, an informed laity, and a loyal clergy, as well as a guarantee of the church's future in America, the schools were often referred to as the church's jewels, "the apple of her eye." Even synods which did not insist on parochial schools as a necessary aspect of Lutheran church life felt them to be the best solution to the difficult problem of an adequate Christian education for the young.[46] Yet in spite of heavy emphasis on Christian schools, only about 30 percent of Missouri congregations had their own school in 1920 and less than 50 percent of the church's children attended.[47] The expense of the schools, a shortage of teachers, and the heavy burden of work on the pastor who was the only teacher in most of the small schools, kept Missouri from ever realizing its ideal.

The Missouri Synod was slow to employ women as teachers. Although 13 percent of all its teachers in 1918 were women, they were not allowed to attend the teacher-training colleges of the church until 1923 when Concordia College at Seward, Nebraska, admitted a small group. Because state accreditation laws forced many unaccredited pastors to withdraw from teaching in the early twenties, Missouri's 1926 convention approved admission of women at Seward and at Edmonton, Alberta, so long as they did not exceed 20 percent of the student body. Not until 1938 were they admitted to the synod's largest college, Concordia, at River Forest, Illinois.[48] Behind this hesitation regarding women was the unique position of "teacher" in the Missouri Synod. He was to be trained in Lutheran theology as well as in educational methods; he was called to his position, not hired; upon acceptance of the call he enjoyed lifetime tenure, as

43.
Annual financial statistics are in the *Lutheran World Almanac and Encyclopedia*. The gross national product was $89 billion in 1920, $104 billion in 1929. U.S. Bureau of the Census, *Historical Statistics of the United States: Colonial Times to 1957* (Washington, D.C., 1960), p. 139.

44.
Martin A. Haendschke, *The Sunday School Story: The History of the Sunday School in the Lutheran Church—Missouri Synod* (River Forest, Ill.: Lutheran Educational Assoc., 1963), p. 31. Throughout the twenties most Lutherans tended to regard the Sunday school as a missionary and auxiliary agency of the congregation rather than as the prime educational activity.

45.
Missouri Synod, *Synodal-bericht . . . 1923*, p. 148.

46.
Although only a small percentage of the Ohio and Iowa congregations had parochial schools, their leaders regarded the "principle of the parochial school as the correct one" and regretted that they lagged so far behind Missouri. Among the Norwegians such schools were numerous in the early years but faded rapidly between 1900 and World War I. O. M. Norlie, *History of the Norwegian People in America* (Minneapolis: Augsburg Publishing House, 1925), p. 375. Among the Danes, only the Danish Lutheran Church in America had parochial schools. Their emphasis on language was stronger than that of any other church. The Danish language was regarded as the best foundation for "Danish Spiritual life" (Nyholm, *Immigrant History*, p. 253). Even some General Synod leaders envied synods with the parochial-school tradition. See George U. Wenner, *Religious Education and the Public School: An American Problem* (New York: Bonnell, Silver & Co., 1907).

47.
For statistics see Arthur L. Miller, *Educational Administration and Supervision of the Lutheran Schools of the Missouri Synod* (Chicago: University of Chicago Press, 1951), p. 67.

did the pastor. Elevation of women to this position seemed to Synodical Conference synods to violate the biblical injunctions about the subordinate role of women in the church.[49]

Apart from the difficulty of staffing and financing a complete and separate school system, new threats to the legal existence of the private schools came from society at large in the postwar years.[50] Oregon tried to eliminate all private and parochial schools by means of a 1922 law requiring all children between the ages of eight and sixteen to attend public school. In Michigan the Wayne County Civic Association advocated a constitutional amendment requiring all children between the ages of five and sixteen (or until graduation from eighth grade) to attend public school. Similar laws were proposed in California, Ohio, Iowa, Oklahoma, Washington, and Texas. In the face of such threats to religious freedom Missouri determined to fight. A *News Service* informed the synod on all issues relating to its educational welfare. In Michigan the Roman Catholics, of course, exerted the greatest pressure against the amendment, but Lutheran congregations were organized to influence public opinion and public officials. Through handbills, newspaper advertisements, letters, and rallies Michigan Lutherans made their first experience in social action a successful one as the amendment was defeated in the state referendum by a margin of almost two to one.[51] In Oregon the Oregon-Washington District School Board of the Missouri Synod began a campaign to fight the 1922 law, but it needed more financial support than the synod was willing to invest in the cause. Fortunately for the Lutherans, the Society of Sisters of the Holy Name of Jesus and Mary carried their case to the Supreme Court. In their behalf it found that the law "unreasonably interferes with the liberty of parents and guardians to direct the upbringing and education of children under their control."[52] In many other places Missouri Synod people organized "state legislative committees" to keep an eye on upcoming legislative proposals, to keep in touch with legislators, and to inform and enlist the aid of pastors and people in opposing unwanted legislation.[53] After the *Meyer* v. *Nebraska* decision of 1922 and the Oregon decision, the anti-private-school forces retreated in all states.

The effort to bring private schools under the educational standards of the states was also initially opposed by parochial-school advocates as one more governmental intrusion into the affairs of the church. Behind teacher certification requirements, curricular standards, regulation of the length of the school year, school inspections, and health examinations they thought they saw the specter of government control which would eventually undermine the parochial schools. Only when Missouri leaders sensed that a rampant nativism might succeed in outlawing the schools themselves did they make peace with a degree of state regulation.[54] When efforts were made in Washington to establish a national department of education (the Towner-Sterling Bill of 1923) not only Missouri but most other Lutherans opposed it on the grounds that all private schools would be damaged by the inevitable centralization, paternalism, and political

48.
"The calling of regular male graduates of our synodical normal institutions as teachers to our parish schools must by all means remain the rule and order in our Synod. All congregations are therefore urged to call male teachers . . . and to strive that woman teachers are replaced by regularly called male teachers as soon as local conditions will permit . . ." (Missouri Synod, *Proceedings . . . 1929*, pp. 73–74).
49.
On the special character of the ministry of teaching, see Arnold C. Mueller, *The Ministry of the Lutheran Teacher: A Study to Determine the Position of the Lutheran Parish School Teacher Within the Public Ministry of the Church* (St. Louis: Concordia Publishing House, 1964); and Walter H. Beck, *Lutheran Elementary Schools in the United States . . .* (St. Louis: Concordia Publishing House, 1939), pp. 390–92.
50.
Missouri's 1920 convention report mentions legislatures, the Roman church, the sects, the lodges (especially the Masonic), general public opinion, the "reformed church" which wants "one language, one church, one school," the American Education Association, the Religious Education Association, nativist organizations such as the "Americanization Association," the "Security League," and especially the "Independent Order of Builders" whose magazine *The Menace* battled against all private schools. See Missouri Synod, *Synodal-bericht . . . 1920*, pp. 226–35; Beck, *Lutheran Elementary Schools*, pp. 316–59; P. Eickstaedt, "Serious Dangers Confronting Our Parochial School System," *Lutheran School Journal* 57 (April 1922): 99–115.
51.
John Frederick Stach, *A History of the Lutheran Schools of the Missouri Synod in Michigan, 1845-1940* (Ann Arbor, Mich.: Edwards Bros., 1942), esp. pp. 142–60. The Wayne County League's slogan: "One Language, One Flag, and One School." During the Michigan fight, which occurred at the time of the great "Red scare," one Missouri Synod writer argued that "by teaching undivided loyalty to

our government as a part of our religious
duties, [the schools] are . . . a mighty bulwark against modern Radicalism and Bol-
shevism which is so brazenly rearing its
hydra-head in our beloved country, in order to destroy it. We feel confident that as
a true American you have no desire and
therefore will not lend your efforts to destroy an institution that makes for loyalty
and patriotism, and works against the
principles of Radicalism—The Lutheran
Parish Schools!" (Quoted in *Lutheran Standard*, July 17, 1920, p. 450.)

52.
See Anson Phelps Stokes, *Church and State
in the United States*, 3 vols. (New York:
Harper, 1950), 3:453, 631; and Miller,
Educational Administration, pp. 244-53.

53.
Miller, *Educational Administration*, pp. 239ff.,
gives some details of this unusual Lutheran participation in the legislative process.

54.
The Wisconsin Synod's *Theological Journal*
quoted with approval an article from the
Moody Monthly which deplored all efforts
to secure accreditation of church schools;
see *Theologische Quartalschrift* 20 (July
1923): 215-16.

55.
Paul E. Scherer, "Religious Education in
the United States," *Lutheran Church Review*
39 (October 1920): 468-76; H. J. Schuh,
"How Shall We Get More Religious Instruction for Christian Children?" *Lutheran
Standard*, August 18, 1923, pp. 520-21;
idem, "Bibel und Morallehre in den öf-
fentlichen Schulen," *Lehre und Wehre* 62
(January 1916): 19.

56.
News Service, February 1, 1925, p. 2; "Ge-
danken über den christlichen Schulunter-
richt," *Theologische Quartalschrift* 20 (April
1923): 81-87; "Die Mittel der Erzie-
hung," ibid., pp. 125-49.

57.
On developments in religious education
see H. Shelton Smith, "Religious Education," in *Protestant Thought in the Twentieth
Century*, ed. Arnold S. Nash (New York:
Macmillan, 1951), pp. 226-39. One of the
few criticisms of Lutheranism's content-
centered curriculum and educational phi-

control of schools. Other similar bills in Congress (Sterling-Reed of 1924; Curtis-Reed of 1926) were opposed on identical grounds. Lutherans as a whole feared every aspect of federal control of education.

So sensitive were Lutherans on the subject of their children's religious education that they strongly opposed the rising senti- ment before and after World War I for some kind of religious instruction in the public schools. Religious education was to be in the hands of teachers of whose full orthodoxy there was no doubt. To many Lutherans, even moral instruction in public school on any basis other than a fully Christian (i.e., Lutheran) one was worse than totally secular education. Therefore, they favored the "released-time" programs which were being experi- mented with in many communities as a supplement to Sunday schools.[55] Missouri was cautious even of this proposal. It feared that any system other than parochial schools was inadequate and it disliked the proposal that the public school exercise some measure of control over the released-time programs.[56]

As far as theories of religious education were concerned, Lu- therans again resisted the general trend in society and among American Protestants. "Progressive" theories of education af- fected their curricular materials and their methods of teaching but slightly. John Dewey's educational theories as applied to religious education, notably by George Albert Coe, and pro- moted within the churches by the Religious Education Associ- ation seemed theologically so suspect as to win virtually no Lutheran followers. Only Lutherans on the periphery of their church's theological and educational tradition were drawn to the newer ideas—the child's own social activities or interests as the focal point of religious education, the implicit denial of original sin in educational psychology, the personalism which tended to replace ultimate loyalty to Jesus (or to an authorita- tive revelation) with loyalty to persons, and the assumption that discussion of issues should take the place of the old education in the "truth." Some greater concern for the child brought an easing of the catechetical emphasis on memorization, but edu- cation as instruction in God's truth remained in full control.[57]

The Church at Work
Lutherans were able to insulate themselves from some of the trends and currents in society and religion, but not from the need for more fully organized programs in all levels of church life above the congregation. In the twenties "the easy-going church of an earlier day became the . . . more fully organized church-at-work."[58] In higher education, missionary expansion, church management, and public relations the Lutherans be- came genuinely American in the twenties.

Higher Education
Educational trends among colleges in America in the first two decades of the century had only slightly influenced most Lu- theran colleges. Their size, cultural insularity, and emphasis on preparation of men for the seminaries made them relatively

429

immune to the fragmentation of educational philosophy which expressed itself in the widely heralded "elective system" and the stress on departmental rather than total educational planning.[59] Between 1920 and 1930 Lutheran colleges and educators had to evaluate the new philosophy of education. Perhaps the educational revolution had less immediate impact on Lutheran institutions than on schools in general, but the church's colleges could not ignore the "practical" emphases at the expense of the classical, nor could they avoid the great pressures for accreditation which demanded expanded facilities. Most Lutheran colleges in 1920 had a long way to go in the climb to excellence. On the whole, faculty members were not highly trained, although natural gifts and striking devotion turned many into excellent teachers. College facilities were inadequate. The curricula in most schools were virtually identical with those of a generation previous. Among the church's most urgent problems in the twenties, therefore, was the development of the modern church-related college. Sometimes without being aware of the implications, Lutheran educators and officials subconsciously adopted the premise that higher education was the right of every person and that the church ought to expand its educational ministry to include preparation for an almost endless range of vocational choices. With more of their own youth clamoring for what they had to offer, Lutheran educators joined the scramble for educational prestige. The only notable exceptions were found in the Synodical Conference, which continued to limit the church's educational responsibility to the fields of ministry and teaching. Yet even there educational planning and improvement received high priority.

Behind the drive for money, buildings, and growth was the powerful stimulus of the North Central Association of Colleges and Secondary Schools, whose approval was practically a necessity for a college to exist in the twenties. Accreditation became the watchword of the colleges, its attainment the occasion for celebration and publicity. Although association standards (number of departments, teaching load, volumes in library, minimum endowment, Ph.D.'s on the faculty, etc.) did not guarantee quality education, they did prod every college into a program of self-improvement. A series of financial campaigns during the decade was the most visible aspect of the educational revolution,[60] but a number of the churches also began to study their educational task and to evaluate their whole educational ministry through surveys. By far the most comprehensive survey was that of the United Lutheran Church, authorized in 1924 and conducted by Teachers College of Columbia University.[61] On the basis of the possibilities which were opening up to the churches, the ULCA recommended in 1928 that all Lutheran bodies celebrate the year 1930 as an "educational year" and requested that an All-American Lutheran convention, geared to education, be convened in June of 1930.[62]

With the war needs only a memory and European relief no longer exciting to church members, the college campaigns became the movement of the decade as Lutherans spent more

losophy was Paul Harold Heisey's "The Lutheran Graded Series of Sunday School Materials," *Lutheran Quarterly* 53 (October 1923): 438–90; ibid. 54 (October 1924): 440–82.

58.
Otto H. Pannkoke, *A Great Church Finds Itself* (Quitman, Ga., 1966), p. 203.

59.
Russell Brown Thomas, *The Search for a Common Learning* (New York: McGraw-Hill, 1962), pp. 1–75, surveys the educational picture of the early twentieth century.

60.
Pannkoke, *A Great Church*, chaps. 6–8, recounts this aspect of Lutheran history and its importance for the church.

61.
R. J. Leonard et al., *Survey of Higher Education for the United Lutheran Church in America*, 3 vols. (New York: Teachers College, Columbia University, 1929). Surveys by the Norwegian Lutheran Church, the Missouri Synod, and the Augustana Synod were much smaller in scale and done without the professional personnel which ULCA used. Implementation of the recommendations was most difficult when they recommended the closing of some schools.

62.
ULCA, *Minutes . . . 1926*, pp. 338–40; ibid. *1928*, pp. 335–37; ibid. *1930*, p. 348.

time and money on education than on any other phase of church work. These financial campaigns, in addition to unprecedented physical development of campuses, produced significant side effects, such as expansion of curricula in the physical and social sciences and in various areas of preprofessional training, development of a new sense of public relations in and beyond the colleges, and a growing sense of corporate strength which the wartime services and National Lutheran Council campaigns had begun to foster. Significant training in stewardship was given to thousands of laymen through their participation in the financial campaigns. During the decade enrollment in Lutheran colleges rose from 4,000 to over 9,000, their total monetary value from $14 million to over $31 million. Far more important than these external indices of improvement, however, was the new orientation of the churches and the colleges to the needs of society and to preparation of educated Lutheran Christians for participation in society. Part of that broadened vision was higher educational standards for faculty and the importance of degrees from recognized graduate schools.[63] From faculty members trained in such schools came a new willingness to take serious account of social and religious ideas antithetical to Christianity. The religious "hothouse" atmosphere of many Lutheran institutions was in the process of disappearing by 1930.

Lutheran academies, which had served a real social and religious need in an earlier generation, were casualties of the twenties. The increase in the number and quality of public schools tended to make the academies superfluous. Because of this competition, as well as the omnipresent problem of finance and the hesitation of parents to send children of thirteen or fourteen away from home to school, academies declined steadily in number and enrollment between 1920 and 1930. Additional factors in the decline were the virtual halt in the flow of immigrants to whom the schools had catered and the lack of any adequate philosophy of education to justify their separate existence. Only Missouri's preparatory schools, which existed solely as feeders for its seminaries and teachers colleges, survived the decade in thriving condition. The ninety-nine academies of the various Lutheran bodies in 1920 had shrunk to fifty-five in 1930, of which only twenty-eight had more than fifty students. By 1930 the academy movement was in full retreat. The depression was its death.[64]

As far as the education of laymen was concerned, summer conferences of several weeks duration which combined a vacation atmosphere with educational and inspirational programs increased in number and popularity. Permanent summer centers were established in the Poconos of Pennsylvania, the resortland of Michigan, Dutchess County, New York, and at Lake Geneva, Wisconsin. Of even greater educational and theological importance was the start of the Bible School movement within Lutheranism. Seeing the appeal of such fundamentalistic Bible schools as the Moody School in Chicago and the Biblical Institute in Los Angeles, Lutherans established Bible institutes

63.
In the Missouri Synod especially, the question of professors studying at nonsynodical schools became a point of contention (*Synodal-bericht . . . 1926*, p. 318). The Missouri Synod refused to make a general rule, suggesting rather that each case be decided on its own merits by the respective school authorities.

64.
The only exception to the trend was Northwestern Lutheran Academy at Mobridge, S.D., started by the Wisconsin Synod in 1928 as a way to offset its lack of parochial schools. See Martin Lehninger et al., *Continuing in His Word* (Milwaukee: Northwestern Publishing House, 1951), p. 198. On the academies see *Lutheran World Almanac, 1921*, pp. 173–74; and Paul M. Lindberg, "The Academies of the Augustana Lutheran Church," in Dowie, *Swedish Immigrant Community*, pp. 93–106.

in Chicago and Minneapolis just prior to 1920. Through day, evening, and summer courses and conferences, the Bible schools contributed toward a biblically informed laity and stimulated many of their students to enter full-time church vocations. Although their tendency toward fundamentalistic interpretation of Scripture and pietist emphasis on Christian living caused some mild controversy, the Bible schools functioned as renewal centers for both laymen and clergy.[65]

Lutheran students at non-Lutheran colleges and universities far outnumbered those at Lutheran schools. Prior to 1920 only the United Lutheran Church and its synods had an organized ministry to students. In that year the number of Lutherans attending Minnesota, Wisconsin, Ohio State, Michigan, Penn State, and Cornell was greater than the combined total at all Lutheran colleges. The church could not afford to ignore ministry to so many of its members for long. Lutheran work, begun by the General Council in 1907 at Wisconsin, was expanded before the war to the universities of Minnesota, Pennsylvania, Illinois, and Cornell, the latter two being served by the General Synod. Under the United Lutheran Church after 1918, the program expanded rapidly to become one of the outstanding student ministries among American denominations. Of special historical import was the appointment of Mary Markley in 1919 as one of the church's two secretaries for student work. She was the first woman to hold full-time executive office in the Lutheran Church in America. Basic to the work of the United Lutheran Church was the principle that local congregations have the responsibility of integrating students within the range of their parish into the life of the congregation. In 1920 the Missouri Synod started its student ministry and within a few years all major Lutheran groups had become involved either directly or in cooperation with others. During the twenties "student congregations" came into being on some campuses as an alternative approach to the ULCA's emphasis on local congregational responsibility.[66] In connection with student work, the natural concern to conserve the young for the church led to a new interest for Lutherans in the relationship between church and society and in the intellectual challenge to Christian faith.

Organization of Lutheran students came in response to an invitation for a national Lutheran student conference in 1922 from the Lutheran Brotherhood, which changed its emphasis from servicemen to college youth after the end of the war. Student delegates from thirteen non-Lutheran and fifteen Lutheran institutions organized the Lutheran Student Association of America to promote Christian growth, fellowship, and service. Through campus groups, regional conferences, national conventions, and the *American Lutheran Student*[67] these goals were fostered and a new spirit of nonsynodical or suprasynodical Lutheran loyalty was stimulated among the coming generation of Lutheran leaders.

In the twenties change began in the seminaries as well—hardly sudden or drastic changes but a few variations in old patterns, which proved that conservatism had not yet hardened

65.
G. Everett Arden, *Augustana Heritage: A History of the Augustana Lutheran Church* (Rock Island, Ill.: Augustana Press, 1963), pp. 311–15. The *Bible Banner* of the Lutheran Bible Institute of Minneapolis is the best resource on the goals and the spirit of the movement within Lutheranism.

66.
Howard Marion LeSourd, *The University Work of the United Lutheran Church in America: A Study of the Work Among Lutheran Students at Non-Lutheran Institutions* (New York: Teachers College, Columbia University, 1929), covers the work of the ULCA. More comprehensive is Mary E. Markley's *The Lutheran Church and Its Students* (Philadelphia: Muhlenberg Press, 1948). Also valuable are Howard R. Gold's "The Beginnings of Work Among Lutheran Students," *Lutheran Church Quarterly* 9 (October 1936): 388–401; and Clarence P. Shedd's *The Church Follows Its Students* (New Haven: Yale University Press, 1938).

67.
The name was changed in 1949 to *The Campus Lutheran* and in 1954 to *Frontiers*.

68.
Over 90 percent of the Lutheran clergymen had either college or seminary training. The average for Protestant clergymen was 51 percent. See Willard L. Sperry, *Religion in America* (Cambridge: University Press, 1946), p. 176.

69.
The plans and buildings received extensive pictorial coverage in the *Architectural Record*.

70.
Theodore G. Tappert, *History of the Lutheran Theological Seminary at Philadelphia, 1864-1964* (Philadelphia: Lutheran Theological Seminary, 1964), p. 74.

into rigor mortis and which gave promise of greater changes somewhere in the future. What happened in seminaries was even more significant in Lutheranism than in other Protestant churches because seminary graduation was virtually the only path into the Lutheran ministry.[68] Seminaries, like colleges, needed and got new buildings. Beyond that, change in seminaries came only with great difficulty. Wartburg's magnificent new Gothic complex overlooking the rolling hills along the Mississippi's west bank at Dubuque was the first. Within half a dozen years Augustana Seminary had its new home, thanks to the successful financial campaign of 1921, and the seminary at Capital University a new quarter-million-dollar Divinity Hall. In 1929 Wisconsin Synod's seminary moved into its new quarters in Mequon, Wisconsin. The Philadelphia Seminary planned a totally new complex but was upstaged by two other financial appeals to its constituency. By the time its turn came the country was submerged in depression. Dwarfing all the others in beauty, excellence, and cost was the new Concordia Seminary in St. Louis, a monument to the Missouri Synod's reaffirmation of its heritage and confidence for its future. Its dedication ceremonies in 1926, covered widely by the press, attended by 75,000 members who came in by special trains from all over the Midwest and preserved on film for posterity, marked a new stage in Missouri's sense of permanence and mission. Missouri had built the best[69] and was determined to remain the best as far as strict Lutheranism was concerned.

In many seminaries, curricular revisions and teaching changes were more difficult to come by than buildings. Most seminaries continued as they had been, teaching traditional Lutheran orthodox theology according to traditional patterns. The students were to learn the truth as systematized in scholastic categories and to know how to defend it by biblical supports. Theodore G. Tappert's characterization of the faculty at Philadelphia before 1910 could be applied with accuracy to most of the seminaries in the twenties.

[Professors were] intent on restoring a theology and a practice of the past. No matter in what discipline of theology they were teaching, their attention was concentrated on a tradition. Most of their literary work was historical and it was calculated, broadly speaking, to demonstrate the superiority of the orthodoxism of the seventeenth century to the pietism and rationalism of the eighteenth century or the revivalism of the nineteenth century. Since there was a tendency to be rather uncritical in the adoption of them, there was actually more of a spirit of romantic repristination at work than there was of disciplined historical inquiry. This is especially evident in the refusal to employ the historical method in biblical study and a reluctance to depart from an exegesis which was imbedded in the doctrinal and liturgical tradition which was embraced.[70]

Some seminaries tried to introduce elective courses and to adjust part of the curriculum to some modern human problems,

433

but faculty and financial shortages kept changes to a minimum. At seminaries where German was still the medium for instruction, the professor sometimes dictated basic material to the class, elaborated on it in a lecture, and had students recite it back at the next session. At Philadelphia and a few other seminaries, concern began to develop about teaching men to think rather than to recite, but the teaching burden and the absence of serious theological quest and exchange among the professors themselves hindered any real improvement. At Capital University most of the theological professors ordered no books for the library with which they were not in complete theological agreement. For Concordia (St. Louis) the Missouri Synod, which had spent over $3 million for new buildings, could provide only $100 per year for books and nothing for a librarian.[71] When a full-time librarian was appointed in 1926 he pleaded for the school to buy the theological books which the professors were criticizing in class so that students could decide for themselves whether they agreed or disagreed.

In most of the twenty-five Lutheran seminaries, certain trends are discernible: a gradual decline in the emphasis on classical languages; greater emphasis on study of the English Bible; addition of so-called practical courses, especially in religious education and missions;[72] the desire, often unimplemented, of introducing courses in sociology or the sociology of religion. No Lutheran seminary in the twenties had any of the specialized courses of the more liberal schools in "the city church," "the rural church," or "the church and industry." In all Lutheran seminaries except Philadelphia and Gettysburg, the course of study was totally prescribed. Organization of the curriculum by departments had been initiated by most seminaries, but in some schools professors with greatest seniority chose each year which courses they preferred to teach; those with least seniority got the leftovers.[73] Everywhere, however, the trend was toward a less rigidly prescribed curriculum, toward more pastoral courses, toward professorships in specific theological disciplines, and toward graduate theological study for professorial prospects in non-Lutheran or non-American universities and seminaries.[74] The ferment of change was starting to work beneath the surface in seminaries, but the twenties brought little of it to the surface. In all synods, the assumption that theological professors were guardians of the tradition, not critics or pioneers, kept excitement and controversy from seminary doorsteps.[75] And the tendency of doctrinal watchdogs to see "modernism" behind all variation from the ways of the fathers intimidated all but the most nonconformist. Only in the United Lutheran Church and, at the very close of the decade, in Augustana was there any vocal and open agitation to forsake the old approach to theological education.[76]

Missions

Much remained unchanged in Lutheran home missions following the war. Salaries were still meager, averaging only $800 per year in 1920. Except in the United Lutheran Church the gath-

71.
Carl S. Meyer, *Log Cabin to Luther Tower: Concordia Seminary . . . 1839-1964* (St. Louis: Concordia Publishing House, 1965), pp. 286-90.
72.
In Lutheran seminaries the religious-education courses were almost all of the catechetics and pedagogics type, in contrast to the growing number of courses in other Protestant seminaries which emphasized the psychological and educational theories of the progressive school. See Robert L. Kelly, *Theological Education in America* (New York: Doran, 1924), pp. 422-33.
73.
Professors such as J. Michael Reu of Wartburg Seminary eventually taught every course in the school; some developed amazing facility in almost every area of theology.
74.
The Missouri Synod was most opposed to such training because it feared the intrusion of the "modernistic poison." On the views of Theodore Graebner, see Meyer, *Log Cabin*, p. 110. For changes at Concordia Seminary, St. Louis, in the twenties, see ibid., pp. 263-66, 278-79.
75.
The controversy at the Lutheran Seminary in Chicago was mainly a matter of personalities and an administrative clash between faculty and board.
76.
In 1930 Knubel said ministers should be trained to be witnesses of the Word rather than conservers of the "true faith" (ULCA, *Minutes . . . 1930*, p. 86). In the ULCA Charles M. Jacobs advocated changes in theological approach which had inevitable educational consequences. He saw the limitations of Lutheran scholastic theology and emphasized the Scriptures as living witness rather than a system of inerrant propositions. To him, theology was "not static but dynamic, not a science fixed and complete and comprised in formulas that must be handed down as infallible tradition, but a science ever growing, ever learning from the Word of God, ever seeking new forms in which to express eternal truth" (Tappert, *History*, p.

ering of immigrants and first-generation Americans was still the bread-and-butter activity of home missions. Until the mid-twenties most Lutherans still hoped for a quick resumption of the heavy immigration which had turned their church into a major American denomination in a little more than a generation. But one thing changed drastically—every church body except the most foreign knew that it could not remain a cohesive immigrant community, not even an English-speaking cohesive immigrant community, and hope to survive. Naturally, all the churches found it easier to talk about evangelizing all types of Americans than to actually evangelize them. English speech and English worship did not automatically mean a harvest of nonimmigrant converts. But talk had to be the first step. The harvest came slowly as Lutheran young people brought their non-Lutheran spouses with them, as pastors overcame their hesitation to participate in community life and as they learned methods of evangelization, as church bodies began the first moves toward a mission strategy to replace the random planting of missions wherever opportunity and manpower happened to coincide.

435

Not that the "gathering" function disappeared in 1917 or even in 1920. In learning to use statistics during the great change, Lutherans discovered that less than one-fourth of the Americans and Canadians of Lutheran heritage were actually members of Lutheran churches.[77] In addition, the unrestricted immigration that poured into Canada in the twenties included a heavy proportion of Lutherans. Understandably, no amount of propagandizing for missions to *all* Americans could keep the Scandinavians in America and all Lutheran groups in Canada and in the Northwest from planting the church among these "brethren." The romantic appeal of man against nature on the Canadian frontier and the image of sacrificial devotion in the face of great odds had a greater psychological impact than the size of the new immigration actually warranted, especially in the manner with which the missionary venture was presented in the regular church paper reports. Therefore, long after the itinerant home missionaries were an anachronism their memory deterred somewhat the necessary change in strategy to meet the needs of a more urban land into which immigration had all but ceased.[78]

As was the case just prior to the war, three different kinds of fields—the exploding cities, the great Northwest,[79] and Canada—constituted the greatest mission challenges. The Central and Upper Midwest, with its greater Lutheran population than all the rest of the United States and its rapidly expanding cities, also called for hundreds of new congregations. The urban centers of the East and the promised lands of Florida and California had to be served. By the late twenties the 540 Lutheran congregations in New York City and its suburbs had made Lutheranism the strongest Protestant church in the area, but calls for more congregations arose from its suburbs and from every urban area. Every Lutheran body regularly heard reports on fields which could not be entered because of the shortage of men and

94). On the start of change in Augustana, see G. Everett Arden, *The School of the Prophets: History of Augustana Theological Seminary* (Rock Island, Ill.: Augustana Theological Seminary, 1960), pp. 230-32.
77.
The 1916 census revealed that there were 17,314,376 Americans of Lutheran heritage but only 4,012,490 members of Lutheran congregations. In the 1921 Canada census 287,484 Canadians claimed to be Lutheran but only 75,000 belonged to Lutheran congregations. See *Lutheran World Almanac, 1926*, p. 83; ibid. *1928*, p. 279.
78.
On the tension between the old and the new see A. N. Graebner, "Acculturation," pp. 163-73. In the case of Missouri, attention to mission policy was urgent because in 1919 there showed a net loss of members for the first time. Of course, the war experience had much to do with that loss.
79.
"This is now the storm and stress center of the States. If we conquer here by the grace of God, then the whole of our vast country will be possessed; if we lose, then for all time our western wing will be weak and open to attack by antagonistic spiritual forces" (*Lutheran Standard*, May 3, 1919, p. 277).

money.[80] For manpower, only Missouri of all the major synods seemed to have an adequate supply thanks to its effective recruiting institutions, the parochial and preparatory schools. In numbers of mission pastors, Missouri continued far in the lead, 648 pastors serving 1,364 stations in 1920, 755 serving 1,684 stations in 1930.[81]

In adopting new missionary methods, community canvassing, Lenten house-to-house visitations, evangelism committees, tract distribution to nonmembers, and concentrated drives for adult membership classes became part of the life of the urban churches.[82] Full-time field secretaries for mission planning relieved some of the pressure on district and synod presidents who had traditionally borne this responsibility often in addition to their own parish duties. Where the need for new approaches was most urgent, such as cooperative planning for most effective use of resources, virtually no progress was made. In Minnesota, where twenty different Lutheran bodies had congregations in 1920, the need was greatest, but the extent of the problem is evident in the fact that ten or more bodies were simultaneously at work in seventeen of the forty-eight states in 1920. The missionary intent of conferences such as those in 1919 and 1920 was sidetracked on doctrine and practice as was that of the intersynodical committees during the twenties. The fruitless struggle to find some basis for full mutual recognition had its most pathetic results at the level where mission pastors and people prayed and worked. Duplication and friction not only took the joy out of the work but also became an offense and a barrier to those whom Lutherans said they were anxious to win. Occasionally, local initiative refused to wait for intersynodical agreements, as in Iowa where pastors of the United Lutheran, Iowa, Ohio, Augustana, Norwegian Lutheran, United Danish, and Danish churches organized the Lutheran Committee for Home Missions and Consultation of Iowa in 1928.[83] Seldom, however, were local relationships cordial enough or influential enough with denominational officials to make local comity a functioning reality.

The emphasis on a ministry to English-speaking Americans did not cause the earlier linguistic variety in Lutheranism to disappear in the twenties. Among Spanish-speaking citizens of New York City and among some enclaves of Estonians, Slovaks, and Italians in a number of large cities, mission work actually increased. On the whole, however, the so-called linguistic missions remained quite stable, largely due to the perennial problem of finding bilingual pastors. The hope of the United Lutheran Church's immigrant mission board that restriction of immigration would give Lutheranism a chance to catch up with the foreign-language groups could not be realized because pastors with facility in these languages simply were not available.[84] Even young men who could have worked in foreign languages often neglected to cultivate them. The anti-foreign-language prejudice of the war and the superpatriotism of the postwar years had done their work well enough to deprive Lutheranism of much of its inherent language potential.

80.
The Norwegian Lutheran Church's aggressive mission program regularly spent considerably more than its income— $300,000 over receipts in the twenties. This was made possible by the almost unlimited credit available to it in Minneapolis banks. Nelson, *Lutheran Church Among Norwegian-Americans*, 2:267.

81.
Lutheran World Almanac, 1930, p. 172. The *Almanac* is the only source of statistical information on all of Lutheranism during this period. In 1920 the ULCA had 365 English-speaking mission parishes; no definite number of German-speaking parishes is given (ULCA, *Minutes . . . 1920*, pp. 197–99). The total number in 1928 was 578 (ibid. *1928*, p. 213).

82.
Where "evangelistic services" were held in Lutheran congregations, as in parts of the Norwegian Lutheran Church, they usually aimed at "quickening" or "saving" people who were already members of the church. In 1923 the Norwegian church had three evangelists who conducted such services. See Nelson, *Lutheran Church Among Norwegian-Americans*, 2:261.

83.
Lutheran World Almanac, 1930, p. 47. At the invitation of the ULCA a Lutheran Home Missions Council was formed in March 1930 by representatives of the ULCA, Norwegian Lutheran Church, American Lutheran Church, Augustana Synod, and United Danish Church. Its purposes were comity, coordination of work, elimination of duplication. See ibid. *1931–33*, pp. 87–88.

84.
The ULCA's Board of American Missions hoped as late as 1930 for one central seminary which would train bilingual pastors to serve in these difficult ministries. The report warned that such a seminary should not be located where students would get used to the luxury of the cities (ULCA, *Minutes . . . 1930*, pp. 226–27). Other denominations were also trying hard to reach the foreign-language groups. See H. N. Morse, *Home Missions Today and Tomorrow* (New York: Home Missions Council, 1934).

Table 5

**Growth of Lutheranism
During the Twenties**

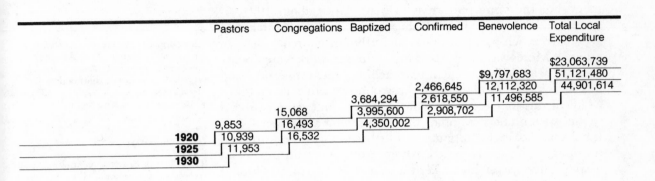

	Pastors	Congregations	Baptized	Confirmed	Benevolence	Total Local Expenditure
1920	9,853	15,068	3,684,294	2,466,645	$9,797,683	$23,063,739
1925	10,939	16,493	3,995,600	2,618,550	12,112,320	51,121,480
1930	11,953	16,532	4,350,002	2,908,702	11,496,585	44,901,614

Like all other Christians, Lutherans showed an upsurge of interest in evangelizing the world in the early twenties. The increased interest was undoubtedly due to the National Lutheran Council's appeals for the orphaned missions of the European churches and to the extensive publicity for its financial campaigns. Lutheran interest held steadier during the decade than did that of the Protestants behind the Interchurch World Movement, but the same pattern is evident. Until about 1924, finances and volunteers were on the ascent; afterward both began a decline which was less sharp in Lutheran churches than in others.[85] Moreover, the goals of the Lutheran work were always more closely tied to preaching, teaching, and conversion and less to social service than were those of many other Protestants. Medical missions received some emphasis but general social service with no purpose other than improving the physical and intellectual lot of the nationals got little support from Lutheran missionaries or home boards. Absence of any significant social gospel influence at home kept Lutheranism in a traditional missionary mentality which had no sympathy for the reorientation of mission philosophy expressed in William Ernest Hocking's *Rethinking Missions.*[86]

Instead of expanding their work into new areas of the world, most of the Lutheran effort was invested in fields already occupied, especially in India, China, and Japan. Consultation and some cooperation, easier to attain in foreign than in home missions, was carried on through the Lutheran Foreign Missions Conference of North America, but its major activity was discussion and cultivation of cordial relations between boards and societies rather than joint work on foreign fields. In proportion to size, the Norwegian Lutheran Church in the twenties supported the largest missionary program with thriving fields in China, Madagascar, and South Africa. The United Lutheran Church, much larger in membership, was close behind with work in India, Japan, Liberia, Argentina, British Guiana, and China. The Missouri Synod's work in India had difficulty in retaining its personnel, partly because of an internal controversy over which name to use for God,[87] and never grew beyond the stage of early infancy. The Missouri board's policy of allowing no cooperation or cordial relationships with other Lutherans or Christians worked hardship on many missionaries in both fields. In China, Elmer L. Arndt protested and sometimes ignored the position of his synod. In India, Adolph A. Brux's participation in household devotions with Presbyterians led to his suspension. The attitude of Missouri toward other Lutherans on the foreign field is shown in its decision to drop the name which all other Lutherans in China used, Faith-Righteousness Church, in favor of Gospel-Doctrine Lutheran Church. Its reason was that Lutherans who are "more or less given to unionism" used the other name.[88] By the decade's end the prevalent postwar sentiment for evangelizing the world had given way to a spirit that was half-disillusioned by the difficulty of making even a few converts

85.
For information on Protestant volunteers see Robert T. Handy, "The American Religious Depression," *Church History* 29 (1960): 4–5. Lutheran contributions for foreign missions were $822,201 in 1920, $1,827,639 in 1924, and $1,749,220 in 1930.
86.
New York: Harper, 1932.
87.
The "Shen vs. Shang-ti" controversy. Full records are at Concordia Historical Institute, St. Louis.
88.
Dean Lueking, *Mission in the Making* (St. Louis: Concordia Publishing House, 1964), p. 267.

and half-preoccupied by the home mission task. The depression brought both to a virtual halt. The time of grace had been short.

Lutherans and Other Christians

Behind the inability of Lutherans in America to agree on the right attitude toward other Christians lay important questions about the nature of the church. Is doctrine the one great responsibility of the church? Is Lutheran doctrine so perfect that Lutherans must separate from the rest of Christendom in a basic stance of judgment and isolation? Or is there enough common affirmation of truth to warrant occasional common action and enough possibility of complementarity within imperfection to make contact with other Christians beneficial to Lutherans? Is separation from those with whom one has disagreements the only or most effective way of witnessing to one's convictions? Does all cooperation between churches whose confessions differ imply recognition of the other's teaching?

No progress was made in the twenties toward resolution of the deep differences among Lutherans on these questions. All Lutheran groups continued to be confident of their church's doctrinal uniqueness and none shared the growing assumption of Protestants that concern over doctrinal details was passé. All felt that Christendom would be stronger if all others accepted the Lutheran approach to such key doctrines as justification; the nature of the Christian life; the way God works through the written, spoken, and sacramental word; the nature of the kingdom of God, the church, and church organization; the relationship of the church and society, church and government. All felt a responsibility to witness to Lutheran convictions and to do nothing which implied that doctrinal issues were of secondary importance.

Only the United Lutheran Church and, to a lesser degree, the Augustana Synod saw the possibilities of cordial relationships with other Christians without compromising Lutheran principles. On the basis of its Washington Declaration of 1920, the United Lutheran Church tried to evaluate each opportunity for cooperation on its own merits, to see whether the churches involved adhered to the basic doctrinal principles of the declaration, whether the proposed cooperation was a legitimate sphere of "church" activity, and whether participation would permit the United Lutheran Church freedom to witness to its understanding of the Christian faith. Augustana operated in similar fashion but somewhat more hesitantly and without a formal statement of guiding principles. Occasionally, Lutheran Free Church pastors and lay people cooperated in local evangelistic or service projects, and the Norwegian merger of 1917 had permitted an ecumenical "Interpretation" of its strictly worded constitution. The rest of Lutheranism was opposed in principle to all consultation and cooperation with non-Lutherans, whether by congregations or church bodies. Both the "middle synods" and the Synodical Conference insisted that "real Lutherans" would be completely separate from non-Lutherans on the official level and would prohibit all joint worship, all pulpit exchange, and all communing of non-Lutherans in Lutheran churches.

Reaction to the major interchurch movements of the twenties illustrates the caution common to all Lutherans as well as the differences in approach. In spite of heavy pressures from Protestant leaders, all Lutheran bodies were categorically opposed to the Interchurch World Movement[89] on the grounds of its doctrinal unconcern and its enthusiasm about attaining unity by administrative manipulations. Both the dream and the methods elicited considerable Lutheran scorn—consolidation of all denominational programs and budgets and achievement of a federation of all evangelical churches in five years, extensive and expensive nationwide publicity, a one-billion-dollar financial goal, the assumption that America as a whole would respond to a great "Christian" crusade to change society and the world.[90] When the interchurch bubble burst in 1921 and 1922, due to the economic recession and the postwar shift in the American mood from idealism and internationalism to disenchantment with altruistic schemes, Lutherans made little effort to hide their "we-told-you-so" attitude.

Because most Lutherans severely criticized the Washington Declaration of the United Lutheran Church and charged it with "unionism," a brief look at that church's procedure on interchurch relations is in order. In harmony with the principle that each venture should be evaluated separately, the ULCA devoted considerable time in its conventions to interchurch affairs. In 1920 it declined to support the Interchurch World Movement and the Lord's Day Alliance, while commending the American Bible Society to congregations and giving tentative permission to the boards of the church to associate with representative interdenominational councils.[91] After careful study of the Federal Council of Churches, the 1922 convention declined to join because the Federal Council did not see the need for unity in faith and confession, failed to distinguish legitimate cooperation between differing churches from the actions of a united church, and inclined toward programs which "compel-[led] men by law to obey the law of Christ." Pastors and boards were warned to be careful in the use of literature emanating from the Federal Council, and some restrictions were placed on the 1920 permission for church boards to participate in interdenominational groups. Yet the convention found enough unity among Federal Council members in basic Christian doctrine, and enough guarantees of its own autonomy and freedom of witness, to permit a "consultative" affiliation with the council— voice but not vote, and cooperation in selected projects.[92] The geographical synods of the church were, however, advised not to affiliate with state councils, and congregations were advised to limit their cooperation in local councils to those areas in which the United Lutheran Church cooperated with the Federal Council. The church's participants in cooperative ventures were

440

89.
See John H. Oldham, "The Interchurch World Movement: Its Problems and Possibilities," *International Review of Missions* 9 (1920): 182–99; and Eldon G. Ernst, "The Interchurch World Movement of North America, 1919–1920" (Ph.D. diss., Yale University, 1968).

90.
R. C. H. Lenski's comment was typical: "It will be an ecclesiastical Noahs-ark housing all sorts of animals. The little bit of Gospel which is still to be found here and there will vanish—it will only be in the way" ("Das Interchurch Ungestüm," *Lutherische Kirchenzeitung*, June 19, 1920, p. 386). See also *Lutheran Witness*, May 25, 1920, p. 167.

91.
ULCA, *Minutes . . . 1920*, p. 86–87; Dorris A. Flesner, "The Role of the Lutheran Churches of America in the Formation of the World Council of Churches" (Ph.D. diss., Hartford Seminary Foundation, Hartford, Conn., 1956), p. 26.

92.
UCLA, *Minutes . . . 1922*, pp. 72–88. The following areas of cooperation were approved: study of church unity, military chaplaincy, general surveys, statistics, disaster relief, general publicity, transportation arrangements, consultation on departmental planning, some phases of educational work, and declarations on matters of public concern.

repeatedly encouraged to work for recognition of the principle that in interchurch affairs only official representatives, and not "co-opted, free-lance individuals who represent only themselves," should have powers of decision.[93]

In spite of recurring criticism of some aspects of the Federal Council, especially its efforts to influence legislation, the United Lutheran Church regularly reaffirmed its consultative relationship as a legitimate way to benefit from and to influence other American Protestants. All other Lutherans roundly condemned the Federal Council as a modernistic organ of social-gospel interests. As it became evident that the fundamentalists were losing their battle to exclude the liberals from the major denominations, antipathy to the Federal Council became even stronger. In instances where particular special interests of some Lutheran bodies coincided with views of the Federal Council (e.g., on prohibition, pacifism, antagonism to the Roman Catholic Church) specific utterances of the council might be cited with approval, but on the essential question of cooperation in the council there was no yielding.

The same attitudes determined Lutheran response to the great international ecumenical conferences of the twenties. In 1922 Frederick H. Knubel declined an invitation to appoint representatives to the 1922 meeting on arrangements for the 1925 Life and Work Conference. In 1924, however, the United Lutheran Church decided that representation at the Life and Work and the Faith and Order conferences were within the principles of the Washington Declaration.[94] Augustana, the only other American Lutheran body officially represented at Stockholm, was probably more influenced by its Swedish loyalties and its regard for Life and Work's founder, Nathan Soderblom, than by agreement in principle with the aims of the movement.[95] Except for one unofficial Lutheran Free Church delegate at both Stockholm and Lausanne and a co-opted representative of the Norwegian Lutheran Church at Lausanne, all other American Lutheran bodies remained aloof from the conferences, still sure that they needed no great conferences to learn about the doctrines of other churches, still suspicious of anything that looked like a scheme to propagandize for episcopacy, and totally skeptical of any effort for a sensational corporate Christian witness to society.[96]

The United Lutheran Church evaluated the results of the two conferences more carefully than nonparticipants, who usually dismissed the results as either superficial or false. United Lutheran Church delegates admitted that their own high expectations of some new insight into the mind of Christ had not been realized, but they praised the Stockholm conference's contribution toward a clearer conception of the world's needs and the church's responsibilities and the Lausanne conference's willingness to face openly the harsh realities blocking Christian unity. Recognition by both conferences of the essentially spiritual character of the church's resources in all crises virtually guaranteed continued support. Decision on future participation

441

93.
Ibid., p. 70; ibid. *1926,* p. 29.
94.
Ibid. *1924,* pp. 534–36. Dr. Knubel's reasons had been: (1) The need for Lutherans first to determine a common position in an international Lutheran convention; (2) the fear that too many such conferences would distract the church and consume its manpower; (3) the danger of mere display; (4) the dangerous disregard of the representative principle; (5) the need for longer conferences and fewer of them; (6) the neglect of the content of faith and its confession (ibid. *1922,* pp. 93–94).
95.
Flesner strains to prove otherwise, "Role of the Lutheran Churches," pp. 304–5.
96.
Nonparticipants rejoiced to see that the conferences did not live up to some of the expectations of those who attended, and they deplored the readiness of some Lutherans to fall for "deceptions" such as the Life and Work movement. See *Theological Monthly* 6 (March 1926): 91; "Interdenominational Cooperation by the ULCA," *Pastors' Monthly* 3 (April 1925): 251–52; "Die Stockholmer Weltkirchenkonferenz," *Kirchliche Zeitschrift* 49 (September 1925): 576–82. Editors of the Midwestern synods saw the conferences as a "tremendous and subtle attack by combined modernistic Protestantism upon confessional fidelity. . . . If we are in earnest about Lutheran cooperation and union in America, why hurt one another by flirting with modernists?" (Johann C. K. Preus, "The Stockholm Conference: An Evaluation," *Pastors' Monthly* 4 [March 1926]: 137). For further reactions see Fred W. Meuser, *The Formation of the American Lutheran Church* (Columbus, Ohio: Wartburg Press, 1958), pp. 263–71.

was to be determined by the church's executive board on the basis of conference programs and the response of their planners to the United Lutheran Church's principle of official representation. Because European Lutheran representation was much greater at both conferences than the American, the strongest influence of the movements came into American Lutheranism through its contacts with Europeans at subsequent meetings of the Lutheran World Convention.[97]

97.
The program of the Second Lutheran World Convention shows considerable evidence of the growing social concern. The Second Lutheran World Convention, *The Minutes, Addresses, and Discussions of the Convention at Copenhagen, Denmark, June 26 to July 4, 1929* (Philadelphia: United Lutheran Publication House, 1930).

Lutherans and Lutherans

Without reverting to the hostilities of the prewar period, Lutheran church bodies in the twenties reverted to a more cautious spirit. Within the "middle synods" there were some significant organizational changes—a cooperative conference and a merger, but these were no more than natural fruits of earlier developments, as bodies which had learned to trust each other drew closer together. No important progress was made in settling old issues between the three "families" of Lutherans or in overcoming the mistrust which had developed in the National Lutheran Council. Spadework was being done which might later bear fruit and limited cooperation between the middle groups and the ULCA continued, but the twenties simply had few external incentives to force Lutherans together.

Vocational and Professional Associations

Only one area saw notable progress in inter-Lutheran relationships. As never before, Lutherans from all groups consulted together along lines of vocational or professional interest. When they did not need to ask, "What separates our church organizations?" but only, "What common interests and problems do we share on which we might be of help to each other?" inter-Lutheran contacts multiplied. Editors of church papers had met together annually since 1910, college students with a missionary interest (Lutheran Student Missionary Association) since 1911, Lutheran educators since 1914, those with responsibility in statistics since 1917, Lutheran laymen interested in general service to their church since 1918. All such groups prospered in the twenties and expanded greatly in number. The Lutheran Foreign Missions Boards began meeting together annually in 1919, inner missions personnel in 1922, college students in 1922, seminary students in 1928, college professors in 1910. Even members of the Synodical Conference occasionally took part. In assuming goodwill and unity of faith, the annual conferences of dozens of special-interest organizations contributed greatly to understanding and mutual acceptance. Few formal requests for specific action on Lutheran unity were submitted to church bodies by these groups; they did not regard this as their purpose. Yet their very existence reflected the assumption that Lutherans belong together. Such annual gatherings of Lutherans, some of whom also attended conventions of their church bodies, some of whom shaped the minds of the coming generation of leaders, some of whom were the coming leaders, had a great deal more to do with post-1930 progress than their minutes could reflect.

The American Lutheran Conference

Organizationally, the most notable event of the decade was the establishment by the Midwestern synods of a measure of the kind of cooperation which the National Lutheran Council had hoped would develop out of its activities. In the unsuccessful joint conferences on doctrine and practice of 1919 and 1920, the presidents of the Joint Synod of Ohio and the Norwegian Lutheran Church opposed the effort of the United Lutheran Church to define Lutheran relationships to non-Lutheran churches in other than negative terms. They feared the Knubel-Jacobs emphasis on catholicity as one more instance of the United Lutheran Church's careless attitude on Lutheran doctrine (further evidence for which was ULCA failure to adopt the Galesburg Rule), equivocation about membership of Lutherans in secret societies, and the absence of official affirmation of the Scriptures as verbally inspired and inerrant. Before the end of 1920, leaders of Ohio, the Norwegians, Iowa, and Augustana had agreed unofficially that closer relationships should be established between these synods.[98]

Probably because of change in the presidencies of both the Joint Ohio Synod and the Norwegian Lutheran Church in the early twenties, formal action toward the desired goal of fellowship was not taken until November 19, 1925, when Carl C. Hein, the new Ohio president, and Johan A. Aasgaard, successor to Hans G. Stub, convened the Minneapolis Colloquy, attended by representatives of Iowa and Buffalo as well. Major voices were those of Hein, Stub, Aasgaard, and J. Michael Reu (Iowa). The purpose was not to discover whether fellowship was possible, for the participants had already been assured about that, but to draw up a statement which the churches could adopt as a basis for fellowship and cooperation. Its decisions, the Minneapolis Theses, were designed at key points as a witness against the United Lutheran Church. After affirming the Chicago Theses of 1919 as a basic indication of doctrinal agreement, the representatives adopted additional statements on Scripture, the confessions, church fellowship, and secret societies. Each one by design went beyond the position of the United Lutheran Church.

In the light of subsequent developments in American Lutheranism, the major issue of the Minneapolis Theses was the question of the inspiration and inerrancy of the Bible. The Norwegians, to their dismay, discovered that Reu was in their judgment a liberal because he considered the infallibility of Scripture limited to its message of salvation. Reu's view did not prevail and the colloquy adopted what was essentially the position of Stub and Hein: the Scriptures "as a whole, and in all their parts, [are] the divinely inspired, revealed, and inerrant Word of God. . . ." In regard to the confessions, the whole of

98.
Archival materials and original records are in the Archives of the American Lutheran Church: American Lutheran Conference Minutes and Colloquies to 1930. The most complete analysis of the formation of the conference is in Meuser, *American Lutheran Church*, pp. 235–49. On the background of the joint conferences of 1919 and 1920, which Meuser omits, see Nelson, *Lutheran Church Among Norwegian-Americans*, 2:288–302.

their doctrinal content was asserted: "without exception or limitation in all articles and parts, no matter whether a doctrine is specifically cited as a confession or incidentally introduced for the purpose of elucidating or proving some other doctrine" (Article II, 2). In contrast to the United Lutheran Church's recognition of the Christian character of all churches which confess basic Christian doctrine, an article on church fellowship merely stated that "true Christians are found in every denomination which has so much of divine truth . . . that children of God can be born in it," and that mutual recognition, pulpit and altar fellowship, and "cooperation in the strictly essential work of the church presupposes unanimity in the pure doctrine of the Gospel and in the confession of the same in word and deed" (III, 1). In striking contrast to the clarity of the ULCA declaration, no further definition was given of the "strictly essential work of the church." Obviously, the intent was to draw the line against all cooperation of Lutherans with other churches. Restriction of Lutheran pulpits and altars to Lutherans only (part 1 of the Galesburg Rule) was also affirmed as a necessary implication of Scripture and Lutheran doctrine. A final article on secret societies asserted that neither individuals nor congregations could have fellowship with societies whose principles or practice conflicted in any way with Christian doctrine and (with the small minority of ULCA pastors who belonged to such societies in mind) "that a Lutheran synod should not tolerate pastors who have affiliated themselves with any anti-Christian society" (V, 4). Pastors were to witness against such groups and to persuade Lutherans to sever their connections with them. In contrast to the Missouri Synod position, the Minneapolis Theses did not absolutely prohibit laymen from belonging, nor did they prescribe church discipline and possible excommunication. Hein's plan to include a statement on predestination and conversion in the hope of allaying the Missouri Synod's misgivings about the Norwegians did not materialize because the Norwegians refused to risk reopening a doctrinal controversy which had been settled with difficulty hardly a dozen years before.[99] At the end of the one-day meeting, the participants agreed to ask the Augustana Synod, the Lutheran Free Church, and the United Danish Church to join them in seeking approval of their synods for the theses.[100] In a variety of ways all gave their endorsement between 1925 and 1930, and the American Lutheran Conference was established in Minneapolis, October 29–31, 1930.

The purposes of the American Lutheran Conference were cooperation in those areas of worship, work, and witness where full unity of doctrine is a prerequisite: home missions, parochial education, higher education, service to students in nonchurch schools, publication of religious literature, exchange of theological professors, and joint planning toward greater Lutheran unity. This amalgamation of various national backgrounds and divergent trends in piety, culture, and language reflected a degree of Americanization far greater than that before World War I. Inasmuch as the United Lutheran Church was the only National Lutheran Council body excluded from the American

99.
Hein sensed that without a clear statement that disposed of the ambiguities of the 1912 Madison Agreement, the Missouri Synod would never drop its charge of doctrinal error against the Norwegians. More than any other factor, this issue torpedoed any chance for fellowship between Missouri and the Ohio and Iowa synods. See Meuser, *American Lutheran Church*, pp. 240–41, 251–53.

100.
The Joint Synod of Ohio had some misgivings about including Augustana because of its long association with the General Council and its friendly gestures to Archbishop Nathan Soderblom in 1925, and about the Lutheran Free Church because of its antipathy to doctrinal statements other than the Lutheran confessions (ibid., pp. 243–47; Nelson, *Lutheran Church Among Norwegian-Americans*, 2:305, n. 64).

Lutheran Conference, it was well aware of the antagonism behind the conference's birth and also fearful lest the conference further jeopardize the National Lutheran Council.[101] Although the conference's cooperative program never developed to the extent its architects had hoped, it did draw the church bodies, with the partial exception of Augustana, into greater working harmony in the post-1930 years.

The Intersynodical Theses

445

A second concurrent effort to promote unity among Midwestern groups grew out of the St. Paul pastoral meeting which had produced the St. Paul Theses in 1916. So favorable had been their reception by pastors and so widespread the hope for settlement of the dispute and establishment of pulpit and altar fellowship that Missouri, Wisconsin, Joint Ohio, and Iowa all appointed official "intersynodical committees" to seek official agreement on the issues of the predestination controversy. Although the Norwegians had tackled their troublesome issues by having committees discuss the problem areas and compose theses of agreement, the Midwestern synods had not heretofore had sufficient trust in each other to try this approach. Because the St. Paul Theses were regarded as inadequate, new theses and antitheses were to be composed by the committee on the basis of Scripture and the Lutheran confessions. Taking their cue from the pastors' conferences, the Intersynodical Committee refused to try to determine who had been more right and more wrong in the earlier stage of the controversy. In order to guarantee that the discussions focused on the doctrines and not the controversy, no theologian was to be cited who had lived after the compilation of the Book of Concord in 1580. As a further indication of their determination not to get bogged down in polemical minutiae, each synod appointed more pastors than professional theologians to its committee.[102] Carl C. Hein's charge of 1917, that the theologians were keeping apart pastors and people who believed alike, was being taken seriously. None of these synods, however, accepted the ULCA's position that no doctrinal agreements other than the Lutheran confessions were necessary. The charges and counter charges of heresy over the years made closer examination of the actual biblical and confessional teaching a necessity. It was the only way to allay the fears of each side that the other harbored dangerous doctrinal views.

Meeting two or three times a year for three days at a time, the committee made significant progress on those issues where discussion had previously always increased antagonism—conversion, the reasons for the conversion of some and the nonconversion of others, the role of man's will, what it means that God elects individuals to salvation. From the start, it was evident that the committee sought no compromise, but rather a precise formulation of the various theological issues on which they could all agree. Agreement was attained early on election, conversion, the confessions, church fellowship, the church, the ministry, the Antichrist, the Last Things, the days and forms for worship, and "open questions." On all of these Missouri had had a long-

101.
President Knubel held that the principles of the Minneapolis Theses were basically sectarian rather than Lutheran, largely because they restricted the "Church" too much to a particular brand of Lutheranism. "[The theses] cannot live ultimately in the life of American Lutheranism for they do not represent Lutheranism. Some day . . . although not while you and I are alive, American Lutheranism will cast those things aside" (letter of Frederick H. Knubel to J. K. Jensen, September 16, 1930, quoted in Nelson, *Lutheran Church Among Norwegian-Americans*, 2:308).
102.
Most of the records of the committee are in the American Lutheran Church Archives, Dubuque, Iowa, or in the Concordia Historical Institute Archives, St. Louis, but few have been sorted or catalogued.

standing conflict with Iowa and to a lesser degree with Ohio. A thesis on the verbal inspiration of Scripture was also added, not because of controversy between these synods but because the current disagreements within Protestantism seemed to require a clear "Lutheran" statement.

As theses on the various points of doctrine were completed they were distributed to pastors and lay leaders of the synods for examination and criticism. Especially in Missouri, but also in the other synods, discussion of the correctness and adequacy of the Intersynodical Theses was a standard part of pastoral conferences and district and synod conventions throughout the twenties. No less than full unity of interpretation on all aspects of these doctrines seemed to be within reach.

The single most important agreement by the committee was that God's "election" of men to salvation has not taken place on the basis of his foreknowledge that certain individuals would come to faith *(intuitu fidei)*. God's foreknowledge is not denied, but nothing in man, not even his faith, is made the basis of God's "election." Faith is seen as the result, not the cause, of God's gracious decree to save. On any other basis, the individual is said to be deprived of the full comfort and assurance that God wills his salvation and will perfect it. On the other hand, every emphasis or formulation which would in any way make God the cause of the reprobation of the lost is vigorously denied.[103] The traditional emphasis of Ohio and Iowa on an election based on foreknowledge is thus renounced. And the fear that Missouri was skirting too close to the edge of a Calvinistic decree of reprobation was allayed.

Hope of fellowship among Ohio, Iowa, Missouri, and Wisconsin declined as the decade progressed. Ohio's fellowship, on the one hand, with the Norwegians who had united on a compromise statement regarding election and its committee work with Missouri and Wisconsin, on the other, seemed grossly inconsistent to Missouri. Repeated efforts were made by Ohio to dispel Missouri's antipathy to the Norwegians and by Missourians to persuade Ohio to give up this friendship or to insist on Norwegian acceptance of the Intersynodical Theses. Further tensions developed over the National Lutheran Council, the Lutheran World Convention, the Lutheran Brotherhood, conferences of foreign mission boards, editors, educators, and over the old question of how to deal with lodge members. All of these were, to Missouri, evidence of a compromising doctrinal spirit in Ohio and Iowa. "By their practice" (wrote Theodore Graebner in 1925) they "prove beyond the shadow of a doubt that their conception of church fellowship is different from our own. . . . Undoubtedly, both are engaged in unionistic undertakings. And when they draw out of these it will be because interest is exhausted, not because the thing is wrong. The Synod [*sic*] are drifting into a middle-of-the-road policy which would spell ruin to our Synod and ultimately must destroy Lutheranism. . . . [I] will bring out this fact so clearly that none can misunderstand, not our laymen either."[104]

103.
See "The Intersynodical (Chicago) Theses," in *Doctrinal Declarations: A Collection of Official Statements on the Doctrinal Position of Various Lutheran Synods in America* (St. Louis: Concordia Publishing House, 1936), pp. 24–41. Richard C. Wolf's *Documents of Lutheran Unity in America* (Philadelphia: Fortress Press, 1966), pp. 361–69, has excerpts of the theses, but omits the antitheses and a very important "Separate Declaration" entirely. The latter, by two Ohio members of the committee, refuses to renounce *intuitu fidei* as a legitimate way of teaching about election. Their misgivings gave opponents of the theses in Missouri additional reason to reject the idea of fellowship with Ohio.
104.
Letter of Theodore Graebner to Theodore Engelder, November 27, 1925, in the William Arndt File, Concordia Historical Institute Archives.

Missouri's 1929 convention delivered the coup de grace. A preconvention report on the theses by faculty members of Concordia Seminary (Springfield, Ill.) had called the theses unclear, ambiguous, and inadequate. They recommended that the theses be discarded and that intersynodical committee work cease. To no one's surprise the convention rejected the theses as a basis for doctrinal unity even though no specific errors of theology were mentioned. How much attitudes had deteriorated was reflected by Missouri's return to the practice of referring to the other synods as "our opponents."[105]

At the end of the twenties it was obvious not only that hopes for unification of all Lutherans were totally unrealistic but also that the Midwestern synods, so alike in general theological assumptions, were still far from recognizing each other as truly Lutheran. The American Lutheran Conference bodies were ready to accept the Synodical Conference (but not the United Lutheran Church) as brothers, but the Synodical Conference insisted that a host of theological and practical issues still needed resolution. Lutheranism's divisions would continue for the foreseeable future. The questions "Who is Lutheran?" or "What are the standards of Lutheranism?" were as undecided in America as ever. Was it those who accepted Scripture and the confessions? Those who, in addition, defined a variety of specific theological questions in precisely the same way? Or only those who in addition to the first two characteristics affirmed identical principles and achieved identical observance of them in the overall life of the church?

American Lutheran Church

While little progress was made in the twenties on major issues dividing Lutherans, one portion of Midwestern Lutheranism was able to unify organizationally. Participants in the American Lutheran Church merger of 1930 were the Iowa and Joint Ohio synods, which had consulted off and on since 1883, the synod in Texas which functioned as a district of the Iowa Synod but was legally a separate body, and the very small Buffalo Synod.[106] All were confessionally conservative, anxious for doctrinal agreement with Missouri, and suspicious of the kind of self-confident "at-homeness" among American Protestants which they thought they saw in the United Lutheran Church. Territorially, Iowa's strength in the Mississippi Valley and Ohio's farther to the east did not exactly overlap, but both were present in enough localities to make continued organizational division seem unnecessary after the doctrinal agreements of 1893 and 1907.[107] When the only barrier to fellowship, Iowa's halfway membership in the General Council, was removed by Iowa's renunciation of the United Lutheran Church merger, fellowship was officially declared by the Joint Synod of Ohio in 1918. Agitation for merger began at once, especially in areas where both had congregations. Iowa's resignation from the National Lutheran Council in 1920 made Ohio's leadership somewhat cautious about rushing into merger, but by 1925 misgivings had

105.
Missouri Synod, *Synodal-bericht . . . 1929*, pp. 110–13. See also J. Buenger, *Missouri, Iowa, and Ohio: The Old and the New Differences* (1928); and Charles F. Bunzel, "The Missouri Synod and the Chicago (Intersynodical) Theses" (S.T.M. thesis, Concordia Seminary, St. Louis, 1964); Wisconsin Synod, *Proceedings . . . 1929*, p. 47. For an interpretation of the events from a Missouri Synod point of view, see H. W. Romoser, "The Historical Background of the Lutheran Churches of America," *The Confessional Lutheran* 14 (December 1955): 141. Iowa had adopted the sections on conversion and predestination in 1926. Buffalo approved the full statement in 1929. Ohio took no action in 1926 because no official English translation was available, and none in 1929 because all hope of positive action by Missouri had vanished. See Meuser, *American Lutheran Church*, pp. 251–53.
106.
On Ohio: Clarence V. Sheatsley, *History of the Evangelical Lutheran Joint Synod of Ohio and Other States* (Columbus, Ohio: Lutheran Book Concern, 1918). On Iowa: Gerhard S. Ottersberg, "The Evangelical Lutheran Synod of Iowa and Other States, 1854–1904" (Ph.D. diss., University of Nebraska, 1949), and George J. Zeilinger, *A Missionary Synod with a Mission* (Chicago: Wartburg Publishing House, 1929). On Texas: H. G. Ziehe, *A Centennial History of the Lutheran Church in Texas*, 2 vols. (Seguin, Tex.: South Texas Printing Co., 1951–54).
107.
The Michigan City Theses and the Toledo Theses.

been laid to rest and a Joint Merger Commission began working on organizational plans. To the surprise of both churches, a serious disagreement developed over the article on Scripture in the constitution for the new church. For several years this "inspiration controversy" threatened the merger. Because it had implications far beyond these church bodies the controversy deserves attention.

Lutheranism had always prided itself on faithfulness to the Reformation's principle of Scripture alone, and it saw behind the distinctive teachings of other churches doctrinal influences other than Scripture, mainly tradition and reason. Even though the constitutions of all Lutheran groups in affirming Scripture as the only authority and standard of the church's belief and practice differed little from that of many other Protestant churches, Lutherans regarded them as adequate statements of Scripture's absolute authority. As various Midwestern synods sought to unite in the American Lutheran Conference and the American Lutheran Church, their pledge to Scripture came up for renewed attention mainly because of the growing popularity of liberal doctrinal ideas in Protestantism, all of which seemed to the conservative Lutherans to grow out of an equivocal attitude to Scripture. As Lutherans hammered out new theological statements and constitutions, in the setting of the struggle between fundamentalists and liberals, many Lutherans saw strong reasons to make their own pledge to Scripture more categorical than ever by affirming the total inerrancy of Scripture. Without a clear statement of the plenary inspiration and total inerrancy of the Bible, many Lutherans felt the door would be left open to modernistic views which would eventually undermine all of the faith. For decades many Lutherans had been appealing to this idea as the only bulwark against the corrupting influences of evolution, biblical criticism, and the social gospel's reinterpretations of Christian faith. To be sure, the United Lutheran Church had not written total inerrancy into its constitution in 1918, but, as noted above, the first article of the Minneapolis Theses of 1925 unequivocally affirmed the equation of verbal inspiration and inerrancy. The Intersynodical Theses maintained "over against modern theology . . . [that] no errors or contradictions of any sort" are found in Scripture. Total inerracy seemed to be the basis of all doctrinal integrity and a particularly pertinent doctrine amid the infidelity of the twenties. Therefore, when the Joint Commissioners of Iowa, Ohio, and Buffalo[108] suggested that the constitution for the new church accept Scripture as "the inspired and inerrant Word of God" they had no idea of the turmoil which the proposal would generate.[109]

J. Michael Reu of Wartburg Seminary led the opposition to the proposed wording, not because he personally thought Scripture contained error but on the ground that the Bible's own statements about its reliability always referred to matters pertaining to salvation, faith, and Christian living. According to Reu, therefore, the church had no right to make total inerrancy a *doctrine* of the church or to make acceptance of inerrancy a

448

108.
Texas did not negotiate as a fourth synod but recognized Iowa's representation as sufficient.
109.
A detailed study of the controversy is chap. 6, "The Inspiration Controversy," in Meuser, *American Lutheran Church*, pp. 177–230. For an understanding of Reu's early soteriological or instrumental approach to Scripture see his chapter in Vergilius Ferm, ed., *What Is Lutheranism?* (New York: Macmillan, 1930). At no point does he use the word "inerrancy" nor argue from the a priori of an errorless Bible. His emphasis is on Scripture as a "means" of grace, as the "bearer" of God's Word and presence.

determinant of church fellowship. Among churches and individual Christians there may be legitimate variety on details of inspiration and questions such as the inerrancy of Scripture, so long as its reliability and complete authority for the faith, doctrine, and practice of the church is maintained. No particular theory of inspiration or deduction regarding inerrancy in matters not affecting the faith may be elevated to the status of doctrine. In the four-year debate which followed, most of the disputants missed Reu's point about the nature of Scripture itself and concentrated instead on theoretical or practical arguments in behalf of inerrancy. In their views of Scripture most Lutherans in America were unaffected by the insights of recent biblical studies and by the various options to verbal inspiration and inerrancy which some conservative Lutherans in Europe and America were beginning to adopt.[110]

449

Reu was on the way to gaining the full support of the Iowa Synod for his view when Ohio made total inerrancy a categorical condition of merger. In the face of such pressure Iowa wilted and the merged church adopted the view that the original manuscripts of the biblical authors were without error of any kind. All minor errors, discrepancies, variants, and difficulties were ascribed to the process of transmission. Only in this manner could the church be preserved from the virus of modern theology. And thus a major barrier was raised against the United Lutheran Church, which refused to allow its definition of Lutheranism to be narrowed down to a particular theory of inspiration. Missouri was pleased by the position which the American Lutheran Church had adopted, but somewhat skeptical about the church's will to enforce compliance on the part of teachers and pastors.

Other characteristics of the ALC had already been determined by the intersynodical events of the previous decade. It thought of itself as a possible mediating force within Lutheranism to bring the ULCA to a more strict position on doctrine and interchurch relations and to influence Missouri, with whom it had contacts closer than any other Lutheran group outside the Synodical Conference, to recognize fellow Lutherans as brothers.

By the time the American Lutheran Church was born in August of 1930, American society was already in the first throes of depression which aggravated all the problems of a young church and subjected the whole American religious community to a series of shocks which reoriented a great deal of energy from doctrinal issues to the struggle for survival itself.

110.
The inaugural address of Charles M. Jacobs in 1927 is the first declaration of an approach to Scripture that made headway in the ULCA from the beginning of the century. It was published in *Lutheran Church Review* 46 (1927): 207–25. The Baltimore Declaration of 1938 made this view official in the church.

E. Clifford Nelson

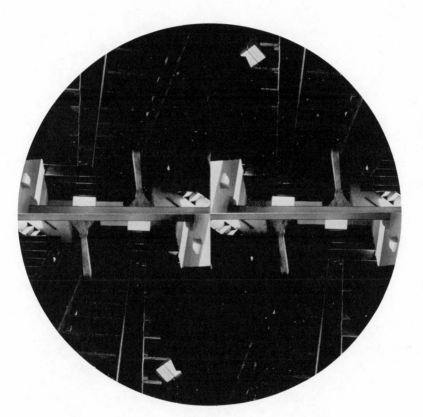

1.
The Crisis of the Old Order, vol. 1 of *The Age
of Roosevelt* (Boston: Houghton Mifflin Co.,
1957), p. 3. Cited in Harvey Swados, ed.,
The American Writer and the Great Depression
(Indianapolis: Bobbs-Merrill, 1966), p.
xii.

All segments of American society experienced the turbulence **453** that characterized the decade prior to the outbreak of World War II. The churches were no exception and American Lutheran denominations shared the lot of all ecclesiastical groups. In fact, Lutheranism in the 1930s can be understood only with difficulty apart from the vicissitudes that plagued the nation between the two world wars. Money—or rather the lack of it— theological reconstruction, and interchurch relationships were issues crying for attention as Lutherans moved beyond the watershed year of 1929.

The Trauma of the Depression
To understand the effects of the Great Depression on the churches following the crash of 1929, one needs to recall the economic, social, and political situation in America during that period. Because the prosperity of the twenties had not prepared men for economic collapse or for such a pervasive and lasting depression, many of the long-accepted basic institutions of society—especially the family, the schools, and the government— underwent drastic changes. The situation in which millions of people faced hunger, malnutrition, unemployment, and loss of morale was graphically described by Arthur Schlesinger, Jr., when he said that "the fog of despair hung over the land."[1]

In such circumstances family life was threatened by the need for relief programs, the loss of homes, the depletion and exhaustion of resources, and concomitant psychological destitution. The schools witnessed the narrowing of the tax base with resultant reductions in budgets, unemployment among teachers, the deterioration of physical facilities, and a lowered quality of education. Government, too, was threatened. Though not faced with the chaotic situations which obtained in Germany, Italy, and Russia, people were dissatisfied and restive. There were, for example, demonstrations by the unemployed and the Bonus Army March on Washington in 1932. Reform, recovery, and a new outlook were finally initiated by the marshaling of the total resources of the federal government in Roosevelt's New Deal. By the end of the thirties there were some economic and social gains, but one must recognize that American industry and agriculture were being transformed into an "arsenal of democracy" necessitated by the overwhelming international developments in the last years of the decade.

The effects of the depression on religious life have been assessed in various ways. Writing about their famous "Middletown," sociologists Robert and Helen Lynd concluded that the influence of the depression on religious life had been negligible and that there was no depression-born religious revival.[2] The hope for a spiritual renewal in the midst of adversity had been expressed by numerous churchmen. For the Lutheran churches the effects of the depression were clear as their annual reports dealt with budget reductions, curtailment of missionary and educational enterprises, and retrenchment in the local and general work of the churches.

Frequent articles and editorials in the official denominational periodicals indicated that the churches were aware of and involved in the suffering and tragedies occurring on all sides.[3] Though these articles were honest in their appraisal of difficulties, they were not without a note of hope in appealing for united action in faith and love for the relief of suffering among the poor and unemployed.

Articulate in voicing the need for an effective social ministry were such churchmen as Sylvester C. Michelfelder, Gustavus H. Bechtold, and Ambrose Hering. In light of the desperate needs Hering, especially, urged the church to a program of action based on a sense of collective social responsibility. Having served the church through social ministries in the Minneapolis-St. Paul area as well as in New York City, he understood the plight of the industrial East as well as that of the Midwest where the agricultural depression had antedated the general collapse by almost a decade. This area had in addition been stricken by drought and dust storms. It was Hering's contention that social and economic planning was imperative and that it would require the highest kind of ethical commitment by the churches to serve the general welfare.[4]

Some authorities demonstrated that there was a religious as well as an economic depression. Robert T. Handy came to this conclusion for the main-line Anglo-American Protestant churches.[5] Other writers saw a similar trend among Lutherans. For example, in a statistical study made of the United Lutheran Church based on communing membership figures, Edward Traill Horn III showed that 1925 marked the beginning of a "religious depression" in that church body.[6] An historical seminar conducted at the Philadelphia Lutheran Seminary presented evidence of a "religious depression," if by that phrase was meant lowered membership, decreased attendance, and reduced income.[7] The same report implied that not a few Lutherans saw a causal relationship between irreligion and depression. The executive secretary of the National Lutheran Council, Ralph H. Long, said that only a spiritual rebirth would restore economic stability.[8] Similarly, Walter A. Maier assured his listeners on "The Lutheran Hour" that all would be well if America would turn to Christ.[9] Long's favorable reaction to the widely read Babson report echoed the view that the business of the church was not to involve itself in public issues but to change the hearts of men. It is clear through hindsight that many American Lutherans did not understand the implications of Lutheran theology for social ethics.

In spite of the undeniable statistical depression which showed that all church bodies suffered loss of income, resulting in re-

2.
Middletown in Transition: A Study in Cultural Conflicts (New York: Harcourt, Brace & Co., 1937), pp. 295ff.
3.
The minutes and proceedings of the major Lutheran churches for the first few years of the depression carry the same story. The reports of church presidents and executive boards are virtually identical: drastically cut budgets and emergency appeals for funds.
4.
Ambrose Hering, "Again God Is to Be Found in a Stable," *The Lutheran*, December 15, 1932, pp. 8–9.
5.
Church History 29 (March 1960): 3–16.
6.
"A Serious Trend Downward: A Statistical Analysis," *The Lutheran*, December 7, 1933, pp. 8–9, 22–23.
7.
Theodore G. Tappert et al., "Lutherans in the Great Depression," *Lutheran Quarterly* 7 (May 1955): 145–54.
8.
Letter to Ambrose Hering, November 12, 1931, Long Papers, Box 1, Archives of Cooperative Lutheranism, Lutheran Council/U.S.A., New York.
9.
This theme occurs repeatedly in Maier's collected radio sermons. See, e.g., his *Christ for the Nation* (St. Louis: Concordia Publishing House, 1936), pp. 28–37.

trenchment in home and world missions and a cutback in the support of educational institutions, there were other statistics that showed a rise in church and Communion attendance in some areas and the appearance of numerous new "religious activities."

In the early thirties the member bodies of the National Lutheran Council and of the Synodical Conference found themselves in increasingly desperate financial straits. Many parishes were thrust into a moral crisis as they struggled with huge debts which tempted them to use for home needs funds specially designated for extracongregational benevolences and missions. In order to alleviate the financial shortage brought on by the too ambitious home missions programs of the twenties, the Norwegian Lutheran Church, for example, curtailed its administrative staff and transferred additional duties to the president of the church body. The Missouri Synod found itself altering (perhaps unconsciously) its traditional polity regarding congregational autonomy with movement toward centralization. The Augustana Synod likewise underwent a thoroughgoing centralizing of administrative activity in Minneapolis. All of these moves, calculated to meet the needs of the moment, had long-range implications for the future development of the churches.

455

One positive effect of the economic squeeze was the furthering of cooperation among the home mission boards, organized into an informal group called the Lutheran Home Missions Council of America. This cooperation transcended ethnic boundaries in home mission work and implied tacit acceptance of the "orthodoxy" of other Lutheran bodies, an understanding which led ultimately to pulpit and altar fellowship among most of the Lutheran churches.

Like other denominations in the United States and Canada, Lutherans had in the nineteenth century established many church schools on all levels, but the depression forced the churches to examine their far-flung educational programs. While the Missouri Synod's parochial-school system survived the storm, most Lutheran academies and junior colleges were forced to close, and all the church bodies authorized programs of consolidation or discontinuance of their schools. The United Lutheran Church and the American Lutheran Church especially faced serious problems in maintaining their theological seminaries.[10] A significant development in ministerial training during the thirties was the adoption of an internship period between the second and final year of seminary study. This came about partly as a calculated curricular change and partly as a way of meeting the problem of ministerial oversupply.

Despite the "statistical depression," Lutherans fared better than the liberal Anglo-American Protestant denominations. Figures quoted in a study by Samuel Kinchloe indicate that the growth of Lutheran churches was proportionately greater than that of the main-line Protestant churches and than that of Roman Catholicism, but less than that of "fundamentalist groups."[11] Even more significant than the steady growth of all Lutheran bodies was the fact that the Lutheran church mem-

10.
ULCA, *Minutes . . . 1932*, pp. 453–54; ibid. *1940*, pp. 484, 496; *Lutheran World Almanac, 1934-1937*, p. 49.
11.
Research Memorandum on Religion in the Depression (New York: Social Science Research Council, 1937), p. 7.

bers contributed *proportionately* considerably more during 1931–35 than during the more affluent forties and fifties.

The thirties marked the emergence of numerous phenomena which could be called signs of new life. As we shall note later, a theological renaissance and a new ecumenical awareness surfaced in American Lutheranism during those years. Moreover, there was an upsurge in an active ministry to youth and students as represented in the Luther Leagues, the Walther League, the Choral Union, and the Bible Camp Movement. These programs were directed to the cultivation and deepening of spiritual life through Bible study, music, service, counseling, and recreation. Though sometimes criticized, these programs had on the whole salutary effects. Moreover, campus ministries developed and prospered during the depression. The work in Lutheran student centers on college and university campuses had been begun in the 1920s by the United Lutheran Church. In 1938 the American Lutheran Conference added its strength to campus work by appointing a director for its ministry to students. By 1945 the National Lutheran Council had created a Commission on Student Service. The Missouri Synod, however, preferred to carry on its ministry to students in its own organization.

Closely allied with the official campus ministry was the Lutheran student movement. Organized in 1922, the Lutheran Student Association of America (LSAA) became the local campus fellowship and was the seedbed for many future leaders of the church.[12] The Missouri Synod had its counterpart to the Lutheran Student Association in the Gamma Delta, which in 1969 seemed prepared to unite its work with that of the LSAA in the newly organized Lutheran Student Movement.[13]

Other far-reaching programs in the search for spiritual resources were to be found in the publication of aids for family devotions and in radio broadcasting for evangelistic purposes. Most notable of the radio preachers was Walter A. Maier, who achieved worldwide acclaim with his "Lutheran Hour."[14] The National Broadcasting Company broadened its "National Radio Pulpit" by inviting the president of the United Lutheran Church, Frederick H. Knubel, to conduct what was first known as "The Knubel Hour." Knubel shortly relinquished his place in the National Radio Pulpit to Paul E. Scherer. Though never as popular as Maier, Scherer nevertheless received a wide and sympathetic hearing.[15] The Lutheran radio ministry, so auspiciously begun and developed by "The Lutheran Hour," was enhanced by the National Lutheran Council's assistance to the Columbia Broadcasting System in the selection of Lutheran speakers for its well-known "Church of the Air."

Another depression-born spiritual resource was the liturgical movement which sprang up in the 1930s from a desire on the part of many Lutherans to give expression to a growing appreciation for the richness of the liturgical and sacramental tradition that Lutherans shared, in part at least, with the pre-Reformation church. The influence of two associations, the Society of St. James and the Society of St. Ambrose, was far-reaching. Though their activities subsequently declined, they had gener-

12.
Among them were such persons as Fredrik A. Schiotz, Carl E. Lund-Quist, Donald Heiges, Kent S. Knutson, and Albert E. Anderson.
13.
Lutheran Standard, September 16, 1969, p. 30. The Gamma Delta was apparently in 1973 still independent of the Lutheran Student Movement. The report of the annual convention of the LSM included a resolution seeking "closer cooperation with Gamma Delta." See News Bureau Release, Lutheran Council/U.S.A., August 20, 1973.
14.
For a careful treatment of Maier's radio career see Paul L. Maier, *A Man Spoke, A World Listened: The Story of Walter A. Maier* (New York: McGraw-Hill, 1963).
15.
See W. S. Gertner, "Paul E. Scherer: Preacher and Homiletician" (Ph.D. diss., Wayne University, Detroit, 1967).

ated a movement of liturgical renewal that was to continue for the next forty years.[16]

Lutherans in North America had been subjected to profound shock and severe trial by the depression. Certain weaknesses, especially theological, ethical, and ecumenical, were laid bare. But strengths also emerged as Lutherans became more aggressive and self-confident by probing their theological and religious heritage. A new interpretation of their tradition was in the making, one which would have abiding effects in the ecumenical movement, in American society as a whole, as well as within "the household of faith."

457

Theological Reconstruction

Despite the depression-born cares that demanded so much of the attention of churchmen, the post-World War I theological revival associated with such names as Karl Barth, Emil Brunner, and the Niebuhr brothers began to be felt increasingly in American church circles. The new theology attacked both fundamentalism on the right and liberalism and modernism on the left. At the same time, it emphasized familiar Reformation themes such as God's sovereign transcendence, the demonic power of sin, the biblical revelation, and justification by grace through faith.

Conservative Christians, including many American Lutherans, found themselves in an ambivalent position regarding this "new orthodoxy." They responded gratefully to the general Reformation emphases, but they were nervous about the use of historical criticism of the Scriptures, the emphasis on ecumenism, and the social and public role of Christianity as taught especially by Reinhold Niebuhr. In fact, it was only when they became aware that similar ideas had appeared as fruits of the Luther renaissance occurring in Germany's Neo-Lutheranism and Sweden's Lundensianism that American Lutherans began to take a positive attitude toward the new theology. Before observing the details of the Lutheran theological reconstruction that began to take form in the twenties and the thirties, a look at the stance of the major Lutheran bodies in 1930 is necessary.

The Theological Attitude of the Churches

As the decade began, it was evident that Lutheran church bodies presented a picture of theological diversity within a confessional community. The earlier and continuing movement toward the union of Lutheran churches in America had been hindered by strong sociological and cultural factors, notably the ethnic backgrounds of the ecclesiastical bodies. By the opening of the 1930s such nontheological factors had begun to recede. But as one set of factors began to lessen, another set—the parallel theological problems—began to assume prominence. The questions which disturbed American Lutherans centered about the varying definitions of confessional unity. All the churches identified themselves as Lutheran by their subscription to the confessional writings of Lutheranism; that is, they were united in their confession of the doctrine of the gospel. This made them

16.
For an objective account of the liturgical revival see David L. Scheidt, "The 'High Church Movement' in American Lutheranism," *Lutheran Quarterly* 9 (November 1957): 343-49. A liturgical renewal in other denominations occurred at about the same time. Cf. E. B. Koenker, *The Liturgical Renaissance in the Roman Catholic Church* (Chicago: University of Chicago Press, 1954); and Massey H. Shepperd, Jr., ed., *The Liturgical Renewal of the Church* (New York: Oxford University Press, 1960).

a confessional community. The question that remained unanswered was whether confessional unity required theological uniformity. Some answered the question in the language of the confessions themselves: for the unity of the church it is enough to agree concerning the doctrine of the gospel and the administration of the sacraments (Augsburg Confession, Article VII). Others insisted that confessional unity meant theological uniformity, that there could be no church unity until it could be demonstrated that the churches agreed in theology and practice. As these differing points of view continued to separate the churches organizationally, the two positions received sharper delineation in a few carefully worded statements (see table 6). From these documents it became apparent that the major issues within the American branch of the Lutheran confessional family were threefold: First, how was the authority of the Bible to be assured? (the question of inspiration and inerrancy); second, what constituted "unionism"? (the question of pulpit and altar fellowship); and third, what was the proper attitude of the church toward secret societies? (the lodge-membership question).

By 1930 the largest American Lutheran body, the United Lutheran Church, had addressed itself to the ecclesiological problems expressed in unionism and lodge membership by means of its 1920 Washington Declaration. Although a definitive statement on the Scriptures was not presented until 1938 (the Baltimore Declaration), many theological professors were affirming that the "orthodox" teaching regarding the inerrancy of the Bible was really neither Lutheran nor orthodox. Using the method of historical criticism without guilt or fear, they taught that the Bible's authority rested in its message, the Word of God concerning salvation communicated through the words of Scripture. Though they carefully distinguished between Scripture and the Word of God, they did not thereby separate the one from the other.

It became apparent, therefore, in the twenties and early thirties that the United Lutheran Church had assumed an "ecumenical" stance within the Lutheran confessional frame of reference; that it urged an "evangelical," not a legalistic, attitude toward lodge membership; and that it taught that the Bible received its authority from its unique message, the Word of God.[17]

The other major churches in the National Lutheran Council, especially the Augustana Synod, the Norwegian Lutheran Church, and the newly formed American Lutheran Church, were not ready in 1930 to affirm the position of the United Lutheran Church. The Augustana Synod, reflecting a religious heritage that was an amalgam of pietism and theological conservatism, maintained cordial relations with the United Lutheran Church but cast its lot with four other Midwestern Lutheran churches in the recently organized federation called the American Lutheran Conference (1930). It should be noted, however, that Augustana stood on the threshold of a new theological era that was to change the course of the church.[18] From that time

17.
A useful collection of documents has been assembled in Richard C. Wolf, *Documents of Lutheran Unity in America* (Philadelphia: Fortress Press, 1966); see esp. pp. 292-93, 301-12, 345-55. Cf. Charles M. Jacobs, "Inaugural Address," *Lutheran Church Review* 46 (July 1927): 216-21; and articles by John O. Evjen, Henry F. Offermann, and Abdel Ross Wentz in *What Is Lutheranism?* ed. Vergilius Ferm (New York: Macmillan, 1930), esp. pp. 25, 57, 88.
18.
G. Everett Arden, *Augustana Heritage: A History of the Augustana Lutheran Church* (Rock Island, Ill.: Augustana Press, 1963), p. 284.

Table 6

**Documents
of Lutheran Unity
1919-1940**

Emphasis One: Sufficiency of Confessions		Emphasis Two: Confessional Unity Means Theological Uniformity
1919 The Essentials of the Catholic Spirit in the Church		Chicago Theses
1920 The Washington Declaration		
1925		The Minneapolis Theses
1925-28		Intersynodical [Chicago] Theses
1932		A Brief Statement
1934	The Savannah Declaration	
1938		The Baltimore Declaration
	Emphasis Three: Attempt at Compromise	
1939-40	The Pittsburgh Agreement	

on Augustana began to affirm in its own way the theological position articulated by the United Lutheran Church. Continuing its new orientation with its tradition of friendship for the United Lutheran Church, Augustana saw itself as the bridge-builder between the two groups in the National Lutheran Council.

Next to the United Lutheran Church, the Norwegian Lutheran Church was, numerically speaking, the ranking member of the National Lutheran Council. A merger of three Norwegian-background bodies (1917), it represented a combination of the tendencies in the uniting groups: Norwegian Lutheran pietism and confessionalism, Missouri Lutheran "orthodoxy," and incipient ecumenism.[19] In 1930 this church looked askance at the theological position of the United Lutheran Church. It preferred to view the Bible as verbally inspired and hence inerrant; "unionism" and "lodgery" were considered major problems preventing inter-Lutheran fellowship. Conservative Norwegian Lutherans were dismayed by modernism and liberalism and saw evidences of the latter in the stance of the United Lutheran Church. Accepting uncritically the presupposition of fundamentalism on the authority of Scripture, they found theological security, along with the recently formed American Lutheran Church, in the orthodoxist-fundamentalist Minneapolis Theses (1925) that had become the basis for the establishment of the American Lutheran Conference (1930).

The four German-background Midwestern Lutheran synods that united to form the American Lutheran Church in 1930[20] reflected much the same pattern as that found in the Norwegian Lutheran Church. The notable exception was the absence of some pietistic attitudes that characterized other bodies, especially those of Scandinavian origin. On the other question—the inerrancy of Scripture, the binding nature of the confessions, and "unionism" with both Lutherans and non-Lutherans—the outlook of this church from its founding was "orthodox." But like the Augustana Synod[21] it liked to regard itself as a bridge, not between the two groups in the National Lutheran Council but between eastern ("liberal") German Lutheranism and Missouri ("orthodox") German Lutheranism. This somewhat illusive role as the bridge-builder within Lutheranism was bequeathed to the *second* American Lutheran Church in the 1960 merger.

The Missouri Synod and the Wisconsin Synod in 1930 continued to be the most influential partners in the Synodical Conference, the members of which were easily the most conservative and isolated ecclesiastical groups in the American Lutheran family. The Wisconsin Synod, one-third the size of Missouri, numbered about 300,000 members and became in time Missouri's "loyal opposition" within the Synodical Conference.

The chief architect of Missouri's theological position was Franz Pieper, professor at Concordia Seminary and author of the synod's guide to dogmatic rectitude.[22] Pieper viewed the Lutheran confessions through the eyes of the seventeenth-century dogmaticians who were "repristinated" by an anti-

460

19.
For a discussion of these see E. Clifford Nelson and Eugene L. Ferold, *The Lutheran Church Among Norwegian-Americans*, 2 vols. (Minneapolis: Augsburg Publishing House, 1960), 2:229–40.

20.
See Fred W. Meuser, *The Formation of the American Lutheran Church* (Columbus, Ohio: Wartburg Press, 1958), pp. 177–253, 272–78.

21.
See Arden, *Augustana Heritage*, p. 280.

22.
Franz Pieper, *Christian Dogmatics*, 3 vols. (St. Louis: Concordia Publishing House, 1950–53); trans. T. Engelder from the original *Christliche Dogmatik* (St. Louis, 1917–20). For an assessment of Pieper see Leigh D. Jordahl, "The Theology of Franz Pieper: A Resource for Fundamentalistic Thought Modes Among American Lutherans," *Lutheran Quarterly* 23 (May 1971): 118–37.

Schleiermacherian group of German Lutherans about mid-nineteenth century. The advocates of "repristination theology" felt that true Lutheranism could only be secured by asserting the inerrancy of a verbally inspired Bible and a dogmatic use of the confessions. Pieper rose to defend this position by saying,

The claim is made that by identifying Scripture and the Word of God our theology will lead to intellectualism. . . . I considered it necessary to refute the unwarranted charge and to remove any misgivings concerning "repristination theology," and have therefore set forth . . . the religious life of a church body which is definitely committed to the "repristination theology."[23]

461

Pieper effectively shaped Missouri's attitude toward biblical criticism, evolution, ecumenism, social action, and numerous other questions until well after World War II. Missouri remained into the 1960s sharply divided on the matter of allegiance to repristination theology as epitomized in the so-called Brief Statement (1932) whose main author was Pieper.[24]

In addition to the major churches in the two Lutheran groupings (the National Lutheran Council and the Synodical Conference), one must note that the smaller bodies generally assumed the "orthodox" theological outlook. Exceptions were the American Evangelical Lutheran Church, the Icelandic Synod, and the Slovak Zion Synod.

In 1930 among the smaller ethnic churches were numbered two Danish groups (the United Evangelical Lutheran Church and the American Evangelical Lutheran Church); four of Norwegian background (the Lutheran Free Church and the Norwegian Synod of the American Evangelical Lutheran Church, the Church of the Lutheran Brethren and the Eielsen Synod); one Icelandic Lutheran Synod; two of Finnish background (the Suomi Synod and the Finnish Evangelical Lutheran National Church); and two of Slovak background (the Slovak Evangelical Lutheran Zion Synod and the Slovak Evangelical Lutheran Synod of the U.S.A.).[25]

The Role of the American Lutheran Conference

American Lutheranism in 1930 existed not only in the two organizational groups (the National Lutheran Council and the Synodical Conference) but also in two theological camps. Unfortunately for ease of understanding these were not coterminous with the National Lutheran Council on the one hand and the Synodical Conference on the other. For example, some churches (especially the American Lutheran Church and the Norwegian Lutheran Church) associated with the United Lutheran Church in the National Lutheran Council were, at least in their attitude toward biblical authority and church unity, sympathetic to the Missourian viewpoint and distrustful of the United Lutheran Church. This cleft within the National Lutheran Council, detected as early as 1919, took on institutional structure by the formation in 1930 of the American Lutheran Conference. The five Midwestern Lutheran churches of the conference continued their membership in the National Luther-

23.
Pieper, *Christian Dogmatics*, vol. 1, preface, ix. Pieper includes the Wisconsin Synod and the German theologian Franz Delitzsch as supporters of this view; see his discussion, pp. 160-86.

24.
For a detailed account see Carl S. Meyer, "The Historical Background of 'A Brief Statement,'"*Concordia Theological Monthly* 32 (July, August, and September, 1961): 403-28, 466-82, 526-42.

25.
For articles on each group see *The Encyclopedia of the Lutheran Church*, ed. Julius Bodensieck, 3 vols. (Minneapolis: Augsburg Publishing House, 1965). Careful book-length histories have been published on some of these churches. See esp. Eugene L. Fevold, *The Lutheran Free Church* (Minneapolis: Augsburg Publishing House, 1969); John M. Jensen, *The United Evangelical Lutheran Church* (Minneapolis: Augsburg Publishing House, 1964); Enok Mortensen, *The Danish Lutheran Church in America* (Philadelphia: Board of Publication, LCA, 1967); Paul C. Nyholm, *A Study in Immigrant History: The Americanization of the Danish Lutheran Churches in America* (Copenhagen: Institute for Danish Church History, 1963); and George Dolak, *A History of the Slovak Evangelical Lutheran Church . . . 1902-1927* (St. Louis: Concordia Publishing House, 1955).

an Council. These churches were *practically* related to the United Lutheran Church by the agency of the National Lutheran Council but were *ideologically* and *sociologically* more akin to the Missouri Synod.[26]

That the American Lutheran Conference possessed the character of a defensive alliance particularly over against the United Lutheran Church can hardly be denied. When the latter published the Washington Declaration, the Norwegians and the Ohio and Iowa Germans were convinced that United Lutherans lacked theological orthodoxy. The American Lutheran Conference and its Minneapolis Theses declared to Lutheranism in general that the event of 1930 was a "protest against the ULCA position."[27]

In relation to the Missouri Synod the new conference felt no need to be defensive, because to influential elements in the American Lutheran Conference the doctrinal position of the Missouri Synod was aggressively and pleasingly Lutheran. The task was rather to convince Missouri of the doctrinal orthodoxy of the arbitrarily designated middle group. Exhibit A, as supporting evidence, was the "orthodox" Minneapolis Theses.

The reaction to the new federation among the leaders of the United Lutheran Church was one of profound regret and no little frustration. Although the church withheld comment on the American Lutheran Conference, Frederick Knubel's article "What Does the United Lutheran Church in America Stand For?" included a staunch apology for the orthodoxy of his church. Veiled in this was the fact that he and his church had taken umbrage at the obvious exclusion of the United Lutheran Church from the American Lutheran Conference.[28]

Despite the historical circumstances out of which the American Lutheran Conference emerged, once under way it served good purposes. The bringing together of Lutherans of diverse national origins was significant. The vigorous student service program at tax-supported universities and colleges, and the farsighted all-Lutheran seminars were particularly praiseworthy. It should be noted, however, that these were activities customarily identified in the ex post facto rationalization of those who found it necessary to justify the existence of the conference. At times overlooked was the fact that these purposes have been or could have been accomplished as effectively through the National Lutheran Council.

As the decade moved on it became apparent that the American Lutheran Conference, as the National Lutheran Council, was of two minds on theological issues and church relations. In order to understand subsequent developments in American Lutheranism, especially as they impinged on the question of church unity, it is necessary to describe briefly the advent of a new theological outlook in some Lutheran quarters.

The Beginnings of Theological Reconstruction

Our brief survey of the theological stance of the churches at the beginning of the thirties showed that American Lutheranism found difficulty in meeting the problems posed by liberalism

26.
For accounts of the formation of the American Lutheran Conference see Meuser, *American Lutheran Church*, pp. 235–49; and Nelson, *Lutheran Church Among Norwegian-Americans*, 2:287–308.
27.
Meuser, *American Lutheran Church*, p. 240.
28.
The Lutheran, October 9, 1930, pp. 5–7.

and fundamentalism. All Lutherans by the beginning of the twentieth century were committed to a confessional viewpoint. The debates that took place were largely limited to problems within this tradition. As has been pointed out above, the first intimation of change appeared in the United Lutheran Church. For the first time on American soil a major church body definitely committed to the Lutheran confessions sought to take an evangelical position in relation to contemporary questions.

The modernist-fundamentalist controversy of the mid-twenties forced the issue of biblical criticism. Was the choice that lay before Lutherans who wished to be loyal to the gospel limited to two alternatives, either to repristinate an "orthodox" view of Scripture (as did traditional Roman Catholicism and Protestant fundamentalism) or to abandon Lutheran confessionalism? Some concluded these were the only choices, and as far as Scripture was concerned they found it impossible to disassociate themselves from the viewpoint that affirmed the verbally inspired inerrancy of the Bible.[29] The Synodical Conference, the American Lutheran Conference, and a large number of people and pastors in the United Lutheran Church rested in this kind of attitude. But several professors in United Lutheran seminaries had found that Luther himself had liberated them from orthodoxism and led them to a Christ-centered and soteriological view of Scripture. The Bible's authority lay not in its inerrancy but in its religious message, the Word of God concerning God's self-disclosure in history, in the people of Israel, and ultimately in Jesus Christ.

Meanwhile, the Augustana Synod, as indicated above, had moved into a new theological climate. Historian Everett Arden has summarized the change at the synod's seminary as follows:

It should be noted that the new theological outlook was not "repristination theology," in the sense that it did not seek simply to reproduce a seventeenth-century interpretation of sixteenth-century doctrine. And yet the new outlook was conservatively confessional in the sense that it made the Word of God normative for faith and practice, and accepted the historic symbols of the Lutheran Church as correct and faithful expositions of God's Word. Its conception, however, of what makes Scripture the Word of God differed markedly from the viewpoint implicit in the "Minneapolis Theses." . . . The new outlook also repudiated the Missourian insistence that Lutheran unity must be achieved on the basis of a common acceptance of certain theological refinements added to the historic confessions, and on strict uniformity in church practice. There remained, however, in the new outlook a certain Rosenian piety which insisted that Christian faith is more than intellectual assent to doctrinal formulation, that it is above all else the experience of the redeeming grace of God in Christ. . . . These various characteristics are clearly articulated in the writings of the new theological mentors of the Augustana Church.[30]

29.
It has been correctly pointed out that even the most conservative Lutherans are not correctly classified as fundamentalists. There are many theological issues to which orthodoxist Lutherans give an answer different from that of the fundamentalists, for example, the doctrine of the church and sacraments. But on the inerrancy of Scripture they are identical. For a discussion see Milton L. Rudnick, *Fundamentalism and the Missouri Synod* (St. Louis: Concordia Publishing House, 1966).
30.
Arden, *Augustana Heritage*, pp. 288–89.

It was no secret that the other major bodies were suspicious of the "new theology." In the American Lutheran Church one theologian who had maintained some openness to Neo-Lutheranism and to the historical orientation of the Erlangen school in Germany was J. Michael Reu (1869-1943), professor at Wartburg Seminary, Dubuque, Iowa. In the twenties and early thirties his views were deemed mildly liberal because he taught the infallibility of Scripture in terms of its soteriological message.[31] Before 1934, however, Reu had undergone a change that led him increasingly to sympathize with the viewpoint of the Missouri Synod. His metamorphosis was complete by 1943, when he wrote *Luther and the Scriptures* in which he alleged that the Reformer was an advocate of inerrancy. No significant changes were to appear in the American Lutheran Church until after World War II, but even then they were not sufficient to remove suspicions of "ULCA theology."

Within the Norwegian Lutheran Church a similar attitude prevailed, despite the fact that a few professors before World War I gave evidence of uneasiness about scholastic Lutheranism. Markus O. Bockman and E. Kristian Johnsen, for example, represented an historical and exegetical, rather than scholastic, approach to theology, but their contribution to a new outlook was cautious and minimal. In 1930 Thaddaeus F. Gullixson (1882-1969) succeeded Bockman as president of the church's seminary and brought to his task a wide range of gifts. A remarkable preacher, a socially conscious pastor and churchman, a Lincolnesque personality—all of these were controlled by an overriding theological conservatism and a churchly pietism. With this kind of leadership it was patent that neither German Neo-Lutheranism nor Swedish Lundensianism would find a welcome in the second largest Lutheran seminary in America. The broad-gauged views and prophetic pleas of Lars W. Boe, long an advocate of Lutheran unity, failed to alter the "orthodox" stance of his colleagues in the Norwegian Lutheran Church.[32]

Virtually no signs of theological reconstruction were apparent in the smaller bodies of the National Lutheran Council and certainly none in the Synodical Conference.[33] As far as the Missouri Synod was concerned, the Brief Statement became more and more the touchstone of orthodoxy and the symbol of authority. Theologically secure, the synod carried on a broad missionary and educational program during the decade before World War II, despite the ravages of the depression. Vitality of faith and vigor in action made it possible for the church to transcend the sterility implicit in its doctrinal status quo. Even the quantitative homiletical application of the law-gospel dialectic as exhibited in Maier's radio sermons did not impede the remarkable growth of "The Lutheran Hour."[34] The best-known theological nonconformists in the Missouri Synod during these years were a missionary, Adolph A. Brux, who was charged with heresy for praying with other Christians in India, and a maverick churchman, Otto H. Pannkoke, who counted scores of

31.
See Meuser, *American Lutheran Church*, p. 229. Reu's soteriological approach to Scripture was spelled out in 1930 in Ferm, *What Is Lutheranism?* pp. 102-15.

32.
Lars W. Boe, "God's Moment and the Next Step in American Lutheranism," in *The Lutheran Church: A Series of Occasional Papers of General Interest to the Entire Lutheran Church* (Minneapolis: Augsburg Publishing House, 1934), p. 5. See also letter of Boe to Johan A. Aasgaard, October 29, 1942, Lars W. Boe Papers, St. Olaf College Archives, Northfield, Minn.

33.
An exception may be noted in the Wisconsin Synod where the Protéstant Conference sought to perpetuate in the twenties the historical-exegetical and nonscholastic theology of John P. Koehler. See Leigh D. Jordahl, "The Protéstant Conference," *Encyclopedia of the Lutheran Church*, 3:1978-79.

34.
See P. L. Maier, *A Man Spoke*, pp. 204-5.

friends in the National Lutheran Council churches and, like Boe, expressed himself as being in favor of immediate steps to church unity.[35]

Interchurch Relationships

Although no spectacular theological and ecumenical awakening took place in the thirties, certain tentative beginnings were made. It should be noted, however, that despite the fact of a minor breakthrough, Lutheran reconstructionists remained solidly confessional and exhibited an anxiety about modernism. A case in point was the attitude of the Board of Foreign Missions of the United Lutheran Church toward the famous Hocking Report (1932), which had brought the entire concept of "missions" under attack. Although missionaries were commended for educational and philanthropic ventures, they were rebuked for engaging in conscious and direct evangelization. To this the United Lutheran Board made a careful reply, thus adding its voice to that of numerous other denominations that sharply criticized the document. Approving "constructive criticisms," the board seriously opposed evidence of liberalism. It concluded its evaluation with these words: "Our board replies that we know as the foundation of our faith no other religion than that which finds its forgiveness, joy and life in the person of Jesus Christ, the Son of God, who died that we might live and who lives that men may never die."[36]

Other evidences of this antiliberal attitude were often seen. Harry Emerson Fosdick's radio sermons, for example, were attacked, not only by the Missouri Synod, but also by the "liberal" United Lutheran Church.[37] Nathan Soderblom, who had been enthusiastically welcomed to America by the Augustana Synod in 1923, was charged by other Lutherans with a lack of concern for confessional Lutheranism. Six years later Augustana president G. A. Brandelle gave assurances that the synod's reception of Soderblom did not imply an endorsement of his theology.[38] Furthermore, when the United Lutheran Church rejected a fundamentalist view of Scripture this did not mean an approval of modernism. As a matter of fact, " . . . Modernism is rationalistic, and corrects the emaciated Bible which it uses, by modern scientific hypotheses and modern philosophic speculations. In part, it revamps old rationalism."[39] Despite the obvious overall conservative climate in American Lutheranism, the acceptance of biblical criticism as a scholarly method and the rejection of orthodoxism's theory of verbal inspiration by some Lutherans was to lead to a theological polarization and regrettable hostility.

Meanwhile, however, the new climate carried with it at least four additional features: (1) a revived interest in the theology of Luther and the thought of Soren Kierkegaard; (2) a deepened understanding of the Lutheran confessions, not as legally binding documents but as historically conditioned writings which were needed to safeguard the church's proclamation; (3) a growing recognition that Lutheran theology provided a founda-

465

35.
On the Brux affair see Dean Lueking, *Mission in the Making* (St. Louis: Concordia Publishing House, 1964), pp. 270–76. Pannkoke's memoirs were published under the title *A Great Church Finds Itself* (Quitman, Ga., 1966).
36.
"A Statement of the Board of Foreign Missions of the United Lutheran Church in America," *The Lutheran*, February 23, 1933, p. 2.
37.
"Across the Desk," ibid., January 15, 1931, p. 15.
38.
Arden, *Augustana Heritage*, pp. 274–77. Cf. Meuser, *American Lutheran Church*, p. 243.
39.
John A. W. Haas, "Where Does the Lutheran Church Stand?" *The Lutheran*, October 27, 1932, p. 14; cf. idem, "The Word and the Bible," ibid., December 8, 1932, p. 7.

tion not only for personal, individual ethics, but social ethics as well; and (4) an openness to the new ecumenical movement. The last two items require further elaboration.

It must be admitted that American Lutheran theology prior to the depression had little room for social ethics.[40] The "social-gospel" era made Lutherans generally suspicious of all attempts to "Christianize the social order." The task of the church was to proclaim the gospel which would save men from sin, death, and the power of the devil. Christ was primarily interested in individuals. Therefore, the way "for the church to reform the world was to reform people rather than programs, to change the individual rather than his environment."[41] The social gospel, with all its recognized shortcomings, was not yet seen as one of the ways by which the church was being awakened to *social action*. This was to come, but it took the depression and World War II to usher it in. Meanwhile, Christian welfare was directed largely "to rescuing individuals, the lost, the homeless, the straying . . . the least of Christ's brethren."[42]

One of the first steps in the direction of social concern was taken by the National Lutheran Council in 1933 when, in response to Ralph Long's recommendation, it established a Committee on Social Trends. Modest in its challenges, the committee received council approval for statements on liquor, films, the causes of war, and national loyalty in the face of the outbreak of World War II. In 1940 the committee was made a part of the council's new Department of Welfare. Henceforth, social welfare was decidedly more prominent than social action. In fact, the latter concerns lay dormant until a few years after World War II.

Two churches within the National Lutheran Council, namely, the United Lutheran Church and the Augustana Synod, moved considerably ahead of the council in social action, while the American Lutheran Church and the Norwegian Lutheran Church lagged behind. Likewise, when the American Lutheran Conference, pressured by the Augustana Synod, established a Commission on Social Relations (1934), the American Lutherans and the Norwegian Lutherans largely ignored the new group, while Augustana pushed ahead of the Conference.[43] Lloyd Svendsbye's analysis of these four major churches from the early thirties to the early forties reveals an interesting progression regarding the church's role in social action: Of the four major National Lutheran Council church bodies, the Norwegian Lutheran Church reflected the least social concern and the Augustana and the United Lutheran churches the largest. The American Lutheran Church lay somewhere in the middle.[44]

The second aspect of the new climate in the thirties was openness to the ecumenical movement. Once again the United Lutheran Church and the Augustana Synod led the way. The former, because of the cooperation of the General Synod in the Federal Council of Churches, quickly found it necessary to formulate its attitude toward other Christian churches (the Washington Declaration) and consequently maintained a "con-

466

40.
The best historical study of the development of a social ethics in American Lutheranism is Lloyd Svendsbye's "The History of a Developing Social Responsibility Among Lutherans in America from 1930 to 1960 . . ." (Th.D. diss., Union Theological Seminary, New York, 1966). I am indebted to this study for much of what follows.
41.
Ibid., p. 18.
42.
Nelson, *Lutheran Church Among Norwegian-Americans*, 2:112.
43.
Svendsbye, "Social Responsibility," pp. 56–65.
44.
Ibid., 2d précis, p. 2.

sultative membership" in the Federal Council to whose quadrennial meetings it sent "visitors."[45]

Both the United Lutheran and Augustana churches were represented officially at the second World Conference on Faith and Order at Edinburgh in 1937, but only Augustana had sent delegates to the second World Conference on Life and Work at Oxford the previous month.[46] The World Council of Churches was to emerge from these two conferences. The question of Lutheran membership in the proposed council was considered during the next decade, and the principle of confessional representation was put forth in 1945 and 1946. The roots of this principle can be traced back to the Washington Declaration and to the Lutheran World Convention's 1936 statement, "Lutherans and the Ecumenical Movement."[47] This document, drafted by Abdel Ross Wentz at the request of President Knubel and Bishop August Marahrens of Hannover, Germany, and reworked by the author with the help of the executive secretary-elect of the Lutheran World Convention, Hanns Lilje, became the Lutheran platform for ecumenical relationships. Substantial portions of the Washington Declaration were incorporated verbatim into the Lutheran World Convention document. Of special note was the fact that the celebrated confessional principle which later guided some American Lutherans into the World Council of Churches (1948) and the National Council of Churches of Christ (1950) was a reflection of the United Lutheran Church's insistence that ecumenical organizations must be constituted only of official representatives of church bodies, not of co-opted individuals.[48]

Thus, by the mid-thirties some American Lutherans had adopted the positive attitude of their European brethren toward the emerging ecumenical movement, asserting the essentially ecumenical character of Lutheranism and urging participation in the unity movement as a part of the church's stewardship of the gospel. Meanwhile, however, the confessional principle was being tested on the very doorstep of the churches by attempts to bring about a greater degree of unity within American Lutheranism itself.

The Confessional Principle and Lutheran Unity Efforts, 1934–40

As has already been pointed out, two views concerning what was necessary for unity among Lutherans dominated interchurch relations. The United Lutheran Church's position had been expressed in these words of the Washington Declaration: "In the case of those Church Bodies calling themselves Evangelical Lutheran, and subscribing to the Confessions which have always been regarded as the standard of Evangelical Lutheran doctrine, the United Lutheran Church in America recognizes no doctrinal reasons against complete cooperation and organic union with such bodies."[49] The Missouri Synod posited the necessity of theological and practical uniformity. It insisted that confessional subscription was not sufficient for the unity of the church, and further that the integrity of the confession must be

45.
"Across the Desk," *The Lutheran*, April 9, 1931, pp. 4, 14–15. Cf. "United Lutheran Consultative Relationships . . . ," ibid., March 2, 1933, pp. 2, 23.

46.
Abdel Ross Wentz, *A Basic History of Lutheranism in America* (Philadelphia: Fortress Press, 1964), pp. 364–65 (*The Lutheran*, February 4, 1937, carried an explanation of why the United Lutheran Church in America was not at Oxford); and Arden, *Augustana Heritage*, p. 305. Augustana carried on a brief dialogue with the Protestant Episcopal Church in 1935. Agreement on Scripture, the sacraments, and the creed was reached. The ministry (the historic episcopate) proved to be the main stumbling block. See "Lutherans Meet Episcopalians," *Lutheran Companion*, January 11, 1936, pp. 38–39. Cf. Ernest E. Ryden, "A Beginning of Dialogue: Lutherans and Anglicans," *Lutheran Forum*, May 1967, pp. 8–10.

47.
The most thorough study of Lutherans and the World Council of Churches has been made by Dorris A. Flesner, "The Role of the Lutheran Churches of America in the Formation of the World Council of Churches" (Ph.D. diss., Hartford Seminary Foundation, Hartford, Conn., 1956). The 1936 document is in *Lutheran World Almanac, 1934-1937*, pp. 35–38.

48.
Flesner, "Role of the Lutheran Churches," pp. 72–77.

49.
Wolf, *Documents,* p. 350. This view had been expressed officially by the Conference for the Norwegian-Danish Evangelical Lutheran Church during its controversy with Missourianism in the 1870s and 1880s. Cf. Nelson and Fevold, *Lutheran Church Among Norwegian-Americans*, 1:302–35.

validated. A major mark of sincerity was the fact that theological uniformity would be accompanied by uniformity in teaching and practice. Therefore, it was incumbent upon theologians to seek agreement by the method of writing doctrinal theses or extraconfessional theological statements. This was to be followed up by the exercise of ecclesiastical discipline upon those whose "practice" and proclamation did not conform to the accepted theses. "The Missourian Way to Unity"[50] produced numerous sets of these extraconfessional theses, the names of which we have already encountered. Despite the enormous amount of theological discussion, the demonstration of dialectical skill, and the unquestioned good intentions of theologians, the production of theses did not assure the evangelical character of the church. Ironically, most of the theses proved, in the end, to be divisive rather than unifying. Because the attitudes made clear in the decade of the thirties persisted into the sixties and seventies and were the cause of no little exacerbation in the interchurch relations,[51] an examination of the inter-Lutheran doctrinal discussions leading to 1940 may prove illuminating.

Between 1936 and 1939 the United Lutheran Church Commission on Relationships to American Lutheran Church Bodies held several separate meetings with representatives of the Missouri Synod and the American Lutheran Church for the purpose of overcoming the obstacles to Lutheran fellowship and unity in America.[52] The discussions with the Missouri Synod theologians began and ended on the subject of biblical authority. The Missourians insisted that the Bible's authority rested on its verbal inspiration and consequent inerrancy. The United Lutheran commissioners maintained that the Bible is authoritative because it communicates God's saving message or the Word of God. Through this Word or gospel the Holy Spirit calls, gathers, enlightens, and sanctifies the church. God's gospel (Christ) or Word is the means of grace and gives the Bible its authority. The Missouri Synod felt that the United Lutheran position was in reality a denial of the Bible as the Word of God. At this point the atmosphere became chilly and discussions broke off.[53]

The conversations with the representatives of the American Lutheran Church, though more prolonged and detailed, were in the end only a little less barren. Having reached an understanding on the troublesome questions of lodge membership and "unionism," the two groups addressed themselves to the problem of Scripture. The main American Lutheran Church spokesmen, Carl C. Hein and J. Michael Reu, like the Missouri Synod theologians, were concerned with the question of verbal inspiration and inerrancy. Hein, for example, sought unsuccessfully to make the following statement from the Minneapolis Theses the basis for discussion and agreement: "The synods . . . accept without exception all the canonical books of the Old and New Testament as a whole, and in all their parts, as the divinely inspired, revealed, and inerrant Word of God, and submit to this as the only infallible authority in all matters of faith and life."[54]

50.
The phrase is Georg Sverdrup's. See "The Struggle for Unity," in *The Heritage of Faith: Selections from the Writings of Georg Sverdrup*, trans. M. A. Helland (Minneapolis: Augsburg Publishing House, 1969), pp. 65–80.
51.
The new ALC (1960) and the Missouri Synod concluded doctrinal discussions directed toward pulpit and altar fellowship in 1967. The LCA declined repeated invitations to participate, basing its decision on its confessional principle.
52.
A detailed account is in E. Clifford Nelson's "A Case Study in Lutheran Unity Efforts: ULCA Conversations with Missouri and ALC, 1936–1940," in *The Maturing of American Lutheranism*, ed. H. T. Neve and B. A. Johnson (Minneapolis: Augsburg Publishing House, 1968), pp. 201–23.
53.
Ibid., pp. 205–6.
54.
Wolf, *Documents*, p. 340. This statement from 1925 was made an unalterable part of the constitution of the second ALC (1960). Its fundamentalistic language proved to be an embarrassment and provoked church leaders to make "interpretations" which were not in accord with the historical circumstances and intentions out of which the statement grew in the twenties and later in the forties and fifties.

The United Lutheran theologians understandably opposed this formulation of the problem. After some sparring it was agreed, at the suggestion of Knubel, that a joint statement on scriptural authority be prepared. Charles M. Jacobs (United Lutheran Church) and J. Michael Reu (American Lutheran Church) were chosen to make the draft. Due to Jacobs's illness and other circumstances, it was impossible for the two theologians to ready a common statement for the next conference. Subsequent meetings of the commissioners, therefore, were faced with two statements, one by Reu, the other by Jacobs. Reu's statement focused on the nature of the Bible and its inspiration, citing the familiar proof-passages, 2 Timothy 3:16 and 2 Peter 1:21, and urging the causal relationship between verbal inspiration and inerrancy. Jacobs, however, asserted that the phrase "Word of God" was used in more than one sense, and that the significant matter was to see the relation between the Word of God and the Scriptures. First, he said, the Word of God meant the gospel; second, the Word of God was the historical self-revelation of God completed in Jesus Christ and interpreted by men chosen and inspired by God; third, because God continued to make himself known in the Holy Scriptures of which Christ was the center, the Bible was properly called the Word of God. Inspiration, he continued, was a fact of which "our faith in God, through Christ, assures us." The mode or manner of inspiration, however, was beyond human definition.[55]

Hein responded by saying that he was certain the American Lutheran Church would have to reject the Jacobs statement because it did not adequately address the problem of inspiration and inerrancy. For this reason the Reu statement was to be preferred; it, said Hein, dealt with "the real problem." To remove the phrases on inerrancy, as Jacobs and Knubel urged, would be "to strike a blow at the very heart and center of the matter."

Discussions between the two groups continued until 1939. Meanwhile, both Hein and Jacobs died. Subsequent meetings pitted Knubel and Henry F. Offermann (a colleague of Jacobs at the Philadelphia Seminary) against Reu, but no softening or alteration of positions was achieved. Therefore, it was agreed in March 1938 that each commission would report to its church body, giving the exact situation and revealing the point where agreement could not be reached. The commissions would then reassemble in February 1939.

The reports were made, but each church body, aware of the cleft, took action to articulate its own view in an official "declaration." The United Lutheran Church adopted the Jacobs statement, revised in a few details; this came to be known as the Baltimore Declaration (1938). The American Lutheran Church did the same with Reu's statement, and it came to be known as the Sandusky Declaration. The Missourian orientation of the latter—the American Lutheran Church was simultaneously holding conversations with the Missouri Synod—was evident in the church's immediate offer of fellowship to the Missouri Synod: ". . . we believe that the Brief Statement

55.
Nelson, "Case Study," p. 214. For insight into the Lutheran understanding of the Word of God see Theodore G. Tappert, "The Word of God According to the Lutheran Confessions," in *Maturing of American Lutheranism*, pp. 58–70.

[Missouri] viewed in the light of our [Sandusky] Declaration is not in contradiction to the Minneapolis Theses which are the bases of membership in the American Lutheran Conference."[56] This was a correct observation; all three statements reflected the "orthodox" view of inspiration and inerrancy.

Despite the sharp divergence between the United Lutheran and American Lutheran churches made evident at the 1938 conventions, the 1939 meeting of the commissioners was held on schedule. Knubel, eager to see some fruit of the years of negotiations, suggested to Reu and his colleagues that, although the United Lutheran Church would never accept a fundamentalistic interpretation of inerrancy (he said his church held to the *doctrinal* perfection of the Scriptures centering in Christ; the Word of God, the gospel of salvation, was without error), in order to break the impasse they might agree that the books of the Bible, taken together, "constitute a complete, *errorless* [italics added], unbreakable whole of which Christ is the center." When Knubel assured the reluctant Reu that this went beyond the Baltimore Declaration, the joint meeting accepted the compromise and gave birth to the Pittsburgh Agreement, which some United Lutheran theologians soon labeled "the Pittsburgh Disagreement."

The conventions of 1940 revealed that the churches were quite aware of the persisting theological differences. The American Lutheran Church accepted the Pittsburgh Agreement but failed to approve fellowship with the United Lutheran Church because there was a general feeling that one ought to wait and see if the latter "lived up to" its agreement. Though the United Lutheran Church also accepted the Pittsburgh Agreement, its action was hedged by a preamble which said that if the Pittsburgh document seemed to be in conflict with the church's earlier declarations (Washington, 1920; Savannah, 1934; and Baltimore, 1938), the latter were to have priority. A large and significant minority, led by the young pastor Franklin Clark Fry, voted against approval despite the "assurances" in the preamble.[57]

The year 1940 was in some respects a watershed. The American Lutheran Church turned more and more to the Norwegian Lutheran Church (Evangelical Lutheran Church, 1946) and the Missouri Synod. With the latter it worked out a Common Confession, Part I, in 1949, that was adopted by both churches in 1950. Part II, issued in 1952 and adopted by the American Lutheran Church in 1953, was accepted by the Missouri Synod in 1956 not as a doctrinally operative document but as a "significant historic statement."[58] Meanwhile, the American Lutheran Church moved toward a merger with some of the churches of the American Lutheran Conference. This eventuated in the formation of the new American Lutheran Church in 1960. The United Lutheran Church, smarting under the experiences culminating in the 1940 conventions, replied to subsequent overtures regarding fellowship and union that "no further definitions of doctrine are necessary . . . and beyond the Lutheran Confessions we will submit . . . no tests of Lutheranism."[59]

56.
Wolf, *Documents*, p. 401.
57.
Nelson, "Case Study," pp. 219–21. For an interesting treatment of Fry see Robert H. Fischer, ed., *Franklin Clark Fry: A Palette for a Portrait*, supplementary number of the *Lutheran Quarterly*, vol. 24 (1972).
58.
Wolf, *Documents*, p. 437.
59.
Ibid., pp. 484–85.

The question that had disturbed American Lutheranism since the twenties and thirties—Does confessional unity require theological uniformity?—remained unresolved into the seventies. The United Lutheran Church and, after 1962, the Lutheran Church in America said no; the American Lutheran Church (1960) and the Missouri Synod said yes. There the problem posed by Lutheranism's confessional principle resided until the late sixties and early seventies.

471

20   The Church
in War and in Peace

When Hitler came to power in 1933, the first impulse of many Americans was to prevent the United States from becoming involved in the problems of Europe. By 1939, however, only small pockets of the population were neutral regarding Hitler. Any earlier "wait-and-see" hesitation about his objectives was dissipated by the invasion of Poland, the crushing of France, the Battle of Britain, and the takeover of Denmark and Norway.

Prewar Attitudes Among Lutherans

On the whole, Lutherans in America reacted to international political events quite as did other Americans. First, there was profound concern; second, there was the mood "let's not get involved in Europe's problems"; third, there was growing fear of German Nazism and Japanese militarism; and fourth, there was a general commitment to the Allied cause, especially when Jews, Catholics, and fellow Lutherans were persecuted. The invasion of Lutheran Scandinavia in 1940 and the bombing of Pearl Harbor were both "days of infamy" that removed any vestige of hesitation regarding the righteousness of the Allied cause.

Although Lutherans generally followed the response pattern of other religious groups in America, there were a few things that set them apart from most other Protestants. There was the basic fact that Germany was the home of the Lutheran Reformation. The strong confessional loyalties within Lutheranism had long demonstrated the fact that its interpretation and proclamation of the gospel transcended geographic and ethnic limits. Naturally, German-American Lutherans were confused and upset by the rise of Hitler; and the others, though never predominantly Germanophiles, recognizing the religious and cultural debt that many of them owed to the land of Martin Luther, were willing for a time to "wait-and-see." This questioning hesitation in America among Scandinavian Lutherans and central European Lutheran minorities quickly turned to righteous wrath in 1939–40.

The thirties posed a particular confessional and ecclesio-political problem for American Lutherans. While college and seminary professors were trying to understand the "theology of crisis," a new crisis—an ecclesiastical one—was developing right under their noses. Articles in church papers, addresses by leading churchmen, and official as well as private correspondence by well-known Lutheran personalities reflected the confusion in the minds of many.[1]

By the spring of 1933 the *Lutheran* was carrying articles and editorials on the rise of Hitlerism and the emergence of the

1.
In what follows I am greatly indebted to Helen M. Knubel, archivist for the Lutheran Council/U.S.A., to Frederick K. Wentz's "The Reaction of the Religious Press in America to the Emergence of Naziism" (Ph.D. diss., Yale University, 1954), and to John G. Mager's "Nazis, Jews, and the War: What the *Lutheran Witness* Said, 1934–1945," *American Lutheran* 47 (November 1964): 10–13. Helpful in understanding the German church situation is Stewart W. Hermann's *It's Your Souls We Want* (New York: Harper, 1943).

2.
The Lutheran, April 20, 1933, p. 4.
3.
Wentz, "Reaction of the Religious Press,"
p. 94.
4.
Mager, "Nazis, Jews, and the War," pp.
10–13.
5.
Augustana Synod, *Minutes . . . 1939,* p.
266.
6.
Ibid. *1941,* p. 234.
7.
Ibid. *1942,* p. 233.
8.
NLCA, *Annual Report . . . 1940,* p. 9.

Nazi-supported movement known as the "German Christians" (*Deutsche Christen*). The periodical felt that the latter, though committed to Nazi purposes, desired "to remain definitely Christian."[2] Generally speaking, however, the *Lutheran* and other major non-Synodical Conference periodicals (the *Lutheran Standard,* the *Lutheran Herald,* and the *Lutheran Companion*) reflected an increasing antipathy toward Hitler's Germany. The *Lutheran,* especially between 1934 and 1937, showed a significant editorial shift from identification with the German *church* to an attitude of anti-Nazism. Nazism was not socialism but fascism and as such quite as evil as communism.[3]

The Missouri Synod's official organ, the *Lutheran Witness,* withheld criticism of Hitler and the Nazis for several years. Between 1934 and 1939 the *Witness* carried articles that reflected "starry-eyed approval of the Nazi regime" and silence regarding the persecution of the Jews. It was not until 1945 that the *Witness* opened its columns, and then only to a non-Lutheran, to a denunciation of the paganism and inhumanity of Nazism. After a lapse of twenty years, these facts caused a Missouri Synod scholar to raise the question "whether the church can remain silent in the presence of monstrous evil and still preserve its integrity. Can the church . . . abandon its role as a light and as conscience to the world and still remain the church?"[4]

Among the National Lutheran Council churches, the Augustana Synod reacted to totalitarianism by opposing all forms of militarism, American as well as European. During the thirties the *Lutheran Companion* frequently printed editorials and articles in support of the peace movement, and even after World War II broke out in 1939 the *Companion* continued to urge a policy of neutrality and peace. This attitude prevailed until Pearl Harbor. Two years before the outbreak of the war, the synod endorsed the Life and Work (Oxford, 1937) statement: "War is a particular demonstration of the power of sin in the world, and a defiance of the righteousness of God as revealed in Jesus Christ and Him crucified. No justification of war must be allowed to minimize or conceal this fact."[5] Shortly before Pearl Harbor, the synod went on record in support of conscientious objectors: "We ask exemption from all forms of combatant military service for all conscientious objectors who may be members of the Augustana Synod."[6] When America officially entered the war, Augustana's resolution of loyalty to the nation was followed by the caveat: "The Synod urges its members to remain loyal to Christ, to be on guard lest the sanction of the Church be given to anything which is contrary to the spirit of Christ."[7]

The attitude of the Norwegian Lutheran Church of America was marked by a sharp contrast. In 1938, for example, there was no mention of the struggle going on in Europe or the problem of war and peace. Two years later, however, the presidential message began with these words: "Today, the land of our fathers . . . is not a free land. . . . Our feelings and emotions are moved at the thought that a country that has desired to live in peace and amity with its neighbors down through the decades should reap such a harvest."[8] The reference, of course, was to the Nazi invasion of Denmark and Norway, April 1940, which generated among the ordinarily peaceloving Danish- and Norwegian-Americans a spirit of deep hostility toward the invader. It was to be expected that the church would adopt the following strong resolution after America became involved:

We recognize that in the present titanic struggle there are principles involved that are essential to human welfare and closely allied with the freedom of conscience and of worship that we value so highly. Therefore, we urge our members to manifest their loyalty by giving full support to the war efforts of their country with their substance and, if necessary, with their lives.[9]

The Churches' Response to War

One cannot think of the wartime activity of the churches apart from the National Lutheran Council. It should be noted that this agency all but collapsed in the early thirties when the American Lutheran Conference was organized by five council churches. This act, which drew a sharp line between the United Lutheran Church and the Midwestern churches that constituted the American Lutheran Conference, threatened to split the council and to place its role in American Lutheranism in jeopardy. As a result, one historian observed, the National Lutheran Council stood at a crossroads in 1937. Should it quietly recede into the background, or should it assert itself by seizing opportunities for service on behalf of the churches before the occasions were lost?

That the National Lutheran Council chose the latter path and did not disintegrate was due in large measure to the wise and effective leadership of its executive director, Ralph H. Long, who almost singlehandedly shaped an aggressive and forward-looking program.[10] This was accomplished despite the strained relationships between the United Lutheran Church and the American Lutheran Conference, and the inhibiting regulations that the churches had imposed on the council. There were four such working "rules": (1) the National Lutheran Council was merely an "agency" for participating bodies. It was not a church nor a federation of churches, but an "agency" through which "participating" bodies could do *specific* tasks; (2) the council could act for the "participating" churches in emergencies that demanded a common front; (3) the council could not assume responsibility for initiating or furthering Lutheran unity or union; only "churches" could negotiate with each other; and (4) council activities were carefully circumscribed by the principle of "cooperation in externals." The distinction between *res externae* and *res internae* was always difficult to maintain. Where was the boundary between "external" and "internal"? What could be done cooperatively without prior doctrinal agreement?[11] Actually, the distinction proved artificial and therefore untenable, but it was strategically retained as a protection against what Missourian-influenced Lutherans called "sinful unionism." It was soon admitted openly that the cliché had become an obstacle to faith and action; it was simply im-

9.
Ibid. *1942*, p. 29.
10.
Osborne Hauge, *Lutherans Working Together: A History of the National Lutheran Council, 1918-1943* (New York: National Lutheran Council, 1945), p. 72. Cf. Frederick K. Wentz, *Lutherans in Concert* (Minneapolis: Augsburg Publishing House, 1968), pp. 77-80.
11.
Lauritz Larsen, "Unity," *Lutheran Church Herald*, April 1, 1919, p. 194. Cf. Hauge, *Lutherans Working Together*, pp. 39-40.

possible to engage in any evangelical action without transgressing the rule. Therefore, Long concluded, if cooperative work was to be carried out, the principles had to be disregarded, or, as Frederick K. Wentz euphemistically described it, the council had to "transcend the rules."[12] Lars W. Boe summarized the history of the National Lutheran Council in two sentences: " . . . The Lord has never permitted it [the NLC] to be only an agency for cooperation in external affairs. Time and again we re-wrote the constitution and regulations . . . to safeguard this line that we arbitrarily set up, . . . but the Lord . . . pushed us across the line every time."[13]

When World War II broke out, the National Lutheran Council, thanks to Long and other farsighted churchmen, was "tooled up" for action. In fact, even before 1939, at least two areas of wartime service had been entered. At the request of the Federal Council's General Committee on Army and Navy Chaplains, the United Lutheran Church had assumed responsibility for recruiting Lutheran chaplains and for serving as liaison between the chaplains and their respective churches. By 1934 its executive board moved to place this ministry into the hands of the National Lutheran Council.[14] This was done, and the council developed its program in cooperation with the Federal Council's General Committee until 1939 when the National Lutheran Council began direct negotiations with the chief of chaplains. Meanwhile the Missouri Synod, unable to cooperate with the council churches, inaugurated its own program in the mid-thirties, and through its Army and Navy Commission built up a corps of highly qualified chaplains.[15] Thus when the National Defense Program was effectuated in 1940, the number of Lutheran chaplains in the armed services approached the assigned quota.

A second area that the National Lutheran Council had already entered was the support of what was called orphaned missions. American Lutherans had been aiding European mission societies ever since the First World War, but the situation became critical in 1936–37 when the Nazi government imposed currency regulations that tended to cut off German mission support.[16] By June 1939 the German fields were completely orphaned. If they were to survive, American Lutherans would have to assume responsibility for them. Representatives of the churches met on October 2, 1939, to coordinate and direct efforts to maintain the orphaned missions of Germany and Finland, the latter having been invaded by Russia. In this manner, the National Lutheran Council and the American Section of the Lutheran World Convention (which for all practical purposes was coextensive with the National Lutheran Council) undertook a Lutheran Emergency Appeal. Under the direction of Otto C. Mees the campaign raised $238,000 by the spring of 1940.[17]

Although America was not at war, the members of National Lutheran Council churches in Canada were, of course, immediately involved. This prompted Long to call a conference of Canadian Lutherans at Winnipeg, April 2, 1940. At this meet-

12.
Wentz, *Lutherans in Concert*, pp. 84, 90.
13.
Letter to Johan A. Aasgaard, October 29, 1942, Lars W. Boe Papers, St. Olaf College Archives, Northfield, Minn.
14.
ULCA, *Minutes . . . 1938*, p. 615; ibid. *1932*, p. 446; ibid. *1934*, p. 56. Cf. Hauge, *Lutherans Working Together*, pp. 64–65.
15.
F. C. Proehl, *Marching Side by Side* (St. Louis: Concordia Publishing House, 1945), pp. 1–11.
16.
It has been estimated that over $200,000 had been given by the NLC to the Gossner Mission (India) alone after World War I and in the late thirties.
17.
Wentz, *Lutherans in Concert*, pp. 106–7; cf. Hauge, *Lutherans Working Together*, p. 73.

ing the Canadian Lutheran Commission was organized to supervise the wartime service of the Canadian churches. Approved by all groups except the Missouri Synod, the commission undertook a broad-gauged ministry, including services for German prisoners of war in Canadian camps. Initially, the project received financial subsidies from the National Lutheran Council, but by 1942 it was self-supporting.[18]

The service to men in the armed forces and the support of war-orphaned missions soon became parts of a massive overall project. The Lutheran Emergency Appeal of 1940 had been undertaken primarily for the benefit of orphaned missions. Consequently, there were no funds at hand to engage in a ministry to men and women in the armed services. In 1941 the annual meeting of the National Lutheran Council heard a report of a survey trip made by Nils M. Ylvisaker and Clarence E. Krumbholz among forty-two military camps and forty-eight communities adjacent to the camps. On the basis of the report the council voted to initiate a comprehensive program and named Ylvisaker as director. Thus, almost overnight the council was embarked on what was soon to be a far-reaching program of wartime services masterfully supervised by its energetic director.[19] The responsibilities of the Service Commission included maintaining close touch with the chaplains, establishing centers for servicemen and women (in 1944 there were forty-four full-time pastors at these centers), and encouraging local parishes to keep in touch with their members in the armed services.[20]

The decision of the National Lutheran Council in 1941 to raise $500,000, one-half of which was to be used for the newly formed Service Commission, the remainder to support orphaned missions and the program of aid to war refugees, resulted in what was called Lutheran World Action (LWA). The supervision and direction of the latter fell chiefly upon the shoulders of two of the ablest men in American Lutheranism, executive secretary Ralph H. Long and his newly appointed assistant, Paul C. Empie. The latter had served on a part-time basis until he was elected assistant director of the National Lutheran Council in 1944. Thereafter, Lutheran World Action was Empie's full responsibility, one which he discharged with imagination, efficiency, and dedication. When Long died unexpectedly in 1948, it was only natural for Empie to succeed him. Under Empie, Lutheran World Action became a household word in the congregations, the vast majority of which gladly cooperated in the program.

Symbolized by a strong arm thrusting the cross forward ("Love's Working Arm"), Lutheran World Action appeals became annual events for the next quarter of a century. By 1965 almost $80 million had been raised and distributed as aid to thousands of people in seventy-five countries around the world.[21] This became the Lutheran churches' "Marshall Plan" during the postwar reconstruction. Together with Lutheran World Relief (not an incorporated part of the National Lutheran Council), which was the material aid program of the council, and the Missouri Synod's Board of World Relief (after 1953),

18.
Hauge, *Lutherans Working Together*, p. 75.
19.
Ibid., p. 76. The Norwegian Lutheran Church appropriated $100,000 for immediate use by the council. These funds were a balance carried over from the Soldiers' and Sailors' appeal in World War I. It is interesting to note that the NLCA made no demand in 1941, as it had done in 1919, for doctrinal agreement before it could engage in "churchly cooperation." This was a clear example of what Boe meant when he said the Lord had not permitted the NLC to stay within the rule marking a distinction between *res externae* and *res internae*. Moreover, it must not be forgotten that *Norway* had been invaded! Cf. NLCA, *Report . . . 1941*, pp. 8–9; ibid. *1942*, p. 21; ibid. *1943*, p. 9.
20.
Wentz, *Lutherans in Concert*, pp. 100–101.
21.
Ibid., p. 128. For a brief history of Lutheran World Action see Rollin G. Shaffer, *LWA: A Quarter Century of Christian Compassion* (New York: Lutheran World Action, 1966).

Figure 1

**LWA—
expressing a quarter-century
of Christian compassion
through sharing**

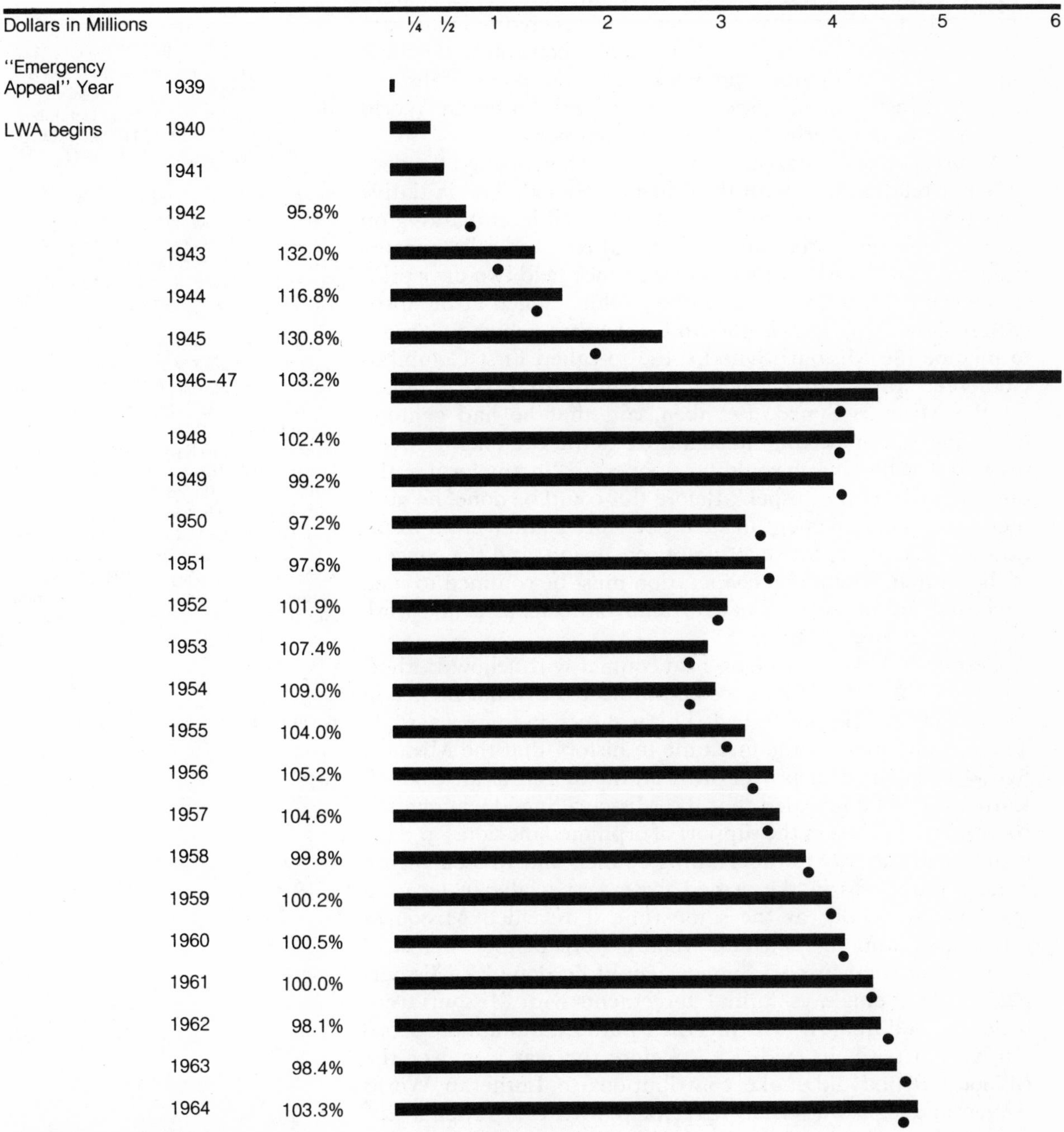

| Dollars in Millions | | | ¼ ½ 1   2   3   4   5   6 |

"Emergency Appeal" Year	1939	
LWA begins	1940	
	1941	
	1942	95.8%
	1943	132.0%
	1944	116.8%
	1945	130.8%
	1946–47	103.2%
	1948	102.4%
	1949	99.2%
	1950	97.2%
	1951	97.6%
	1952	101.9%
	1953	107.4%
	1954	109.0%
	1955	104.0%
	1956	105.2%
	1957	104.6%
	1958	99.8%
	1959	100.2%
	1960	100.5%
	1961	100.0%
	1962	98.1%
	1963	98.4%
	1964	103.3%

LWA goals and receipts for the years 1939–64 are compared in this graph. The bar shows the accomplishment of the churches in relation to the goal, marked by a dot. In 1946–47 a two-year appeal for $10 million was conducted. Interpretation of this graph should take into consideration the factor of inflation.

Source: Rollin G. Shaffer, *LWA: A Quarter Century of Christian Compassion* (New York: Lutheran World Action, 1966), pp. 10-11.

Lutheran World Action elicited the admiration of both ecclesiastical and governmental leaders. In fact, the manner in which American Lutheranism mobilized its resources for overseas aid both during and after the war did as much as anything else to enhance its stature in ecumenical circles. Voices in Asia, Africa, the Near East, and Western Europe were raised in unstinted gratitude and praise. A few were critical of what they termed American Lutheranism's "confessional imperialism." The well-known Martin Niemoeller, for example, was credited with saying, "*Cuius dollar eius religio*" ("Religion is controlled by those who supply the money; 'he who pays the piper, calls the tune'"). Most people, however, recognized Lutheran World Action as an outpouring of Christian compassion.

As has been observed, common calamity had opened the door to better relationships with the Missouri Synod. The initiative displayed by the National Lutheran Council in embarking on such an ambitious program in 1941 had received solid encouragement from an All-Lutheran Conference held two days prior to the council meeting in Columbus, Ohio. Called at the instigation of the American Lutheran Conference, which was eager to include the Missouri Synod,[22] the so-called First Columbus Conference produced a policy statement by John W. Behnken for the Missouri Synod. Behnken said that he had genuine misgivings about affixing his signature to the call for this meeting and that his church could not cooperate "in any form in the dissemination of the gospel." Before this could be done, he said, there must be agreement in such doctrines as the verbal inspiration of Scripture, the doctrine of conversion, and the concept of the church. Therefore, cooperation must be confined to such "externals" as physical relief to orphaned missionaries and work among soldiers and sailors.[23]

Despite Behnken's backing into contact with fellow Lutherans, the Columbus Conference accomplished a minor breach in the wall of the Missouri Synod. This was seen in three ways: (1) The meeting marked the first time in history that the Missouri Synod had joined in prayer with National Lutheran Council Lutherans; (2) it revealed that the Missouri Synod was open to coordinating efforts in the support of orphaned missions; and (3) it prepared the way for dovetailing council and Missouri work among Lutherans in the armed forces, especially in locating service centers. But at the same time it revealed Missouri's traditional caution: "spiritual welfare work in the interest of members of the Missouri Synod" would be done by Missouri pastors. As Wentz says, formal agreements with Missouri were little changed from the World War I pattern, but a more cooperative spirit was in evidence.[24] Before the war was over the Missouri Synod did make contributions to Lutheran World Action and signed a formal agreement with the National Lutheran Council to establish a common Lutheran Commission for Prisoners of War.[25]

One cannot fully assess the role of the National Lutheran Council during the war years by looking only at those areas that were directly associated with its war-shaped ministries. Several

22.
"Convention Proceedings," *Journal of Theology of the American Lutheran Conference* 6 (January 1941): 85–86. The meeting, including Missouri, was held at Columbus, Ohio, on January 20, 1941. The NLC met there on January 22–23, 1941.

23.
"Report of Representatives to an Intersynodical Lutheran Conference," January 20, 1941, Columbus, Ohio. J. K. Jensen Papers, Northwestern Lutheran Seminary Library, St. Paul, Minn. Cf. ULCA, *Minutes . . . 1942*, pp. 117–19.

24.
"The Twenty Third Annual Meeting of the NLC," *Journal of Theology of the American Lutheran Conference* 6 (April 1941): 387. Cf. E. E. Ryden, "The Birth and Youth of the Council," *National Lutheran* 34 (December 1966): 6. Ryden informed Behnken that the ULCA would attend on one condition, that the conference be opened with prayer. Behnken offered no objection. Cf. George V. Schick, "The Columbus Conference and Its Repercussions," *Lutheran Witness*, May 13, 1941; "Coordination with the National Lutheran Council," ibid., p. 172. Cf. Wentz, *Lutherans in Concert*, p. 102.

25.
Wentz, *Lutherans in Concert*, p. 108. Cf. Augustana Synod, *Report . . . 1944*, "The National Lutheran Council," p. 299.

domestic programs should be noted, among them social welfare and American missions.

The social welfare department of the council, under the leadership of Clarence E. Krumbholz, was primarily engaged in the problems of welfare rather than in direct social action. In fact, the latter, somewhat cautiously undertaken in the thirties by the council's Social Trends Committee, was not pursued with vigor until the fifties.[26] This is not to denigrate the work of the department, which, as a matter of fact, was engaged in a huge humanitarian enterprise expressing the Christian concern of the churches. Serving as the Lutheran World Convention's contact for war refugees, the department was also in close contact with Lutheran welfare or inner mission societies across America; furthermore, it kept the churches informed of social legislation and provided invaluable assistance to Lutheran welfare institutions. Wentz summarizes: "To indicate the size of the field within which the department operated, the following statistics . . . are instructive: including the Missouri Synod, there were 461 benevolent organizations (in 1945), contacting more than a million people with services, spending $16½ million, involving more than 18,000 people as employees, board members, and volunteers."[27]

Another aspect of the council's domestic program fell under the general rubric of American Missions. As noted earlier, World War I had focused attention on the necessity of missionary work in the new defense-industry communities. Home mission conferences during the twenties were the occasion for the National Lutheran Council to recommend that a Lutheran Home Missions Council of North America be established. Since the various American mission boards were not yet ready to entrust this work to the National Lutheran Council, some agency was needed to coordinate their activities. With this in mind, the Home Missions Council came into being in 1931 and functioned with some effectiveness until 1942. In that year, at the prodding of the National Lutheran Editors' Association, consideration was given to closer domestic cooperation. This was the background of the council's action in the fall of 1942 to organize a Commission on American Missions. Although it came on the scene under wartime conditions, the commission soon transcended its "emerging" nature and became a permanent Division of American Missions in the council's new constitutional structure (1945).[28]

The major work of the Division of American Missions, beyond the "temporary ministries" in defense industry areas, was to foster comity among National Lutheran Council Lutherans in establishing new congregations. The Missouri Synod and other Synodical Conference churches did not participate in the comity arrangements nor in the division's regional home missions councils. Nevertheless, as years went on some Missouri Synod pastors cooperated with the council "in local urban self-study workshops."[29] Of no little interest in this connection was the fact that through the work of this division the National Lutheran Council was unmistakably involved in a "churchly"

479

26.
Lloyd Svendsbye, "The History of a Developing Social Responsibility Among Lutherans . . . " (Th.D. diss., Union Theological Seminary, New York, 1966), p. 58. Cf. Wentz, *Lutherans in Concert*, p. 181.
27.
Wentz, *Lutherans in Concert*, p. 98.
28.
Ralph H. Long, "Today and Tomorrow," in Hauge, *Lutherans Working Together*, pp. 100-102; Helen M. Knubel, "National Lutheran Council," in *The Encyclopedia of the Lutheran Church*, ed. Julius Bodensieck, 3 vols. (Minneapolis: Augsburg Publishing House, 1965), 3:1705; and Wentz, *Lutherans in Concert*, pp. 105-6, 122-24, 148-51.
29.
Paul C. Empie, "A Case Study in Lutheran Cooperation," unpublished manuscript (New York, 1963), p. 5.

ministry. In no sense could its activity be interpreted as merely cooperation "in externals." The executive secretary of the Division of American Missions, H. Conrad Hoyer, recalling the wartime services, wrote: ". . . in these ministries we often had pastors . . . of different Church Bodies. . . . In fact, the Synodical affiliation of the pastors in relation to the area was rarely taken into account, and it was never decisive. . . . [Pastors] were elected by our Division, paid by us, supervised by us, and the services which they conducted were considered chaplaincy services in the area."[30]

The Church: Acids and Assets in Wartime

America's equivocal position at the outbreak of World War II had changed abruptly on December 7, 1941. The shock of Pearl Harbor thrust deep into the American body ecclesiastic, both in its local and national manifestations.

On the local level, the life of the church was traditionally rooted in the worshiping community. All activities, theoretically at least, were adjuncts to and fruits of the life of worship. Sunday schools, adult education, community outreach, visitations, buildings and grounds, auxiliary organizations, fund-raising, church boards—all these and more were the accouterments of the congregation. When the war came, there was no material change in the general contour of the local church. Rather, there was a deepening of mood in the life of worship, a perceptible drawing together around Word and sacrament, a growing sense of interdependence and community. When sons and daughters of the congregation were drawn inevitably into the armed forces, star-bedecked "service flags" were hung in the churches. As the war lengthened, increasing numbers of blue stars were changed to gold. Each time this happened the congregation mourned with the bereaved and renewed its prayers for peace and justice.

New problems, social acids which began to ulcerate spiritual vitality, soon appeared. America's vast industrial-military complex demanded more and more workers, women as well as men. Overnight "Rosie the Riveter" became a familiar sight in defense plants throughout the nation. The disruption of homes, not only by the military draft and enlistments, but also by the unprecedented movement of wives and mothers into factories, offices, and schools placed unaccustomed stresses on family life. With fathers working one shift and mothers another, children soon became the victims of familial instability. Social workers and pastors added a new phrase to their vocabularies: juvenile delinquency. To be sure, young people had gotten into trouble before, but the war years saw an unhappy enlargement of the problem. But this was not all; increased paychecks and wives with independent incomes produced a new freedom, and the new freedom often led to excesses. In many cases, moral patterns broke down, divorce increased, and alcoholism surfaced with an alarming frequency.

Pastoral responsibilities, already extended by the decreased

30.
Letter of H. Conrad Hoyer to E. Clifford Nelson, April 17, 1959, Archives of Cooperative Lutheranism, Lutheran Council/U.S.A., New York, Division of American Missions.

480

number of clergymen available for civilian ministries (the Lutheran church supplied hundreds of chaplains and service-center pastors) multiplied parochial duties almost beyond human endurance. Moreover, the colleges and seminaries of the church were graduating fewer and fewer men. Several colleges "went to war" by making a portion of their facilities available to the federal government for special military purposes such as the V-12 and other programs. Accelerated education, especially on the seminary level, occupied faculties virtually on a year-round basis, resulting in exhausted teachers and inadequately prepared and immature graduates.

Meanwhile, the "war boom" economy was reflected in higher church income. Many congregations whose prewar plans for new churches and educational units were interrupted by government-ordered stoppages used the building hiatus to husband funds for postwar construction opportunities. Other congregations, carrying indebtedness from the depression era, were able to burn mortgages and bring their financial houses into order.

The income of the church at large also mounted. In addition to the large sums raised for Lutheran World Action, contributions to home and foreign missions, charities and welfare, and education showed substantial increments. The funds for American (home) missions were expended on programs of expansion that burgeoned in all the major bodies during the forties. The fact that missions in Japan, China, and Southeast Asia were cut off from American churches for several years made it necessary for boards of world missions to invest a portion of wartime receipts until such a time as reactivation of some Asian missions and the opening of new fields could be undertaken. American Lutherans, like all other citizens, awaited eagerly the cessation of hostilities in order that the ways of peace might be resumed and reconstruction for a new day might enlist the energies of all loyal churchmen.

Postwar Church Life

Millions of words have been written in an attempt to describe and evaluate the postwar "religious boom" in America. Although no definitive interpretation has appeared, it is now a commonplace in American religious historiography to refer to "the revival of the fifties." One is hard put to judge the American "revival." Was "true religion" absent from the popular acclaim? Was biblical faith necessarily and always confined to "the remnant"? Wasn't "the remnant" quite as vulnerable to demonic perversion as "mass Christendom"? Was the self-righteousness of the "little flock" less a denial of God than the superficiality of bourgeois religion? Whatever the answer, Lutherans participated in the "boom."

Lutheranism and the "Revival"

Theodore Roosevelt said, "The Lutheran Church is destined to become one of the two or three greatest and most important churches in the United States. . . ."[31] Others spoke of Lutheran-

31.
Theodore Roosevelt, *Presidential Addresses and State Papers* . . . (New York: Review of Reviews Co., 1910), 3:206–7.

ism in America as a sleeping giant that began to wake up between the two world wars. Whatever the validity of these observations and whatever may be the future of American Lutheranism, there is no doubt that it experienced a huge expansion in the postwar period. In the first place, each of the major church bodies reported advances in membership and church attendance. Of the major churches the conservative Missouri Synod showed the greatest gains.[32] That there was no correlation between Lutheran "orthodoxy" and rapid growth—a conclusion sometimes drawn—could be seen right within the Synodical Conference where the Missouri Synod's even more conservative partner, the Wisconsin Synod, experienced the smallest increase (see fig. 2).

It can hardly be denied that, measured by secular "success" criteria alone, Lutheranism's missionary expansion in North America was remarkable. When President Oliver Harms of the Missouri Synod was asked in 1968 what developments in the Missouri Synod merited preservation in the collective memory of American Lutheranism, he unhesitatingly placed "missionary outreach" high on his list.[33] Other church leaders could have said the same. At its peak the mission program produced one new congregation every fifty-four hours! Although this rapid expansion no doubt shared and reflected some of the undesirable aspects of the "revival of the fifties," in its major thrust it was without the frothy superficiality of the much heralded "return to religion" via "positive thinking" or "revival." Billy Graham's influence upon American Lutheranism would be difficult to assess. Individuals and groups were attracted by his widely acclaimed "crusades." Moreover, churchmen expressed gratitude for Graham's evangelical emphasis. On the whole, however, Lutherans found his techniques questionable and his message truncated. The absence of a sacramental and social dimension prevented many from giving him their whole-hearted approbation.

In most instances, Lutheran evangelism was the missionary projection of a solidly based doctrinal and catechetical emphasis rooted in congregations. An example of the churches' interest in parish-centered evangelism was a proposal in 1947 by President Emmanuel Poppen of the American Lutheran Church, for inter-Lutheran cooperation in evangelism.[34] The Lutheran Evangelism Council, composed of representatives of the National Lutheran Council churches, sponsored evangelistic missions nicknamed "PTRs" (Preaching-Teaching-Reaching) after the successful program begun in 1952 by the Evangelical Lutheran Church.[35] The Missouri Synod also adopted this type of mission, saying that it "represents one of the most effective and fruitful evangelism programs ever undertaken in the Lutheran church."[36] The evangelical thrust generated a new interest in the apostolate of the laity. "The United Lutheran Church," it was reported, "has never been so stirred to its depths by any previous undertaking as by the Lutheran Evangelism Mission."[37] Lutherans were concerned that evangelism center

482

32.
For annual tabulations see Archives of Cooperative Lutheranism and Office of Research, Statistics and Archives, Lutheran Council/U.S.A., New York.
33.
Interview, Harms and E. Clifford Nelson, St. Louis, August 28, 1968. The Missouri Synod had a notable growth. For over twenty consecutive years after 1945 the synod had the highest numerical growth of all Lutherans. The greatest advance on a percentage basis for most of these same years was made by the ELC. See the annual analysis of Lutheran statistics released by News Bureau, NLC and Lutheran Council/U.S.A., 1952-68.
34.
ULCA, *Minutes . . . 1948*, pp. 241-42.
35.
ELC, *Report . . . 1953*, p. 10.
36.
LC—MS, *Proceedings . . . 1956*, p. 377.
37.
ULCA, *Minutes . . . 1956*, p. 1113.

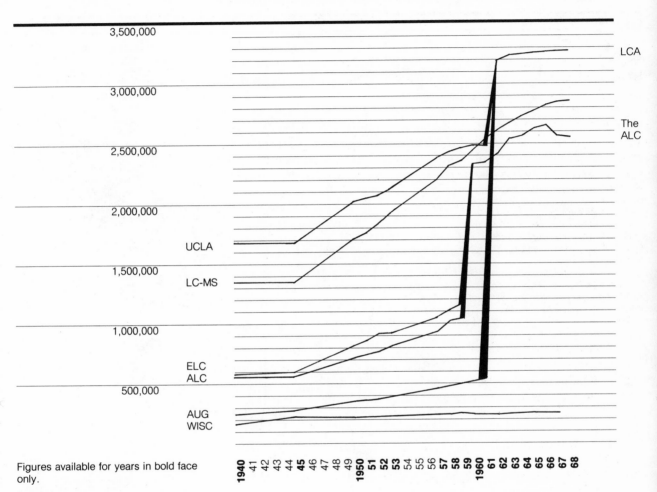

Figure 2

**Lutheran Membership
(Baptized)
1940–68**

LCA

The
ALC

3,500,000

3,000,000

2,500,000

2,000,000

UCLA

1,500,000

LC-MS

1,000,000

ELC
ALC

500,000

AUG
WISC

1940 41 42 43 44 **45** 46 47 48 49 **1950** **51** **52** **53** 54 55 56 **57** **58** **59** **1960** **61** 62 63 64 65 66 **67** **68**

Figures available for years in bold face
only.

Data supplied by Office of Research,
Statistics and Archives, Lutheran
Council/U.S.A., N.Y.

Figure 3

**Lutheran Churches
1850**

Number of churches
per county

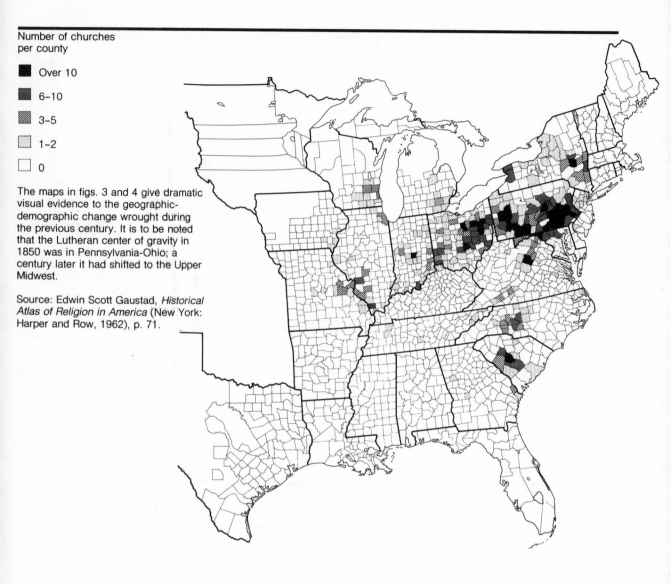

Over 10

6–10

3–5

1–2

0

The maps in figs. 3 and 4 give dramatic
visual evidence to the geographic-
demographic change wrought during
the previous century. It is to be noted
that the Lutheran center of gravity in
1850 was in Pennsylvania-Ohio; a
century later it had shifted to the Upper
Midwest.

Source: Edwin Scott Gaustad, *Historical
Atlas of Religion in America* (New York:
Harper and Row, 1962), p. 71.

Figure 4

**Lutherans as
Percentages of Total
Population in the
United States, 1970**

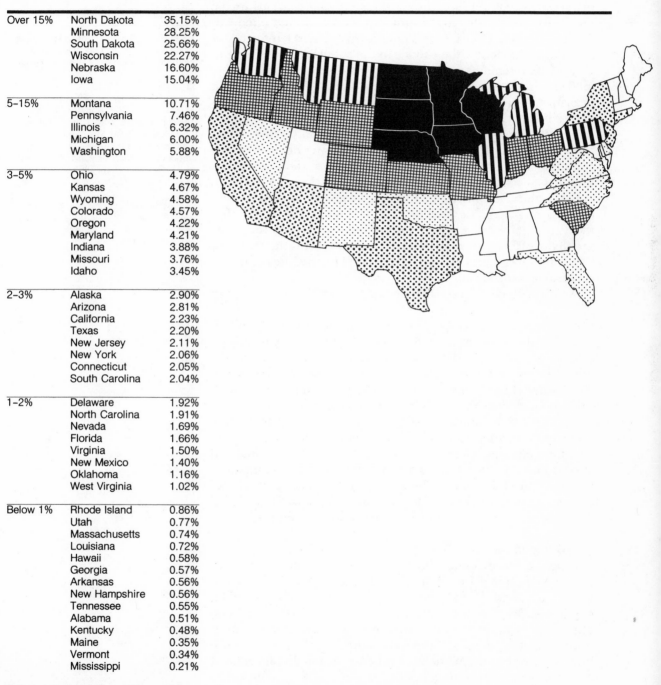

Over 15%	North Dakota	35.15%
	Minnesota	28.25%
	South Dakota	25.66%
	Wisconsin	22.27%
	Nebraska	16.60%
	Iowa	15.04%
5–15%	Montana	10.71%
	Pennsylvania	7.46%
	Illinois	6.32%
	Michigan	6.00%
	Washington	5.88%
3–5%	Ohio	4.79%
	Kansas	4.67%
	Wyoming	4.58%
	Colorado	4.57%
	Oregon	4.22%
	Maryland	4.21%
	Indiana	3.88%
	Missouri	3.76%
	Idaho	3.45%
2–3%	Alaska	2.90%
	Arizona	2.81%
	California	2.23%
	Texas	2.20%
	New Jersey	2.11%
	New York	2.06%
	Connecticut	2.05%
	South Carolina	2.04%
1–2%	Delaware	1.92%
	North Carolina	1.91%
	Nevada	1.69%
	Florida	1.66%
	Virginia	1.50%
	New Mexico	1.40%
	Oklahoma	1.16%
	West Virginia	1.02%
Below 1%	Rhode Island	0.86%
	Utah	0.77%
	Massachusetts	0.74%
	Louisiana	0.72%
	Hawaii	0.58%
	Georgia	0.57%
	Arkansas	0.56%
	New Hampshire	0.56%
	Tennessee	0.55%
	Alabama	0.51%
	Kentucky	0.48%
	Maine	0.35%
	Vermont	0.34%
	Mississippi	0.21%

Data supplied by Office of Research,
Statistics and Archives, Lutheran
Council/U.S.A., N.Y.

in and proceed from congregations rather than from "revival" crusades.

The Changing Face of the Churches

While the churches were experiencing the postwar boom, some noteworthy changes occurred in the visage of the church. At the parish level in urban centers, for example, the so-called flight to the suburbs took on huge proportions.[38] Congregations in the inner city and on the edge of the city's central area often suffered large losses of members. Some congregations felt forced for relocate and to follow the exodus to the suburbs. Those congregations that remained were either weakened to the point of ineffectiveness or were led to reorient both their mission and priorities. For most Protestant denominations these years marked the beginning of a new understanding of the church's role in the inner city, something which Roman Catholics had been engaged in for several years with varying degrees of success. The most urban of the Lutheran groups, the United Lutheran Church, quickly asked its Board of Social Mission to make a study of Christian social responsibility and to address itself to metropolitan problems. It was soon discovered that racial and cultural relations were intertwined with the other problems of the inner city church and, as a result, tentative beginnings were made in the integration of nonwhites into congregational worship and life.[39]

Another phase of postwar religious interest was to be seen in the revitalization of church colleges. The depression and the war had all but closed the doors of many colleges. But the G.I. Bill of Rights brought a flood of veterans to Lutheran colleges as it did to all American campuses. The general religious climate throughout the country served also to strengthen the church ties of most church-related schools. Hand in hand with this came a noticeable improvement in the financial status of the colleges. New buildings rose, endowments were augmented, and faculty salaries increased. Typical of the interest developed was the Christian Higher Education Year (CHEY) financial appeal in the United Lutheran Church and similar campaigns in other churches. Despite these successful efforts, however, the colleges soon found it necessary to utilize the newly authorized government loans for financing construction of buildings.[40]

The Campus Ministry

During the forties student ministries were conducted by three groups, the United Lutheran Church, the American Lutheran Conference, and the Missouri Synod. Between 1942 and 1944, Fredrik A. Schiotz, director of the Student Service Commission of the American Lutheran Conference, urged that the campus ministries of the United Lutheran Church and the conference be transferred to the National Lutheran Council. The council created a Commission on Student Service in 1945 and called its first executive in 1946. In this way, the church prepared itself to meet the heavy increase of postwar college enrollments. About one-half of the students in 1946 were war veterans, a circum-

486

38.
See Gibson Winter, *The Suburban Captivity of the Churches* (New York: Doubleday, 1960), for an analysis of this transformation.

39.
See ULCA, *Minutes . . . 1948*, pp. 300–308; ibid. *1954*, pp. 709–12; ibid. *1958*, pp. 732–66. Under the direction of the Board of Social Missions a scholarly symposium was published in three volumes entitled *Christian Social Responsibility*, ed. H. C. Letts (Philadelphia: Muhlenberg Press, 1957).

40.
ULCA, *Minutes . . . 1948*, pp. 353–58; ibid. *1954*, pp. 912–17; ELC, *Report . . . 1948*, p. 54; ibid. *1954*, p. 69.

stance that allowed the council to appropriate emergency funds from Lutheran World Action to provide facilities for campus ministries at crowded state and Lutheran colleges.

By 1949 the National Lutheran Council granted "division status" to the campus ministry and in 1956 altered its name to the Division of College and University Work (DCUW). A noticeable change in program occurred shortly. The earlier ministry was geared primarily to "preserve Lutheran students in the faith." This was enlarged to a "mission to the university," an attempt by the church to relate the Christian faith to the academic world. Moreover, a reorientation in the life of worship took place after 1950. Initially the students had been encouraged to worship in established congregations near the campus. In the fifties the trend was to hold services on the campus led by the campus pastor, or to organize campus congregations. In addition, under the new executive secretary (Donald R. Heiges succeeded Morris Wee in 1950), the DCUW conducted annual staff conferences, aided the Lutheran Student Association of America in its national assemblies, and embarked on a program of aid to foreign students and arranged study-work projects in Europe. Heiges reported in 1952 that the ministry of the DCUW "touched 600 of the 1800 colleges and universities in the United States. . . ."[41]

Service to War Refugees

One of the most dramatic stories in recent church history was the action of the churches to aid war refugees. Programs developed by Jews, Catholics, and Lutherans were rooted in the fact that a large majority of the refugees were co-religionists of these groups. Parallel but less extensive relief work was done on an interdenominational basis by Church World Service, with which the Lutheran program was coordinated. American Lutherans, as noted earlier, had begun raising funds in 1940. Lutheran World Action money together with material aid gathered by Lutheran World Relief after 1945 amounted to over $250 million.[42] It was a severe, and perhaps necessary, blow to Lutheran pride in this considerable achievement when American Jews, only about half as numerous as Lutherans, raised $100 million in a single year! Nevertheless, the funds and material aid provided by Lutherans made it possible to bring hope and new life to thousands of families and individuals uprooted by the tragedies of war.

Before the war was over, early in 1945, Ralph Long and Peter O. Bersell, representing the National Lutheran Council, and Lawrence Meyer, representing the Missouri Synod, visited Europe to lay plans for relief and reconstruction and to reactivate the war-disrupted Lutheran World Convention. The latter effort met with little enthusiasm from the Scandinavians (there was yet no contact with Germans); and the Missouri Synod, having no official connection with the convention, exhibited no interest in its rebirth. But when the team visited the Geneva staff of the World Council of Churches (in process of formation) it received good news from General Secretary W. A. Visser

41.
This section is largely a summary of the account found in Wentz, *Lutherans in Concert*, pp. 118–22.
42.
For accounts of the service to refugees and related actions see Richard W. Solberg, *As Between Brothers: The Story of Lutheran Response to World Need* (Minneapolis: Augsburg Publishing House, 1957). Cf. also Wentz, *Lutherans in Concert*; articles in *The Encyclopedia of the Lutheran Church*, 3 vols. (Minneapolis: Augsburg Publishing House, 1965); Stewart W. Herman, "Lutheran Service to Refugees," *Lutheran Quarterly* 2 (February 1950): 3–16; and "Lutheran Service to Immigrants," unpublished report of Lutheran Refugee Service, New York, October 1957, addendum to Agenda of NLC, Division of Welfare, September 19–21, 1956, Archives of Cooperative Lutheranism, Lutheran Council/U.S.A. The writer has also had access to the invaluable two-volume unpublished documentary account edited by Howard Hong, St. Olaf College, Northfield, Minn. (see n. 45, below).

t'Hooft: the World Council would be happy to work out an agreement to coordinate Lutheran relief efforts with the newly established World Council Department of Church Reconstruction. To facilitate this a Lutheran representative, Sylvester C. Michelfelder, was sent by the American Section of the Lutheran World Convention to Geneva to establish an office on the World Council precinct. On the same ship which carried Michelfelder to Europe in July 1945 was Stewart Herman, another American Lutheran, who was to join the World Council staff as its officer in charge of establishing contact with the German churches. A third American Lutheran, who was to be a pioneer in the refugee program, was Howard V. Hong, St. Olaf College professor of philosophy and budding Kierkegaard specialist. He arrived in Europe in December 1945 under the auspices of the World's YMCA program for prisoners of war.

Meanwhile, the American Section of the Lutheran World Convention sent Ralph Long, Franklin Clark Fry, and Johan A. Aasgaard to Europe in the fall of 1945. Their task was to assess the conditions among the churches and to reassemble the executive committee of the Lutheran World Convention at Copenhagen in December. This group received the resignation of Bishop Marahrens, president of the Lutheran World Convention, and appointed the Swedish archbishop, Erling Eidem, as acting president and Michelfelder as secretary. An officially called meeting of the executive committee was then arranged for Uppsala in July 1946.

President Fry also participated in the simultaneous study commission appointed by the Federal Council of Churches. Other members were Methodist bishop G. Bromley Oxnam and Episcopal bishop Henry Knox Sherrill. This commission, given a "guided tour" by American officials—who were inclined to say "the Germans are getting what they deserve"— returned with a report that gave little hope that American Protestants could be of much assistance because there was a ban on private relief shipments to Germany. To this Fry was utterly and furiously opposed and found it necessary publicly to denounce the American use of "starvation as an instrument of foreign policy." President Truman finally lifted the ban and thus opened the way to CRALOG (Council of Relief Agencies Licensed to Operate in Germany) of which Lutheran World Relief (established in 1945) was a chief member.

In this manner, the way was prepared for additional American Lutherans to join those already in Germany. Clifford Ansgar Nelson arrived to serve as short-term assistant to Michelfelder. Carl Schaffnit became the Lutheran representative for CRALOG. Julius Bodensieck, president of Wartburg Seminary, served as commissioner to Germany for the Lutheran World Convention, American Section; and his remarkable wife was soon engaged in service to Displaced Peoples (DPs).

It was the so-called spiritual ministry to DPs which engaged the attention of Michelfelder and his associates at the outset. In April 1946 he and Hong made contact with the United Nations

Relief and Rehabilitation Administration headquarters. Nelson surveyed the needs of the DPs and the Lutheran churches in exile. Schaffnit, completing his assignment with CRALOG, moved directly into DP work. Mrs. Bodensieck, now attached to the World Council staff, was similarly engaged. Hong had returned to St. Olaf in September 1946 to resume his teaching duties. The following January the annual meeting of the National Lutheran Council (American Section of the Lutheran World Convention) in Detroit approved a recommendation from Michelfelder that a permanent Service to Refugees be established and that Hong be appointed director, to take up his duties in June 1947.[43] The intervening months afforded Hong time to project some plans, one of which was to gather a cadre of volunteers to serve in Germany. One month after his appointment, the Lutheran World Convention/American Section approved his proposal to use college and seminary student volunteers to staff the program. During Hong's imaginative administration eighteen volunteer workers joined the refugee service.

Before the Service to Refugees was to get under way, the long-delayed meeting of the executive committee of the Lutheran World Convention (Uppsala, July 1946) had determined to reactivate and reorganize the world body. A constitution was drafted, a new name was chosen (Lutheran World Federation, proposed twenty-seven years earlier by John A. Morehead), and a place and date for a world assembly was selected (Lund, 1947). When the Lund Assembly made the refugee program an official responsibility of the Lutheran World Federation, the next step was to secure recognition and cooperation from the Allied occupation forces. Through Michelfelder's initiative—he had been elected the first executive secretary of the Lutheran World Federation—the LWF received a written agreement from the Preparatory Commission of the International Refugee Organization to open the door for Lutheran work among the refugees. In Richard Solberg's words, the Lutheran World Federation thus "began a long and mutually fruitful relationship with the IRO. . . ."[44]

With most of the essential preliminaries out of the way, Hong and his assistants plunged into the inchoate mass of forlorn refugees. The first task was to revive hope and to secure the religious moorings of the new "churches-in-exile," as the DP Lutherans were called. Refugee pastors were sought out and enabled to minister to their own people. Bicycles and motorcycles provided transportation to and from scattered congregations. Teachers and supplies for newly organized Sunday schools were brought in. Supplementary food was provided. But basic to the whole "spiritual ministry," as it was called, was the Lutheran World Federation/Service to Refugees objective to aid the DPs in ministering to their own people. One of the boldest and most fruitful of Hong's projects was the establishment of two study centers, one at Imbshausen near Goettingen, the other at Berchtesgaden in the Bavarian Alps, to provide

43.
Johan A. Aasgaard, president of the ELC and member of the LWC Executive Committee, called Hong from Detroit and intisted that he accept. Interview, Hong and E. Clifford Nelson, November 13, 1969.
44.
As Between Brothers, p. 138.

retreat facilities, conference opportunities, and year-round courses for pastors, Sunday school and Bible teachers, and student workers.[45]

One of the resolutions passed at the 1947 assembly in Lund urged that plans be devised for resettlement of the refugees. Hong was not slow to carry out this resolution. Once the spiritual program among the 227,750 Lutheran and non-German DPs in Germany and Austria was under way, he presented (December 1947) the U.S.A. Committee of the Lutheran World Federation with a proposal that the federation begin resettlement work in earnest. No action was taken, so in February 1948 he submitted a carefully worked out resettlement plan which asked the Lutheran World Federation to establish in Geneva under an executive officer a Resettlement and Emigration Division for non-German DPs and the ethnic Germans and German expellees. Area offices and reception centers were to be coordinated by Geneva. A revolving fund of $500,000 would be needed for overseas passage loans to the emigrants.[46] In May, Hong and Michelfelder were asked to come to New York to discuss the details of the plan and in June the U.S.A. Committee approved it, appointing Stewart Herman to be the first executive officer. The same month the U.S. Congress passed its DP Act and a year later legislation made it possible to include ethnic Germans for resettlement. Thus, when Hong had to return to his professional duties in 1949 he had the satisfaction of knowing that immense steps had been taken to cope with an even more immense problem.

By this time, Lutheran World Federation/Service to Refugees had become a global undertaking directed by Stewart Herman with vitality and efficiency. His vision and energies were dedicated not only to the immediate problem of the refugees but also to strengthening the Lutheran churches in every continent by the lines established in the resettlement activity. The American end of the program, including the enlisting of sponsors, settling legal problems, and developing cooperation at national and congregational levels, was chiefly the result of the genius and energy of Cordelia Cox, on the staff of the National Lutheran Council. Hardly an American congregation was without some lively involvement in this action, many of them "adopting" refugee families and individuals in order that they might begin life anew. Even the Missouri Synod expressed its desire to cooperate with the National Lutheran Council after Congress passed the Refugee Relief Act of 1953. The Lutheran Refugee Service, organized in 1954, thus became a joint National Lutheran Council–Missouri Synod program.[47]

Although statistics are a poor illustration of the human drama in which American Lutherans had engaged themselves, they nevertheless provide some indication of the magnitude of the enterprise. In 1952 it had been estimated that Lutheran World Federation/Service to Refugees had assisted almost 90,000 Lutheran emigrants, 37,000 of whom had been fully sponsored. By the sixties it was reported that 70,000 immigrants had been settled in the United States alone; Canada had received more

45.
A fascinating account of this project is found in Howard Hong, ed., "Lutheran World Federation Service to Refugees, 1947–1949," vol. 1, pp. 273–307.

46.
The original document is in ibid., pp. 309–16.

47.
Solberg, *As Between Brothers*, p. 154.

than 22,000, and Australia another 20,000. The program had involved 265 full-time workers plus innumerable others both in Europe and the receiving countries. Beyond the resettlement program, the not inconsiderable refugee work in Hong Kong and the Middle East together with the continuing support of orphaned missions had elicited the generous support of the churches. The direct overall cost to the Lutheran World Federation was above $4 million.[48]

In some ways, this vast missionary and refugee work, spearheaded by American Lutherans, was the high point of postwar church life. Although this was coterminous with the "religious boom," most, if not all, churchmen looked upon it as being something much more profound than a mass demonstration of religiosity.

491

Reorientation in World Missions

The nineteenth-century pattern of "doing foreign missions" persisted well into the present century. The church building, the school, and the hospital were the ordinary fruits as well as loci of missionary work. Preaching (church), teaching (school), and healing (hospital), accompanied in many instances by "agricultural" and "industrial" missions, reflected the main concerns of the American churches as they sought to obey the Great Commission in Asia and Africa.

At the end of World War II missiologists and church boards were placing the missionary enterprise under close scrutiny. Some of the concerns of the earlier Laymen's Foreign Mission Inquiry and the Hocking report, "Re-Thinking Missions" (1932), were surfacing in Lutheran circles without the accompaniment of responses conditioned by theological liberalism. Without cutting the evangelical nerve of missions, men were nevertheless asking substantive questions which, though present before, were being raised with a new intensity. Mid-twentieth century saw a revitalizing of the great non-Christian religions of the Orient and a ferment in the Islamic and Arab world. What was the relation of Christianity to other religions? Was the classical concept of revelation in need of reinterpretation? How should the church establish contact with the non-Christian religions? What were the best ways of proclaiming the gospel to them? Moreover, as far as the "mission" and "younger churches" were concerned, the turbulence of the post-World War II era was pushing new problems to the fore. How could indigenization be speeded? What kind of ecclesiastical constitutions were proper to non-Western churches unacquainted with the democratic tradition? In the face of new nationalisms, how could "younger churches" escape the stigma of being outposts of Western "imperialism" and rise above the charge of being little more than "ecclesiastical Western colonies"? What was the relation of the Western missionary to the younger churches? Was he really needed any longer? Furthermore, was it necessary or good for a Lutheran mission church to adopt the Lutheran confessions of the sixteenth century, when these confessions were hardly an existential part of its tradition? Would it not be more

48.
Encyclopedia of the Lutheran Church, 1:711–12; Wentz, *Lutherans in Concert,* pp. 139, 162; cf. E. Theodore Bachmann, *Epic of Faith* (New York: National Lutheran Council, 1952), p. 40. Accurate statistics on retention of refugees for the Lutheran church are impossible to obtain at this time.

honest to prepare new confessions, such as a *Confessio Africana* rather than a *Confessio Augustana*? Was it not the evangelical witness to the truth, embodied *in* the original confessions, that ought now be "confessed" in words and ways appropriate to the "younger churches"?[49] In addition to all these problems, the churches in the sixties confronted the question: In the face of the violent social and political changes in Africa, Asia, and Latin America, what is the role of the church in nation-building and economic development?

The questions that appeared with such sharpness during and after World War II have persisted with an unyielding tenacity to the present. All the answers were not in because all the questions had not been asked. One thing, however, emerged with clarity: the Lutheran churches in America were facing a reorientation in world missions. Future historians will have the task of describing and interpreting the change; for the present, it is necessary only to report on work that was being carried on by the major church bodies (ca. 1965) and their efforts at cooperation as the world moved into the last third of the twentieth century.

1. The American Lutheran Church (1960). The old American Lutheran Church (1930-60) brought three thriving mission fields into the merger of 1960: the India mission, the Lutheran Mission of New Guinea, and the Ethiopia mission. The Evangelical Lutheran Church (1917-60), with strong mission work reaching back into the nineteenth century, was operating in eight fields: Nationalist China and Hong Kong (the residuum of a large work on the mainland up to the Communist takeover in 1949); Madagascar; Zululand and the Cameroun in Africa; Colombia and Brazil in South America; Japan; and Mexico (administered by the Board of American Missions). The Lutheran Free Church (1897-1963) work was in three areas: Madagascar, Taiwan and Hong Kong, and Japan. The United Evangelical Lutheran Church supported missionaries in Japan and India (Santal).

2. The Lutheran Church in America (1962). The United Lutheran Church in America (1918-62) did mission work in eight countries: Argentina, British Guiana, Hong Kong, India, Japan, Liberia, Malaya, and Uruguay. Augustana (1860-1962) operated in India, Taiwan and Hong Kong, Tanganyika, North Borneo, Japan, and Uruguay. The American Evangelical Lutheran Church (1872-1962) and the Suomi Synod (1890-1962) operated in India (Santal) and Japan respectively. By 1970 Chile and Trinidad (1966) and Indonesia (1970) had been added to the Lutheran Church in America mission areas.

3. The Lutheran Church—Missouri Synod (1847). Beginning world missions in 1893, the Missouri Synod's outreach included India, Hong Kong and Taiwan, the Philippines, Japan, New Guinea, Korea, Brazil, Argentina, Chile, Central America, the Middle East, and Nigeria (a Synodical Conference undertaking).

4. The Wisconsin Evangelical Lutheran Synod (1892). A relatively small amount of overseas work was carried on by the

49.
A recognition of the problem and an evangelical resolution of it occurred in 1951 when the Batak Protestant Christian Church (Huria Kristen Batak Protestant [HKBP]) applied for membership in the LWF. The Hannover Assembly of the LWF (1952) admitted the Batak Church on *the basis of its own confession of faith* and its traditional *use* of Lutheran confessional literatures, especially Luther's Small Catechism. See R. B. Manikam, "Lutherans in Asia," in *Lutheran Churches of the World* (Minneapolis: Augsburg Publishing House, 1957), p. 203.

Wisconsin Synod in Nigeria (Synodical Conference), Northern Rhodesia, and Japan.

5. The National Lutheran Council. A program in Tanganyika (Tanzania) for the American Lutheran Church and the Lutheran Church in America was administered by the National Lutheran Council. This was a continuation of support begun under "orphaned missions" during and after World War II. Although administration of personnel was under the jurisdiction of the Lutheran Church in America, both churches subsidized the program.

6. Independent Organizations. A half-dozen groups, each drawing support from "interested friends" rather than a church body, were at work in various parts of the world: the Latin American Lutheran Mission (Mexico); the Lutheran Orient Mission (Kurdistan in northern Iran and Iraq); the Santal Board (India); the World Mission Prayer League (Bolivia, Ecuador, Mexico, India, Nepal, and West Pakistan); and the World Brotherhood Exchange. The World Brotherhood Exchange, later to become a part of the Lutheran Council in the U.S.A., was essentially a recruiting agency seeking skilled men and women (craftsmen, physicians, nurses, dentists, farmers, etc.) to donate their time and talents to mission fields and underdeveloped areas.

World War II had marked a turn in the road for world missions as well as for other church activities. For example, some churches, cut off from their prewar China fields, began work in Japan, Hong Kong, and Taiwan. New interests were developed in Latin America and Africa. All of the churches, as observed earlier, became involved in the support of German, Finnish, Norwegian, and Danish missions orphaned by the war. Between 1939 and 1947 orphaned missions received more than $2½ million from American Lutherans. To administer these and subsequent funds, the National Lutheran Council organized the Commission on Younger Churches and Orphaned Missions (CYCOM) in 1948. During the next five years another $3½ million were provided for this work, the scope of which exceeded both in activity and budget the work of the International Missionary Council with other Protestant orphaned missions. Not only was the work immense, it was also dramatic. For example, at the time of the division of Palestine CYCOM's representative, United Lutheran Church of America pastor Edwin Moll, with great courage and devotion ministered to the fleeing Arab refugees and began a program of service that attracted international interest. Meanwhile, another CYCOM representative, Fredrik A. Schiotz, arranged a partial compensation for Lutheran church properties taken over by the Israelis. In another part of the world, exciting rescues and hair-breadth escapes were negotiated by Evangelical Lutheran Church missionary Daniel Nelson, using a reconditioned airplane to evacuate church workers from areas being overrun by advancing Chinese Communists.

By 1955 the major portion of CYCOM's work was transferred to the Lutheran World Federation Department of World Mis-

493

sion because an international agency with headquarters in Switzerland was in a more favorable position to deal with international issues than an American office in New York City. CYCOM's contribution has been described in glowing terms by Frederick Wentz: "[CYCOM produced] a network of mutually valuable associations that bound together in Christian service the people of many nations on many continents, helping Lutheranism to be truly worldwide."[50] The guiding hand and animating spirit of CYCOM from 1948 to 1954 belonged to Fredrik A. Schiotz. Two years after Schiotz left CYCOM (1954) to become president of the Evangelical Lutheran Church, the National Lutheran Council restructured itself (1956) and created a Division of Lutheran World Federation Affairs that included a Department of World Missions Cooperation, the successor to CYCOM.

The impact of World War II on American Lutheranism was unquestionably deeper and more far-reaching than any chronicle can convey. The rise of European totalitarianism in the thirties and the emergence of controlled capitalism associated with the New Deal in America were the nonmusical overture to the cacaphony of the twenty years following 1939. The explosion of World War II, the trauma-producing agonies of the era, the nuclear sudden-death at Hiroshima, the alternating heating up and cooling off of the Cold War, and the launching of the space race by Russia's Sputnik (1957)—all of these apocalyptic events gave to the age the character of a classical drama moving with predestinarian relentlessness to its tragic end. Was the postwar religious boom, in which American Lutherans shared, really only some deux ex machina introduced to take men's minds off unveiled horrors still to be revealed? Or was the restless ferment, the widespread seriousness, more than a momentary exhilarating religiosity? Was it indeed a "Voice from the other side" calling for judgment beginning in the household of faith and for renewed proclamation by Word and deed that death shall not prevail against the body of Christ?

50.
Lutherans in Concert, p. 141.

21   The Struggle for Union

The desire to express the unity of the church was present among American Lutherans from their first years in the New World. Incongruous as it may have been, the theological controversy that marked so much of the Lutheran story emerged in large measure from a conscientious desire for church unity. What was debatable—and debated—was the definition of unity. Alongside this theological issue was the sociological problem of acculturation. The theological and the cultural walked side by side but not often hand in hand. Even within the national groupings, culture or ethos was not enough to assure unity. Most of the ethnic Lutheran islands were sadly fragmented by doctrinal and religious attitudes, some of which had been transplanted from Europe and often aggravated in America.

The story of the coming together of the various bodies of Lutherans in North America is a long and confusing one. This chapter will provide a comprehensive and comprehensible narrative of the main stages through which the drama unfolded after 1940. However, it would be wise to first take note of certain forces and factors that paralleled the union movement and, in fact, wove in and out of the movement itself, shaping it, conditioning it, and even changing its direction.

The Milieu of the Union Movement

The new climate during the forties and fifties possessed ingredients that both fostered and inhibited the union movement. Among these were influences from World War II and the changing theological atmosphere.

World War II Influences

The influence of World War II, like the Great Depression, will perhaps never be fully understood nor adequately assessed. The very profundity of the effects precludes anything but a simple pointing out of the obvious results that lay on the surface for all to see.

The inter-Lutheran cooperation that was born of the death and destruction of World War II was one of the forces for unity. The marshaling of resources within American Lutheranism not only brought new life to the enfeebled National Lutheran Council but helped to break down barriers between the cooperating groups within the council. Even the Missouri Synod, which had a long and unbroken tradition of isolation from Lutherans outside the Synodical Conference, found itself drawn irresistibly into a measure of involvement. Although Missouri hedged its cooperation with various and sundry conditions, the net result was ultimately to shatter the Synodical Conference and to bring the Missouri Synod into closer relationship with the churches of the National Lutheran Council.

Beyond improving inter-Lutheran relationships, the impact of World War II fostered Lutheran participation in the ecumenical movement. The only major National Lutheran Council church to remain outside the World Council of Churches during the latter's early years was the Evangelical Lutheran Church (Norwegian), which, by 1956, finally overcame its reluctance to join other Lutherans in the ecumenical world.

One aspect of wartime which must not be overlooked in seeking to measure the influence of those years on the union movement was the unprecedented mobility of population, both civilian and military. Wartime job opportunities drew thousands of men and women from small towns and rural areas into the industrial cities of the nation. As these people sought new church homes, they exhibited a noticeable lack of concern whether congregations were United Lutheran, American Lutheran, Augustana Lutheran, or Evangelical Lutheran. Many of the churches, they discovered, simply identified themselves as belonging to the National Lutheran Council. Missouri Synod migrants, however, were often kept for Missouri congregations by the refusal of letters of transfer to non-Missouri Lutheran congregations. Even so, many Missouri members found their way into other than Missouri congregations and vice versa. What eventually happened to institutional loyalties goes without saying.

A similar pattern emerged among those who served in the armed forces. Few if any Lutherans in uniform inquired as to the church affiliation of a Lutheran chaplain before participating in Holy Communion. As a matter of fact, intercommunion was practiced among Lutherans in the military decades before the official ecclesiastical proclamation of pulpit and altar fellowship. Again, it goes without saying what this did to the general attitude of Private Joe Doaks who might sometimes have worn a "Lutheran" dogtag in addition to his regular Protestant identification.

The dynamics of the wartime situation simply did not permit Lutherans to live in isolation from each other or, in many cases, from non-Lutherans. The problem, which many leaders were unwilling or unprepared to admit, was not Lutheran union but rather Lutheran particularity in a religious pluralism. Lutheran union was already long overdue; the question that now clamored for an answer was how to maintain a Lutheran identity and yet participate honestly in the ecumenical movement.

The Changing Theological Climate

It has been said with justification that American Lutherans contributed little or nothing to the theological renaissance during the thirties and forties. Many Protestants, having been thrust from the agonies of the depression into the pathos of World War II, were rediscovering the perennial relevance of Reformation theology. Dissatisfied with and disillusioned by liberalism's "ballet of bloodless categories," they were prepared to listen to European evangelical theologians who saw the contemporaneity of such Reformation themes as the theology of the cross, salvation by pure grace received through personal faith, the authority of the Word of God in sermon and sacrament, and the believer's participation in the priesthood of Christ.[1] American Lutherans, who in large measure had retained these treasures, albeit in the earthen vessels of an unhistorical confessionalism and an intellectualistic orthodoxy, had not heeded the cry of a theologically exhausted Anglo-American Protestantism to come over and help.[2] Most American Lutheran theologians were either reproducing what they firmly believed was the faith of the fathers or attempting to introduce the churches to the vast field of biblical research via the historical method and thus to provide a new approach to biblical and confessional theology. Those who sought to uphold biblical inerrancy and generally to repristinate "orthodoxy" might be called Old Lutherans; those who sought to relate contemporary theology and the Luther renaissance to American Lutheranism, Neo-Lutherans. All, however, were speaking *within* Lutheranism.

It was the position of Old Lutheranism on infallibility which the American Lutheran Conference churches in the National Lutheran Council sought to protect in the Minneapolis Theses (1925) and which the Missouri Synod enunciated in its Brief Statement (1932). The Neo-Lutherans preferred to speak of the infallibility of the message ("the Word of God") of the Scriptures, thus distinguishing between the Word of God and the Scriptures but not separating them. It was primarily here that the battle was joined in the union movement from the forties to 1962, and resumed by parties within the Missouri Synod between 1962 and 1973.

Intimately associated with the theological climate of Lutheranism, of course, was the attitude of colleges and seminaries. Religion departments in the colleges tended to be conservative into the forties, largely because they were staffed by men educated in the categories of Old Lutheranism. There were individual professors in some colleges who were liberal, judged by prevailing ideas, but they were generally exceptions to the rule. It has been pointed out in a previous chapter that Neo-Lutheranism began to manifest itself in United Lutheran seminaries as early as the twenties. At Augustana Seminary the break with Old Lutheranism began in 1931. Before World War II Luther Theological Seminary gave only infrequent hints of breaking out of the circle of prevailing "orthodoxy." When this did occasionally occur it was largely the result of pietistic dissatisfaction with orthodoxism. A discernible change appeared about 1947 when some professors began to approach the Scriptures theologically and historically rather than with the a priori of inerrancy and verbal inspiration. What was a small voice in 1947 became a large noise within a decade.

In due course, groups of alarmed defenders of the faith in all churches began to form in order to protest the encroachment of "liberalism." The flinging of charges of "neo-orthodoxy," "existentialism," "heresy," and "modernism" at the colleges and

1.
For a careful statement of this rediscovery see Sydney E. Ahlstrom, "Continental Influences on American Theology Since World War I," *Church History* 27 (September 1958): 256–72. Cf. also idem, *Theology in America* (Indianapolis: Bobbs-Merrill, 1967), pp. 77–84.
2.
"Lutheran Isolation," *Christian Century*, November 4, 1942, pp. 1342–43.

seminaries became the hallmark of self-styled "Confessional Lutherans" and "Lutherans Alert." It was evident that a theological ferment of some magnitude had taken the scene. Indebted in some ways to neo-orthodoxy or dialectical theology, the leadership of the "liberal" movement insisted that it was unequivocally Lutheran.

It would be asking too much of readers to plunge into the maze of Lutheran unity efforts in the forties and fifties without some understanding of the developments described above. But with this sketchy orientation the ecclesiastical politics of those years ought to be somewhat less baffling and forbidding.

Lutheranism and Ecumenism

If one defined ecumenism as the striving for unity, the Lutheran role in it, like Gaul, was divided into three parts: (1) the Lutheran unity movement in the United States, (2) the Canadian sector, and (3) American Lutherans and international ecumenism.

The Unity Movement in the United States

Before World War II the pace of progress toward Lutheran unity was leisurely. As described earlier, the burst of enthusiasm that accompanied the 400th anniversary of the Reformation and the cooperative spirit forged by World War I produced the Norwegian Lutheran Church (ELC) in 1917, the United Lutheran Church in 1918, and the National Lutheran Council, likewise in 1918. Two main groupings of Lutherans in America, the Synodical Conference (1872) and the newly established National Lutheran Council, represented somewhat imprecisely the polarization within confessional Lutheranism.

We have seen that by 1920 the National Lutheran Council, despite the fact that the Missouri Synod was not a member, reflected two theological points of view. Although all council churches were unhappy with the exclusivism of Missouri, some felt that Missourians were "more Lutheran" than United Lutherans. Thus, many Midwestern Lutherans in the council began to move closer together. Between 1925 and 1930 these churches, without separating from the National Lutheran Council, had given themselves organizational expression in the American Lutheran Conference (1930).[3]

We have already described the unsuccessful attempts of the United Lutheran Church to further Lutheran unity by its conversations in the thirties with the Missouri Synod and the old American Lutheran Church (1930). The polarities between Neo-Lutheranism and Old Lutheranism, evident in these discussions, were destined to continue for at least two decades. Furthermore, as noted already, the American Lutheran Church, while holding talks with the United Lutherans, had also been negotiating with the Missouri Synod. The Common Confession, which it worked out with the latter, was a dressed-up version of Old Lutheranism calculated to make it attractive to the American Lutheran Church and acceptable to Missouri because no substantive alteration of Old Lutheranism was in-

3.
For a discussion of this see chapter 19. Cf. Fred W. Meuser, *The Formation of the American Lutheran Church* (Columbus, Ohio: Wartburg Press, 1958), pp. 235–49; and E. Clifford Nelson, *The Lutheran Church Among Norwegian-Americans* (Minneapolis: Augsburg Publishing House, 1960), 2:281–312.

4.
E. C. Fendt, "The Theology of the 'Common Confession,'" *Lutheran Quarterly* 2 (August 1950): 308–23. Fendt declared: "The aim is not to say anything new, but to state the old faith in modern language" (p. 311).
5.
American Lutheran Church, *Reports and Actions of the Constituting Convention*, April 22–24, 1960, p. 98.
6.
American Lutheran Conference, "Proceedings . . . 1940," *Journal of Theology of the American Lutheran Conference* 6 (1941): 85–86, 90–91.
7.
Ibid., pp. 312–13; and ibid. 7 (1942): 388–90, 457–65, 542–54.
8.
Ibid. 7 (1942): 860.
9.
Ibid. 8 (January 1943). This issue is devoted to this important meeting, including reports, minutes, and addresses.

tended.[4] After the formation of the new American Lutheran Church (1960), the agreement between the old American Lutheran Church and Missouri in the Common Confession was often advanced as a reason for the new American Lutheran Church to seek pulpit and altar fellowship with the Missouri Synod. The constituting convention of the new American Lutheran Church was informed: "The American Lutheran Church has instructed its Standing Committee on Relations to Lutheran Churches to 'continue official negotiations already established by the united Churches.' . . ."[5]

The year 1940 had marked a definite turning point in inter-Lutheran relations. One need but recall the fate of the Pittsburgh Agreement and the attempt of the former American Lutheran Church to seek closer ties with Missouri. Meanwhile, the pressures of World War II began to thrust massive responsibilities on the whole of American Lutheranism. In this setting the American Lutheran Conference in 1940 asked for a meeting of all Lutherans to consider the problem of war-orphaned missions and other "matters of common interest." At the same time it sought a redefinition of the objectives of the conference to promote the "welfare of Lutherans in America as a whole."[6]

Subsequently, several significant meetings were held: the First Columbus All-Lutheran Conference, January 20, 1941; the National Lutheran Council and Editors Meeting, Pittsburgh, January 28–29, 1942; and the Second Columbus Conference, May 14–15, 1942.[7] The consensus of all these meetings, in which representatives of Missouri took some part, was the urgency of greater Lutheran unity and cooperation. The National Lutheran Council proposed a Lutheran federation; the Second Columbus Conference urged the enlargement of the American Lutheran Conference and the calling of a "free conference" by the National Lutheran Council. Meanwhile, the American Lutheran Church declared its willingness to establish fellowship with "either or both" the United Lutheran Church and the Missouri Synod.[8] This latter declaration was susceptible to several interpretations: (1) the American Lutheran Church was eager to be the bridge between the United Lutherans and Missouri; (2) the American Lutheran Church was ignorant of or disregarded the basic theological difference between the United Lutheran Church and Missouri; or (3) the American Lutheran Church hoped to swing the United Lutheran Church into the Old Lutheranism which both the Pittsburgh Agreement and the Brief Statement enunciated. Whatever motives or combination of motives existed, it was apparent on all sides in 1942 that strenuous efforts were being made to advance the cause of Lutheran unity.

In this atmosphere of heightened interest in a broader expression of Lutheran unity, the American Lutheran Conference met in Rock Island, Illinois (November 11–12, 1942).[9] Its Commission on Lutheran Unity, created in 1938, said, ". . . the American Lutheran Conference must leave the door open, as far as it is concerned, for all Lutheran bodies." It further asked that "the Executive Committee . . . be instructed to negotiate with all

499

other Lutheran bodies, looking toward a more inclusive organization. . . . As a necessary step to this end this Conference urges its constituent members to invite into pulpit and altar fellowship those Lutheran groups with whom they are not now in fellowship."[10] This resolution, it should be noted, was largely the work of Augustana Synod leaders Ernest E. Ryden (president of the conference), synod president Peter O. Bersell, and Conrad Bergendoff. Ryden and Bersell had advanced the idea of expanding the conference at the first and second Columbus meetings; Bergendoff was the author of the sentence on offering pulpit and altar fellowship. What does not appear in the minutes was the resistance of two Norwegian Lutheran leaders to what they considered Augustana Synod pressure to include the United Lutheran Church in the American Lutheran Conference. Johan A. Aasgaard resented the "pushiness of the Swedes" (the sociological factor of Norwegian-Swedish tension is not to be underestimated in inter-Lutheran relations), and Thaddaeus F. Gullixson feared the inclusion of the United Lutheran Church because of its "liberal" theological position. Lars W. Boe, a close personal friend of both the aforementioned, took a broader view of the situation; his primary concern was to preserve the National Lutheran Council as the forum for Lutheran unity. In order to facilitate the union movement he, like Bergendoff, urged an immediate declaration of pulpit and altar fellowship.[11] His plea went unheeded and a short time later he died.

Meanwhile, the conference executive committee, which had been instructed to *negotiate* with other Lutherans and to *invite* all into pulpit and altar fellowship, met in Minneapolis, January 26, 1943. The action of the committee represented a subtle shift from the intention of the 1942 Rock Island resolution. The dominating figure in the executive committee was Gullixson (Bersell was absent) and largely through his influence the committee determined that before it could carry out the instructions of the conference it would need to know what conditions would be necessary preliminary to negotiations and the invitation to pulpit and altar fellowship. Thereupon, the executive committee charged the commission "with a study of the minimum basis for pulpit and altar fellowship." In other words, the invitation to pulpit and altar fellowship with the United Lutheran Church (which would accept) and the Missouri Synod (which would reject) would be delayed. As a matter of fact, it was effectively delayed, by subsequent events, for more than a quarter of a century, until 1969.

The Commission on Lutheran Unity turned to J. Michael Reu to prepare a statement of the "minimum basis," a task which his death prevented him from completing.[12] The commission then turned to Gullixson and Harold Yochum, president of the American Lutheran Church's Michigan District, to draft a document. Largely the work of the former,[13] the statement was called the "Overture on Lutheran Unity." Together with a copy of the Minneapolis Theses (1925) and parts of the Chicago Theses (1919), it was sent to all Lutheran bodies in America.[14] Although reaction within the Missouri Synod was favorable—

10.
Ibid., p. 84.

11.
Letter to Aasgaard, October 29, 1942, Lars W. Boe Papers, St. Olaf College Archives, Northfield, Minn.

12.
Reu's obituary in *Lutheran Outlook*, November 1943, p. 264.

13.
Gullixson told the writer that Reu's statement was too heavily weighted with academic theology; therefore, in the interest of simplification, Gullixson wrote a new draft which Yochum approved with minor changes (interview, August 25, 1955). Cf. "Forgotten History in Lutheran Unity," *Lutheran Outlook*, January 1944, pp. 4–5.

14.
American Lutheran Conference, *Convention Report . . . November 15-17, 1944*, pp. 7–8, 15–20. The entire document is found in *Lutheran Outlook*, January 1944, pp. 10–12.

in some instances enthusiastic—the synod itself took no notice of it. One observer said it was "sidetracked." The synod did, however, consider membership in the National Lutheran Council, but expectedly it was voted down.[15]

The United Lutheran Church's Commission on Relations to American Lutheran Church Bodies reported at the Minneapolis convention (1944) that it had received the Overture. Its comment was: "This document was deemed neither forward-looking, fruitful, nor necessary as an approach to our common problem. In the Washington Declaration we already have . . . a better statement, already approved by us, of the real tests of evangelicalism."[16] From the point of view of emerging Neo-Lutheranism this was indeed true; from the point of view of Old Lutheranism it was grossly inadequate. An examination of the contents of the Overture reveals the specific reason that it was not warmly received. The document warned against doctrinal latitudinarianism, insisted on "genuine" acceptance of the confessions, and asserted the necessity of extraconfessional doctrinal theses as testimonies to unity—all of which were clear references to what some, perhaps a majority, of the American Lutheran Conference considered to be United Lutheran Church faults. However, the Overture continued, on the basis of the Minneapolis Theses (American Lutheran Conference), the Brief Statement (Missouri Synod), and the Pittsburgh Agreement (United Lutheran Church–American Lutheran Church), pulpit and altar fellowship could be established among Lutherans.[17] The reason for such a hope, it was declared, was that those three documents were "in essential accord with one another." Here was the key phrase in the document and, as a matter of fact, in the whole carefully calculated unity strategy. The Overture observed correctly and forthrightly that the American Lutheran Conference could have no fellowship with the United Lutheran Church on the basis of its Washington (1920), Savannah (1934), and Baltimore (1938) declarations, all three of which addressed the problems of ecumenism, lodge membership, confessional integrity, and scriptural authority in ways unacceptable to Old Lutheranism.

Just as the years 1919-25 had revealed the presence of two sharply defined attitudes within the National Lutheran Council, the years 1940-44 demonstrated the presence of precisely the same attitudes within the American Lutheran Conference. The Augustana Synod, not a partner in the original negotiations that produced the American Lutheran Conference but nevertheless drawn into its membership before the influence of its new theological professors could be felt, wished to include all Lutherans in fellowship. Practically speaking, this meant extending fellowship to the United Lutheran Church only, because the intransigence of the Missourians eliminated any realistic hope of unity with them. Opposing this were the other members of the conference, notably the Norwegian Church, which feared the United Lutheran Church[18] and preferred the Missouri Synod. Any fellowship with this church should be balanced by fellowship with Missouri, but only on the basis of

15.
For reactions and "action" on the Overture, see *Lutheran Outlook,* January 1944, pp. 69, 131–32, 163–64, 234–35.

16.
ULCA, *Minutes . . . Minneapolis, October 11-17, 1944,* pp. 240–42. The convention, assembled in Central Lutheran Church, a congregation of the Norwegian Lutheran Church of America, softened the unnecessarily candid language of the committee lest the rejection of the Overture be a slap at NLCA hospitality.

17.
The statements are available for comparison in Richard C. Wolf, *Documents of Lutheran Unity in America* (Philadelphia: Fortress Press, 1966). For a history of the Pittsburgh Agreement see E. Clifford Nelson, "A Case Study in Lutheran Unity Efforts," in *The Maturing of American Lutheranism,* ed. H. T. Neve and B. A. Johnson (Minneapolis: Augsburg Publishing House, 1968), pp. 207–21.

18.
The United Lutheran Church was regarded by many to be liberal not only in theology but in its practice. It was judged as too lax about lodge membership, too casual about the use of alcoholic beverages, and too permissive about certain amusements, especially social dancing. Missouri and American Lutheran Church attitudes toward drinking and dancing were not unlike those of the United Lutheran Church, but the Norwegian Lutheran Church was strangely silent in this regard.

501

assurances, such as the Overture proposed, that there would be "genuine and wholehearted" acceptance of Old Lutheranism. In 1944 the Norwegian Lutheran Church (ELC in 1946) surprisingly declared itself ready for fellowship with all Lutherans because it felt that the doctrinal statements of the American Lutheran Conference (Minneapolis and Chicago Theses) were in "essential agreement" with the position of the United Lutheran Church and Missouri. Therefore, it continued, "we believe no additional theses, statements, or agreements are necessary for fellowship among American Lutherans." This seemingly advanced position must be seen in light of and as a response to the Overture and not as an evidence of Neo-Lutheranism.[19] That this was true could be seen in the attitude of its official organ, the *Lutheran Herald*. Editor Olaf G. Malmin commented that his church was prepared for fellowship with the Missouri Synod but not with the United Lutheran Church. The latter, he said, called into question the inspiration of Holy Writ ("as we understand it"), was soft on "unionism," and tolerant of pastors who were lodge members.[20]

The next four years saw no basic change in this pattern. Although a project for a common hymnal and service book was successfully launched (the Evangelical Lutheran Church hesitated to participate because it feared that the spirit and theology of the United Lutheran Church would dominate the venture), the basic problems reaching back to 1919 continued to be identified as obstacles to unity.

The decade following 1947 saw the organizational crystallization of the two attitudes. In the process, three members of the American Lutheran Conference (the American Lutheran Church, the Evangelical Lutheran Church, and the United [Danish] Evangelical Lutheran Church) merged to establish the American Lutheran Church (1960). Later (1963) the latter received the Lutheran (Norwegian) Free Church into its membership. Subsequently, the United Lutheran Church drew to itself three other churches (Augustana, the Finnish Suomi Synod, and the Danish American Evangelical Lutheran Church); together they formed the Lutheran Church in America (1962).

The story of this decade revolves almost exclusively around the churches of the National Lutheran Council. The Synodical Conference was beginning to experience stress and strain that eventually led to its demise and left Missouri trying to bring itself into relationship with others. Meanwhile, Missouri stood in the wings while the drama on the National Lutheran Council stage became two separate actions. Although the chronicle of events has been recorded elsewhere, it is well to mention them here in this broader frame of reference.[21]

Three National Lutheran Council member bodies met in June 1948—the Evangelical Lutheran Church, the Augustana Lutheran Church, and the United Evangelical Lutheran Church. Two other major groups, the United Lutheran Church and the American Lutheran Church, met in October. Moreover, the American Lutheran Conference convened in Novem-

19.
NLCA, *Report . . . 1944*, pp. 404–5.
20.
Lutheran Herald, July 4, 1944, pp. 540–41. He said that if the United Lutheran Church was sincere in its profession of the Pittsburgh Agreement, that would change the case.
21.
What follows is largely based on the account in Nelson, *Lutheran Church Among Norwegian-Americans*, 2:315–22. Full documentation is in the footnotes of that volume and is not repeated here.

ber. In all of these meetings Lutheran unity was a paramount issue.

The first group to meet was the Augustana Church. In response to a memorial from one of its regional conferences, the synod requested its executive council to invite all National Lutheran Council churches to discuss organic merger of the council or federation as an intermediate step.

The Evangelical Lutheran Church, meeting the same week, anticipated an invitation from the United Evangelical Lutheran Church (meeting the following week) to begin merger conversations. Unofficial overtures from United Evangelical Lutheran Church leaders led T. F. Gullixson to present a "resolution of friendship" for the United Evangelical Lutheran Church and to ask the Evangelical Lutheran Church to name a union committee to negotiate with the United Evangelical Lutheran Church and "other constituent bodies of the American Lutheran Conference." It should be noted that the resolution excluded the possibility of conversations with the United Lutheran Church.[22]

The president of the United Evangelical Lutheran Church, Niels C. Carlsen, urged merger with the Evangelical Lutheran Church, but his synod feared that its small Danish-background constituency would be completely swallowed up by the much larger Evangelical Lutheran Church (Norwegian background). Consequently, a new proposal was adopted: that the United Evangelical Lutheran Church invite two or more bodies of the American Lutheran Conference to discuss organic union.

When the American Lutheran Conference met in Detroit, November 10-12, 1948, unity resolutions were passed calling for an all-Lutheran free conference under the auspices of the National Lutheran Council and commending the various efforts for unity being initiated within the conference and the council. Following the convention the five presidents—J. A. Aasgaard (Evangelical Lutheran Church), P. O. Bersell (Augustana), T.O. Burntvedt (Lutheran Free Church), N. C. Carlsen (United Evangelical Lutheran Church), and E. Poppen (American Lutheran Church)—met to consider further steps. Two decisions were reached: (1) that the National Lutheran Council be petitioned to call a free conference; and (2) that dates be determined for meetings which Bersell and Carlsen were contemplating calling in order to implement the resolutions of their churches. It was decided that a meeting of council representatives be held at the Augustana headquarters in Minneapolis on January 4, 1949, and that the American Lutheran Conference presidents meet in the Evangelical Lutheran Church headquarters, also in Minneapolis, the next day, January 5, 1949.

Considerable tension developed around the calling of these meetings. The Evangelical Lutheran Church officials maintained that the Augustana proposal came as a surprise and seemed intended to undercut the meeting of January 5. Bersell, however, said that Carlsen had "graciously" agreed to allow the National Lutheran Council meeting to precede the January 5 conference.[23] This was verified by Carlsen's letter to the editor

22.
Prominent leadership in this matter was given by Ole G. Malmin, editor of the *Lutheran Herald*. See John M. Jensen, "An Old Soldier Who Will Not Fade Away," *Lutheran Standard*, January 10, 1967, p. 9.
23.
Interview, Bersell and E. Clifford Nelson, May 20, 1959.

of the *Lutheran Standard* (American Lutheran Church) who had inquired about the matter. Carlsen reported that the Detroit meeting of conference presidents decided on the dates for the discussions. "Dr. Bersell seemed to be quite concerned about getting the meeting which he was calling the day before we had ours. *No objections were made* [italics added]."[24]

The meetings of January 4 and 5, 1949, proved to be fateful for a large majority of American Lutheranism. In response to Augustana's invitation representatives of the eight National Lutheran Council bodies (henceforth known as "the Committee of Thirty-Four") convened according to schedule. The Evangelical Lutheran Church representatives (Aasgaard, Gullixson, and Mr. Sigurd H. Holstad) were present only as observers because they maintained that no mandate had been given them by their church.

The proposal before the group was two-pronged: (1) organic merger of the bodies in the National Lutheran Council, or (2) federation of the National Lutheran Council as an intermediate step. After a full day of discussion, Emmanuel Poppen offered the following resolution: "Resolved, that it is the sense of this group that a closer organizational affiliation of the participating bodies in the National Lutheran Council is desirable and should be sought by all proper means."[25]

In the discussion, Franklin Clark Fry of the United Lutheran Church argued forcefully in favor of "a Church with strong federative aspects." Henry F. Schuh, an American Lutheran Church representative, not only pleaded for such action but insisted that a definite time be indicated when a federation should become an organic union. "What are we waiting for?" he asked. "We are already cooperating here at home and in all parts of the world."[26] When a ballot was taken on the resolution, not a dissenting vote was cast. The group then voted to appoint a committee of fifteen to prepare a structural plan and report to the full Committee of Thirty-Four the next autumn.

Although the records show only unanimous support for the above proposals, at least two churches voiced their objections. President Carlsen of the United Evangelical Lutheran Church pointed out that his church would hesitate taking such steps because of the laxity in practice within the United Lutheran Church regarding dancing, drinking, and lodge membership of pastors. Gullixson then objected to Schuh's intimation that the National Lutheran Council, as it now existed, had outlived its usefulness. Moreover, if there was to be union it must be on the basis of doctrinal agreement, especially since there were evidences that United Lutheran Church seminaries were teaching views on Scripture that were contrary to what had been held in the Evangelical Lutheran Church for the last one hundred years.

The next day, January 5, 1949, the representatives of the American Lutheran Conference met in the Evangelical Lutheran Church headquarters under the chairmanship of Carlsen. An informal approach had been made to secure Missouri Synod support and presence at this meeting by inviting Theodore

504

24.
Letter to E. W. Schramm, January 11, 1950, American Lutheran Church Archives, Wartburg Seminary, Dubuque, Iowa.
25.
See "Minutes, Conference on Lutheran Unity, Augustana Church Headquarters, Minneapolis, Minn., Jan. 4, 1949," J. K. Jensen Papers, Northwestern Lutheran Seminary Library, St. Paul, Minn.
26.
"A Move Toward Unity," *Lutheran Outlook* 14 (February 1949): 55-56.

Graebner, editor of the *Lutheran Witness*. Although it proved abortive, the gesture indicated the direction in which the group—with the exception of Bersell—wished to move.[27] During the meeting considerable discussion was devoted to the action of the previous day. Gullixson spoke critically and at length about the United Lutheran Church. He specifically attacked Joseph Sittler's recently published book, *The Doctrine of the Word*, which criticized the Old Lutheran view of verbal inspiration.[28] At the conclusion of the day the group adopted a resolution that every effort should be made to bring about the plans of the previous day's meeting but that there ought to be no objection to lesser approaches to unity within the conference.

During the next year the gap between the two groups in the council widened and soon became unbridgeable. In 1950 the plan proposed by the Committee of Thirty-Four (merger or federation of the council) was defeated.[29] This meant that the only remaining union movement was that initiated by the United Evangelical Lutheran Church with behind-the-scenes encouragement from the Evangelical Lutheran Church. Since the original resolution included all members of the American Lutheran Conference, invitations were extended to the Augustana Church and the Lutheran Free Church. Both accepted, but with some reservations. The Augustana Church naturally preferred its own larger proposal, while the Free Church was nervous about losing its "freedom."

The stage was now set for the organic union of the American Lutheran Conference. In 1952 the Joint Union Committee of the five churches presented for action a statement on faith and life called "The United Testimony," which was a curious blend—or, more correctly, juxtapositioning—of Old Lutheranism and Neo-Lutheranism.[30] The ambivalence in the United Testimony was completely erased in the "Confession of Faith," Article IV of the constitution (1956) for the new church (1960). It defined the authority of the Scriptures in the language of the Minneapolis Theses (" [the Church] accepts all the canonical books of the Old and New Testaments as a whole and in all their parts as the divinely inspired, revealed, and inerrant Word of God . . .").[31]

The events of the decade from 1952 to 1962 had all the ingredients of a Greek drama moving irreversibly to its denouement. The Augustana Church withdrew from the conference merger movement because it was "not open to all Lutheran general bodies and . . . did not include the consideration of the subject of ecumenical relations."[32] It now turned toward the United Lutheran Church. In 1954 the American Lutheran Conference was officially dissolved in de facto recognition of the existing circumstances in American Lutheranism. The Lutheran Free Church, as a result of congregational referendums in 1955 and 1957, found it necessary to remove itself from the projected union. But later (1961), affirmative results of a third referendum paved the way for the Free Church to join the American Lutheran Church in 1963. Dissenters who claimed the name Lutheran Free Church were denied this by the courts.

505

27.
See Niels C. Carlsen Papers, American Lutheran Church Archives. A letter from Herbert Lindemann to Carlsen (December 31, 1948) said that Graebner had requested him to attend the meeting. But because of the roundabout manner of invitation, Lindemann expressed hesitation about being present. Who approached Graebner and why? Why was not Behnken asked?

28.
Sittler's book was considered heretical by Old Lutherans. E. C. Fendt noted that the United Lutheran Church did not discipline Sittler for his views. He continued, "In the ALC the president of the Church would have him immediately charged with heresy." See Minutes, Special Commission on Relations to American Lutheran Bodies of the ULCA and the Commission on Union and Fellowship of the ALC, March 13, 1952, p. 8, American Lutheran Church Archives.

29.
National Lutheran 19 (September 1950): 12.

30.
Wolf, *Documents*, p. 501. Interview, Bernhard Christensen and E. Clifford Nelson, May 28, 1957. Cf. Arden, *Augustana Heritage*, pp. 388-94.

31.
Wolf, *Documents*, pp. 532-33.

32.
Augustana Church, *Report . . . 1953*, pp. 340-43.

They renamed themselves the Association of Free Lutheran Congregations.[33]

In 1955 the United Lutheran Church and Augustana invited all Lutherans to "consider such an organic union as will give real evidence of our unity in the faith, and to proceed to draft a constitution and devise organizational procedures to effect union." The Missouri Synod declined on the basis of existing doctrinal differences; the Joint Union Committee declined because the three bodies (American Lutheran Church, United Evangelical Lutheran Church, and Evangelical Lutheran Church) were committed to their own union.[34] This was consummated at the constituting convention of the American Lutheran Church which took place in Minneapolis, April 22-24, 1960.[35] The new church began official operations January 1, 1961. Its first president, Fredrik A. Schiotz, told the *Christian Century* that the new body "would not want another organic union unless it included both the Missouri Synod and the forthcoming Lutheran Church in America. . . . Failure to include the Missouri Synod . . . would create 'complications.' . . ."[36]

Meanwhile, the Lutheran Church in America was quickly taking shape. The United Lutheran–Augustana invitation had been accepted by the American Evangelical Lutheran Church (Danish) and the Finnish Evangelical Lutheran Church (Suomu Synod), and together these four created the Joint Commission on Lutheran Unity (JCLU) to prepare the necessary documents for organic union. In 1956 United Lutheran Church President Franklin Clark Fry delivered a statement on Lutheran unity which was immediately recognized as an unofficial charter for the new church and as a guide to the joint commission. Speaking of the two principles of unity and truth, he urged that those churches seeking unity should not neglect the truth and that those intent on upholding the truth must not neglect unity. Both principles, rooted in the biblical witness, must be viewed as centering in the Word of God which creates the church.[37]

The doctrinal statement, approved by the four churches, affirmed the Christ-centered and soteriological character of the Scriptures, which as such "are normative for the faith and life of the church." The catholic creeds were described as "true declarations of the faith of the Church." The unaltered Augsburg Confession and Luther's Small Catechism were seen as "true witnesses to the Gospel," and the other symbols of Lutheranism were said to be "further valid interpretations of the confession of the Church."[38]

Lutheran unity efforts in the twentieth century had usually foundered on three or four major problems: the relation of the Word of God to the Scriptures and confessions (addressed in the above statement), "unionism," ecumenism, and membership of pastors in lodges. The Statement of Agreement and the constitution met the latter problems. The new church would acknowledge as one with it in faith and doctrine "all churches that . . . accept the teachings of these symbols [unaltered Augsburg Confession and Luther's Small Catechism]." Moreover, it would

33.
Eugene L. Fevold, *The Lutheran Free Church* (Minneapolis: Augsburg Publishing House, 1969), pp. 272–302.
34.
Wolf, *Documents*, pp. 543–45.
35.
To distinguish itself from the American Lutheran Church of 1930, the new church capitalized the definite article "The." Objections were subsequently raised and requests were made to use the lower case. A decision was reached that "The" would have to be used in all legal documents and official designation. But there would be no objection to the use of the lower case in mass media and popular references. See ALC, *Reports and Actions . . . 1968*, pp. 92–93, 461.
36.
"A.L.C., E.L.C., U.E.L.C.—T.A.L.C.!" *Christian Century*, May 11, 1960, pp. 574–76.
37.
ULCA, *Minutes . . . 1956*, pp. 29–38.
38.
Wolf, *Documents*, pp. 554–56.

39.
ULCA, *Minutes . . . 1958*, pp. 696–99. Cf. Fry's statement in *The Lutheran*, October 8, 1958, and A. D. Mattson's "Where Does the ULCA Stand?" *Lutheran Companion*, November 12, 1958. An extensive file on the debate is in the Franklin Clark Fry Papers, Box I, Folder: Joint Commission on Lutheran Unity (JCLU), the Lodge Question, 1957–58. The minutes of the JCLU, vol. 1, contain numerous references to the discussion. Fry's papers and the JCLU minutes are in the LCA Archives, Lutheran School of Theology, Chicago, Ill.
40.
Wolf, *Documents,* pp. 555, 567, 569, 570–71.
41.
LCA, *Minutes of Constituting Convention . . . 1962,* pp. 279–93.

"strive for the unification of all Lutherans" and "participate in ecumenical Christian activities, contributing its witness and works and cooperating with other churches which confess God the Father, Son and Holy Ghost." The sensitive problem of lodge membership caused Augustana leaders to question "lax" United Lutheran Church attitudes. This led to an extended debate.[39] Finally, at the insistence of the Augustana Church, the Joint Commission on Lutheran Unity adopted the following statement:

After the organization of the Lutheran Church in America no person, who belongs to any organization which claims to possess in its teachings and ceremonies that which the Lord has given solely to His Church, shall be ordained or otherwise received into the ministry of this church, nor shall any person so ordained or received by this church be retained in its ministry if he subsequently joins such an organization. Violation of this rule shall make such minister subject to discipline.[40]

Though certain phrases met sharp criticism—for example, "any organization which claims to possess in its teaching and ceremonies that which the Lord has given solely to His Church . . ."—the paragraph was calculated to resolve the issue in the new church.

The four churches approved the union documents and voted favorably on the constitution. Having thus affirmed the merger, the constituting convention was held in Detroit, June 28—July 1, 1962. The Lutheran Church in America began its actual operation as a corporate entity on January 1, 1963.[41]

Thus by the early sixties the two points of view that had come to light in the National Lutheran Council as early as 1919 found organizational expression in these two church bodies. The forces—overt and covert—which produced them included differing theological stances as well as conflicting viewpoints of what constituted the Christian life. In addition, personality clashes, sociological factors, and unvarnished power politics were all in evidence. In the welter of circumstances a few judgments are already self-evident. It is clear, for example, that a major change had taken place in American Lutheranism since World War I. Call it "acculturation," "Americanization," "theological renaissance," or whatever, the difficulty all along had been to understand the transformation *while it was taking place.* The failure to perceive that change was occurring and inaccurate interpretation of the transformation when it occurred led to unjust accusations and serious distortions on both sides. Moreover, the description of the Lutheran Church in America as "liberal," the American Lutheran Church as "middle-of-the-road," and Missouri as "orthodox" was a palpably egregious cliché. American Lutheranism was institutionally tripartite, but theologically it was bipartite. Lutheranism had not suffered the erosions of late-nineteenth and early-twentieth-century theological liberalism. It remained loyal to its confessional interpretation of the gospel, but theological differences had divided the denomination into two camps, Old Lutherans and Neo-Lutherans, both of whom were found in varying numbers in all three church bodies, the Lutheran Church in America, the American Lutheran Church, and the Lutheran Church—Missouri Synod.

One of the major hypothetical questions of American Lutheran history remained unanswered and unanswerable in the sixties. What would have happened in the years after 1950 had the National Lutheran Council become a federation with an open door to Missouri rather than a crystallization of two theologically and structurally different organic mergers? Educated guesses are not the proper ingredients of historiography. However much historians, like others, may have opinions, their craft limits them to the historical record. Therefore, table 7 simply attempts to trace the ecclesio-theological lines manifested in the records since World War I.

The Canadian Scene

Canadian Lutheranism developed along lines parallel to those that had emerged in the States. This was only natural because each of the major Lutheran bodies included Canadian districts or synods as integral parts of their organizational structure. With the advent of World War II, Lutherans in Canada showed a growing sense of being a distinct, recognizable Canadian entity. Like Canada itself, Lutheranism there was declaring its independence of things American.

It should be recalled that before the United States was drawn into World War II Canada had been immediately involved (1939). This had implications for Canadian Lutherans, especially those who were associated with the National Lutheran Council. In recognition of this fact, Ralph H. Long, executive director of the National Lutheran Council, had called a conference for April 2, 1940, in Winnipeg. A commission to direct wartime services of Canadian Lutherans was created. Called the Canadian Lutheran Commission, it was approved by all except the Missouri Synod.[42]

In 1944 representatives of the American Lutheran Church, Augustana Synod, Canada Synod of the United Lutheran Church, Lutheran Free Church, Manitoba Synod of the United Lutheran Church, Norwegian Lutheran Church, and United Danish Lutheran Church agreed that there was "unity in doctrine" and that a Canadian Lutheran Council, patterned after the National Lutheran Council, should be formed. Negotiations continued for several years. By 1947 a constitution was drafted, but the Missouri Synod, which had joined the negotiations, and the American Lutheran Church cast the deciding votes against the proposed council. The Evangelical Lutheran Church, the Augustana Church, the United Evangelical Lutheran Church, and the United Lutheran Church supported the motion. Finally, in December 1952, after further deliberations, the Canadian Lutheran Council came into being with six participating bodies: the American Lutheran Church, Augustana Church, Evangelical Lutheran Church, Lutheran Free Church, United Evangelical Lutheran Church, and United Lutheran Church.[43]

42.
Osborne Hauge, *Lutherans Working Together* (New York: National Lutheran Council, 1945), p. 75.
43.
Wolf, *Documents*, p. 574.

508

Table 7

Lutheran Confessionalism in the National Lutheran Council and the Synodical Conference 1918–1970

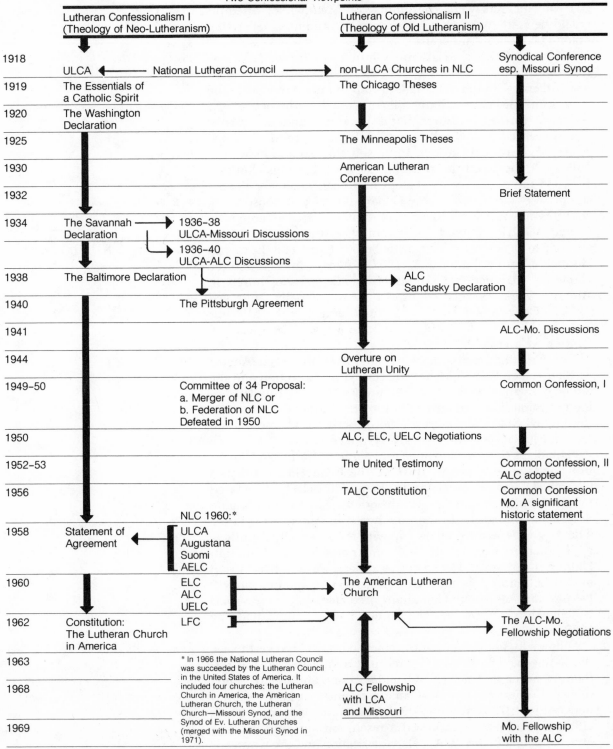

Two Confessional Viewpoints

Lutheran Confessionalism I (Theology of Neo-Lutheranism)

Lutheran Confessionalism II (Theology of Old Lutheranism)

1918 — ULCA ← National Lutheran Council → non-ULCA Churches in NLC — Synodical Conference esp. Missouri Synod

1919 — The Essentials of a Catholic Spirit — The Chicago Theses

1920 — The Washington Declaration

1925 — The Minneapolis Theses

1930 — American Lutheran Conference

1932 — Brief Statement

1934 — The Savannah Declaration → 1936–38 ULCA-Missouri Discussions / 1936–40 ULCA-ALC Discussions

1938 — The Baltimore Declaration — ALC Sandusky Declaration

1940 — The Pittsburgh Agreement

1941 — ALC-Mo. Discussions

1944 — Overture on Lutheran Unity

1949–50 — Committee of 34 Proposal: a. Merger of NLC or b. Federation of NLC Defeated in 1950 — Common Confession, I

1950 — ALC, ELC, UELC Negotiations

1952–53 — The United Testimony — Common Confession, II ALC adopted

1956 — TALC Constitution — Common Confession Mo. A significant historic statement

NLC 1960:*

1958 — Statement of Agreement ← ULCA, Augustana, Suomi, AELC

1960 — ELC, ALC, UELC → The American Lutheran Church

1962 — Constitution: The Lutheran Church in America — LFC — The ALC-Mo. Fellowship Negotiations

1963

* In 1966 the National Lutheran Council was succeeded by the Lutheran Council in the United States of America. It included four churches: the Lutheran Church in America, the American Lutheran Church, the Lutheran Church—Missouri Synod, and the Synod of Ev. Lutheran Churches (merged with the Missouri Synod in 1971).

1968 — ALC Fellowship with LCA and Missouri

1969 — Mo. Fellowship with the ALC

While the Canadian Lutheran Council was emerging, hopes for a united Lutheran Church in Canada were frequently expressed and discussions were occasionally held. Recognizing that Canadian Lutheranism would have to wait on developments in the United States during the fifties, it was decided in 1959 that union negotiations be postponed until after the two stateside mergers were consummated. Meanwhile, attempts would be made to reach a basis for pulpit and altar fellowship among Canadian Lutherans.[44]

When the American Lutheran Church was formed (1960) its Canada District took steps to incorporate itself as the Evangelical Lutheran Church of Canada. From the point of view of the American Lutheran Church, it remained a district of the American Lutheran Church, but as far as its Canadian charter was concerned it was a "church." The new president of the American Lutheran Church, addressing the Canada District in July 1960, suggested the possibility of an indigenous church.[45] By 1966 the necessary legal steps had been taken for the assumption of autonomy by the Canada District. A constituting convention was held in Regina (November 1966) whereby the Canada District severed itself from the American Lutheran Church to become the first autonomous Canadian Lutheran church, effective January 1, 1967.[46] Meanwhile, the three Canadian jurisdictional synods of the Lutheran Church in America were coordinated into a constitutionally approved "LCA—Canada Section,"[47] and similar action in the Missouri Synod led its Canadian affiliate to be known as "The Lutheran Church—Canada."[48]

The Canadian Lutheran Council was reorganized August 31–September 1, 1966, to include this Missouri section and the Synod of Evangelical Lutheran Churches (Slovak), thus becoming the Canadian counterpart to the new Lutheran Council in the United States of America (1966). Both the Canadian and U.S.A. councils became operative January 1, 1967.

Canadians continued to hope that a united Lutheran Church in Canada would emerge. By 1968 the Evangelical Lutheran Church of Canada (American Lutheran Church) had declared pulpit and altar fellowship with the others. The LCA—Canada Section continued the Lutheran Church in America tradition. The Missourians voted fellowship with the Evangelical Lutheran Church in Canada in 1969, but not with the Lutheran Church in America. The major roadblock was the Missourian or Old Lutheran view of the Bible's inspiration and inerrancy.[49] Despite this, optimistic Canadians predicted that there would be fellowship by 1971 and one Lutheran church in Canada by 1978.

Fellowship, however, was not achieved by 1971. Nevertheless, the Evangelical Lutheran Church in Canada invited the Lutheran Church in America—Canada Section and the Missouri-related Lutheran Church—Canada to enter merger negotiations. At its 1973 convention the Lutheran Church in America affiliate unanimously approved a resolution agreeing to bring about a merger of the LCA—Canada Section and the Evangeli-

44.
Ibid., pp. 585–86.
45.
ALC, *Reports and Actions . . . 1964*, p. 457.
46.
Ibid. 1966, pp. 90–91. Documents relative to the new church are to be found in ibid. *1964*, pp. 458–82.
47.
LCA, *Minutes . . . 1964*, p. 308.
48.
LC—MS, *Proceedings . . . 1962*, p. 131.
49.
N. E. Berner, "Crossroads in Canada," *The Lutheran*, September 28, 1966, pp. 13–15. Cf. Erich R. W. Schultz, "Tragedy and Triumph in Canadian Lutheranism," *Concordia Historical Institute Quarterly* 38 (July 1965): 55–72.

cal Lutheran Church in Canada. The Missouri Synod's Canadian arm refused merger but agreed to talks that could center on "doctrinal consensus sufficient for altar and pulpit fellowship." The LCA—Canada Section eventually approved a plan to enter merger discussions under these conditions, but only because its concern for one Canadian church overrode its often stated conviction that a basis for altar and pulpit fellowship already existed.[50]

50.
"Canada: Lutheran Union . . . by 1978," *Lutheran Forum,* February 1969, p. 21. An insightful essay on Canadian Lutheranism is Walter Freitag's "Lutheran Tradition in Canada," in *The Churches and the Canadian Experience . . .*, ed. J. W. Grant (Toronto: Ryerson Press, 1963), pp. 94-101. "Lutherans in Canada Make Fellowship an Early Goal," News Bureau Release, Lutheran Council/U.S.A., December 18, 1969, p. 7; ibid., June 29, 1973.
51.
Abdel Ross Wentz, *A Basic History of Lutheranism in America* (Philadelphia: Fortress Press, 1964), p. 333.
52.
LWF, *Proceedings . . . Lund . . . 1947,* pp. 15-19, 29, 32-33.

American Lutheran and International Ecumenism

The Lutheran World Federation. Ever since 1923 the majority of American Lutherans had participated in the movement to bring world Lutheranism into closer fellowship. Two world wars and the work of the National Lutheran Council enlarged the world-consciousness of American Lutherans. World assemblies had been held in 1923 (Eisenach), 1929 (Copenhagen), and 1935 (Paris). After the Paris convention the executive committee announced that the next assembly would be held in Philadelphia in 1940. Because of World War II the contemplated assembly was canceled. In 1946, however, the executive committee of the Lutheran World Convention, meeting in Sweden, planned an assembly for the summer of 1947. Held at Lund, Sweden, the assembly brought forty-four official delegates from American churches in the National Lutheran Council. Several Missouri Synod observers were also present.

Much of the leadership of the Lund assembly fell upon American Lutherans who had the financial resources and administrative know-how to cope with the massive postwar exigencies. One of the two most memorable accomplishments of the convocation was the adoption of the proposed constitution for the Lutheran World Federation, which was defined as "a free association of Lutheran churches" to serve as an agency for autonomous member churches. Its constitutionally stated purposes proved to be such as to lead it into activities beyond those of a mere agency. Regardless of protestations to the contrary, the federation often found itself engaged in definitely churchly matters. This meant that the Lutheran World Federation was involved from its beginning in a problem closely akin to the one that had plagued the National Lutheran Council, that is, how to avoid cooperation in "internals" while cooperating in "externals." The distinction was impossible to maintain. Nevertheless, the adoption of the constitution marked what has been called "a turning-point in the history of world Lutheranism. The constitution provided [Lutheranism] with more systematic and more durable integration than [it] had ever known before."[51]

The first president of the Lutheran World Federation was Anders Nygren (Sweden) and its executive secretary was Sylvester C. Michelfelder (U.S.A.). American members of the executive committee were Johan A. Aasgaard, Franklin Clark Fry, Ralph H. Long, and Abdel Ross Wentz.[52]

The Second Assembly of the Lutheran World Federation, Hannover, July 25–August 3, 1952, took on the air of a religious folk-festival when thousands of Germans and American visitors joined the delegates and official visitors in mass rallies. Once again the Missouri Synod sent unofficial representatives, twenty in number. The prominent role of Americans was in evidence at Hannover as at Lund. In order to expedite the carrying out of tasks that had fallen to the federation since 1947, its structure was modified by the creation of three departments, theology, world service, and world mission. To fill the vacancy created by the death of Michelfelder, the federation elected Carl E. Lund-Quist, another American, to be its executive secretary. Bishop Hanns Lilje (Hannover) was elected president.[53]

The Third Assembly of the Federation, upon invitation of the U.S.A. National Committee (the National Lutheran Council), was held in Minneapolis, August 15-25, 1957. Marking the tenth anniversary of the federation, the assembly struck a strong theological and ecumenical note. Under the direction of the president-elect, Franklin Clark Fry, world-renowned theologians produced a remarkable document sometimes called the Fifty-One Minneapolis Theses on the assembly theme, "Christ Frees and Unites." The broad ecumenical outreach of the assembly was indicated by the presence of official visitors from the Lutheran Church—Missouri Synod, world confessional bodies other than Lutheran (Presbyterian, Baptist, Methodist, Congregational), the World Council of Churches, and several other international Christian associations. In retrospect, perhaps the most significant ecumenical gesture was the proposal by the German National Committee to initiate conversations with the Roman Catholic Church. Without any knowledge of the upcoming Second Vatican Council, world Lutherans anticipated the age of dialogue by appointing a Special Commission on Inter-Confessional Research, which in 1963 became the Foundation for Inter-Confessional Research. President-elect Fry summarized federation history by characterizing each assembly: "At Lund we learned to walk together; at Hannover we learned to pray together; at Minneapolis we learned to think together." Not long after the Minneapolis Assembly the health of the executive secretary, Carl E. Lund-Quist, began to fail. Obliged to resign in 1961, he was succeeded by Kurt-Schmidt Clausen of Germany. Lund-Quist died in 1965, an offering not unlike that of great American Lutherans before him: John A. Morehead, Lauritz Larsen, Lars W. Boe, Ralph H. Long, and Sylvester C. Michelfelder.[54]

The World Council of Churches. Guidelines for Lutheran participation in the ecumenical movement had been articulated as early as 1936. American Lutherans were present at both the Faith and Order and the Life and Work conferences in Edinburgh and Oxford (1937). Frederick H. Knubel and Ralph H. Long represented American Lutherans at Utrecht (1938) when a provisional constitution for a World Council of Churches was drafted. After the war, President Fry of the United Lutheran Church called a meeting (September 6, 1945) of representatives of American Lutheran churches to achieve a "common understanding with reference to the World Council of Churches." The meeting decided to press for "Lutheran representation on

53.
For the account of this assembly see LWF, *Proceedings . . . Hannover . . . 1952*, pp. 11, 103, 168–98.
54.
An inadequate account of the third assembly is in LWF, *Proceedings . . . Minneapolis . . . 1957* (Minneapolis: Augsburg Publishing House, 1957).

a confessional basis" and sought the assistance of the executive committee of the Lutheran World Convention. Having obtained this, the Lutheran position was presented by Abdel Ross Wentz to the Committee on Arrangements for the First Assembly of the World Council. Meeting in England in August 1946, the committee finally agreed to change the World Council of Churches constitution which had called for allocation of seats on a geographical rather than confessional basis. With "confessional representation" as one of the assured factors in determining allocation of seats, most of American Lutheranism was prepared to consider joining the World Council. Johan A. Aasgaard predicted enthusiastically that all but one (the Missouri Synod) church would affiliate.[55] His remarkable gifts of leadership, however, did not make him clairvoyant; his own church, the Evangelical Lutheran, rejected a resolution to join the council. Nevertheless, encouraged by developments spearheaded by Wentz and Fry, five churches voted to affiliate and sent delegates to the First Assembly at Amsterdam in 1948: the American Lutheran Church, the American Evangelical Lutheran Church, the Augustana Lutheran Church, the United Evangelical Lutheran Church, and the United Lutheran Church in America.

In addition to the churches of the Synodical Conference, three National Lutheran Council churches delayed membership: the Suomi Synod, the Lutheran Free Church, and, as already noted, the Evangelical Lutheran Church. The latter was to be painfully divided over the issue for a whole decade, but in 1956 the church voted decisively—1,434 to 685—to apply for membership in the World Council.[56]

An incomplete but perhaps helpful explanation of the altered attitude in the Evangelical Lutheran Church is to be found in the following factors: (1) Some of the misinformation and misrepresentation of the World Council had, in the meantime, been corrected. The new president, Fredrik A. Schiotz, for example, was able to present from personal experience a complete and accurate picture of the council; this had the effect of allaying many fears. (2) The churches with which the Evangelical Lutheran Church was planning to merge, the American Lutheran Church and the United Evangelical Lutheran Church, were charter members of the World Council. This fact led many to question the reasons given for continued Evangelical Lutheran Church opposition. (3) Between 1946 and 1956 the seminary had graduated 723 students. Many of these men were convinced of the wisdom of affiliating with the World Council and now added their voting strength to the supporters of the ecumenical movement.

The eventual presence of most American Lutheran churches in the World Council helped to make the Lutheran church the largest confessional group in the council. This, however, was temporary, for in 1961 the Russian Orthodox Church was received into membership at the New Delhi Assembly, thus making the Orthodox communion the ranking ecclesiastical family in the council.

55.
Dorris A. Flesner, "The Role of the Lutheran Churches of America in the Formation of the World Council of Churches" (Ph.D. diss., Hartford Seminary Foundation, Hartford, Conn., 1956), p. 154.
56.
Congressman Albert Quie from Minnesota was largely instrumental in winning lay support for World Council membership.

In conclusion, it ought to be observed that by 1973 two-thirds of American Lutheranism (the Lutheran Church in America and the American Lutheran Church) belonged to the World Council. The Missouri Synod, having voted down membership in the Lutheran World Federation for over two decades, could hardly be expected to look favorably on the World Council. The synod's Denver convention (1969) decisively rejected a resolution to join the federation and then refused to consider World Council membership. Despite the absence of this vigorous and theologically concerned body, American Lutheranism has supplied high-quality leadership to the ecumenical movement. It is difficult to exaggerate, for example, the contribution of Franklin Clark Fry, who for many years was the highly respected chairman of the powerful Central Committee of the World Council and one of the chief architects of the National Council of Churches of Christ (1950). Without immodesty, the Lutheran churches of America can rejoice in Fry's leadership that accepted ecumenical responsibility for viewing the church and her role in the world under the aspect of the gospel as witnessed to in the Holy Scriptures and explicated in the Lutheran confessions. Erik W. Modean, head of the Lutheran Council News Bureau, writing Fry's obituary (June 7, 1968), said: "Nothing was more important, he believed, than to preach the gospel and administer the sacraments. . . . Many things contributed to his stature as a giant of modern Christianity, but above all was the clear, strong evangelical witness that marked him as a dedicated man of God."

22 American Lutheranism
to the 1970s

1.
See official reports and comments in the three bodies: LCA, *Minutes . . . 1964,* pp. 39–40; *The Lutheran,* March 19, 1969, p. 26; ALC, *Reports and Actions . . . 1964,* pp. 230–33; News Bureau Release, no. 69–93, Lutheran Council/U.S.A., p. 2; LC—MS *Proceedings . . . 1965,* pp. 22–28; and ibid. *1967,* p. 75.

By the sixties, Lutherans faced an identity crisis not unlike that in the early years of the nineteenth century. Numerous questions seemed to demand answers. For example: Within the spectrum of American Christianity did Lutheranism have a viable future as a separate confessional church? In the face of the so-called great issues of the last third of the twentieth century was there anything unique, and therefore worthy of preservation, about Lutheranism? Much serious reflection during the decade had not provided a resolution with sharply defined contours recognizably Lutheran and ecumenical and practical. This item on the Lutheran agenda remained unfinished business as the future rushed in upon the church, whose profile and prospect in the sixties and early seventies conclude this study.

The General Work of the Churches

Traditionally, American Protestant denominations have carried out their "general" work under categories such as missions (home and foreign), welfare and charities, and education. This work has required special boards, executives, and, of course, money, customarily called benevolence funds among Lutherans. The several branches of Lutheranism have followed this pattern with remarkably little deviation and measured growth or noted failure against the criteria within each category.

Missions

American Missions. By the mid-sixties it was clear that the "revival" of the previous decade was coming to an end. Statistics revealed that the rapid growth of the churches was ending; the statistical curve began to move downward. Although Lutheran church bodies in North America had a combined membership in 1968 of 9,239,274, ranking third behind Baptists and Methodists, one conclusion was evident: the Lutheran churches differed only slightly from typical main-line Protestant churches in the experience of slow growth in the mid- and late-sixties. Of the three major bodies, the Lutheran Church—Missouri Synod had shown the highest numerical growth for a quarter of a century. By mid-decade, however, even this church was being informed that a decline had set in.[1] It was small consolation that the Roman Catholic Church, which like the Missouri Synod had earlier experienced remarkable growth, was now also suffering decline. Church membership as a whole in America, though still showing slight increase, was not keeping pace with population growth.

World Missions. In preparation for the 1968 convention of the American Lutheran Church, its Board of World Missions raised several probing questions which indicated that Lutherans were engaged in a latter-day "Re-thinking Missions." The questions focused the attention of the decision-making body on the problems that contemporary circumstances were forcing Christians in all churches to face. Was there a basic difference between world missions and home missions and/or social missions? Were theological emphases in the sixties obfuscating the gospel? What should the future program of the churches be?[2]

It was unquestionable that the prototype missionary of popular imagination was all but gone. No longer did this dominating figure reflect the contemporary situation in which leadership was increasingly in the hands of indigenous churchmen. Rather, a growing proportion of missionaries filled specific posts that required skills still not common in the less developed countries.

Moreover, the theological climate, like the changing political and social situation around the world, had brought Lutheranism as well as other churches to what the Lutheran Church in America missions executive Arne Sovik and the Lutheran scholar and theologian Conrad Bergendoff agreed was a crisis for Christian missions.[3] Lutherans, said Bergendoff, had no call to Lutheranize the world; their charge was to proclaim the central doctrine of justification by grace through faith, the gospel of the forgiveness of sins through Christ. The institutional form must follow function lest the form become mere propaganda and not genuine mission.

During the triennium 1962–65, Martin L. Kretzmann, a long-time Missouri Synod missionary and theological professor in India, conducted a "Mission Self-Study and Survey." Kretzmann's report, submitted to the synodical board of directors, examined the theological basis, administration, areas of ministry, finances, and missionary education for the mission of Christ by the whole church. Certain vigorous "affirmations" or resolutions, based on his report, were adopted by the church. As a sample of the affirmations the following is cited:

Resolved, **That we affirm as Lutheran Christians that the Evangelical Lutheran Church is chiefly a confessional movement within the total body of Christ rather than a denomination emphasizing institutional barriers of separation. The Lutheran Christian uses the Lutheran Confessions for the primary purpose for which they were framed: to confess Christ and His Gospel boldly and lovingly to all Christians. *While the Confessions seek to repel all attacks against the Gospel, they are not intended to be a kind of Berlin wall to stop communication with other Christians. . . .*[4] [Italics added]**

An indication of the forward-looking and unity-minded attitude of the three major Lutheran world mission boards was the establishment of a joint preservice missionary orientation program. Replacing a school of missions operated by the Lutheran Church in America since 1957, its sessions were to be conducted

516

2.
ALC, *Pre-Convention Report . . . 1968,* p. 343.

3.
The installation (February 11, 1968) of Arne Sovik, former director of the World Mission Department (LWF), as executive secretary of LCA World Missions became the occasion for a consultation in depth on world missions. The entire issue of *World Encounter* 5 (July 1968), publication of the LCA Board of World Missions, was devoted to this subject.

4.
LC—MS, *Proceedings . . . 1965,* p. 80. "The Kretzmann Report" in its entirety is printed in *Convention Workbook . . . 1965,* pp. 112–40. Note how closely the main ideas parallel the ULCA's Washington Declaration (1920) and Savannah Declaration (1934).

5.
Lutheran Standard, July 7, 1969; and News Bureau Release, no. 68–75, Lutheran Council/U.S.A., November 26, 1968.
6.
"A Proposal for the Establishment of a World Church Institute," published statement (Geneva, June 1969). No authors are listed, but the director of the Summer Institute informed the writer that three men collaborated: Martin L. Kretzmann, Wayne Ewing, and Donald C. Flatt.
7.
Ronald L. Johnstone, *The Effectiveness of the Lutheran Elementary and Secondary Schools as Agencies of Christian Education* (St. Louis: Concordia Seminary, 1966), p. 146. See William A. Kramer, "The Johnstone Study of Lutheran Schools," *Concordia Theological Monthly* 38 (January 1967): 23–36; and Ronald L. Johnstone, "A Response to the Kramer Review," ibid., pp. 37–38. Cf. criticism of Roman Catholic parochial education: Mary Perkins Ryan, *Are Parochial Schools the Answer?* (New York: Holt, Rinehart, and Winston, 1964).
8.
ULCA, *Minutes . . . 1942,* pp. 395–96.
9.
The published statement was *Parish Education: A Statement of Basic Principles and a Program of Christian Education* (Philadelphia: Board of Parish Education, ULCA, 1954–55). See the board report in ULCA, *Minutes . . . 1956,* pp. 716–50.

successively in Chicago (1969), in St. Louis (1970), and in St. Paul (1971), providing summer courses for missionary candidates from all three churches. The director was also to supervise continuing study by first-term missionaries on the field.[5] To complement this, the boards in 1969 laid plans for a World Church Institute, a center for missiological research which would undertake to stimulate and carry on a "massive attack on the problems which face the church in its understanding of its missionary obedience," and to anticipate the "probable need for radical change in the thought patterns of the whole missionary movement."[6] After initial consideration of an independent institute closely related to a theological school, the decision was made in April 1970, to commit the project to the new Division of Mission and Ministry of the Lutheran Council/U.S.A.

In the face of the intricate and widespread unrest and profound need for missionary reorientation, American Lutherans gradually realized that institutional disunity had to be put aside. The nature of the church as Christ's mission to the whole world, to the whole body of Christians, and to the whole of society required united efforts in planning, in implementation, and in organization.

Christian Education

Parish Level. The Lutheran church traditionally laid heavy stress on education and was actively engaged at every level: elementary, secondary, college and university, and seminary. Any profile of American Lutheranism in the sixties, therefore, must include the church's continuing role in education.

Although Lutheran parochial schools were under criticism,[7] it should be remembered that less than one-third of American Lutheranism maintained a parochial system. Parish education, however—including Sunday schools, catechetical instruction, vacation schools—was common to all Lutheran bodies. It was in this area that cooperation among the main churches was to develop. The old American Lutheran Church and the Augustana Synod had expressed (prior to 1942) an interest in the joint preparation and publication (with the United Lutheran Church of America) of a new series of graded curricular materials. An agreement was reached whereby these three churches would produce what was to be known as *The Christian Growth Series.*[8] About 1950, the Parish and Church School Board of the United Lutheran Church began to think in terms of developing a long-range plan of parish education for the congregations. In December 1954 the board adopted a document setting forth the basic principles for a long-range program.[9] At the outset the partners in the enterprise urged the participation of other National Lutheran Council churches. In response to a subsequent invitation, an eight-church venture was begun on the basis of a document called "A Proposal for Cooperation in a Long Range Program of Parish Education." The program was divided into four phases: (1) the study and development of general and age-group objectives; (2) the study and development of curriculum to fulfill the objectives; (3) the production and promotion of materials to implement the curriculum design; and (4) the field-testing and use of materials.[10] Phase 1 was to be completed by December 31, 1957; phase 2, by mid-1960; phase 3's materials should begin to appear by January 1963, but the nature of phase 4 made it impossible to project a completion date.[11]

In due course, representatives of the eight bodies met in Columbus, Ohio, on January 8-9, 1957, organizing a joint board committee which would be the functioning body for all the churches. At this meeting the Evangelical Lutheran Church, with support from the American Lutheran Church and the United Evangelical Lutheran Church (the partners in the tri-partite merger of 1960), pointed out certain difficulties in accepting the long-range program. Largely because of this the Joint Union Committee (ELC, ALC, UELC) voted that it could not commit the American Lutheran Church (1960) to the project.[12] A short time later, however, it was resolved that the ELC, UELC, and ALC take "immediate steps" to provide the new ALC with its *own* parish curriculum by 1965.[13]

Meanwhile, the two church mergers came about and the two parish education curricula—LCA and the ALC—were in process. To the credit of a durable goodwill and an uncommon common sense that survived the tensions of 1956-60, there were persistent efforts in the late fifties and early sixties to find ways in which the two churches could cooperate in parish education. Subsequent negotiations disclosed several potentially fruitful areas for cooperative work, and resolutions were prepared to implement a common program in the future.[14] It was hoped that the first elements of a total parish education program for the LCA/ALC would be ready for introduction by 1975.[15] Although attempts were made to bring the Lutheran Church—Missouri Synod into the new enterprise, and although some strong Missouri support was won, the project did not receive the synod's approval.[16]

Two projects in which the Missouri Synod was able to cooperate were the revision of the intersynodical translation of Luther's Small Catechism and the study of the theology and practice of confirmation.[17] The latter grew out of the widespread interest within American Lutheranism generated by the work of the Lutheran World Federation Commission on Christian Education. In 1964, representatives of each of the three major churches formed the Joint Commission on the Theology and Practice of Confirmation, which after four years issued a "Report for Study" (December 28, 1967) and published a study book on confirmation and Communion.[18] The report made two significant recommendations: (1) that baptized children be admitted to Communion during the latter part of the fifth grade and (2) that confirmation, defined as a "pastoral and educational ministry . . . designed to help baptized children identify with the life and mission of the adult Christian community . . . ," should take place in the latter part of the tenth grade. This was a sharp reversal of traditional Lutheran practice that looked upon confirmation as an educational ministry prior to Communion.

10.
ULCA, *Minutes . . . 1956,* pp. 731-33.
11.
A Program for Long Range Cooperation in Parish Education (n.p., n.d.), pp. 15-16.
12.
Interview, C. Richard Evenson and E. Clifford Nelson, August 21, 1968; W. Kent Gilbert and E. Clifford Nelson, April 6, 1970. The ULCA's position was partially explained by the fact that it had already invested large sums and a decade of study in the LRP. Moreover, the ULCA feared that the ELC and the new ALC would use supplementary materials to "correct" the ULCA theology. Cf. Joint Union Committee, "Minutes, October 2-4, 1957," pp. 171-72, Permanent Merger File, vol. 2, 1957, Augsburg Publishing House, Minneapolis.
13.
ELC, *Annual Report . . . 1958,* pp. 107-8. The old ALC was reluctant to withdraw. Its convention in 1958 requested the JUC to reconsider inter-Lutheran cooperation in parish education. A similar spirit had been expressed by E. W. Schramm, editor of the ALC's official organ. Cf. Joint Union Committee, "Minutes, November 13-14, 1958"; and *Lutheran Standard,* November 30, 1957, p. 21.
14.
LCA, *Minutes . . . 1964,* pp. 394-96; ALC, *Reports and Actions . . . 1964,* pp. 328-33. Interview, W. Kent Gilbert and E. Clifford Nelson, April 6, 1970.
15.
The following documents supplied by the ALC Office of Parish Education and Lloyd Svendsbye, Augsburg editor-in-chief (1966-71), have been consulted: "A Plan for Developing a Comprehensive Program of Parish Education . . . ALC and LCA, April 30, 1969"; "A Central Objective for Educational Ministry . . . ALC and LCA, September 1, 1969"; "Minutes, Joint Program Coordinating Committee . . . September 23, 1969"; and "Subcommittee on Parish Education, Joint Program Coordinating Committee, November 6-7, 1969."

The proposal, as intended, evoked immediate and sharp discussion among pastors and congregations. Pastors, having been provided guidance, were asked to conduct congregational study sessions during 1969. In November, the Joint Commission considered the results of the parish-level evaluation and began the preparation of a final report and recommendations to be submitted to the churches. The·Lutheran Church in America and the American Lutheran Church took favorable action at their conventions in 1970. The Missouri Synod found itself divided over the issue and therefore recommended that congregations "study their practice" of confirmation and Communion.

College Education. The profile of American Lutheranism would be inadequate without a glance at its program of higher education, not least because Lutheranism in America has placed such stress on its colleges and seminaries. In the late sixties there were seventy-five educational institutions related to the Lutheran church: thirty-six senior colleges and universities, nineteen junior colleges, and twenty seminaries. Despite this broad interest in higher education, there was an understandable reluctance to begin new institutions. The primary reason was economic; the cost of higher education boggled the minds of those who would venture anew into this realm. The most recently founded college (1961, in California), despite the support of both the Lutheran Church in America and the American Lutheran Church, had encountered problems that illustrated the legitimate hesitation of educational leaders to ask churches to leap into fiscal waters beyond their depth. The Lutheran Church—Missouri Synod, however, voted in 1971 to construct a four-year college in southern California.

Enrollments in Lutheran colleges since World War II and especially during the sixties continued to rise. The rate of growth was not as dramatic as that in tax-supported schools, but nevertheless the church-related colleges were bursting at the seams. According to the annual statistical report of the National Lutheran Educational Conference, Washington, D.C., the academic year 1960–61 showed a total of 47,347 in Lutheran colleges and universities. The next year the figure had risen to 50,592. By 1969 the total was 53,444 full-time undergraduates. With the reckoning of part-time students, graduate students, and those engaged in other programs the figure stood at 77,812.[19] Figure 5 shows college enrollment figures by church bodies during the 1960s.

The sixties witnessed a continuing expansion of physical facilities and faculties in order to meet rising enrollments. The general economic inflation meant rising costs in new buildings and increased instructional and general education budgets. Although financial support from the church bodies with which the colleges were associated rose somewhat, the support was wholly inadequate to meet the new needs. This usually meant two things: (1) increased tuitions and (2) broader extrachurch sources of support. The former tended to limit the student bodies to young people of relatively affluent parents, despite large-scale student aid and loan programs. Most of the colleges,

16.
Lutheran Standard, June 10, 1969, p. 23. Through the assistance of Gilbert, Evenson, and Svendsbye the writer has had access to unpublished minutes and papers which present the Joint Program of Parish Education in detail.
17.
LC—MS, *Proceedings . . . 1965,* pp. 157–58; and ALC, *Reports and Actions . . . 1966,* p. 376.
18.
Frank W. Klos, *Confirmation and First Communion: A Study Book* (Philadelphia, Minneapolis, St. Louis: Augsburg Publishing House; Board of Publication, LCA; Concordia Publishing House, 1968); the "Report for Study" is bound as a supplement.
19.
See National Lutheran Educational Conference, "Lutheran Schools Experience Large Enrollment Increases," January 7, 1962, pp. 1, 3–6; and News Bureau Release, Office of Research, Statistics and Archives, Lutheran Council/U.S.A., January 3, 1968, pp. 1, 3; and ibid., January 8, 1970, pp. 1–2.

519

founded by Lutherans to educate Lutherans, never intended to exclude the young people of the church for whose benefit the colleges in every instance were founded. The latter tended to attenuate ties to the parent church body. With the increasing costs and the possibility of reduction in contributions from individuals and foundations, Lutheran colleges along with other private colleges faced a crisis of the first magnitude.[20]

Seminary Education. The numerical strength of Lutheran theological schools in the sixties is illustrated in figure 6. It should be noted that the Lutheran Church in America with eight seminaries counted over 1,450 students; the Missouri Synod with two, over 1,590; and the American Lutheran Church with three, about 1,240.[21] Beyond these external features, Lutheran theological education exhibited some problems that were common to all divinity schools, Protestant and Roman Catholic. Granted that the task of the seminary was to prepare men for the ministry of the church in today's world, several questions were to the fore. One concerned the definition of terms. In the light of today's world, which some said was writing the agenda for the church, what was meant by "ministry"? Moreover, what was the "church"? And if one could define "ministry" and "church," was the education which seminarians were receiving "relevant" to the needs of society? The specifically Lutheran aspect of the common problem brought traditional theological formulations and the concept of the functioning ministry under examination.

All schools worked at curriculum revision. The traditional departments were Bible (including Introduction, Exegesis, and Theology), History (including Church History and History of Christian Thought), Systematic Theology (including Introduction, Dogmatics, and Ethics), and Practical Theology (including Liturgics and Music, Homiletics, Catechetics, Pastoral Care, Clinical or Field Work). Some curricula remained relatively unchanged. Others were adjusted and rearranged within the traditional framework with the purpose of better integration and the reduction of required courses and the increase of elective offerings. Still others sought change to provide an entirely new way of theological education, deemed necessary for a ministry relevant to the world.[22]

Among the seminary problems that remained as unfinished business at the end of the decade were the ever-present ones of adequate financing, selection of teaching personnel, confessional and academic standards, continuing education and graduate programs, student recruitment (male and female), inter-Lutheran and ecumenical (churchly and secular) relations. These and other issues confronted each of the seminaries in particular and would provide in years to come the working agendas for consultations and task forces on theological education.[23]

Theological Scholarship. Closely related to college and seminary education was the development in the post-World War II era of an academic community of scholars. The names of earlier American Lutherans such as Charles Porterfield Krauth, C. F.

520

20.
Hartwick College (LCA, Oneonta, N.Y.) terminated its ties with the church in 1968 in order to be eligible for New York state aid. See News Bureau Release, no. 68-109, Lutheran Council/U.S.A., November 12, 1968, pp. 1-2. Wagner College, Staten Island, N.Y., and Waterloo Lutheran University, Waterloo, Ont., have since broken their ties with the LCA. See *The Lutheran*, July 11, 1973, p. 37.
21.
The statistical reports are from the Office of Research, Statistics and Archives, Lutheran Council/U.S.A., News Bureau Releases nos. 68-121 and 70-2.
22.
Carl T. Uehling, "Fantastic!" *The Lutheran*, June 18, 1969, pp. 5-9; cf. *The Lutheran*, July 16, 1969, p. 49: "I would like to know how it [curriculum revision] works in the areas of language, hermeneutics, and how it equips a future pastor for bringing people . . . to Christ, which is really the touchstone of the whole effort."
23.
ALC, *Reports and Actions . . . 1968*, pp. 413-17. Cf. "The Future of Our Seminaries," *Lutheran Quarterly* 18 (November 1966). Cf. News Bureau Release, no. 70-92, Lutheran Council/U.S.A., August 20, 1970, pp. 1-2.

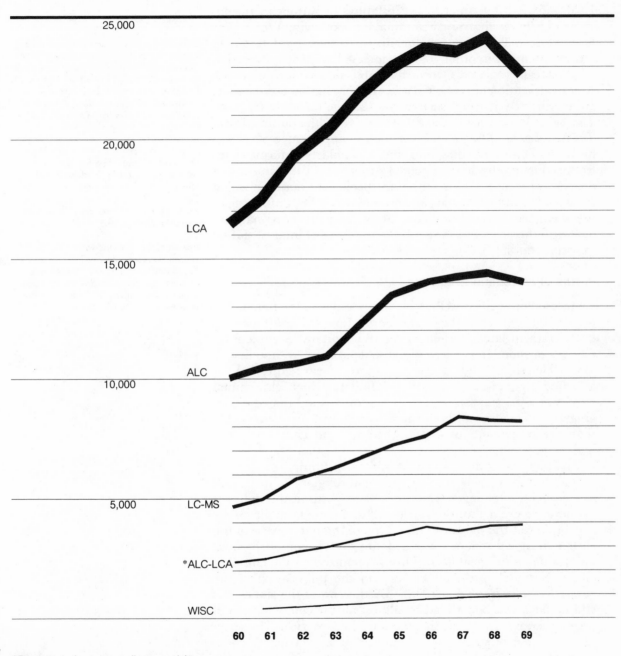

Figure 5

Four-Year College
Enrollments
(Undergraduate)
1960–69

25,000

20,000

LCA

15,000

ALC

10,000

5,000   LC-MS

*ALC-LCA

WISC

60 61 62 63 64 65 66 67 68 69

*Represents four-year college receiving
support from both ALC and LCA.

Data supplied by Office of Research,
Statistics and Archives, Lutheran
Council/U.S.A., N.Y.

W. Walther, Franz Pieper, Georg Sverdrup, Henry Eyster Jacobs, Conrad Lindberg, and J. Michael Reu were little known beyond American Lutheranism. However, the rebirth of theological interest fostered by the emergence of Neo-Lutheranism associated with such names as Charles M. Jacobs, G. A. Voigt, Herbert C. Alleman, James W. Richard, Henry F. Offermann, and Abdel Ross Wentz was nourished in large measure between 1920 and 1945 by American translations of European theologians, chiefly German and Scandinavian. Following World War II, American Lutheran scholarship in its own right began to attract attention in other communions.[24] The joint publication (by Fortress Press and Concordia Publishing House) of a new American edition of *Luther's Works,* the reading by non-Lutherans of scholarly journals such as the *Lutheran Quarterly, Concordia Theological Monthly, Dialog,* and *Lutheran World,* the publication of *The Encyclopedia of the Lutheran Church,* the appearance of critical histories of church bodies, and similar scholarly enterprises introduced men outside the circle of American Lutheranism to a deeper appreciation of a Lutheran theological heritage which transcended the scholastic categories of an earlier day. At first, the themes that received major attention were doctrinal and historical theology, but in the sixties the focus of interest shifted to social ethics.

Forms of Worship and Service

Congregational Life and Piety. It was popular in the first half of the 1960s to denigrate the local congregation. It was attacked as irrelevant, outdated, and no longer an adequate instrument for Christ's mission. It was a vestigial anachronism, a "medieval" form which simply did not correspond to present reality.[25] After a period of masochistic self-flagellation in which churchmen cried *mea culpa, mea magna culpa,* it was discovered that the congregation was after all both more sturdy and more malleable than the proponents of secular theology and churchmanship had judged it.[26]

The piety of Lutherans was exhibited in liturgy, music, arts and architecture, as well as in "personal religion," church and Communion attendance. Despite differing liturgical emphases, Lutherans were not antiliturgical. All had some form for public worship, even the most informal. One of the outgrowths of the earlier liturgical renewal was a desire for a common hymnal and common liturgical form. This was realized for the churches of the National Lutheran Council in the publication of the *Service Book and Hymnal* in 1958.[27] By the end of the sixties this church book was being used by almost all the congregations of the Lutheran Church in America and the American Lutheran Church. Like other hymnals before it, it served the cause of unity at the congregational level in a manner which no amount of theological treatises could ever have accomplished. Liturgically, the commission for the *Service Book and Hymnal* felt no obligation to repristinate the Common Service. However, working from this Lutheran base and other Lutheran services, it

24.
Some of the better-known names were Conrad Bergendoff, Joseph Sittler, T. A. Kantonen, Theodore G. Tappert, Jaroslav J. Pelikan, Edgar M. Carlson, Warren A. Quanbeck, Martin J. Heinecken, Jerald C. Brauer, Martin E. Marty, Sydney E. Ahlstrom, and George W. Forell.
25.
A spate of books and articles with titles such as "Where in the World?" "What in the World?" and "The Secular City" were directed to the problem of "relevancy."
26.
LCA, *Minutes . . . 1966,* pp. 539–64. See also ibid. *1964,* p. 39.
27.
For an account of the work of the joint commissions see Edward T. Horn III, "Preparation of the Service Book and Hymnal," in *Liturgical Reconnaissance,* ed. Edgar S. Brown, Jr. (Philadelphia: Fortress Press, 1968), pp. 91–101.

Figure 6

**Seminary Enrollments
1960–69**

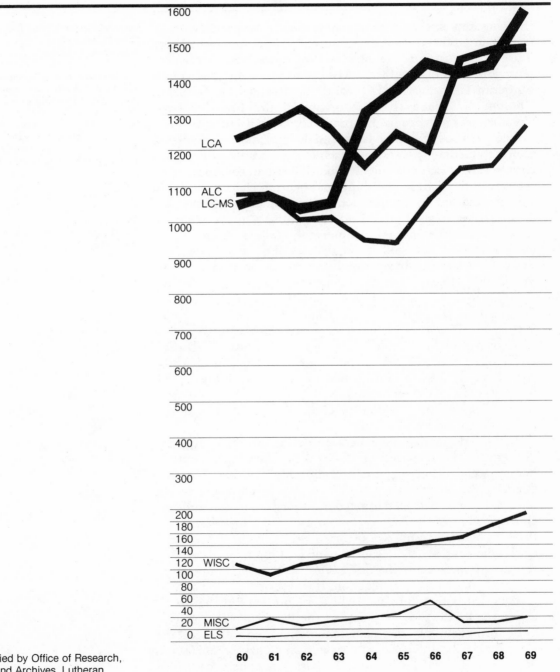

Data supplied by Office of Research,
Statistics and Archives, Lutheran
Council/U.S.A., N.Y.

recovered for use some pertinent forms from the early church, thus blending the liturgical tradition of the Eastern and Western churches.

With the publication and general use of the new book of worship, weaknesses—such as occasional rigid traditionalism and theological vacuities hitherto not noted—began to be recognized, and the question was inevitably raised as to the need for a completely new hymnal. Moreover, the Lutheran Church—Missouri Synod was now being drawn closer to other churches and expressed its desire in 1965 to cooperate with all American Lutheran bodies "in developing hymnological and liturgical materials."[28] At the invitation of the Missouri Synod, representatives of the LCA, ALC, the Synod of Evangelical Lutheran Churches (SELC), and the Evangelical Lutheran Church of Canada (ELCC) organized the Inter-Lutheran Commission on Worship, February 11, 1966.

The work of the Inter-Lutheran Commission on Worship almost immediately addressed itself to the question of liturgical change which was agitating the whole Christian community. By the end of the decade one thing had become clear: renewal in worship had to face the question of the relation between continuity and change—formal and substantive—in the common desire to be contemporary, ecumenical, and Lutheran.

New Ministries, Evangelism, Auxiliaries. The decade also saw the continuation of trends apparent in the immediate post-World War II years. The rapidly changing social scene led the churches to set up commissions to study the nature and function of ministry in the modern world.[29] So-called experimental ministries, mobile ministries, inner city/suburban ministries, and intercongregational or merged pastorates were essayed. Conferences were held on "town and country" problems because churchmen had become disturbed by what was happening to religious life in rural sections of mid-America.[30] All these areas reflected the serious efforts of the churches to fulfill their ministerial role in the turbulent sixties.

The allied question of evangelism per se naturally came under scrutiny. Did evangelism require a new face in the contemporary scene? Congregational ("churchly") evangelism and "personal" evangelism continued to receive emphasis in the official reports of evangelism commissions in most Lutheran church bodies as the sixties drew to a close.[31] However, a "rethinking of evangelism" was being called for by theologians and churchmen as the new decade dawned.[32] One major issue that repeatedly surfaced in the discussion was the relation between personal religion and social action. It was the conviction of most leaders that both emphases ought to be present but that social action was hardly to be described as another form of evangelism.

Important in all the above-mentioned ministries of the church was the role of auxiliary and ancillary organizations oriented to special lay groups. In past years there had been organized men's groups, women's societies, and youth associations, all of which altered with the times. The history of these auxiliaries showed that men's organizations (e.g., Lutheran

28.
A. R. Kretzmann, "The Definition of the Task Before Us," in *Liturgical Reconnaissance*, pp. 131–33.
29.
See William Larsen, "Specialized Ministries for Clergymen," *Lutheran Quarterly* 18 (May 1966): 136–43; this issue focuses on "Ministry and Ministries."
30.
E. W. Mueller and Giles Ekola, eds., *The Silent Struggle for Mid-America* (Minneapolis: Augsburg Publishing House, 1963).
31.
See, for example, ALC, *Reports and Actions . . . 1968*, pp. 448–54.
32.
H. George Anderson, "Evangelism in a New Climate," *Lutheran Quarterly* 21 (November 1969): 384, 390–91.

33.
Paul L. Maier, *A Man Spoke, A World Listened: The Story of Walter A. Maier* (New York: McGraw-Hill, 1963), p. 113 and passim.
34.
See News Bureau Release, Lutheran Council/U.S.A., August 10, 1973.
35.
See Will Herberg, *Protestant, Catholic, Jew* (Magnolia, Mass.: Peter Smith, 1955); Martin E. Marty, *The New Shape of American Religion* (New York: Harper & Row, 1959); Peter Berger, *The Noise of Solemn Assemblies* (Garden City, N.Y.: Doubleday, 1968).

Brotherhood, Lutheran Laymen's League, Lutheran Churchmen) functioned best when there were specific projects to be undertaken. The Lutheran Laymen's League, for example, flourished as an auxiliary of the Missouri Synod when it was challenged to provide financial support for "The Lutheran Hour."[33] The men's groups in the other bodies filled a similar if less spectacular role. It must be admitted, however, that the congregational men's clubs were something less than the pulsebeat of the church.

It was a different story with the women's groups. In all Lutheran bodies the original purpose of the women's organizations was largely the support of foreign missions. In due course, however, the women's societies expanded their understanding of "mission" to include support of home missions, the churches' educational and charitable institutions, and, especially in the Lutheran Church in America and the American Lutheran Church, the social action programs of the churches.

The youth program of the churches, like that of other auxiliary enterprises, underwent considerable alteration in the post-World War II years. Prior to the fifties the youth organizations, known as Luther Leagues in the LCA and the ALC and the Walther League (named after C. F. W. Walther) in the Missouri Synod, were primarily programs for church young people planned and directed by adult personnel in national offices. In later years, however, the youth work in all branches of American Lutheranism underwent changes that saw the leadership move more and more from adults to young people themselves. The inability and disinterest of high-school young people to administer organizations which, in the past, adults and young adults had created and effectively managed, and the desire for local service and action ministries rather than structured programming from "above," led to a new understanding of youth work that recognized young people as an integral part of the people of God and not as an entity known as "the church of the future." This was calculated to give responsibility for leadership and decision-making to the young people. A harbinger of things to come was the cooperation by the youth ministries of the three major churches (LCA, ALC, LC—MS). An all-Lutheran youth gathering in August 1973 brought over 20,000 young people to a convention labeled "Discovery 73" in Houston, Texas.[34]

Church and World. The religious revival of the 1950s was submitted to a severe critique by numerous sociologists and historians of religion in America.[35] The common charge was that religion was in danger of being too closely allied with "the American way of life." To be American was to be identified with some church. The resultant "culture-religion" was generally content with the status quo.

Theoretically, Lutherans were opposed to all forms of culture-religion, assuming in some instances a position described by H. Richard Niebuhr's phrase, "Christ against culture." They defended their attitude by pointing to the eschatological theme of the Bible and by putting divine transcendence against immanence, the latter being a hallmark of liberalism. In so doing they misinterpreted, or at least gave one-sided emphasis to, a facet of Lutheran theology, and they did not escape captivity to culture-religion by minimizing the public and prophetic role of the church. As a matter of fact, Lutheran congregations across the land in the prosperous fifties gave evidence that they were enamoured of the desire for popular approval and success. Accepting uncritically the approbation of middle-class America, Lutheranism was in danger of becoming what its theology did not allow, a culture-religion.

In the sixties, however, the church like the rest of American society was involved in rapid and, at times, overwhelming change. Politically, American Lutherans no longer felt the need to vote against a Catholic candidate for the presidency. In fact, the official organ of the conservative Missouri Synod carried an article which, though it warned against Roman Catholic political power, insisted that John F. Kennedy should have the right to seek the presidency.[36] Some consternation occurred when a group of prominent Lutheran theologians issued a preelection endorsement of Kennedy.[37] Nevertheless, the Kennedy candidacy, like the problems of the depression years, led the Lutherans to face the question of the public political role of the churches.

In like manner, the churches found it necessary to react to profound issues raised by the problems of racial integration and civil rights in the first half of the sixties and "Black power" and urban riots and violence in the remainder of the decade. Added to this was the social turmoil engendered by the war in Southeast Asia, the subsequent campus unrest, and conscientious objection to the government's Vietnam policy and war in general. The deterioration of American cities, especially in the ghettos, the growing problem of poverty, and the increasing dismay over ecological imbalance and the population explosion—all these and more were questions which pressed themselves upon the churches, forcing churchmen to face the sober reality that continuance of life on earth might be in jeopardy.

Increasingly aware of criticism that they were guilty of social ethical quietism, and yet unwilling to capitulate to pressures for a "social gospel," Lutheran theologians and boards of social action began to define the public role of the church in terms of a descholasticized Lutheran doctrine of "the two realms," which taught that through the presently available eschatological gospel of forgiveness and reconciliation God frees believers to cooperate with all men, Christian and non-Christian, in God's "kingdom of the left" to establish peace and justice in the *seculum*. It was asserted that the ultimate character of righteousness by grace through faith does not separate a Christian from seeking penultimate righteousness on earth, but rather encourages him to cast himself with abandon into the problems of the so-called secular world. At the same time, it was reiterated that the individual does not become a Christian by social action ("works"), but by grace appropriated through faith in the Word of the gospel.

36.
"Is There a Religious Issue in the Presidential Campaign?" *Lutheran Witness*, September 20, 1960, p. 5.
37.
Ibid., December 13, 1960, p. 17.

With this kind of theological undergirding, the major branches of American Lutheranism issued position papers on social and political problems, encouraged new ministries, and channeled increasing sums of money into direct social action.[38] This did not meet with unanimous support. In fact, the churches on both the national and local levels were being polarized into "left" and "right" elements. The "left," insofar as they were theologically motivated, charged Lutheranism with being ethically listless and unable to face the radical demands of a "political theology." The "right," unable to appreciate the Lutheran dialectic that kept evangelical proclamation and social action in tension, charged that the "spiritual" character of the church was being eroded by a new "liberalism." As the sixties ended, these polarities were compounded by decline in church attendance and financial support, all of which served to magnify the potentially explosive nature of the unresolved problems that Lutherans shared with other Christians. However, an unexpected, and therefore somewhat surprising, mood of calm seemed to be descending on the churches during the first years of the new decade. As if in weariness from the recent turbulence, church leaders appeared to welcome a respite from earlier tensions and to focus their energies on intrachurch issues such as constitutional revisions and institutional restructuring. These problems, coupled with the evaluation of the growing charismatic movement and a hiatus in the efforts toward Lutheran unity, characterized much of the mood of the early seventies.

527

Inter-Lutheran Relations

By the late fifties it was apparent that the two large associations of Lutherans in America—the National Lutheran Council and the Synodical Conference—no longer corresponded to reality. As a result of the merger movement the council was reduced from eight member churches to but two, the American Lutheran Church and the Lutheran Church in America, a fact which immediately challenged the continued existence of the National Lutheran Council. Between 1958 and 1966 a successor organization, the Lutheran Council in the United States of America (Lutheran Council/U.S.A.), which embraced the Lutheran Church—Missouri Synod and the Synod of Evangelical Lutheran Churches (SELC), as well as the two members of the former National Lutheran Council, was established.[39]

Meanwhile, the Synodical Conference was experiencing difficulty because of the Missouri Synod's cautious but growing openness to other Lutherans. As noted earlier, World War II brought the Missouri Synod into numerous contacts with the churches of the National Lutheran Council. Though reluctant to enter into official cooperation, which according to Missouri required complete doctrinal agreement, there were several areas in which boards or agencies—not the synod itself—found it expedient to associate with others. Some of these contacts evolved into formal and official synodical relationships, such as Lutheran World Relief, the Lutheran Service Commission, Lu-

38.
The minutes and proceedings of the ALC, LCA, and LC—MS during the 1960s, especially the last five years, give ample documentation to the public posture of the church.

39.
For an account of the steps leading up to the establishment of the Lutheran Council/U.S.A. see Richard C. Wolf, *Documents of Lutheran Unity in America* (Philadelphia: Fortress Press, 1966), pp. 614–37; and Frederick K. Wentz, *Lutherans in Concert* (Minneapolis: Augsburg Publishing House, 1968), pp. 171–74. Doctrinal essays, reports, and decisions were published jointly by the Missouri Synod and the NLC under the titles *Essays on the Lutheran Confessions Basic to Lutheran Cooperation* and *Toward Cooperation Among American Lutherans* (St. Louis and New York, 1961). The first collection dealt with "The Doctrine of the Gospel" and "The Significance of Confessional Subscription"; the second, "What Kind of Cooperation Is Possible in View of the Discussions to Date?" The essayists were Conrad Bergendoff, Martin Franzmann, Theodore G. Tappert, Herbert Bouman, and Alvin Rogness.

theran Immigration Service, and Lutheran Church Productions, Inc., the latter being responsible for the highly successful film *Martin Luther.* Two of Missouri's partners in the Synodical Conference—the Wisconsin Evangelical Lutheran Synod and the Evangelical Lutheran Synod (Norwegian)—repeatedly charged Missouri with "unionism." Although the latter made efforts to maintain ties with its attackers, in time fellowship was broken and the Synodical Conference existed only in name.[40]

Against this two-faceted development within American Lutheranism the inter-Lutheran relations of the late fifties and the sixties must be placed.

Change in Missouri. During the thirty years between 1932 and 1962 the Missouri Synod not only changed its name to "the Lutheran Church—Missouri Synod" (1947) but its attitude toward other Lutherans. The change in attitude was accompanied by a partial relaxing of Missouri's doctrinal rigidity. The Brief Statement (1932), which had become its standard for measuring doctrinal orthodoxy and which had virtually been given confessional status in 1959,[41] was subjected to increasing criticism by a number of theologians.[42] The synodical convention of 1962, though disciplining one of the "guilty" theologians,[43] recognized that it was unconstitutional to bind pastors and professors to anything but the Scriptures and the Lutheran confessions.[44]

The events of those years gave evidence that the theological faculty at St. Louis was divided into two schools, the old-line Missourians and a growing minority of progressives or moderates. The latter were not strong enough to control the synod but were sufficiently influential by 1962 to cause the right wing to organize itself to thwart what was deemed a dangerous move to the "left."

To replace the retiring president (Behnken), the synod elected Oliver Harms who was destined in the next seven years to lead Missouri into closer relationships with other Lutherans, including membership in the new Lutheran council, despite uneasiness among the traditionalists. Other actions that revealed a spirit of openness were approval of Missouri's participation in the Lutheran-Presbyterian dialogue and permission to commissions and boards, under carefully prescribed limits, to cooperate with divisions of the National Council of Churches.[45]

Subsequent to the 1962 convention (Cleveland), it became common knowledge that a vigorous right-wing element in the church was organizing itself as a political force to direct future decisions of the synod. Membership on and even control of certain important boards and committees placed the conservatives in a position of strength. The effect of this tactic was evident already at the 1965 convention (Detroit) and even more so at the 1967 convention (New York). Between 1967 and 1969 this activity was to produce a serious challenge to the leadership of President Harms.

The ALC-Missouri Fellowship Negotiations. Earlier accounts have shown that there were strong Missouri-oriented elements in the Evangelical Lutheran Church and the former American

40.
An objective historical account of inner-Synodical Conference developments is in *Lutheran Witness,* March 7, 1961, pp. 11-17. The documentary data are to be found in Wolf, *Documents,* pp. 429-55. See also LC—MS, *Proceedings . . . 1965,* pp. 104-5; ibid. *1967,* p. 99.
41.
LC—MS, *Proceedings . . . 1959,* p. 191.
42.
"A Statement" was published in the *American Lutheran* (November 1945) and in the *Lutheran Outlook* (December 1945). It challenged the attitude as well as the doctrinal stance of Missouri. The document has been included in Carl S. Meyer, ed., *Moving Frontiers: Readings in the History of the Lutheran Church—Missouri Synod* (St. Louis: Concordia Publishing House, 1964), pp. 422-24. Behnken describes his distress over the "Statement" in *This I Recall,* pp. 190-93. His official report and the synod's official action are recorded in Missouri Synod, *Proceedings . . . 1947,* pp. 15-16, 523. See also *This I Recall,* p. 192.
43.
LC—MS, *Proceedings . . . 1962,* pp. 106-7.
44.
The controversial resolution actually required subscription to statements additional to those specified in the synod's constitution (Scriptures and the confessions), and therefore had the effect of amending the constitution by simple resolution. See LC—MS, *Proceedings . . . 1962,* pp. 122-23; and ibid., pp. 105-6. Cf. Herbert T. Mayer, "The Triangle of Tension," *Concordia Theological Monthly* 34 (July 1963): 389.
45.
Martin E. Marty, "Head First But Not Headlong," *Lutheran Standard,* August 14, 1962, pp. 2-5, 12.

Lutheran Church. As a matter of fact, the 1949 proposal for a merger or a federation of National Lutheran Council churches died a-borning because some strategists and merger-makers had in mind forming a church which Missouri would find less repelling than the United Lutheran and Augustana bodies. In view of this, contacts between the Missouri Synod and the projected American Lutheran Church were made in the late fifties. This produced in turn an official statement from the Joint Union Committee (ALC, ELC, UELC) to the Missouri Synod that an invitation to "conduct doctrinal discussions looking to pulpit and altar fellowship" would be welcomed.[46] The Missouri Synod replied by voting such an invitation in 1959. It was accepted by the American Lutheran Church at its constituting convention in April 1960.[47]

When expressions of concern were made that a Missouri-ALC alliance would strain the already frayed relations between the new American Lutheran Church and the new Lutheran Church in America,[48] invitations were extended to the LCA to join the negotiations.[49] The latter declined on the grounds that it was already officially committed to inter-Lutheran fellowship and saw no need to engage in doctrinal discussions. To insist on such discussions as a prerequisite to fellowship *among Lutherans* was considered redundant.[50] This was not to say that all Lutherans were in theological accord. In fact, numerous issues needed airing and clarification, but such issues were not or ought not to be divisive of fellowship among those who affirmed Article VII of the Augsburg Confession. Moreover, to rest the case for Lutheran unity on formal confessional subscription was not to admit theological bankruptcy nor to capitulate to a theological rigor mortis. Rather, this was to declare that the church could say *satis est* confessionally but not theologically; it could affirm that within confessional unity there must be room for theological diversity. Or, to put it another way, the theology in which agreement in "the doctrine of the gospel" (Augsburg Confession, VII) is stated should be an adiaphoron. Therefore, it was argued, the unresolved theological problems could best be discussed in an atmosphere of confessional unity which all American Lutherans possessed.

The Missouri Synod and the American Lutheran Church, unwilling to admit the adequacy of this position (perhaps for different reasons) decided in January 1964 to proceed with pulpit and altar negotiations. Opposition within the ALC found focus in a memorial to the 1964 convention requesting that the ALC declare immediately that it was in fellowship with all Lutherans. The president, nettled by this action, took sharp issue with those who opposed his leadership in promoting the Missouri negotiations. He asserted that for the ALC to declare fellowship with the LCA "might have disastrous effects" upon the Missouri Synod and its future relations with the ALC.[51] The convention supported the president, who had promised that no "new doctrinal statements" would be produced.[52]

In this atmosphere, talks between the representatives of the American Lutheran Church and the Lutheran Church—Mis-

46.
Wolf, *Documents*, pp. 622–23.
47.
LC—MS, *Proceedings . . . 1959*, pp. 196–97; ALC, *Reports and Actions . . . 1960*, p. 98.
48.
Editorial, *Lutheran World*, May 1962, p. 168.
49.
ALC, *Reports and Actions . . . 1962*, pp. 375–76.
50.
The same view was expressed not only by an increasing number of persons in the ALC, but also by some in the Missouri Synod. See "We Have a Basis," *American Lutheran*, March 1964, p. 5.
51.
ALC, *Reports and Actions . . . 1964*, pp. 80–81, 658. Schiotz called those opposed to his policies "self-appointed critics" whose organized activities would dash his hopes for ALC-Missouri fellowship indefinitely—at least for another decade. He took particular exception to an essay by associate editor Kent S. Knutson, "Article VII and the Fellowship Question Among Lutherans," *Dialog* 3 (Summer 1964): 223–25.
52.
ALC, *Reports and Actions . . . 1964*, p. 485. The Synod of Evangelical Lutheran Churches (Slovak) joined the discussions in April 1965.

souri Synod were conducted from November 1964 to January 1966. Three doctrinal statements dealing with grace, the Scriptures, and the church according to Lutheran confessions were prepared and distributed among the participating bodies. Subsequently a "Joint Statement and Declaration," purporting to show the existence of doctrinal agreement, was adopted by the Missouri Synod in 1967 and by the ALC in 1968.[53] The LCA looked upon these doctrinal statements, whether officially adopted or not, as going beyond confessional requirements for fellowship and the true unity of the church.

That the LCA fears were not groundless had been made evident when President Harms of the Missouri Synod in 1966 reissued the invitation to the LCA to join the discussions in order that "a *formal and clear statement* [italics added] of some issues which are not treated explicitly in the historic Lutheran confessions" be prepared.[54] The wording of the invitation made it transparent that agreement in extraconfessional statements was being sought as a prerequisite to fellowship, not least on the thorny question of biblical inerrancy.[55] Therefore, the confessional affirmation regarding the "true unity" of the church was, according to the LCA, being undercut.[56] In this situation, the ALC, embarrassed by Missouri's insistence on extraconfessional statements which allegedly had been eschewed by both parties, voted in 1968 to approve ALC President Schiotz's 1966 suggestion that the church vote fellowship with both the LCA and the Missouri Synod.[57]

The Missouri Synod approached its 1969 convention in the knowledge that it faced a crisis compounded of numerous elements: (1) a widening gap between traditionalists and progressives; (2) the 1967 decision to join the new Lutheran Council in the U.S.A.; (3) the 1967 approval of the "Joint Statement and Declaration" as a green light for fellowship with the ALC; and (4) the 1968 consultation with unofficial representatives of the LCA. All of the latter were interpreted by an increasing number of old-line Missourians as the encroachment of liberalism. Harms, who had led the church in a new direction, was severely criticized by the right wing, the spokesmen of which soon mounted a campaign to replace him with a conservative president. It was hoped that such action would return Missouri to its traditional moorings.[58] A sharply divided church met in synod at Denver in the summer of 1969 and elected Jacob A. O. Preus, Jr., as its new president. The convention then turned about-face and, despite the objections of its new president, voted by a margin of eighty-four to declare fellowship with the American Lutheran Church.[59]

Post-Denver developments indicated that changes in policy and personnel were being made in keeping with the attitude of the new administration. The elimination of prominent "moderates" from important posts and the announcement of an investigation of alleged "liberalism" in the faculty at Concordia Seminary in St. Louis made it clear that the Lutheran Church—Missouri Synod in 1970 was confronted with a major task of internal reconciliation.[60] Its 1971 Milwaukee convention,

53.
LC—MS, *Proceedings . . . 1967,* pp. 102–3; ALC, *Reports and Actions . . . 1968,* pp. 636–38.
54.
LCA, *Minutes . . . 1966,* p. 711.
55.
Lutheran Witness Reporter, July 3, 1966, p. 3.
56.
LCA, *Minutes . . . 1966,* p. 712.
57.
ALC, *Reports and Actions . . . 1968,* pp. 636–38.
58.
The official organs of the Missouri Synod were not open to the attacks from the right, so the latter used the columns of an ecclesiastically independent paper, the *Lutheran News* (later, the *Christian News*). Widely circulated, this theologically conservative paper unquestionably served to widen the rift in the Missouri Synod.
59.
News Releases, Dept. of Public Relations, LC—MS, July 12 and 14, 1969. Cf. LC—MS, *Proceedings . . . 1969,* pp. 20, 22. News Release, LC—MS, Dept. of Public Relations, July 15, 1969. Preus quoted "an ALC theologian" to the effect that the problem of Scripture had not been faced head-on.
60.
Lutheran Witness Reporter, October 5, 1969, p. 2. Cf. *Christian News,* September 29, 1969, p. 3. News Bureau Release, Lutheran Council/U.S.A., October 30, 1969, pp. 1–2. Cf. *Minneapolis Star,* November 22, 1969. Preus later blocked Jungkuntz's appointment to the St. Louis faculty. Cf. *Christian Century,* February 25, 1970, p. 230. Jungkuntz subsequently became provost of Pacific Lutheran University, an institution supported by the ALC and LCA in Tacoma, Wash. See News Bureau Release, Lutheran Council/U.S.A., June 1, 1970, p. 5. See president's desk letter, "Brother to Brother," Pentecost 1970; and *Lutheran Witness Reporter,* November 1, 1970. Cf. "Hunting Lutheran Heretics," *Newsweek,* August 3, 1970, p. 47; "Missouri Lutheran Leader Eyes Liberal Clergy, Teachers," *Washington Post,* July

the theme of which was "Sent to Reconcile," left the distinct impression that the two wings in the church remained unreconciled.[61] As a matter of fact, the next biennium revealed that the two opposing parties were on a collision course, and there seemed to be little disposition on either side to avoid the confrontation. The collision occurred at the New Orleans convention in the summer of 1973 (July 6-13).

American church historians look at the modernist-fundamentalist controversy of the 1920s and the current internal conflict in Catholicism as evidences of the monumental furor capable of being engendered by theological and ecclesiastical differences, but neither of these episodes matched the spiritual carnage that took place at what some observers called "the Second Battle of New Orleans." Not in the twentieth century, said Martin E. Marty, "has a large church been so savagely torn."[62]

The leaders of the two parties were Jacob A. O. Preus, president of the synod and unyielding advocate of Missouri traditionalism, and John H. Tietjen, president of the St. Louis Concordia Seminary, forty-five of whose fifty-member faculty were under fire from the conservative forces. Central to the conflict was the continuing question of biblical authority couched in the now familiar Old Lutheran terminology of verbal inspiration and inerrancy. The conservatives insisted that doctrinal purity was imperiled by the Neo-Lutheran view that the Bible's authority rested on its character as the bearer of the primary witness to the gospel, the divine message of the gracious forgiveness of sins and of the gift of new life in the Spirit. This Word of God was and is infallible; moreover, it is not jeopardized by the use of the historical-critical method of biblical study. Preus and the conservatives charged Tietjen and the faculty majority with "Gospel reductionism," that is, restricting scriptural authority to the gospel but not to scientific, geographic, or historical matters found in the Bible. The Scriptures must be factually inerrant if they are to be the norm for the faith and life of the church. Each of the other major Lutheran bodies had in greater or lesser degree faced the problem of the Bible; hence, much of the ground that the Missouri Synod was covering had been traveled before. But of the three major bodies Missouri alone was driven to a position that forced a vote on the issue at its biennial convention.

Shortly after the Milwaukee (1971) convention, the religion editor of the *New York Times* had interviewed Preus's brother, Robert Preus, a member of the faculty minority. Preus had admitted that no other major denomination "had managed to pull off what he and his brother were seeking." He argued that this action was "the only way to preserve doctrinal purity. Whether it is possible," he added, "is another matter."[63] Events leading up to New Orleans indicated that the preservation of "doctrinal purity," as defined by the Preus forces, was not only impossible but also incapable of keeping the contending parties from holding in reverence the biblical injunction to "speak the truth in love."

531

27, 1970; "Investigation Stirs Tempest," *Lutheran Standard,* August 18, 1970, p. 22; *St. Louis Globe Democrat* and *St. Louis Post-Dispatch,* July 13, 1970; David Runge, "Progressives Raise Flurry About Synod," *Milwaukee Journal,* November 15, 1969; Herbert T. Mayer, "The Task Ahead," *Concordia Theological Monthly* 40 (September 1969); and "Unsettled Missouri," *Lutheran Forum,* December 1969, pp. 13-14.
61.
See LC—MS, *Proceedings . . . 1971,* pp. 51-61, 117-20, 130-39, and passim.
62.
"Missouri's Inner Struggle," *The Lutheran,* November 15, 1972, p. 8.
63.
Edward B. Fiske, "Lutherans: A Leader Who Has Sharply Divided His Flock," *New York Times,* July 18, 1972.

For both parties, the New Orleans convention was crucial and each side made its plans accordingly. Preus was seeking reelection to another four-year term. If successful, he would look upon the decision of the synod as a vote of confidence and as a mandate to carry through his program of securing the synod in its traditional Missourianism. The moderates naturally saw their hopes, humanly speaking, resting in their ability to enlist delegate support for a candidate who might be able to unseat the incumbent. Jacob Preus, in many circles, was looked upon as a parvenu. He was not of German-Missourian background; his family had for a century been associated with Norwegian Lutheranism in America—that branch of which, however, that was sympathetic to Missourianism; he had received his education at schools of the Norwegian Lutheran Church of America (Luther College in Iowa, Luther Seminary in St. Paul); he, together with his brother Robert, had left the Evangelical Lutheran (Norwegian) Church and joined the "little Norwegian Synod" (the Norwegian minority [Evangelical Lutheran Synod] which rejected the union of Norwegian synods in 1917); he and his brother were instrumental in causing this synod to break fellowship with the Missouri Synod in 1955; and then suddenly and dramatically in 1957 and 1958 both men accepted professorships in Missouri schools, Robert at Concordia Seminary in St. Louis, and Jacob at Concordia Seminary in Springfield, Illinois.

The task of the "liberals," it seemed, was to find a moderate but classical Missourian who would attract the confidence of the majority and yet one who would not foreclose the possibility of Missouri's turning away from Lutheran scholasticism toward the position of Neo-Lutheranism now being advocated by the majority of the faculty at Concordia Seminary, St. Louis.

The choice of the moderates was Oswald C. J. Hoffmann, the widely known and noncontroversial "Lutheran Hour" radio evangelist.[64] Meanwhile, Hoffmann noted that the synod's election procedures, adopted in 1971 at Milwaukee, required a candidate to "reply within 10 days as to his willingness to serve if elected." Consequently he asked that his name be dropped from consideration: "I cannot express at this time a willingness to serve if elected, since I believe that does violence to the call I now have as speaker on The Lutheran Hour."[65] Although the moderates hoped that Hoffmann might be nominated from the convention floor, his withdrawal all but guaranteed a Preus victory. At the opening business session at New Orleans, Preus was reelected on the first ballot, 606 to 451.[66] This vote was a harbinger of actions to be taken on most of the other crucial issues. Preus's forces formed a solid phalanx to push through the Preus program demonstrating an approximate 6-to-4 control of the convention.

An examination of the vast literature that flooded the congregations between 1971 and 1973 shows that the subject matter of virtually all the articles and pamphlets dealt with the question of biblical authority and the role of the St. Louis faculty in upholding or undercutting that authority. It was to be expected,

64.
"Mo. Synod Moderates Support Dr. Hoffmann for Presidency," News Bureau Release, Lutheran Council/U.S.A., September 19, 1972, pp. 1–3.
65.
"Dr. Hoffmann Questions New Election Procedure . . . ," ibid., April 9, 1973, pp. 1–3.
66.
Lutheran Witness, "The New Orleans Convention," August 5, 1973, p. 6. Even had Hoffmann remained in the contest it is questionable whether he could have won. The secret congregational nominating ballots, revealed at the convention, showed Preus with 2,678 votes, Hoffmann with 1,172. The next highest managed 46! Ibid., p. 7.

therefore, that the major resolutions before the New Orleans convention were distillations of these concerns.

The first significant vote was to reaffirm Missouri's earlier—especially 1959 and 1971—decisions concerning the binding nature of synodically adopted doctrinal statements.[67] Encouraged by this action, the conservative majority elevated to doctrinal status the Preus-authored "Statement of Scriptural and Confessional Principles," while hundreds of delegates, simultaneously weeping and singing "The Church's One Foundation," streamed to the podium to register their negative votes. Next came resolutions condemning the theological stance held by the faculty majority at Concordia Seminary and referring charges against its president to the institution's board of control. The latter action faced President Tietjen with the likely prospect of dismissal.[68]

All of these events had implications for Missouri's relations with other Lutherans. Although LCA President Robert Marshall addressed the convention and was politely received, there was no action to renew discussions with the LCA such as those initiated by Presidents Fry and Harms in 1967-68.[69] The new president of the American Lutheran Church, David Preus, a cousin of Missouri's Jacob Preus, expressed confidence that "God-pleasing solutions to our relatively *peripheral differences*" (italics added) would be found and that ALC-Missouri fellowship would be continued.[70] This statement was made in the face of a resolution to declare the existing fellowship "to be in a state of suspension." Were the synod to act in character, the expected result would be adoption of the resolution. In a surprise move involving what some called carefully staged parliamentary confusion, a motion to table was passed during the closing hour of the convention. The explanation of this decision lay in the close personal ties between the two Preuses. The Missouri Preus, despite his theological convictions, had promised the ALC Preus that he would not support suspension of fellowship.[71] The final day also saw Missouri's threatened relationship with the Lutheran Council in the U.S.A., together with numerous unconsidered resolutions, referred to the board of directors of the synod.[72]

The trauma of the 1973 synod produced wounds, bitterness, and deep sorrow, not only within the Lutheran Church—Missouri Synod, but throughout the ecclesiastical world. Lutheran leaders, lay and clerical, expressed their dismay at the spectacle. Questions were asked: Will there be a schism? Are the faculty members going to be dismissed and will such action mean the shutting down of the world's largest Lutheran theological seminary? Will Tietjen be dismissed and who will replace him? Is it possible for inter-Lutheran and ecumenical relations to recover momentum or has the unity movement been set back another generation?

Of necessity, most of these questions must remain unanswered, but two issues quickly surfaced after New Orleans. One was the decision of the minority (representing roughly one-million people) to reject schism—but to continue within the

533

67.
"LCMS Reaffirms Position on Doctrinal Statements," News Bureau Release, Lutheran Council/U.S.A., July 13, 1973, pp. 6-7. At this writing, the official proceedings of the LC—MS (1973) have not been published. Hence, documentation is limited to news releases and published reports in church periodicals.
68.
"Domination by Conservatives . . . ," ibid., July 16, 1973, pp. 1-7; and "Dr. Tietjen Faces Ouster," ibid., July 17, 1973, pp. 1-3.
69.
For a brief account see E. Clifford Nelson, *Lutheranism in North America, 1914-1970* (Minneapolis: Augsburg Publishing House, 1972), pp. 265-68.
70.
Lutheran Witness, August 5, 1973, p. 9.
71.
"LCMS Tables Suspension of Fellowship with ALC," News Bureau Release, Lutheran Council/U.S.A., July 17, 1973, pp. 4-5. Letter of David W. Preus to E. Clifford Nelson, November 13, 1973, St. Olaf College Archives, Northfield, Minn. This letter and subsequent developments led some observers to comment that "blood is thicker than theology."
72.
"Time Runs Out . . . ," News Bureau Release, Lutheran Council/U.S.A., July 17, 1973, pp. 6-7.

Missouri Synod as a "confessing movement." The group, meeting in Chicago (August 28-29, 1973) adopted a document in which they protested the "unconstitutional actions" of the New Orleans synod and urged the synod to retract the "errant actions" of the majority.[73] President Preus, writing in the official organ of the synod, the *Lutheran Witness,* described the meeting of the moderates as "a rebellion not only against our Synod and its recent convention, but, more importantly, against God's holy, inspired, and inerrant Word." The "insurgents" (Preus's word) had "misunderstood the Synod's constitution."[74]

The second issue to emerge from the rubble at New Orleans was the future of the seminary and its president. The conservative-dominated board of control voted on August 18, 1973, to suspend Tietjen but to "delay implementation" of the suspension until legal opinions on the ouster could be obtained. Procedural debates and contemplated doctrinal conversations between Tietjen and his main accusers complicated matters to the point that the seminary board voted at its September meeting to "vacate" the earlier suspension in order to begin dismissal proceedings anew, that is, to "revert to the first step."[75] Moreover, despite Preus's denunciation of forty-five faculty members for rebellion and defiance of the synod and creating "an intolerable situation at the seminary," 600 seminarians began classes in September 1973, with Tietjen still in office as president and the faculty members teaching their usual courses.[76]

The reaction of the Christian world, apart from those churches sympathetic to an untinctured fundamentalism, was one of stunned dismay and disbelief. Some impartial outsiders saw the whole conflict as a needless internecine feud between mild conservatives and extreme conservatives. Others judged the Preus army as winning a Pyrrhic victory and engaging in a costly but temporary flirtation with the past. Ironically, Roman Catholic biblical scholars looked "with horror and pity" on the spectacle of a Christian community controlled by "militant fundamentalists."[77] Meanwhile, within the American Lutheran family there were signs that the posture of "waiting for Missouri," an attitude which had characterized so much of American Lutheran history, was once again impeding the move toward Lutheran unity. The notion that steps toward Lutheran unity without Missouri would be harmful or even unchristian, led to suggestions that the time had come for church bodies to occupy themselves with their own internal development.

"The problem of Missouri" was clearly unresolved in 1973. The rest of Lutheranism, however, had to give an answer "without horns [reservations] and without teeth [backbiting]" to the question: Does Missouri write the agenda for American Lutheranism?

It may be academic and pointless to speculate "what would have happened if. . . ." Nevertheless, the interesting question regarding the "kairotic moment" which confronted American Lutheranism in 1949-50 poses the possibility that history would have taken a different course had the churches of the National Lutheran Council acted at that time to form a national feder-

73.
Forum Letter, September 1973, pp. 2-3. The document of "confession" and "protest," entitled "In the Name of Jesus Christ and for the Sake of the Gospel," was included as a supplement to ibid., October 1973.

74.
"LCMS Leader Terms Meeting . . . 'A Rebellion,' " News Bureau Release, Lutheran Council/U.S.A., September 18, 1973, p. 7.

75.
"Concordia Board Delays Action . . . ," ibid., August 20, 1973, pp. 9-10; "Tietjen Suspension Vacated . . . ," ibid., October 5, 1973, pp. 1-2; and "LCMS Pastors to Meet Again with Seminary President," ibid., October 24, 1973, p. 4.

76.
"Preus Calls Opponents Insurgents and Rebels," *The Lutheran,* October 17, 1973, p. 20. Tietjen was "suspended" in January 1974. This action was followed by the dismissal of 45 of 50 faculty members. About 400 of 600 seminarians withdrew and, together with the dismissed faculty, formed "Concordia Seminary in Exile" (Seminex). Sympathizers organized themselves as "Evangelical Lutherans in Mission" (ELIM) to support Seminex.

77.
"The Scholars Fight Back," *Christian Century,* October 24, 1973, p. 1045.

78.
Originally, the invitation of the North America Area of the World Alliance of Reformed Churches Holding the Presbyterian Order was addressed to its counterpart, the U.S.A. National Committee (NLC) of the LWF. The latter expressed the desire that the Missouri Synod, though not a member of the NLC-LWF, participate in the conversations. The Missouri Synod agreed to do this. See ALC, *Reports and Actions . . . 1962*, pp. 442–43.
79.
See *Marburg Revisited*, ed. Paul C. Empie and James I. McCord (Minneapolis: Augsburg Publishing House, 1966), p. 191.
80.
Reports of the Lutheran-Roman Catholic dialogue have been published: U.S.A. National Committee of the LWF and the Bishops' Commission for Ecumenical Affairs, *The Status of the Nicene Creed as Dogma of the Church* (Washington: National Catholic Welfare Conference, 1965); *One Baptism for the Remission of Sins* (New York and Washington: U.S.A. Committee of the LWF and NCWC, 1966); *The Eucharist as Sacrifice* (New York and Washington: U.S.A. Committee of the LWF and United States Catholic Conference, 1967); and *Lutherans and Catholics in Dialogue IV: Eucharist and Ministry* (New York and Washington: U.S.A. Committee of the LWF and the Committee on Ecumenical and Interreligious Affairs, National Conference of Catholic Bishops, 1970). Cf. News Bureau Releases, nos. 70–109, 70–112, Lutheran Council/U.S.A., October 30, 1970. Interview, E. Clifford Nelson and Warren Quanbeck (member of the Lutheran "team"), October 30, 1973.

ation rather than to foster a climate that was to lead to the birth of two organic merger movements within the NLC.

Knowing the options that existed in 1950 and being aware of the historical developments in the twenty years that followed, the contemporary observer quite understandably might raise certain questions. For example, would the confessional basis for the true unity of the church (Augsburg Confession, Article VII) have been recognized more rapidly had the National Lutheran Council become a federation rather than being forced out of existence by the formation of two new churches? Would the Missouri Synod have been nearer the solution of its internal problems without the "help" of well-intentioned outsiders? Did the ALC wooing of Missouri between 1959 and 1968 produce a backlash against "moderates" who were coming into positions of leadership? Did in fact the ALC create the phenomena of Jacob Preus and New Orleans? In other words, could the present (1973) polarization in Missouri have been avoided? Would the problem of organizational unity for the whole of American Lutheranism have been nearer solution? No one, of course, knows the answers, but the questions persist.

Lutherans in the Ecumenical Movement

The ecumenical movement of the sixties had moved into the so-called age of dialogue. The Lutheran World Federation at its Minneapolis Assembly in 1957, without any foreknowledge of Pope John's 1959 dramatic announcement of his intention to convoke the Second Vatican Council, had taken action to establish a special commission on interconfessional research. Its initial purpose was to encourage scholarly studies of contemporary Roman Catholicism with the hope that interconfessional conversations might result. This fortuitous action placed Lutherans in the forefront of the dialogical activity that blossomed in the next decade.

Although this initial move was oriented toward Roman Catholicism, it was but natural that Lutherans accept the invitation of their Protestant cousins in the Calvinist (Presbyterian) tradition to engage in bilateral conversations.[78] Following several theological consultations beginning in 1962 and extending to 1965, representatives of the two groups published an official report which contended that "no insuperable obstacles to pulpit and altar fellowship" existed. This statement took on special significance because the Missouri Synod had participated in this and subsequent dialogues.[79]

Unlike the Lutheran-Reformed consultation, the Catholic-Lutheran dialogue, which began in 1965, found, quite understandably, that the historically divisive issues did not yield to rapid solution. By the end of 1973, seventeen meetings had produced four separate volumes on the Nicene Creed, baptism, the Eucharist as sacrifice, and the especially difficult question of the Eucharist and ministry. A fourth volume, on primacy in the church, was in preparation.[80] These reports indicated that surprising progress in mutual understanding had been achieved. *Time* magazine observed wryly that, while the possibility of

535

Lutheran and Roman Catholic intercommunion had reached "an advanced stage," Lutherans had not been able to establish fellowship among themselves.[81]

Representatives of American Lutheranism were also engaged in three other dialogues during the second half of the sixties: with the Eastern Orthodox churches, with the Protestant Episcopal Church, and with the American Jewish Committee. Although significant conversations were held with each party, it must be noted that the major advances in ecumenical understanding had emerged most notably from the dialogue with the Reformed, Roman Catholic, and Anglican traditions. The encounters with Orthodoxy and the Jewish community provided no discernible contours as the decade of the 1970s began.

Beyond these bilateral dialogues, other ecumenical developments should be mentioned. On the international level American Lutherans, for example, were among the official Lutheran World Federation-appointed observers at Vatican II. Moreover, the membership of international committees for dialogue with other churches included American theologians and churchmen. On the national level of ecumenical interchange, the Lutheran Church in America was a full member of the National Council of Churches, while the American Lutheran Church and the Missouri Synod found it expedient to remain outside and yet to accept the invitation to be represented in committees and commissions of their choice.[82] With regard to the Consultation on Church Union (COCU), which grew out of the well-publicized "Blake Proposal," the Lutheran churches preferred the status of observers to that of participants. In 1968, the Lutheran Council/U.S.A. appointed "observer-consultants" to represent the member bodies. The council's general secretary reported that Lutherans, Roman Catholics, Eastern Orthodox, and other confessional communions would experience increasing difficulty with COCU in the light of its deliberate avoidance of confessional issues and its generous use of theologically ambiguous terminology.[83] The fact that Lutherans did not enter the COCU negotiations indicated that they viewed their history and confessional tradition as justifying their remaining an identifiable confessional group within the spectrum of American Christianity. Thus, as the decade of the seventies dawned the most promising ecumenical developments seemed to lie in the Lutheran attraction for those churches that reflected the classical western tradition, the Roman Catholic, the Reformed, and the Anglican communions.

The Issues in the 1970s

In 1968 the Lutheran Church in America received three published reports from its "Task Group for Long Range Planning."[84] Recognizing that the sixties had been marked by rapid and sometimes radical change, the church had determined that "an assessment of current trends" was needful as the seventies approached. This was done in full knowledge of the historical insight and consequent caveat of Elson Ruff, editor of *The Lutheran:* "We'll have to wait for the church historians of the 22nd

536

81.
Time, May 25, 1970, p. 76.
82.
Both the LCA and the ALC published statements on the NCCC. LCA, *The Lutheran Church in America and the National Council of the Churches of Christ* . . . (Philadelphia: Board of Publication, LCA, 1964); ALC, "The American Lutheran Church and Inter-Church Relations," memorandum from the president, Minneapolis, n.d. (1969?).
83.
"COCU Too Vague About Creeds . . . ," *The Lutheran,* March 5, 1969, p. 29.
84.
The reports were entitled: *Significant Issues for the 1970s, Theology,* and *Social Change* (Philadelphia: Fortress Press, 1968).

century to figure out the dominant trends in church life in the 1970s."[85]

One of the reports made the judgment that contemporary thought gave little emphasis to such traditional Lutheran concerns as the significance of Word and sacrament as means of grace, the nature (not mission) of the church itself, and the concept of the church as the custodian and proclaimer of the gospel.[86] That this observation could be applied to all Lutherans or even to all members of the Lutheran Church in America (LCA) would be highly problematical. Nevertheless, it raised the interesting question: what were the major issues that seemed to be surfacing as the churches entered the decade of the seventies? This "concluding unscientific postscript" (with apologies to Soren Kierkegaard) will single out a few of the more obvious questions facing Lutherans.

First and foremost is the nature of the gospel. The late president of the American Lutheran Church, Kent S. Knutson, emphasized in his report to the church (1971) that the heart of Lutheran theology was its confession of the gospel. Few Lutheran theologians would disagree with his assertion that "the Lutheran confessions define and preserve the gospel in a way which is unparalleled in Christian history."[87] As true as this is, large numbers of Lutherans in all age groups and all social, economic, and educational strata have difficulty in articulating the central thrust of Christianity. The gospel is often confused with law; "being a Christian" is often described as "obeying the Ten Commandments," or "living by the Golden Rule," or "loving your neighbor," or "being relevant to social needs." Despite carefully designed curricula in parish education, serious catechetical instruction, and generally evangelical preaching, the central confession that man is saved by grace through faith in Jesus Christ is blurred and indistinct. Mesmerized by an enchantingly "modern" Pelagianism (i.e., man saves himself, or contributes to his salvation, by his good activities), Lutherans in all walks of life have been de-Lutheranized by an unevangelical moralism, social and individual. Luther's teaching that the gospel is really identical with "justification by faith" (the gift of forgiveness of sin and new life) and that this same gift is bestowed in the sacraments (Luther said of the Lord's Supper, "Where there is the forgiveness of sins there is also life and salvation") is in many instances only vaguely understood. If it is true that justification is "the article of a standing and falling church," and if "God's Word and Gospel are interchangeable terms" (Edmund Schlink's phrase),[88] the Lutheran churches in America are in no little spiritual danger. Clarity regarding the gospel appears, therefore, to be high on the working agenda in the 1970s, not least when one considers the ecumenical appeal of the Lutheran confession: "For the true unity of the church it is enough *to agree concerning the teaching of the gospel* [italics added] and the administration of the sacraments" in accordance with the gospel (Augsburg Confession, Article VII).

Second, and closely related to the above, is the question of confessional integrity in an ecumenical age. Lutheran convictions regarding the

---

85.
The Lutheran, July 15, 1970, p. 50.

86.
Significant Issues, pp. 8–9.

87.
Knutson was elected by the ALC during its convention at San Antonio, Tex., October 21–27, 1970. (In autumn of 1972 Knutson became ill and died on March 12, 1973; he was succeeded by David W. Preus.) The other two major Lutheran bodies likewise had new presidents: the LCA chose Robert J. Marshall to succeed the deceased Franklin Clark Fry; the LC—MS in 1969 elected Jacob A. O. - Preus, Jr., a cousin of the ALC's David Preus, over incumbent Oliver Harms. See also Kent S. Knutson, "The State of the Church: Hope and Anxiety," in his *Report of the President* (Minneapolis: American Lutheran Church, 1971), p. 2.

88.
The Theology of the Lutheran Confessions, trans. P. F. Koehneke and H. J. A. Bouman (Philadelphia: Muhlenberg Press, 1961), p. 139.

content of the gospel are not without the attendant dangers of institutional pride and "morphological fundamentalism." That such attitudes have been present in the past and are an ever-present possibility cannot be denied. A basic misreading of the confessions has too often led to confessional legalism and Lutheran sectarianism. And there is no guarantee that such things will not happen again. Nowhere in the confessions, however, is there a "great commission" to go into all the world and make Lutherans of all nations. The confessions are not self-conscious; they are evangel-conscious. The confessions are not concerned with denominational survival but with confessional integrity vis-à-vis the catholic and apostolic faith. Their chief concern is to safeguard the proclamation of the gospel by the church. It is this conviction that has led serveral Lutheran theologians to ask pointedly what the role of American Lutheranism is in an ecumenical age. Jaroslav Pelikan put the question: "American Lutheranism: Denomination or Confession?"[89] Warren A. Quanbeck described the problem in an essay, "Confessional Integrity and Ecumenical Dialogue," in which he urged consideration of the historical context and doxological character of the Lutheran confession. He argued that the Lutheran confession "is confession in the primary biblical sense of the word, the praise of God in the heralding forth of his mighty saving deeds. It . . . calls attention to the way God has acted for human salvation in Christ, and how he continues to act in the life and witness of his church."[90] James A. Scherer called it "The Identity Crisis in Contemporary Lutheranism," and commented:

It is an unpleasant but undeniable fact that Lutheran identity today consists mostly of the cultivation of Lutheran adiaphora [hymnal, liturgical practice, model constitutions, education materials, centralized boards, etc.]. So pervasive is our sense of Lutheran . . . identity at this level that we are apt to think that it is the main thing about our churchmanship. We are, in short, most identifiably Lutheran precisely at the point where the reformers said there should be the greatest liberty.

In light of this huge irony, Scherer charges that the issue of Lutheran identity has been left largely in the hands of administrators who have tended to make it a pragmatic rather than a theological problem. And insofar as this has happened "Lutheranism today has either lost or temporarily misplaced the central concerns of the Reformation."[91]

These kinds of searching questions and criticisms led the late president of the American Lutheran Church to say, "This is the decade [the 1970s] in which Lutherans must reach some decisions about themselves."[92] What these decisions will be remains unknown, but it is certain that they will have implications for understanding the church's nature and mission, its unity, and its structure.

This leads to a third issue: the church and its purposes. A theological answer to questions about the nature of the church and its function is a necessity if the church is to meet the challenges

89.
Christian Century, December 25, 1963, pp. 1608–10.
90.
A Reexamination of Lutheran and Reformed Traditions—IV, ed. Paul C. Empie and James I. McCord (New York: North American Area, World Alliance of Reformed Churches and U.S.A. National Committee of the LWF, 1966), pp. 41–47.
91.
Context: Journal of the Lutheran School of Theology at Chicago, Autumn 1967, pp. 34–41, 55–56.
92.
Kent S. Knutson quoted in News Bureau Release, Lutheran Council/U.S.A., September 17, 1970, p. 8.

growing out of the historical situation. There is nothing novel about this affirmation; it has always been true that the church's self-understanding has shaped its mission. The question of ministry and mission cannot be separated from the question of the church's being. Hence, what the church is and what it does have a reciprocal relationship.

The recent discussion about "secularity" has caused some to assert that the "world writes the agenda for the church." Therefore, it is argued, one must seek and find God in the world. In the light of this, it is asked, is the definition of the church as the assembly of believers "among whom the gospel is preached in its purity and the holy sacraments are administered according to the gospel" (Augsburg Confession, Article VII) adequate for our day? Rather than being "the people of God" to whom has been entrusted the kerygmatic Word, it is said that the church is a "Christian presence" in the world. This "presence" affirms that all efforts seeking the liberation of men, equality and justice for all, eradication of hunger, disease, pain, and oppression are tokens of the "redemptive" activity of the cosmic Christ. The church consists, according to this view, of all those who recognize and cooperate with this "christic" action in the world and celebrate this presence by means of table fellowship and eucharistic offering.

Against this view is that which asserts that the church is indeed "the people of God" serving the world, but under the mandate "to bring men the word of the living God in judgment and mercy, to call them to repentance, to assure them of forgiveness, to free men for their work in the world. . . ." The church is not "to exhaust itself in . . . activities in which . . . it has no special competence and for which it has no monopoly of compassion. Its task must center on what others have no competence in doing nor any mandate. . . ."[93] It is here that the emerging struggle between two views of the church and its mission is joined. It is here, too, that the adequacy or inadequacy of Luther's teaching concerning "the two realms" of God's action (the realm of civil righteousness and the realm of righteousness by faith) comes under scrutiny.

Closely related to this is the fourth issue: the question of the church's unity. If Christ is present in all men of goodwill who have concern for humanity, it naturally follows that "secular ecumenism" is the expression of the church's unity. If Christ's presence, however, is marked by the ministry of the church-creating Word and sacraments, then the unity of "the people of God" is confessional. Lutherans have seen both their identity and unity in their confession of Christ's presence in the world through Word and sacrament. It is this conviction that has made the divisions in Lutheranism so painful and needless. One of the main questions confronting confessional Lutherans currently is not their unity—the Missouri Synod to the contrary notwithstanding—but their particularity in the ecumenical scene. Lutheran unity, fifty years overdue, will come eventually because Missouri cannot forever escape the implications of its own confession. But

93.
Martin J. Heinecken, "The 'Hidden' Church and How the 'Hidden' Life of Love Must Be Known by Its Fruits," *Lutheran Quarterly*, November 1969, p. 325.

meanwhile a burden of concern rests upon those who see the ecumenical heart of the Lutheran confession of the gospel as God's Word to the whole world.

The fifth and final item is the question of structure. Lutheran ecclesiology has always taught that structure is not constitutive of the church. But this is not to say that polity is a matter of indifference. Central to Lutheran ecclesiology is the conviction that structure must always assume the form of a servant; any other form would be inappropriate to the gospel. Though structure is of God, it is not in itself divine. It is a creature, but as a creature it is subject to the temptation of becoming an end in itself. Having reminded themselves of this danger, Lutherans nevertheless believe that God uses visible and tangible means to carry forward his work in the world. Hence, the church is constantly seeking a proper institutional embodiment.

In 1973 over 95 percent of American Lutherans were members of three institutional groupings: the Lutheran Church in America, the American Lutheran Church, and the Lutheran Church—Missouri Synod. Moreover, these three had created an additional structure, the Lutheran Council in the United States of America, to serve as an agency for cooperative ventures. The question that requires the attention of the churches as they prepare for full pulpit and altar fellowship is: What form should the united Lutheran church of the future assume? Is a national merger of the three—patterned after one of them or on some combination of elements from all three to produce a structural mishmash in an attempt to please everyone—a genuine solution? It has been suggested that the long-range-planning commissions of all three bodies work together to produce a new model that would provide regional churches uniting all Lutheran congregations in a given geographic area.[94] Whether the present Lutheran Council in the U.S.A. can become the structure to embody the church at a national level is a moot question. The council was created as an "agency" in the hopes of *furthering* cooperation rather than as *the national form* of the church. Established primarily in order to facilitate the participation of the Missouri Synod in some pan-Lutheran enterprises, the council was a cart-before-the-horse arrangement that evoked criticism even before it got wheels. Current comment recognizes the necessity of "a checkup, and possible overhaul."[95] Some would insist that Lutheran unity at the national level must be ecclesial; the visible form of confessional fellowship should be "church" and not "agency."

Although the issue of structure does not lie at the heart of Lutheran theology, it is patent that the "body and soul" of the church are inextricably conjoined. The congregation of God's people seeks visible expression at all levels—parochial, regional, national, and global. The structure will be ministerial, not magisterial; confessional, not triumphal, affirming its confidence that "one holy church is to continue forever" (Augsburg Confession).

The historian of Christianity or the historian of anything, for that matter, knows both the temptation and the folly of forsak-

540

94.
Such a proposal was published in the early sixties in *Lutheran World* 9 (May 1962): 169; it was elaborated on in "Does American Lutheranism Need a New Forum?" *Dialog* 4 (Winter 1965): 47–53. Cf. Kent S. Knutson, "Musings on the Future of American Lutheranism," *Lutheran Quarterly* 21 (February 1969): 46–48; and idem, *Report of the President*, p. 11.
95.
"Time for a Checkup," *Lutheran Standard*, March 2, 1971, pp. 15–16.

ing his role *qua* historian and assuming the mantle of seer. Moreover, the Christian historian, no more than the historian of Christianity, is privy to no special revelation about the future. Like all believers, he is limited to affirmations of faith when he speaks about tomorrow's church. He rests content in saying that believers cannot know *what* is in the future; they can only say *Who* is in the future. In the seventies, American Lutherans continue to confess that Christ is present now and in the future through Word and sacrament. At the same time they are learn- ing to see the catholic dimension of their confession: "Where Christ is there is the catholic church" (Ignatius).

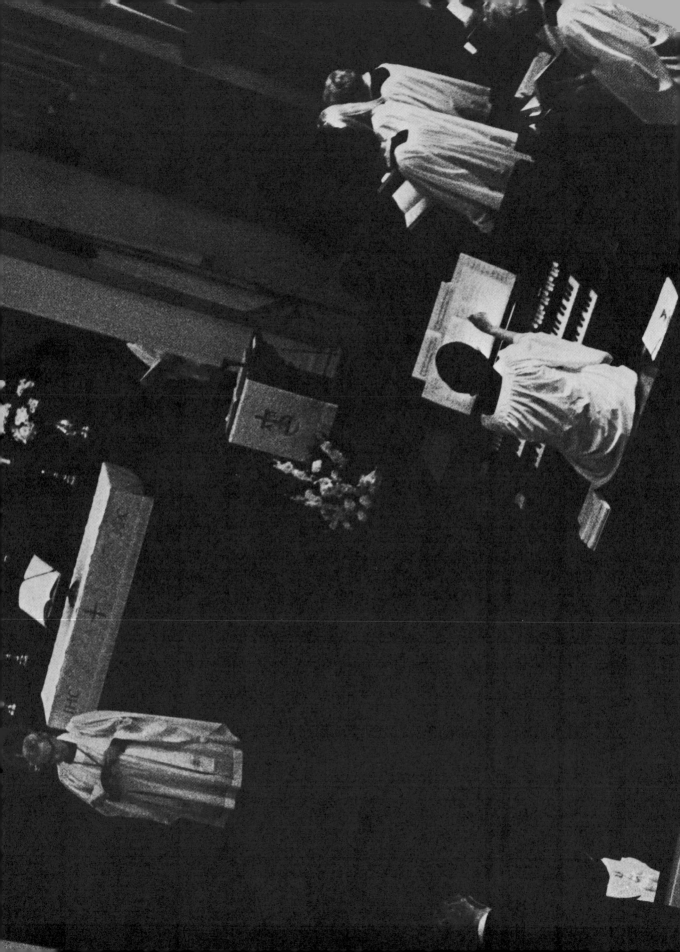